OVERVIEW OF BIBLE HISTORY

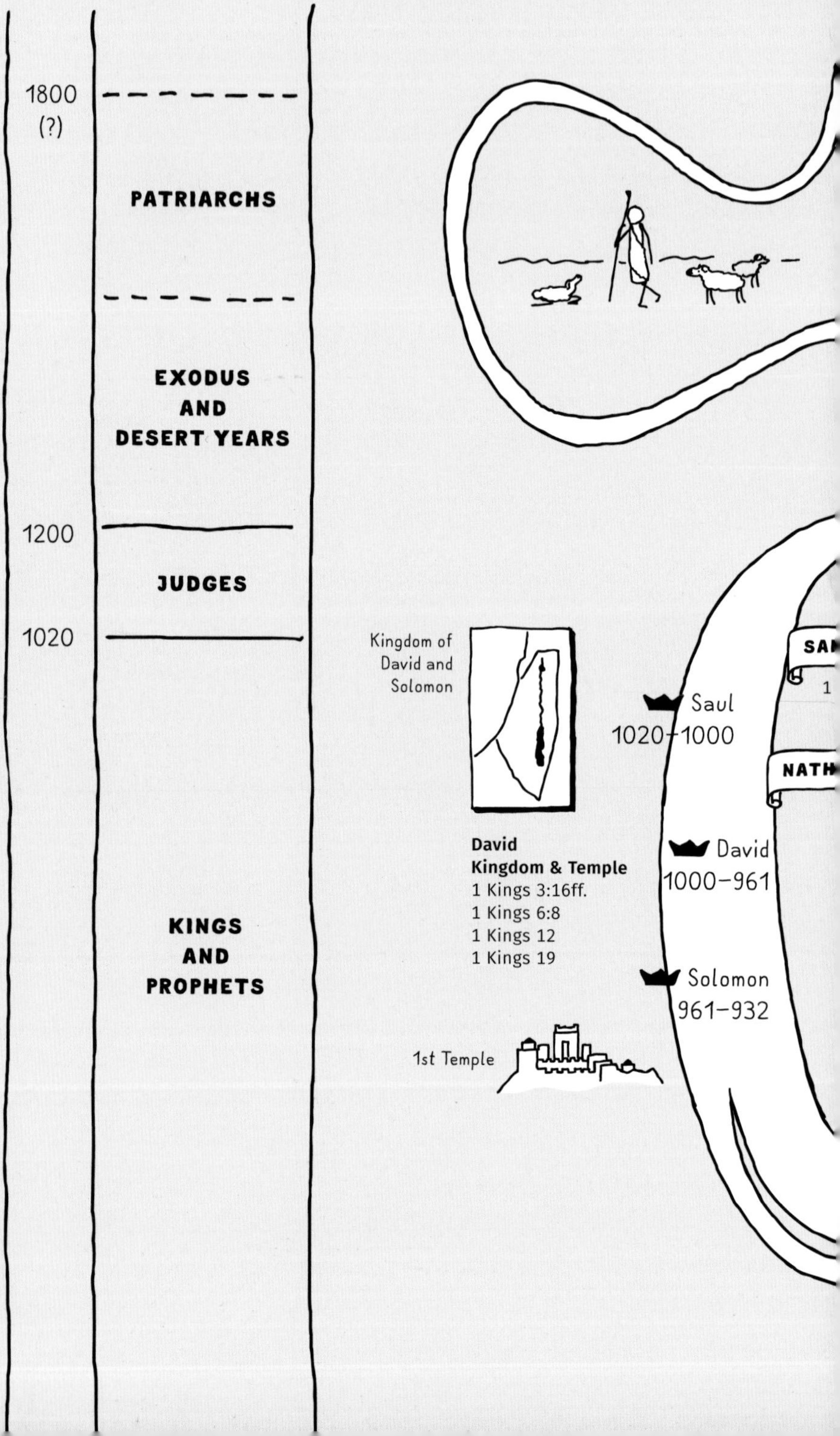
1800
(?)
PATRIARCHS
EXODUS
AND
DESERT YEARS
1200
JUDGES
1020
KINGS
AND
PROPHETS
Kingdom of
David and
Solomon
Saul
1020–1000
David
1000–961
Solomon
961–932
David
Kingdom & Temple
1 Kings 3:16ff.
1 Kings 6:8
1 Kings 12
1 Kings 19
1st Temple

Original graphics by Robert Saam

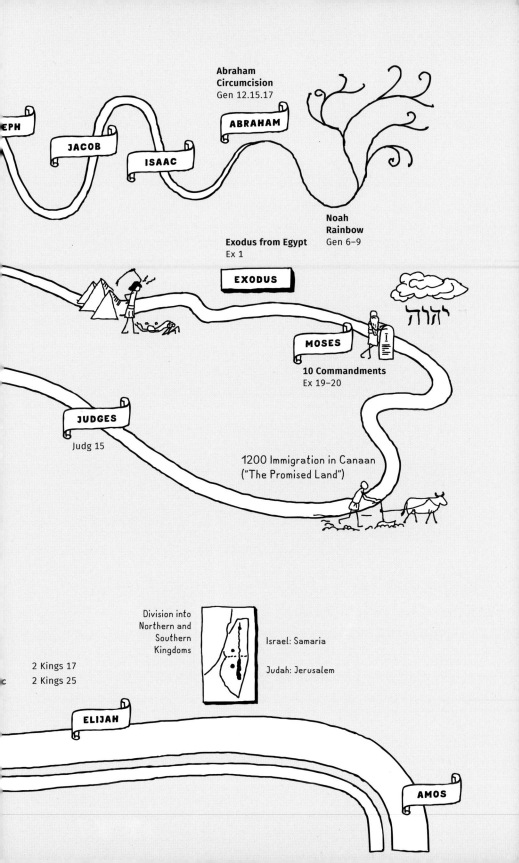

BIBLE

Youth Bible
of the Catholic Church

with a Preface by
Pope Francis

An introduction to the Bible
with selected biblical texts

YOUCAT
FOUNDATION

IGNATIUS PRESS   SAN FRANCISCO

These selections from the Bible were published originally in
German by the
Austrian Conference of Bishops

This book, including the selection of Bible passages, was prepared
in collaboration with young people by
Prof. Michael Langer, Regensburg (coordination)
Prof. Georg Fischer, S.J., Innsbruck (Old Testament)
Prof. Dominik Markl, S.J., Rome (Old Testament)
Prof. Thomas Söding, Bochum (New Testament)

Editor-in-chief: Bernhard Meuser
Editorial coordinator: Clara Steber

Original German edition © 2015 YOUCAT Foundation, a non-profit
corporation, Augsburg.
The English edition is based on the 3rd revised and expanded
German edition (2016):
Scripture passages from The Holy Bible, Revised Standard Version,
Second Catholic Edition;
non-scriptural texts translated by Michael J. Miller.

Nihil Obstat: Reverend Patrick Hartin, Ph.D.
Imprimatur: + Most Reverend Salvatore J. Cordileone, Archbishop
of San Francisco
March 20, 2017

Cover design, layout, illustrations, and typographic design:
Alexander von Lengerke, Cologne

The publishing house YOUCAT Verlag is wholly owned by the
non-profit YOUCAT Foundation gGmbH, with headquarters in König-
stein im Taunus. The YOUCAT trademark is used with permission of
the publisher of YOUCAT, the Austrian Conference of Bishops.
YOUCAT© is an internationally protected trademark and logo.
Registered under GM: 011929131.

Content

Preface Pope Francis 6

How to Read the Bible 8

The Bible Is Unique 11

The Old Testament 14

The New Testament 248

Preface

Dear Young Friends,

If you were to see my Bible, you might not think that it was particularly impressive. "What?! That is the Pope's Bible! Such an old, worn-out book!" You could give me a new one as a present, one that cost a thousand dollars, but I would not want it. I love my old Bible, which has been with me for half of my life. It witnessed my priestly jubilee and has been sprinkled by my tears. It is my most precious treasure. My life depends on it. I would not give it up for anything in the world.

I like very much the Youth Bible that you have just opened. It is so colorful, so rich in testimonies—the testimonies of saints, the testimonies of young people—and it entices the reader to start reading it from the beginning and not to stop until the last page. And then …? And then you put it away. It disappears on the bookshelf, back in the third row. It collects dust. Your children sell it someday at the flea market. No, that must not happen!

I want to tell you something: Today there are more persecuted Christians than in the early centuries of the Church. And why are they being persecuted? They are being persecuted because they wear a cross and give witness to Jesus. They are condemned because they own a Bible. The Bible is therefore an extremely dangerous book. So dangerous that in many countries its owners are treated as though they were storing hand grenades in the wardrobe. It was a non-Christian, Mahatma Gandhi, who once said: "You Christians look after a document containing enough dynamite to blow all civilization to pieces, turn the world upside down, and bring peace to a battle-torn planet. But you treat it as though it were nothing more than a piece of literature."

What, then, are you holding in your hands? A piece of literature? A few nice old stories? Then we would have to say to the many Christians who let themselves be locked up and tortured for the Bible: "How stupid you were; after all, it is only a piece of literature!" No, through the Word of God, light came into the world. And it will never again be extinguished. In *Evangelii gaudium* (175), I said: "We do not blindly seek God, or wait for him to speak to us first, for 'God has already spoken, and there is nothing further that we need to know, which has not been revealed to us.' Let us receive the sublime treasure of the revealed word."

So you are holding something divine in your hands: a book that is like fire! A book through which God speaks. So keep in mind: the Bible is not something to be put on a bookshelf but, rather, to be kept on hand, so you can read from it often, every day, both alone and together. After all, you play sports together or go shopping together. Why not read the Bible together, two, three, or four of you at a time? Outdoors in nature, in the woods, on the beach, in the evening, by the light of a few candles.... You will have a powerful experience! Or are you afraid to make fools of yourselves in front of others with such a suggestion?

Read attentively. Do not remain on the surface, as with a comic book. Never just flip through the Word of God! Ask yourselves: "What does it say to my heart? Is God speaking to me through this passage? Is he touching me in the depths of my yearning? What must I do?" Only in that way can the Word of God display its power. Only then can our lives change and become great and beautiful.

I want to tell you how I read in my old Bible! Often I take it out and read a little in it, then I put it away and let the Lord look at me. I do not look at the Lord, but HE looks at me. Indeed, HE is there. I let him gaze at me. And I perceive—this is not just sentimentality—I perceive very deeply the things that the Lord says to me. Sometimes he does not speak. Then I feel nothing, only emptiness, emptiness, emptiness.... But I remain there patiently, and so I wait. I read and pray. I pray seated, because it hurts me to kneel down. Sometimes I even fall asleep while praying. But that makes no difference. I am like a son in his father's house, and that is the important thing.

Do you want to make me happy? Read the Bible.

Yours truly,

Franciscus

Pope Francis

How to Read the Bible

The Bible is written for you. By reading it, you can let God's Word become a part of your life. The following ten rules for reading can help that to happen.

Read the Bible ...

... and pray.

The Bible is Sacred Scripture. Therefore it is good to pray, before reading, to ask God for his Holy Spirit and, after reading to thank him. How can you pray? Simply start with this short prayer: "Your word is a lamp to my feet and a light to my path" (Ps 119:105).

... and allow yourself to be surprised.

The Bible is a book full of surprises. Even though you have heard many of the stories already, give them a second chance. And yourself, too! The Bible shows you the all-surpassing breadth and greatness of God.

... and be glad.

The Bible is a great love story with a happy ending: death does not have a chance. Life wins. You find this Good News again and again in all passages of the Bible. Look for it—and be glad when you have found it.

... and do it regularly.

The Bible is the book for your life. If you read from it every day, even if it is only a verse or a short paragraph, you may realize that the book does you a lot of good. Just as with sports and music: you make progress only by constant practice—and once you have acquired a few skills, it is really fun.

... and do not read too much.

The Bible is a gigantic treasure. You receive it as a free gift. You do not have to unpack it all right away. Read only as much as you can take in well. If something speaks to you in a special way, write it out for yourself and learn it by heart.

... and allow yourself time.

The Bible is an ancient book that is eternally young and new. It is not supposed to be read from start to finish without a break. It is good to pause as you read. That way you can reflect and become aware of what God wants to say to you. And once you have read through the Bible, just start over again from the beginning. You will again discover completely different aspects of it.

❞ Reading the Bible should be a form of prayer. The Bible should be read in God's presence and as the unfolding of His mind. It is not just a book, but God's love letter to you.

PETER KREEFT (b. 1937), American philosopher and spiritual writer

... and be patient.

The Bible is a book full of profound wisdom, but occasionally it seems puzzling and strange. You will not understand everything right away. Then, too, much can be understood only in terms of the time or the historical situation. Have patience with yourself and with the Bible. When something is not clear to you, then look at the context or at other passages that deal with the same subject. Your Bible gives you a lot of support.

... and read it with others.

You can share with others what the Bible says to you. And what others have discovered in the Bible can help you to understand it better. If you speak with others about the Bible, make sure that God's Word remains central and does not get talked to death. The Bible is never a weapon to use against others; it is a bridge for peacemakers.

... and open your heart.

The Bible is a matter of the heart. Someone who reads the Bible cannot leave it at that. God opens his heart. His Word continues to be written in your life, and you can celebrate it in the liturgy. You are being invited to read the Bible with an open heart.

... and go on your way.

The Bible is the compass for your life. It shows you how things ought to be. You yourself walk the path of your life. But you do not travel it alone. Think of the disciples on the road to Emmaus (Lk 24:13–35). At first they did not recognize Jesus, who accompanied them in their grief. But then they asked themselves: "Did not our hearts burn within us while he talked to us on the road, while he opened to us the Scriptures?" (Lk 24:32).

The Bible
is unique.

The Bible is unique. It is the most widely circulated book in the world. No other book has been translated into as many different languages. No other book in human history has had a greater influence. For all Christians, the Bible is Sacred Scripture.

The Bible is world literature. It contains wonderful stories. Many biblical writings are of great poetical beauty, for example the Book of Job and a whole series of psalms from the Old Testament or the great hymn of love (1 Cor 13) and the Revelation of John from the New Testament. Often the Bible is disturbing. It is critical. Many times it strikes contemporary readers as odd. It may take years to understand a particular passage from Sacred Scripture. But it is worthwhile to keep trying. For all Christians, it is the charter of the faith.

And more than that: the Bible is the "Word of God". It expresses it with human words and in human language. But it is a revelation. It was written because men listened to God's Word and wrote it down in their own words. It was handed down, because others believed that those people did not just invent something but really had a message from God to convey.

The Bible is meant to move people. It ought to motivate readers to a life of striving for good. This life should combine love for God and love for one's neighbors. That is why we cannot just read

the Bible and leave it at that. Praying is part of it, helping others, reflecting on the faith—and in all this there is the joy that God exists, who gives us life.

B Hear, O Israel: The Lord our God is one Lord; and you shall love the Lord your God with all your heart, and with all your soul, and with all your might. And these words which I command you this day shall be upon your heart; and you shall teach them diligently to your children, and shall talk of them when you sit in your house, and when you walk by the way, and when you lie down, and when you rise.

Deut 6:4–7

The Old Testament

HISTORICAL BOOKS

TORAH

GENESIS · EXODUS · LEVITICUS · NUMBERS · DEUTERONOMY

JOSHUA · JUDGES · RUTH · SAMUEL · KINGS · CHRONICLES · EZRA/NEHEMIAH · TOBIT · JUDITH · ESTHER · MACCABEES

Christians call the first part of the Bible the Old Testament. It is a collection of writings that give testimony to the creation and God's care for mankind before Jesus came to earth. "Old" does not mean "out-of-date" but, rather, "original".

This "Old Testament" was Jesus' Bible. He knew, loved, and often quoted it. It is the basis for his proclamation. Jesus sees his task as transforming the message of the Old Testament in a new spirit.

Many hands contributed to the writing of the Old Testament. Only about a few books do we know precisely who wrote them, when, and where. Most of the books of the Old Testament were composed in Hebrew—some in Aramaic and Greek. Most of the books originated in Israel, though several were perhaps composed outside the Holy Land. It took centuries for the Old Testament to come into being and to take its present form.

For those of the Jewish faith, the Old Testament is all of Sacred Scripture. The New Testament is not recognized in Judaism. According to the Jewish tradition, the Hebrew Bible has three parts: the Torah, the Prophets, and the Writings. The Torah is made up of the first five books of the Bible (Genesis through Deuteronomy). The Prophets include both many historical books (from Joshua on) and the so-called "literary prophets", among which are numbered Isaiah, Jeremiah, and Ezekiel, as well as the twelve minor prophets (from Hosea to Malachi). All the remaining works written in Hebrew, for example the Psalms, belong to the category of "Writings".

The Christian Old Testament is subdivided somewhat differently. After the "Pentateuch" (Genesis through Deuteronomy) come the Historical Books, then the Wisdom Books, and finally the Prophets, including the Book of Daniel. Moreover, in the Old Testament of the Eastern Christian and Roman Catholic tradition, there are more books than in the Jewish Bible: Sirach, Baruch, Tobit, Judith, 1 and 2 Maccabees, Wisdom.

 Your word is a lamp to my feet and a light to my path.
Ps 119:105

 The New Testament lies hidden in the Old, and the Old is made plain in the New.
AUGUSTINE OF HIPPO (A.D. 354-430), Father of the Church and philosopher

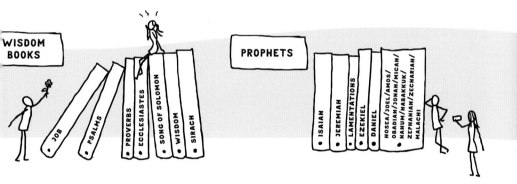

The writings of the Old Testament reflect a revolution in the history of the religions of mankind. While almost all the peoples in the vicinity of Israel feared a multitude of gods, in Israel the belief developed that there is only one God of the entire universe. Judaism, Christianity, and Islam are characterized by this fundamental conviction.

The Old Testament contains passages that speak very often about violence. Sometimes God himself appears to be violent. This shows, on the one hand, that the Bible looks realistically at the difficult and painful sides of reality, too. God has to do with all aspects of life. On the other hand, we must read these passages very carefully and try to understand them. Biblical passages must never be misunderstood as justification for destructive violence. God is above all the God of life (Gen 1–2) and of mercy (Ex 34:6–7).

The Torah

The Hebrew word "Torah" means "teaching, instruction". It designates the first five books of the Bible (Genesis, Exodus, Leviticus, Numbers, Deuteronomy). Just as the Gospels in the New Testament loom large and important by their position at the beginning, so too does the Torah in the Old Testament. It is the foundation on which all the rest is based. In the Christian Old Testament, the Torah is called "the Law" because it contains the revelation of the Law to Moses on Mount Sinai, with the Decalogue (the Ten Commandments) at the head.

The Torah follows a long narrative arc from the creation (Genesis 1–2) to the death of Moses (Deuteronomy 34). The so-called Primordial History (Gen 1–11) is followed by stories about the patriarchs and matriarchs (starting with Abraham and Sarah, Gen 12–50), the liberation of the People Israel from Egypt (Exodus 1–15), the long encounter with God on Mount Sinai (from Exodus 19 to Numbers 10), the further travels through the desert toward the Promised Land (from Numbers 10 on), and the lengthy speeches of Moses on the last day of his life, as found in the Book of Deuteronomy.

The Torah thus presents a sort of "pre-history", before the life of the People Israel begins in the Holy Land. With the creation, the deliverance from Egypt, and the gift of the Law, it lays the foundation for belief in God, both in Judaism and in Christianity.

THE BOOK OF

Genesis

The first book of the Bible begins with God's creation of the world and of man (Gen 1–2); it ends with the stay of the large family of Jacob (who also bears the name Israel) in Egypt. Later the Israelites will set out from there again, which is described in the following Book of Exodus.

In the first eleven chapters, the Book of Genesis is centered on creation and all mankind. In this way it shows that the biblical God is all-embracing and present throughout the universe. With Noah he makes a covenant with all living things (Gen 9) and gives them his blessing. The sign of this covenant is the rainbow (Gen 9:12–17).

In the following chapters, Genesis shows how God enters into relationships with men: he accompanies them and promises them his strong assistance. Abraham, Isaac, and Jacob with their wives and children experience this in a special way, even in difficult situations. Famine, personal failure, conflicts, living in foreign lands—in all their needs, God proves to be their helper.

TWO CREATION ACCOUNTS (GEN 1–2)

The first two chapters of the Bible are a testimony of faith: God is the Creator of the world and of mankind. The Bible does not intend to explain scientifically how the universe came into being. Rather, it intends to show the sense, the deeper meaning, and important connections of the cosmos. It does this on the basis of the world view at that time, but in a unique way: everything that exists has its origin in God and owes its life to him. The first account depicts an ordered, good creation. It has two goals: the creation of man (Gen 1:26f.) and God's rest on the seventh day (Gen 2:1–3), the Sabbath.

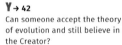

Great are You, O Lord, and greatly to be praised. And man, this tiny part of Your creation, desires to praise You. You move us to delight in praising You; for You have formed us for Yourself, and our hearts are restless till they find rest in You.

AUGUSTINE

The first account (Gen 1:1–2:4a)

1 ¹ In the beginning God created the heavens and the earth. ² The earth was without form and void, and darkness was upon the face of the deep; and the Spirit of God was moving over the face of the waters.

³ And God said, "Let there be light"; and there was light.⁴And God saw that the light was good; and God separated the light from the darkness.⁵ God called the light Day, and the darkness he called Night. And there was evening and there was morning, one day.

⁶ And God said, "Let there be a firmament in the midst of the waters, and let it separate the waters from the waters."⁷And God made the firmament and separated the waters which were under the fir-

mament from the waters which were above the firmament. And it was so. ⁸ And God called the firmament Heaven. And there was evening and there was morning, a second day.

⁹ And God said, "Let the waters under the heavens be gathered together into one place, and let the dry land appear." And it was so.¹⁰ God called the dry land Earth, and the waters that were gathered together he called Seas. And God saw that it was good.¹¹ And God said, "Let the earth put forth vegetation, plants yielding seed, and fruit trees bearing fruit in which is their seed, each according to its kind, upon the earth." And it was so.¹² The earth brought forth vegetation, plants yielding seed according to their own kinds, and trees bearing fruit in which is their seed, each according to its kind. And God saw that it was good.¹³ And there was evening and there was morning, a third day.

¹⁴ And God said, "Let there be lights in the firmament of the heavens to separate the day from the night; and let them be for signs and for seasons and for days and years, ¹⁵ and let them be lights in the firmament of the heavens to give light upon the earth." And it was so. ¹⁶ And God made the two great lights, the greater light to rule the day, and the lesser light to rule the night; he made the stars also. ¹⁷ And God set them in the firmament of the heavens to give light upon the earth, ¹⁸ to rule over the day and over the night, and to separate the light from the darkness. And God saw that it was good. ¹⁹ And there was evening and there was morning, a fourth day.

Y → 42
Can someone accept the theory of evolution and still believe in the Creator?

²⁰ And God said, "Let the waters bring forth swarms of living creatures, and let birds fly above the earth across the firmament of the heavens." ²¹ So God created the great sea monsters and every living creature that moves, with which the waters swarm, according to their kinds, and every winged bird according to its kind. And God saw that it was good. ²² And God blessed them, saying, "Be fruitful and multiply and fill the waters in the seas, and let birds multiply on the earth." ²³ And there was evening and there was morning, a fifth day.

²⁴ And God said, "Let the earth bring forth living creatures according to their kinds: cattle and creeping things and beasts of the earth according to their kinds." And it was so. ²⁵ And God made the beasts of the earth according to their kinds and the cattle according to their kinds, and everything that creeps upon the ground according to its kind. And God saw that it was good. ²⁶ Then God said, "Let us make man in our image, after our likeness; and let them have dominion over the fish of the sea, and over the birds of the air, and over the cattle, and over all the earth, and over every creeping thing that creeps upon the earth." ²⁷ So God created man in his own image, in the image of God he created him; male and female he created

▶ "Image" and "likeness" (v. 26) show that man is very close to God. In every human being God is visible. This constitutes our dignity and our worth.

▶ Our life is characterized by the fact that we are equal as human beings yet different as man and woman. It challenges us to have great respect for every person and to accept our diversity (↗ Is 49:15).

them.²⁸ And God blessed them, and God said to them, "Be fruitful and multiply, and fill the earth and subdue it; and have dominion over the fish of the sea and over the birds of the air and over every living thing that moves upon the earth." ²⁹ And God said, "Behold, I have given you every plant yielding seed which is upon the face of all the earth, and every tree with seed in its fruit; you shall have them for food. ³⁰ And to every beast of the earth, and to every bird of the air, and to everything that creeps on the earth, everything that has the breath of life, I have given every green plant for food." And it was so. ³¹ And God saw everything that he had made, and behold, it was very good. And there was evening and there was morning, a sixth day.

▶ "Subdue" and "have dominion" (v. 28) do not mean to rule recklessly but, rather, to manage responsibly, as God's representatives.

▶ God's assessment (v. 31) shows how positively the Bible views creation: It is ordered and well done.

The second creation account completes the first. It is focused on man: he is created as the work of God's hands and has the breath of God within him (Gen 2:7). He has a relation to the ground from which he is taken (Gen 2:7). But this is the man who will be driven out of Paradise.

2 Thus the heavens and the earth were finished, and all the host of them.² And on the seventh day God finished his work which he had done, and he rested on the seventh day from all his work

Y → 43
Is the world a product of chance?

which he had done.[3] So God blessed the seventh day and hallowed it, because on it God rested from all his work which he had done in creation. [4a] These are the generations of the heavens and the earth when they were created.

The second account (Gen 2:4b–25)
[4b] In the day that the LORD God made the earth and the heavens, [5] when no plant of the field was yet in the earth and no herb of the field had yet sprung up—for the LORD God had not caused it to rain upon the earth, and there was no man to till the ground; [6] but a mist went up from the earth and watered the whole face of the ground— [7] then the LORD God formed man of dust from the ground, and breathed into his nostrils the breath of life; and man became a living soul. [8] And the LORD God planted a garden in Eden, in the east; and there he put the man whom he had formed.... [15] The Lord GOD took the man and put him in the garden of Eden to till it and keep it. [16] And the LORD God commanded the man, saying, "You may freely eat of every tree of the garden; [17] but of the tree of the knowledge of good and evil you shall not eat, for in the day that you eat of it you shall die."

▶ "Eden", the Hebrew word "delight", stands for Paradise. It is above all to be understood as a symbolic place of original happiness. Verses 9–14 go on to describe, among other things, its rivers.

💡 "Woman" and "man" (vv. 23) are a play on words in Hebrew as well (*ishshah* and *ish*). This shows that they belong together—they are created for each other.

▶ These verses were often misunderstood and interpreted as the subordination of the woman. Yet "helper" (v. 18, 20) in Hebrew also means rescuer and protector, and "fit for him" expresses the equality of the two sexes. The man confirms this in his first statement in v. 23. The image of making from a "rib" shows that man and woman originally belong together.

[18] Then the LORD God said, "It is not good that the man should be alone; I will make him a helper fit for him." [19] So out of the ground the LORD God formed every beast of the field and every bird of the air, and brought them to the man to see what he would call them; and whatever the man called every living creature, that was its name. [20] The man gave names to all cattle, and to the birds of the air, and to every beast of the field; but for the man there was not found a helper fit for him. [21] So the LORD God caused a deep sleep to fall upon the man, and while he slept took one of his ribs and closed up its place with flesh; [22] and the rib which the LORD God had taken from the man he made into a woman and brought her to the man.[23] Then the man said,
"This at last is bone of my bones
and flesh of my flesh;
she shall be called Woman,
because she was taken out of Man."
[24] Therefore a man leaves his father and his mother and clings to his wife, and they become one flesh. [25] And the man and his wife were both naked, and were not ashamed.

"" Jesus Christ goes Adam's route, but in reverse. In contrast to Adam he is really "like God". ... Because he does not go the route of power but that of love, he can descend into the depths of Adam's lie, into the depths of death, and there raise up truth and life. →

The end of paradise (Gen 3:1–24)
3 Now the serpent was more subtle than any other wild creature that the LORD God had made. He said to the woman, "Did God

say, 'You shall not eat of any tree of the garden'?" ² And the woman said to the serpent, "We may eat of the fruit of the trees of the garden; ³ but God said, 'You shall not eat of the fruit of the tree which is in the midst of the garden, neither shall you touch it, lest you die.' " ⁴ But the serpent said to the woman, "You will not die. ⁵ For God knows that when you eat of it your eyes will be opened, and you will be like God, knowing good and evil." ⁶ So when the woman saw that the tree was good for food, and that it was a delight to the eyes, and that the tree was to be desired to make one wise, she took of its fruit and ate; and she also gave some to her husband, and he ate. ⁷ Then the eyes of both were opened, and they knew that they were naked; and they sewed fig leaves together and made themselves aprons.

⁸ And they heard the sound of the LORD God walking in the garden in the cool of the day, and the man and his wife hid themselves from the presence of the LORD God among the trees of the garden. ⁹ But the LORD God called to the man, and said to him, "Where are you?" ¹⁰ And he said, "I heard the sound of you in the garden, and I

Thus Christ is the new Adam, with whom mankind begins anew. The Son, who is by nature relationship and relatedness, reestablishes relationships. His arms, spread out on the cross, are an open invitation to relationship, which is continually offered to us.

JOSEPH RATZINGER (POPE BENEDICT XVI), *In the Beginning...: A Catholic Understanding of the Story of Creation and the Fall*, 1986.

Nature-lovers hug trees. Christians, too, have a "tree of life" that they are supposed to embrace: the Cross. On the tree of the Cross, life started over again.

was afraid, because I was naked; and I hid myself." ¹¹ He said, "Who told you that you were naked? Have you eaten of the tree of which I commanded you not to eat?" ¹² The man said, "The woman whom you gave to be with me, she gave me fruit of the tree, and I ate." ¹³ Then the LORD God said to the woman, "What is this that you have done?" The woman said, "The serpent beguiled me, and I ate." ¹⁴ The LORD God said to the serpent,

"Because you have done this, cursed are you above all cattle, and above all wild animals; upon your belly you shall go, and dust you shall eat all the days of your life. ¹⁵ I will put enmity between you and the woman, and between your seed and her seed; he shall bruise your head, and you shall bruise his heel."

¹⁶ To the woman he said, "I will greatly multiply your pain in childbearing; in pain you shall bring forth children, yet your desire shall be for your husband, and he shall rule over you."

¹⁷And to Adam he said, "Because you have listened to the voice of your wife, and have eaten of the tree of which I commanded you, 'You shall not eat of it,' cursed is the ground because of you; in toil you shall eat of it all the days of your life; ¹⁸ thorns and thistles it shall bring forth to you; and you shall eat the plants of the field. ¹⁹ In the sweat of your face you shall eat bread till you return to the ground, for out of it you were taken; you are dust, and to dust you shall return."

▶ The tree of the knowledge of good and evil, in the figurative sense, stands for an attitude whereby people try to decide on their own, without God, what is right and what is wrong.

But where sin increased, grace abounded all the more, so that, as sin reigned in death, grace also might reign through righteousness to eternal life through Jesus Christ our Lord.

Rom 5:20b–21

O God, to turn away from you is to fall. To turn toward you is to stand up. To remain in you is to have steady support.

AUGUSTINE

▶ God cares about people even when they have acted against his will. He clothes Adam and Eve so that they no longer need to be ashamed.

²⁰ The man called his wife's name Eve, because she was the mother of all living. ²¹ And the LORD God made for Adam and for his wife garments of skins, and clothed them.

²² Then the Lord GOD said, "Behold, the man has become like one of us, knowing good and evil; and now, lest he put forth his hand and take also of the tree of life, and eat, and live for ever"— ²³ therefore the Lord GOD sent him forth from the garden of Eden, to till the ground from which he was taken. ²⁴ He drove out the man; and at the east of the garden of Eden he placed the cherubim, and a flaming sword which turned every way, to guard the way to the tree of life.

In the following chapter 4, evil spreads: Cain kills his brother, Abel. In Gen 6, violence on earth has increased so much that God wants to put an end to the escalating evil and sends a flood to cover the face of the earth. Only the just man Noah (Gen 6:9) with his family and representatives of all living creatures are saved from it. After the flood is over, God blesses mankind, gives them new precepts, and offers them a lasting relationship.

> **"** The Hebrew term for a rainbow is the same term used for a hunting or military bow. Some see the rainbow as a sign of peace. They picture God hanging up his bow in the sky, retiring it from service and signifying that he has ended his battle with the sinful world.
>
> **SCOTT HAHN** and **CURTIS MITCH**, *Ignatius Catholic Study Bible*

God's covenant with all living things (Gen 9:8–16)

▶ "Covenant" is a key theme in the Bible (↗ Gen 15; Ex 19; Jer 31). Jesus said, "This is my blood of the covenant, which is poured out for many" (Mk 14:24). It signifies that God enters into a lasting union with mankind and thus shows his desire for a relationship with us.

▶ By the "bow", the biblical author means the rainbow. The sunlight that breaks through after heavy rain refracts the colors of the spectrum into the atmosphere, suggesting the union of heaven and earth and, symbolically, their reconciliation.

9 ⁸ Then God said to Noah and to his sons with him, ⁹ "Behold, I establish my covenant with you and your descendants after you, ¹⁰ and with every living creature that is with you, the birds, the cattle, and every beast of the earth with you, as many as came out of the ark. ¹¹ I establish my covenant with you, that never again shall all flesh be cut off by the waters of a flood, and never again shall there be a flood to destroy the earth." ¹² And God said, "This is the sign of the covenant which I make between me and you and every living creature that is with you, for all future generations: ¹³ I set my bow in the cloud, and it shall be a sign of the covenant between me and the earth. ¹⁴ When I bring clouds over the earth and the bow is seen in the clouds, ¹⁵ I will remember my covenant which is between me and you and every living creature of all flesh; and the waters shall never again become a flood to destroy all flesh. ¹⁶ When the bow is in the clouds, I will look upon it and remember the everlasting covenant between God and every living creature of all flesh that is upon the earth."

Gen 10 depicts all mankind as a big family of seventy nations, all of which are descended from Noah's three sons. This chapter tries thereby to express their intrinsic connectedness, their fullness and equal dignity, but at the same time their multiplicity and diversity as well. The very next story tells of the destruction of this harmony.

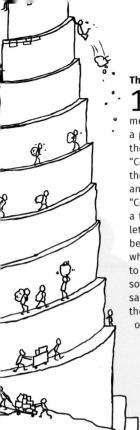

The Tower of Babel (Gen 11:1–9)

11 ¹ Now the whole earth had one language and few words. ² And as men migrated from the east, they found a plain in the land of Shinar and settled there. ³ And they said to one another, "Come, let us make bricks, and burn them thoroughly." And they had brick for stone, and bitumen for mortar. ⁴ Then they said, "Come, let us build ourselves a city, and a tower with its top in the heavens, and let us make a name for ourselves, lest we be scattered abroad upon the face of the whole earth." ⁵ And the LORD came down to see the city and the tower, which the sons of men had built. ⁶ And the LORD said, "Behold, they are one people, and they have all one language; and this is only the beginning of what they will do; and nothing that they propose to do will now be impossible for them. ⁷ Come, let us go down, and there confuse their language, that they may not understand one another's speech." ⁸ So the LORD scattered them abroad from there over the face of all the earth, and they left off building the city. ⁹ Therefore its name was called Ba'bel, because there the LORD confused the language of all the earth; and from there the LORD scattered them abroad over the face of all the earth.

💡 Esperanto combats the consequences of the Tower of Babel: this artificial language, which is easy to learn, was created in the nineteenth century to facilitate international understanding. What Esperanto did not achieve, Pentecost accomplished.

▶ Human megalomania and ambition ("making a name") rarely bring a community together. More often they are the source of conflicts and division. The following verses depict this connection as divine intervention.

▶ The narrative ironically connects "Babel" with the verb "to confuse" (in Hebrew, *balal*); on the other hand, in the language of the Babylonians, "Babel" means "Gate of God".

💡 In Babylon there really was a tall tower: It was a many-tiered temple tower constructed on a base measuring approximately 91 x 91 meters [300 x 300 feet]. Nothing remains of the tower except the foundations.

STORIES ABOUT ABRAHAM AND SARAH (GEN 12–25)

With Abram, who is later named Abraham, God begins a history of special elections. Abraham means "Father of a Multitude" (Gen 17:4–5). This name is a program. Election is not only a privilege, but also a promise, which is coupled with requirements. To leave one's homeland means to give up much security, but it also offers the opportunity to mature and to sense more and more of the breadth that characterizes God himself.

God's call to Abram (Gen 12:1–5)

12 ¹ Now the LORD said to Abram, "Go from your country and your kindred and your father's house to the land that I will show you. ² And I will make of you a great nation, and I will bless you, and make your name great, so that you will be a blessing. ³ I will bless those who bless you, and him who curses you I will curse; and by you all the families of the earth shall bless themselves."

▶ "Blessing" is the great gift and the task given to Abraham. His intensive relationship with God is supposed to and does become fruitful for others. So God prepares for him a "name", a reputation, in contrast to human ambition (cf. Gen 11:4).

> **99** God often grants in a single moment what he has long refused to give. For the Lord pours out graces where he finds empty vessels.
>
> **THOMAS À KEMPIS** (ca. 1380–1471), mystic

⁴ So Abram went, as the LORD had told him; and Lot went with him. Abram was seventy-five years old when he departed from Haran. ⁵ And Abram took Sar'ai his wife, and Lot his brother's son, and all their possessions which they had gathered, and the persons that they had gotten in Haran; and they set forth to go to the land of Canaan.

In Gen 13, Abraham generously allows his nephew to choose in which part of the land he will dwell. One chapter later, he courageously frees him and many others who have been kidnapped from the hands of their abductor. In this way he already fulfills God's promise to him in Gen 12 that he would be a blessing.

Believing in God (Gen 15:1–6)

▶ Having no child and a promise of countless offspring is like dividing by zero to get infinity. This is how the Bible explains what it means to "believe" in God, to hold fast to him.

15 ¹ After these things the word of the LORD came to Abram in a vision, "Fear not, Abram, I am your shield; your reward shall be very great." ² But Abram said, "O Lord GOD, what will you give me, for I continue childless, and the heir of my house is Elie'zer of Damascus?" ³ And Abram said, "Behold, you have given me no offspring; and a slave born in my house will be my heir." ⁴ And behold,

> **📖** Now faith is the assurance of things hoped for, the conviction of things not seen.
>
> Heb 11:1

the word of the LORD came to him, "This man shall not be your heir; your own son shall be your heir." ⁵ And he brought him outside and said, "Look toward heaven, and number the stars, if you are able to number them." Then he said to him, "So shall your descendants be." ⁶ And he believed the LORD; and he reckoned it to him as righteousness.

Ten and twenty-five years pass before God's promise begins to be fulfilled and Abraham's sons Ishmael and Isaac are born. Right before that Abraham proves to be the perfect host.

💡 At the age of ninety-nine (Gen 17:24), at the hour for the siesta, when it is hottest, Abraham rushes out to greet travelers and to invite them to a meal. Thus he embodies the ideal of hospitality. In the Semitic system of values, hospitality still ranks high today; it goes without saying that you should treat a guest regally, even when you yourself do not have much.

Extraordinary hospitality (Gen 18:1–15)

18 ¹ And the LORD appeared to him by the Oaks of Mamre, as he sat at the door of his tent in the heat of the day. ² He lifted up his eyes and looked, and behold, three men stood in front of him. When he saw them, he ran from the tent door to meet them, and bowed himself to the earth, ³ and said, "My lord, if I have found favor in your sight, do not pass by your servant. ⁴ Let a little water be brought, and wash your feet, and rest yourselves under the tree, ⁵ while I fetch a morsel of bread, that you may refresh yourselves, and after that you may pass on—since you have come to your servant." So they said, "Do as you have said." ⁶ And Abraham hastened into the tent to Sarah, and said, "Make ready quickly three measures of fine meal, knead it, and make cakes." ⁷ And Abraham ran to the herd, and took a calf, tender and good, and gave it to the servant, who hastened to prepare it. ⁸ Then he took curds, and milk, and the calf which he had prepared, and set it before them; and he stood by them under the tree while they ate.

⁹ They said to him, "Where is Sarah your wife?" And he said, "She is in the tent." ¹⁰ The LORD said, "I will surely return to you in the spring, and Sarah your wife shall have a son." And Sarah was listening at the tent door behind him. ¹¹ Now Abraham and Sarah were old, advanced in age; it had ceased to be with Sarah after the manner of women. ¹² So Sarah laughed to herself, saying, "After I have grown old, and my husband is old, shall I have pleasure?" ¹³ The LORD said to Abraham, "Why did Sarah laugh, and say, 'Shall I indeed bear a child, now that I am old?' ¹⁴ Is anything too hard for the LORD? At the appointed time I will return to you, in the spring, and Sarah shall have a son." ¹⁵ But Sarah denied, saying,
"I did not laugh"; for she was afraid.
He said, "No, but you did laugh."

▶ In Gen 17:15, God changed the name "Sarai" to "Sarah" (= princess). A *seah* in Hebrew (18:6) is a dry measure. It is the equivalent of at least 7 but probably a good 12 liters [6 to 11 quarts]. The quantity noted amounts to 20 or even 35 kilograms [44–77 pounds] of dough—a superabundant meal.

▶ The Hebrew word for "laugh" (*zahaq*) is the root of the child's name, Isaac (in Hebrew, Jizhaq, Gen 21:2–3).

▶ The rhetorical question indicates that God can do everything (↗ also Jer 31:17, 27). Nothing is "impossible" or too marvelous for him.

Abraham's intercession on behalf of Sodom and Gomorrah right after his hospitality (Gen 18:22–33) obtains from God the promise to spare both cities if there are ten righteous souls in them; but not even that small number can be found, and only Lot's family is saved in Gen 19. Two chapters later, Isaac is born, and Sarah insists on sending away his older half-brother, Ishmael (the child of a different mother), whereupon he is in danger of dying in the desert. In parallel to this, the life of her son, too, is threatened in Gen 22.

An extreme test (Gen 22:1–14)

22 ¹ After these things God tested Abraham, and said to him, "Abraham!" And he said, "Here am I." ² He said, "Take your son, your only-begotten son Isaac, whom you love, and go to the land of Mori'ah, and offer him there as a burnt offering upon one of the mountains of which I shall tell you." ³ So Abraham rose early in the morning, saddled his donkey, and took two of his young men with him, and his son Isaac; and he cut the wood for the burnt offering, and arose and went to the place of which God had told him. ⁴ On the third day Abraham lifted up his eyes and saw the place afar off. ⁵ Then Abraham said to his young men, "Stay here with the donkey; I and the lad will go yonder and worship, and come again to you." ⁶ And Abraham took the wood of the burnt offering, and laid it on Isaac his son; and he took in his hand the fire and the knife. So they went both of them together. ⁷ And Isaac said to his father Abraham, "My father!" And he said, "Here am I, my son." He said, "Behold, the fire and the wood; but where is the lamb for a burnt offering?"

▶ This introductory sentence, "God tested Abraham", gives the decisive key to understanding the story. God does not want the death of Isaac; rather, he is putting the boy's father to the test.

” God tests everyone, one with wealth, another with poverty. A rich man is tested in whether he extends an arm of support to those who need it; a poor man in whether he bears all his sufferings without discontent and with obedience.
TALMUD

▶ The expression "to fear God" (v. 12) occurs here for the first time. It shows that Abraham has passed the test. It means "respect, reverence" that puts God in first place in everything, even ahead of close personal relationships. Jesus says something similar in Mt 10:37: "He who loves father or mother more than me is not worthy of me..."

▶ The term *"Yahweh-yireh"* (v. 14) mentions the biblical name of God and actually means "YHWH sees." This explanation complements the idea that God can be experienced in a special way on mountains (↗ Ex 19).

⁸Abraham said, "God will provide himself the lamb for a burnt offering, my son." So they went both of them together.

⁹When they came to the place of which God had told him, Abraham built an altar there, and laid the wood in order, and bound Isaac his son, and laid him on the altar, upon the wood. ¹⁰Then Abraham put forth his hand, and took the knife to slay his son. ¹¹But the angel of the Lᴏʀᴅ called to him from heaven, and said, "Abraham, Abraham!" And he said, "Here am I." ¹²He said, "Do not lay your hand on the lad or do anything to him; for now I know that you fear God, seeing you have not withheld your son, your only-begotten son, from me." ¹³And Abraham lifted up his eyes and looked, and behold, behind him was a ram, caught in a thicket by his horns; and Abraham went and took the ram, and offered it up as a burnt offering instead of his son. ¹⁴So Abraham called the name of that place The Lᴏʀᴅ will provide; as it is said to this day, "On the mount of the Lᴏʀᴅ it shall be provided."

After the test, God's messenger gives Abraham further promises of blessings (Gen 22:15–19). Shortly afterward, Sarah (Gen 23) and Abraham (Gen 25) die. Their son Isaac marries Rebecca; after twenty years she bears twins: Esau, the ancestor of the Edomites, and Jacob, who receives the name Israel. Even in their mother's womb, they fight for pre-eminence. Finally, in Gen 27, when Jacob fools his blind father and tricks Esau out of the blessing that he expected as the firstborn, the family breaks apart, and Jacob has to flee. Along the way God appears to him at night.

STORIES ABOUT JACOB AND HIS FAMILY (GEN 25–50)

The dream in Bethel (Gen 28:10–22)

28 ¹⁰Jacob left Be'er-she'ba, and went toward Haran. ¹¹And he came to a certain place, and stayed there that night, because the sun had set. Taking one of the stones of the place, he put it under his head and lay down in that place to sleep. ¹²And he dreamed that there was a ladder set up on the earth, and the top of it reached to heaven; and behold, the angels of God were ascending and descending on it! ¹³And behold, the Lᴏʀᴅ stood above it and said, "I am the Lᴏʀᴅ, the God of Abraham your father and the God of Isaac; the land on which you lie I will give to you and to your descendants; ¹⁴and your descendants shall be like the dust of the earth, and you shall spread abroad to the west and to the east and to the north and to the south; and by you and your descendants shall all the families of the earth bless themselves. ¹⁵Behold, I am with you and will keep you wherever you go, and will bring you back to this land; for I will not leave you until I have done that of which I have spoken to you." ¹⁶Then Jacob awoke from his sleep and said, "Surely the Lᴏʀᴅ is in this place; and I did not know it." ¹⁷And he was afraid, and said, "How awesome is this place! This is none other than the house of God, and this is the gate of heaven."

▶ What men in Babel tried in their megalomania to do ("let us build ourselves ... a tower with its top in the heavens", Gen 11:4) but did not accomplish has long since been a work of God: a ladder joins heaven and earth, and his messengers ("angels") maintain two-way contact.

▶ These promises are extraordinary, especially because God gives them to someone who has failed seriously. He does not abandon even a guilty man and promises him great things.

▶ Beth-El means "House of God" (see v. 17) and was a famous pilgrimage shrine north of Jerusalem.

¹⁸So Jacob rose early in the morning, and he took the stone which he had put under his head and set it up for a pillar and poured oil on the top of it. ¹⁹He called the name of that place Bethel; but

the name of the city was Luz at the first. ²⁰ Then Jacob made a vow, saying, "If God will be with me, and will keep me in this way that I go, and will give me bread to eat and clothing to wear, ²¹ so that I come again to my father's house in peace, then the LORD shall be my God, ²² and this stone, which I have set up for a pillar, shall be God's house; and of all that you give me I will give the tenth to you."

God stands by his promise. So while staying in a foreign land with his deceitful uncle and father-in-law, Laban, Jacob is able to found his own family and to acquire a large flock. After more than twenty years he sets out for his homeland, and again God meets him in the night along the way.

Nocturnal wrestling (Gen 32:22–32)

32 ²² The same night he arose and took his two wives, his two maids, and his eleven children, and crossed the ford of the Jabbok. ²³ He took them and sent them across the stream, and likewise everything that he had. ²⁴ And Jacob was left alone; and a man wrestled with him until the breaking of the day. ²⁵ When the man saw that he did not prevail against Jacob, he touched the hollow

▶ The identity of the "man" (v. 25) remains uncertain; yet it is possible to assume that God himself was Jacob's adversary.

of his thigh; and Jacob's thigh was put out of joint as he wrestled with him. ²⁶ Then he said, "Let me go, for the day is breaking." But Jacob said, "I will not let you go, unless you bless me." ²⁷ And he said to him, "What is your name?" And he said, "Jacob." ²⁸ Then he said, "Your name shall no more be called Jacob, but Israel, for you have striven with God and with men, and have prevailed." ²⁹ Then Jacob asked him, "Tell me, I pray, your name." But he said, "Why is it that you ask my name?" And there he blessed him. ³⁰ So Jacob called the name of the place Peni'el, saying, "For I have seen God face to face, and yet my life is preserved." ³¹ The sun rose upon him as he passed Penu'el, limping because of his thigh. ³² Therefore to this day the Israelites do not eat the sinew of the hip which is upon the hollow of the thigh, because he touched the hollow of Jacob's thigh on the sinew of the hip.

▶ "Israel" (v. 29) means "God strives" and is Jacob's new name of blessing. He does not have to use every means to gain acceptance himself, but God himself stands at his side and supports him.

▶ Peni'el (v. 31) means "the face of God", a reminder of Jacob's encounter by night.

▶ This story explains a custom in Israel: again by this prohibition against eating a particular muscle of animals, the people should remember their forefather Jacob and also his encounter with God.

His nocturnal wrestling changes Jacob, and not only his name. Immediately afterward, he is able to run to meet Esau submissively, and the latter very emotionally accepts him again as a brother (Gen 33:1–10). This long process leading to reconciliation is repeated in the next generation among Jacob's sons.

The so-called story of Joseph (Gen 37–50) is one of the most suspenseful narratives in the Bible. It is about how a family breaks up and comes together again. Gen 37 shows how complicated relationships in the family are. Everyone makes mistakes. Joseph is young and gifted, but also naïve and arrogant. His brothers react aggressively and cruelly. It takes many years for them to mature through difficult experiences and to realize their mistakes. The story shows how important it is to become more mature in one's own family and to resolve old conflicts if possible. It is worthwhile reading the whole story in an unabridged Bible!

Getting rid of a difficult brother (Gen 37)

▶ "Brought an ill report of them" (v. 2); the original Hebrew actually says "wrongfully accused them".

A troubling story! At first I was unsure with which of the characters I could best identify, which was emotionally confusing for me. I have trouble with dreams of dominance or wielding power

37 [2] Joseph, being seventeen years old, was shepherding the flock with his brothers; he was a lad with the sons of Bilhah and Zilpah, his father's wives; and Joseph brought an ill report of them to their father. [3] Now Israel loved Joseph more than any other of his children, because he was the son of his old age; and he made him a long robe with sleeves. [4] But when his brothers saw that their father loved him more than all his brothers, they hated him, and could not speak peaceably to him.

[5] Now Joseph had a dream, and when he told it to his brothers they only hated him the more. [6] He said to them, "Hear this dream which I have dreamed: [7] behold, we were binding sheaves in the field, and behold, my sheaf arose and stood upright; and behold, your sheaves gathered round it, and bowed down to my sheaf." [8] His brothers said

→ I am jealous when someone seems to be called to a higher position than mine. Jealousy gnaws away at me, and I lose sight of my own God-given abilities.

NICK

❞ Trifles light as air / are to the jealous confirmations strong / as proofs of Holy Writ.
WILLIAM SHAKESPEARE (1564–1616), English playwright

▶ Literally Joseph says in v. 13 "See me!" Actually he does not do his father's bidding, and therefore Jacob must tell him again (v. 14).

to him, "Are you indeed to reign over us? Or are you indeed to have dominion over us?" So they hated him yet more for his dreams and for his words. [9] Then he dreamed another dream, and told it to his brothers, and said, "Behold, I have dreamed another dream; and behold, the sun, the moon, and eleven stars were bowing down to me." [10] But when he told it to his father and to his brothers, his father rebuked him, and said to him, "What is this dream that you have dreamed? Shall I and your mother and your brothers indeed come to bow ourselves to the ground before you?" [11] And his brothers were jealous of him, but his father kept the saying in mind.

[12] Now his brothers went to pasture their father's flock near She'chem. [13] And Israel said to Joseph, "Are not your brothers pasturing the flock at She'chem? Come, I will send you to them." And he said to him, "Here I am." [14] So he said to him, "Go now, see if it is well with your brothers, and with the flock; and bring me word again." So he sent him from the valley of He'bron, and he came to She'chem. [15] And a man found him wandering in the fields; and the man asked him, "What are you seeking?" [16] "I am seeking my brothers," he said, "tell me, I beg you, where they are pasturing the flock." [17] And the man said, "They have gone away, for I heard them say, 'Let us go to Do'than.' " So Joseph went after his brothers, and found them at Do'than. [18] They saw him afar off, and before he came near to them they conspired against him to kill him. [19] They said to one another, "Here

comes this dreamer. ²⁰ Come now, let us kill him and throw him into one of the pits; then we shall say that a wild beast has devoured him, and we shall see what will become of his dreams." ²¹ But when Reuben heard it, he delivered him out of their hands, saying, "Let us not take his life."... ²³ So when Joseph came to his brothers, they stripped him of his robe, the long robe with sleeves that he wore; ²⁴ and they took him and cast him into a pit. The pit was empty, there was no water in it.

²⁵ Then they sat down to eat; and looking up they saw a caravan of Ish'maelites coming from Gilead, with their camels bearing gum, balm, and myrrh, on their way to carry it down to Egypt. ²⁶ Then Judah said to his brothers, "What profit is it if we slay our brother and conceal his blood? ²⁷ Come, let us sell him to the Ish'maelites, and let not our hand be upon him, for he is our brother, our own flesh." And his brothers heeded him. ²⁸ Then Mid'ianite traders passed by; and they drew Joseph up and lifted him out of the pit, and sold him to the Ish'maelites for twenty shekels of silver; and they took Joseph to Egypt....

³¹ Then they took Joseph's robe, and killed a goat, and dipped the robe in the blood; ³² and they sent the long robe with sleeves and

> The brethren of Joseph were free to toss him into a well, but from that point on Joseph was in God's hands. Rightly did he say to his brethren: "You intended it for evil, but God for good."
> **FULTON J. SHEEN** (1895–1979), Bishop of Rochester, N.Y.; Titular Archbishop of Neoportus

▶ What Judah says seems to be "reasonable" (v. 27), but his plan is also inhumane. Because Joseph is "our brother", he is "merely" sold, and at the same time the brothers can profit from it.

brought it to their father, and said, "This we have found; see now whether it is your son's robe or not." ³³ And he recognized it, and said, "It is my son's robe; a wild beast has devoured him; Joseph is without doubt torn to pieces." ³⁴ Then Jacob tore his garments, and put sackcloth upon his loins, and mourned for his son many days. ³⁵ All his sons and all his daughters rose up to comfort him; but he refused to be comforted, and said, "No, I shall go down to Sheol to my son, mourning." Thus his father wept for him....

💡 American English has the expression "sold down the river (as a slave)". The brothers get twenty pieces of silver for Joseph (v. 28). Judas receives thirty pieces of silver for betraying his Lord with a kiss.

Contrary to the brothers' expectations, Joseph becomes a powerful political figure in Egypt. When they have to buy grain in Egypt because of a famine, they stand in his presence several times without recognizing him. Finally it appears as though their youngest brother, Benjamin, has stolen a valuable goblet. But now Joseph's brothers and especially Judah no longer behave as they did in Gen 37.

Judah's plea (Gen 44:18–34)

44 ¹⁸ Then Judah went up to him and said, "O my lord , let your servant, I beg you, speak a word in my lord's ears, and let not your anger burn against your servant; for you are like Pharoah himself. ¹⁹ My lord asked his servants, saying, 'Have you a father, or a brother?' ²⁰ And we said to my lord , 'We have a father, an old man, and a young brother, the child of his old age; and his brother is dead, and he alone is left of his mother's children; and his father

▶ The brothers had assumed that Joseph would not survive his fate as a slave in Egypt. Moreover, Judah mentions here the fact that his father, Jacob, is especially fond of the youngest brother, Benjamin.

▶ Joseph's demand had forced his father, Jacob, to give up his unhealthy, biased, preferential "love" for his youngest son.

B Honor your father and your mother, that your days may be long in the land which the LORD your God gives you.

Ex 20:12

▶ Judah frankly addresses the inequality in the family. "My wife" means Rachel, whereas Jacob's other wife, Leah, Judah's mother, does not count as much. The fact that Judah can repeat his father's words exactly shows that he has a sympathetic understanding of his father's thinking, although he was slighted by him many times.

loves him.' ²¹ Then you said to your servants, 'Bring him down to me, that I may set my eyes upon him.' ²² We said to my lord , 'The lad cannot leave his father, for if he should leave his father, his father would die.' ²³ Then you said to your servants, 'Unless your youngest brother comes down with you, you shall see my face no more.' ²⁴ When we went back to your servant my father we told him the words of my lord. ²⁵ And when our father said, 'Go again, buy us a little food,' ²⁶ we said, 'We cannot go down. If our youngest brother goes with us, then we will go down; for we cannot see the man's face unless our youngest brother is with us.' ²⁷ Then your servant my father said to us, 'You know that my wife bore me two sons; ²⁸ one left me, and I said, Surely he has been torn to pieces; and I have never seen him since. ²⁹ If you take this one also from me, and harm befalls him, you will bring down my gray hairs in sorrow to Sheol.' ³⁰ Now therefore, when I come to your servant my father, and the lad is not with us, then, as his life is bound up in the lad's life, ³¹ when he sees that the lad is not with us, he will die; and your servants will bring down the gray hairs of your servant our father with sorrow to Sheol. ³² For your servant became surety for the lad to my

▶ Thus Judah is ready to take upon himself the same fate that he imposed on Joseph in Gen 37.

B "Can a woman forget her sucking child, that she should have no compassion on the son of her womb? Even these may forget, yet I will not forget you."

Is 49:15

▶ The brothers' alarm is understandable. Their brother, whom they considered dead and against whom they had committed a serious crime, suddenly stands in front of them.

▶ Joseph's maturity is evident in this interpretation of his cruel lot. Regarding past →

father, saying, 'If I do not bring him back to you, then I shall bear the blame in the sight of my father all my life.' ³³ Now therefore, let your servant, I beg you, remain instead of the lad as a slave to my lord; and let the lad go back with his brothers. ³⁴ For how can I go back to my father if the lad is not with me? I fear to see the evil that would come upon my father."

Joseph's answer (Gen 45:1–15)

45 ¹ Then Joseph could not control himself before all those who stood by him; and he cried, "Make every one go out from me." So no one stayed with him when Joseph made himself known to his brothers. ² And he wept aloud, so that the Egyptians heard it, and the household of Pharaoh heard it. ³ And Joseph said to his brothers, "I am Joseph; is my father still alive?" But his brothers could not answer him, for they were dismayed at his presence.

⁴ So Joseph said to his brothers, "Come near to me, I beg you." And they came near. And he said, "I am your brother, Joseph, whom you sold into Egypt. ⁵ And now do not be distressed, or angry with yourselves, because you sold me here; for God sent me before you to preserve life. ⁶ For the famine has been in the land these two years; and there are yet five years in which there will be neither plowing nor harvest. ⁷ And God sent me before you to preserve for you a remnant on earth, and to keep alive for you many survivors.

8 So it was not you who sent me here, but God; and he has made me a father to Pharoah, and lord of all his house and ruler over all the land of Egypt. 9 Make haste and go up to my father and say to him, 'Thus says your son Joseph, God has made me lord of all Egypt; come down to me, do not tarry; 10 you shall dwell in the land of Go'shen, and you shall be near me, you and your children and your children's children, and your flocks, your herds, and all that you have; 11 and there I will provide for you, for there are yet five years of famine to come; lest you and your household, and all that you have, come to poverty.' 12 And now your eyes see, and the eyes of my brother Benjamin see, that it is my mouth that speaks to you. 13 You must tell my father of all my splendor in Egypt, and of all that you have seen. Make haste and bring my father down here." 14 Then he fell upon his brother Benjamin's neck and wept; and Benjamin wept upon his neck. 15 And he kissed all his brothers and wept upon them; and after that his brothers talked with him.

▶ injustice and dire need from God's perspective as a way to salvation (see also vv. 7–8) is the key to a new understanding and a conciliatory encounter.

▶ Joseph's love and desire for reconciliation are demonstrated by his concern for the well-being of his father and the survival of his extended family.

▶ Benjamin, too, was a child of Rachel and thus Joseph's only full brother. .

Subsequently Jacob, in fact, moves with his extended family to Egypt and meets his son Joseph again (Gen 46). Jacob comprehensively and sincerely blesses his offspring before his death (Gen 48–49).

Joseph's consolation and encouragement for his brothers (Gen 50:15–21)

50 15 When Joseph's brothers saw that their father was dead, they said, "It may be that Joseph will hate us and pay us back for all the evil which we did to him." 16 So they sent a message to Joseph, saying, "Your father gave this command before he died, 17 'Say to Joseph, Forgive, I beg you, the transgression of your brothers and their sin, because they did evil to you.' And now, we pray you, forgive the transgression of the servants of the God of your father." Joseph wept when they spoke to him. 18 His brothers also came and fell down before him, and said, "Behold, we are your servants." 19 But Joseph said to them, "Fear not, for am I in the place of God? 20 As for you, you meant evil against me; but God meant it for good, to bring it about that many people should be kept alive, as they are today. 21 So do not fear; I will provide for you and your little ones." Thus he reassured them and comforted them.

▶ Like Judah in Gen 44, now the other brothers, too, are ready to accept the same fate that they imposed on Joseph in Gen 37.

▶ Joseph's reply here is a key to Genesis and to God's activity in general. When men plan and carry out evil, God can turn it around and, in the long term, bring good out of it.

Joseph dies in Egypt and is buried there. But he promises his family a return to Israel. That is their home.

THE BOOK OF

Exodus

The Book of Exodus (a Greek term that means "road out" or
"emigration"), tells the story of the founding of the people of
God, Israel. The family of Jacob (= Israel) becomes a great nation
in Egypt. A new Pharaoh oppresses the Israelites because they
are foreigners (Ex 1). Moses is rescued as a baby (Ex 2). God
commissions him to free Israel from Egypt (Ex 3–4). He succeeds
only after a long power struggle with the Pharaoh (Ex 5–11). The
People of Israel celebrates the first Passover (Ex 12). God leads
Israel through the Red Sea, in which the Egyptian army perishes
(Ex 14). Israel celebrates the victory (Ex 15) but soon must under-
go its first trials in the desert (Ex 16–18). When the people arrive
at Mount Sinai, God makes a covenant with them (Ex 19–24). As
he does so, he appears in a storm and an earthquake (Ex 19)
and promulgates the Ten Commandments (Ex 20) and other laws
(Ex 21–31). While Moses is on the mountain, the people make
a golden calf for themselves and reverence it (Ex 32). After a
difficult crisis, God allows himself to be reconciled by Moses, and
he forgives the people (Ex 34) so they can build the tabernacle in
which God intends to accompany Israel (Ex 35–40).

In the Book of Exodus, God reveals his Name (Ex 3); he proclaims
the Ten Commandments (Ex 20); he declares his infinite willingness to forgive sin (Ex 34). The Book of Exodus shows how concerned God is about us. He would like to encounter us spiritually,
yet he also offers practical support for political freedom and
social justice. He has grown fond of us.

The dictator and the strong women (Ex 1:8–22)

1 [8] Now there arose a new king over Egypt, who did not know Joseph. [9] And he said to his people, "Behold, the sons of Israel are too many and too mighty for us. [10] Come, let us deal shrewdly with them, lest they multiply, and, if war befall us, they join our enemies and fight against us and escape from the land." [11] Therefore they set taskmasters over them to afflict them with heavy burdens; and they built for Pharaoh store-cities, Pithom and Ra-am'ses. [12] But the more they were oppressed, the more they multiplied and the more they spread abroad. And the Egyptians were in dread of the sons of Israel. [13] So they made the sons of Israel serve with rigor, [14] and made their lives bitter with hard service, in mortar and brick, and in all kinds of work in the field; in all their work they made them serve with rigor.

[15] Then the king of Egypt said to the Hebrew midwives, one of whom was named Shiphrah and the other Puah, [16] "When you serve as midwife to the Hebrew women, and see them upon the birth-stool, if it is a son, you shall kill him; but if it is a daughter, she shall live." [17] But the midwives feared God, and did not do as the king of

💡 Starting in 1619, ten million Africans were deported as slaves to America. They were forced, often with a whip, to work on tobacco and cotton plantations. They gave expression to their suffering and their hope for freedom in songs based on biblical stories and images. One of the most well-known of these spirituals is "When Israel Was in Egypt's Land", which is about the liberation recounted in the Book of Exodus.

▶ The Pharaoh is not named—but two ordinary women are (v. 15). In the Bible, people like you and me become heroes when they respect God.

Egypt commanded them, but let the male children live. [18] So the king of Egypt called the midwives, and said to them, "Why have you done this, and let the male children live?" [19] The midwives said to Pharaoh, "Because the Hebrew women are not like the Egyptian women; for they are vigorous and are delivered before the midwife comes to them." [20] So God dealt well with the midwives; and the people multiplied and grew very strong. [21] And because the midwives feared God he gave them families. [22] Then Pharaoh commanded all his people, "Every son that is born to the Hebrews you shall cast into the Nile, but you shall let every daughter live."

▶ Sacred Scripture is full of parallels. Here Moses is rescued as a little child, so as to become a liberator later on. Similarly, Matthew relates that Jesus as a baby was rescued from the massacre of the children (↗ Mt 2:13). Like Moses, Jesus himself becomes a savior, too.

The rescue of Moses from the Nile and his flight into the desert (Ex 2:1–25)

2 [1] Now a man from the house of Levi went and took to wife a daughter of Levi. [2] The woman conceived and bore a son; and when she saw that he was a goodly child, she hid him three months. [3] And when she could hide him no longer she took for him a basket made of bulrushes, and daubed it with bitumen and pitch; and she put the child in it and placed it among the reeds at the river's brink. [4] And his sister stood at a distance, to know what would be done to him. [5] Now the daughter of Pharaoh came down to bathe at the river, and her maidens walked beside the river; she saw the basket among the reeds and sent her maid to fetch it. [6] When she opened it

▶ The Levites (descendants of Levi) later become priests, like Moses' brother Aaron.

▶ Moses does not have an easy childhood. He grows up in the home of stepparents. His birth parents live in another world. Probably he feels torn. But, meanwhile, he learns a lot that he will need later to perform his duties.

she saw the child; and behold, the baby was crying. She took pity on him and said, "This is one of the Hebrews' children." ⁷ Then his sister said to Pharaoh's daughter, "Shall I go and call you a nurse from the Hebrew women to nurse the child for you?" ⁸ And Pharaoh's daughter said to her, "Go." So the girl went and called the child's mother. ⁹ And Pharaoh's daughter said to her, "Take this child away, and nurse him for me, and I will give you your wages." So the woman took the child and nursed him. ¹⁰ And the child grew, and she brought him to Pharaoh's daughter, and he became her son; and she named him Moses, for she said, "Because I drew him out of the water."

¹¹ One day, when Moses had grown up, he went out to his people and looked on their burdens; and he saw an Egyptian beating a Hebrew, one of his people. ¹² He looked this way and that, and seeing no one he killed the Egyptian and hid him in the sand. ¹³ When he went out the next day, behold, two Hebrews were struggling together; and he said to the man that did the wrong, "Why do you strike your fellow?" ¹⁴ He answered, "Who made you a prince and a judge over us? Do you mean to kill me as you killed the Egyptian?" Then Moses was afraid, and thought, "Surely the thing is known." ¹⁵ When Pharaoh heard of it, he sought to kill Moses.

💡 Really clever, how the women here secretly work together and outwit Pharaoh and his murderous plans. One of God's crafty devices: Moses' sister rescues her brother.

▶ Just as Moses is saved from the Nile, so too Israel is saved from the Red Sea (Ex 14). Similarly Jesus, too, is rescued as a child (↗ Mt 2:13–15) and becomes a savior himself.

But Moses fled from Pharaoh, and stayed in the land of Mid'ian; and he sat down by a well. ¹⁶ Now the priest of Mid'ian had seven daughters; and they came and drew water, and filled the troughs to water their father's flock. ¹⁷ The shepherds came and drove them away; but Moses stood up and helped them, and watered their flock. ¹⁸ When they came to their father Reu'el, he said, "How is it that you have come so soon today?" ¹⁹ They said, "An Egyptian delivered us out of the hand of the shepherds, and even drew water for us and watered the flock." ²⁰ He said to his daughters, "And where is he? Why have you left the man? Call him, that he may eat bread." ²¹ And Moses was content to dwell with the man, and he gave Moses his daughter Zippo'rah. ²² She bore a son, and he called his name Gershom; for he said, "I have been a sojourner in a foreign land."

²³ In the course of those many days the king of Egypt died. And the sons of Israel groaned under their bondage, and cried out for help, and their cry under bondage came up to God. ²⁴ And God heard their groaning, and God remembered his covenant with Abraham, with Isaac, and with Jacob. ²⁵ And God saw the sons of Israel, and God knew their condition.

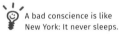

😊 A bad conscience is like New York: It never sleeps.

▶ Although Moses himself is a foreigner, he fights with the native machos and stands up for the young women. That makes a good impression on them....

😊 Man meets woman at the well: in the Old Testament, it always has the deeper meaning of "bridegroom meets bride". So it is with Isaac and Rebecca (↗ Gen 24), Jacob and Rachel (Gen 29), Moses and Zipporah (↗ Ex 2).

▶ God hears and sees: God is especially attentive to people for whom things are not going well.

As young people, we experience moments when we sense that we must take responsibility, undertake a difficult task. Then anxieties often arise and many questions: Can I do this? What will the others think about me? Do I have to do all this alone? A decisive question is: What task is God giving me with this new challenge? Moses' call is the most detailed account of a vocation in the Bible. It spells out important questions and God's answers.

Moses' call—a great responsibility (Gen 3–4)

3 [1] Now Moses was keeping the flock of his father-in-law, Jethro, the priest of Mid'ian; and he led his flock to the west side of the wilderness, and came to Horeb, the mountain of God. [2] And the angel of the LORD appeared to him in a flame of fire out of the midst of a bush; and he looked, and behold, the bush was burning, yet it was not consumed. [3] And Moses said, "I will turn aside and see this great sight, why the bush is not burnt." [4] When the LORD saw that he turned aside to see, God called to him out of the bush, "Moses, Moses!" And he said, "Here am I." [5] Then he said, "Do not come near; put off your shoes from your feet, for the place on which you are standing is holy ground." [6] And he said, "I am the God of your father,

> [God] came down from glory to speak with Moses. Moses had known about God. In fact, he was living with a priest who worshiped God. But at the burning bush, God introduced himself to Moses by name. And the whole relationship changed.
>
> **STEVE RAY** Catholic convert, author, and speaker

▶ Removing one's shoes means to sense the ground under one's feet, to be humble, a servant. It expresses reverence for what is holy.

▶ In many passages of the OT, it seems dangerous to come close to God. Not because God might harm man, but rather because the presence of the Holy One is so different and intense that too close an encounter is overwhelming.

👤 I am created to do something or to be something for which no one else is created; I have a place in God's counsels, in God's world, which no one else has; whether I be rich or poor, ... God knows me and calls me by my name.

JOHN HENRY NEWMAN (1801–1890), English cardinal

the God of Abraham, the God of Isaac, and the God of Jacob." And Moses hid his face, for he was afraid to look at God.

[7] Then the LORD said, "I have seen the affliction of my people who are in Egypt, and have heard their cry because of their taskmasters; I know their sufferings, [8] and I have come down to deliver them out of the hand of the Egyptians, and to bring them up out of that land to a good and broad land, a land flowing with milk and honey, to the place of the Canaanites, the Hittites, the Am'orites, the Per'izzites, the Hi'vites, and the Jeb'usites. [9] And now, behold, the cry of the sons of Israel has come to me, and I have seen the oppression with which the Egyptians oppress them. [10] Come, I will send you to Pharaoh that you may bring forth my people, the sons of Israel, out of Egypt." [11] But Moses said to God, "Who am I that I should go to Pharaoh, and bring the sons of Israel out of Egypt?" [12] He said, "But I will be with you; and this shall be the sign for you, that I have sent you: when you have brought forth the people out of Egypt, you shall serve God upon this mountain."

[13] Then Moses said to God, "If I come to the sons of Israel and say to them, 'The God of your fathers has sent me to you,' and they ask me, 'What is his name?' what shall I say to them?" [14] God said to Moses, "I AM WHO I AM." And he said, "Say this to the sons of Israel, 'I AM

has sent me to you.'" ¹⁵ God also said to Moses, "Say this to the sons of Israel, 'The LORD, the God of your fathers, the God of Abraham, the God of Isaac, and the God of Jacob, has sent me to you': this is my name for ever, and thus I am to be remembered throughout all generations....

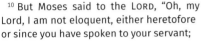 God's name is mysterious. Another possible translation: "I will be who(ever) I will be." God does not allow himself to be pinned down with mere words.

4 ¹ Then Moses answered, "But behold, they will not believe me or listen to my voice, for they will say, 'The LORD did not appear to you.'" ² The LORD said to him, "What is that in your hand?" He said, "A rod." ³ And he said, "Cast it on the ground." So he cast it on the ground, and it became a serpent; and Moses fled from it. ⁴ But the LORD said to Moses, "Put out your hand, and take it by the tail"—so he put out his hand and caught it, and it became a rod in his hand— ⁵ "that they may believe that the LORD, the God of their fathers, the God of Abraham, the God of Isaac, and the God of Jacob, has appeared to you."...

¹⁰ But Moses said to the LORD, "Oh, my Lord, I am not eloquent, either heretofore or since you have spoken to your servant;

▶ Jews do not pronounce the name "Yahweh", as a sign of respect for this holy Name. Instead, they say *Adonai* (Lord) or *HaShem* (the Name). The four Hebrew letters with which the Name of God is written, יהוה (YHWH), are also referred to by the Greek word *tetragrammaton* (= four-lettered).

but I am slow of speech and of tongue." ¹¹ Then the LORD said to him, "Who has made man's mouth? Who makes him mute, or deaf, or seeing, or blind? Is it not I, the LORD ? ¹² Now therefore go, and I will be with your mouth and teach you what you shall speak." ¹³ But he said, "Oh, my Lord, send, I pray, some other person." ¹⁴ Then the anger of the LORD was kindled against Moses and he said, "Is there not Aaron, your brother, the Levite? I know that he can speak well; and behold, he is coming out to meet you, and when he sees you he will be glad in his heart. ¹⁵ And you shall speak to him and put the words in his mouth; and I will be with your mouth and with his mouth, and will teach you what you shall do. ¹⁶ He shall speak for you to the people; and he shall be a mouth for you, and you shall be to him as God. ¹⁷ And you shall take in your hand this rod, with which you shall do the signs."

¹⁸ Moses went back to Jethro his father-in-law and said to him, "Let me go back, I beg, to my kinsmen in Egypt and see whether they are still alive." And Jethro said to Moses, "Go in peace."

▶ Moses thinks that he cannot speak well, or at least he uses this as an excuse. Nevertheless he becomes the greatest orator in the Old Testament (especially in the Book of Deuteronomy).

▶ God's "anger" here is not destructive. God is depicted as having strong feelings because this is an important matter, and he does everything possible to win Moses over.

 Aaron, God's media spokesman!

When Moses and Aaron present God's plan to their people, the first reaction is agreement (end of Ex 4). Yet Pharaoh stonewalls and oppresses the Israelites even more harshly (Ex 5). God encourages Moses once again (Ex 6). Then comes the big battle for deliverance with the so-called ten Egyptian plagues, which in the Bible are called signs and wonders (Ex 7–12). Through swarms of frogs, gnats, grasshoppers, and other misfortunes, God tries to force Pharaoh to let Israel go. Yet Pharaoh stubbornly refuses. Finally God resorts to the most severe expedient—all the oldest sons of the Egyptians must die (Ex 12).

The feast of the lamb and the deliverance (Ex 12–15)

12 [21] Then Moses called all the elders of Israel, and said to them, "Select lambs for yourselves according to your families, and kill the Passover lamb. [22] Take a bunch of hyssop and dip it in the blood which is in the basin, and touch the lintel and the two doorposts with the blood which is in the basin; and none of you shall go out of the door of his house until the morning. [23] For the LORD will pass through to slay the Egyptians; and when he sees the blood on the lintel and on the two doorposts, the LORD will pass over the door, and will not allow the destroyer to enter your houses to slay you. [24] You shall observe this rite as an ordinance for you and for your sons for ever. [25] And when you come to the land which the LORD will give you, as he has promised, you shall keep this service.

▶ To this day, the Passover, or Paschal Feast, is for Jews the great celebration of their deliverance. For Christians, it became the feast of Easter: Jesus was slain like a Passover lamb (↗ 1 Cor 5:7). By raising him to new life, God freed mankind from the power of death.

[26] And when your children say to you, 'What do you mean by this service?' [27] you shall say, 'It is the sacrifice of the LORD's Passover, for he passed over the houses of the sons of Israel in Egypt, when he slew the Egyptians but spared our houses.'" And the people bowed their heads and worshiped.

[28] Then the sons of Israel went and did so; as the LORD had commanded Moses and Aaron, so they did.

[29] At midnight the LORD struck all the first-born in the land of Egypt, from the first-born of Pharaoh who sat on his throne to the first-born of the captive who was in the dungeon, and all the first-born of the cattle. [30] And Pharaoh rose up in the night, he, and all his servants, and all the Egyptians; and there was a great cry in Egypt, for there was not a house where one was not dead. [31] And he summoned Moses and Aaron by night, and said, "Rise up, go forth from among my people, both you and the sons of Israel; and go, serve the LORD, as you have said. [32] Take your flocks and your herds, as you have said, and be gone; and bless me also!"

[33] And the Egyptians were urgent with the people, to send them out of the land in haste; for they said, "We are all dead men." [34] So the people took their dough before it was leavened, their kneading bowls being bound up in their mantles on their shoulders. [35] The sons of Israel had also done as Moses told them, for they had asked of the Egyptians jewelry of silver and of gold, and clothing....

" This is the night, when once you led our forebears, Israel's children, from slavery in Egypt and made them pass dry-shod through the Red Sea. This is the night that with a pillar of fire banished the darkness of sin. This is the night that even now, throughout the world, sets Christian believers apart from worldly vices and from the gloom of sin, leading them to grace and joining them to his holy ones. This is the night when Christ broke the prison bars of death and rose victorious from the underworld.

From the "Exsultet", a hymn at the Easter Vigil that praises God in the salvation history of his People Israel.

We hear the following story of deliverance as one of the readings at the Easter Vigil. The Egyptian military was one of the largest armed forces in the ancient world. The story intends to encourage all refugees: God is greater than the strongest human army.

14 ⁵ When the king of Egypt was told that the people had fled, the mind of Pharaoh and his servants was changed toward the people, and they said, "What is this we have done, that we have let Israel go from serving us?" ⁶ So he made ready his chariot and took his army with him, ⁷ and took six hundred picked chariots and all the other chariots of Egypt with officers over all of them....

¹⁹ Then the angel of God who went before the host of Israel moved and went behind them; and the pillar of cloud moved from before them and stood behind them, ²⁰ coming between the host of Egypt and the host of Israel. And there was the cloud and the darkness; and the night passed without one coming near the other all night.

²¹ Then Moses stretched out his hand over the sea; and the LORD drove the sea back by a strong east wind all night, and made the sea dry land, and the waters were divided. ²² And the sons of Israel went into the midst of the sea on dry ground, the waters being a wall

▶ "Despoiled" would be better translated as "recovered their lost wages from. ..." The Israelites receive farewell gifts from the Egyptians. Relations between the two peoples are friendly; only the dictator and his armed forces are violent and hostile.

💡 Chariots were like the tanks and fighter jets of the ancient world.

to them on their right hand and on their left. ²³ The Egyptians pursued, and went in after them into the midst of the sea, all Pharaoh's horses, his chariots, and his horsemen. ²⁴ And in the morning watch the LORD in the pillar of fire and of cloud looked down upon the host of the Egyptians, and discomfited the host of the Egyptians, ²⁵ clogging their chariot wheels so that they drove heavily; and the Egyptians said, "Let us flee from before Israel; for the LORD fights for them against the Egyptians." ²⁶ Then the LORD said to Moses, "Stretch out your hand over the sea, that the water may come back upon the Egyptians, upon their chariots, and upon their horsemen." ²⁷ So Moses stretched forth his hand over the sea, and the sea returned to its usual flow when the morning appeared; and the Egyptians fled into it, and the LORD routed the Egyptians in the midst of the sea. ²⁸ The waters returned and covered the chariots and the horsemen and all the host of Pharaoh that had followed them into the sea; not so much as one of them remained. ²⁹ But the sons of Israel walked on dry ground through the sea, the waters being a wall to them on their right hand and on their left.

³⁰ Thus the LORD saved Israel that day from the hand of the Egyptians; and Israel saw the Egyptians dead upon the seashore. ³¹ And Israel saw the great work which the LORD did against the Egyptians,

In 1947, over 4,000 Jewish refugees traveled to Palestine on the ship *Exodus* from Europe. Many of the refugees were survivors of the Holocaust. In his novel *Exodus*, the author Leon Uris distills the dramatic events, in which many readers saw a reflection of the biblical deliverance of the people of God.

B Turn to me and be saved,
all the ends of the earth!
For I am God, and there is no
other.

Is 45:22

▶ "The Egyptians": in the
Hebrew text, literally "Egypt".
This is not only about men
but about the destruction of a
military power.

▶ The Song about the Red Sea
is the first "hymn" in the Bible.
This poem praises God for the
deliverance in the Exodus. It
emphasizes that God is unique
(v. 11) and for the first time
calls him "king" (v. 18). Against
this background, Jesus preaches about the "kingdom of God".

and the people feared the LORD; and they believed in the LORD and
in his servant Moses.

15 Then Moses and the sons of Israel sang this song to the LORD,
saying,
"I will sing to the Lord, for he has triumphed gloriously;
the horse and his rider he has thrown into the sea.
² The Lord is my strength and my song,
and he has become my salvation;
this is my God, and I will praise him,
my father's God, and I will exalt him.
³ The LORD is a man of war;
the LORD is his name.
⁴ "Pharaoh's chariots and his host he cast into the sea;
and his picked officers are sunk in the Red Sea.
⁵ The floods cover them;
they went down into the depths like a stone.
⁶ Your right hand, O LORD, glorious in power,
your right hand, O LORD, shatters the enemy.

⁷ In the greatness of your majesty you overthrow your
adversaries;
you send forth your fury, it consumes them like stubble.
⁸ At the blast of your nostrils the waters piled up,
the floods stood up in a heap;
the deeps congealed in the heart of the sea.
⁹ The enemy said, 'I will pursue, I will overtake,
I will divide the spoil, my desire shall have its fill of
them.
I will draw my sword, my hand shall destroy them.'
¹⁰ You blew with your wind, the sea covered them;
they sank as lead in the mighty waters.
¹¹ "Who is like you, O LORD, among the gods?
Who is like you, majestic in holiness,
terrible in glorious deeds, doing wonders?...
¹⁸ The LORD will reign for ever and ever."...
²⁰ Then Miriam, the prophetess, the sister of Aaron, took
a timbrel in her hand; and all the women went out after her with timbrels and dancing. ²¹ And Miriam sang to
them:
"Sing to the Lord, for he has triumphed gloriously;
the horse and his rider he has thrown into the sea."

The prophetess Miriam: a fearless woman.
With Moses and Aaron she leads the
procession of the people of God, singing
and dancing, a tambourine in her hand
and the praise of God, their deliverer from
oppression, on her lips.

The journey through the desert is an image for major challenges. The Israelites contend with hunger (Ex 16), thirst, and a hostile people (Ex 17). Often they want to go back to Egypt—slavery was, after all, more pleasant and safer than the desert. Ultimately, however, this is a great test of their trust.

Water from the rock (Ex 17)

17 ¹All the congregation of the sons of Israel moved on from the wilderness of Sin by stages, according to the commandment of the LORD, and camped at Reph'idim; but there was no water for the people to drink. ²Therefore the people found fault with Moses, and said, "Give us water to drink." And Moses said to them, "Why do you find fault with me? Why do you put the LORD to the test?" ³But the people thirsted there for water, and the people murmured against Moses, and said, "Why did you bring us up out of Egypt, to kill us and our children and our cattle with thirst?" ⁴So Moses cried to the LORD, "What shall I do with this people? They are almost ready to stone me." ⁵And the LORD said to Moses, "Pass on before the people, taking with you some of the elders of Israel; and take in your hand the rod with which you struck the Nile, and go. ⁶Behold, I will stand before you there on the rock at Horeb; and you shall strike the rock, and water shall come out of it, that the people may

After graduating from high school, I wanted to work as a schoolteacher. I was accepted into an elementary education program in my favorite city, and through student teaching it became clear to me that this was right for me. Yet during the course of my studies, many problems came up, and I wondered why they were making it so difficult for me. Did God have other plans for me? After a midwifery course, though, it became clear to me in prayer that God still had a teaching career in mind for me. From then on I stopped worrying. I have been working for three years now at my dream job.

MICHAELA

drink." And Moses did so, in the sight of the elders of Israel. ⁷And he called the name of the place Massah and Mer'ibah, because of the fault-finding of the sons of Israel, and because they put the LORD to the test by saying, "Is the LORD among us or not?"...

B Jesus said to her [the Samaritan woman], "Every one who drinks of this water will thirst again, but whoever drinks of the water that I shall give him will never thirst.

Jn 4:13–14a

Israel now arrives at Mount Sinai, a fascinating desert landscape with high mountain peaks of reddish-brown granite. This specific landscape is a fitting backdrop for the decisive phase in which Israel becomes God's special people and receives his commandments.

The Decalogue and the Covenant at the burning mountain (Ex 19–24)

19 ¹On the third new moon after the sons of Israel had gone forth out of the land of Egypt, on that day they came into the wilderness of Sinai. ²And when they set out from Reph'idim and came into the wilderness of Sinai, they encamped in the wilderness; and there Israel encamped before the mountain. ³And Moses went up to God, and the LORD called to him out of the mountain, saying, "Thus you shall say to the house of Jacob, and tell the sons of Israel: ⁴You have seen what I did to the Egyptians, and how I bore you on eagles' wings and brought you to myself. ⁵Now therefore, if you will obey my voice and keep my covenant, you shall be my own posses-sion among all peoples; for all the earth is mine, ⁶and you shall be

Y → 348–468
All of these questions are about the "Decalogue" (Ten Commandments).

▶ On eagle's wings: a vivid image for the way in which God defends his people and brings them like a fledgling to a safe nest on a mountain.

B He found him in a desert land, and in the howling waste of the wilderness; he encircled him, he cared for him, he kept him as the apple of his eye. Like an eagle that stirs up its nest, that flutters over its young, spreading out its wings, catching them, bearing them on its pinions, the LORD alone did lead him, and there was no foreign god with him.

Deut 32:10–12

▶ All the people agree in v. 8 and accept God's commandments (↗ Ex 24:3, 7). That is an early idea of democracy. The legal constitution of a nation is valid because the whole people consent to it. God's commandments are not validated by the people's consent. But, at the same time, the people as a whole agree to obey the commandments.

to me a kingdom of priests and a holy nation. These are the words which you shall speak to the children of Israel."

⁷ So Moses came and called the elders of the people, and set before them all these words which the LORD had commanded him. ⁸ And all the people answered together and said, "All that the LORD has spoken we will do." And Moses reported the words of the people to the LORD. ⁹ And the LORD said to Moses, "Behold, I am coming to you in a thick cloud, that the people may hear when I speak with you, and may also believe you for ever."

Then Moses told the words of the people to the LORD. ¹⁰ And the LORD said to Moses, "Go to the people and consecrate them today and tomorrow, and let them wash their garments, ¹¹ and be ready by the third day; for on the third day the LORD will come down upon Mount Sinai in the sight of all the people. ¹² And you shall set bounds for the people round about, saying, 'Take heed that you do not go up into the mountain or touch the border of it; whoever touches the mountain shall be put to death; ¹³ no hand shall touch him, but he shall be stoned or shot; whether beast or man, he shall not live.' When the trumpet sounds a long blast, they shall come up to the mountain." ¹⁴ So Moses went down from the mountain to the

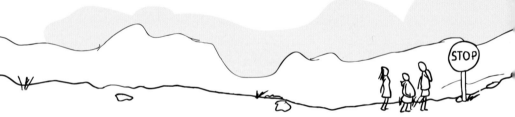

▶ Men and women should not sleep together before the great manifestation of God. Not because sex is bad, but because the relationship with God—like a human relationship of love—often requires undivided attention.

If we accept wholeheartedly the tables of the Ten Commandments, we will live fully by the law which God has placed in our hearts and we will have a share in the salvation which the Covenant made on Mount Sinai between God and his people revealed, and which the Son of God through his work of redemption offers to us.

POPE JOHN PAUL II, 2000

▶ God does not visit the iniquity of the fathers on innocent children, but only when the latter "hate me" (v. 5). Ex 34:7, too, should be understood with this proviso.

people, and consecrated the people; and they washed their garments. ¹⁵ And he said to the people, "Be ready by the third day; do not go near a woman."

¹⁶ On the morning of the third day there was thunder and lightning, and a thick cloud upon the mountain, and a very loud trumpet blast, so that all the people who were in the camp trembled. ¹⁷ Then Moses brought the people out of the camp to meet God; and they took their stand at the foot of the mountain. ¹⁸ And Mount Sinai was wrapped in smoke, because the LORD descended upon it in fire; and the smoke of it went up like the smoke of a kiln, and the whole mountain quaked greatly....

20 ¹ And God spoke all these words, saying, ² "I am the LORD your God, who brought you out of the land of Egypt, out of the house of bondage.

³ "You shall have no other gods before me.

⁴ You shall not make for yourself a graven image, or any likeness of anything that is in heaven above, or that is in the earth beneath, or that is in the water under the earth; ⁵ you shall not bow down to them or serve them; for I the LORD your God am a jealous God, visiting the iniquity of the fathers upon the children to the third and the fourth generation of those who hate me, ⁶ but showing mercy

to thousands of those who love me and keep my commandments.
⁷ "You shall not take the name of the LORD your God in vain; for the LORD will not hold him guiltless who takes his name in vain.

⁸ "Remember the sabbath day, to keep it holy. ⁹ Six days you shall labor, and do all your work; ¹⁰ but the seventh day is a sabbath to the LORD your God; in it you shall not do any work, you, or your son, or your daughter, your manservant, or your maidservant, or your cattle, or the sojourner who is within your gates; ¹¹ for in six days the LORD made heaven and earth, the sea, and all that is in them, and rested the seventh day; therefore the LORD blessed the sabbath day and hallowed it.

¹² "Honor your father and your mother, that your days may be long in the land which the LORD your God gives you.

▶ "Jealous" here means "passionate": God is thoroughly committed to this relationship. He cares when injustice occurs, and with everlasting fidelity he intervenes on behalf of all who strive for justice.

¹³ "You shall not kill.
¹⁴ "You shall not commit adultery.
¹⁵ "You shall not steal.
¹⁶ "You shall not bear false witness against your neighbor.
¹⁷ "You shall not covet your neighbor's house; you shall not covet your neighbor's wife, or his manservant, or his maidservant, or his ox, or his donkey, or anything that is your neighbor's."

The people are afraid and can no longer bear God's appearance. God communicates the following laws, the so-called Book of the Covenant (Ex 21–23), to Moses on the mountain. Very old laws of Israel are reflected in the narrative. It is often difficult to understand them without a good commentary, because they were written for people in a completely different world.

24 ³ Moses came and told the people all the words of the LORD and all the ordinances; and all the people answered with one voice, and said, "All the words which the LORD has spoken we will do." ⁴ And Moses wrote all the words of the LORD. And he rose early in the morning, and built an altar at the foot of the mountain, and twelve pillars, according to the twelve tribes of Israel. ⁵ And he sent young men of the sons of Israel, who offered burnt offerings and sacrificed peace offerings of oxen to the LORD. ⁶ And Moses took

B He who says "I know him" but disobeys his commandments is a liar, and the truth is not in him.

1 Jn 2:4

▶ "Blood of the covenant" (v. 8): The blood is the sign that Israel is allied most intimately with God, with its whole life. Jesus refers to this during the Last Supper: "This is my blood of the covenant" (Mt 26:28).

▶ This covenant celebration is unique in the OT. "To see" God is otherwise impossible.

half of the blood and put it in basins, and half of the blood he threw against the altar. ⁷ Then he took the book of the covenant, and read it in the hearing of the people; and they said, "All that the LORD has spoken we will do, and we will be obedient." ⁸ And Moses took the blood and threw it upon the people, and said, "Behold the blood of the covenant which the LORD has made with you in accordance with all these words."

⁹ Then Moses and Aaron, Na'dab, and Abi'hu, and seventy of the elders of Israel went up, ¹⁰ and they saw the God of Israel; and there was under his feet as it were a pavement of sapphire stone, like the very heaven for clearness. ¹¹ And he did not lay his hand on the chief men of the people of Israel; they beheld God, and ate and drank....

God calls Moses again to the mountain, where he remains for forty days and nights. God describes for him the sanctuary that the people are supposed to build (Ex 25–31; ↗ commentary below on Ex 40). In it God wishes to remain close to Israel. But meanwhile ...

99 The worship of the ancient golden calf (cf. Ex 32:1–35) has returned in a new and ruthless guise in the idolatry of money and the dictatorship of an impersonal economy lacking a truly human purpose.

POPE FRANCIS, *Evangelii Gaudium*, 55

▶ Idolatry contradicts the first of the Ten Commandments (Ex 20:2).

99 Only a believer is obedient, and only the obedient believe.

DIETRICH BONHOEFFER (1906–1945), Lutheran theologian and martyr

The golden calf—the first major crisis (Ex 32–34)

32 ¹ When the people saw that Moses delayed to come down from the mountain, the people gathered themselves together to Aaron, and said to him, "Up, make us gods, who shall go before us; as for this Moses, the man who brought us up out of the land of Egypt, we do not know what has become of him." ² And Aaron said to them, "Take off the rings of gold which are in the ears of your wives, your sons, and your daughters, and bring them to me." ³ So all the people took off the rings of gold which were in their ears, and brought them to Aaron. ⁴ And he received the gold at their hand, and fashioned it with a graving tool, and made a molten calf; and they said, "These are your gods, O Israel, who brought you up out of the land of Egypt!" ⁵ When Aaron saw this, he built an altar before it; and Aaron made proclamation and said, "Tomorrow shall be a feast to the LORD." ⁶ And they rose up early the next day, and offered burnt offerings and brought peace offerings; and the people sat down to eat and drink, and rose up to play.

⁷ And the LORD said to Moses, "Go down; for your people, whom

you brought up out of the land of Egypt, have corrupted themselves; [8] they have turned aside quickly out of the way which I commanded them; they have made for themselves a molten calf, and have worshiped it and sacrificed to it, and said, 'These are your gods, O Israel, who brought you up out of the land of Egypt!'" [9] And the LORD said to Moses, "I have seen this people, and behold, it is a stiff-necked people; [10] now therefore let me alone, that my wrath may burn hot against them and I may consume them; but of you I will make a great nation."

[11] But Moses begged the LORD his God, and said, "O LORD, why does your wrath burn hot against your people, whom you have brought forth out of the land of Egypt with great power and with a mighty hand? [12] Why should the Egyptians say, 'With evil intent he brought them forth, to slay them in the mountains, and to consume them

> When we see the face of God we shall know that we have always known it.

CLIVE STAPLES LEWIS
(1898–1963), British author and literary scholar

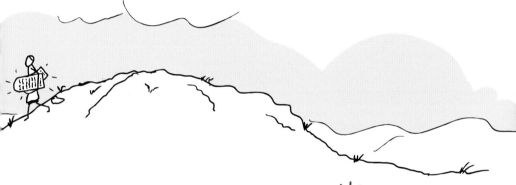

from the face of the earth'? Turn from your fierce wrath, and repent of this evil against your people. [13] Remember Abraham, Isaac, and Israel, your servants, to whom you swore by your own self, and said to them, 'I will multiply your descendants as the stars of heaven, and all this land that I have promised I will give to your descendants, and they shall inherit it for ever.'" [14] And the LORD repented of the evil which he thought to do to his people....

"God repented of something." This is a Hebrew way of speaking anthropomorphically about God. God is very near to us; he sees and hears and understands what we feel. God takes his friends seriously. Awesome!

Moses sees the golden calf and in anger breaks the stone tablets on which God has written. After a major crisis with the people, Moses climbs the mountain again to negotiate with God.

33

[18] Moses said, "I beg you, show me your glory." [19] And he said, "I will make all my goodness pass before you, and will proclaim before you my name 'The LORD'; and I will be gracious to whom I will be gracious, and will show mercy on whom I will show mercy. [20] But," he said, "you cannot see my face; for man shall not see me and live." [21] And the LORD said, "Behold, there is a place by me where you shall stand upon the rock; [22] and while my glory passes by I will put you in a cleft of the rock, and I will cover you with my hand until I have passed by; [23] then I will take away my hand, and you shall see my back; but my face shall not be seen."

They deceive themselves who believe that union with God consists in ecstasies or raptures, and in the enjoyment of Him. For it consists in nothing except →

→ the surrender and subjection of our will—with our thoughts, words, and actions—to the will of God.

TERESA OF AVILA (1515–1582), Spanish Carmelite, mystic and Doctor of the Church

▶ God reveals in v. 6 his innermost being. God speaks about himself and declares his willingness to be reconciled, his everlasting mercy and fidelity: a high point of the story, which is cited in many other books of the Bible.

99 This is the time of mercy. It is important that the lay faithful live it and bring it into different social environments. Go forth!

POPE FRANCIS announcing the Holy Year 2016

34 ⁴ So Moses ... rose early in the morning and went up on Mount Sinai, as the Lᴏʀᴅ had commanded him, and took in his hand two tables of stone. ⁵ And the Lᴏʀᴅ descended in the cloud and stood with him there, and proclaimed the name of the Lᴏʀᴅ. ⁶ The Lᴏʀᴅ passed before him, and proclaimed, "The Lᴏʀᴅ, the Lᴏʀᴅ, a God merciful and gracious, slow to anger, and abounding in mercy and faithfulness, ⁷ keeping merciful love for thousands, forgiving iniquity and transgression and sin, but who will by no means clear the guilty, visiting the iniquity of the fathers upon the children and the children's children, to the third and the fourth generation." ⁸ And Moses made haste to bow his head toward the earth, and worshiped....

²⁸ And he was there with the Lᴏʀᴅ forty days and forty nights; he neither ate bread nor drank water. And he wrote upon the tables the words of the covenant, the ten commandments.

²⁹ When Moses came down from Mount Sinai, with the two tables of the covenant in his hand as he came down from the mountain, Moses did not know that the skin of his face shone because he had been talking with God....

▶ People who are in contact with God often have a special radiance.

God forgave Israel. So the people can build the sanctuary. It is a pattern for the later Temple in Jerusalem. In the middle of it, in the Holy of Holies, stands the Ark of the Covenant, a gilded wooden container holding the two stone tablets with the Ten Commandments. In front of it stand altars, a table, and a seven-branched candlestick.

99 God hides himself. He does not dazzle us with the brilliance of his glory; he does not make us bow the knee before his power. He wishes to make real between him and us the mystery of love which presupposes freedom.

POPE BENEDICT XVI

God's glory Fills the sanctuary (Ex 40)

40 ¹⁶ Thus did Moses; according to all that the Lᴏʀᴅ commanded him, so he did. ¹⁷ And in the first month in the second year, on the first day of the month, the tabernacle was erected. ¹⁸ Moses erected the tabernacle; he laid its bases, and set up its frames, and put in its poles, and raised up its pillars; ¹⁹ and he spread the tent over the tabernacle, and put the covering of the tent over it, as the Lᴏʀᴅ had commanded Moses. ²⁰ And he took the covenant and put it into the ark, and put the poles on the ark, and set the mercy seat above on the ark; ²¹ and he brought the ark into the tabernacle, and set up the veil of the screen, and screened the ark of the covenant; as the Lᴏʀᴅ had commanded Moses....

³⁴ Then the cloud covered the tent of meeting, and the glory of the Lᴏʀᴅ filled the tabernacle. ³⁵ And Moses was not

able to enter the tent of meeting, because the cloud abode upon it, and the glory of the LORD filled the tabernacle. [36] Throughout all their journeys, whenever the cloud was taken up from over the tabernacle, the sons of Israel would go onward; [37] but if the cloud was not taken up, then they did not go onward till the day that it was taken up. [38] For throughout all their journeys the cloud of the Lord was upon the tabernacle by day, and fire was in it by night, in the sight of all the house of Israel.

I think that it would be super if I could see God. But God happens to be invisible. Although he does not show himself to my eyes, I can still sense that he is there somehow. Often I even feel very clearly God's hand over me, which is simply there, protecting and guiding me in my life.

MARTIN

When Israel went forth from Egypt,
the house of Jacob from a people
of strange language,
Judah became his sanctuary,
Israel his dominion.
The sea looked and fled, Jordan turned back.
The mountains skipped like rams,
the hills like lambs.
What ails you, O sea, that you flee?
O Jordan, that you turn back?
O mountains, that you skip like rams?
O hills, like lambs?
Tremble, O earth,
at the presence of the LORD,
at the presence of the God of Jacob,
who turns the rock into a pool of water,
the flint into a spring of water.
Psalm 114

This psalm sings of the miracles of the Exodus. Israel becomes God's holy people ("sanctuary", → Ex 19:6). The miracle at the Red Sea, the water from the rock, the quaking ("skipping") of Mount Sinai, and the miracle at the Jordan River as they entered the Promised Land (Josh 3)—all this summons the whole world to "tremble", or, as the word could also be translated, to "dance".

THE BOOK OF
Leviticus

The third book of the Bible is at the center of the Torah. It takes its name from the Levites, the assistants at divine worship. Everything revolves around the encounter with God: sacrifice, worship services, priests, feast days. God's holiness should be reflected also, however, in his people's food, clothing, behavior, and, not least important, in their love for their neighbor and for the stranger (Lev 19). To make this possible, once a year, on the so-called Day of Atonement (in Hebrew, *Yom Kippur*, for Jews the highest holiday), God forgives the whole community their guilt. Thus God's mercy, which he promised Israel after their sin with the golden calf (Ex 34:6–7), is made concrete. Aaron, as high priest, has a particularly important role. The celebration shows symbolically how God grants forgiveness.

The day of atonement (Lev 16)

▶ In order for the priest to be able to pray for forgiveness of the sins of the community, he himself must first be freed from his sin.

16 ¹¹ Aaron shall present the bull as a sin offering for himself, and shall make atonement for himself and for his house; he shall kill the bull as a sin offering for himself....

¹⁵ "Then he shall kill the goat of the sin offering which is for the people, and bring its blood within the veil, and do with its blood as he did with the blood of the bull, sprinkling it upon the mercy seat and before the mercy seat; ¹⁶ thus he shall make atonement for the holy place, because of the uncleannesses of the sons of Israel, and because of their transgressions, all their sins; and so he shall do for the tent of meeting, which abides with them in the midst of their uncleannesses....

▶ With that the priest has performed the essential rituals (in vv. 18–19 for the altar, too). An additional gesture symbolizes the removal of guilt (vv. 21–22).

²¹ and Aaron shall lay both his hands upon the head of the live goat, and confess over him all the iniquities of the sons of Israel, and all their transgressions, all their sins; and he shall put them upon the head of the goat, and send him away into the wilderness by the hand of a man who is in readiness. ²² The goat shall bear all their iniquities upon him to a solitary land; and he shall let the goat go in the wilderness...

💡 People we can no longer send off into the desert: neighbors, children, parents, teachers, politicians, coworkers, scientists, Church leaders ...

²⁹ "And it shall be a statute to you for ever that in the seventh month, on the tenth day of the month, you shall afflict yourselves, and shall do no work, either the native or the stranger who sojourns among you; ³⁰ for on this day shall atonement be made for you, to

cleanse you; from all your sins you shall be clean before the LORD. ³¹ It is a sabbath of solemn rest to you, and you shall afflict yourselves; it is a statute for ever....

> Three chapters later, God tells the people how to be guided by him in everyday life, so as to become holy:

Rules for the community (Lev 19)

19 ¹ And the LORD said to Moses, ² "Say to all the congregation of the sons of Israel, You shall be holy; for I the LORD your God am holy. ³ Every one of you shall revere his mother and his father, and you shall keep my sabbaths: I am the LORD your God....

⁹ "When you reap the harvest of your land, you shall not reap your field to its very border, neither shall you gather the gleanings after your harvest. ¹⁰ And you shall not strip your vineyard bare, neither shall you gather the fallen grapes of your vineyard; you shall leave them for the poor and for the sojourner: I am the LORD your God.

¹¹ "You shall not steal, nor deal falsely, nor lie to one another. ¹² And you shall not swear by my name falsely, and so profane the name of your God: I am the LORD.

A fresh start! How liberating, when a whole society has a chance to start over, whatever may have happened in the past.

We must accept and love our imperfection and no longer work to become saints, but strive only to please God. **THÉRÈSE OF LISIEUX** (1873–1897), Carmelite and Doctor of the Church

▶ In the Decalogue, the Sabbath is mentioned before parents and the father before the mother (↗ Ex 20:8–12). Both are in reverse order here.

¹³ "You shall not oppress your neighbor or rob him. The wages of a hired servant shall not remain with you all night until the morning. ¹⁴ You shall not curse the deaf or put a stumbling block before the blind, but you shall fear your God: I am the LORD.

¹⁵ "You shall do no injustice in judgment; you shall not be partial to the poor or defer to the great, but in righteousness shall you judge your neighbor. ¹⁶ You shall not go up and down as a slanderer among your people, and you shall not stand forth against the life of your neighbor: I am the LORD.

¹⁷ "You shall not hate your brother in your heart, but you shall reason with your neighbor, lest you bear sin because of him. ¹⁸ You shall not take vengeance or bear any grudge against the sons of your own people, but you shall love your neighbor as yourself: I am the LORD.

¹⁹ "You shall keep my statutes. You shall not let your cattle breed with a different kind; you shall not sow your field with two kinds of seed; nor shall there come upon you a garment of cloth made of two kinds of stuff. ...

²⁹ "Do not profane your daughter by making her a harlot, lest the land fall into harlotry and the land become full of wickedness...

³¹ "Do not turn to mediums or wizards; do not seek them out, to be defiled by them: I am the LORD your God.

³² "You shall rise up before the hoary head, and honor the face of an old man, and you shall fear your God: I am the LORD.

❝❞ Just as the commandment "Thou shalt not kill" sets a clear limit in order to safeguard the value of human life, today we also have to say "thou shalt not" to an economy of exclusion and inequality. Such an economy kills. **POPE FRANCIS,** *Evangelii Gaudium,* 53

▶ Our willingness to be reconciled and to love our neighbor is especially important for Jesus, too (↗ Mt 18:21–35; 22:34–40).

▶ It destroys any society when people are abused, when sexuality has nothing to do with a relationship, and when people are respected less just because they are women or men.

THE LORD'S FEAST DAYS / BIBLICAL FEASTS

SPRING FESTIVALS

PASSOVER   UNLEAVENED   FIRST FRUITS   SHAVUOT
            BREAD

³³ "When a stranger sojourns with you in your land, you shall not do him wrong. ³⁴ The stranger who sojourns with you shall be to you as the native among you, and you shall love him as yourself; for you were strangers in the land of Egypt: I am the LORD your God.

³⁵ "You shall do no wrong in judgment, in measures of length or weight or quantity. ³⁶ You shall have just balances, just weights, a just *ephah*, and a just *hin*: I am the LORD your God, who brought you out of the land of Egypt....

▶ *Ephah*, around 22 liters [6.3 bushels]; *hin*, approx. 3.5 liters [3.7 quarts]

> Worldwide and in many societies, inequality is increasing. Often the rich and the powerful succeed in working the system so as to maximize their own profit, while paying little attention to sustainability, fairness, and the dignity of those who are weaker. To counter such forces, which destroy both nature and social unity, God introduced two special years for his People Israel:

Sabbatical Year and Jubilee Year (Lev 25)

25 ¹ The LORD said to Moses on Mount Sinai, ² "Say to the sons of Israel, When you come into the land which I give you, the land shall keep a sabbath to the LORD. ³ Six years you shall sow your field, and six years you shall prune your vineyard, and gather in its fruits; ⁴ but in the seventh year there shall be a sabbath of solemn rest for the land, a sabbath to the LORD; you shall not sow your field or prune your vineyard. ⁵ What grows of itself in your harvest you shall not reap, and the grapes of your undressed vine you shall not gather; it shall be a year of solemn rest for the land. ⁶ The sabbath of the land shall provide food for you, for yourself and for your male and female

▶ Verse 10, "jubilee": The Hebrew word *jobel* refers to the "ram's horn", which from prehistoric time was used as a wind instrument.

FALL FESTIVALS

AST OF   DAY OF   FEAST OF   JOY OF THE
JMPETS   ATONEMENT   TABERNACLES   TORAH

> Life is more than work, however important our work is. God gave Israel the various Sabbaths to create a space of time for him to form their identity as his people. Israel was to "guard" or "keep" the Sabbath from work and ordinary concerns and activities.

DR. TIM GRAY author, President of the Augustine Institute, and Professor of Sacred Scripture

▶ Just as the people rest every seventh day, so too the ground is allowed to "rest" every seven years (v. 4). Such a time of "lying fallow" is important for the fields, so as to replenish nutrients. At the same time, it is a sign that fruitfulness ultimately comes from God and that it is not a question of "maximizing performance".

slaves and for your hired servant and the sojourner who lives with you; ⁷ for your cattle also and for the beasts that are in your land all its yield shall be for food.

⁸ "And you shall count seven weeks of years, seven times seven years, so that the time of the seven weeks of years shall be to you forty-nine years. ⁹ Then you shall send abroad the loud trumpet on the tenth day of the seventh month; on the day of atonement you shall send abroad the trumpet throughout all your land. ¹⁰ And you shall hallow the fiftieth year, and proclaim liberty throughout the land to all its inhabitants; it shall be a jubilee for you, when each of you shall return to his property and each of you shall return to his family....

²³ The land shall not be sold in perpetuity, for the land is mine; for you are strangers and sojourners with me. ²⁴ And in all the country you possess, you shall grant a redemption of the land.

²⁵ "If your brother becomes poor, and sells part of his property, then his next of kin shall come and redeem what his brother has sold....

³⁵ "And if your brother becomes poor, and cannot maintain himself with you, you shall maintain him; as a stranger and a sojourner he shall live with you. ³⁶ Take no interest from him or increase, but fear your God; that your brother may live beside you....

⁵⁵ For to me the sons of Israel are servants, they are my servants whom I brought forth out of the land of Egypt: I am the Lᴏʀᴅ your God....

▶ A general forgiveness of debts was supposed to put an end to the societal differences, especially impoverishment and dependency, that had arisen in 49 years (three generations in those days).

▶ A "redeemer" (v. 25) was the term for the nearest relation, who was obliged to take responsibility for a relative who had fallen into misfortune. He was supposed to buy back lost land and pay off debts if a relative was about to be sold as a slave. Some biblical passages assign this role to God in a figurative sense (for the first time in Ex 6:6).

THE BOOK OF

Numbers

The numbers in the title refer to the censuses of able-bodied men in the People of Israel mentioned in Numbers 1. In Hebrew, this book is called "In the Wilderness", which establishes the location of the first verse.

The fourth book of the Bible describes the departure from Sinai (Num 1–10) and the journey of the people toward the Promised Land. This takes Israel—according to Ex 15–19—through the wilderness again (Num 10–21), and once again conflicts arise. They show that the people were far from having attained the ideal of "holiness" presented in Leviticus. In contrast to the "grumbling" in the Book of Exodus, some people rebel after they have encountered God at Mount Sinai; accordingly, the consequences are more severe in Numbers.

Before they set out, God gives the people instructions in Num 6 for a special way of consecrating their life to God and a formula that the priests are supposed to recite, the so-called "Aaronic blessing", which also had considerable influence on the Christian liturgy (Num 6:22–27).

From Num 22 on, the land comes noticeably into view. The foreign visionary Balaam blesses Israel (Num 23–24), Joshua is appointed Moses' successor (Num 27:12–23), and the region east of the Jordan is divided up (Num 32). In this way, everything is prepared for the entrance into the Promised Land, before which nothing remains but the great farewell discourse of Moses, the Book of Deuteronomy.

There are still "Nazirites" even today. Many Rastafarians with their dreadlocks take the vow that appeared already in the Book of Numbers. A vow is a solemn promise to God to perform a good work or to renounce something (for a definite time or forever).

▶ The untrimmed hair symbolizes vitality that comes from God; one example is Samson in Judg 16:17.

Nazirites and priestly blessing (Num 6)

6 And the LORD said to Moses, ² "Say to the sons of Israel, When either a man or a woman makes a special vow, the vow of a Naz'irite, to separate himself to the LORD, ³ he shall separate himself from wine and strong drink; he shall drink no vinegar made from wine or strong drink, and shall not drink any juice of grapes or eat grapes, fresh or dried. ⁴ All the days of his separation he shall eat nothing that is produced by the grapevine, not even the seeds or the skins.

⁵ "All the days of his vow of separation no razor shall come upon his head; until the time is completed for which he separates himself to the LORD, he shall be holy; he shall let the locks of hair of his head grow long.

⁶ "All the days that he separates himself to the LORD he shall not go near a dead body....

When the time of his vow has passed, the Nazirite is supposed to come with sacrificial offerings to the sanctuary; his hair, the sign of his devotion during that phase of his life, is then cut off and burned in the fire. Then he may drink wine again (vv. 13–20).

▶ God not only grants blessings, he also appoints individuals who are to impart blessings(↗ Gen 12:1). →

The repetition of "face" emphasizes his personal care. The final word, shalom (translated "peace" or "salvation"), shows that God wishes to grant peace and happiness. Incidentally, anyone may bless: a mother her child, a boyfriend his girlfriend..., although certain formal blessings are reserved for bishops, priests, and deacons.

²² The LORD said to Moses, ²³ "Say to Aaron and his sons, Thus you shall bless the sons of Israel: you shall say to them,
²⁴ The LORD bless you and keep you:
²⁵ The LORD make his face to shine upon you, and be gracious to you:
²⁶ The LORD lift up his countenance upon you, and give you peace.
²⁷ "So shall they put my name upon the sons of Israel, and I will bless them."

FROM SINAI ON THE JOURNEY THROUGH THE WILDERNESS TO THE PROMISED LAND (FROM NUM 11)

In contrast to the ideal image of Israel as the holy people sketched in Leviticus (→ Lev 19), many conflicts and difficulties arise among the people from the moment they set out from Mount Sinai and continue their journey to the Promised Land. This is already evident in Num 11:

▶ "Taberah" means "fire" and recalls the consequences of this first rebellion.

Lots of problems (Num 11)

11 ¹ And the people complained in the hearing of the LORD about their misfortunes; and when the LORD heard it, his anger was kindled, and the fire of the LORD burned among them, and consumed some outlying parts of the camp. ² Then the people cried to

Moses; and Moses prayed to the LORD, and the fire abated. ³ So the name of that place was called Tab'erah, because the fire of the LORD burned among them.

⁴ Now the rabble that was among them had a strong craving; and the people of Israel also wept again, and said, "O that we had meat to eat! ⁵ We remember the fish we ate in Egypt for nothing, the cucumbers, the melons, the leeks, the onions, and the garlic; ⁶ but now our strength is dried up, and there is nothing at all but this manna to look at."...

¹⁰ Moses heard the people weeping throughout their families, every man at the door of his tent; and the anger of the LORD blazed hotly, and Moses was displeased. ¹¹ Moses said to the LORD, "Why have you dealt ill with your servant? And why have I not found favor in your sight, that you lay the burden of all this people upon me? ¹² Did I conceive all this people? Did I bring them forth, that you should say to me, 'Carry them in your bosom, as a nurse carries the sucking child,' to the land which you swore to give their fathers? ¹³ Where am I to get meat to give to all this people? For they weep before me and say, 'Give us meat, that we may eat.' ¹⁴ I am not able to carry all this people alone, the burden is too heavy for me. ¹⁵ If you will deal thus with me, kill me at once, if I find favor in your sight, that I may not see my wretchedness."

Egypt was so cool! The food and everything.... Suddenly the Israelites look back on their time under Pharaoh's rule through rose-colored glasses, although they had been oppressed and enslaved in Egypt.

▶ The chronic discontent of the people wears Moses down, since he bears the greatest responsibility. He in turn puts pressure on God.

🙶🙶 A few days ago a great Italian artist said that it was easier for the Lord to take the Israelites out of Egypt than to take Egypt out of the heart of the Israelites.

POPE FRANCIS, December 31, 2014

¹⁶ And the LORD said to Moses, "Gather for me seventy men of the elders of Israel, whom you know to be the elders of the people and officers over them; and bring them to the tent of meeting, and let them take their stand there with you. ¹⁷ And I will come down and talk with you there; and I will take some of the spirit which is upon you and put it upon them; and they shall bear the burden of the people with you, that you may not bear it yourself alone. ¹⁸ And say to the people, 'Consecrate yourselves for tomorrow, and you shall eat meat; for you have wept in the hearing of the LORD, saying, "Who will give us meat to eat? For it was well with us in Egypt." Therefore the LORD will give you meat, and you shall eat. ¹⁹ You shall not eat one day, or two days, or five days, or ten days, or twenty days, ²⁰ but a whole month, until it comes out at your nostrils and becomes loathsome to you, because you have rejected the LORD who is among you, and have wept before him, saying, "Why did we come forth out of Egypt?"'" ²¹ But Moses said, "The people among whom I am number six hundred thousand on foot; and you have said, 'I will give them meat, that they may eat a whole month!' ²² Shall flocks and herds be slaughtered for them, to satisfy them? Or shall all the fish of the sea be gathered together for them, to satisfy them?" ²³ And the LORD said to Moses, "Is the LORD's hand shortened? Now you shall see whether my word will come true for you or not."

❓ Do I accept the dry spells that God sends in my life? What is my "Egypt", for which I yearn nostalgically? Do I know better than God what is good for me?

▶ God relieves Moses of a burden by dividing up the responsibility, and God confronts the Israelites by giving them exactly what they want: meat, all they can eat! So much so that they get sick of it!

▶ What is possible for God far surpasses our human thought. (↗ the promise to Sarah in Gen 18.)

The wind [i.e., the Spirit] blows where it will.

Jn 3:8

 The unspiritual man does not receive the gifts of the Spirit of God, for they are folly to him, and he is not able to understand them because they are spiritually discerned.

1 Cor 2:14

▶ The Spirit of God cannot be controlled. That annoys many people.

[24] So Moses went out and told the people the words of the LORD; and he gathered seventy men of the elders of the people, and placed them round about the tent. [25] Then the LORD came down in the cloud and spoke to him, and took some of the spirit that was upon him and put it upon the seventy elders; and when the spirit rested upon them, they prophesied. But they did so no more.

[26] Now two men remained in the camp, one named Eldad, and the other named Medad, and the spirit rested upon them; they were among those registered, but they had not gone out to the tent, and so they prophesied in the camp. [27] And a young man ran and told Moses, "Eldad and Medad are prophesying in the camp." [28] And Joshua the son of Nun, the minister of Moses, one of his chosen men, said, "My lord Moses, forbid them." [29] But Moses said to him, "Are you jealous for my sake? Would that all the LORD's people were prophets, that the LORD would put his spirit upon them!"...

In the next chapter, Moses is attacked by his siblings:

▶ It is possible that the wife mentioned here is Zipporah (↗ Ex 2:21). Usually, though, "Cush" refers to regions in modern-day Sudan or Ethiopia.

 As the deer longs for flowing streams, so longs my soul for you, O God. My soul thirsts for God, for the living God. When shall I come and behold the face of God? My tears have been my food day and night, while men say to me continually, "Where is your God?"

Ps 42:1–3

❞❞ God knows the human heart. He knows that those who reject him have not recognized his true Face, and so he never ceases to knock at our door like a humble pilgrim in search of hospitality.

POPE BENEDICT XVI, December 1, 2007

Moses' unique closeness to God (Num 12)

12 [1] Miriam and Aaron spoke against Moses because of the Cushite woman whom he had married, for he had married a Cushite woman; [2] and they said, "Has the LORD indeed spoken only through Moses? Has he not spoken through us also?" And the LORD heard it. [3] Now the man Moses was very meek, more than all men that were on the face of the earth. [4] And suddenly the LORD said to Moses and to Aaron and Miriam, "Come out, you three, to the tent of meeting." And the three of them came out. [5] And the LORD came down in a pillar of cloud, and stood at the door of the tent, and called Aaron and Miriam; and they both came forward. [6] And he said, "Hear my words: If there is a prophet among you, I the LORD make myself known to him in a vision, I speak with him in a dream. [7] Not so with my servant Moses; he is entrusted with all my house. [8] With him I speak mouth to mouth, clearly, and not in dark speech; and he beholds the form of the LORD. Why then were you not afraid to speak against my servant Moses?"

[9] And the anger of the LORD was kindled against them, and he departed; [10] and when the cloud removed from over the tent, behold, Miriam was leprous, as white as snow. And Aaron turned towards Miriam, and behold, she was leprous....

To prepare for their entrance into the Promised Land, the Israelites send men ahead to bring back information about it. The scouts report that the land is fruitful, but they extravagantly exaggerate the dangers in the land (Num 13:32–33). Thus they discourage the people and stir up resistance:

Clarifications (Num 14)

14 ¹ Then all the congregation raised a loud cry; and the people wept that night. ² And all the sons of Israel murmured against Moses and Aaron; the whole congregation said to them, "Would that we had died in the land of Egypt! Or would that we had died in this wilderness! ³ Why does the LORD bring us into this land, to fall by the sword? Our wives and our little ones will become a prey; would it not be better for us to go back to Egypt?"

⁴ And they said to one another, "Let us choose a captain, and go back to Egypt." ⁵ Then Moses and Aaron fell on their faces before all the assembly of the congregation of the sons of Israel. ⁶ And Joshua the son of Nun and Caleb the son of Jephun'neh, who were among those who had spied out the land, tore their clothes, ⁷ and said to all the congregation of the sons of Israel, "The land, which we passed through to spy it out, is an exceedingly good land. ⁸ If the LORD delights in us, he will bring us into this land and give it to us, a

▶ The accusations of the people (v. 3) now become much worse: They want to undo God's deliverance and rebel against Moses, who was delegated by God.

💡 Grumbling, slander, and grousing are a common ailment, that is found even in the Bible. The saints, too, fought against it: Benedict of Nursia expected "good zeal" from his monks. It is "pleasing to God and beneficial for men" when a task is performed "with a glad heart" and "not timidly, … indifferently, or else with grumbling and contradiction".

land which flows with milk and honey. ⁹ Only, do not rebel against the LORD; and do not fear the people of the land, for they are bread for us; their protection is removed from them, and the LORD is with us; do not fear them." ¹⁰ But all the congregation said to stone them with stones.

Then the glory of the LORD appeared at the tent of meeting to all the sons of Israel. ¹¹ And the LORD said to Moses, "How long will this people despise me? And how long will they not believe in me, in spite of all the signs which I have wrought among them? ¹² I will strike them with the pestilence and disinherit them, and I will make of you a nation greater and mightier than they."

¹³ But Moses said to the LORD, "Then the Egyptians will hear of it, for you brought up this people in your might from among them, ¹⁴ and they will tell the inhabitants of this land. They have heard that you, O LORD, are in the midst of this people; for you, O LORD, are seen face to face, and your cloud stands over them and you go before them, in a pillar of cloud by day and in a pillar of fire by night. ¹⁵ Now if you kill this people as one man, then the nations who have heard your fame will say, ¹⁶ 'Because the LORD was not able to bring this people into the land which he swore to give to them, therefore he has slain them in the wilderness.' ¹⁷ And now, I beg you, let the power of the LORD be great as you have promised, saying, ¹⁸ 'The LORD is slow to anger, and abounding in mercy, forgiving iniquity and transgression, but he

▶ Joshua and Caleb are the names of the two scouts who report true marvels about the land of Canaan: "Milk and honey" are said to flow there. They show (compared with ↗ Num 13:32–33) how differently "specialists" may view the same question.

▶ Moses reminds God of his solemn promise of reconciliation, in which God presented himself as being extremely merciful (Ex 34:6–7).

▶ God reacts in three ways to Moses' intercession: he forgives in principle (v. 20). However, there are also consequences for the guilty (vv. 21–23), because they have repeatedly rebelled. They will die, yet their children, who bore no responsibility for it, will come into the land after forty years (vv. 31–34). An exception is made for Caleb, who is innocent and is praised (→ so is Joshua, vv. 6–9, 24, 38).

will by no means clear the guilty, visiting the iniquity of fathers upon children, upon the third and upon the fourth generation.' ¹⁹ Pardon the iniquity of this people, I beg you, according to the greatness of your mercy, and according as you have forgiven this people, from Egypt even until now."

²⁰ Then the LORD said, "I have pardoned, according to your word; ²¹ but truly, as I live, and as all the earth shall be filled with the glory of the LORD, ²² none of the men who have seen my glory and my signs which I wrought in Egypt and in the wilderness, and yet have put me to the proof these ten times and have not hearkened to my voice, ²³ shall see the land which I swore to give to their fathers; and none of those who despised me shall see it. ²⁴ But my servant Caleb, because he has a different spirit and has followed me fully, I will bring into the land into which he went, and his descendants shall possess it...."

There is no end to conflicts among the people and with Moses and Aaron. This corresponds to a realistic picture of communities. Before the land comes ever more plainly into view (Num 21 ff.), two more incidents occur.

▶ The people had already been thirsty once before and complained about it in Ex 17. But since then they have come to know God and experienced his care for them. That is why their rebellion and lack of trust are more serious now.

❞❞ Have we lost the gift of tears? I remember that in the old Missals from another era, there was a beautiful prayer asking for the gift of tears. "Lord, who commanded Moses to strike the rock so that water might gush forth, strike the stone of my heart so that tears...." It was very beautiful. But how many of us weep when we see the suffering of a child, the breakup of a family, so many people who do not find the path?... Do you weep?

POPE FRANCIS, March 6, 2014

Those in charge fail (Num 20)

20 ² Now there was no water for the congregation; and they assembled themselves together against Moses and against Aaron. ³ And the people contended with Moses, and said, "Would that we had died when our brethren died before the LORD! ⁴ Why have you brought the assembly of the LORD into this wilderness, that we should die here, both we and our cattle? ⁵ And why have you made us come up out of Egypt, to bring us to this evil place? It is no place for grain, or figs, or vines, or pomegranates; and there is no water to drink." ⁶ Then Moses and Aaron went from the presence of the assembly to the door of the tent of meeting, and fell on their faces. And the glory of the LORD appeared to them, ⁷ and the LORD said to Moses, ⁸ "Take the rod, and assemble the congregation, you and Aaron your brother, and tell the rock before their eyes to yield its water; so you shall bring water out of the rock for them; so you shall give drink to the congregation and their cattle." ⁹ And Moses took the rod from before the LORD, as he commanded him.

¹⁰ And Moses and Aaron gathered the assembly together before the rock, and he said to them, "Hear now, you rebels; shall we bring forth water for you out of this rock?" ¹¹ And Moses lifted up his hand and struck the rock with his rod twice; and water came forth abundantly, and the congregation drank, and their cattle. ¹² And the LORD said to

Moses and Aaron, "Because you did not believe in me, to sanctify me in the eyes of the sons of Israel, therefore you shall not bring this assembly into the land which I have given them." ¹³ These are the waters of Mer'ibah, where the sons of Israel contended with the LORD, and he showed himself holy among them....

The bronze serpent (Num 21:4–9)

21 ⁴ From Mount Hor they set out by the way to the Red Sea, to go around the land of E'dom; and the people became impatient on the way. ⁵ And the people spoke against God and against Moses, "Why have you brought us up out of Egypt to die in the wilderness? For there is no food and no water, and we loathe this worthless food." ⁶ Then the LORD sent fiery serpents among the people, and they bit the people, so that many sons of Israel died. ⁷ And the people came to Moses, and said, "We have sinned, for we have spoken against the LORD and against you; pray to the LORD, that he take away the serpents from us." So Moses prayed for the people. ⁸ And the LORD said to Moses, "Make a fiery serpent, and set it up as a sign; and every one

▶ Moses speaks to the people aggressively; he emphasizes his own and Aaron's role in the miracle ("we"), as though he were the star; and he makes a theatrical production out of his actions (vv. 10–11). As we see in v. 8, God prefers a different style.

▶ The above-mentioned differences are the reason for God's judgment (v. 12). Even toward his close friends, to whom he has given responsibility, he behaves clearly and properly; he does not allow himself to be "swayed".

▶ On September 14, the Church celebrates the feast of the "Exaltation of the Cross", which makes a connection between this Old Testament passage and the conquest over death on the Cross.

who is bitten, when he sees it, shall live." ⁹ So Moses made a bronze serpent, and set it up as a sign; and if a serpent bit any man, he would look at the bronze serpent and live....

B O come, let us worship and bow down,
let us kneel before the LORD, our Maker!
For he is our God,
and we are the people of his pasture,
and the sheep of his hand.
O that today you would listen to his voice!
Harden not your hearts, as at Mer'ibah,
as on the day at Massah in the wilderness,
when your fathers tested me,
and put me to the proof, though they had seen my work.
For forty years I was wearied of that generation
and said, "They are a people who err in heart,
and they do not regard my ways."
Therefore I swore in my anger
that they should not enter my rest.

Ps 95:6–11

B As Moses lifted up the serpent in the wilderness, so must the Son of man be lifted up, that whoever believes in him may have eternal life.

Jn 3:14–15

THE BOOK OF

Deuteronomy

In the book of Deuteronomy, Moses gives his farewell speeches to the People of Israel in the land of Moab (in modern-day Jordan), shortly before the entrance into the land that God had promised to Israel (Deut 1–30). He appoints Joshua as his successor (Deut 31:7–8), writes down the Torah, and entrusts it to the leaders of the people (Deut 31:9). After Moses' hymn (Deut 32) and blessing (Deut 33), God lets him see the Promised Land from Mount Nebo; he may not enter in himself, however, but dies (Deut 34).

In his extensive speeches, Moses summarizes what the People of Israel ought to learn from their past for the future. He admonishes the people, on account of all their experiences on their journey through the wilderness, to listen to God (e.g., ↗ Deut 1–3). Moses repeats, explains, and interprets the laws that he received from God on Mount Horeb (called "Sinai" in Exodus) (↗ Deut 5–26). This is necessary, because almost all the Israelites who were at Sinai had to die in the wilderness (↗ Num 14). Moses makes God's Law comprehensible to the younger generation and thereby shows how in the future their religion must be expounded and understood anew. The changed circumstances of a new era require us to reflect on the wisdom of former times and to apply them to the present. This message of the Book of Deuteronomy is especially important for the present time.

Before repeating the commandments, Moses states the "Greatest Commandment": Israel should "hear"; and it should "love" the one and only true God (↗ Deut 6:4f.). This commandment is fundamental also for Jesus and Christianity.

Although Moses begs God for this grace, he himself may not set foot on the Promised Land. He may only have a glimpse of it before his death. In order to remember that time, Jews today celebrate Sukkot, the Feast of Tabernacles. They build a booth with branches on the balcony or in the garden and eat their meals in it.

Allowed to see the land (Deut 3:23–29)

> The essential point of all Moses' sermons is simple. It is the message of Psalm 1, the message of the two ways. Two and only two ways are open to us in this life: the way of obedience to God and the way of disobedience. … The way of obedience is divinely guaranteed to lead to inheriting all God's promises. The way of disobedience is equally guaranteed to result in misery and failure.
>
> **PETER KREEFT**

3 23 "And I begged the LORD at that time, saying, 24 'O Lord GOD, you have only begun to show your servant your greatness and your mighty hand; for what god is there in heaven or on earth who can do such works and mighty acts as yours? 25 Let me go over, I pray, and see the good land beyond the Jordan, that excellent hill country, and Lebanon.'

26 But the LORD was angry with me on your account, and would not listen to me; and the LORD said to me, 'Let it satisfy you; speak no more to me of this matter. 27 Go up to the top of Pisgah, and lift up your eyes westward and northward and southward and eastward, and behold it with your eyes; for you shall not go over this Jordan. 28 But charge Joshua, and encourage and strengthen him; for he shall go over at the head of this people, and he shall put them in possession of the land which you shall see.' 29 So we remained in the valley opposite Beth-pe'or.

In this first long sermon, Moses shows what Israel's experience at Mount Horeb (Sinai) means for the people. There God appointed Moses as teacher. In the manifestation of God (in Greek, "theophany"), the people saw no figure—therefore God must not be depicted in images. Israel is special on account of its unique encounter with God and his Torah.

▶ Verse 2 shows one of the first steps on the long journey in which the biblical books were collected and recognized as the canon (Greek for "standard").

▶ "Teach": Moses teaches what he himself learned from God on Mount Horeb (Deut 4:14). Consequently, the people should learn from him (↗ Deut 6:7; 31:12).

The unique experience on Horeb (Deut 4:1–40)

4 1 "And now, O Israel, give heed to the statutes and the ordinances which I teach you, and do them; that you may live, and go in and take possession of the land which the LORD, the God of your fathers, gives you. 2 You shall not add to the word which I command you, nor take from it; that you may keep the commandments of the LORD your God which I command you….

5 Behold, I have taught you statutes and ordinances, as the LORD my God commanded me, that you should do them in the land which you are entering to take possession of it. 6 Keep them and do them; for that will be your wisdom and your understanding in the sight of the peoples, who, when they hear all these statutes, will say, 'Surely this great nation is a wise and understanding people.' 7 For what great nation is there that has a god so near to it as the LORD our God is to us, whenever we call upon him? 8 And what great nation is there, that

has statutes and ordinances so righteous as all this law which I set before you this day?

⁹ "Only take heed, and keep your soul diligently, lest you forget the things which your eyes have seen, and lest they depart from your heart all the days of your life; make them known to your children and your children's children— ¹⁰ how on the day that you stood before the LORD your God at Horeb, the LORD said to me, 'Gather the people to me, that I may let them hear my words, so that they may learn to fear me all the days that they live upon the earth, and that they may teach their children so.' ¹¹ And you came near and stood at the foot of the mountain, while the mountain burned with fire to the heart of heaven, wrapped in darkness, cloud, and gloom. ¹² Then the LORD spoke to you out of the midst of the fire; you heard the sound of words, but saw no form; there was only a voice. ¹³ And he declared to you his covenant, which he commanded you to perform, that is, the ten commandments; and he wrote them upon two tables of stone. ¹⁴ And the LORD commanded me at that time to teach you statutes and ordinances, that you might do them in the land which you are going over to possess.

 Don't forget your roots! My roots are what I am handing down to my children. Someday, hopefully, it will be a source of strength for them. When I practice forgiveness and act justly, I do not lose sight of God. That is the life-style that I would like to send my children off with on their journey. It is so important that God reminds me of my roots! God cares for me. So I, too, treat life with care.

ROSE

Y → 351
Aren't the Ten Commandments outmoded?

¹⁵ "Therefore take good heed to yourselves. Since you saw no form on the day that the LORD spoke to you at Horeb out of the midst of the fire, ¹⁶ beware lest you act corruptly by making a graven image for yourselves, in the form of any figure, the likeness of male or female, ¹⁷ the likeness of any beast that is on the earth, the likeness of any winged bird that flies in the air, ¹⁸ the likeness of anything that creeps on the ground, the likeness of any fish that is in the water under the earth. ¹⁹ And beware lest you lift up your eyes to heaven, and when you see the sun and the moon and the stars, all the host of heaven, you be drawn away and worship them and serve them, things which the LORD your God has allotted to all the peoples under the whole heaven. ²⁰ But the LORD has taken you, and brought you forth out of the iron furnace, out of Egypt, to be a people of his own possession, as at this day. ²¹ Furthermore the LORD was angry with me on your account, and he swore that I should not cross the Jordan, and that I should not enter the good land which the LORD your God gives you for an inheritance. ²² For I must die in this land, I must not go over the Jordan; but you shall go over and take possession of that good land. ²³ Take heed to yourselves, lest you forget the covenant of the LORD your God, which he made with you, and make a graven

▶ No images of God: Moses emphasizes this prohibition so strongly because among all the other peoples of the ancient world it was quite normal to have many statues of gods and to be very afraid of their power. The sun, the moon, and the stars were also considered to be gods, which ruled the life of men. Modern astrology developed out of this notion.

▶ "Devouring fire" (v. 24) is a central image for God in the Old Testament. God is never cold or lukewarm, but always alive and intense. This fire, however, is extraordinary, because it does not necessarily destroy—the burning bush shows this (Ex 3:2). Concerning "jealous" (↗ Ex 20:5).

▶ Moses foretells the Exile. The Babylonians conquered Jerusalem in the sixth century B.C. (↗ 2 Kings 25) and took many inhabitants into exile.

image in the form of anything which the LORD your God has forbidden you. ²⁴ For the LORD your God is a devouring fire, a jealous God.

²⁵ "When you beget children and children's children, and have grown old in the land, if you act corruptly by making a graven image in the form of anything, and by doing what is evil in the sight of the LORD your God, so as to provoke him to anger, ²⁶ I call heaven and earth to witness against you this day, that you will soon utterly perish from the land which you are going over the Jordan to possess; you will not live long upon it, but will be utterly destroyed. ²⁷ And the LORD will scatter you among the peoples, and you will be left few in number among the nations where the LORD will drive you. ²⁸ And there you will serve gods of wood and stone, the work of men's hands, that neither see, nor hear, nor eat, nor smell. ²⁹ But from there you will seek the LORD your God, and you will find him, if you search after him with all your heart and with all your soul. ³⁰ When you are in tribulation, and all these things come upon you in the latter days, you will return to the LORD your God and obey his voice, ³¹ for the LORD your God is a merciful God; he will not fail you or destroy you or forget the covenant with your fathers which he swore to them.

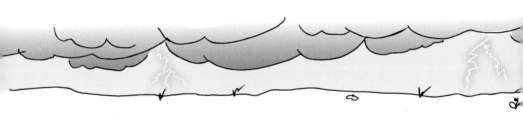

▶ "No other" (v. 35 and v. 39). This passage is one of the strongest testimonies to faith in God as the one God of the universe (the Greek term for this is "monotheism"; ↗ also Is 45:5–6).

▶ Moses says explicitly here for the first time in the Bible that God loves the Israelites. Therefore they, too, can love God (↗ Deut 6:5).

🅱 Do not think that I have come to abolish the law and the prophets; I have come not to abolish them but to fulfil them.

Mt 5:17

³² "For ask now of the days that are past, which were before you, since the day that God created man upon the earth, and ask from one end of heaven to the other, whether such a great thing as this has ever happened or was ever heard of. ³³ Did any people ever hear the voice of God speaking out of the midst of the fire, as you have heard, and still live? ³⁴ Or has God ever attempted to go and take a nation for himself from the midst of another nation, by trials, by signs, by wonders, and by war, by a mighty hand and an outstretched arm, and by great terrors, according to all that the LORD your God did for you in Egypt before your eyes? ³⁵ To you it was shown, that you might know that the LORD is God; there is no other besides him. ³⁶ Out of heaven he let you hear his voice, that he might discipline you; and on earth he let you see his great fire, and you heard his words out of the midst of the fire. ³⁷ And because he loved your fathers and chose their descendants after them, and brought you out of Egypt with his own presence, by his great power, ³⁸ driving out before you nations greater and mightier than yourselves, to bring you in, to give you their land for an inheritance, as at this day; ³⁹ know therefore this day, and lay it to your heart, that the LORD is God in heaven above and on the earth beneath; there is no other. ⁴⁰ Therefore you shall keep his statutes and his commandments, which I command you this

day, that it may go well with you, and with your children after you, and that you may prolong your days in the land which the LORD your God gives you for ever."

MOSES EXPLAINS THE LAWS GIVEN AT HOREB (DEUT 5–26)

Moses' second great speech is the longest speech in the Bible (Deut 5–26). First Moses repeats the Ten Command-ments (→ Ex 20:2–17 and Deut 5:6–21). Even in this fundamental passage, he introduces his own new emphases. As the reason for the commandment about the Sabbath, he cites, not the seventh day of creation (Ex 20:11), but the deliverance in the Exodus (Deut 6:15). Thus he stresses that the Sabbath serves to bring about the equality of all men in God's sight. In Deut 6–11, Moses preaches mainly about the First Commandment: Israel has only one God and must not allow itself to be led astray to serve other gods. Then Moses sets out the laws that the people are to keep in the Promised Land (Deut 12–26). In doing so, he changes a few laws from the form in which they appeared in the Book of the Covenant that he presented to Israel at Mount Sinai (Ex 20:22–23, 33). The Bible thus shows that it is necessary to adapt laws to new conditions.

The Covenant is relevant today (Deut 5:2–3)

5 ² The LORD our God made a covenant with us in Horeb. ³ Not with our fathers did the LORD make this covenant, but with us, who are all of us here alive this day.

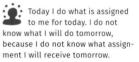 Today I do what is assigned to me for today. I do not know what I will do tomorrow, because I do not know what assignment I will receive tomorrow.

FRANCIS DE SALES (1567–1622), French bishop, mystic, founder of a religious order, and Doctor of the Church

The *Shema Yisrael* and the question from a young man (Deut 6)

6 ⁴ Hear, O Israel: The LORD our God is one LORD; ⁵and you shall love the LORD your God with all your heart, and with all your soul, and with all your might.

⁶ And these words which I command you this day shall be upon your heart; ⁷ and you shall teach them diligently to your children, and shall talk of them when you sit in your house, and when you walk by the way, and when you lie down, and when you rise. ⁸ And you shall bind them as a sign upon your hand, and they shall be as frontlets between your eyes. ⁹ And you shall write them on the doorposts of your house and on your gates....

²⁰ "When your son asks you in time to come, 'What is the meaning of the decrees and the statutes and the ordinances which the LORD our God has commanded you?' ²¹ then you shall say to your son, 'We were Pharaoh's slaves in Egypt; and the LORD brought us out of Egypt with a mighty hand; ²² and the LORD showed signs and wonders, great and grievous, against Egypt and against Pharaoh and all his household, before our eyes; ²³ and he brought us out from there, that he might bring us in and give us the land which he swore to give to our fathers. ²⁴ And the LORD commanded us to do all these statutes, to fear the LORD our God, for our good always, that he might preserve us alive, as at this day....

▶ "Hear, O Israel", in Hebrew, *Shema Yisrael*, is the name for the passage Deut 6:4–9. It is the fundamental profession of faith for Jews. They repeat this verse in their prayers every day.

▶ "Heart" (v. 5) means not only feelings, but also thinking and understanding. As the Bible sees it, one can think properly only with the heart.

▶ "Doorposts", in Hebrew, *mezuzot*: When you come to a Jewish residence, you see on the doorpost a little box containing a little scroll with the *Shema Yisrael* (↗ Deut 6:4) and other passages from the Torah. The purpose of this little box is to fulfill the command in Deut 6:9, and accordingly it is called a *mezuzah*.

Blessed are those who hunger and thirst for righteousness, for they shall be satisfied.

Mt 5:6: Jesus, in the Sermon on the Mount

Y → 523
Why does man not live on bread alone?

When we sin by pride, we are telling God that we are independent of everything.

JEAN-MARIE VIANNEY
(1786–1859), French priest (the Curé of Ars)

Man does not live by bread alone (Deut 8:2–3)

8 ² And you shall remember all the way which the LORD your God has led you these forty years in the wilderness, that he might humble you, testing you to know what was in your heart, whether you would keep his commandments, or not. ³ And he humbled you and let you hunger and fed you with manna, which you did not know, nor did your fathers know; that he might make you know that man does not live by bread alone, but that man lives by everything that proceeds out of the mouth of the LORD.

God is unique (Deut 10:14–22)

10 ¹⁴ Behold, to the LORD your God belong heaven and the heaven of heavens, the earth with all that is in it; ¹⁵ yet the LORD set his heart in love upon your fathers and chose their descendants after them, you above all peoples, as at this day.

¹⁶ Circumcise therefore the foreskin of your heart, and be no longer stubborn. ¹⁷ For the LORD your God is God of gods and LORD of lords, the great, the mighty, and the terrible God, who is not partial and takes no bribe. ¹⁸ He executes justice for the fatherless and the widow, and loves the sojourner, giving him food and clothing. ¹⁹ Love the sojourner therefore; for you were sojourners in the land of Egypt.

God is partial. He has a weakness for foreigners! Moses stresses this point for good reasons, as we see today in societies where there are many religions and immigrants.

▶ "As the stars in heaven": God fulfilled his promise to Abraham (→ Gen 15:5).

▶ "Brother": Moses would like a spirit of fraternal unity to prevail among the Israelites.

" The poor provide us with a concrete opportunity to encounter Christ himself, and to touch his suffering flesh.

POPE FRANCIS, in his Message to World Youth Day 2014

²⁰ You shall fear the LORD your God; you shall serve him and cling to him, and by his name you shall swear. ²¹ He is your praise; he is your God, who has done for you these great and terrible things which your eyes have seen. ²² Your fathers went down to Egypt seventy persons; and now the LORD your God has made you as the stars of heaven for multitude.

Thoughts in the heart (Deut 15:7–11)

15 ⁷ "If there is among you a poor man, one of your brethren, in any of your towns within your land which the LORD your God gives you, you shall not harden your heart or shut your hand against your poor brother, ⁸ but you shall open your hand to him, and lend him sufficient for his need, whatever it may be. ⁹ Take heed lest there be a base thought in your heart, and you say, 'The seventh year, the year of release is near,' and your eye be hostile to your poor brother, and you give him nothing, and he cry to the LORD against you, and it be sin in you. ¹⁰ You shall give to him freely, and your heart shall not be grudging when you give to him; because for this the LORD your God will bless you in all your work and in all that you undertake.

[11] For the poor will never cease out of the land; therefore I command you, You shall open wide your hand to your brother, to the needy and to the poor, in the land.

 You have one teacher, and you are all brethren.
Mt 23:8

Moses declares that the Passover together with the Feast of the Unleavened Bread (→ Ex 12:1–25) should be celebrated by all Israelites together in Jerusalem (Deut 16:1–9), without mentioning the name of the city (→ below at Deut 16:11). The same is true for the Feast of Pentecost and the Feast of Tabernacles. On the basis of this rule, Jesus and his disciples went for the Passover feast to Jerusalem, where Jesus was crucified.

Divine worship—gladness and equality in God's sight (Deut 16:10–17)

16 [10] Then you shall keep the feast of weeks to the LORD your God with the tribute of a freewill offering from your hand, which you shall give as the LORD your God blesses you; [11] and you shall rejoice before the LORD your God, you and your son and your daughter, your manservant and your maidservant, the Levite who is within your towns, the sojourner, the fatherless, and the widow who are among you, at the place which the LORD your God will choose, to make his name dwell there. [12] You shall remember that you were a slave in Egypt; and you shall be careful to observe these statutes.

[13] "You shall keep the feast of booths seven days, when you make your ingathering from your threshing floor and your wine press; [14] you shall rejoice in your feast, you and your son and your daughter, your manservant and your maidservant, the Levite, the sojourner, the fatherless, and the widow who are within your towns. [15] For seven days you shall keep the feast to the LORD your God at the place which the LORD will choose; because the LORD your God will bless you in all your produce and in all the work of your hands, so that you will be altogether joyful.

[16] "Three times a year all your males shall appear before the LORD your God at the place which he will choose: at the feast of unleavened bread, at the feast of weeks, and at the feast of booths. They shall not appear before the LORD empty-handed; [17] every man shall give as he is able, according to the blessing of the LORD your God which he has given you.

▶ The "place" means the Temple in Jerusalem. The fact that God's "Name" will "dwell" there means that God wishes to be present there in a special way. Moses mysteriously does not specify where that will be. Although Jerusalem is of central importance for Israel, this name does not occur anywhere in the Pentateuch.

There we shall rest [i.e., observe the holy day of rest] and see, we shall see and love, we shall love and praise. Behold what will be at the end without end.

ST. AUGUSTINE →

The prophet like Moses (Deut 18:15-18)

18 [15] The LORD your God will raise up for you a prophet like me from among you, from your brethren—him you shall heed— [16] just as you desired of the LORD your God at Horeb on the day of

▶ "Appear before": literally, "behold the face of". Like the "Name" of God, so also his "Face" stands for his personal presence.

▶ The prophet like Moses: Jeremiah is described in this way—God places his words on his lips (↗ Jer 1:9). Jesus, too, was regarded as this prophet who was foretold (↗ Jn 6:14; Rev 3:22–23).

One must lend an ear to God's voice in order to discern the signs of his will. And once his will is recognized, one must do it, whatever it is and whatever it may cost.
CHARLES DE FOUCAULD (1858–1916), French explorer, officer, priest, and hermit

Tenderness has the right of way! The Bible knows what young lovers need: a lot of time to discover each other and a protected, undisturbed space, so that their delight in each other may unfold.

the assembly, when you said, 'Let me not hear again the voice of the LORD my God, or see this great fire any more, lest I die.' ¹⁷ And the LORD said to me, 'They have rightly said all that they have spoken. ¹⁸ I will raise up for them a prophet like you from among their brethren; and I will put my words in his mouth, and he shall speak to them all that I command him.

Respect: more than strict justice (Deut 24:5–22)

24 ⁵ When a man is newly married, he shall not go out with the army or be charged with any business; he shall be free at home one year, to be happy with his wife whom he has taken.

⁶ "No man shall take a mill or an upper millstone in pledge; for he would be taking a life in pledge....

¹⁰ "When you make your neighbor a loan of any sort, you shall not go into his house to fetch his pledge. ¹¹ You shall stand outside, and the man to whom you make the loan shall bring the pledge out to you. ¹² And if he is a poor man, you shall not sleep in his pledge; ¹³ when the sun goes down, you shall restore to him the pledge that he may sleep in his cloak and bless you; and it shall be righteousness to you before the LORD your God.

▶ This rule has nothing to do with mere economic justice. It is a matter of respect for the poor.

❞ To defraud anyone of wages that are his due is a great crime which cries to the avenging anger of Heaven. "Behold, [says the Holy Spirit in Sacred Scripture,] the hire of the laborers ... which by fraud has been kept back by you, crieth; and the cry of them hath entered into the ears of the LORD of Sabaoth." The rich must ... refrain from cutting down the workmen's earnings, whether by force, by fraud, or by usurious dealing.
POPE LEO XIII, Encyclical *Rerum Novarum* (1891), 20.

Awesome! What is left over belongs to those who have nothing. A principle that turns the world upside-down.

¹⁴ "You shall not oppress a hired servant who is poor and needy, whether he is one of your brethren or one of the sojourners who are in your land within your towns; ¹⁵ you shall give him his hire on the day he earns it, before the sun goes down (for he is poor, and sets his heart upon it); lest he cry against you to the LORD, and it be sin in you....

¹⁹ "When you reap your harvest in your field, and have forgotten a sheaf in the field, you shall not go back to get it; it shall be for the sojourner, the fatherless, and the widow; that the LORD your God may bless you in all the work of your hands. ²⁰ When you beat your olive trees, you shall not go over the boughs again; it shall be for the sojourner, the fatherless, and the widow. ²¹ When you gather the grapes of your vineyard, you shall not glean it afterward; it shall be for the sojourner, the fatherless, and the widow. ²² You shall remember that you were a slave in the land of Egypt; therefore I command you to do this.

COVENANT AT MOAB, TRANSFER OF POWER, AND MOSES' DEATH (DEUT 29–34)

Before Moses hands over authority to his successor (Deut 31) and dies (Deut 34), Moses makes in the land of Moab another covenant with Israel, as God commanded him (Deut 28:69 in Hebrew = Deut 29:1). Moses concludes his covenant speech (Deut 29–30) with the solemn admonition that Israel should commit itself to God and his Torah (Deut 30:15–20). Scripture does not tell us Israel's answer. But we read the answer that we should give even earlier in the mysterious verse Deut 29:29:

29 [28] The secret things belong to the LORD our God; but the things that are revealed belong to us and to our children for ever, that we may do all the words of this law.

▶ "Law"—in Hebrew, *Torah*. "This Torah" refers here primarily to Moses' teaching in the Book of Deuteronomy. The expression is often used, however, in reference to all five books from Gen to Deut.

A life-or-death decision (Deut 30)

30 [1] "And when all these things come upon you, the blessing and the curse, which I have set before you, and you call them to mind among all the nations where the LORD your God has driven you, [2] and return to the LORD your God, you and your children, and obey his voice in all that I command you this day, with all your heart and with all your soul; [3] then the LORD your God will restore your fortunes, and have compassion upon you, and he will gather you

▶ Blessing and curse (v. 1) are set forth in Deut 28. In ancient Eastern Middle Eastern treaties, it was customary to specify in writing blessings for those

again from all the peoples where the LORD your God has scattered you. [4] If your outcasts are in the uttermost parts of heaven, from there the LORD your God will gather you, and from there he will fetch you; [5] and the LORD your God will bring you into the land which your fathers possessed, that you may possess it; and he will make you more prosperous and numerous than your fathers. [6] And the LORD your God will circumcise your heart and the heart of your offspring, so that you will love the LORD your God with all your heart and with all your soul, that you may live. [7] And the LORD your God will put all these curses upon your foes and enemies who persecuted you. [8] And you shall again obey the voice of the LORD, and keep all his commandments which I command you this day. [9] The LORD your God will make you abundantly prosperous in all the work of your hand, in the fruit of your body, and in the fruit of your cattle, and in the fruit of your ground; for the LORD will again take delight in prospering you, as he took delight in your fathers, [10] if you obey the voice of the LORD your God, to keep his commandments and his statutes which are written in this book of the law, if you turn to the LORD your God with all your heart and with all your soul.

who keep the treaty and curses in case someone breaks it. The curses of the Book of Deuteronomy interpret the Exile as a curse that strikes Israel because it has not kept the Torah (↗ Deut 4:25–27; 28:64; 29:24–27).

▶ Circumcision of the male foreskin is the sign of the covenant with Abraham (Gen 17:11). Circumcision of the heart (↗ Deut 6:4; 10:16) refers to a conversion of heart so that one will be dedicated to God from within.

▶ As Israel "returns" to the Lord by inner conversion, so God will let the people return to their land. In Hebrew, this play on words runs through Deut 30:1–10.

[11] "For this commandment which I command you this day is not too hard for you, neither is it far off. [12] It is not in heaven, that you should say, 'Who will go up for us to heaven, and bring it to us, that we may hear it and do it?' [13] Neither is it beyond the sea, that you should say, 'Who will go over the sea for us, and bring it to us, that we may hear it and do it?' [14] But the word is very near you; it is in your mouth and in your heart, so that you can do it.

[15] "See, I have set before you this day life and good, death and evil. [16] If you obey the commandments of the LORD your God which I command you this day, by loving the LORD your God, by walking in his ways, and by keeping his commandments and his statutes and his ordinances, then you shall live and multiply, and the LORD your God will bless you in the land which you are entering to take possession of it. [17] But if your heart turns away, and you will not hear, but are drawn away to worship other gods and serve them, [18] I declare to you this day, that you shall perish; you shall not live long in the land which you are going over the Jordan to enter and possess. [19] I call heaven and earth to witness against you this day, that I have set before you life and death, blessing and curse; therefore choose life, that you and your descendants may live, [20] loving the LORD your God, obeying his voice, and clinging to him; for that means life to you and

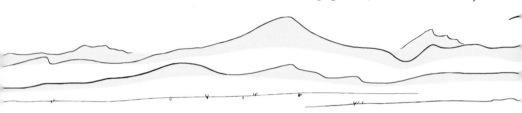

length of days, that you may dwell in the land which the LORD swore to your fathers, to Abraham, to Isaac, and to Jacob, to give them.'"

Moses hands over leadership and the Torah (Deut 31:7–13)

31 [7] Then Moses summoned Joshua, and said to him in the sight of all Israel, "Be strong and of good courage; for you shall go with this people into the land which the LORD has sworn to their fathers to give them; and you shall put them in possession of it. [8] It is the LORD who goes before you; he will be with you, he will not fail you or forsake you; do not fear or be dismayed."

[9] And Moses wrote this law, and gave it to the priests the sons of Levi, who carried the ark of the covenant of the LORD, and to all the elders of Israel. [10] And Moses commanded them, "At the end of every seven years, at the set time of the year of release, at the feast of booths, [11] when all Israel comes to appear before the LORD your God at the place which he will choose, you shall read this law before all Israel in their hearing. [12] Assemble the people, men, women, and little ones, and the sojourner within your towns, that they may hear and learn to fear the LORD your God, and be careful to do all the words of this law, [13] and that their children, who have not known it, may hear and

learn to fear the LORD your God, as long as you live in the land which you are going over the Jordan to possess."

Moses climbs Mount Nebo and dies (Deut 34)

34 [1] And Moses went up from the plains of Moab to Mount Nebo, to the top of Pisgah, which is opposite Jericho. And the LORD showed him all the land, Gilead as far as Dan, [2] all Naph'tali, the land of E'phraim and Manas'seh, all the land of Judah as far as the western sea, [3] the Neg'eb, and the Plain, that is, the valley of Jericho the city of palm trees, as far as Zoar. [4] And the LORD said to him, "This is the land of which I swore to Abraham, to Isaac, and to Jacob, 'I will give it to your descendants.' I have let you see it with your eyes, but you shall not go over there." [5] So Moses the servant of the LORD died there in the land of Moab, according to the word of the LORD, [6] and he buried him in the valley in the land of Moab opposite Beth-pe'or; but no man knows the place of his burial to this day. [7] Moses was a hundred and twenty years old when he died; his eye was not dim, nor

Many of the greatest scientists, artists, and thinkers have been Jews: the author Franz Kafka, the composer Felix Mendelssohn-Bartholdy, the psychologist Sigmund Freud, the philosopher Ludwig Wittgenstein, the saint Edith Stein, the painter Marc Chagall, the physicist Albert Einstein, the violinist Yehudi Menuhin. Being spiritually alert is part of their religion and tradition. With practice beginning in early childhood, they come to enjoy the experience of reading and learning.

his natural force abated. [8] And the sons of Israel wept for Moses in the plains of Moab thirty days; then the days of weeping and mourning for Moses were ended.

[9] And Joshua the son of Nun was full of the spirit of wisdom, for Moses had laid his hands upon him; so the sons of Israel obeyed him, and did as the LORD had commanded Moses. [10] And there has not arisen a prophet since in Israel like Moses, whom the LORD knew face to face, [11] none like him for all the signs and the wonders which the LORD sent him to do in the land of Egypt, to Pharaoh and to all his servants and to all his land, [12] and for all the mighty power and all the great and terrible deeds which Moses wrought in the sight of all Israel.

▶ "According to the word of the Lord" (v. 5), literally "upon the Lord's mouth". Therefore one rabbinical tradition says that Moses died "at the kiss" of God.

The Historical Books

The Torah dealt with the prehistory of Israel and laid the foundations for the common life of the people. Now the Historical Books show how this program is carried out only partially in various epochs and describe the resulting problems.

An initial phase begins with Joshua, Moses' successor, and leads through the time of the "judges" and the prophet Samuel to the kings in the Southern Kingdom of Judah and in the Northern Kingdom of Israel. It depicts the slow process by which the people became firmly rooted in the land, but it also shows how it ultimately declined on account of many failures, especially of its leaders. The capture of Samaria in 720 B.C. by the Assyrians and the destruction of Jerusalem in 587 B. C. by the Babylonians meant for a long time the end of its political autonomy.

Chronicles depicts this past time from a hopeful perspective, with an emphasis on Temple, priests, Levites, and divine worship. This leads to a new beginning in the Persian period, which becomes especially evident in Ezra and Nehemiah.

The increasing importance of the individual, and in particular of women, also, is reflected in a few shorter books that highlight individual persons. Ruth, which follows Judges and precedes Samuel, emphasizes the extraordinary solidarity of a Moabite woman. The angel Raphael in Tobit is an example of God's protective accompaniment. Esther and Judith assign to courageous women a key role in saving their people.

The two Books of the Maccabees deal with the conflicts in the second century B.C., when pious Jews who practiced their religion experienced oppression and rose up against it. In all, the "Historical Books" of the Old Testament span more than a millennium and show how God always and in entirely different ways accompanies people who trust in him.

Joshua

The books Joshua through Kings are called in Judaism the "former prophets", because in them prophets play the most important role. The Book of Joshua tells of how Moses' successor, Joshua, conquers the Promised Land with the People of Israel (Josh 1–12) and divides it among the twelve tribes (Josh 13–22). Before Joshua dies, he renews the covenant between Israel and God (Josh 23–24). In this way, God fulfills his promise to give the land of Canaan to Abraham's posterity ↗ especially Gen 12:1–7; Ex 3:8).

In Deuteronomy, Moses had commanded the Israelites to kill mercilessly the former inhabitants of the land during the conquest. Joshua is therefore a very warlike and problematic book. Yet we must consider: there never was a bloody conquest of the land. The city of Jericho (Josh 6) was not inhabited at all at that time. The stories of battle are supposed to show how God protects his people from all dangers. Moreover, these accounts are supposed to deter Israel from adopting the religions and practices of the peoples of Canaan: child sacrifices should never again occur in Israel (↗ Deut 12:31). The Historical Books must not be misused to justify violence in God's name.

God's fidelity (Josh 1:1–8)

1 ¹ After the death of Moses the servant of the LORD, the LORD said to Joshua the son of Nun, Moses' minister, ² "Moses my servant is dead; now therefore arise, go over this Jordan, you and all this people, into the land which I am giving to them, to the sons of Israel. ³ Every place that the sole of your foot will tread upon I have given to you, as I promised to Moses. ⁴ From the wilderness and this Lebanon as far as the great river, the river Euphrates, all the land of the Hittites to the Great Sea toward the going down of the sun shall be your territory. ⁵ No man shall be able to stand before you all the days of your life; as I was with Moses, so I will be with you; I will not fail you or forsake you. ⁶ Be strong and of good courage; for you shall cause this people to inherit the land which I swore to their fathers to give them. ⁷ Only be strong and very courageous, being careful to do according to all the law which Moses my servant commanded you; turn not from it to the right hand or to the left, that you may have good success wherever you go. ⁸ This book of the law shall not depart out of your mouth, but you shall meditate on it day and night, that you may be careful to do according to all that is written in it; for then you shall make your way prosperous, and then you shall have good success.

▶ The name "Joshua" means "God saves." "Jesus" is the Greek and Latin form of this name. In his native language, Jesus' name was actually "Yoshua".

▶ According to Joshua's words, the land is supposed to extend from the Euphrates River (in modern-day Iraq) to the Mediterranean—a considerable exaggeration! It is supposed to show how generous God is.

▶ The sort of "meditation" meant here (v. 8) is the repetition, over and over again, of words that have been learned by heart so as to assimilate them spiritually.

Rahab saves the spies (Josh 2:1–15)

2 ¹ And Joshua the son of Nun sent two men secretly from Shittim as spies, saying, "Go, view the land, especially Jericho." And they went, and came into the house of a harlot whose name was Ra'hab, and lodged there. ² And it was told the king of Jericho, "Behold, certain men of Israel have come here tonight to search out the land." ³ Then the king of Jericho sent to Ra'hab, saying, "Bring forth the men that have come to you, who entered your house; for they have come to search out all the land." ⁴ But the woman had taken the two men and hidden them; and she said, "True, men came to me, but I did not know where they came from; ⁵ and when the gate was to be closed, at dark, the men went out; where the men went I do not know; pursue them quickly, for you will overtake them." ⁶ But she had brought them up to the roof, and hid them with the stalks of flax which she had laid in order on the roof. ⁷ So the men pursued after them on the way to the Jordan as far as the fords; and as soon as the pursuers had gone out, the gate was shut.

⁸ Before they lay down, she came up to them on the roof, ⁹ and said to the men, "I know that the LORD has given you the land, and that the fear of you has fallen upon us, and that all the inhabitants of the land melt away before you. ¹⁰ For we have heard how the LORD dried up the water of the Red Sea before you when you came out of Egypt, and what you did to the two kings of the Am'orites that were

▶ This story makes a prostitute the heroine. The Bible shows that even people on the margins of society play a role in God's plans and can even be especially close to him.

▶ If Rahab were to report the spies, they would be in mortal danger. Instead, she herself incurs a great risk.

💡 During the Second World War, between 3,000 and 5,000 Jews were preserved from death in the gas chambers because brave contemporaries hid them, thus risking their own lives. After the war, many of these rescuers—who were often very simple people—were designated "Just among nations" in Israel's memorial Yad Vashem.

▶ Although Rahab is a foreigner, she professes faith in the all-embracing power of the God of the Israelites. Already in this incident, the faith crosses the boundary between peoples (↗ Naaman also in 2 Kings 5:17).

▶ One woman rescues two men. Although ancient Israel was a patriarchal society, women assume important roles in the Bible.

beyond the Jordan, to Si'hon and Og, whom you utterly destroyed. [11] And as soon as we heard it, our hearts melted, and there was no courage left in any man, because of you; for the LORD your God is he who is God in heaven above and on earth beneath. [12] Now then, swear to me by the LORD that as I have dealt kindly with you, you also will deal kindly with my father's house, and give me a sure sign, [13] and save alive my father and mother, my brothers and sisters, and all who belong to them, and deliver our lives from death." [14] And the men said to her, "Our life for yours! If you do not tell this business of ours, then we will deal kindly and faithfully with you when the LORD gives us the land."

[15] Then she let them down by a rope through the window, for her house was built into the city wall, so that she dwelt in the wall.

Israel crosses the Jordan (Josh 3:14–17)

3 [14] So, when the people set out from their tents, to pass over the Jordan with the priests bearing the ark of the covenant before the people, [15] and when those who bore the ark had come to the Jordan, and the feet of the priests bearing the ark were dipped in the brink of the water (the Jordan overflows all its banks throughout

▶ The Jordan River flows from the Lake of Gennesaret into the Dead Sea (called here the "Salt Sea"). Jericho is located in the Jordan Valley, around ten kilometers (6 miles) distant from the Dead Sea, today in the Palestinian West Bank. Jericho is one of the oldest cities in the world.

▶ The miracle at the Jordan duplicates the miracle at the Red Sea (↗ Ex 14:21; Ps 114:3, 5) and continues it. Both at the deliverance from Egypt and at the entrance into the Promised Land, God shows that he rules the powers of nature so as to protect his people.

▶ Shechem is located near the modern Palestinian city of Nablus and not far from ancient Samaria. Gen 12:6 relates that Shechem was the first place that Abraham visited in the land of Canaan.

the time of harvest), [16] the waters coming down from above stood and rose up in a heap far off, at Adam, the city that is beside Zar'ethan, and those flowing down toward the sea of the Ar'abah, the Salt Sea, were wholly cut off; and the people passed over opposite Jericho. [17] And while all Israel were passing over on dry ground, the priests who bore the ark of the covenant of the LORD stood on dry ground in the midst of the Jordan, until all the nation finished passing over the Jordan.

A new decision in Shechem (Josh 24)

24 [1] Then Joshua gathered all the tribes of Israel to She'chem, and summoned the elders, the heads, the judges, and the officers of Israel; and they presented themselves before God. [2] And Joshua said to all the people, "Thus says the LORD, the God of Israel, 'Your fathers lived of old beyond the Euphrates, Te'rah, the father of Abraham and of Na'hor; and they served other gods. [3] Then I took your father Abraham from beyond the River and led him through all the land of Canaan, and made his offspring many. I gave him Isaac; [4] and to Isaac I gave Jacob and Esau. And I gave Esau the hill country of Se'ir to possess, but Jacob and his children went down to Egypt. [5] And I sent Moses and Aaron, and I plagued Egypt with what I did in the midst of it; and afterwards I

brought you out.... . ¹³ I gave you a land on which you had not labored, and cities which you had not built, and you dwell therein; you eat the fruit of vineyards and oliveyards which you did not plant.'

¹⁴ "Now therefore fear the LORD, and serve him in sincerity and in faithfulness; put away the gods which your fathers served beyond the River, and in Egypt, and serve the LORD. ¹⁵ And if you be unwilling to serve the LORD, choose this day whom you will serve, whether the gods your fathers served in the region beyond the River, or the gods of the Am′orites in whose land you dwell; but as for me and my house, we will serve the LORD."

¹⁶ Then the people answered, "Far be it from us that we should forsake the LORD, to serve other gods; ¹⁷ for it is the LORD our God who brought us and our fathers up from the land of Egypt, out of the house of bondage, and who did those great signs in our sight, and preserved us in all the way that we went, and among all the peoples through whom we passed; ¹⁸ and the LORD drove out before us all the peoples, the Am′orites who lived in the land; therefore we also will serve the LORD, for he is our God."

¹⁹ But Joshua said to the people, "You cannot serve the LORD; for he is a holy God; he is a jealous God; he will not forgive your trans-

▶ Abraham's family was originally from Babylon in modern-day Iraq (↗ Gen 11:31). The "River" meant here is the Euphrates.

I believe in my God. He exists. I accept that and feel good about it. That's it. I don't care what other people think about it. I have reached my own conviction: My God is with me.

ZORAN

🙷 I want to serve God, and I want to make up for the mistakes that I have made and the pain that I have caused. I recommend the same for everyone.

MARK WAHLBERG (*1971), Hollywood-actor

gressions or your sins. ²⁰ If you forsake the LORD and serve foreign gods, then he will turn and do you harm, and consume you, after having done you good." ²¹ And the people said to Joshua, "No; but we will serve the LORD." ²² Then Joshua said to the people, "You are witnesses against yourselves that you have chosen the LORD, to serve him." And they said, "We are witnesses." ²³ He said, "Then put away the foreign gods which are among you, and incline your heart to the LORD, the God of Israel."

²⁹ After these things Joshua the son of Nun, the servant of the LORD, died, being a hundred and ten years old. ³⁰ And they buried him in his own inheritance at Tim′nath-se′rah, which is in the hill country of E′phraim, north of the mountain of Ga′ash.

³¹ And Israel served the LORD all the days of Joshua, and all the days of the elders who outlived Joshua and had known all the work which the LORD did for Israel....

▶ Joshua summarizes Israel's history and challenges the people to make a decision.

The Book of Joshua tells how they chose the Lord at Shechem.... In the religious awareness of the Old Testament, this choice increasingly takes the form of a rigorous and universalistic monotheism.... The universal salvific will transforms human history into a great pilgrimage of peoples towards one destination, Jerusalem, but without loss of any of their ethnic-cultural differences (↗ Rev 7:9).

POPE JOHN PAUL II, April 21, 1999

THE BOOK OF

Judges

The judges in this book are not only officials who administer justice but also leaders of the people. Generally they rescue it from dangers. Examples of famous judges are Deborah, Gideon, Jephthah, and finally Samson (Judg 13–16).

Several times the book treats critically the issues of leading a community and the relation between women and men. It shows good insight into problems, such as the ones involved in introducing the kingship in Israel in Judg 9:

▶ Jerubbaal (= contender with Baal, a nickname given to him because he destroyed the altar of Baal), also named Gideon, saved Israel from the threat of the Midianites (Judg 6–8) but refused to rule over the people. On Shechem, → Josh 24:1.

▶ Intrigue, bribery, a god of power ("Baal" in v. 4 means "Lord"), a band of criminals, multiple murders—that cannot be a good basis for a community. As a matter of fact, as the story continues (from v. 22 on) there are further acts of violence. Shechem is destroyed, and Abimelech, too, must die.

Taking power with violence (Judg 9:1–6)

9 ¹ Now Abim'elech the son of Jerubba'al went to She'chem to his mother's kinsmen and said to them and to the whole clan of his mother's family, ² "Say in the ears of all the citizens of She'chem, 'Which is better for you, that all seventy of the sons of Jerubba'al rule over you, or that one rule over you?' Remember also that I am your bone and your flesh." ³ And his mother's kinsmen spoke all these words on his behalf in the ears of all the men of She'chem; and their hearts inclined to follow Abim'elech, for they said, "He is our brother." ⁴ And they gave him seventy pieces of silver out of the house of Ba'al-be'rith with which Abim'elech hired worthless and reckless fellows, who followed him. ⁵ And he went to his father's house at Oph'rah, and slew his brothers the sons of Jerubba'al, seventy men, upon one stone; but Jo'tham the youngest son of Jerubbaal was left, for he hid himself. ⁶ And all the citizens of She'chem came together, and all Beth-mil'lo, and they went and made Abim'elech king, by the oak of the pillar at Shechem.

Jotham's speech (Judg 9:7–15)

⁷ When it was told to Jo'tham, he went and stood on the top of Mount Ger'izim, and cried aloud and said to them, "Listen to me, you men of She'chem, that God may listen to you. ⁸ The trees once went forth to anoint a king over them; and they said to the olive tree, 'Reign over us.' ⁹ But the olive tree said to them, 'Shall I leave my fatness, by which gods and men are honored, and go to sway over the trees?' ¹⁰ And the trees said to the fig tree, 'Come you, and reign over us.' ¹¹ But the fig tree said to them, 'Shall I leave my sweetness and my good fruit, and go to sway over the trees?' ¹² And the trees said to the vine, 'Come you, and reign over us.' ¹³ But the vine said to them, 'Shall I leave my wine which cheers gods and men, and go to sway over the trees?' ¹⁴ Then all the trees said to the bramble, 'Come you, and reign over us.' ¹⁵ And the bramble said to the trees, 'If in good faith you are anointing me king over you, then come and take refuge in my shade; but if not, let fire come out of the bramble and devour the cedars of Lebanon.'

▶ Jotham told a fable (a story in which plants or animals stand for human beings). It is full of subtle irony: the trees that in themselves are useful refuse to rule over the others, whereas the unfruitful bramble, which provides neither shade nor fruit, is willing to do so and also immediately threatens destruction. Jotham thereby very sharply criticizes Abimelech and kingship in general, which he makes even clearer in the following verses (16–21).

99 We are meant to serve God with the gifts He has given us.

MOTHER DOLORES HART O.S.B. (b. 1938), former movie star who became a Benedictine nun

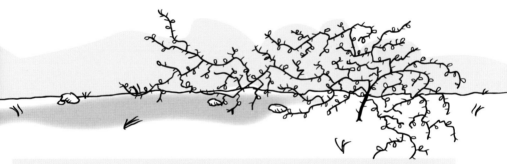

Judges highlights the roles of women more than almost any other book of the Bible. They have quite different roles: Deborah and Jael are heroines (Judg 4–5), Jephthah's daughter is a victim of her father's stupidity (Judg 11:34–40), Delilah is sly (Judg 16). Judg 13 shows us two very dissimilar parents:

Prediction of Samson's birth (Judg 13:1–8)

13 ¹ And the sons of Israel again did what was evil in the sight of the Lord; and the Lord gave them into the hand of the Philis'tines for forty years.

² And there was a certain man of Zorah, of the tribe of the Da'nites, whose name was Mano'ah; and his wife was barren and had no children. ³ And the angel of the Lord appeared to the woman and said to her, "Behold, you are barren and have no children; but you shall conceive and bear a son. ⁴ Therefore beware, and drink no wine or strong drink, and eat nothing unclean, ⁵ for behold, you shall conceive and bear a son. No razor shall come upon his head, for the boy shall be a Naz'irite to God from birth; and he shall begin to deliver Israel from the hand of the Philis'tines." ⁶ Then the woman came and told her husband, "A man of God came to me, and his countenance was like the countenance of the angel of God, very terrible; I did not ask him where he was from, and he did not tell me his name; ⁷ but he

▶ The husband's name means "rest" and suits his easygoing nature (→ the different kinds of movement in vv. 10–11).

▶ The instructions for the Nazirite vow (see Num 6) are divided up here between the mother and her son: she must refrain from alcohol, and his hair must not be cut.

> Angels are God's messengers. They bring God to men, they open heaven and thus open earth. Precisely because they are with God, they can also be very close to man. Indeed, God is closer to each one of us than we ourselves are. The Angels speak to man of what constitutes his true being, of what in his life is so often concealed and buried.
>
> **POPE BENEDICT XVI**, September 29, 2007

said to me, 'Behold, you shall conceive and bear a son; so then drink no wine or strong drink, and eat nothing unclean, for the boy shall be a Naz'irite to God from birth to the day of his death.'" [8] Then Mano'ah entreated the LORD, and said, "O, LORD, I beg you, let the man of God whom you sent come again to us, and teach us what we are to do with the boy that will be born."

The Angel comes again (Judg 13:9–15)

[9] And God listened to the voice of Mano'ah, and the angel of God came again to the woman as she sat in the field; but Mano'ah her husband was not with her. [10] And the woman ran in haste and told her husband, "Behold, the man who came to me the other day has appeared to me." [11] And Mano'ah arose and went after his wife, and came to the man and said to him, "Are you the man who spoke to this woman?" And he said, "I am." [12] And Mano'ah said, "Now when your words come true, what is to be the boy's manner of life, and what is he to do?" [13] And the angel of the LORD said to Mano'ah, "Of all that I said to the woman let her beware. [14] She may not eat of anything that comes from the vine, neither let her drink wine or strong drink,

▶ Again God comes to the woman and thus shows preference for her as a conversation partner rather than her husband. This contradicts the usual picture in this patriarchal society. The story thus underscores even more the religious position of women.

▶ The divine messenger reacts laconically to Manoah's questions (v. 11); he repeats himself (vv. 13f., cf. vv. 3–5) and keeps his distance twice (v. 16, 18). He shows thereby that these questions are inappropriate; God has already communicated all that is important to his wife.

or eat any unclean thing; all that I commanded her let her observe." [15] Mano'ah said to the angel of the LORD, "Please, let us detain you, and prepare a kid for you."

The angel's secret (Judg 13:16–18)

[16] And the angel of the LORD said to Mano'ah, "If you detain me, I will not eat of your food; but if you make ready a burnt offering, then offer it to the LORD." (For Manoah did not know that he was the angel of the LORD.) [17] And Mano'ah said to the angel of the LORD, "What is your name, so that, when your words come true, we may honor you?" [18] And the angel of the LORD said to him, "Why do you ask my name, seeing it is wonderful?"

Manoah's sacrifice (Judg 13:19–23)

[19] So Mano'ah took the kid with the cereal offering, and offered it upon the rock to the LORD, to him who works wonders. [20] And when the flame went up toward heaven from the altar, the angel of the LORD ascended in the flame of the altar while Mano'ah and his wife looked on; and they fell on their faces to the ground.

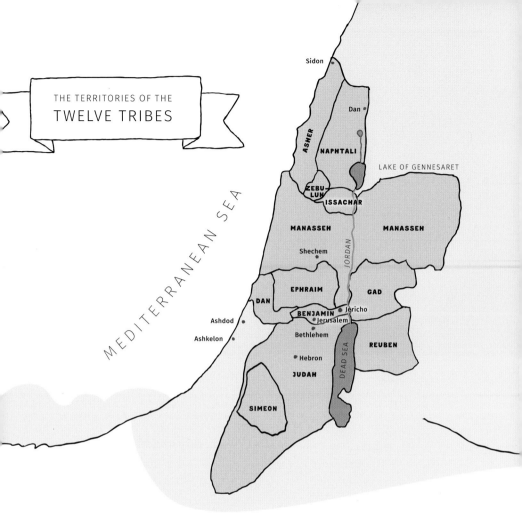

THE TERRITORIES OF THE
TWELVE TRIBES

Map labels: Sidon, Dan, ASHER, NAPHTALI, LAKE OF GENNESARET, ZEBU-LUN, ISSACHAR, MANASSEH, MANASSEH, Shechem, JORDAN, MEDITERRANEAN SEA, EPHRAIM, GAD, DAN, Ashdod, BENJAMIN, Jericho, Jerusalem, Ashkelon, Bethlehem, DEAD SEA, REUBEN, Hebron, JUDAH, SIMEON

---

²¹ The angel of the LORD appeared no more to Mano'ah and to his wife. Then Mano'ah knew that he was the angel of the LORD. ²² And Mano'ah said to his wife, "We shall surely die, for we have seen God." ²³ But his wife said to him, "If the LORD had meant to kill us, he would not have accepted a burnt offering and a cereal offering at our hands, or shown us all these things, or now announced to us such things as these."

Samson Is born (Judg 13:24–25)

²⁴ And the woman bore a son, and called his name Samson; and the boy grew, and the LORD blessed him. ²⁵ And the Spirit of the LORD began to stir him in Ma'haneh-dan, between Zorah and Esh'ta-ol.

Anyone who performs a work contrary to obedience, however good and holy it may be in itself, does not act by God's inspiration.

TERESA OF AVILA

▶ The name "Samson" (in Hebrew, *Shimshon*) (v. 24) is probably related originally to the word "sun" (in Hebrew, *shemesh*). Later chapters show how Samson is pulled in different directions: on the one hand, he has the great mission of saving Israel; on the other hand, he feels strongly attracted to women and often forgets his responsibility.

Ruth

Ruth is the daughter-in-law of Naomi. The story named after her is mainly about the friendship between these two women, who together cope with difficult challenges. In their faithful friendship, God, too, shows his fidelity. Whereas in most biblical stories men play the main roles, this book is told from the point of view of women. It plays out in the time of the judges and therefore is listed after the Book of Judges. At the end, the reader learns that Ruth is one of the ancestors of King David—and consequently of Jesus, too.

The background story (Ruth 1:1–5)

1 ¹ In the days when the judges ruled there was a famine in the land, and a certain man of Bethlehem in Judah went to sojourn in the country of Moab, he and his wife and his two sons. ² The name of the man was Elim'elech and the name of his wife Na'omi, and the names of his two sons were Mahlon and Chil'ion; they were Eph'rathites from Bethlehem in Judah. They went into the country of Moab and remained there. ³ But Elim'elech, the husband of Na'omi, died, and she was left with her two sons. ⁴ These took Moabite wives; the name of the one was Orpah and the name of the other Ruth. They lived there about ten years; ⁵ and both Mahlon and Chil'ion died, so that the woman was bereft of her two sons and her husband.

Naomi goes home (Ruth 1:6–22)

⁶ Then she started with her daughters-in-law to return from the country of Moab, for she had heard in the country of Moab that the LORD had visited his people and given them food. ⁷ So she set out from the place where she was, with her two daughters-in-law, and they went on the way to return to the land of Judah. ⁸ But Na'omi said to her two daughters-in-law, "Go, return each of you to her mother's house. May the LORD deal kindly with you, as you have dealt with

▶ Moab (v. 2) is located east of the Jordan River, in modern-day Jordan (↗ the Book of Deuteronomy). Famines often compel people to emigrate to another country (↗ Gen 45:9–11)—to this day in Africa.

▶ Elimelech means "my God is king." Mahlon and Chilion mean "sickly" and "frail". All the names in the short Book of Ruth have a symbolic meaning.

▶ Bethlehem means "House of Bread"—in stark contrast to the famine there (v. 1). David's family, too, originated in Bethlehem (↗ 1 Sam 16), and Jesus, too (according to the account in Mt 2:6), is born there (↗ Mic 5:1 in the background).

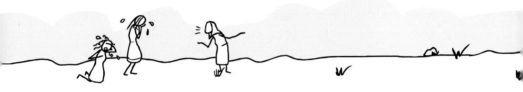

the dead and with me. ⁹ The LORD grant that you may find a home, each of you in the house of her husband!" Then she kissed them, and they lifted up their voices and wept. ¹⁰ And they said to her, "No, we will return with you to your people." ¹¹ But Na'omi said, "Turn back, my daughters, why will you go with me? Have I yet sons in my womb that they may become your husbands? ¹² Turn back, my daughters, go your way, for I am too old to have a husband. If I should say I have hope, even if I should have a husband this night and should bear sons, ¹³ would you therefore wait till they were grown? Would you therefore refrain from marrying? No, my daughters, for it is exceedingly bitter to me for your sake that the hand of the LORD has gone forth against me." ¹⁴ Then they lifted up their voices and wept again; and Orpah kissed her mother-in-law, but Ruth clung to her.

¹⁵ And she said, "See, your sister-in-law has gone back to her people and to her gods; return after your sister-in-law." ¹⁶ But Ruth said, "Entreat me not to leave you or to return from following you; for where you go I will go, and where you lodge I will lodge; your people shall be my people, and your God my God; ¹⁷ where you die I will die, and there will I be buried. May the LORD do so to me and more also if even death parts me from you." ¹⁸ And when Na'omi saw that she was determined to go with her, she said no more.

¹⁹ So the two of them went on until they came to Bethlehem. And when they came to Bethlehem, the whole town was stirred because

99 We thank God for the grace of our conversion to Jesus Christ and the Catholic Church which he founded; for it is only by the most amazing grace of God that we could ever have found our way home.
SCOTT AND KIMBERLY HAHN, Catholic converts

▶ According to the general custom, a brother of a deceased husband was supposed to marry the widowed wife (↗ Deut 25:5–10).

99 What could be more beautiful for us than walking with our people? … When I think of the parish priests who knew the names of their parishioners, who went to visit them; even as one of them told me: "I know the name of each family's dog". Imagine that!
POPE FRANCIS, October 4, 2013

In the evening of this life, I shall appear before You with empty hands, for I do not ask You, Lord, to count my works. All our justice is stained in Your eyes. I wish, then, to be clothed with Your own *Justice* and to receive from Your *Love* the eternal possession of Yourself.

THÉRÈSE OF LISIEUX

of them; and the women said, "Is this Na'omi?" ²⁰ She said to them, "Do not call me Na'omi, call me Mara, for the Almighty has dealt very bitterly with me. ²¹ I went away full, and the LORD has brought me back empty. Why call me Na'omi, when the LORD has afflicted me and the Almighty has brought calamity upon me?"

²² So Na'omi returned, and Ruth the Moabitess her daughter-in-law with her, who returned from the country of Moab. And they came to Bethlehem at the beginning of barley harvest.

Ruth in Boaz's field (Ruth 2:1–23)

2 ¹ Now Na'omi had a kinsman of her husband's, a man of wealth, of the family of Elim'elech, whose name was Boaz. ² And Ruth the Moabitess said to Na'omi, "Let me go to the field, and glean among the ears of grain after him in whose sight I shall find favor." And she said to her, "Go, my daughter." ³ So she set forth and went and gleaned in the field after the reapers; and she happened to come to the part of the field belonging to Boaz, who was of the family of Elim'elech. ⁴ And behold, Boaz came from Bethlehem; and he said to the reapers, "The LORD be with you!" And they answered, "The LORD bless you." ⁵ Then Boaz said to his servant who was in charge of the reapers, "Whose maiden is this?" ⁶ And the servant who was in charge

▶ The Book of Deuteronomy expressly commands that widows and other needy people may gather what is left over at the harvest (Deut 24:21).

of the reapers answered, "It is the Moabite maiden, who came back with Na'omi from the country of Moab. ⁷ She said, 'Please, let me glean and gather among the sheaves after the reapers.' So she came, and she has continued from early morning until now, without resting even for a moment."

⁸ Then Boaz said to Ruth, "Now, listen, my daughter, do not go to glean in another field or leave this one, but keep close to my maidens. ⁹ Let your eyes be upon the field which they are reaping, and go after them. Have I not charged the young men not to molest you? And when you are thirsty, go to the vessels and drink what the young men have drawn." ¹⁰ Then she fell on her face, bowing to the ground, and said to him, "Why have I found favor in your eyes, that you should take notice of me, when I am a foreigner?" ¹¹ But Boaz answered her, "All that you have done for your mother-in-law since the death of your husband has been fully told me, and how you left your father and mother and your native land and came to a people that you did not know before. ¹² The LORD recompense you for what you have done, and a full reward be given you by the LORD, the God of Israel, under whose wings you have come to take refuge!" ¹³ Then she said, "You are most gracious to me, my lord, for you have comforted me and spoken kindly to your maidservant, though I am not one of your maidservants."

▶ Usually a man leaves his father and mother in order to marry (Gen 2:24).

▶ "Under his wings" is a metaphor for protection and security (↗ Ps 63:7, p. GT158). In ancient Egypt, tutelary gods were often represented with this image.

[14] And at mealtime Boaz said to her, "Come here, and eat some bread, and dip your morsel in the wine." So she sat beside the reapers, and he passed to her parched grain; and she ate until she was satisfied, and she had some left over. [15] When she rose to glean, Boaz instructed his young men, saying, "Let her glean even among the sheaves, and do not reproach her. [16] And also pull out some from the bundles for her, and leave it for her to glean, and do not rebuke her." [17] So she gleaned in the field until evening; then she beat out what she had gleaned, and it was about an ephah of barley.

[18] And she took it up and went into the city; she showed her mother-in-law what she had gleaned, and she also brought out and gave her what food she had left over after being satisfied. [19] And her mother-in-law said to her, "Where did you glean today? And where have you worked? Blessed be the man who took notice of you." So she told her mother-in-law with whom she had worked, and said, "The name of the man with whom I worked today is Boaz." [20] And Na'omi said to her daughter-in-law, "Blessed be he by the LORD, whose kindness has not forsaken the living or the dead!"

Na'omi also said to her, "The man is a relative of ours, one of our nearest kin."

> Jesus saw the love of God flowing into and expanding the love of neighbor while the love of neighbor flowed back into and expanded the love of God.
> **ROBERT SPITZER, S.J.**

▶ "Beat out" means to strike the ground with sheaves of grain so that the kernels fall out. An ephah is at least 22 liters [6.3 bushels], and therefore a large quantity.

▶ "Kindness" is in Hebrew the same word as the love that Ruth showed to Naomi (1:8). Just as Ruth did not forsake Naomi, so too God has not forsaken "the living or the dead": the Moabite woman Ruth illustrates the faithfulness of the God of Israel.

[21] And Ruth the Moabitess said, "Besides, he said to me, 'You shall keep close by my servants, till they have finished all my harvest.'" [22] And Na'omi said to Ruth, her daughter-in-law, "It is well, my daughter, that you go out with his maidens, lest in another field you be molested." [23] So she kept close to the maidens of Boaz, gleaning until the end of the barley and wheat harvests; and she lived with her mother-in-law.

Nocturnal meeting with Boaz (Ruth 3:1–18)

3 [1] Then Na'omi her mother-in-law said to her, "My daughter, should I not seek a home for you, that it may be well with you? [2] Now is not Boaz our kinsman, with whose maidens you were? See, he is winnowing barley tonight at the threshing floor. [3] Wash therefore and anoint yourself, and put on your best clothes and go down to the threshing floor; but do not make yourself known to the man until he has finished eating and drinking. [4] But when he lies down, observe the place where he lies; then, go and uncover his feet and lie down; and he will tell you what to do." [5] And she replied, "All that you say I will do."

[6] So she went down to the threshing floor and did just as her mother-in-law had told her. [7] And when Boaz had eaten and drunk, and his heart was merry, he went to lie down at the end of the heap of

▶ A "redeemer" has the duty to help a relative who is in dire need. That may mean buying back parcels of land. According to the precept in Deut 25:5–10, the brother of a deceased husband should marry the widow who is left behind.

▶ In "winnowing", grain was thrown into the air so that the wind carried off the chaff and the clean grain fell on the ground again.

▶ "To anoint" also means "to perfume".

> The secret of happiness is to be able to find one's joy in the joy of another.
> **GEORGES BERNANOS** (1888–1948), French writer

Not one of the five mothers in the genealogy of Jesus (Mt 1:1–17)—Tamar, Rahab, Ruth, Bathsheba, and Mary—has a conventional life story: they are either cunning, given to prostitution, commit adultery, come from paganism, or else an angel announces that they will give birth without a man. But they play a decisive role in God's master plan.

▶ Although Ruth makes herself attractive for Boaz, he is very stand-offish: He intends to proceed quite properly and, in keeping with tradition, give a closer relative a chance to marry Ruth (↗ Deut 25:5). And he protects her reputation by allowing her to go home early enough.

grain. Then she came softly, and uncovered his feet, and lay down. [8] At midnight the man was startled, and turned over, and behold, a woman lay at his feet! [9] He said, "Who are you?" And she answered, "I am Ruth, your maidservant; spread your garment over your maidservant, for you are next of kin." [10] And he said, "May you be blessed by the LORD, my daughter; you have made this last kindness greater than the first, in that you have not gone after young men, whether poor or rich. [11] And now, my daughter, do not fear, I will do for you all that you ask, for all my fellow townsmen know that you are a woman of worth. [12] And now it is true that I am a near kinsman, yet there is a kinsman nearer than I. [13] Remain this night, and in the morning, if he will do the part of the next of kin for you, well; let him do it; but if he is not willing to do the part of the next of kin for you, then, as the LORD lives, I will do the part of the next of kin for you. Lie down until the morning."

[14] So she lay at his feet until the morning, but arose before one could recognize another; and he said, "Let it not be known that the woman came to the threshing floor." [15] And he said, "Bring the mantle you are wearing and hold it out." So she held it, and he measured out

If happiness is not a goddess but, in reality, a gift of God, then we must seek that God who can give it.

AUGUSTINE

six measures of barley, and laid it upon her; then she went into the city. [16] And when she came to her mother-in-law, she said, "How did you fare, my daughter?" Then she told her all that the man had done for her, [17] saying, "These six measures of barley he gave to me, for he said, 'You must not go back empty-handed to your mother-in-law.'" [18] She replied, "Wait, my daughter, until you learn how the matter turns out, for the man will not rest, but will settle the matter today."

Boaz marries Ruth (Ruth 4:1–12)

▶ The gate of a city is the place where men gather to discuss important questions and also to make legal decisions (↗ Ps 127:5).

▶ Ten men (v. 2) constitute a council capable of making decisions (↗ also Gen 18:32). To this day, it takes ten Jewish men to celebrate an official worship service in a synagogue.

[1] And Boaz went up to the gate and sat down there; and behold, the next of kin, of whom Boaz had spoken, came by. So Boaz said, "Turn aside, friend; sit down here"; and he turned aside and sat down. [2] And he took ten men of the elders of the city, and said, "Sit down here"; so they sat down. [3] Then he said to the next of kin, "Na'omi, who has come back from the country of Moab, is selling the parcel of land which belonged to our kinsman Elim'elech. [4] So I thought I would tell you of it, and say, Buy it in the presence of those sitting here, and in the presence of the elders of my people. If you will redeem it, redeem it; but if you will not, tell me, that I may know, for there is no one besides you to redeem it, and I come after you." And he said, "I will redeem it." [5] Then Boaz said, "The day you buy the field from the hand of Na'omi, you are also buying Ruth the Moabi-

tess, the widow of the dead, in order to restore the name of the dead to his inheritance." ⁶ Then the next of kin said, "I cannot redeem it for myself, lest I impair my own inheritance. Take my right of redemption yourself, for I cannot redeem it."

⁷ Now this was the custom in former times in Israel concerning redeeming and exchanging: to confirm a transaction, the one drew off his sandal and gave it to the other, and this was the manner of attesting in Israel. ⁸ So when the next of kin said to Boaz, "Buy it for yourself," he drew off his sandal. ⁹ Then Boaz said to the elders and all the people, "You are witnesses this day that I have bought from the hand of Na'omi all that belonged to Elim'elech and all that belonged to Chil'ion and to Mahlon. ¹⁰ Also Ruth the Moabitess, the widow of Mahlon, I have bought to be my wife, to perpetuate the name of the dead in his inheritance, that the name of the dead may not be cut off from among his brethren and from the gate of his native place; you are witnesses this day." ¹¹ Then all the people who were at the gate, and the elders, said, "We are witnesses. May the LORD make the woman, who is coming into your house, like Rachel and Leah, who together built up the house of Israel. May you prosper in Eph'rathah and be renowned in Bethlehem; ¹² and may your house be like the house of Per'ez, whom Ta'mar bore to Judah, because of the children that the LORD will give you by this young woman."

The word "to redeem", "redeemer", or "redemption" occurs twenty times in the Book of Ruth. When we call Jesus the "Redeemer", this is the same biblical word. The Son of man, as Matthew, for instance, puts it, "came not to be served but to serve, and to give his life as a ransom for many" (Mt 20:28).

▶ Rachel and Leah, Jacob's wives, are the mothers of the People of Israel. Perez is a son of Judah and Tamar (↗ Gen 38:29) and an ancestor of Boaz (↗ Ruth 4:18–21). Tamar had disguised herself as a harlot, so that Judah slept with her and thus begot Perez (→ Gen 38). Despite this morally dubious story, Perez becomes a proverbial blessing.

And she bore a child (Ruth 4:13–22)

¹³ So Boaz took Ruth and she became his wife; and he went in to her, and the LORD gave her conception, and she bore a son. ¹⁴ Then the women said to Na'omi, "Blessed be the LORD, who has not left you this day without next of kin; and may his name be renowned in Israel! ¹⁵ He shall be to you a restorer of life and a nourisher of your old age; for your daughter-in-law who loves you, who is more to you than seven sons, has borne him." ¹⁶ Then Na'omi took the child and laid him in her bosom, and became his nurse. ¹⁷ And the women of the neighborhood gave him a name, saying, "A son has been born to Na'omi." They named him O'bed; he was the father of Jesse, the father of David.

¹⁸ Now these are the descendants of Per'ez: Perez was the father of Hezron, ¹⁹ Hezron of Ram, Ram of Ammin'adab, ²⁰ Ammin'adab of Nahshon, Nahshon of Salmon, ²¹ Salmon of Boaz, Boaz of O'bed, ²² O'bed of Jesse, and Jesse of David.

The Bible has a soft spot for strong, unusual women. In many religions, families, and societies to this day, a son counts more than a daughter. The Book of Ruth is very keenly opposed to such a notion.

▶ This genealogy shows that the Moabite Ruth became the great-grandmother of King David and, thus, also an ancestor of Jesus (Mt 1:5).

Samuel

The prophet Samuel, the son of Hannah and Elkanah, plays a major role in the books named after him. He anoints the first two kings of Israel, Saul and David, whose stories are likewise recounted here (David dies in 1 Kings 2:10). Samuel is thus situated in a critical phase of Israel's history, at the transition from rather informal rule by judges (the so-called pre-governmental period) to the kingdom of Israel (ca. 1000 B.C.).

Although Samuel on behalf of God warns the people about the dangers of a monarchy, they insist on their wish for a king, which Samuel grants against his better judgment (1 Sam 8). In the long term, this path leads to ruin, which becomes clearly evident in the following Books of the Kings (2 Kings 24–25). A survey of this history provides insights into what is really important in life and in a community.

The stories in the Books of Samuel, like the story of Joseph, are among the most lively and suspenseful in the Bible. They show how people fight in faith against their mistakes and weaknesses and how God always walks with them despite it all.

FIRST BOOK OF SAMUEL

By oversleeping, you can miss a class, a date, or a driver's test. But you can also miss God's voice by oversleeping.

Open your heart wide, to receive what God gives!

CHARLES DE FOUCAULD

The call of Samuel (1 Sam 3)

3 [1] Now the boy Samuel was ministering to the LORD under Eli. And the word of the LORD was rare in those days; there was no frequent vision.

[2] At that time Eli, whose eyesight had begun to grow dim, so that he could not see, was lying down in his own place; [3] the lamp of God had not yet gone out, and Samuel was lying down within the temple of the LORD, where the ark of God was. [4] Then the LORD called, "Samuel! Samuel!" and he said, "Here I am!" [5] and ran to Eli, and said, "Here I am, for you called me." But he said, "I did not call; lie down again." So he went and lay down. [6] And the LORD called again, "Samuel!" And Samuel arose and went to Eli, and said, "Here I am, for you called me." But he said, "I did not call, my son; lie down again." [7] Now Samuel did not yet know the LORD, and the word of the LORD had not yet been revealed to him. [8] And the LORD called Samuel again the third time. And he arose and went to Eli, and said, "Here I am, for you called me."

Then Eli perceived that the LORD was calling the boy.

▶ God did not give up but waited until Samuel could understand him. God is patient. We must develop and mature. God gives us the time we need for that.

99 I will never forget that day, 21 September—I was seventeen years old—when, after stopping in the Church of San José de Flores to go to confession, I first heard God calling me. Do not be afraid of what God asks of you! It is worth saying "yes" to God. In him we find joy! Dear young people, some of you may not yet know what you will do with your lives. Ask the Lord, and he will show you the way. The young Samuel kept hearing the voice of the Lord who was calling him, but he did not understand or know what to say, yet with the help →

[9] Therefore Eli said to Samuel, "Go, lie down; and if he calls you, you shall say, 'Speak, LORD, for your servant hears.'" So Samuel went and lay down in his place.

[10] And the LORD came and stood forth, calling as at other times, "Samuel! Samuel!" And Samuel said, "Speak, for your servant hears." [11] Then the LORD said to Samuel, "Behold, I am about to do a thing in Israel, at which the two ears of every one that hears it will tingle. [12] On that day I will fulfil against Eli all that I have spoken concerning his house, from beginning to end. [13] And I tell him that I am about to punish his house for ever, for the iniquity which he knew, because his sons were blaspheming God, and he did not restrain them. [14] Therefore I swear to the house of Eli that the iniquity of Eli's house shall not be expiated by sacrifice or offering for ever."

[15] Samuel lay until morning; then he opened the doors of the house of the LORD. And Samuel was afraid to tell the vision to Eli. [16] But Eli called Samuel and said, "Samuel, my son." And he said, "Here I am." [17] And Eli said, "What was it that he told you? Do not hide it from me. May God do so to you and more also, if you hide anything from me of all that he told you."

[18] So Samuel told him everything and hid nothing from him. And he said, "It is the LORD; let him do what seems good to him."

[19] And Samuel grew, and the LORD was with him and let none of his

words fall to the ground. ²⁰ And all Israel from Dan to Be'er-she'ba knew that Samuel was established as a prophet of the LORD. ²¹ And the LORD appeared again at Shiloh, for the LORD revealed himself to Samuel at Shiloh. ...

→ of the priest Eli, in the end he answered: Speak, Lord, for I am listening.
POPE FRANCIS, July 28, 2013

In the following chapters, Samuel proves that he is up to his task. He judges the people, helps them, intercedes for Israel with God, and anoints Saul as its first king. The latter is a failure, however, partly because of psychological problems, but also because he does not listen to God (1 Sam 15). God therefore chooses a new king.

The anointing of David (1 Sam 16)

16 ¹ The LORD said to Samuel, "How long will you grieve over Saul, seeing I have rejected him from being king over Israel? Fill your horn with oil, and go; I will send you to Jesse the Bethlehemite, for I have provided for myself a king among his sons."

² And Samuel said, "How can I go? If Saul hears it, he will kill me."

And the LORD said, "Take a heifer with you, and say, 'I have come to sacrifice to the LORD.' ³ And invite Jesse to the sacrifice, and I will show you what you shall do; and you shall anoint for me him whom I name to you."

⁴ Samuel did what the LORD commanded, and came to Bethlehem. The elders of the city came to meet him trembling, and said, "Do you come peaceably?"

⁵ And he said, "Peaceably; I have come to sacrifice to the LORD; consecrate yourselves, and come with me to the sacrifice." And he consecrated Jesse and his sons, and invited them to the sacrifice.

⁶ When they came, he looked on Eli'ab and thought, "Surely the LORD's anointed is before him."

⁷ But the LORD said to Samuel, "Do not look on his appearance or on the height of his stature, because I have rejected him; for the LORD sees not as man sees; man looks on the outward appearance, but the LORD looks on the heart."

⁸ Then Jesse called Abin'adab, and made him pass before Samuel. And he said, "Neither has the LORD chosen this one." ⁹ Then Jesse made Shammah pass by. And he said, "Neither has the LORD chosen this one."

¹⁰ And Jesse made seven of his sons pass before Samuel. And Samuel said to Jesse, "The LORD has not chosen these."

¹¹ And Samuel said to Jesse, "Are all your sons here?" And he said, "There remains yet the youngest, but behold, he is keeping the sheep." And Samuel said to Jesse, "Send and fetch him; for we will not sit down till he comes here."

▶ The fear of the town leaders (v. 4) is proof of their great respect for the prophet. His appearance is a direct consequence of God's command, which often brings about changes that are not welcomed by everyone.

▶ "Consecrate" here means to prepare for communion with God in a religious festival (↗ Ex 19:10, 14).

▶ No other passage in the Bible describes so poignantly the difference between human and divine perception. Even the prophet Samuel judges by externals, and God has to correct him.

▶ God chooses an unexpected "surprise candidate": the youngest son, who at first is not even present because he is tending the sheep—at that time a typical chore for children. Yet he, of all people, is particularly suited to the task. He is attractive and has special talents. As a musician, he can have a positive influence on the mood of the people (in the case of Saul, vv. 14–23); as a warrior, he relies on courage and strategy (in the case of Goliath, 1 Sam 17).

▶ The servant tactfully describes Saul's affliction and politely suggests something that might help Saul. His strategy is successful.

¹² And he sent, and brought him in. Now he was ruddy, and had beautiful eyes, and was handsome. And the LORD said, "Arise, anoint him; for this is he." ¹³ Then Samuel took the horn of oil, and anointed him in the midst of his brothers; and the Spirit of the LORD came mightily upon David from that day forward. And Samuel rose up, and went to Ra'mah.

¹⁴ Now the Spirit of the LORD departed from Saul, and an evil spirit from the LORD tormented him. ¹⁵ And Saul's servants said to him, "Behold now, an evil spirit from God is tormenting you. ¹⁶ Let our lord now command your servants, who are before you, to seek out a man who is skilful in playing the lyre; and when the evil spirit from God is upon you, he will play it, and you will be well."

¹⁷ So Saul said to his servants, "Provide for me a man who can play well, and bring him to me." ¹⁸ One of the young men answered, "Behold, I have seen a son of Jesse the Bethlehemite, who is skilful in playing, a man of valor, a man of war, prudent in speech, and a man of good presence; and the LORD is with him." ¹⁹ Therefore Saul sent messengers to Jesse, and said, "Send me David your son, who is with the sheep." ²⁰ And Jesse took a donkey laden with bread, and a skin of wine and a kid, and sent them by David his son to Saul. ²¹ And David came to Saul, and entered his service.

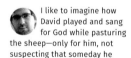

I like to imagine how David played and sang for God while pasturing the sheep—only for him, not suspecting that someday he would be king. →

And Saul loved him greatly, and he became his armor-bearer. ²² And Saul sent to Jesse, saying, "Let David remain in my service, for he has found favor in my sight." ²³ And whenever the evil spirit from God was upon Saul, David took the lyre and played it with his hand; so Saul was refreshed, and was well, and the evil spirit departed from him.

As a youth, David comes to the battle between Israel and the Philistines. The latter send the giant Goliath ahead as their representative, against whom no one has the courage to fight.

→ As a musician, I want to be like David; at the piano I would like to "pray in tones", as I like to call my music-making; I would like to convey in tones and sounds this indescribable love of God.

TOBIAS

99 Courage is being scared to death but saddling up anyway.

JOHN WAYNE (1907–1979)

David and Goliath (1 Sam 17)

17 ³² And David said to Saul, "Let no man's heart fail because of him; your servant will go and fight with this Philis'tine." ³³ And Saul said to David, "You are not able to go against this Philis'tine to fight with him; for you are but a youth, and he has been a man of war from his youth." ³⁴ But David said to Saul, "Your servant used to keep sheep for his father; and when there came a lion, or a bear, and took a lamb from the flock, ³⁵ I went after him and struck him and delivered it out of his mouth; and if he arose against me, I caught him by his beard, and struck him and killed him. ³⁶ Your servant has killed both lions and bears; and this uncircumcised Philis'tine shall be like one of them, seeing he has defied the

armies of the living God." ³⁷ And David said, "The LORD who delivered me from the paw of the lion and from the paw of the bear, will deliver me from the hand of this Philis'tine." And Saul said to David, "Go, and the LORD be with you!" ³⁸ Then Saul clothed David with his armor; he put a helmet of bronze on his head, and clothed him with a coat of mail. ³⁹ And David belted on his sword over his armor, and he tried in vain to go, for he was not used to them. Then David said to Saul, "I cannot go with these; for I am not used to them." And David put them off. ⁴⁰ Then he took his staff in his hand, and chose five smooth stones from the brook, and put them in his shepherd's bag or wallet; his sling was in his hand, and he drew near to the Philis'tine.

⁴¹ And the Philis'tine came on and drew near to David, with his shield-bearer in front of him. ⁴² And when the Philis'tine looked, and saw David, he disdained him; for he was but a youth, ruddy and comely in appearance. ⁴³ And the Philis'tine said to David, "Am I a dog, that you

come to me with sticks?" And the Philistine cursed David by his gods. ⁴⁴ The Philis'tine said to David, "Come to me, and I will give your flesh to the birds of the air and to the beasts of the field." ⁴⁵ Then David said to the Philis'tine, "You come to me with a sword and with a spear and with a javelin; but I come to you in the name of the LORD of hosts, the God of the armies of Israel, whom you have defied. ⁴⁶ This day the LORD will deliver you into my hand, and I will strike you down, and cut off your head; and I will give the dead bodies of the host of the Philis'tines this day to the birds of the air and to the wild beasts of the earth; that all the earth may know that there is a God in Israel, ⁴⁷ and that all this assembly may know that the LORD saves not with sword and spear; for the battle is the LORD's and he will give you into our hand."

⁴⁸ When the Philis'tine arose and came and drew near to meet David, David ran quickly toward the battle line to meet the Philistine. ⁴⁹ And David put his hand in his bag and took out a stone, and slung it, and struck the Philis'tine on his forehead; the stone sank into his forehead, and he fell on his face to the ground.

⁵⁰ So David prevailed over the Philis'tine with a sling and with a stone, and struck the Philistine, and killed him; there was no sword in the hand of David. ⁵¹ Then David ran and stood over the Philis'tine,

When the heroes of Israel saw the giant Goliath, they freaked out and said: "He is way too big; he will pulverize us." Only David thought: "He is just the right size; you can't miss him." It all depends on how you look at things.

And now, let us inquire who is our Goliath? Who is it we have to contend with? The answer is plain; the devil is our Goliath: we have to fight Satan, who is far more fearful and powerful than ten thousand giants, and who would to a certainty destroy us were not God with us; but praised be His Name, He is with us. "Greater is He that is with us, than he that is in the world."

BLESSED JOHN HENRY NEWMAN

B I have fought the good
fight, I have finished the
race, I have kept the faith.
The apostle Paul in 2 Tim 4:7

and took his sword and drew it out of its sheath, and killed him, and
cut off his head with it. When the Philistines saw that their champion
was dead, they fled.

> David's successes in battle with the Philistines make Saul jealous, and he goes mad with anger. He persecutes David
> and tries several times to kill him. Saul's children, however, have great esteem for David: Jonathan, Saul's oldest son,
> becomes close friends with David. And Michal, Saul's daughter, becomes his wife and saves his life (1 Sam 19:10–17).

99 Friendship should be a
joy that is given gratu-
itously, like the joys of art or of
life. It is a kind of grace.
SIMONE WEIL (1909–1943),
French philosopher

99 Envy is the stupidest sin
in the world. It never
caused a single person a single
moment of joy, even false or
fake joy, as most other sins do.
PETER KREEFT

Jonathan's friendship with David (1 Sam 18–20)

18 [1] When he had finished speaking to Saul, the soul of Jonathan
was knit to the soul of David, and Jonathan loved him as his
own soul. [2] And Saul took him that day, and would not let him return
to his father's house.

[3] Then Jonathan made a covenant with David, because he loved him
as his own soul. [4] And Jonathan stripped himself of the robe that was
upon him, and gave it to David, and his armor, and even his sword
and his bow and his belt. [5] And David went out and was successful
wherever Saul sent him; so that Saul set him over the men of war.
And this was good in the sight of all the people and also in the sight
of Saul's servants.

99 Envy harms most the
one who harbors it in
his heart, and others very little.
Just as rust consumes iron, so
envy consumes the envious.
BASIL THE GREAT (ca. 330–379),
Cappadocian ascetic, bishop, and
Doctor of the Church

99 Jealousy leads to murder.
Envy leads to murder. …
The Bible says: "Through the
envy of the devil, evil entered
the world." Jealousy and envy
open the doors to all evil
things. It also divides the community. A Christian community,
when some of its members
suffer from envy, jealousy, it
ends up divided: one against
the other. This is a powerful
poison.
POPE FRANCIS, January 23, 2014

[6] As they were coming home, when David returned from slaying the
Philis'tine, the women came out of all the cities of Israel, singing and
dancing, to meet King Saul, with timbrels, with songs of joy, and with
instruments of music. [7] And the women sang to one another as they
made merry,

"Saul has slain his thousands,
and David his ten thousands."

[8] And Saul was very angry, and this saying displeased him; he said,
"They have ascribed to David ten thousands, and to me they have
ascribed thousands; and what more can he have but the kingdom?"
[9] And Saul eyed David from that day on.

[10] And the next day an evil spirit from God rushed upon Saul, and
he raved within his house, while David was playing the lyre, as he
did day by day. Saul had his spear in his hand; [11] and Saul cast the
spear, for he thought, "I will pin David to the wall." But David evaded
him twice.

[12] Saul was afraid of David, because the LORD was with him but had
departed from Saul.…

19 [1] And Saul spoke to Jonathan his son and to all his servants,
that they should kill David. But Jonathan, Saul's son, delighted much in David. [2] And Jonathan told David, "Saul my father seeks
to kill you; therefore take heed to yourself in the morning, stay in a

secret place and hide yourself; ³ and I will go out and stand beside my father in the field where you are, and I will speak to my father about you; and if I learn anything I will tell you." ⁴ And Jonathan spoke well of David to Saul his father, and said to him, "Let not the king sin against his servant David; because he has not sinned against you, and because his deeds have been of good service to you;

⁵ for he took his life in his hand and he slew the Philis'tine, and the LORD wrought a great victory for all Israel. You saw it, and rejoiced; why then will you sin against innocent blood by killing David without cause?"

⁶ And Saul listened to the voice of Jonathan; Saul swore, "As the LORD lives, he shall not be put to death." ⁷ And Jonathan called David, and Jonathan showed him all these things. And Jonathan brought David to Saul, and he was in his presence as before.

▶ A fine example of action that brings about reconciliation.

▶ Jonathan is doubly loyal: to his father, whom he courageously contradicts and helps to realize the injustice that he is plotting and to give it up; and to David, whom he warns about the danger and for whom he intercedes.

In the same chapter, Saul tries to kill David again. David flees from him. In 1 Sam 20, the situation worsens. During a banquet, which David does not attend because of the threat, Saul confronts his son Jonathan:

20 ²⁷ But on the second day, the next day after the new moon, David's place was empty. And Saul said to Jonathan his son, "Why has not the son of Jesse come to the meal, either yesterday or today?"

²⁸ Jonathan answered Saul, "David earnestly asked leave of me to go to Bethlehem; ²⁹ he said, 'Let me go; for our family holds a sacrifice in the city, and my brother has commanded me to be there. So now, if I have found favor in your eyes, let me get away, and see my brothers.' For this reason he has not come to the king's table."

³⁰ Then Saul's anger was kindled against Jonathan, and he said to him, "You son of a perverse, rebellious woman, do I not know that you have chosen the son of Jesse to your own shame, and to the shame of your mother's nakedness?

³¹ For as long as the son of Jesse lives upon the earth, neither you nor your kingdom shall be established. Therefore send and fetch him to me, for he shall surely die." ³² Then Jonathan answered Saul his father, "Why should he be put to death? What has he done?" ³³ But Saul cast his spear at him to strike him; so Jonathan knew that his father was determined to put David to death.

³⁴ And Jonathan rose from the table in fierce anger and ate no food the second day of the month, for he was grieved for David, because his father had disgraced him. ...

99 God of love, show us our place in this world
as channels of your love
for all the creatures of this earth,
for not one of them is forgotten in your sight.
Enlighten those who possess power and money
that they may avoid the sin of indifference,
that they may love the common good, advance the weak,
and care for this world in which we live.

POPE FRANCIS,
Prayer from *Laudato Si*, 218

99 No violence lasts.
LEONARDO DA VINCI
(1452–1519), Italian painter

► Despite their close family tie, Jonathan opposes his father, Saul, because the latter is wrong. In doing so, he risks his life.

[41] And as soon as the lad had gone, David rose from beside the stone heap and fell on his face to the ground, and bowed three times; and they kissed one another, and wept with one another, until David recovered himself. [42] Then Jonathan said to David, "Go in peace, for as much as we have sworn both of us in the name of the LORD, saying, 'The LORD shall be between me and you, and between my descendants and your descendants, for ever.'" And he rose and departed; and Jonathan went into the city.

Saul does not stop his attempts on the life of his son-in-law, David, because he sees him as a rival and a threat to his family's kingdom.

► En-gedi is an oasis on the western shore of the Dead Sea.

David spares his persecutor Saul (1 Sam 24)

24 [1] When Saul returned from following the Philis'tines, he was told, "Behold, David is in the wilderness of En-ge'di." [2] Then Saul took three thousand chosen men out of all Israel, and went to seek David and his men in front of the Wildgoats' Rocks.

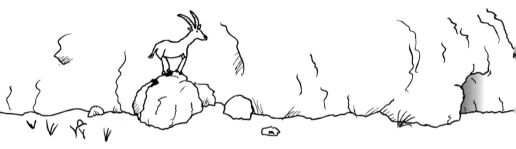

► Saul's eyes are accustomed to the dazzling sunlight outside; he cannot perceive David and his men in the darkness.

► Although his own people encourage him to kill Saul, invoking the name of "God" ("the Lord said to you", v. 4), David protects the king. He still sees Saul as God's "Anointed" (v. 6), even though he has become his mortal enemy.

99 At each sincere stirring of charity, the Gospel triumphs, Christianity is already effective.

HENRI DE LUBAC (1928–2015), French theologian and cardinal

[3] And he came to the sheepfolds by the way, where there was a cave; and Saul went in to relieve himself. Now David and his men were sitting in the innermost parts of the cave. [4] And the men of David said to him, "Here is the day of which the LORD said to you, 'Behold, I will give your enemy into your hand, and you shall do to him as it shall seem good to you.'" Then David arose and stealthily cut off the skirt of Saul's robe. [5] And afterward David's heart struck him, because he had cut off Saul's skirt.

[6] He said to his men, "The LORD forbid that I should do this thing to my lord, the LORD's anointed, to put forth my hand against him, seeing he is the LORD's anointed." [7] So David persuaded his men with these words, and did not permit them to attack Saul. And Saul rose up and left the cave, and went upon his way.

[8] Afterward David also arose, and went out of the cave, and called after Saul, "My lord the king!" And when Saul looked behind him, David bowed with his face to the earth, and did obeisance. [9] And David said to Saul, "Why do you listen to the words of men who say, 'Behold, David seeks your hurt'?

[10] Behold, this day your eyes have seen how the LORD gave you today into my hand in the cave; and some bade me kill you, but I spared you. I said, 'I will not put forth my hand against my lord; for he is the LORD's anointed.' [11] See, my father, see the skirt of your robe in my hand; for by the fact that I cut off the skirt of your robe,

and did not kill you, you may know and see that there is no wrong or treason in my hands. I have not sinned against you, though you hunt my life to take it.

¹² May the LORD judge between me and you, may the LORD avenge me upon you; but my hand shall not be against you. ¹³ As the proverb of the ancients says, 'Out of the wicked comes forth wickedness'; but my hand shall not be against you....

¹⁶ When David had finished speaking these words to Saul, Saul said, "Is this your voice, my son David?" And Saul lifted up his voice and wept.

King Saul's tears (1 Sam 24:17–22)

¹⁷ He said to David, "You are more righteous than I; for you have repaid me good, whereas I have repaid you evil. ¹⁸ And you have declared this day how you have dealt well with me, in that you did not kill me when the LORD put me into your hands. ¹⁹ For if a man finds his enemy, will he let him go away safe? So may the LORD reward you with good for what you have done to me this day. ²⁰ And now, behold, I know that you shall surely be king, and that the kingdom of Israel

▶ David refers many times to God's judgment and sentence (in vv. 12 and 15) and thus shows that he relies on divine justice. That keeps him from taking revenge personally.

▶ Saul has to acknowledge David's honesty. It reduces him to tears but does not prevent him from persecuting David once again two chapters later (1 Sam 26). Saul is torn inside.

O my brothers, when we die, God will not accuse us of performing no miracles or of not being theologians or mystics, but we will surely have to give him an accounting of why we did not bewail our sins tirelessly.

JOHN CLIMACUS (d. 649), Christian monk

shall be established in your hand. ²¹ Swear to me therefore by the LORD that you will not cut off my descendants after me, and that you will not destroy my name out of my father's house." ²² And David swore this to Saul. Then Saul went home; but David and his men went up to the stronghold.

> Saul and his sons, Jonathan too, die in the battle against the Philistines (1 Sam 31), while David with God's help continues to move up and becomes king over all Israel (2 Sam 5). Out of gratitude, he wants to build a house for God:

SECOND BOOK OF SAMUEL

God's promise to David (2 Sam 7)

7 ¹ Now when the king dwelt in his house, and the LORD had given him rest from all his enemies round about, ² the king said to Nathan the prophet, "See now, I dwell in a house of cedar, but the ark of God dwells in a tent." ³ And Nathan said to the king, "Go, do all that is in your heart; for the LORD is with you."

⁴ But that same night the word of the LORD came to Nathan, ⁵ "Go and tell my servant David, 'Thus says the LORD: Would you build me a house to dwell in? ⁶ I have not dwelt in a house since the day I brought up the sons of Israel from Egypt to this day, but I have been

▶ The biblical God is "mobile" and cannot be pinned down (cf. 1 Kings 8:27). He accompanies us without being bound to a particular place—that is one of his distinctive features.

B I was glad when they said to me, "Let us go to the house of the LORD!" Our feet have been standing within your gates, O Jerusalem! Jerusalem, built as a city which is bound firmly together, to which the tribes go up, the tribes of the LORD, as was decreed for Israel, to give thanks to the name of the LORD. There thrones for judgment were set, the thrones of the house of David. Pray for the peace of Jerusalem! May they prosper who love you!

Ps 122:1–6

▶ "House" also means "family", here the royal dynasty (↗ also in English history, e.g., "the House of Tudor").

moving about in a tent for my dwelling. ⁷ In all places where I have moved with all the sons of Israel, did I speak a word with any of the judges of Israel, whom I commanded to shepherd my people Israel, saying, "Why have you not built me a house of cedar?'"

⁸ Now therefore thus you shall say to my servant David, 'Thus says the LORD of hosts, I took you from the pasture, from following the sheep, that you should be prince over my people Israel; ⁹ and I have been with you wherever you went, and have cut off all your enemies from before you; and I will make for you a great name, like the name of the great ones of the earth…. Moreover the LORD declares to you that the LORD will make you a house.

¹² When your days are fulfilled and you lie down with your fathers, I will raise up your offspring after you, who shall come forth from your body, and I will establish his kingdom.

¹³ He shall build a house for my name, and I will establish the throne of his kingdom for ever.

¹⁴ I will be his father, and he shall be my son. When he commits iniquity, I will chasten him with the rod of men, with the stripes of the sons of men; ¹⁵ but I will not take my merciful love from him, as I took it from Saul, whom I put away from before you.

▶ David prays and seeks to be close to God. God promises him a dynasty that is to lead Israel in the future forever. These promises are central to the Bible, because many other passages refer to them (as early as 1 Kings 2:4). One reason for this is that the rule of David's descendants was ended by the Babylonian Exile (2 Kings 25). Many passages ask whether and how God can nevertheless fulfill his promise (e.g., Ps 89, 132). This gave rise to the idea of someone anointed by God, the Messiah of the House of David (e.g., Is 11; Jer 33:15–21). In this sense, the NT calls Jesus the "Son of David" (Mt 1:1; 20:30).

¹⁶ And your house and your kingdom shall be made sure for ever before me; your throne shall be established for ever.'"

¹⁷ In accordance with all these words, and in accordance with all this vision, Nathan spoke to David.

¹⁸ Then King David went in and sat before the LORD, and said, "Who am I, O Lord GOD, and what is my house, that you have brought me thus far?

¹⁹ And yet this was a small thing in your eyes, O Lord GOD; you have spoken also of your servant's house for a great while to come, and have shown me future generations, O Lord GOD!

²⁰ And what more can David say to you? For you know your servant, O Lord GOD! ²¹ Because of your promise, and according to your own heart, you have wrought all this greatness, to make your servant know it.

²² Therefore you are great, O Lord GOD; for there is none like you, and there is no God besides you, according to all that we have heard with our ears.

²³ What other nation on earth is like your people Israel, whom God went to redeem to be his people, making himself a name, and doing for them great and terrible things, by driving out before his people a nation and its gods?…

Although David is united with God and very successful, he allows himself to be seduced by his own power.

Davids adultery with Bathsheba (2 Sam 11)

11 [1] In the spring of the year, the time when kings go forth to battle, David sent Jo'ab, and his servants with him, and all Israel; and they ravaged the Am'monites, and besieged Rabbah. But David remained at Jerusalem.

[2] It happened, late one afternoon, when David arose from his couch and was walking upon the roof of the king's house, that he saw from the roof a woman bathing; and the woman was very beautiful.

[3] And David sent and inquired about the woman. And one said, "Is not this Bathshe'ba, the daughter of Eli'am, the wife of Uri'ah the Hittite?"

[4] So David sent messengers, and took her; and she came to him, and he lay with her. (Now she was purifying herself from her uncleanness.) Then she returned to her house. [5] And the woman conceived; and she sent and told David, "I am with child."

[6] So David sent word to Jo'ab, "Send me Uri'ah the Hittite." And Joab sent Uriah to David. [7] When Uri'ah came to him, David asked how

You shall not commit adultery.

Ex 20:14 (Sixth Commandment in the Decalogue)

▶ While his soldiers risk their lives for him, David enjoys a comfortable life in the capital. In the afternoon, he indulges in a long siesta.

Jo'ab was doing, and how the people fared, and how the war prospered.

[8] Then David said to Uri'ah, "Go down to your house, and wash your feet." And Uriah went out of the king's house, and there followed him a present from the king.

[9] But Uri'ah slept at the door of the king's house with all the servants of his lord, and did not go down to his house. [10] When they told David, "Uri'ah did not go down to his house," David said to Uriah, "Have you not come from a journey? Why did you not go down to your house?"

[11] Uri'ah said to David, "The ark and Israel and Judah dwell in booths; and my lord Jo'ab and the servants of my lord are camping in the open field; shall I then go to my house, to eat and to drink, and to lie with my wife? As you live, and as your soul lives, I will not do this thing."

[12] Then David said to Uri'ah, "Remain here today also, and tomorrow I will let you depart." So Uriah remained in Jerusalem that day, and the next. [13] And David invited him, and he ate in his presence and drank, so that he made him drunk; and in the evening he went out to lie on his couch with the servants of his lord, but he did not go down to his house.

99 David gives in to temptation. … This can happen to any of us. Temptation is our daily bread. If one of us were to say, "I have never been tempted," the right response would be, "either you're a cherub, or you're a little stupid."
POPE FRANCIS, January 31, 2014

99 Political leaders can sin by committing adultery. If a politician breaks his marriage vows, he also compromises the people's trust that he will keep his oath of office as well. The issue is not just about sexual infidelity but includes the ability to trust people in power.
MITCH PACWA S.J. (b. 1949), Scripture scholar and EWTN host

▶ Uriah is a foreigner (v. 3) and yet stands in exemplary solidarity with the soldiers at the front. David, on the other hand, tries to hush up his adultery: he wants Uriah to sleep with Bathsheba so that Uriah will seem to be the child's father. Through stark contrasts, the Bible shows the differences between characters

▶ The rich man in this story is not satisfied with what he has; furthermore, he cannot imagine the value that the lamb has for the poor man.

[14] In the morning David wrote a letter to Jo'ab, and sent it by the hand of Uri'ah. [15] In the letter he wrote, "Set Uri'ah in the forefront of the hardest fighting, and then draw back from him, that he may be struck down, and die."

God's reaction (2 Sam 12)

12 [1] And the LORD sent Nathan to David. He came to him, and said to him, "There were two men in a certain city, the one rich and the other poor. [2] The rich man had very many flocks and herds; [3] but the poor man had nothing but one little ewe lamb, which he had bought. And he brought it up, and it grew up with him and with his children; it used to eat of his morsel, and drink from his cup, and lie in his bosom, and it was like a daughter to him. [4] Now there came a traveler to the rich man, and he was unwilling to take one of his own flock or herd to prepare for the wayfarer who had come to him, but he took the poor man's lamb, and prepared it for the man who had come to him." [5] Then David's anger was greatly kindled against the man; and he said to Nathan, "As the LORD lives, the man who has done this de-

👤 To bear patiently injustice that is done to another is a sign of imperfection and a real sin.
THOMAS AQUINAS (1225–1274), Italian Dominican friar, philosopher, theologian, and Doctor of the Church

▶ Nathan's parable translates David's behavior into an allegory. In this way, David can see it as a disinterested party and, therefore, more objectively. When he looks at it from outside, David is capable of judging correctly. The Law prescribes in Ex 21:37 that a stolen, slaughtered sheep must be replaced fourfold.

serves to die; [6] and he shall restore the lamb fourfold, because he did this thing, and because he had no pity."

[7] Nathan said to David, "You are the man. Thus says the LORD, the God of Israel, 'I anointed you king over Israel, and I delivered you out of the hand of Saul; [8] and I gave you your master's house, and your master's wives into your bosom, and gave you the house of Israel and of Judah; and if this were too little, I would add to you as much more. [9] Why have you despised the word of the LORD, to do what is evil in his sight? You have struck down Uri'ah the Hittite with the sword, and have taken his wife to be your wife, and have slain him with the sword of the Am'monites. [10] Now therefore the sword shall never depart from your house, because you have despised me, and have taken the wife of Uri'ah the Hittite to be your wife.'...

[13] David said to Nathan, "I have sinned against the LORD." And Nathan said to David, "The LORD also has put away your sin; you shall not die. [14] Nevertheless, because by this deed you have utterly scorned the LORD, the child that is born to you shall die."

[15] Then Nathan went to his house. And the LORD struck the child that Uri'ah's wife bore to David, and it became sick.

[16] David therefore besought God for the child; and David fasted, and went in and lay all night upon the ground.

¹⁷ And the elders of his house stood beside him, to raise him from the ground; but he would not, nor did he eat food with them.

¹⁸ On the seventh day the child died. And the servants of David feared to tell him that the child was dead; for they said, "Behold, while the child was yet alive, we spoke to him, and he did not listen to us; how then can we say to him the child is dead? He may do himself some harm."

¹⁹ But when David saw that his servants were whispering together, David perceived that the child was dead; and David said to his servants, "Is the child dead?" They said, "He is dead."

²⁰ Then David arose from the earth, and washed, and anointed himself, and changed his clothes; and he went into the house of the LORD, and worshiped; he then went to his own house; and when he asked, they set food before him, and he ate.

²¹ Then his servants said to him, "What is this thing that you have done? You fasted and wept for the child while it was alive; but when the child died, you arose and ate food."

▶ The prophet unsparingly confronts the king with his guilt, which he had previously repressed, and with God's judgment. Only now does David see that he has sinned (v. 13).

▶ The king is transformed: after he has acknowledged his guilt (v. 13), he again seeks union with God and shows sorrow for the suffering child.

▶ Unlike before (in 2 Sam 11), David again senses what motivates other people. In one week, during which he lay on the ground and fasted, he has become compassionate again.

²² He said, "While the child was still alive, I fasted and wept; for I said, 'Who knows whether the LORD will be gracious to me, that the child may live?'

²³ But now he is dead; why should I fast? Can I bring him back again? I shall go to him, but he will not return to me."

²⁴ Then David comforted his wife, Bathshe'ba, and went in to her, and lay with her; and she bore a son, and he called his name Solomon. And the LORD loved him, ²⁵ and sent a message by Nathan the prophet; so he called his name Jedidi'ah, because of the LORD ....

▶ Without wanting to, Bathsheba had become pregnant by David and on account of her guilt had also lost the child. On the other hand, God has a special love for their second child, Solomon, whom he therefore calls "Jedidiah", which means "beloved of Yah". Yah is the short form of the biblical name for God ↗ note on "hallelujah" at Ps 104:35).

THE BOOKS OF

Kings

After the Books of Samuel relate the history of the first kings of
Israel, Saul and David, the Books of the Kings deal with the remaining history of the kingdom until its fall. Solomon reigns as
the first king over all Israel and builds the Temple in Jerusalem
(1 Kings 1–11). Under his son Rehoboam, the government splits
into the Northern Kingdom f Israel (King Omri founds Samaria
as his capital, 1 Kings 16:24), and the Southern Kingdom of
Judah with its capital, Jerusalem. The reigns of the kings of both
kingdoms are narrated in parallel, until the Northern Kingdom
is conquered and destroyed by the Assyrians in 720 B.C. (1
Kings 12–2 Kings 17). The history of the Southern Kingdom of
Judah ends when the Babylonian King Nebuchadnezzar destroys
Jerusalem and has part of the population deported from Judah
into exile in Babylon (2 Kings 24–25).

The Books of the Kings intend to show that these
catastrophes took place because many kings were unfaithful to
God and disobedient, although God sent several prophets. The
prophets Elijah and Elisha (1 Kings 17 – 2 Kings 13) and Isaiah
(2 Kings 19–20) are God's messengers. They are also prefigurations of Jesus.

FIRST BOOK OF KINGS

Solomon's wisdom (1 Kings 3)

▶ Solomon is loved by God (↗ 2 Sam 12:25), and he loves God.

💡 A "modern" politician: King Solomon enlarges his kingdom, divides it into districts, and organizes a smooth-running administration. Militarily, too, it must be the newest and the best. For example, he introduces the chariots that we know from films like *Ben Hur*.

▶ "An understanding mind" [in some translations, "a discerning heart"] combines two decisive key words from the *Shema Yisrael*, "Hear [understand], O Israel" (↗ Deut 6:4–5).

3 ³ Solomon loved the LORD, walking in the statutes of David his father; only, he sacrificed and burnt incense at the high places. ⁴ And the king went to Gib'eon to sacrifice there, for that was the great high place; Solomon used to offer a thousand burnt offerings upon that altar. ⁵ At Gib'eon the LORD appeared to Solomon in a dream by night; and God said, "Ask what I shall give you." ⁶ And Solomon said, "You have shown great and merciful love to your servant David my father, because he walked before you in faithfulness, in righteousness, and in uprightness of heart toward you; and you have kept for him this great and merciful love, and have given him a son to sit on his throne this day. ⁷ And now, O LORD my God, you have made your servant king in place of David my father, although I am but a little child; I do not know how to go out or come in.

⁸ And your servant is in the midst of your people whom you have chosen, a great people, that cannot be numbered or counted for multitude. ⁹ Give your servant therefore an understanding mind to govern your people, that I may discern between good and evil; for who is able to govern this great people of yours?"

¹⁰ It pleased the LORD that Solomon had asked this. ¹¹ And

▶ God is glad that Solomon does not think of himself above all else but, rather, about how he can perform his duties for other people as well as possible.

Grant me, O Lord, an ever-watchful heart that no frivolous thought can lure away from you; a noble heart that no base love can sully; an upright heart that no perverse intention can lead astray; an invincible heart that no distress can overcome; an unfettered heart that no impetuous desires can enchain. Grant me, O Lord my God, a mind to know you, a heart to seek you, wisdom to find you.

Prayer of **THOMAS AQUINAS** for wisdom

God said to him, "Because you have asked this, and have not asked for yourself long life or riches or the life of your enemies, but have asked for yourself understanding to discern what is right, ¹² behold, I now do according to your word. Behold, I give you a wise and discerning mind, so that none like you has been before you and none like you shall arise after you. ¹³ I give you also what you have not asked, both riches and honor, so that no other king shall compare with you, all your days. ¹⁴ And if you will walk in my ways, keeping my statutes and my commandments, as your father David walked, then I will lengthen your days."

¹⁵ And Solomon awoke, and behold, it was a dream. Then he came to Jerusalem, and stood before the ark of the covenant of the LORD, and offered up burnt offerings and peace offerings, and made a feast for all his servants.

¹⁶ Then two harlots came to the king, and stood before him. ¹⁷ The one woman said, "Oh, my lord, this woman and I dwell in the same house; and I gave birth to a child while she was in the house. ¹⁸ Then on the third day after I was delivered, this woman also gave birth; and we were alone; there was no one else with us in the house, only we two were in the house. ¹⁹ And this woman's son died in the night, because she lay on it. ²⁰ And she arose at midnight, and took my son from beside me, while your maidservant slept, and laid it in her bosom, and laid her dead son in my bosom. ²¹ When I rose in the

morning to nurse my child, behold, it was dead; but when I looked at it closely in the morning, behold, it was not the child that I had borne." ²² But the other woman said, "No, the living child is mine, and the dead child is yours." The first said, "No, the dead child is yours, and the living child is mine." Thus they spoke before the king.

²³ Then the king said, "The one says, 'This is my son that is alive, and your son is dead'; and the other says, 'No; but your son is dead, and my son is the living one.'"

²⁴ And the king said, "Bring me a sword." So a sword was brought before the king. ²⁵ And the king said, "Divide the living child in two, and give half to the one, and half to the other." ²⁶ Then the woman whose son was alive said to the king, because her heart yearned for her son, "Oh, my lord, give her the living child, and by no means slay it." But the other said, "It shall be neither mine nor yours; divide it."

²⁷ Then the king answered and said, "Give the living child to the first woman, and by no means slay it; she is its mother."

²⁸ And all Israel heard of the judgment which the king had rendered; and they stood in awe of the king, because they perceived that the wisdom of God was in him, to render justice.

The playwright Bertolt Brecht adapted the story about Solomon's wise judgment in his play *The Caucasian Chalk Circle* (1948). In his story, however, the mother does not get her child back.

▶ Solomon not only listens to what the woman says, but scrutinizes the emotions that prompt her. An "understanding mind" senses the feelings of other people.

▶ In this proverbial "Solomonic judgment", Solomon resorts to a trick in order to find out who the real mother is.

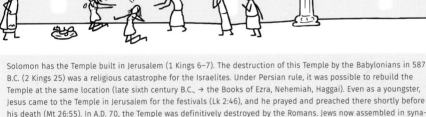

Solomon has the Temple built in Jerusalem (1 Kings 6–7). The destruction of this Temple by the Babylonians in 587 B.C. (2 Kings 25) was a religious catastrophe for the Israelites. Under Persian rule, it was possible to rebuild the Temple at the same location (late sixth century B.C., → the Books of Ezra, Nehemiah, Haggai). Even as a youngster, Jesus came to the Temple in Jerusalem for the festivals (Lk 2:46), and he prayed and preached there shortly before his death (Mt 26:55). In A.D. 70, the Temple was definitively destroyed by the Romans. Jews now assembled in synagogues. Christians understood themselves as a spiritual temple (→ 1 Peter 2:5), since they no longer worshipped God at a particular place but rather in spirit and in truth (Jn 4:23). On the spot of the ruins of the Temple in Jerusalem, Muslims built the Dome of the Rock in the eighth century A.D. They believe that Mohammed ascended from there into heaven. For Jews, the Western Wall of the Temple area, the so-called "Wailing Wall", is an important place to pray. After the Temple construction is completed, Solomon has the Ark of the Covenant (→ Ex 40) brought into it, and then God's presence is manifested in the Temple under the sign of the cloud.

Solomon's Temple and his prayer (1 Kings 8)

8 ¹⁰ And when the priests came out of the holy place, a cloud filled the house of the LORD, ¹¹ so that the priests could not stand to minister because of the cloud; for the glory of the LORD filled the house of the LORD ....

²² Then Solomon stood before the altar of the LORD in the presence of all the assembly of Israel, and spread forth his hands toward heaven; ²³ and said, "O LORD, God of Israel, there is no God like you, in heaven above or on earth beneath, keeping covenant and showing mercy to your servants who walk before you with all their

B As God's glory filled the tabernacle on Mount Sinai, so now it fills the Temple.
↗ Ex 40:34–35

▶ People in entirely different cultures pray in this posture. It widens one's view of God's greatness and expresses openness.

heart; ²⁴ who have kept with your servant David my father what you declared to him; yes, you spoke with your mouth, and with your hand have fulfilled it this day....

²⁷ "But will God indeed dwell on the earth? Behold, heaven and the highest heaven cannot contain you; how much less this house which I have built!

²⁸ Yet have regard to the prayer of your servant and to his supplication, O Lord my God, listening to the cry and to the prayer which your servant prays before you this day; ²⁹ that your eyes may be open night and day toward this house, the place of which you have said, 'My name shall be there,' that you may listen to the prayer which your servant offers toward this place.

³⁰ And hear the supplication of your servant and of your people Israel, when they pray toward this place; yes, hear in heaven your dwelling place; and when you hear, forgive....

⁴¹ "Likewise when a foreigner, who is not of your people Israel, comes from a far country for your name's sake ⁴² (for they shall hear of your great name, and your mighty hand, and of your outstretched arm), when he comes and prays toward this house, ⁴³ hear in heaven your dwelling place, and do according to all for which the foreigner

God has his ear on your heart.
AUGUSTINE

Solomon even asks God to hear and answer the prayers of foreigners. Whoever prays to the God of the universe gains great breadth and openness to mankind as a whole.

calls to you; in order that all the peoples of the earth may know your name and fear you, as do your people Israel, and that they may know that this house which I have built is called by your name....

⁴⁶ "If they sin against you—for there is no man who does not sin— and you are angry with them, and give them to an enemy, so that they are carried away captive to the land of the enemy, far off or near; ⁴⁷ yet if they lay it to heart in the land to which they have been carried captive, and repent, and make supplication to you in the land of their captors, saying, 'We have sinned, and have acted perversely and wickedly'; ⁴⁸ if they repent with all their mind and with all their heart in the land of their enemies, who carried them captive, and pray to you toward their land, which you gave to their fathers, the city which you have chosen, and the house which I have built for your name;

⁴⁹ then hear in heaven your dwelling place their prayer and their supplication, and maintain their cause ⁵⁰ and forgive your people who have sinned against you, and all their transgressions which they have committed against you; and grant them compassion in the sight of those who carried them captive, that they may have compassion on them....

⁵⁴ Now as Solomon finished offering all this prayer and supplication to the Lord, he arose from before the altar of the Lord, where he had knelt with hands outstretched toward heaven....

The name "Solomon" is connected with shalom, "peace, salvation". This amounts to a program for Solomon's reign (↗ 1 Kings 5:4). He gets his ability as a politician to ensure peace and well-being from the wisdom for which he asked God (1 Kings 3:8).

ISRAEL, JUDAH
AND THE SURROUNDING
NATIONS

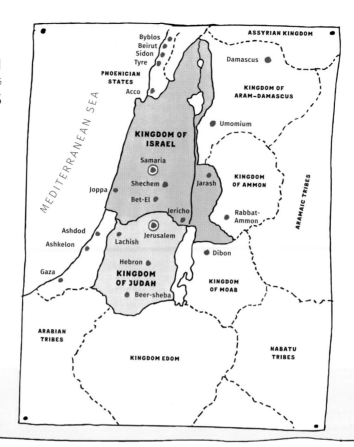

ASSYRIAN KINGDOM

Byblos
Beirut
Sidon
Tyre

PHOENICIAN
STATES

Acco

Damascus

KINGDOM OF
ARAM–DAMASCUS

MEDITERRANEAN SEA

KINGDOM OF
ISRAEL

Samaria

Umomium

Shechem

Jarash

KINGDOM
OF AMMON

ARAMAIC TRIBES

Joppa

Bet-El

Jericho

Rabbat-
Ammon

Ashdod

Ashkelon

Lachish

Jerusalem

Dibon

Hebron

Gaza

KINGDOM
OF JUDAH

KINGDOM
OF MOAB

Beer-sheba

ARABIAN
TRIBES

KINGDOM EDOM

NABATU
TRIBES

ELIJAH AND ELISHA

The stories about the prophets Elijah and Elisha take place in the ninth century B.C. Elijah (1 Kings 17 – 2 Kings 2:12) works during the time of Ahab, king over the Northern Kingdom of Israel, whereas his successor, Elisha (2 Kings 2:13–13:20), serves under several later kings. Elijah and Elisha heal people and even bring the dead back to life. In this way they are prefigurations of Jesus. Both actively support foreigners (the widow in Zarephath in 1 Kings 17, the Syrian Naaman in 2 Kings 5). Jesus refers to this in the synagogue in his hometown of Nazareth (Lk 4:25–27).

Elijah and the widow of Zarephath (1 Kings 17)

17 [1] Now Eli'jah the Tishbite, of Tishbe in Gilead, said to A'hab, "As the LORD the God of Israel lives, before whom I stand, there shall be neither dew nor rain these years, except by my word." [2] And the word of the LORD came to him, [3] "Depart from here and turn eastward, and hide yourself by the brook Cherith, that is east of the Jordan. [4] You shall drink from the brook, and I have commanded the ravens to feed you there." [5] So he went and did according to the word of the LORD; he went and dwelt by the brook Cherith that is east of the Jordan. [6] And the ravens brought him bread and meat in the morning, and bread and meat in the evening; and he drank from the brook.

[7] And after a while the brook dried up, because there was no rain in the land. [8] Then the word of the LORD came to him. [9] "Arise, go to

Remarkably often, people who are united to God also have a special relationship with animals. One example is Saint Francis of Assisi.

▶ Sidon (like Tyre and Byblos) was a rich seaport of the Phoenicians on the Mediterranean coast, in modern-day Lebanon.

▶ Under normal circumstances, in this culture, one would always offer guests refreshment (↗ Gen 18:1–5). The woman apologizes, therefore, and explains her dire situation.

▶ The woman gives all that she has left. In this way, she saves her own life and her son's.

Zar'ephath, which belongs to Si'don, and dwell there. Behold, I have commanded a widow there to feed you." ¹⁰ So he arose and went to Zar'ephath; and when he came to the gate of the city, behold, a widow was there gathering sticks; and he called to her and said, "Bring me a little water in a vessel, that I may drink." ¹¹ And as she was going to bring it, he called to her and said, "Bring me a morsel of bread in your hand." ¹² And she said, "As the LORD your God lives, I have nothing baked, only a handful of meal in a jar, and a little oil in a pitcher; and now, I am gathering a couple of sticks, that I may go in and prepare it for myself and my son, that we may eat it, and die."

¹³ And Eli'jah said to her, "Fear not; go and do as you have said; but first make me a little cake of it and bring it to me, and afterward make for yourself and your son. ¹⁴ For thus says the LORD the God of Israel, 'The jar of meal shall not be spent, and the pitcher of oil shall not fail, until the day that the LORD sends rain upon the earth.'" ¹⁵ And she went and did as Eli'jah said; and she, and he, and her household ate for many days. ¹⁶ The jar of meal was not spent, neither did the pitcher of oil fail, according to the word of the LORD which he spoke by Eli'jah.

¹⁷ After this the son of the woman, the mistress of the house, became ill; and his illness was so severe that there was no breath left

▶ This shows that God has power over life and death and that Elijah really is his prophet. A similar story is told later about Elisha (compare 1 Kings 17 with 2 Kings 4). When Jesus raises the dead, this also revives the memory of Elijah and Elisha (↗ Mk 5:21–37; Lk 7:11–17; Jn 11).

Two essential parts of a prayer of petition are confidence that one's prayer will be answered and the total abandonment of one's own plans as to how it should be answered.

AUGUSTINE

in him. ¹⁸ And she said to Eli'jah, "What have you against me, O man of God? You have come to me to bring my sin to remembrance, and to cause the death of my son!" ¹⁹ And he said to her, "Give me your son." And he took him from her bosom, and carried him up into the upper chamber, where he lodged, and laid him upon his own bed. ²⁰ And he cried to the LORD, "O LORD my God, have you brought calamity even upon the widow with whom I sojourn, by slaying her son?" ²¹ Then he stretched himself upon the child three times, and cried to the LORD, "O LORD my God, let this child's soul come into him again." ²² And the LORD listened to the voice of Eli'jah; and the soul of the child came into him again, and he revived. ²³ And Eli'jah took the child, and brought him down from the upper chamber into the house, and delivered him to his mother; and Elijah said, "See, your son lives." ²⁴ And the woman said to Eli'jah, "Now I know that you are a man of God, and that the word of the LORD in your mouth is truth."

Elijah is a hotheaded guy and takes a radical stand for his faith in God, as related in 1 Kings 18: he challenges the prophets of foreign gods to a competition, proves to them that his God is the only true God, and has them all killed.

Elijah at God's mountain, Horeb (1 Kings 19:1–13)

19 ¹ A'hab told Jez'ebel all that Eli'jah had done, and how he had slain all the prophets with the sword. ² Then Jez'ebel sent a messenger to Eli'jah, saying, "So may the gods do to me, and more also, if I do not make your life as the life of one of them by this time tomorrow." ³ Then he was afraid, and he arose and went for his life, and came to Be'er-she'ba, which belongs to Judah, and left his servant there.

⁴ But he himself went a day's journey into the wilderness, and came and sat down under a broom tree; and he asked that he might die, saying, "It is enough; now, O Lᴏʀᴅ, take away my life; for I am no better than my fathers." ⁵ And he lay down and slept under a broom tree; and behold, an angel touched him, and said to him, "Arise and eat." ⁶ And he looked, and behold, there was at his head a cake baked on hot stones and a jar of water. And he ate and drank, and lay down again. ⁷ And the angel of the Lᴏʀᴅ came again a second time, and touched him, and said, "Arise and eat, else the journey will be too great for you." ⁸ And he arose, and ate and drank, and walked in the strength of that food forty days and forty nights to Horeb the mount of God.

⁹ And there he came to a cave, and lodged there; and behold, the word of the Lᴏʀᴅ came to him, and he said to him, "What are you doing here, Eli'jah?" ¹⁰ He said, "I have been very jealous for the Lᴏʀᴅ, the God of hosts; for the sons of Israel have forsaken your

▶ Horeb (Sinai) is the place where God made his covenant with Israel (→ Ex 19; Deut 5:2–3). "Forty days and nights" alludes to the time that Moses spent on Mount Sinai (Ex 24:18; 34:28). Jesus, too, fasted that long in the desert (Mt 4:2; Mk 1:13; Lk 4:1).

covenant, thrown down your altars, and slain your prophets with the sword; and I, even I only, am left; and they seek my life, to take it away." ¹¹ And he said, "Go forth, and stand upon the mount before the Lᴏʀᴅ." And behold, the Lᴏʀᴅ passed by, and a great and strong wind tore the mountains, and broke in pieces the rocks before the Lᴏʀᴅ, but the Lᴏʀᴅ was not in the wind; and after the wind an earthquake, but the Lᴏʀᴅ was not in the earthquake; ¹² and after the earthquake a fire, but the Lᴏʀᴅ was not in the fire; and after the fire a still small voice.¹³ And when Eli'jah heard it, he wrapped his face in his mantle and went out and stood at the entrance of the cave....

Elisha becomes Elijah's successor (1 Kings 19:19–21)

¹⁹ So he departed from there, and found Eli'sha the son of Sha'phat, who was plowing, with twelve yoke of oxen before him, and he was with the twelfth. Eli'jah passed by him and cast his mantle upon him. ²⁰ And he left the oxen, and ran after Eli'jah, and said, "Let me kiss my father and my mother, and then I will follow you." And he said to him, "Go back again; for what have I done to you?" ²¹ And he returned from following him, and took the yoke of oxen, and slew them, and boiled their flesh with the yokes of the oxen, and gave it to the people, and they ate. Then he arose and went after Eli'jah, and ministered to him. ...

💡 Martin Buber poetically translated the Hebrew original about "a still, small voice" as "the voice of hovering silence".

▶ Elijah notices that God manifests himself very gently (v. 13). This is in stark contrast to the extreme zeal with which he slew the prophets of Baal (1 Kings 18).

💡 Jesus is in more of a hurry. In Lk 9:62, he says to one man who would like to go home quickly to say goodbye: "No one who puts his hand to the plow and looks back is fit for the kingdom of God."

SECOND BOOK OF KINGS

> Everyone must be able to rely on something by which he will not be abandoned.

LAO TZU (ca. 4th–6th century B.C.), Chinese philosopher

> True apostles and prophets don't send themselves; they are chosen and sent by God. Sometimes God works through others to send his leaders. This is true of apostolic succession: Jesus chose the apostles, the apostles chose the bishops, who themselves appointed other bishops, down to our own day.

STEVE RAY

▶ Three times Elijah tries to send Elisha away without saying goodbye properly. He is a character with rough edges with which his disciple Elisha has to cope. Elisha's attachment shows how much he likes his teacher (↗ Ruth 1:16), but also that he knows exactly what he wants.

2 [1] Now when the LORD was about to take Eli'jah up to heaven by a whirlwind, Elijah and Eli'sha were on their way from Gilgal. [2] And Eli'jah said to Eli'sha, "Tarry here, I beg you; for the LORD has sent me as far as Bethel." But Elisha said, "As the LORD lives, and as you yourself live, I will not leave you." So they went down to Bethel. [3] And the sons of the prophets who were in Bethel came out to Eli'sha, and said to him, "Do you know that today the LORD will take away your master from over you?" And he said, "Yes, I know it; hold your peace."

[4] Eli'jah said to him, "Eli'sha, tarry here, I beg you; for the LORD has sent me to Jericho." But he said, "As the LORD lives, and as you yourself live, I will not leave you." So they came to Jericho. [5] The sons of the prophets who were at Jericho drew near to Eli'sha, and said to him, "Do you know that today the LORD will take away your master from over you?" And he answered, "Yes, I know it; hold your peace."

[6] Then Eli'jah said to him, "Tarry here, I beg you; for the LORD has sent me to the Jordan." But he said, "As the LORD lives, and as you yourself live, I will not leave you." So the two of them went on. [7] Fifty men of the sons of the prophets also went, and stood at some distance from them, as they both were standing by the Jordan. [8] Then

▶ As earlier in 1 Kings 19:8, 13, this scene, too, compares Elijah with Moses (↗ Ex 14:21).

Eli'jah took his coat, and rolled it up, and struck the water, and the water was parted to the one side and to the other, till the two of them could go over on dry ground.

[9] When they had crossed, Eli'jah said to Eli'sha, "Ask what I shall do for you, before I am taken from you." And Elisha said, "I beg you, let me inherit a double share of your spirit." [10] And he said, "You have asked a hard thing; yet, if you see me as I am being taken from you, it shall be so for you; but if you do not see me, it shall not be so." [11] And as they still went on and talked, behold, a chariot of fire and horses of fire separated the two of them. And Eli'jah went up by a whirlwind into heaven. [12] And Eli'sha saw it and he cried, "My father, my father! the chariots of Israel and its horsemen!" And he saw him no more.

Then he took hold of his own clothes and tore them in two pieces.

▶ This story is the reason why in early Judaism the idea arose that Elijah had not really died and would come back to earth again. Jesus was therefore taken for Elijah (↗ Mt 11:14; 16:14). During the Passover, Jews to this day keep a place free for Elijah.

▶ "Chariots ...horsemen." Elisha is saying that Elijah (and not the king) was the real leader for the People of Israel.

Elisha heals the Aramean Naaman (2 Kings 5)

5 [1] Na'aman, commander of the army of the king of Syria, was a great man with his master and in high favor, because by him the LORD had given victory to Syria. He was a mighty man of valor, but he was a leper. [2] Now the Syrians on one of their raids had carried off a little maid from the land of Israel, and she waited on Na'aman's wife. [3] She said to her mistress, "Would that my lord were with the prophet who is in Samar'ia! He would cure him of his leprosy." [4] So Na'aman went in and told his lord, "Thus and so spoke the maiden from the land of Israel." ⁵ And the king of Syria said, "Go now, and I will send a letter to the king of Israel."

So he went, taking with him ten talents of silver, six thousand shekels of gold, and ten festal garments. ⁶ And he brought the letter to the king of Israel, which read, "When this letter reaches you, know that I have sent to you Na'aman my servant, that you may cure him of his leprosy." ⁷ And when the king of Israel read the letter, he tore his clothes and said, "Am I God, to kill and to make alive, that this man sends word to me to cure a man of his leprosy? Only consider, and see how he is seeking a quarrel with me."

⁸ But when Eli'sha the man of God heard that the king of Israel had torn his clothes, he sent to the king, saying, "Why have you torn your clothes? Let him come now to me, that he may know that there is a prophet in Israel." ⁹ So Na'aman came with his horses and chariots, and halted at the door of Eli'sha's house. ¹⁰ And Eli'sha sent a messenger to him, saying, "Go and wash in the Jordan seven times, and your flesh shall be restored, and you shall be clean."

¹¹ But Na'aman was angry, and went away, saying, "Behold, I thought that he would surely come out to me, and stand, and call on the name of the LORD his God, and wave his hand over the place, and

▶ "Leprosy" can mean various skin diseases.

▶ The girl is concerned about her master, even though she was abducted from her homeland and enslaved.

💡 In the world of the Bible, tearing one's clothing is a wild gesture of lamentation and sorrow. Saint Francis, too, tore the clothes from his body on the marketplace of Assisi as a sign that he did not belong to the old world and was beginning a new life of following Christ.

cure the leper. ¹² Are not Aba'na and Pharpar, the rivers of Damascus, better than all the waters of Israel? Could I not wash in them, and be clean?" So he turned and went away in a rage. ¹³ But his servants came near and said to him, "My father, if the prophet had commanded you to do some great thing, would you not have done it? How much rather, then, when he says to you, 'Wash, and be clean'?" ¹⁴ So he went down and dipped himself seven times in the Jordan, according to the word of the man of God; and his flesh was restored like the flesh of a little child, and he was clean.

¹⁵ Then he returned to the man of God, he and all his company, and he came and stood before him; and he said, "Behold, I know that there is no God in all the earth but in Israel; so accept now a present from your servant." ¹⁶ But he said, "As the LORD lives, whom I serve, I will receive none." And he urged him to take it, but he refused. ¹⁷ Then Na'aman said, "If not, I beg you, let there be given to your servant two mules' burden of earth; for henceforth your servant will not offer burnt offering or sacrifice to any god but the LORD. ¹⁸ In this matter may the LORD pardon your servant: when my master goes into the house of Rimmon to worship there, leaning on my arm, and I bow myself in the house of Rimmon, when I bow myself in the house of Rimmon, the LORD pardon your servant in this matter." ¹⁹ He said to him, "Go in peace."

▶ The story of Naaman offers an early example of a foreigner who begins to believe in the God of Israel. Around the time of Jesus, many Greeks [Gentiles] were fascinated by the religion of Judaism. In the NT they are called "those who fear God" (↗ Acts 13:16). Many of them became Christians.

▶ Naaman apologizes that for career reasons he must participate in another cult. Elisha understands this; he is far-seeing and religiously tolerant.

But when Na'aman had gone from him a short distance, ²⁰ Geha'zi, the servant of Eli'sha the man of God, said, "See, my master has spared this Na'aman the Syrian, in not accepting from his hand what he brought. As the LORD lives, I will run after him, and get something from him."

▶ Gehazi swears with the same exclamation, "As the Lord lives!" with which Elisha had refused to accept every gift (v. 16), that he himself will take something in exchange for what his boss did.

²¹ So Geha'zi followed Na'aman. And when Naaman saw some one running after him, he alighted from the chariot to meet him, and said, "Is all well?" ²² And he said, "All is well. My master has sent me to say, 'There have just now come to me from the hill country of E'phraim two young men of the sons of the prophets; please, give them a talent of silver and two festal garments.'" ²³ And Na'aman said, "Be pleased to accept two talents." And he urged him, and tied up two talents of silver in two bags, with two festal garments, and laid them upon two of his servants; and they carried them before Geha'zi. ²⁴ And when he came to the hill, he took them from their hand, and put them in the house; and he sent the men away, and they departed. ²⁵ He went in, and stood before his master, and Eli'sha said to him, "Where have you been, Geha'zi?" And he said, "Your servant went nowhere." ²⁶ But he said to him, "Did I not go with you in spirit when the man turned from his chariot to meet you? Was it a time to

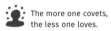

The more one covets, the less one loves.

THOMAS AQUINAS

▶ Gehazi hides himself like a coward behind Elisha's authority (v. 22), lies to him, too (v. 25), and shamelessly lets others serve him (vv. 23–24); this behavior is unhealthy (v. 27). Elisha must endure an unacceptable servant, while Naaman has exemplary servants (v. 13).

accept money and garments, olive orchards and vineyards, sheep and oxen, menservants and maidservants?
²⁷ Therefore the leprosy of Na'aman shall cling to you, and to your descendants for ever." So he went out from his presence a leper, as white as snow.

THE DEFEAT OF ISRAEL AND JUDAH

The downfall of the Northern Kingdom of Israel (2 Kings 17) and the Southern Kingdom of Judah (2 Kings 25) was a consequence of the power politics of the Assyrians and the Babylonians. The Assyrians had their heartland in the northern part, the Babylonians in the southern part of the region drained by the Euphrates and Tigris Rivers, in modern-day Iraq. During the 9th–7th centuries B.C., the Assyrians built an empire by conquering the surrounding kingdoms with brutal methods: they deported hundreds and thousands of people over hundreds of miles. These compulsory resettlements destroyed the original structures of the smaller states, so that the simple population could easily be forced to pay high taxes. Around 720 B.C. the Assyrians definitively conquered the capital Samaria and thus the Northern Kingdom Israel and carried off a large part of the population to modern-day Iraq. In the 7th century B.C., the Babylonians took over the power and the methods of the Assyrians. In 597 B.C., under King Nebuchadnezzar, they captured Jerusalem for the first time. In 587 B.C., they destroyed the city and the Temple and led many inhabitants of Judah into the Babylonian Exile (2 Kings 25).

Downfall of the Northern Kingdom of Israel (2 Kings 17:1–24)

17 ¹ In the twelfth year of A'haz king of Judah Hoshe'a the son of E'lah began to reign in Samar'ia over Israel, and he reigned nine years. ² And he did what was evil in the sight of the LORD, yet not as the kings of Israel who were before him. ³ Against him came up Shalmane'ser king of Assyria; and Hoshe'a became his vassal, and paid him tribute. ⁴ But the king of Assyria found treachery in Hoshe'a; for he had sent messengers to So, king of Egypt, and offered no tribute to the king of Assyria, as he had done year by year; therefore the king of Assyria shut him up, and bound him in prison. ⁵ Then the king of Assyria invaded all the land and came to Samar'ia, and for three years he besieged it. ⁶ In the ninth year of Hoshe'a the king of Assyria captured Samar'ia, and he carried the Israelites away to Assyria, and placed them in Ha'lah, and on the Ha'bor, the river of Gozan, and in the cities of the Medes.

⁷ And this was so, because the sons of Israel had sinned against the LORD their God, who had brought them up out of the land of Egypt from under the hand of Pharaoh king of Egypt, and had feared other gods ⁸ and walked in the customs of the nations whom the LORD drove out before the sons of Israel, and in the customs which the kings of Israel had introduced....

¹³ Yet the LORD warned Israel and Judah by every prophet and every seer,

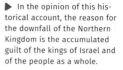

▶ In the opinion of this historical account, the reason for the downfall of the Northern Kingdom is the accumulated guilt of the kings of Israel and of the people as a whole.

🅱 The kings of the Gentiles exercise lordship over them; and those in authority over them are called benefactors. But not so with you. ...

Lk 22:25–26

▶ The people of the Medes lived in areas of modern-day Iran.

🅱 Those who choose another god multiply their sorrows; their libations of blood I will not pour out or take their names upon my lips.

Ps 16:4

saying, "Turn from your evil ways and keep my commandments and my statutes, in accordance with all the law which I commanded your fathers, and which I sent to you by my servants the prophets." ¹⁴ But they would not listen, but were stubborn, as their fathers had been, who did not believe in the LORD their God. ¹⁵ They despised his statutes, and his covenant that he made with their fathers, and the warnings which he gave them. They went after false idols, and became false, and they followed the nations that were round about them, concerning whom the LORD had commanded them that they should not do like them. ¹⁶ And they forsook all the commandments of the LORD their God, and made for themselves molten images of two calves; and they made an Ashe'rah, and worshiped all the host of heaven, and served Ba'al. ¹⁷ And they burned their sons and their daughters as offerings, and used divination and sorcery, and sold themselves to do evil in the sight of the LORD, provoking him to anger.... ²³ ...until the LORD removed Israel out of his sight, as he had spoken by all his servants the prophets. So Israel was exiled from their own land to Assyria until this day.

²⁴ And the king of Assyria brought people from Babylon, Cu'thah, Avva, Ha'math, and Sepharva'im, and placed them in the cities of Samar'ia instead of the sons of Israel; and they took possession of Samaria, and dwelt in its cities.

▶ The downfall does not come out of the clear blue sky; several generations prepared the way for it. Similarly, in order to understand the causes of the World Wars and the Holocaust, we must study developments that go back decades and centuries. What we do today can cause or prevent catastrophes in future generations.

▶ Bulls and calves were a widespread symbol for strength and fertility, and in Egypt and in the ancient Middle East they stood for various deities. Similarly, the sun, moon, and stars were often revered as deities (↗ commentary on Gen 1:16 and Deut 4:19. Concerning Baal, ↗ Judg 9:6).

King Josiah has the Temple in Jerusalem renovated. During the construction, the priest Hilkiah finds a book.

The Book in the Temple and Josiah's reform (2 Kings 22)

22 [10] Then Sha'phan the secretary told the king, "Hilki'ah the priest has given me a book." And Shaphan read it before the king.

[11] And when the king heard the words of the book of the law, he tore his clothes. [12] And the king commanded Hilki'ah the priest, and Ahi'kam the son of Sha'phan, and Achbor the son of Micai'ah, and Shaphan the secretary, and Asai'ah the king's servant, saying, [13] "Go, inquire of the LORD for me, and for the people, and for all Judah, concerning the words of this book that has been found; for great is the wrath of the LORD that is kindled against us, because our fathers have not obeyed the words of this book, to do according to all that is written concerning us."

[14] So Hilki'ah the priest, and Ahi'kam, and Achbor, and Sha'phan, and Asai'ah went to Huldah the prophetess...and they talked with her. [15] And she said to them, "Thus says the LORD, the God of Israel: 'Tell the man who sent you to me, [16] Thus says the LORD, Behold, I

▶ "Book of the Law", literally "Book of the Torah". This refers to the Book of Deuteronomy (↗ Deut 29:28; 31:9).

▶ Huldah is a biblical prophetess (↗ also Deborah in Judg 4:4 or Hannah in Lk 2:36). God distributes religious gifts equally between women and men, as the holy women and men among Christians demonstrate.

99 The humble person is perceived as someone who gives up, someone defeated, someone who has nothing to say to the world. Instead, this is the royal road, and not only because humility is a great human virtue but because, in the first place, it represents God's own way of acting. It was the way chosen by Christ, the Mediator of the New Covenant.

POPE BENEDICT XVI, September 2, 2007

will bring evil upon this place and upon its inhabitants, all the words of the book which the king of Judah has read. [17] Because they have forsaken me and have burned incense to other gods, that they might provoke me to anger with all the work of their hands, therefore my wrath will be kindled against this place, and it will not be quenched. [18] But as to the king of Judah, who sent you to inquire of the LORD, thus shall you say to him, Thus says the LORD, the God of Israel: Regarding the words which you have heard, [19] because your heart was penitent, and you humbled yourself before the LORD, when you heard how I spoke against this place, and against its inhabitants, that they should become a desolation and a curse, and you have torn your clothes and wept before me, I also have heard you, says the LORD. [20] Therefore, behold, I will gather you to your fathers, and you shall be gathered to your grave in peace, and your eyes shall not see all the evil which I will bring upon this place.'" And they brought back word to the king.

Josiah takes the words of the Book very seriously and carries out a religious reform in keeping with the Book of Deuteronomy: he orders the altars of foreign gods destroyed. Nevertheless, he cannot stop the downfall of Jerusalem.

The destruction of Jerusalem and the Babylonian Exile (2 Kings 25)

25 And Zedeki'ah rebelled against the King of Babylon. [1] And in the ninth year of his reign, in the tenth month, on the tenth day of the month, Nebuchadnez'zar king of Babylon came with all his army against Jerusalem, and laid siege to it; and they built siege-works against it round about. [2] So the city was besieged till the eleventh year of King Zedeki'ah. [3] On the ninth day of the fourth month the famine was so severe in the city that there was no food for the people of the land. [4] Then a breach was made in the city; the king with all the men of war fled by night by the way of the gate between the two walls, by the king's garden, though the Chalde'ans were around the city. And they went in the direction of the Ar'abah. [5] But the army of the Chalde'ans pursued the king, and overtook him in the plains of Jericho; and all his army was scattered from him. [6] Then they captured the king, and brought him up to the king of Babylon at Rib'lah, who passed sentence upon him. [7] They slew the sons of Ze-deki'ah before his eyes, and put out the eyes of Zedekiah, and bound him in fetters, and took him to Babylon.

[8] In the fifth month, on the seventh day of the month—which was the nineteenth year of King Nebuchadnez'zar, king of Babylon—Ne-

▶ "Chaldeans" refers to the Babylonian army. Like a cowardly captain, the king secretly abandons the sinking ship (v. 4).

bu''zarad'an, the captain of the bodyguard, a servant of the king of Babylon, came to Jerusalem. [9] And he burned the house of the LORD, and the king's house and all the houses of Jerusalem; every great house he burned down. [10] And all the army of the Chalde'ans, who were with the captain of the guard, broke down the walls around Jerusalem. [11] And the rest of the people who were left in the city and the deserters who had deserted to the king of Babylon, together with the rest of the multitude, Nebu''zarad'an the captain of the guard carried into exile. [12] But the captain of the guard left some of the poorest of the land to be vinedressers and plowmen....

[27] And in the thirty-seventh year of the exile of Jehoi'achin king of Judah, in the twelfth month, on the twenty-seventh day of the month, E'vil-mer'odach king of Babylon, in the year that he began to reign, graciously freed Jehoi'achin king of Judah from prison; [28] and he spoke kindly to him, and gave him a seat above the seats of the kings who were with him in Babylon. [29] So Jehoi'achin put off his prison garments. And every day of his life he dined regularly at the king's table; [30] and for his allowance, a regular allowance was given him by the king, every day a portion, as long as he lived.

B Judah has gone into exile because of affliction and hard servitude; she dwells now among the nations, but finds no resting place; her pursuers have all overtaken her in the midst of her distress. The roads to Zion mourn, for none come to the appointed feasts; all her gates are desolate, her priests groan; her maidens have been dragged away, and she herself suffers bitterly. Her foes have become the head, her enemies prosper, because the LORD has made her suffer for the multitude of her transgressions; her children have gone away, captives before the foe. From the daughter of Zion has departed all her majesty.

Lam 1:3–6a

Later the Books of Ezra and Nehemiah tell how the Jews were able to return to the land and rebuild Jerusalem.

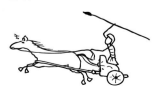

Chronicles

These two books are generally thought to come from the period of around 350–300 B.C. They reflect a concern about presenting the history of Israel once again in a new way. They refer back to the Books of Samuel and the Kings, but have new emphases and supplement them with additional passages, especially for religious reasons. Themes like the Temple, divine worship, and the activities of priests and Temple singers are developed here in much greater detail. The next two excerpts are examples of these new aspects in the portrayal of history:

💡 The whereabouts of the Ark of the Covenant is a riddle that has inspired many fantasies. Steven Spielberg had Indiana Jones look for it in *Raiders of the Lost Ark*. The Bible mentions it in describing the construction of the Temple in Jerusalem under King Solomon. Jeremiah speaks of the Ark ceasing to be part of Jewish worship after the Exile (Jer 3:16). According to 2 Mac 2:5-8, Jeremiah had the Ark hidden in a cave on Mount Nebo. Nevertheless, various legends arose concerning the Ark's location. The Samaritans think that it is found in a hiding place near their holy Mount Gerizim. Ethiopian →

The transfer of the Ark to the City of David: the preparations (1 Chron 15:1–16:3)

15 ¹ David built houses for himself in the city of David; and he prepared a place for the ark of God, and pitched a tent for it. ² Then David said, "No one but the Levites may carry the ark of God, for the LORD chose them to carry the ark of the LORD and to minister to him for ever."

³ And David assembled all Israel at Jerusalem, to bring up the ark of the LORD to its place, which he had prepared for it. ⁴ And David gathered together the sons of Aaron and the Levites: ⁵ of the sons of Ko'hath, Uri'el the chief, with a hundred and twenty of his brethren; ⁶ of the sons of Merar'i, Asai'ah the chief, with two hundred and twenty of his brethren; ⁷ of the sons of Gershom, Joel the chief, with a hundred and thirty of his brethren; ⁸ of the sons of Eliza'phan, Shemai'ah the chief, with two hundred of his brethren; ⁹ of the sons of He'bron, Eli'el the chief, with eighty of his brethren; ¹⁰ of the sons of Uz'ziel, Ammin'adab the chief, with a hundred and twelve of his

brethren. ¹¹ Then David summoned the priests Za'dok and Abi'athar, and the Levites Uri'el, Asai'ah, Joel, Shemai'ah, Eli'el, and Ammin'ad-ab, ¹² and said to them, "You are the heads of the fathers' houses of the Levites; sanctify yourselves, you and your brethren, so that you may bring up the ark of the LORD, the God of Israel, to the place that I have prepared for it....

The entrance of the Ark (1 Chron 15:25–29)

²⁵ So David and the elders of Israel, and the commanders of thousands, went to bring up the ark of the covenant of the LORD from the house of O'bed-e'dom with rejoicing. ²⁶ And because God helped the Levites who were carrying the ark of the covenant of the LORD, they sacrificed seven bulls and seven rams. ²⁷ David was clothed with a robe of fine linen, as also were all the Levites who were carrying the ark, and the singers, and Chenani'ah the leader of the music of the singers; and David wore a linen ephod. ²⁸ So all Israel brought up the ark of the covenant of the LORD with shouting, to the sound of the horn, trumpets, and cymbals, and made loud music on harps and lyres.

→ Christians (80 million of them) believe that the Ark arrived in Ethiopia via Egypt and that it is preserved in Axum to this day. In thousands of Ethiopian churches, a replica of the Ark is revered. In Judaism, the scroll of the Torah took over from the Ark of the Covenant as the most sacred object in the synagogue. Similarly, Sacred Scripture is revered in the Christian liturgy as well. Just as David dances before the Ark of the Covenant, African Christians dance at Mass before the reading from Sacred Scripture.

²⁹ And as the ark of the covenant of the LORD came to the city of David, Michal the daughter of Saul looked out of the window, and saw King David dancing and making merry; and she despised him in her heart.

16 And they brought in the ark of God, and set it inside the tent which David had pitched for it; and they offered burnt offerings and peace offerings before God. ² And when David had finished offering the burnt offerings and the peace offerings, he blessed the people in the name of the LORD, ³ and distributed to all Israel, both men and women, to each a loaf of bread, a portion of meat, and a cake of raisins.

Exemplary treatment of prisoners of war (2 Chron 28:8–15)

28 ⁸ The men of Israel took captive two hundred thousand of their kinsfolk, women, sons, and daughters; they also took much spoil from them and brought the spoil to Samar'ia. ⁹ But a prophet of the LORD was there, whose name was O'ded; and he went

▶ The historical background is a fratricidal war in the eighth century B.C. The Northern Kingdom of Israel was stronger than the South, Judah.

Disobedience comes from pride, which issues from self-love, depriving the soul of humility.

CATHERINE OF SIENA (1347–1380), Third Order Dominican, mystic, spiritual writer, and Doctor of the Church

▶ Military victories are not a blank check for violence and enslavement. God's spokesman Oded reminds the Jews that "winners" have the responsibility not to exploit their superiority unjustly.

▶ Verses 14–15 read like an early anticipation of the ideas of Henry Dunant, the founder of the Red Cross; they even →

out to meet the army that came to Samar'ia, and said to them, "Behold, because the LORD, the God of your fathers, was angry with Judah, he gave them into your hand, but you have slain them in a rage which has reached up to heaven.

[10] And now you intend to subjugate the people of Judah and Jerusalem, male and female, as your slaves. Have you not sins of your own against the LORD your God?

[11] Now hear me, and send back the captives from your kinsfolk whom you have taken, for the fierce wrath of the LORD is upon you."

[12] Certain chiefs also of the men of E'phraim, Azari'ah the son of Joha'nan, Berechi'ah the son of Meshil'lemoth, Jehizki'ah the son of Shallum, and Ama'sa the son of Hadlai, stood up against those who were coming from the war, [13] and said to them, "You shall not bring the captives in here, for you propose to bring upon us guilt against the LORD in addition to our present sins and guilt. For our guilt is already great, and there is fierce wrath against Israel."

[14] So the armed men left the captives and the spoil before the princes and all the assembly.

→ go much farther. The prisoners receive caring treatment that restores their dignity ("clothing"), and they are allowed to return home after a very short time. The border city of Jericho is the place where they are handed over.

[15] And the men who have been mentioned by name rose and took the captives, and with the spoil they clothed all that were naked among them; they clothed them, gave them sandals, provided them with food and drink, and anointed them; and carrying all the feeble among them on donkeys, they brought them to their kinsfolk at Jericho, the city of palm trees. Then they returned to Samar'ia.

In the last chapter the Books of the Chronicles, like the Books of the Kings that preceded them, offer a view of the downfall of Jerusalem in the year 587 B.C. Yet 2 Chron 36 concentrates more than 2 Kings 25 does on the reasons for the catastrophe and—unlike Kings—gives a hopeful prospect at the end.

End and beginning (2 Chron 36:11–23)

36 [11] Zedeki'ah was twenty-one years old when he began to reign, and he reigned eleven years in Jerusalem. [12] He did what was evil in the sight of the LORD his God. He did not humble himself before Jeremi'ah the prophet, who spoke from the mouth of the LORD. [13] He also rebelled against King Nebuchadnez'zar, who had made him swear by God; he stiffened his neck and hardened his heart against turning to the LORD, the God of Israel. [14] All the leading priests and the people likewise were exceedingly unfaithful, follow-

On deaf ears, any sermon is wasted.

Folk saying

ing all the abominations of the nations; and they polluted the house of the LORD which he had hallowed in Jerusalem.

¹⁵ The LORD, the God of their fathers, sent persistently to them by his messengers, because he had compassion on his people and on his dwelling place; ¹⁶ but they kept mocking the messengers of God, despising his words, and scoffing at his prophets, till the wrath of the LORD rose against his people, till there was no remedy.

¹⁷ Therefore he brought up against them the king of the Chalde'ans, who slew their young men with the sword in the house of their sanctuary, and had no compassion on young man or virgin, old man or aged; he gave them all into his hand.

¹⁸ And all the vessels of the house of God, great and small, and the treasures of the house of the LORD, and the treasures of the king and of his princes, all these he brought to Babylon. ¹⁹ And they burned the house of God, and broke down the wall of Jerusalem, and burned all its palaces with fire, and destroyed all its precious vessels.

 Son of man, you dwell in the midst of a rebellious house, who have eyes to see, but see not, who have ears to hear, but hear not; for they are a rebellious house.

Ezek 12:2–3a

▶ Chronicles sees the main cause of the downfall as disobedience to God and those whom he sends; Jeremiah is mentioned in particular (v. 21 also). The rejection of God's message is many times a reason for the misfortune that strikes mankind.

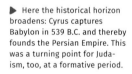

²⁰ He took into exile in Babylon those who had escaped from the sword, and they became servants to him and to his sons until the establishment of the kingdom of Persia, ²¹ to fulfil the word of the LORD by the mouth of Jeremi'ah, until the land had enjoyed its sabbaths. All the days that it lay desolate it kept sabbath, to fulfil seventy years.

²² Now in the first year of Cyrus king of Persia, that the word of the LORD by the mouth of Jeremi'ah might be accomplished, the LORD stirred up the spirit of Cyrus king of Persia so that he made a proclamation throughout all his kingdom and also put it in writing:

²³ "Thus says Cyrus king of Persia, 'The LORD, the God of heaven, has given me all the kingdoms of the earth, and he has charged me to build him a house at Jerusalem, which is in Judah. Whoever is among you of all his people, may the LORD his God be with him. Let him go up.'"

▶ Here the historical horizon broadens: Cyrus captures Babylon in 539 B.C. and thereby founds the Persian Empire. This was a turning point for Judaism, too, at a formative period.

 Then the land shall rest and enjoy its sabbaths.

Lev 26:34

▶ Verses 22–23 cite Ezra 1:1–3. These key verses signal a turning point: it becomes possible to go back home, the destroyed Temple can be rebuilt, and even the ruler of the empire supports all this benevolently.

THE BOOKS OF

Ezra

AND

Nehemiah

The Books of Ezra and Nehemiah belong together. They deal with the return of the Jews from the Babylonian Exile and the rebuilding of the Temple and the city wall of Jerusalem. The Persian King Cyrus made this possible through a decree in the year 539 B.C. Both books begin with the plan to rebuild the Temple or the city, which with God's help is carried out successfully.

Ezra was a priest and scribe who probably appeared in the year 398 (Ezra 7:7, "in the seventh year of Artaxerxes", probably Artaxerxes II). Many scholars assume that he was substantially associated with the Torah and its acceptance by the community (see Neh 8).

Nehemiah the governor was concerned about the restoration of Jerusalem and of civic life there. He may have begun to work as early as 445 (Neh 1, "in the twentieth year", probably of Artaxerxes I). The two leaders together are key figures for the renewal of political and religious life in Jerusalem and Judah in the time after the Exile. They continue to make fruitful the developments that had slowly begun with the building of the second Temple (520–515) and the return of the descendants of the exiled inhabitants of the city.

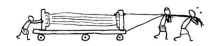

EZRA

▶ Cyrus, a foreign ruler, is inspired by God. ↗ Is 45:1.

99 The infinite God is at the same time the God who is near. He wants to live among us, to be one with us. Jerusalem with its Temple is the place of the meeting between God and his people. The place where he wants to be revered and where he comes to meet us. Since the time of David, Jerusalem is also the place of promise. Jerusalem is connected with the expectation of the Messiah, with the hope that God will come as king into this world and make it his kingdom.

POPE BENEDICT XVI, March 28, 2010

King Cyrus gives the command to build the Temple (Ezra 1)

1 ¹ In the first year of Cyrus king of Persia, that the word of the LORD by the mouth of Jeremi'ah might be accomplished, the LORD stirred up the spirit of Cyrus king of Persia so that he made a proclamation throughout all his kingdom and also put it in writing:
² "Thus says Cyrus king of Persia: The LORD, the God of heaven, has given me all the kingdoms of the earth, and he has charged me to build him a house at Jerusalem, which is in Judah. ³ Whoever is among you of all his people, may his God be with him, and let him go up to Jerusalem, which is in Judah, and rebuild the house of the LORD, the God of Israel—he is the God who is in Jerusalem; ⁴ and let each survivor, in whatever place he sojourns, be assisted by the men of his place with silver and gold, with goods and with beasts, besides freewill offerings for the house of God which is in Jerusalem."

To Jerusalem!

⁵ Then rose up the heads of the fathers' houses of Judah and Benjamin, and the priests and the Levites, every one whose spirit God

▶ Religion and divine worship thrive on generosity (↗ already in the case of the sanctuary set up in the wilderness in Ex 25:1–7; 35:4—36:7).

▶ Susa was an important Persian city (today near the city of Shush in Iran).

B By the waters of Babylon, there we sat down and wept, when we remembered Zion. On the willows there we hung up our lyres. For there our captors required of us songs, and our tormentors, mirth, saying, "Sing us one of the songs of Zion!"

Ps 137:1–3

had stirred to go up to rebuild the house of the LORD which is in Jerusalem; ⁶ and all who were about them aided them with vessels of silver, with gold, with goods, with beasts, and with costly wares, besides all that was freely offered. ⁷ Cyrus the king also brought out the vessels of the house of the LORD which Nebuchadnez'zar had carried away from Jerusalem and placed in the house of his gods....

NEHEMIAH

King Artaxerxes allows Nehemiah to rebuild Jerusalem (Neh 1–2)

1 ¹ The words of Nehemi'ah the son of Hacali'ah. Now it happened in the month of Chis'lev, in the twentieth year, as I was in Susa the capital, ² that Hana'ni, one of my brethren, came with certain men out of Judah; and I asked them concerning the Jews that survived, who had escaped exile, and concerning Jerusalem. ³ And they said to me, "The survivors there in the province who escaped exile are in great trouble and shame; the wall of Jerusalem is broken down, and its gates are destroyed by fire."
⁴ When I heard these words I sat down and wept, and mourned for days; and I continued fasting and praying before the God of heaven.

5 And I said, "O Lord God of heaven, the great and terrible God who keeps covenant and merciful love with those who love him and keep his commandments; 6 let your ear be attentive, and your eyes open, to hear the prayer of your servant which I now pray before you day and night for the sons of Israel your servants, confessing the sins of the sons of Israel, which we have sinned against you. Yes, I and my father's house have sinned. 7 We have acted very corruptly against you, and have not kept the commandments, the statutes, and the ordinances which you commanded your servant Moses. 8 Remember the word which you commanded your servant Moses, saying, 'If you are unfaithful, I will scatter you among the peoples; 9 but if you return to me and keep my commandments and do them, though your dispersed be under the farthest skies, I will gather them from there and bring them to the place which I have chosen, to make my name dwell there.'

10 They are your servants and your people, whom you have redeemed by your great power and by your strong hand. 11 O Lord, let your ear be attentive to the prayer of your servant, and to the prayer

If you do not want to stop praying, then do not stop yearning. Is your yearning constant? Then the cry of your prayer is constant, too. You will be silent only when you stop loving.
AUGUSTINE

▶ In several postexilic books, the authors find it important to acknowledge the guilt of the people that led to their exile: ↗ Dan 9:4–19; Ezra 9:6–15; Neh 9:5–38; Ps 106.

99 God allows us to feel our weakness only so as to give us his strength.
FRANÇOIS FÉNELON (1651–1715), French bishop

of your servants who delight to fear your name; and give success to your servant today, and grant him mercy in the sight of this man."
Now I was cupbearer to the king.

2 In the month of Ni'san, in the twentieth year of King Ar-ta-xe-rx'es, when wine was before him, I took up the wine and gave it to the king. Now I had not been sad in his presence. 2 And the king said to me, "Why is your face sad, seeing you are not sick? This is nothing else but sadness of the heart." Then I was very much afraid. 3 I said to the king, "Let the king live for ever! Why should not my face be sad, when the city, the place of my fathers' sepulchres, lies waste, and its gates have been destroyed by fire?" 4 Then the king said to me, "For what do you make request?" So I prayed to the God of heaven. 5 And I said to the king, "If it pleases the king, and if your servant has found favor in your sight, that you send me to Judah, to the city of my fathers' sepulchres, that I may rebuild it." 6 And the king said to me (the queen sitting beside him), "How long will you be gone, and when will you return?"
So it pleased the king to send me; and I set him a time.

▶ To pray before challenging, important duties as Nehemiah did is a Christian practice to this day. Not everything depends on how well I do something. Often I cannot influence important factors at all, and it is good to entrust them to God.

99 We are responsible not only for what we do, but also for what we do not do.
MOLIÈRE (1622–1673), French dramatist

99 No snowflake in an avalanche ever feels responsible.
STANISLAW JERZY LEC (1909–1966), Polish author

When the most important buildings have been rebuilt, it is a question of strengthening Israel again intellectually and religiously. This happens in festivals and especially by reading the Torah—the Bible at that time—and understanding it correctly.

Reading and understanding God's Word (Neh 8)

▶ Interestingly enough, the desire to hear the Torah of Moses is a grass-roots phenomenon. People actively seek instruction.

Ⱡ → 486
What do Christians express by prayer postures?

8 ¹ And all the people gathered as one man into the square before the Water Gate; and they told Ezra the scribe to bring the book of the law of Moses which the LORD had given to Israel. ² And Ezra the priest brought the law before the assembly, both men and women and all who could hear with understanding, on the first day of the seventh month. ³ And he read from it facing the square before the Water Gate from early morning until midday, in the presence of the men and the women and those who could understand; and the ears of all the people were attentive to the book of the law. ⁴ And Ezra the scribe stood on a wooden pulpit which they had made for the purpose…. ⁵ And Ezra opened the book in the sight of all the people, for he was above all the people; and when he opened it all the people stood.

❓ How do I show my reverence for the Bible? Is it collecting dust on the shelf? Is it within reach? Do I read from it regularly? Do I allow the words of Sacred Scripture to say something to me?

📖 God is faithful.
1 Cor 10:13

👤 Worthy are you, Lord, our God, to receive praise, glory, honor, and worship. … And let us praise and exalt him above all forever.

From a prayer by **FRANCIS OF ASSISI** (1181/2–1226)

⁶ And Ezra blessed the LORD, the great God; and all the people answered, "Amen, Amen," lifting up their hands; and they bowed their heads and worshiped the LORD with their faces to the ground. ⁷ Also Jesh'ua, Ba'ni, Sherebi'ah, Ja'min, Akkub, Shab'bethai, Hodi'ah, Ma-asei'ah, Keli'ta, Azari'ah, Jo'zabad, Ha'nan, Pelai'ah, the Levites, helped the people to understand the law, while the people remained in their places.

⁸ And they read from the book, from the law of God, clearly; and they gave the sense, so that the people understood the reading.

⁹ And Nehemi'ah, who was the governor, and Ezra the priest and scribe, and the Levites who taught the people said to all the people, "This day is holy to the LORD your God; do not mourn or weep." For all the people wept when they heard the words of the law. ¹⁰ Then he said to them, "Go your way, eat the fat and drink sweet wine and send portions to him for whom nothing is prepared; for this day is holy to our LORD; and do not be grieved, for the joy of the LORD is your strength." ¹¹ So the Levites stilled all the people, saying, "Be quiet, for this day is holy; do not be grieved." ¹² And all the people went their way to eat and drink and to send portions and to make great rejoicing, because they had understood the words that were declared to them.

Celebrating the Feast of Booths (Neh 8:13–18)

¹³ On the second day the heads of fathers' houses of all the people, with the priests and the Levites, came together to Ezra the scribe in order to study the words of the law. ¹⁴ And they found it written in the law that the LORD had commanded by Moses that the sons of Israel should dwell in booths during the feast of the seventh month, ¹⁵ and that they should publish and proclaim in all their towns and in Jerusalem, "Go out to the hills and bring branches of olive, wild olive, myrtle, palm, and other leafy trees to make booths, as it is written."

¹⁶ So the people went out and brought them and made booths for themselves, each on his roof, and in their courts and in the courts of the house of God, and in the square at the Water Gate and in the square at the Gate of E'phraim. ¹⁷ And all the assembly of those who had returned from the captivity made booths and dwelt in the booths; for from the days of Jesh'ua the son of Nun to that day the sons of Israel had not done so. And there was very great rejoicing. ¹⁸ And day by day, from the first day to the last day, he read from the book of the law of God. They kept the feast seven days; and on the eighth day there was a solemn assembly, according to the ordinance.

▶ Concerning the Feast of Booths, ↗ Deut 16:13, 16; 31:10. To this day Jews celebrate this feast, remembering the time in the wilderness after the Exodus from Egypt.

You shall dwell in booths for seven days ... that your generations may know that I made the sons of Israel dwell in booths when I brought them out of the land of Egypt: I am the LORD your God.

Lev 23:42–43

Prayer of repentance (Neh 9)

9 ⁶ And Ezra said:"You are the LORD, you alone; you have made heaven, the heaven of heavens, with all their host, the earth and all that is on it, the seas and all that is in them; and you preserve all of them; and the host of heaven worships you. ⁷ You are the LORD, the God who chose Abram and brought him forth out of Ur of the Chalde'ans and gave him the name Abraham; ⁸ and you found his heart faithful before you, and made with him the covenant to give to his descendants the land of the Canaanite, the Hittite, the Am'orite, the Per'izzite, the Jeb'usite, and the Gir'gashite; and you have fulfilled your promise, for you are righteous.

⁹ "And you saw the affliction of our fathers in Egypt and heard their cry at the Red Sea, ¹⁰ and performed signs and wonders against Pharaoh and all his servants and all the people of his land, for you knew that they acted insolently against our fathers; and you got yourself a name, as it is to this day.... ³³ Yet you have been just in all that has come upon us, for you have dealt faithfully and we have acted wickedly....

▶ Prayers of repentance and the confession of the guilt of the whole people become especially important in later books (see also Ezra 9; Dan 9). First, they recall all the good things that God has done for Israel, and, then, they acknowledge their own failure to resolve to be faithful to God again.

Have mercy on me, O God, according to your merciful love; according to your abundant mercy blot out my transgressions. Wash me thoroughly from my iniquity, and cleanse me from my sin! For I know my transgressions, and my sin is ever before me.

Ps 51:1–3

Tobit

Tobit, a pious, righteous man, lives in Assyrian exile in Nineveh. Through an accident, he is blinded. At the same time, Sarah, a young Jewish woman, is suffering in Media (in modern-day Iran) from a demon: all the men whom she married died on their wedding night. Tobit sends his son Tobias to Sarah's father, Gabael, to reclaim money that he had lent. Tobias is accompanied by an angel, through whose help Sarah and Tobit are cured. Tobias and Sarah marry. The Book of Tobit shows how God assists those who strive to live righteously and pray confidently.

Tobias and Raphael start out on their journey (Tob 5:1–4)

5 ¹ Then Tobi'as answered him, "Father, I will do everything that you have commanded me; ² but how can I obtain the money when I do not know the man?" ³ Then Tobit gave him the receipt, and said to him, "Find a man to go with you and I will pay him wages as long as I live; and go and get the money." ⁴ So he went to look for a man; and he found Ra'phael, who was an angel.

The Angel accompanies him (Tob 5:5–22)

⁵ But Tobi'as did not know it. Tobias said to him, "Can you go with me to Ra'ges in Med'ia? Are you acquainted with that region?" ⁶ The angel replied, "I will go with you; I am familiar with the way, and I have stayed with our brother Gab'ael." ⁷ Then Tobi'as said to him, "Wait for me, and I shall tell my father." ⁸ And he said to him, "Go, and do not delay." So he went in and said to his father, "I have found some one to go with me." He said, "Call him to me, so that I may learn to what tribe he belongs, and whether he is a reliable man to go with you."...

¹⁷ But Anna, his mother, began to weep, and said to Tobit, "Why have you sent our child away? Is he not the staff of our hands as he goes in and out before us? ¹⁸ Do not add money to money, but consider it rubbish as compared to our child. ¹⁹ For the life that is given to us by the Lᴏʀᴅ is enough for us."

> **"** God go with you on your way; may he give you strength when you are sick, comfort you when you are sad, and rejoice with you when things go well for you.
>
> Irish travel blessing

▶ "Angel" means "messenger", a messenger from God. "Raphael" means "God heals" (concerning the angel Michael, ↗ Dan 10:13).

²⁰ And Tobit said to her, "Do not worry, my sister; he will return safe and sound, and your eyes will see him. ²¹ For a good angel will go with him; his journey will be successful, and he will come back safe and sound." ²² So she stopped weeping.

The healing of Tobit (11:1–15)

11 ¹ After this Tobi'as went on his way, praising God because he had made his journey a success. And he blessed Rag'uel and his wife Edna.

So he continued on his way until they came near to Nin'eveh. ² Then Ra'phael said to Tobi'as, "Are you not aware, brother, of how you left your father? ³ Let us run ahead of your wife and prepare the house. ⁴ And take the gall of the fish with you." So they went their way, and the dog went along behind them.

⁵ Now Anna sat looking intently down the road for her son. ⁶ And she caught sight of him coming, and said to his father, "Behold, your son is coming, and so is the man who went with him!"

⁷ Ra'phael said to Tobi'as, before they approached his father, "I know that his eyes will be opened. ⁸ Smear the gall of the fish on his eyes, and the medicine will cause the white films to fall away. And your father will regain his sight and see the light."

 All dog-owners are glad that not only an angel accompanies young Tobias on his dangerous journey—his little dog can go along, too, and gets a special mention in the Bible.

 Angels are God's street workers.

👥 Our guardian angel's desire to help us is far greater than our desire to be helped by him.

JOHN DON BOSCO (1815–1888), Italian priest, youth pastor, and founder of a religious congregation

My eyes are dim, so that I cannot see the signs of your presence. You alone can quicken my hearing and purge my sight, and cleanse and renew my heart. Teach me to sit at your feet and to hear your word. Amen.

JOHN HENRY NEWMAN

9 Then Anna ran to meet them, and embraced her son, and said to him, "I have seen you, my child; now I am ready to die." And she wept. 10 Tobit got up, and came stumbling out through the courtyard door. But his son ran to him 11 with the gall of the fish in his hand, and holding him firmly, he blew into his eyes, saying, "Take courage, Father." 12 With this he applied the medicine on his eyes. 13 Next, with both his hands, he peeled off the white films from the corners of his eyes.

14 Then he saw his son and embraced him, and he wept and said, "Here I see my son, the light of my eyes!" Then he said, "Blessed be God, and blessed be his great name, and blessed be all his holy angels. May his holy name be blessed throughout all the ages. 15 Though he afflicted me, he has had mercy on me. Now I see my son Tobi'as!"

Raphael makes himself known (Tob 12:1–17)

12 1 Tobit then called his son Tobi'as and said to him, "My son, see to the wages of the man who went with you; and he must also be given more." 2 He replied, "Father, it would do me no harm to

I am wholeheartedly grateful for all defeats and crises, for they alone drive me to prayer and back into God's arms.

SØREN KIERKEGAARD (1813–1855), Danish philosopher, theologian, and writer

Economic life undoubtedly requires contracts, in order to regulate relations of exchange between goods of equivalent value. But it also needs just laws and forms of redistribution governed by politics, and what is more, it needs works redolent of the spirit of gift.

POPE BENEDICT XVI, *Caritas in Veritate*

give him half of what I have brought back. 3 For he has led me back to you safely, he cured my wife, he obtained the money for me, and he also healed you." 4 The old man said, "He deserves it." 5 So he called the angel and said to him, "Take for your wages half of all that you two have brought back, and farewell."

6 Then the angel called the two of them privately and said to them: "Praise God and give thanks to him; exalt him and give thanks to him in the presence of all the living for what he has done for you. It is good to praise God and to exalt his name, worthily declaring the works of God, and with fitting honor to acknowledge him. Do not be slow to give him thanks. 7 It is good to guard the secret of a king, but gloriously to reveal the works of God, and with fitting honor to acknowledge him. Do good, and evil will not overtake you. 8 Prayer is good when accompanied by fasting, almsgiving, and righteousness. A little with righteousness is better than much with wrongdoing. It is better to give alms than to treasure up gold. 9 For almsgiving delivers from death, and it will purge away every sin. Those who perform deeds of charity and of righteousness will have fulness of life; 10 but those who commit sin are the enemies of their own lives.

11 "I will now declare the whole truth to you and I will not conceal anything from you. I have said, 'It is good to guard the secret of a king, but gloriously to reveal the works of God.' 12 And so, when

you and your daughter-in-law Sarah prayed, I brought a re-minder of your prayer before the Holy One; and when you buried the dead, I was likewise present with you. ¹³ When you did not hesitate to rise and leave your dinner in order to go and lay out the dead, I was sent to test you. ¹⁴ So now God sent me to heal you and your daughter-in-law Sarah. ¹⁵ I am Ra'phael, one of the seven holy angels who present the prayers of the saints and enter into the presence of the glory of the Lord."

¹⁶ They were both alarmed; and they fell upon their fac-es, for they were afraid. ¹⁷ But he said to them, "Do not be afraid; you will be safe. But praise God for ever."

Tobit's song of praise (Tob 13:1–4)

13 ¹ Then Tobit wrote a prayer of rejoicing, and said:
² "Blessed is God who lives for ever,
   and blessed is his kingdom.
For he afflicts, and he shows mercy;

▶ God is like a king who ceaselessly does wonderful things for us, secretly and in a hidden way, throughout the universe. The more we understand about the world, the more we can praise God.

"" Angels and saints place the prayers of the holy on earth at God's feet (Tob 12:12; Rev 5:8, 8:3), which is to say that they support the prayers with their intercessions.

KARL KEATING (b. 1950), Catholic apologist and author

▶ Only at the very end of the story do Tobit and Tobias understand that Raphael is an angel.

he leads down to Hades, and brings up again,
   and there is no one who can escape his hand.
³ Acknowledge him before the nations, O sons of Israel;
   for he has scattered us among them.
⁴ Make his greatness known there,
   and exalt him in the presence of all the living;
⁵ because he is our Lord and God,
   he is our Father for ever.

Y → 54
What are angels?

▶ Tobit sees the scattering of the Jews among the Gentiles (in Greek, "diaspora") as a divine commission for Jews to witness to God in all the nations. He believes that one day all peoples will praise God in a new Jerusalem (Tob 13:10–18, → Is 60; Rev 21:9–27).

? Who has accompanied me in my life? Who is like an angel for me?

> **B** No evil shall befall you,
>   no scourge come near your tent.
> For he will give his angels charge of you
> to guard you in all your ways.
> On their hands they will bear you up,
> lest you dash your foot against a stone.
> You will tread on the lion and the adder,
> the young lion and the serpent you will trample under foot.
> Because he clings to me in love, I will deliver him;
> I will protect him, because he knows my name.
>
> Ps 91:10–14

THE BOOK OF

Judith

This didactic tale may have been composed in Aramaic, but it has been preserved for us only in a Greek translation. The heroine of the book is named Judith, which means "woman of Judah" or "Jewish woman". The name itself indicates her responsibility for her people and her activity: she saves her town, Bethulia, and thus her people from impending destruction by killing the enemy commander through cunning (Jud 13). Previously the local elders had decided to surrender in five days on account of a water shortage—unless God intervened. In this situation, Judith takes action.

▶ The struggle for water existed in the Bible and exists today.

Patience obtains everything.

TERESA OF AVILA

The water shortage in Bethulia (Jud 7)

7 [19] The people of Israel cried out to the Lord their God, for their courage failed, because all their enemies had surrounded them and there was no way of escape from them. [20] The whole Assyrian army, their infantry, chariots, and cavalry, surrounded them for thirty-four days, until all the vessels of water belonging to every inhabitant of Beth"uli'a were empty; [21] their cisterns were going dry, and they did not have enough water to drink their fill for a single day, because it was measured out to them to drink. [22] Their children lost heart, and the women and young men fainted from thirst and fell down in the streets of the city and in the passages through the gates; there was no strength left in them any longer.

[23] Then all the people, the young men, the women, and the children, gathered about Uzzi'ah and the rulers of the city and cried out with a loud voice, and said before all the elders, [24] "God be judge between you and us! For you have done us a great injury in not making peace with the Assyrians. [25] For now we have no one to help us; God has sold us into their hands, to strew us on the ground before them with thirst and utter destruction. [26] Now call them in and surrender the whole city to the army of Hol'ofer'nes and to all his forces, to be plundered. [27] For it would be better for us to be captured by them; for we will be slaves, but our lives will be spared, and we shall not witness the death of our infants before our eyes, or see our wives

and children draw their last breath. [28] We call to witness against you heaven and earth and our God, the Lord of our fathers, who punishes us according to our sins and the sins of our fathers. Let him not do this day the things which we have described!"

[29] Then great and general lamentation arose throughout the assembly, and they cried out to the Lord God with a loud voice. [30] And Uzzi'ah said to them, "Have courage, my brothers! Let us hold out for five more days; by that time the Lord our God will restore to us his mercy, for he will not forsake us utterly. [31] But if these days pass by, and no help comes for us, I will do what you say."

[32] Then he dismissed the people to their various posts, and they went up on the walls and towers of their city. The women and children he sent home. And they were greatly depressed in the city.

God is not to be pressured! (Jud 8)

8 [11] They came to her, and she said to them, "Listen to me, rulers of the people of Beth'uli'a! What you have said to the people today is not right; you have even sworn and pronounced this oath between God and you, promising to surrender the city to our enemies unless the Lord turns and helps us within so many days. [12] Who are you, that have put God to the test this day, and are setting yourselves up in the place of God among the sons of

> When we say "message of salvation", this is not simply a manner of speaking, these are not mere words or empty words like so many today. Mankind truly needs to be saved!
>
> **POPE FRANCIS** to young people in Assisi, October 4, 2013

▶ Judith astutely perceives that people who set conditions for God thereby set themselves above God. We can state conditions when dealing with subordinates or peers; it is not fitting in our relationship with God.

men? [13] You are putting the Lord Almighty to the test—but you will never know anything! [14] You cannot plumb the depths of the human heart, nor find out what a man is thinking; how do you expect to search out God, who made all these things, and find out his mind or comprehend his thought? No, my brethren, do not provoke the Lord our God to anger. [15] For if he does not choose to help us within these five days, he has power to protect us within any time he pleases, or even to destroy us in the presence of our enemies. [16] Do not try to bind the purposes of the Lord our God; for God is not like man, to be threatened, nor like a human being, to be won over by pleading. [17] Therefore, while we wait for his deliverance, let us call upon him to help us, and he will hear our voice, if it pleases him.

[18] "For never in our generation, nor in these present days, has there been any tribe or family or people or city of ours which worshiped gods made with hands, as was done in days gone by.... [25] In spite of everything let us give thanks to the Lord our God, who is putting us to the test as he did our forefathers. [26] Remember what he did with Abraham, and how he tested Isaac, and what happened to Jacob in Mesopota'mia in Syria, while he was keeping the sheep of La'ban, his mother's brother. [27] For he has not tried us with fire, as he did them, to search their hearts, nor has he taken revenge upon us; but the Lord scourges those who draw near to him, in order to admonish them."

▶ In her reasoning, Judith refers to the infinite distance between human and divine knowledge (↗ see also 1 Sam 16:7).

▶ Because Israel had worshipped homemade idols, it had been defeated earlier (→ 2 Kings 17:5–8). Because this is no longer the case, Judith trusts in God's help.

▶ Judith recalls the difficult tests to which their ancestors were put. At the conclusion of her speech, she puts the present crisis in an entirely new light: God is thereby giving them a chance to mature, and they should even thank him for it (v. 25).

THE BOOK OF

Esther

Like the Book of Judith, the Book of Esther is an edifying story. The action takes place in the Persian court. The young Jewish woman Esther marries King Artaxerxes and thus become queen (Esther 2). Haman, a high-ranking Persian official, is planning the destruction of all Jews (Esther 3:6). Through her uncle Mordecai, Esther learns about it and is ready to risk her life for her endangered people and go unbidden to see the king (Esther 4). He welcomes her graciously, and during a banquet she presents her concerns.

Chapter 3 of the Book of Esther describes an archetypal scene: the foreigners in the country give offense, because they are different. Their differentness must be eliminated ...

> Elitist views of personhood have besieged the African American population, caused genocide in Nazi Germany and the former Soviet Union, and lie at the root of virtually every form of bias and prejudice.

ROBERT SPITZER S.J.

> We must preserve the memory of those—whether Jews or non-Jews— who were able to behave in the midst of utter chaos as though the world had not become unhinged.

EMMANUEL LEVINAS (1906–1995), French-Jewish philosopher, whose parents and siblings were killed by the Nazis. His central concern is the human face, which preserves "the otherness of the other" and shouts to mankind: "Thou shalt not kill."

The plan for extermination (Esther 3:7–1)

3 [7] In the first month, which is the month of Ni'san, in the twelfth year of King Ahas'u-e'rus, they cast Pur, that is the lot, before Ha'man day after day; and they cast it month after month till the twelfth month, which is the month of Adar'. [8] Then Ha'man said to King Ahas'u-e'rus, "There is a certain people scattered abroad and dispersed among the peoples in all the provinces of your kingdom; their laws are different from those of every other people, and they do not keep the king's laws, so that it is not for the king's profit to tolerate them. [9] If it please the king, let it be decreed that they be destroyed, and I will pay ten thousand talents of silver into the hands of those who have charge of the king's business, that they may put it into the king's treasuries." [10] So the king took his signet ring from his hand and gave it to Ha'man the Ag'agite, the son of Hammeda'tha, the enemy of the Jews. [11] And the king said to Ha'man, "The money is given to you, the people also, to do with them as it seems good to you."

Wickedness falls back onto its author (Esther 7:1–10)

7 ¹ So the king and Ha'man went in to feast with Queen Esther. ² And on the second day, as they were drinking wine, the king again said to Esther, "What is your petition, Queen Esther? It shall be granted you. And what is your request? Even to the half of my kingdom, it shall be fulfilled." ³ Then Queen Esther answered, "If I have found favor in your sight, O king, and if it please the king, let my life be given me at my petition, and my people at my request. ⁴ For we are sold, I and my people, to be destroyed, to be slain, and to be annihilated. If we had been sold merely as slaves, men and women, I would have held my peace; for our affliction is not to be compared with the loss to the king."

⁵ Then King Ahas'u-e'rus said to Queen Esther, "Who is he, and where is he, that would presume to do this?"

⁶ And Esther said, "A foe and enemy! This wicked Ha'man!"

▶ The Jews are "sold" in a twofold sense: delivered into enemy hands to be slaughtered, so as then to confiscate their property (↗ Esther 3:9).

Then Ha'man was in terror before the king and the queen. ⁷ And the king rose from the feast in wrath and went into the palace garden; but Ha'man stayed to beg his life from Queen Esther, for he saw that evil was determined against him by the king. ⁸ And the king returned from the palace garden to the place where they were drinking wine, as Ha'man was falling on the couch where Esther was;

and the king said, "Will he even assault the queen in my presence, in my own house?" As the words left the mouth of the king, they covered Haman's face. ⁹ Then said Harbo'na, one of the eunuchs in attendance on the king, "Moreover, the gallows which Ha'man has prepared for Mor'decai, whose word saved the king, is standing in Haman's house, fifty cubits high."

¹⁰ And the king said, "Hang him on that." So they hanged Ha'man on the gallows which he had prepared for Mor'decai. Then the anger of the king abated.

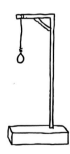

▶ Here the crime that was plotted can be thwarted successfully. The Jews remember this event each year in the Purim Festival. Yet later in the course of history, Jews were persecuted and killed countless times, down to the Holocaust. Other ethnic groups, too, have fallen victim to genocides and slaughters: Armenians in 1915 in Turkey, millions of Ukrainians under Stalin, thousands of Bosnians in 1995 in Srebrenica, millions of Tutsis and Hutus in Rwanda, Burundi, and in the Congo (starting in 1994). What can be done to prevent such massacres from happening again?

Maccabees

These two works are found only in the Greek Bible; they relate the
uprising of Mattathias and his sons against the desecration of the Temple by the Seleucid King Antiochus IV in the year 167 B.C. The latter's
hostile treatment of the traditional religion and its customs precipitat-
ed the violent resistance of pious Jews; decades-long battles followed
and led finally to independence and also to the rule of the Hasmonean
kings. The Second Book of the Maccabees depicts the suffering of those
who remained true to their faith, including the martyrdom of Eleazar
and of a mother together with her seven children (2 Mac 6–7). Despite
the enticements of the hostile king and the sight of the horrible deaths
of his brothers, the youngest son holds fast to God.

Dictatorial regimes often tend to lead people away from their familiar traditions and to reorient them to their ideology. Mattathias resists and thereby launches a rebellion.

Mattathias' resistance (1 Mac 2:15-28)

2 [15] Then the king's officers who were enforcing the apostasy came to the city of Mo'dein to make them offer sacrifice. [16] Many from Israel came to them; and Mattathi'as and his sons were assembled. [17] Then the king's officers spoke to Mattathi'as as follows: "You are a leader, honored and great in this city, and supported by sons and brothers. [18] Now be the first to come and do what the king commands, as all the Gentiles and the men of Judah and those that are left in Jerusalem have done. Then you and your sons will be numbered among the friends of the king, and you and your sons will be honored with silver and gold and many gifts."

[19] But Mattathi'as answered and said in a loud voice: "Even if all the nations that live under the rule of the king obey him, and have chosen to do his commandments, departing each one from the religion of his fathers, [20] yet I and my sons and my brothers will live by the covenant of our fathers. [21] Far be it from us to desert the law and

"White Rose" was the name chosen by an anti-Nazi resistance group made up of young Christian believers. Shortly before their execution, Sophie Scholl, Hans Scholl, and Christoph Probst were allowed to smoke their last cigarette together. "It was only a few minutes, but I think that it meant a lot for them", says Inge Aicher-Scholl, their sister. "I did not know that dying could be so easy", said Christoph Probst. And then: "In a few minutes we will see each other again in eternity." Then they were led away. Sophie went first, standing tall. The executioner said that he had never seen anyone die like that.

the ordinances. [22] We will not obey the king's words by turning aside from our religion to the right hand or to the left."

[23] When he had finished speaking these words, a Jew came forward in the sight of all to offer sacrifice upon the altar in Mo'dein, according to the king's command. [24] When Mattathi'as saw it, he burned with zeal and his heart was stirred. He gave vent to righteous anger; he ran and killed him upon the altar. [25] At the same time he killed the king's officer who was forcing them to sacrifice, and he tore down the altar. [26] Thus he burned with zeal for the law, as Phin'ehas did against Zimri the son of Sa'lu.

[27] Then Mattathi'as cried out in the city with a loud voice, saying: "Let every one who is zealous for the law and supports the covenant come out with me!" [28] And he and his sons fled to the hills and left all that they had in the city.

> So many people are killed [in action] for this regime. It is time for someone to be killed against it.

SOPHIE SCHOLL (*1921), member of the resistance against National Socialism, executed on February 22, 1943

In many societies there are people who set an example. The aged Eleazar is aware that younger men look to him (v. 28). This, too, gives him the strength to make the right decision.

Eleazar's death (2 Mac 6:18–31)

6 ¹⁸ Elea'zar, one of the scribes in high position, a man now advanced in age and of noble presence, was being forced to open his mouth to eat swine's flesh. ¹⁹ But he, welcoming death with honor rather than life with pollution, went up to the rack of his own accord, spitting out the flesh, ²⁰ as men ought to go who have the courage to refuse things that it is not right to taste, even for the natural love of life.

²¹ Those who were in charge of that unlawful sacrifice took the man aside, because of their long acquaintance with him, and privately urged him to bring meat of his own providing, proper for him to use, and pretend that he was eating the flesh of the sacrificial meal which had been commanded by the king, ²² so that by doing this he might be saved from death, and be treated kindly on account of his old friendship with them. ²³ But making a high resolve, worthy of his years and the dignity of his old age and the gray hairs which he had reached with distinction and his excellent life even from childhood, and moreover according to the holy God-given law, he declared himself quickly, telling them to send him to Hades.

► Eleazar does not allow himself to be "bought" (v. 21). For him there is no question of being dishonest.

💡 Eleazar's courage in the face of death has a counterpart in the ancient world in the death of the Greek philosopher Socrates (469–399 B.C.). Accused of "godlessness" because he rejected polytheism, he was sentenced to die by drinking poison. "I respect you, men of Athens, ... but I will →

→ obey God rather than you", Socrates had said in his own defense, but in vain. So he accepted the death sentence: "It is time for us to go—I to die, you to live: but no one except God knows which of us walks the better path."

► The ninety-year-old man has no intention of prolonging his life. His faith in God and his responsibility in his sight give Eleazar the strength to give courageous witness.

❞ If death, though, is like an emigration from here to another place, and if what they say is true, that all who have died find themselves there, what greater happiness could there be than that?

SOCRATES

²⁴ "Such pretense is not worthy of our time of life," he said, "lest many of the young should suppose that Elea'zar in his ninetieth year has gone over to an alien religion, ²⁵ and through my pretense, for the sake of living a brief moment longer, they should be led astray because of me, while I defile and disgrace my old age. ²⁶ For even if for the present I should avoid the punishment of men, yet whether I live or die I shall not escape the hands of the Almighty. ²⁷ Therefore, by manfully giving up my life now, I will show myself worthy of my old age ²⁸ and leave to the young a noble example of how to die a good death willingly and nobly for the revered and holy laws."

When he had said this, he went at once to the rack. ²⁹ And those who a little before had acted toward him with good will now changed to ill will, because the words he had uttered were in their opinion sheer madness. ³⁰ When he was about to die under the blows, he groaned aloud and said: "It is clear to the Lord in his holy knowledge that, though I might have been saved from death, I am enduring terrible sufferings in my body under this beating, but in my soul I am glad to suffer these things because I fear him."

³¹ So in this way he died, leaving in his death an example of nobility and a memorial of courage, not only to the young but to the great body of his nation.

Courage to die (2 Mac 7:24–41)

7 [24] .... The youngest brother being still alive, Antiochus not only appealed to him in words, but promised with oaths that he would make him rich and enviable if he would turn from the ways of his fathers, and that he would take him for his friend and entrust him with public affairs. [25] Since the young man would not listen to him at all, the king called the mother to him and urged her to advise the youth to save himself. [26] After much urging on his part, she undertook to persuade her son. [27] But, leaning close to him, she spoke in their native tongue as follows, deriding the cruel tyrant: "My son, have pity on me. I carried you nine months in my womb, and nursed you for three years, and have reared you and brought you up to this point in your life, and have taken care of you. [28] I beg you, my child, to look at the heaven and the earth and see everything that is in them, and recognize that God did not make them out of things that existed.Thus also mankind comes into being. [29] Do not fear this butcher, but prove worthy of your brothers. Accept death, so that in God's mercy I may get you back again with your brothers."

[30] While she was still speaking, the young man said, "What are you waiting for? I will not obey the king's command, but I obey the

B Set the believers an example in speech and conduct, in love, in faith, in purity.

1 Tim 4:12

▶ The youngest son, too, wants to adhere to the Torah. Faith in God's justice gives him courage.

command of the law that was given to our fathers through Moses. [31] But you,who have contrived all sorts of evil against the Hebrews, will certainly not escape the hands of God. [32] For we are suffering because of our own sins. [33] And if our living Lord is angry for a little while, to rebuke and discipline us, he will again be reconciled with his own servants. [34] But you, unholy wretch, you most defiled of all men, do not be elated in vain and puffed up by uncertain hopes, when you raise your hand against the children of heaven. [35] You have not yet escaped the judgment of the almighty, all-seeing God. [36] For our brothers after enduring a brief suffering have drunk of everflowing life under God's covenant; but you, by the judgment of God, will receive just punishment for your arrogance. [37] I, like my brothers, give up body and life for the laws of our fathers, appealing to God to show mercy soon to our nation and by afflictions and plagues to make you confess that he alone is God, [38] and through me and my brothers to bring to an end the wrath of the Almighty which has justly fallen on our whole nation."

[39] The king fell into a rage, and handled him worse than the others, being exasperated at his scorn. [40] So he died in his integrity, putting his whole trust in the Lord.

[41] Last of all, the mother died, after her sons.

▶ "God did not make them out of things that existed": a literal translation from the Greek; in other words, God made them out of nothing. This is the only passage in the OT that expresses this idea; it thus deepens faith in God as Creator.

B You dismiss us from this present life, but the King of the universe will raise us up to an everlasting renewal of life.

2 Mac 7:9

▶ Here there is an echo of faith in the resurrection and eternal life (↗ v. 29 earlier).

▶ The hopes of the mother and of her sons are fulfilled. Antiochus IV dies, and after a few years the Jews can again practice their religion freely.

The
Wisdom Books

Above and beyond the foundation of community life in the Torah and a critical examination of its history, in which God's instruction was disregarded many times, Israel reflected on its special experiences from several perspectives and collected its insights. The third part of the Hebrew Bible, after the Torah and the Prophets, is called "The Writings". It includes what Christians call "Wisdom Books". (You will recall that Christians generally divide the Old Testament into four parts: the Law, the Historical Books, the Prophets, and the Wisdom Books.)

Job looms large because of the intensity with which it poses the question about innocent suffering, explores solutions in the speeches of the visitors, and finally has God answer in riddles.

The *Psalms* are testimonies to great closeness to God; in them, those who pray bring their personal concerns to him in frank and sometimes even drastic language. They are part of the ev-erlasting treasure of mankind because they help us to speak to God in the most diverse situations and to deepen our relationship with him.

The Book of *Proverbs* consists of several collections that gather up wisdom gained from life and tie it together with faith experiences. They are a compilation of insights that people have had in their everyday lives and with God and wanted to hand on as tried and true.

Ecclesiastes again is the work of a "critical mind" that questions conventional notions and tries to discover the true value of things and behaviors. This leads to unusual perspectives and stimulates a search for what really lasts in life.

The *Song of Solomon* is unsurpassed in the Bible in its portrayal of the love of a man and a woman, which is described as extremely precious, something in which God's power can be perceived.

THE BOOK OF

Job

The Book of Job is one of the most significant books in world literature. It combines the most exalted poetry with a profound spiritual message that is not content with easy answers. It grapples intensely with the question of why innocent people must suffer and how God can allow that. It arrives at a mysterious answer (Job 38–42).

The beginning of the book tells how wealthy, righteous Job loses everything he owns and all his children and then becomes seriously ill, because Satan, the troublemaker in the heavenly council, will not believe that Job is truly just (Job 1–2). Job, together with three friends who have come to console him, silently endures his suffering for seven days (Job 2:11–13), then curses his life (Job 3).

In the discussions that follow, his friends try to convince him that he must have committed some sort of injustice—otherwise such suffering could not have befallen him. Job, however, resists such assumptions and finds his way to a deeper hope in God (e.g., in Job 19:25–27). He yearns for God to manifest himself, and the Lord grants him this favor and justifies him at the end (Job 42:7–17).

It would be better if I had never been born (Job 3:1–26)

3 ¹After this Job opened his mouth and cursed the day of his birth. ²And Job said:

³"Let the day perish wherein I was born,
and the night which said,
'A man-child is conceived.'
⁴Let that day be darkness!
May God above not seek it,
nor light shine upon it.
⁵Let gloom and deep darkness claim it.
Let clouds dwell upon it;
let the blackness of the day terrify it.
⁶That night—let thick darkness seize it!
let it not rejoice among the days of the year,
let it not come into the number of the months.
⁷Yes, let that night be barren;
let no joyful cry be heard in it.
⁸Let those curse it who curse the day,
who are skilled to rouse up Levi'athan.
⁹Let the stars of its dawn be dark;
let it hope for light, but have none,
nor see the eyelids of the morning;

> I believe in the sun, even when it is not shining. I believe in love, even when I do not feel it. I believe in God, even when he is silent.

Written on the wall of a cellar in Cologne where Jews hid during the war.

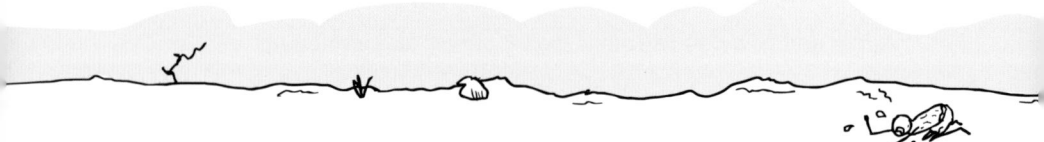

> Job does not wait patiently, but he waits. Job's faith is not sunny and serene, but it is faith. It is not without doubts. ... But Job remains a hero of faith. He waits in faith, and he sees the glory of God. He is blessed in the very waiting, in the dung, in the agony; and he is doubly blessed in the finding, in the end.

PETER KREEFT

▶ Job sees the realm of death as liberation from the injustices of life.

▶ Scarcely any other passage finds such strong words to express the yearning for death of those who suffer.

¹⁰because it did not shut the doors of my mother's womb,
nor hide trouble from my eyes.
¹¹"Why did I not die at birth,
come forth from the womb and expire?
¹²Why did the knees receive me?
Or why the breasts, that I should suck?
¹³For then I should have lain down and been quiet;
I should have slept; then I should have been at rest,
¹⁴with kings and counselors of the earth
who rebuilt ruins for themselves,
¹⁵or with princes who had gold,
who filled their houses with silver.
¹⁶Or why was I not as a hidden untimely birth,
as infants that never see the light?
¹⁷There the wicked cease from troubling,
and there the weary are at rest.
¹⁸There the prisoners are at ease together;
they hear not the voice of the taskmaster.
¹⁹The small and the great are there,
and the slave is free from his master.
²⁰"Why is light given to him who is in misery,
and life to the bitter in soul,
²¹who long for death, but it comes not,

and dig for it more than for hidden treasures;
²² who rejoice exceedingly,
and are glad, when they find the grave?
²³ Why is light given to a man whose way is hidden,
whom God has hedged in?
²⁴ For my sighing comes as my bread,
and my groanings are poured out like water.
²⁵ For the thing that I fear comes upon me,
and what I dread befalls me.
²⁶ I am not at ease, nor am I quiet;
I have no rest; but trouble comes."

 Y → 66
Was it part of God's plan for
men to suffer and die?

Jesus did not come down
from his cross either.
POPE JOHN PAUL II, shortly
before his death in 2005.

In the more than thirty chapters that follow, a debate unfolds between Job and his friends: they represent the traditional view that people suffer on account of their sins, that all men are sinners; Job, therefore, must endure a just
punishment from God. Job, however, insists that he has not sinned. Job addresses his friends with strong words:

My redeemer lives (Job 19:21–27)

19 ²¹ Have pity on me, have pity on me, O you my friends,
for the hand of God has touched me!
²² Why do you, like God, pursue me?
Why are you not satisfied with my flesh?
²³ "Oh, that my words were written!

▶ Job does not hesitate to
accuse God. Today, too, it is
permissible to question God
passionately, and to wrestle
with him.

Oh, that they were inscribed in a book!
²⁴ Oh, that with an iron pen and lead
they were graven in the rock for ever!
²⁵ For I know that my Redeemer lives,
and at last he will stand upon the earth;
²⁶ and after my skin has been thus destroyed,
then from my flesh I shall see God,
²⁷ whom I shall see on my side,
and my eyes shall behold, and not another.
My heart faints within me!

 ▶ "Redeemer" is the same
word as in the Book of Ruth
(↗ Ruth 2:20).

▶ Although Job suffers terribly
and accuses God, he yearns to
meet God. People who come
close to dying often sense this
yearning much more strongly
than those who are well.

The debate between Job and his friends continues without being resolved until God himself finally answers.

Do you send forth the lightning? (Job 38)

38 ¹ Then the LORD answered Job out of the whirlwind:
² "Who is this that darkens counsel by words without
knowledge?
³ Gird up your loins like a man,
I will question you, and you shall declare to me.
⁴ "Where were you when I laid the foundation of the earth?
Tell me, if you have understanding.
⁵ Who determined its measurements—surely you know!

B For my thoughts are not
your thoughts, neither
are your ways my ways, says
the LORD. For as the heavens
are higher than the earth, so
are my ways higher than your
ways and my thoughts than
your thoughts.

Is 55:8–9

📖 My God, my God, why have you forsaken me? Why are you so far from helping me, from the words of my groaning? O my God, I cry by day, but you do not answer; and by night, but find no rest.

Ps 22:2–3

▶ God reacts to Job's accusations with many questions. He speaks aggressively and bitterly, like someone who feels misunderstood and therefore offended.

▶ This poem uses old mythical images for the formation of the earth (↗ e.g., Ps 104:1–9).

Or who stretched the line upon it?
⁶ On what were its bases sunk,
or who laid its cornerstone,
⁷ when the morning stars sang together,
and all the sons of God shouted for joy?
⁸ "Or who shut in the sea with doors,
when it burst forth from the womb;
⁹ when I made clouds its garment,
and thick darkness its swaddling band;
¹⁰ and prescribed bounds for it, and set bars and doors,
¹¹ and said, 'Thus far shall you come, and no farther,
and here shall your proud waves be stayed'?
¹² "Have you commanded the morning since your days began,
and caused the dawn to know its place,
¹³ that it might take hold of the skirts of the earth,
and the wicked be shaken out of it?
¹⁴ It is changed like clay under the seal, and it is dyed like a garment.
¹⁵ From the wicked their light is withheld,
and their uplifted arm is broken.
¹⁶ "Have you entered into the springs of the sea,
or walked in the recesses of the deep?

Most High, all powerful, good Lord, yours are the praises, the glory, the honor, and all blessing. To you alone, Most High, do they belong, and no man is worthy to mention Your name. Be praised, my Lord, through all your creatures, especially through my lord Brother Sun, who brings the day; and you give light through him. And he is beautiful and radiant in all his splendor! Of you, Most High, he bears the likeness.

From the "Canticle of the Sun" by **FRANCIS OF ASSISI**

99 Man, with all his problems, lives in a world with a wisdom which he has not established, but which he cannot exclude from his consideration so that he can relate as an isolated individual to God and thereby play at being "God's censor".

HANS URS VON BALTHASAR
(1905–1988), Swiss theologian and Catholic priest

¹⁷ Have the gates of death been revealed to you,
or have you seen the gates of deep darkness?
¹⁸ Have you comprehended the expanse of the earth?
Declare, if you know all this.
¹⁹ "Where is the way to the dwelling of light,
and where is the place of darkness,
²⁰ that you may take it to its territory
and that you may discern the paths to its home?
²¹ You know, for you were born then,
and the number of your days is great!
²² "Have you entered the storehouses of the snow,
or have you seen the storehouses of the hail,
²³ which I have reserved for the time of trouble,
for the day of battle and war?
²⁴ What is the way to the place where the light is distributed,
or where the east wind is scattered upon the earth?
²⁵ "Who has cleft a channel for the torrents of rain,
and a way for the thunderbolt,
²⁶ to bring rain on a land where no man is,
on the desert in which there is no man;
²⁷ to satisfy the waste and desolate land,
and to make the ground put forth grass?
²⁸ "Has the rain a father, or who has begotten the drops of dew?

²⁹ From whose womb did the ice come forth,
and who has given birth to the hoarfrost of heaven?
³⁰ The waters become hard like stone,
and the face of the deep is frozen.
³¹ "Can you bind the chains of the Plei'ades,
or loose the cords of Ori'on?
³² Can you lead forth the Maz'zaroth in their season,
or can you guide the Bear with its children?
³³ Do you know the ordinances of the heavens?
Can you establish their rule on the earth?
³⁴ "Can you lift up your voice to the clouds, that a flood of waters
may cover you? ³⁵ Can you send forth bolts of lightning, that they
may go and say to you, 'Here we are'?
³⁶ Who has put wisdom in the clouds,
or given understanding to the mists?
³⁷ Who can number the clouds by wisdom?
Or who can tilt the waterskins of the heavens, ³⁸ when the dust
runs into a mass and the clods cling tightly together?
³⁹ "Can you hunt the prey for the lion, or satisfy the appetite of the
young lions, ⁴⁰ when they crouch in their dens,
or lie in wait in their hiding places?
⁴¹ Who provides for the raven its prey, when its young ones cry to
God, and wander about for lack of food?

God guides not only life on earth but even the stars. This recalls the certainties of the philosopher Immanuel Kant: "Two things fill the mind with ever-new and increasing admiration and awe, the more often and steadily we reflect upon them: the starry heavens above me and the moral law within me."

▶ Some translations of Job 38:36 read: "Who has put wisdom in the ibis, or given understanding to the rooster?" The ibis (a bird) and the rooster are capable of predicting the weather. The ibis in Egypt announced the rising of the Nile.

After God has spoken at length and in detail (Job 38–41), Job answers:

Now my eye has seen you! (Job 42:1–7)

42 ¹ Then Job answered the LORD :
² "I know that you can do all things,
and that no purpose of yours can be thwarted.
³ 'Who is this that hides counsel without knowledge?'
Therefore I have uttered what I did not understand,
things too wonderful for me, which I did not know.
⁴ 'Hear, and I will speak; I will question you, and you declare to me.'
⁵ I had heard of you by the hearing of the ear,
but now my eye sees you;
⁶ therefore I despise myself, and repent in dust and ashes."
⁷ After the LORD had spoken these words to Job, the LORD said to
Eli'phaz the Te'manite: "My wrath is kindled against you and against
your two friends; for you have not spoken of me what is right, as my
servant Job has.

 Are not five sparrows sold for two pennies? And not one of them is forgotten before God. Why, even the hairs of your head are all numbered. Fear not; you are of more value than many sparrows.

Lk 12:6–7

 Someone who runs away from a cross will find a larger one on his path.
PHILIP NERI (1515–1595), the "smiling saint", Italian priest, mystic, and founder of the Oratory

▶ Some interpret the Hebrew in Job 42:6 to mean "I am consoled."

The Book of Job gives no direct answer to the question of suffering. But it becomes clear that Job will be content with nothing less than meeting God (→ also Ps 73:25). Although Job takes back what he said about God, God says that he is right—and his friends are not (Job 42:7–8).

THE BOOK OF

Psalms

The Psalms are poems and prayers that are often sung. They give expression in God's presence to the sadness and sorrows, but also to the joy and exultation of life. They are much more than two thousand years old. But to this day they are the greatest treasury of prayer for Jews and Christians. They speak to the hearts of countless believers.

In many psalms, the moods and themes change very drastically, just as the moods in our life are often changeable and contradictory. When we pray with the psalms, we bring before God not only our own life, but the destiny of all mankind.

There are 150 psalms in all; here we introduce only individual special examples. In addition, we have cited a few psalms in the margins of other passages, which respond, as it were, to the themes in them (e.g., Psalm 114 about the miracles of Exodus, p. GT49).

The language of the psalms is poetic and dense, full of imagery and contrasts. It is best to focus on a sentence or an image that speaks to you and bring it into your personal conversation with God. In that way the inexhaustible power of the psalms will be effective for you, too.

The glory of the Creator—the dignity of man (Ps 8)

8 2 O Lᴏʀᴅ, our Lord,
how majestic is your name in all the earth!
You whose glory above the heavens is chanted
² by the mouth of babies and infants,
you have founded a bulwark because of your foes,
to still the enemy and the avenger.
³ When I look at your heavens, the work of your fingers,
the moon and the stars which you have established;
⁴ what is man that you are mindful of him,
and the son of man that you care for him?
⁵ Yet you have made him little less than the angels,
and you have crowned him with glory and honor.
⁶ You have given him dominion over the works of your hands;
you have put all things under his feet,
⁷ all sheep and oxen, and also the beasts of the field,
⁸ the birds of the air, and the fish of the sea,
whatever passes along the paths of the sea.
⁹ O Lᴏʀᴅ, our Lord, how majestic is your name in all the earth!

> 99 In the eyes of God we are the most beautiful thing, the greatest, the best of creation: even the angels are beneath us, we are more than the angels. ...The Lord favors us! We must give thanks to him for this. ...God forgives always, we men forgive sometimes, but creation never forgives and if you don't care for it, it will destroy you!
>
> **POPE FRANCIS**, May 21, 2014

God in the wide universe and in the little word (Ps 19)

19 ¹ The heavens are telling the glory of God;
and the firmament proclaims his handiwork.
² Day to day pours forth speech,
and night to night declares knowledge.
³ There is no speech, nor are there words;
their voice is not heard;
⁴ yet their voice goes out through all the earth,
and their words to the end of the world.
In them he has set a tent for the sun,
⁵ which comes forth like a bridegroom leaving his chamber,
and like a strong man runs its course with joy.
⁶ Its rising is from the end of the heavens,
and its circuit to the end of them;
and there is nothing hidden from its heat.
⁷ The law of the Lᴏʀᴅ is perfect, reviving the soul;
the testimony of the Lᴏʀᴅ is sure making wise the simple;
⁸ the precepts of the Lᴏʀᴅ are right, rejoicing the heart;
the commandment of the Lᴏʀᴅ is pure, enlightening the eyes;
⁹ the fear of the Lᴏʀᴅ is clean, enduring for ever;
the ordinances of the Lᴏʀᴅ are true, and righteous altogether.
¹⁰ More to be desired are they than gold, even much fine gold;
sweeter also than honey and drippings of the honeycomb.

> "The Heavens Are Telling the Glory of God" is one of the most popular movements in the oratorio by Franz Josef Haydn entitled *The Creation*. The eighteenth-century composer was inspired by Psalm 19 and set several verses of it to glorious music for choir and orchestra.

> ▶ "Law" (v. 7) is literally "Torah" (→ p. 16 f.).

> 99 An enlightened eye is a pure eye to which things appear as they are; an eye without falsehood, without ulterior motives, which effortlessly distinguishes light and dark, good and evil. The precepts of the Lord remove all cloudiness from the eye.
>
> **ROBERT SPAEMANN** (b. 1927), German philosopher, from *Meditations of a Christian on the Psalms*

[11] Moreover by them is your servant warned;
in keeping them there is great reward.
[12] But who can discern his errors? Clear me from hidden faults.
[13] Keep back your servant also from presumptuous sins;
let them not have dominion over me!
Then I shall be blameless, and innocent of great transgression.
[14] Let the words of my mouth and the meditation of my heart
be acceptable in your sight, O LORD, my rock and my redeemer.

A cry for deliverance (Ps 22)

22 [1] My God, my God, why have you forsaken me?
Why are you so far from helping me, from the words of my groaning?
[2] O my God, I cry by day, but you do not answer;
and by night, but find no rest.
[3] Yet you are holy, enthroned on the praises of Israel.
[4] In you our fathers trusted; they trusted, and you delivered them.
[5] To you they cried, and were saved;
in you they trusted, and were not disappointed.
[6] But I am a worm, and no man;
scorned by men, and despised by the people.

 I am not aware of anything against myself, but I am not thereby acquitted. It is the Lord who judges me. Therefore do not pronounce judgment before the time, before the Lord comes, who will bring to light the things now hidden in darkness and will disclose the purposes of the heart.

1 Cor 4:4–5

▶ At the hour of his death, Jesus prayed this psalm in Aramaic. In keeping with Jewish tradition, Jesus made the content of the entire psalm his own, not only the cry of abandonment in v. 2.

 At the ninth hour Jesus cried with a loud voice, "Eloi, Eloi, lama sabachthani?"

Mk 15:34

[7] All who see me mock at me,
they make mouths at me, they wag their heads;
[8] "He committed his cause to the LORD; let him deliver him,
let him rescue him, for he delights in him!"
[9] Yet you are he who took me from the womb;
you kept me safe upon my mother's breasts.
[10] Upon you was I cast from my birth,
and since my mother bore me you have been my God.
[11] Be not far from me, for trouble is near and there is none to help.
[12] Many bulls encompass me, strong bulls of Bashan surround me;
[13] they open wide their mouths at me,
like a ravening and roaring lion.
[14] I am poured out like water, and all my bones are out of joint;
my heart is like wax, it is melted within my breast;
[15] my strength is dried up like a potsherd,
and my tongue cleaves to my jaws; you lay me in the dust of death.
[16] Yes, dogs are round about me; a company of evildoers encircle me; they have pierced my hands and feet—
[17] I can count all my bones—they stare and gloat over me;
[18] they divide my garments among them,
and for my clothing they cast lots.
[19] But you, O LORD, be not far off! O my help, hasten to my aid!

💡 God as a "midwife"—a beautiful image! We, too, owe our lives to God. From one second to the next we would sink back into nothingness if God did not keep us in being.

❞ We often forget the bitter dregs at the bottom of the eucharistic chalice, the cup that is the memory of his suffering.

HANS URS VON BALTHASAR

▶ The psalmist praying makes God responsible ("you ..." v. 15) for his situation.

B And they crucified him, and divided his garments among them.

Mk 15:24: Roman soldiers divide Jesus' clothes.

▶ At v. 22, the tone changes completely. All of a sudden, the dire need seems to turn, and a "crescendo of praise" begins, which encompasses all mankind (vv. 27–28), but also the dead (v. 29) and even future generations (vv. 30–31).

▶ Misery can be repulsive, but not for God. He sees the need and helps (↗ also v. 26, the meal for the poor).

²⁰ Deliver my soul from the sword, my life from the power of the dog!

²¹ Save me from the mouth of the lion,
my afflicted soul from the horns of the wild oxen!

²² I will tell of your name to my brethren;
in the midst of the congregation I will praise you:

²³ You who fear the LORD, praise him! All you sons of Jacob, glorify him, and stand in awe of him, all you sons of Israel!

²⁴ For he has not despised or abhorred the affliction of the afflicted;
and he has not hidden his face from him,
but has heard, when he cried to him.

²⁵ From you comes my praise in the great congregation;
my vows I will pay before those who fear him.

²⁶ The afflicted shall eat and be satisfied; those who seek him shall praise the LORD! May your hearts live for ever!

²⁷ All the ends of the earth shall remember
and turn to the LORD; and all the families of the nations
shall worship before him.

²⁸ For dominion belongs to the LORD, and he rules over the nations.

²⁹ Yes, to him shall all the proud of the earth bow down;

We can never trust too much in the kindly, mighty God. We obtain everything from him according to the measure of our trust.

THÉRÈSE OF LISIEUX

99 I have read many intelligent and good books in my life. But in all of them I found nothing that would have made my heart so quiet and glad as the four words from Psalm 23, "You are with me."

IMMANUEL KANT (1724–1804), German philosopher

before him shall bow all who go down to the dust,
and he who cannot keep himself alive.

³⁰ Posterity shall serve him; men shall tell of the Lord to the coming generation,

³¹ and proclaim his deliverance to a people yet unborn,
that he has wrought it.

The Good Shepherd (Ps 23)

23 ¹ The LORD is my shepherd, I shall not want;
²he makes me lie down in green pastures.
He leads me beside still waters; ³ he restores my soul.
He leads me in paths of righteousness for his name's sake.

⁴ Even though I walk through the valley of the shadow of death,
I fear no evil;
for you are with me; your rod and your staff, they comfort me.

⁵ You prepare a table before me in the presence of my enemies;
you anoint my head with oil, my cup overflows.

⁶ Surely goodness and mercy shall follow me
all the days of my life; and I shall dwell in the house of the LORD
for ever.

Ever trusting (Ps 27)

27 The LORD is my light and my salvation; whom shall I fear?
The LORD is the stronghold of my life;
of whom shall I be afraid?

[2] When evildoers assail me, to devour my flesh,
my adversaries and foes, they shall stumble and fall.

[3] Though a host encamp against me, my heart shall not fear;
though war arise against me, yet I will be confident.

[4] One thing have I asked of the LORD, that will I seek after;
that I may dwell in the house of the LORD all the days of my life,
to behold the beauty of the LORD, and to inquire in his temple.

[5] For he will hide me in his shelter in the day of trouble;
he will conceal me under the cover of his tent,
he will set me high upon a rock.

[6] And now my head shall be lifted up above my enemies round about me; and I will offer in his tent sacrifices with shouts of joy;
I will sing and make melody to the LORD.

[7] Hear, O LORD, when I cry aloud, be gracious to me and answer me!

[8] You have said, "Seek my face."
My heart says to you, "Your face, LORD, do I seek."

If God is for us, who is against us?

Rom 8:31; in vv. 38–39, Paul then says that nothing "will be able to separate us from the love of God in Christ Jesus our Lord".

[9] Hide not your face from me. Turn not your servant away in anger,
you who have been my help.
Cast me not off, forsake me not, O God of my salvation!

[10] For my father and my mother have forsaken me,
but the LORD will take me up.

[11] Teach me your way, O LORD; and lead me on a level path
because of my enemies.

[12] Give me not up to the will of my adversaries;
for false witnesses have risen against me,
and they breathe out violence.

[13] I believe that I shall see the goodness of the LORD
in the land of the living!

[14] Wait for the LORD; be strong, and let your heart take courage;
yes, wait for the LORD!

To seek God's face—that is precisely what praying means to me. I do not know whether I have found it yet. Whenever I feel very close to him, I seem so little, and I tell myself that I have no idea what prayer is. I like to converse with God; I tell him about my concerns and joys. Often I wait for a sign from him. I really ought to pray more often with the Bible, because that is God's word to me.

CLAIRE

A path from yearning for God to joy with him (Ps 42)

42 As a deer longs for flowing streams,
so longs my soul for you, O God.

[2] My soul thirsts for God, for the living God.
When shall I come and behold the face of God?

[3] My tears have been my food day and night,
while men say to me continually, "Where is your God?"

▶ Korah belongs to the tribe of Levi and is even a cousin of Moses and Aaron (Ex 6:18–21). The sons of Korah are therefore a priestly family.

▶ The psalmist is torn: on the one hand, he is full of sadness, because others question him (v. 3, 9–10); on the other hand, he remembers the solemn procession with great religious joy (v. 4). In the following refrain (v. 5, also v. 11 and 43:5), this tension is resolved, and he finds inner peace.

▶ Here the inner strife is heightened: the psalmist blames God for the fact that he is close to sinking (v. 7; see also v. 9 and 43:2), yet in the night he sings praise to him (v. 8).

⁴These things I remember, as I pour out my soul:
how I went with the throng, and led them in procession to the house of God, with glad shouts and songs of thanksgiving, a multitude keeping festival.
⁵Why are you cast down, O my soul,
and why are you disquieted within me?
Hope in God; for I shall again praise him, my savior ⁶and my God.
My soul is cast down within me, therefore I remember you
from the land of Jordan and of Hermon, from Mount Mizar.
⁷Deep calls to deep at the thunder of your cataracts;
all your waves and your billows have gone over me.
⁸By day the LORD commands his steadfast love;
and at night his song is with me, a prayer to the God of my life.
⁹I say to God, my rock: "Why have you forgotten me?
Why do I go mourning because of the oppression of the enemy?"
¹⁰As with a deadly wound in my body, my adversaries taunt me, while they say to me continually, "Where is your God?"
¹¹Why are you cast down, O my soul, and why are you disquieted within me? Hope in God; for I shall again praise him, my help and my God.

▶ God's "light and truth" (43:3) lead the psalmist to an ever-greater, immediate closeness: out of distant lands (42:6) to the holy "mountain" in Jerusalem, to the "house" (the Temple), and to the "altar", and finally to "God the joy of my jubilation": that is the literal formulation of v. 4 and at the same time the highest fulfillment that the psalmist experiences.

99 Probably the psalm "Miserere" has been prayed the most often over the course of the last two thousand years. Without God's mercy, we are lost. David, when he prayed the psalm, had destroyed another man. Not because he delighted in destruction, but rather because he followed his spontaneous wishes and, since he was king, could remove →

43 ¹Vindicate me, O God, and defend my cause against an ungodly people; from deceitful and unjust men deliver me!
²For you are the God in whom I take refuge; why have you cast me off? Why do I go mourning because of the oppression of the enemy?
³Oh, send out your light and your truth; let them lead me,
let them bring me to your holy hill and to your dwelling!
⁴Then I will go to the altar of God, to God my exceeding joy;
and I will praise you with the lyre, O God, my God.
⁵Why are you cast down, O my soul,
and why are you disquieted within me?
Hope in God; for I shall again praise him,
my savior and my God.

David prays for forgiveness (Ps 51)

51 ¹Have mercy on me, O God, according to your merciful love; according to your abundant mercy blot out my transgressions.
²Wash me thoroughly from my iniquity, and cleanse me from my sin!
³For I know my transgressions, and my sin is ever before me.
⁴Against you, you only, have I sinned, and done that which is evil in

your sight, so that you are justified in your sentence
and blameless in your judgment.

[5] Behold, I was brought forth in iniquity,
and in sin did my mother conceive me.

[6] Behold, you desire truth in the inward being;
therefore teach me wisdom in my secret heart.

[7] Purge me with hyssop, and I shall be clean;
wash me, and I shall be whiter than snow.

[8] Make me hear joy and gladness;
let the bones which you have broken rejoice.

[9] Hide your face from my sins, and blot out all my iniquities.

[10] Create in me a clean heart, O God,
and put a new and right spirit within me.

[11] Cast me not away from your presence,
and take not your holy Spirit from me.

[12] Restore to me the joy of your salvation,
and uphold me with a willing spirit.

[13] Then I will teach transgressors your ways,
and sinners will return to you.

[14] Deliver me from bloodguilt, O God, O God of my salvation,
and my tongue will sing aloud of your deliverance.

→ the obstacles that got in his way. Do we know what we would do if we were oriental kings? David was a pious man, but he could do what he wanted. That was enough to turn him into a murderer. Only the prophet Nathan opened his eyes. Who opens our eyes to what we perpetrate?

ROBERT SPAEMANN *Meditations of a Christian on the Psalms*

> My God, I am sorry for my sins with all my heart. In choosing to do wrong and failing to do good, I have sinned against you whom I should love above all things. I firmly intend, with your help, to do penance, to sin no more, and to avoid whatever leads me to sin. Our Savior Jesus Christ suffered and died for us. In his name, my God, have mercy. Amen.

AN ACT OF CONTRITION

[15] O Lord, open my lips, and my mouth shall show forth your praise.

[16] For you take no delight in sacrifice;
were I to give a burnt offering, you would not be pleased.

[17] The sacrifice acceptable to God is a broken spirit;
a broken and contrite heart, O God, you will not despise.

[18] Do good to Zion in your good pleasure;
rebuild the walls of Jerusalem,

[19] then will you delight in right sacrifices,
in burnt offerings and whole burnt offerings;
then bulls will be offered on your altar.

> We ask him for what suits us, and he gives us what we need: obviously these are completely different things.

LEON BLOY (1846–1917), French man of letters

To be united with God is most important (Ps 63)

63 [1] O God, you are my God, I seek you,
my soul thirsts for you;
my flesh faints for you, as in a dry and weary land
where no water is.

[2] So I have looked upon you in the sanctuary,
beholding your power and glory.

[3] Because your merciful love is better than life,
my lips will praise you.

[4] So I will bless you as long as I live;
I will lift up my hands and call on your name.

[5] My soul is feasted as with marrow and fat,

▶ "As in a dry and weary land" actually reads in the original: "in a dry and weary land"—an image for the most intense yearning for God. About "thirsting" for God, ↗ Ps 42:1–2.

▶ "Marrow and fat": Since provisions were often scarce in ancient times, foods rich in fat were prized very highly.

The image "shadow of your wings" combines the protection that a mother hen gives to her young with her wings with the "shade" that preserves from the heat—which is especially important in lands of the Middle East. Both are applied here to God metaphorically.

Blessed are the pure of heart, for they shall see God.

Mt 5:8

If I am always striving to do whatever I want, when I want, how I want, and as often as I want, I'm not really free. I actually become a slave—a slave to my selfish desires.

DR. EDWARD SRI, Scripture scholar, theologian, and popular author

and my mouth praises you with joyful lips,
⁶ when I think of you upon my bed,
and meditate on you in the watches of the night;
⁷ for you have been my help,
and in the shadow of your wings I sing for joy.
⁸ My soul clings to you; your right hand upholds me.
⁹ But those who seek to destroy my life
shall go down into the depths of the earth;
¹⁰ they shall be given over to the power of the sword,
they shall be prey for jackals.
¹¹ But the king shall rejoice in God;
all who swear by him shall glory;
for the mouths of liars will be stopped.

No envy of the "happiness" of the wicked! (Ps 73)

73 ¹ Truly God is good to the upright,
to those who are pure in heart.
² But as for me, my feet had almost stumbled,
my steps had well nigh slipped.
³ For I was envious of the arrogant,
when I saw the prosperity of the wicked.

Because wickedness is multiplied, most men's love will grow cold.

Mt 24:12

The pious psalmist finds it difficult to endure the "injustice" (vv. 2–3) that wicked men have success and recognition (vv. 4–10) and, furthermore, mock God disparagingly (v. 11).

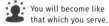
You will become like that which you serve.

CATHERINE OF SIENA

Two things keep the psalmist from imitating the wicked: his solidarity with other believers (v. 15: God's "children") and the insight that he received in the Temple (v. 17).

⁴ For they have no pangs; their bodies are sound and sleek.
⁵ They are not in trouble as other men are;
they are not stricken like other men.
⁶ Therefore pride is their necklace;
violence covers them as a garment.
⁷ Their eyes swell out with fatness,
their hearts overflow with follies.
⁸ They scoff and speak with malice;
loftily they threaten oppression.
⁹ They set their mouths against the heavens,
and their tongue struts through the earth.
¹⁰ Therefore the people turn and praise them;
and find no fault in them.
¹¹ And they say, "How can God know?
Is there knowledge in the Most High?"
¹² Behold, these are the wicked;
always at ease, they increase in riches.
¹³ All in vain have I kept my heart clean
and washed my hands in innocence.
¹⁴ For all the day long I have been stricken,
and chastened every morning.
¹⁵ If I had said, "I will speak thus,"
I would have been untrue to the generation of your children.
¹⁶ But when I thought how to understand this,
it seemed to me a wearisome task,

¹⁷ until I went into the sanctuary of God; then I perceived their end.
¹⁸ Truly you set them in slippery places; you make them fall to ruin.
¹⁹ How they are destroyed in a moment,
swept away utterly by terrors!
²⁰ They are like a dream when one awakes,
on awaking you despise their phantoms.
²¹ When my soul was embittered, when I was pricked in heart,
²² I was stupid and ignorant, I was like a beast toward you.
²³ Nevertheless I am continually with you; you hold my right hand.
²⁴ You guide me with your counsel,
and afterward you will receive me to glory.
²⁵ Whom have I in heaven but you?
And there is nothing upon earth that I desire besides you.
²⁶ My flesh and my heart may fail,
but God is the strength of my heart and my portion for ever.
²⁷ For behold, those who are far from you shall perish;
you put an end to those who are false to you.
²⁸ But for me it is good to be near God;
I have made the Lord GOD my refuge,
that I may tell of all your works.

> I believe that God can and will bring good out of everything, even from what is most wicked. ...I believe that in every calamity God wants to give us as much strength to resist as we need. But he does not give it in advance, so that we do not rely on ourselves, but on him alone.

DIETRICH BON-HOEFFER in the cell where he died

💡 "The strength"—literally, "the rock of my heart": what an incredibly awesome image for God!

Refuge with God (Ps 84)

84 ¹ How lovely is your dwelling place,
O LORD of hosts!
² My soul longs, yes, faints for the courts of the LORD;
my heart and flesh sing for joy to the living God.
³ Even the sparrow finds a home,
and the swallow a nest for herself,
where she may lay her young, at your altars, O LORD of hosts,
my King and my God.
⁴ Blessed are those who dwell in your house,
ever singing your praise!
⁵ Blessed are the men whose strength is in you,
in whose heart are the highways to Zion.
⁶ As they go through the valley of Baca
they make it a place of springs;
the early rain also covers it with pools.
⁷ They go from strength to strength;
the God of gods will be seen in Zion.
⁸ O LORD God of hosts, hear my prayer; give ear, O God of Jacob!
⁹ Behold our shield, O God; look upon the face of your anointed!
¹⁰ For a day in your courts is better than a thousand elsewhere.
I would rather be a doorkeeper in the house of my God
than dwell in the tents of wickedness.

▶ God's house, the Temple, is a source of joy (vv. 1–2) and like a home, even for animals (v. 3).

> I think obviously the saints are people who have fallen in love with God; his grace has knocked them head over heels. Jesus Christ is thenceforward their romance.

MSGR. RONALD KNOX (1888–1957), British priest, theologian, and author

> I have come home. I have dropped anchor. I have taken my place in the Church of the apostles, Fathers, confessors, martyrs, bishops, saints, and all the Catholic faithful.

THOMAS HOWARD (b. 1935), Catholic convert and popular author

▶ Three times Psalm 84 says what makes a person "happy" ("blessed …" in vv. 4, 5, and 12): at the beginning, those who are in the Temple are called blessed (v. 4), but finally only trust is sufficient (v. 12).

▶ God encompasses all times and is beyond the human experience of transience. This contrast is developed intensively here (vv. 2–12) and is connected with divine "wrath" on account of human iniquities (v. 8).

God has promised to forgive your sins if you convert tomorrow. He has not promised you tomorrow.
AUGUSTINE

11 For the Lord GOD is a sun and shield; he bestows favor and honor. No good thing does the LORD withhold
from those who walk uprightly.
12 O LORD of hosts, blessed is the man who trusts in you!

Teach us to number our days (Ps 90)

90 1 LORD, you have been our dwelling place
in all generations.
2 Before the mountains were brought forth,
or ever you had formed the earth and the world,
from everlasting to everlasting you are God.
3 You turn man back to the dust,
and say, "Turn back, O children of men!"
4 For a thousand years in your sight
are but as yesterday when it is past, or as a watch in the night.
5 You sweep men away; they are like a dream,
like grass which is renewed in the morning:
6 in the morning it flourishes and is renewed;
in the evening it fades and withers.

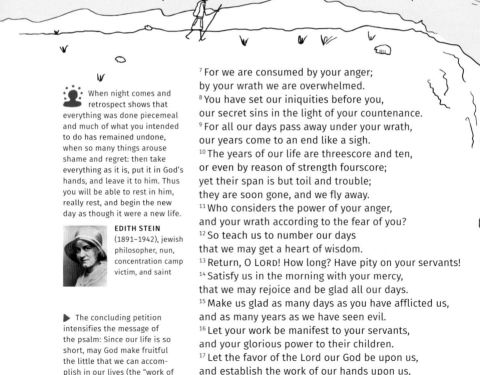

When night comes and retrospect shows that everything was done piecemeal and much of what you intended to do has remained undone, when so many things arouse shame and regret: then take everything as it is, put it in God's hands, and leave it to him. Thus you will be able to rest in him, really rest, and begin the new day as though it were a new life.

EDITH STEIN
(1891–1942), jewish philosopher, nun, concentration camp victim, and saint

▶ The concluding petition intensifies the message of the psalm: Since our life is so short, may God make fruitful the little that we can accomplish in our lives (the "work of our hands").

7 For we are consumed by your anger;
by your wrath we are overwhelmed.
8 You have set our iniquities before you,
our secret sins in the light of your countenance.
9 For all our days pass away under your wrath,
our years come to an end like a sigh.
10 The years of our life are threescore and ten,
or even by reason of strength fourscore;
yet their span is but toil and trouble;
they are soon gone, and we fly away.
11 Who considers the power of your anger,
and your wrath according to the fear of you?
12 So teach us to number our days
that we may get a heart of wisdom.
13 Return, O LORD! How long? Have pity on your servants!
14 Satisfy us in the morning with your mercy,
that we may rejoice and be glad all our days.
15 Make us glad as many days as you have afflicted us,
and as many years as we have seen evil.
16 Let your work be manifest to your servants,
and your glorious power to their children.
17 Let the favor of the Lord our God be upon us,
and establish the work of our hands upon us,
yes, establish the work of our hands.

Assurance of God's protection (Ps 91)

91 [1] He who dwells in the shelter of the Most High,
who abides in the shadow of the Almighty,
[2] will say to the LORD, "My refuge and my fortress;
my God, in whom I trust."
[3] For he will deliver you from the snare of the fowler
and from the deadly pestilence;
[4] he will cover you with his pinions,
and under his wings you will find refuge;
his faithfulness is a shield and buckler.
[5] You will not fear the terror of the night,
nor the arrow that flies by day,
[6] nor the pestilence that stalks in darkness,
nor the destruction that wastes at noonday.
[7] A thousand may fall at your side,
ten thousand at your right hand;
but it will not come near you.
[8] You will only look with your eyes
and see the recompense of the wicked.
[9] Because you have made the LORD your refuge,
the Most High your habitation,

99 God, hear my supplication, / And listen to my prayer. / You saw me from a distance, / I called in dark of night. / Be gracious, Lord, and raise me / On high upon a rock. / I look to you and trust you; / You are my rule and guide. // For you are like a tower / Unconquered by the foe. / No storm can make we waver, / With you I have no fear. / Within your tent forever / You will that I should dwell. / You keep me safe from danger, / Sheltered beneath your wings ....

From a poem by **EDITH STEIN** modeled on Psalm 91.

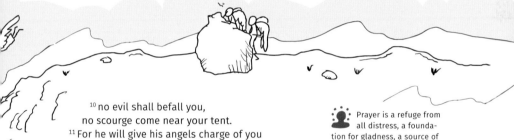

[10] no evil shall befall you,
no scourge come near your tent.
[11] For he will give his angels charge of you
to guard you in all your ways.
[12] On their hands they will bear you up,
lest you dash your foot against a stone.
[13] You will tread on the lion and the adder,
the young lion and the serpent you will trample under foot.
[14] Because he clings to me in love, I will deliver him;
I will protect him, because he knows my name.
[15] When he calls to me, I will answer him;
I will be with him in trouble, I will rescue him and honor him.
[16] With long life I will satisfy him, and show him my salvation.

Prayer is a refuge from all distress, a foundation for gladness, a source of constant happiness, protection against sadness and pettiness of soul.

JOHN CHRYSOSTOM

God, the merciful father (Ps 103)

103 [1] Bless the LORD, O my soul;
and all that is within me, bless his holy name!
[2] Bless the LORD, O my soul, and forget not all his benefits,
[3] who forgives all your iniquity, who heals all your diseases,
[4] who redeems your life from the Pit,
who crowns you with mercy and compassion,
[5] who satisfies you with good as long as you live
so that your youth is renewed like the eagle's.

▶ In vv. 3–5, this hymn in Hebrew uses mostly verbs in the present tense ("forgives, heals..."): God acts in the present, constantly and repeatedly in this way.

▶ In v. 8, the psalmist takes up God's self-revelation in Ex 34:6 (see also Ps 86:15).

▶ The three comparisons in vv. 11–13 show the immense mercy of God.

❝ Once a well-known confessor came to see me: "I have a small scruple, because I know that I forgive too much!" ...And we spoke about mercy. At a certain point he said to me: "You know, when I feel this scruple keenly, I go to the chapel, before the Tabernacle, and I say to Him: Excuse me, but it's Your fault, because you are the one who gave me the bad example! And I go away at peace ...."

POPE FRANCIS, March 6, 2014

⁶ The LORD works vindication and justice for all who are oppressed.
⁷ He made known his ways to Moses,
his acts to the people of Israel.
⁸ The LORD is merciful and gracious,
slow to anger and abounding in mercy.
⁹ He will not always chide, nor will he keep his anger for ever.
¹⁰ He does not deal with us according to our sins,
nor repay us according to our iniquities.
¹¹ For as the heavens are high above the earth,
so great is his mercy toward those who fear him;
¹² as far as the east is from the west,
so far does he remove our transgressions from us.
¹³ As a father pities his children,
so the LORD pities those who fear him.
¹⁴ For he knows our frame; he remembers that we are dust.
¹⁵ As for man, his days are like grass;
he flourishes like a flower of the field;
¹⁶ for the wind passes over it, and it is gone,
and its place knows it no more.
¹⁷ But the mercy of the LORD is from everlasting to everlasting

▶ On the contrast between God and human transience, ↗ Ps 90. Here God's ongoing care ("favor" in v. 17) is emphasized as the grounds for hope.

My wife and I married while we were college students. Afterward we wrote all our thank-you cards by hand the old-fashioned way: we spent an entire day thanking each and every one for all sorts of things. Our thank-you notes gave a lot of people joy. The coolest thing was that our thank-you campaign, which at first seemed stressful, made us noticeably happier and grateful, too. Isn't that interesting? Sometimes the feeling does not come until afterward.

RALPH

upon those who fear him,
and his righteousness to children's children,
¹⁸ to those who keep his covenant
and remember to do his commandments.
¹⁹ The LORD has established his throne in the heavens,
and his kingdom rules over all.
²⁰ Bless the LORD, O you his angels,
you mighty ones who do his word,
hearkening to the voice of his word!
²¹ Bless the LORD, all his hosts, his ministers that do his will!
²² Bless the LORD, all his works, in all places of his dominion.
Bless the LORD, O my soul!

Praise for the works of God in nature (Ps 104)

104 ¹ Bless the LORD, O my soul!
O LORD my God, you are very great!
You are clothed with honor and majesty,
² who cover yourself with light as with a garment,
who have stretched out the heavens like a tent,
³ who have laid the beams of your chambers on the waters,
who make the clouds your chariot,
who ride on the wings of the wind,

⁴ who make the winds your messengers,
fire and flame your ministers.
⁵ You set the earth on its foundations,
so that it should never be shaken.
⁶ You covered it with the deep as with a garment;
the waters stood above the mountains.
⁷ At your rebuke they fled;
at the sound of your thunder they took to flight.
⁸ The mountains rose, the valleys sank down
to the place which you appointed for them.
⁹ You set a bound which they should not pass,
so that they might not again cover the earth.
¹⁰ You make springs gush forth in the valleys;
they flow between the hills,
¹¹ they give drink to every beast of the field;
the wild donkeys quench their thirst.
¹² By them the birds of the air have their habitation;
they sing among the branches.
¹³ From your lofty abode you water the mountains;
the earth is satisfied with the fruit of your work.

▶ In the creation myths of the ancient Near East, the primeval ocean stands for chaos and danger. Divine intervention brings about order and thus makes possible the life of the created world.

Grant me, O Lord, good digestion, and also something to digest. Grant me a healthy body, and the necessary good humor to maintain it. ...Give me a soul that knows not boredom, grumblings, sighs and laments, nor excess of stress, because of that obstructing thing called "I." →

¹⁴ You cause the grass to grow for the cattle,
and plants for man to cultivate,
that he may bring forth food from the earth,
¹⁵ and wine to gladden the heart of man,
oil to make his face shine,
and bread to strengthen man's heart.
¹⁶ The trees of the LORD are watered abundantly,
the cedars of Lebanon which he planted.
¹⁷ In them the birds build their nests;
the stork has her home in the fir trees.
¹⁸ The high mountains are for the wild goats;
the rocks are a refuge for the badgers.
¹⁹ You have made the moon to mark the seasons;
the sun knows its time for setting.
²⁰ You make darkness, and it is night,
when all the beasts of the forest creep forth.
²¹ The young lions roar for their prey, seeking their food from God.
²² When the sun rises, they get them away
and lie down in their dens.
²³ Man goes forth to his work and to his labor until the evening.
²⁴ O LORD, how manifold are your works!
In wisdom you have made them all;

→ Grant me, O Lord, a sense of good humor. Allow me the grace to be able to take a joke to discover in life a bit of joy, and to be able to share it with others.

THOMAS MORE (1478–1535), English Lord Chancellor, philos-opher (*Utopia*), and saint, suffered martyrdom be-cause he resisted Henry VIII.

▶ In the imagination of the ancient Near East, Leviathan is a terrible sea monster. In this psalm, it is only a plaything for God.

▶ The exclamation Hallelujah occurs here for the first time (↗ Ps 145–150). "Hallelujah" means "Praise Yah (= God)!"

the earth is full of your creatures.
²⁵ Yonder is the sea, great and wide,
which teems with things innumerable,
living things both small and great.
²⁶ There go the ships, and Leviathan
which you formed to sport in it.
²⁷ These all look to you, to give them their food in due season.
²⁸ When you give to them, they gather it up;
when you open your hand, they are filled with good things.
²⁹ When you hide your face, they are dismayed;
when you take away their spirit, they die
and return to their dust.
³⁰ When you send forth your Spirit, they are created;
and you renew the face of the earth.
³¹ May the glory of the LORD endure for ever,
may the LORD rejoice in his works,
³² who looks on the earth and it trembles,
who touches the mountains and they smoke!
³³ I will sing to the LORD as long as I live;
I will sing praise to my God while I have being.
³⁴ May my meditation be pleasing to him, for I rejoice in the LORD.
³⁵ Let sinners be consumed from the earth,
and let the wicked be no more!
Bless the LORD, O my soul!
Praise the LORD!

❝❞ Praise of God is a movement or path, so that our heart is purified and drawn away from what is opposed to God.

GEORGE CARDINAL PELL, (b. 1941), Australian cardinal and Prefect for the Secretariat for the Economy

▶ Again and again God makes himself "lowly", although he is infinitely exalted: in his appearance to Moses in the burning bush in Ex 3, in order to deliver Israel; by becoming man in Jesus, in order to save the world; by accompanying people in need in every age.

The Most High bends down to the lowly (Pa 113)

113 ¹ Praise the LORD!
Praise, O servants of the LORD,
praise the name of the LORD!
² Blessed be the name of the LORD
from this time forth and for evermore!
³ From the rising of the sun to its setting
the name of the LORD is to be praised!
⁴ The LORD is high above all nations,
and his glory above the heavens!
⁵ Who is like the LORD our God, who is seated on high,
⁶ who looks far down upon the heavens and the earth?
⁷ He raises the poor from the dust,
and lifts the needy from the ash heap,
⁸ to make them sit with princes, with the princes of his people.
⁹ He gives the barren woman a home,
making her the joyous mother of children.
Praise the LORD!

Trust in God's protection eternally (Ps 121)

121 [1] I lift up my eyes to the hills.
From where does my help come?
[2] My help comes from the LORD, who made heaven and earth.
[3] He will not let your foot be moved,
he who keeps you will not slumber.
[4] Behold, he who keeps Israel will neither slumber nor sleep.
[5] The LORD is your keeper; the LORD is your shade
on your right hand.
[6] The sun shall not strike you by day, nor the moon by night.
[7] The LORD will keep you from all evil; he will keep your life.
[8] The LORD will keep your going out and your coming in
from this time forth and for evermore.

Hope for new rejoicing (Ps 126)

126 [1] When the LORD restored the fortunes of Zion,
we were like those who dream.
[2] Then our mouth was filled with laughter,
and our tongue with shouts of joy;
then they said among the nations,
"The LORD has done great things for them."
[3] The LORD has done great things for us; we are glad.

[4] Restore our fortunes, O LORD, like the watercourses in the Neg'eb!
[5] May those who sow in tears reap with shouts of joy!
[6] He that goes forth weeping, bearing the seed for sowing,
shall come home with shouts of joy,
bringing his sheaves with him.

A cry from the depths (Ps 130)

130 [1] Out of the depths I cry to you, O LORD!
[2] Lord, hear my voice!
Let your ears be attentive to the voice of my supplications!
[3] If you, O Lord, should mark iniquities,
LORD, who could stand?
[4] But there is forgiveness with you, that you may be feared.
[5] I wait for the LORD, my soul waits,
and in his word I hope;
[6] my soul waits for the LORD
more than watchmen for the morning,
more than watchmen for the morning.
[7] O Israel, hope in the LORD! For with the LORD there is mercy,
and with him is plenteous redemption.
[8] And he will redeem Israel from all his iniquities.

 Jesus began to be sorrowful and troubled. Then he said to them, "My soul is very sorrowful, even to death; remain here, and watch with me." ... And he came to the disciples and found them sleeping, and he said to Peter, "So, could you not watch with me one hour?"

Mt 26:37–38, 40. Jesus spent the night before his arrest trembling and praying on the Mount of Olives.

▶ In the ancient Near East, the sun and the moon were considered gods that have power over life.

▶ Verse 1 refers to the return of the Jews from the Babylonian Exile.

▶ The "Negeb" or "southern land" means the desert in southern Palestine. When it rains, the dry rock valleys suddenly turn into a raging torrent.

99 I was choosing a contemplative life because of a desire to seek God in a pure and direct way and because of an instinct that I could neither define nor explain, except to say that it was the Spirit of God pressing me to find Him ...

MOTHER DOLORES HART O.S.B.

My God and Lord, you are my origin and also my goal. You are full of simplicity, full of tranquility and love. Endless is your goodness and glory. You are a glorious light and the highest joy of my heart. You are joy, endless as the ocean, the fullness of all that is good. What can I lack if you are mine?

ALBERT THE GREAT (ca. 1200–1280), Dominican, bishop, polymath (perhaps the most learned man of his time)

▶ Hermon is a high mountain in northern Israel, in modern-day Lebanon, the source of the Jordan. Oil and dew are images for a pleasant, refreshing feeling and for divine blessing.

Like a little child (Ps 131)

131
¹ O Lᴏʀᴅ, my heart is not lifted up,
my eyes are not raised too high;
I do not occupy myself with things
too great and too marvelous for me.
² But I have calmed and quieted my soul,
like a child quieted at its mother's breast;
like a child that is quieted is my soul.
³ O Israel, hope in the Lᴏʀᴅ
from this time forth and for evermore.

Brothers in peace (Ps 133)

133
¹ Behold, how good and pleasant it is
when brothers dwell in unity!
² It is like the precious oil upon the head,
running down upon the beard, upon the beard of Aaron,
running down on the collar of his robes!
³ It is like the dew of Hermon,
which falls on the mountains of Zion!
For there the Lᴏʀᴅ has commanded the blessing,
life for evermore.

Darkness is like light (Ps 139)

139
¹ O Lᴏʀᴅ, you have searched me and known me!
² You know when I sit down and when I rise up;
you discern my thoughts from afar.
³ You search out my path and my lying down,
and are acquainted with all my ways.
⁴ Even before a word is on my tongue,
behold, O Lᴏʀᴅ, you know it altogether.
⁵ You beset me behind and before, and lay your hand upon me.
⁶ Such knowledge is too wonderful for me;
it is high, I cannot attain it.
⁷ Where shall I go from your Spirit?
Or where shall I flee from your presence?
⁸ If I ascend to heaven, you are there!
If I make my bed in Sheol, you are there!
⁹ If I take the wings of the morning
and dwell in the uttermost parts of the sea,
¹⁰ even there your hand shall lead me,
and your right hand shall hold me.
¹¹ If I say, "Let only darkness cover me,
and the light about me be night,"

99 Wherever I go—you! Wherever I stay—you! Only you, you again, always you! You, you, you! If it goes well for me—you! When I feel bad—you! Only you, you again, always you! You, you, you! Heaven—you, earth—you, above—you, below—you, wherever I turn, in every nook, only you, you again, always you! You, you, you!

MARTIN BUBER
poem based on
Ps 139

Adam, Jonah, and Saul— all of them men who turn from God, run away, and hide. All without success.

¹² even the darkness is not dark to you,
the night is bright as the day; for darkness is as light with you.
¹³ For you formed my inward parts,
you knitted me together in my mother's womb.
¹⁴ I praise you, for I am wondrously made.
Wonderful are your works! You know me right well;
¹⁵ my frame was not hidden from you,
when I was being made in secret,
intricately wrought in the depths of the earth.
¹⁶ Your eyes beheld my unformed substance;
in your book were written, every one of them,
the days that were formed for me,
when as yet there was none of them.
¹⁷ How precious to me are your thoughts, O God!
How vast is the sum of them!
¹⁸ If I would count them, they are more than the sand.
When I awake, I am still with you.
¹⁹ O that you would slay the wicked, O God,
and that men of blood would depart from me,
²⁰ men who maliciously defy you,
who lift themselves up against you for evil!
²¹ Do I not hate them that hate you, O LORD ?
And do I not loathe them that rise up against you?
²² I hate them with perfect hatred; I count them my enemies.

 No other passage speaks in such detail about God's work even before birth. God knows Jeremiah even before his conception (Jer 1:5).

O my God, teach me to serve you as you deserve to be served, to give without counting the cost, to fight without fear of being wounded, ... to spend myself without expecting any reward but the knowledge that I am doing your holy will.

IGNATIUS OF LOYOLA

▶ Anyone who "hates" (v. 21) the God of life turns destructively against life and all that is good. The perfect hatred in v. 22 is directed against such an attitude.

²³ Search me, O God, and know my heart!
Try me and know my thoughts!
²⁴ And see if there be any wicked way in me,
and lead me in the way everlasting!

Whereas the early parts of the Psalter consist mainly of prayers that express much sorrow, the last psalms (Ps 145–150) are a grand finale of praise. The last psalm ends with a great concert of praise by the whole universe.

Let everything that breathes praise the Lord! (Ps 150)

150
¹ Praise the LORD!
Praise God in his sanctuary;
praise him in his mighty firmament!
² Praise him for his mighty deeds;
praise him according to his exceeding greatness!
³ Praise him with trumpet sound; praise him with lute and harp!
⁴ Praise him with timbrel and dance;
praise him with strings and pipe!
⁵ Praise him with sounding cymbals;
praise him with loud clashing cymbals!
⁶ Let everything that breathes praise the LORD!
Praise the LORD!

▶ "Sanctuary" means the Temple in Jerusalem; the "mighty firmament" is heaven.

❞ The Christian life, the life of grace, of faith and charity, is necessarily one that proceeds from fullness of being, and is, therefore, a life of thanksgiving: *eucharistia*.

HANS URS VON BALTHASAR

▶ "Cymbals" here are like miniature versions of the cymbals in a drum set.

Proverbs

The wealth of human experience is reflected in this book. The introductory collection (Prov 1–9) invites the younger generation (addressed as son/child) to accept this treasure and thus to gain fundamental insights for a successful life. Three examples illustrate the lines that this education follows:

"Better is a dinner of herbs where love is than a fatted ox and hatred with it" (Prov 15:17). The lesson to be learned here is that kindness in relationships is more important than a good meal.

"As a door turns on its hinges, so does a sluggard on his bed" (Prov 26:14). This drastic comparison is at the same time a warning and motivation not to be lazy.

"Three things are too wonderful for me; four I do not understand: the way of an eagle in the sky, the way of a serpent on a rock, the way of a ship on the high seas, and the way of a man with a maiden" (Prov 30:18–19). These verses contain both attentive observation of particular phenomena and astonishment at the riddles of our world.

These three examples show keen perception and a sound gift of discernment. These two things are keys to leading a good life, and repeatedly they appear in the Book of Proverbs in connection with God, as in the following passage.

> Through my father, our household was imbued with a sound Irish spirituality. The predominant feature in our home was devotion to the Sacred Heart of Jesus, which was very strongly united with Eucharistic devotion and also devotion to the Blessed Virgin.

RAYMOND BURKE (b. 1948), cardinal archbishop and patron of the Sovereign Military Order of Malta

Attentiveness to God and his wisdom (Prov 3:1–18)

3 ¹ My son, do not forget my teaching,
  but let your heart keep my commandments;
² for length of days and years of life
and abundant welfare will they give you.
³ Let not loyalty and faithfulness forsake you;
bind them about your neck,
write them on the tablet of your heart.
⁴ So you will find favor and good repute
in the sight of God and man.

> I have seen the world longer than you have. Not all that glitters is gold, dear son, and I have seen many a star fall from heaven and many a staff that someone relied on break. That is why I want to give you some advice and tell you what I have found and what time has taught me. Nothing is great that is not good; and nothing is true that does not endure.

MATTHIAS CLAUDIUS to his son Johannes

⁵ Trust in the LORD with all your heart,
and do not rely on your own insight.
⁶ In all your ways acknowledge him,
and he will make straight your paths.
⁷ Be not wise in your own eyes;
fear the LORD, and turn away from evil.
⁸ It will be healing to your flesh and refreshment to your bones.
⁹ Honor the LORD with your substance
and with the first fruits of all your produce;
¹⁰ then your barns will be filled with plenty,
and your vats will be bursting with wine.
¹¹ My son, do not despise the LORD's discipline
or be weary of his reproof,
¹² for the LORD reproves him whom he loves,
as a father the son in whom he delights.
¹³ Happy is the man who finds wisdom,
and the man who gets understanding,
¹⁴ for the gain from it is better than gain from silver
and its profit better than gold.
¹⁵ She is more precious than jewels,

▶ All our insight is extremely limited. Someone who thinks he is wise (→ also v. 5) deceives himself and is close to ruin. Only a relationship with God can preserve right judgment.

▶ "Reproves" basically means "trains". In the ancient world, it could also mean corporal punishment.

Among the things that make up knowledge and wisdom in a man, the greatest is that he does not depend entirely on his own opinion.

THOMAS AQUINAS

> **"** He that breaks a thing to find out what it is has left the path of wisdom.
>
> **J. R. R. TOLKIEN**

and nothing you desire can compare with her.
¹⁶ Long life is in her right hand;
in her left hand are riches and honor.
¹⁷ Her ways are ways of pleasantness, and all her paths are peace.
¹⁸ She is a tree of life to those who lay hold of her;
those who hold her fast are called happy.

> Toward the end of the first collection (Prov 1–9), the author personifies Wisdom and has her speak directly to the people. He thereby intensifies in the listeners or the readers the desire to enter into a close relationship with her.

▶ Wisdom introduces herself here as the first creature of God, which accompanied him from the beginning of the world. There is a similarity to what in Gen 1:2 is called his Spirit. "... The Spirit of God was moving over the face of the waters" (Gen 1:2).

Allow your soul the freedom to sing, to dance, to glorify and praise and to love.

TERESA OF AVILA

The child with God (Prov 8:22–31)

8 ²² The LORD created me at the beginning of his work,
the first of his acts of old.
²³ Ages ago I was set up,
at the first, before the beginning of the earth.
²⁴ When there were no depths I was brought forth,
when there were no springs abounding with water....
³⁰ then I was beside him, like a master workman;
and I was daily his delight, rejoicing before him always,
³¹ rejoicing in his inhabited world
and delighting in the sons of men.

The invitation from "Lady" Wisdom (Prov 9:1–6)

▶ Everything is prepared for a festive meal. The "seven columns" presumably refer to the seven collections of sayings that make up Prov, and at the same time they suggest a very large house, in which many people find a place to feast.

9 ¹ Wisdom has built her house,
she has set up her seven pillars.
² She has slaughtered her beasts, she has mixed her wine,
she has also set her table.
³ She has sent out her maids to call
from the highest places in the town,
⁴ "Whoever is simple, let him turn in here!"
To him who is without sense she says,
⁵ "Come, eat of my bread and drink of the wine I have mixed.
⁶ Leave simpleness,and live,
and walk in the way of insight."

> The last chapter of Prov contains instructions of an (unknown) queen mother to her son Lemuel. He must not get drunk (Prov 31:4–5) and should stand up for the rights of the poor (vv. 8–9). An ideal portrait of a wife follows:

A Strong Woman (Prov 31)

▶ The mutual reliance of the couple is a source of strength and security.

31 ¹⁰ Who can find a good wife?
She is far more precious than jewels.
¹¹ The heart of her husband trusts in her,
and he will have no lack of gain.

¹² She does him good, and not harm,
all the days of her life.
¹³ She seeks wool and flax,
and works with willing hands.
¹⁴ She is like the ships of the merchant,
she brings her food from afar.
¹⁵ She rises while it is yet night
and provides food for her household
and tasks for her maidens.
¹⁶ She considers a field and buys it;
with the fruit of her hands she plants a vineyard.
¹⁷ She clothes her loins with strength
and makes her arms strong.
¹⁸ She perceives that her merchandise is profitable.
Her lamp does not go out at night.
¹⁹ She puts her hands to the distaff,
and her hands hold the spindle.
²⁰ She opens her hand to the poor,
and reaches out her hands to the needy.

 Necessary emphasis should be placed on the "genius of women". ... How many women have been and continue to be valued more for their physical appearance than for their skill, their professionalism, their intellectual abilities, their deep sensitivity; in a word, the very dignity of their being! ... In giving themselves to others each day women fulfil their deepest vocation. Perhaps more than men, women acknowledge the person, because they see persons with their hearts. They see them independently of various ideological or political systems. They see others in their greatness and limitations; they try to go out to them and help them.

POPE JOHN PAUL II, Letter to Women

²¹ She is not afraid of snow for her household,
for all her household are clothed in scarlet.
²² She makes herself coverings;
her clothing is fine linen and purple.
²³ Her husband is known in the gates,
when he sits among the elders of the land.
²⁴ She makes linen garments and sells them;
she delivers sashes to the merchant.
²⁵ Strength and dignity are her clothing,
and she laughs at the time to come.
²⁶ She opens her mouth with wisdom,
and the teaching of kindness is on her tongue.
²⁷ She looks well to the ways of her household,
and does not eat the bread of idleness.
²⁸ Her children rise up and call her blessed;
her husband also, and he praises her:
²⁹ "Many women have done excellently,
but you surpass them all."
³⁰ Charm is deceitful, and beauty is vain,
but a woman who fears the LORD is to be praised.
³¹ Give her of the fruit of her hands,
and let her works praise her in the gates.

Tip for men: "A woman is capable of living for two days on nothing more than a nice compliment", says Michèle Morgan, the French film actress.

99 Without love you can chop wood, make bricks, and forge iron. But without love you cannot deal with people.
LEO TOLSTOY

99 Women are called to motherhood, whether it be physical or spiritual.
DR. JANET SMITH, (b. 1950), American classicist and philosopher

▶ The decisive thing is not outward belongings or appearance but a right relationship to God. From it follow all the good deeds listed earlier.

THE BOOK OF

Ecclesiastes

Ecclesiastes is a highly independent, philosophical, thoughtful little book of the Bible. With sober insight into life, it calls into question conventional values such as wealth and career. It advocates simple living, concentrating on important human relationships (Eccles 9:9), and being mindful of God's eternal action (Eccles 3:14–15).

▶ The name Qoheleth is related to the Hebrew word for "gathering"; hence the Greek title Ecclesiastes. As son of David and king of Jerusalem, Qoheleth is identified with Solomon, the legendary wise king (↗ also the "Song of Solomon" following Ecclesiastes).

▶ "Vanity" is an image for transience. The word is repeated five times in v. 2, stating a theme for the entire book.

"Isn't it odd", someone said to his friend, "that every day just as much news happens in the world as fits in the newspaper?"

All is vanity (Eccles 1:1–11)

1 ¹ The words of the Preacher, the son of David, king in Jerusalem.
² Vanity of vanities, says the Preacher,
vanity of vanities! All is vanity.
³ What does man gain by all the toil
at which he toils under the sun?
⁴ A generation goes, and a generation comes,
but the earth remains for ever.
⁵ The sun rises and the sun goes down,
and hastens to the place where it rises.
⁶ The wind blows to the south, and goes round to the north;
round and round goes the wind,
and on its circuits the wind returns.
⁷ All streams run to the sea, but the sea is not full;
to the place where the streams flow, there they flow again.
⁸ All things are full of weariness; a man cannot utter it;
the eye is not satisfied with seeing,
nor the ear filled with hearing.
⁹ What has been is what will be,
and what has been done is what will be done;
and there is nothing new under the sun.
¹⁰ Is there a thing of which it is said, "See, this is new"?
It has been already, in the ages before us.

¹¹ There is no remembrance of former things,
nor will there be any remembrance
of later things yet to happen
among those who come after.

Try to make friends (Eccles 2:1–11)

2 ¹ I said to myself, "Come now, I will make a test of pleasure; enjoy yourself." But behold, this also was vanity.

² I said of laughter, "It is mad," and of pleasure, "What use is it?"

³ I searched with my mind how to cheer my body with wine—my mind still guiding me with wisdom—and how to lay hold on folly, till I might see what was good for the sons of men to do under heaven during the few days of their life.

⁴ I made great works; I built houses and planted vineyards for myself;

⁵ I made myself gardens and parks, and planted in them all kinds of fruit trees.

⁶ I made myself pools from which to water the forest of growing trees.

▶ Gardens (v. 5) in the largely desert Near East were among the greatest luxury items and status symbols of kings. The hanging gardens of Semiramis in Babylon, like the pyramids of Giza, the Colossus of Rhodes or the sculpture of Artemis in Ephesus, were among the seven wonders of the ancient world.

⁷ I bought male and female slaves, and had slaves who were born in my house; I had also great possessions of herds and flocks, more than any who had been before me in Jerusalem.

⁸ I also gathered for myself silver and gold and the treasure of kings and provinces; I got singers, both men and women, and many concubines, man's delight.

⁹ So I became great and surpassed all who were before me in Jerusalem; also my wisdom remained with me.

¹⁰ And whatever my eyes desired I did not keep from them; I kept my heart from no pleasure, for my heart found pleasure in all my toil, and this was my reward for all my toil.

¹¹ Then I considered all that my hands had done and the toil I had spent in doing it, and behold, all was vanity and a striving after wind, and there was nothing to be gained under the sun.

A time for everything (Eccles 3)

3 ¹ For everything there is a season, and a time for every matter under heaven:

² a time to be born, and a time to die;
a time to plant, and a time to pluck up what is planted;

³ a time to kill, and a time to heal;
a time to break down, and a time to build up;

⁴ a time to weep, and a time to laugh;

> 99 If I cling to things, [God] lets me have my things. If I am empty of things, he fills me with himself.

THOMAS DUBAY, S.M. (1921–2010), Catholic priest, author, and spiritual director

For me, property means being able to start a family. Owning things gives me security. I am a romantic, and it is difficult for me not to want to own a lot of things. Then I remember that things do not satisfy. I experience true joy in my relationship with God.

SHARON

The time to seek God is this life. The time to find God is death. The time to possess God is eternity.

FRANCIS DE SALES

> Many people think that to desire our own good and earnestly to hope for the enjoyment of it is a bad thing. ... If we consider the unblushing promises of reward and the staggering nature of the rewards promised in the Gospels, it would seem that Our Lord finds our desires not too strong, but too weak.

C. S. LEWIS

> Anyone can become furious; that is easy. But to become furious about the right thing, to the right degree, at the right time, for the right purpose, and in the right way is difficult.

ARISTOTLE

▶ Literally v. 11 says that God "put eternity in their hearts" (the hearts of men).

a time to mourn, and a time to dance;
⁵ a time to cast away stones, and a time to gather stones together;
a time to embrace, and a time to refrain from embracing;
⁶ a time to seek, and a time to lose;
a time to keep, and a time to cast away;
⁷ a time to tear, and a time to sew;
a time to keep silence, and a time to speak;
⁸ a time to love, and a time to hate;
a time for war, and a time for peace.
⁹ What gain has the worker from his toil?
¹⁰ I have seen the business that God has given to the sons of men to be busy with.
¹¹ He has made everything beautiful in its time; also he has put eternity into man's mind, yet so that he cannot find out what God has done from the beginning to the end.
¹² I know that there is nothing better for them than to be happy and enjoy themselves as long as they live; ¹³ also that it is God's gift to man that every one should eat and drink and take pleasure in all his toil.
¹⁴ I know that whatever God does endures for ever; nothing can be added to it, nor anything taken from it; God has made it so, in order that men should fear before him.

▶ "What has been driven away" (v. 15) probably refers to the past. Maybe this already reflects the psychological insight that many repressed experiences surface again later in life.

¹⁵ That which is, already has been; that which is to be, already has been; and God seeks what has been driven away.

Qoheleth repeatedly explains that everything is passing and many things are a burden for man. In the following verses, however, he encourages his listeners to take a relaxed, cheerful attitude toward life.

B Make the most of the time, because the days are evil.

Eph 5:16

▶ In the earliest parts of the Old Testament the idea of the time after death is usually sober.

Eat your bread joyfully (Eccles 9:3–10)

9 ³ This is an evil in all that is done under the sun, that one fate comes to all; also the hearts of men are full of evil, and madness is in their hearts while they live, and after that they go to the dead. ⁴ But he who is joined with all the living has hope, for a living dog is better than a dead lion. ⁵ For the living know that they will die, but the dead know nothing, and they have no more reward; but the memory of them is lost. ⁶ Their love and their hate and their envy have already perished, and they have no more for ever any share in all that is done under the sun.
⁷ Go, eat your bread with enjoyment, and drink your wine with a merry heart; for God has already approved what you do.

⁸ Let your garments be always white; let not oil be lacking on your head.

⁹ Enjoy life with the wife whom you love, all the days of your vain life which he has given you under the sun, because that is your portion in life and in your toil at which you toil under the sun. ¹⁰ Whatever your hand finds to do, do it with your might; for there is no work or thought or knowledge or wisdom in Sheol, to which you are going.

Think of your Creator (Eccles 11:4–12:1)

11 ⁴ He who observes the wind will not sow;
and he who regards the clouds will not reap.

⁵ As you do not know how the spirit comes to the bones in the womb of a woman with child, so you do not know the work of God who makes everything.

⁶ In the morning sow your seed, and at evening withhold not your hand; for you do not know which will prosper, this or that, or whether both alike will be good.

⁷ Light is sweet, and it is pleasant for the eyes to behold the sun.

⁸ For if a man lives many years, let him rejoice in them all; but

 Be cheerful, do good, and let the sparrows sing!

JOHN DON BOSCO

 A proverb says: "He who cannot enjoy, quickly ceases to be enjoyable." The secret of being a Christian is to enjoy creation gladly and to say thank you to God for everything, even what is difficult.

❞ To be a disciple of Jesus requires discipline, especially self-discipline; what Paul calls self-control.

GEORGE CARDINAL PELL

let him remember that the days of darkness will be many. All that comes is vanity.

⁹ Rejoice, O young man, in your youth, and let your heart cheer you in the days of your youth; walk in the ways of your heart and the sight of your eyes. But know that for all these things God will bring you into judgment.

¹⁰ Remove vexation from your mind, and put away pain from your body; for youth and the dawn of life are vanity.

12 ¹ Remember also your Creator in the days of your youth, before the evil days come, and the years draw nigh, when you will say, "I have no pleasure in them".

 Do your best, and God will do the rest.

JOHN DON BOSCO

 When you are in a good mood, think of how to behave when you are in a bad mood, and gather strength.

IGNATIUS OF LOYOLA, from The Spiritual Exercises

THE SONG OF

Solomon

The Song of Solomon is attributed to King Solomon, although it may not have been written by him. In the Bible he is depicted as a great poet (1 Kings 5:12) and lover (1 Kings 11:1). It is a collection of love poems, in which the voice of the loving woman begins and then alternates with the voice of her beloved. The book expresses young, passionate, sensual love very freely and beautifully—also as an image for the love between God and the human soul. The two dimensions belong together: in human love, God grants us to experience how intensely devoted he is to us and how closely he would like to be united to us. And in divine love, it becomes clear how beautiful the love between a man and a woman is.

▶ The female voice begins the loving conversation and raves about the man's love. In this way, the equal dignity of the partners in the relationship is expressed.

❞ God doesn't make junk. Never forget that. Stop taking your body image cues from images in magazines. No one looks like the models ... even the models themselves. Their flaws are hidden through great photography, lighting, computerized imaging, professional makeup artists, and in many cases plastic surgery.

TERESA TOMEO, radio host and author

ⴿ → 400
What does it mean to say that man is a sexual being?

Sweeter than wine (Song 1:1–17)

1 ¹ The Song of Songs, which is Solomon's.
² O that you would kiss me with the kisses of your mouth!
For your love is better than wine,
³ your anointing oils are fragrant, your name is oil poured out;
therefore the maidens love you.
⁴ Draw me after you, let us make haste.
The king has brought me into his chambers.
We will exult and rejoice in you; we will extol your love more than wine; rightly do they love you.
⁵ I am very dark, but comely, O daughters of Jerusalem,
like the tents of Ke'dar, like the curtains of Solomon.
⁶ Do not gaze at me because I am swarthy, because the sun has scorched me. My mother's sons were angry with me, they made me keeper of the vineyards; but, my own vineyard I have not kept!
⁷ Tell me, you whom my soul loves, where you pasture your flock,
where you make it lie down at noon; for why should I be like one who wanders beside the flocks of your companions?
⁸ If you do not know, O fairest among women,
follow in the tracks of the flock, and pasture your kids
beside the shepherds' tents.
⁹ I compare you, my love, to a mare of Pharaoh's chariots.

¹⁰ Your cheeks are comely with ornaments,
your neck with strings of jewels.
¹¹ We will make you ornaments of gold, studded with silver.
¹² While the king was on his couch, my nard gave forth its fragrance.
¹³ My beloved is to me a bag of myrrh, that lies between my breasts.
¹⁴ My beloved is to me a cluster of henna blossoms
in the vineyards of En-ge'di.
¹⁵ Behold, you are beautiful, my love; behold, you are beautiful;
your eyes are doves.
¹⁶ Behold, you are beautiful, my beloved,
truly lovely. Our couch is green;
¹⁷ the beams of our house are cedar, our rafters dare pine.

▶ Myrrh is an aromatic, sweet-smelling resin that is used also in incense. En-gedi is located on the Dead Sea and was renowned as a producer of perfume.

▶ In the ancient world, doves were considered messengers of love because of their courting rituals.

A lily among thorns! (Song 2:1–17)

2 ¹ I am a rose of Sharon, a lily of the valleys.
² As a lily among brambles, so is my love among maidens.
³ As an apple tree among the trees of the wood,
so is my beloved among young men.
With great delight I sat in his shadow,
and his fruit was sweet to my taste.
⁴ He brought me to the banqueting house,
and his banner over me was love.

The Song of Songs is a marriage song telling of chaste souls in loving embrace, of their wills in sweet accord, of the mutual exchange of the heart's affection.

BERNARD OF CLAIRVAUX (1090-1153), important reformer of medieval monasticism

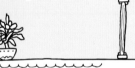

⁵ Sustain me with raisins, refresh me with apples;
for I am sick with love.
⁶ O that his left hand were under my head,
and that his right hand embraced me!
⁷ I adjure you, O daughters of Jerusalem, by the gazelles or the deer of the field, that you stir not up nor awaken love until it please.
⁸ The voice of my beloved! Behold, he comes,
leaping upon the mountains, bounding over the hills.
⁹ My beloved is like a gazelle, or a young stag.
Behold, there he stands behind our wall,
gazing in at the windows, looking through the lattice.
¹⁰ My beloved speaks and says to me:
"Arise, my love, my dove, my fair one, and come away;
¹¹ for behold, the winter is past, the rain is over and gone.
¹² The flowers appear on the earth, the time of pruning has come,
and the voice of the turtledove is heard in our land.
¹³ The fig tree puts forth its figs, and the vines are in blossom;
they give forth fragrance.
Arise, my love, my fair one, and come away.
¹⁴ O my dove, in the clefts of the rock, in the covert of the cliff, let me see your face, let me hear your voice, for your voice is sweet, and your face is comely.

❝❝ Christ takes pleasure in His Church as a husband takes pleasure in his bride. Finding His delight in her, He seeks to share with her all His gifts.

PAUL QUAY, (1924–1994), Catholic priest, author, and professor of physics, philosophy, and theology

▶ The lovers charmingly compare each other to fragrant plants (lily, apple tree), graceful animals (dove, gazelle), and playful creatures (young foxes, v. 15, a metaphor for young men).

¹⁵ Catch us the foxes, the little foxes, that spoil the vineyards, for our vineyards are in blossom."
¹⁶My beloved is mine and I am his, he pastures his flock among the lilies.
¹⁷Until the day breathes and the shadows flee, turn, my beloved, be like a gazelle, or a young stag upon rugged mountains.

Song of praise to the beloved woman (Song 4:1–16)

4 ¹ Behold, you are beautiful, my love, behold, you are beautiful! Your eyes are doves behind your veil.

Your hair is like a flock of goats, moving down the slopes of Gilead.
² Your teeth are like a flock of shorn ewes that have come up from the washing, all of which bear twins, and not one among them is bereaved.
³ Your lips are like a scarlet thread, and your mouth is lovely.

Your cheeks are like halves of a pomegranate behind your veil.
⁴ Your neck is like the tower of David, built for an arsenal, whereon hang a thousand bucklers, all of them shields of warriors.
⁵ Your two breasts are like two fawns, twins of a gazelle, that feed among the lilies.
⁶ Until the day breathes and the shadows flee,

I will hasten to the mountain of myrrh and the hill of frankincense.
⁷ You are all fair, my love; there is no flaw in you.
⁸ Come with me from Lebanon, my bride; come with me from Lebanon. Depart from the peak of Ama'na, from the peak of Se'nir and Hermon, from the dens of lions, from the mountains of leopards.
⁹ You have ravished my heart, my sister, my bride, you have ravished my heart with a glance of your eyes, with one jewel of your necklace.
¹⁰ How sweet is your love, my sister, my bride! how much better is your love than wine, and the fragrance of your oils than any spice!
¹¹ Your lips distil nectar, my bride; honey and milk are under your tongue; the scent of your garments is like the scent of Lebanon.
¹² A garden locked is my sister, my bride, a garden locked, a fountain sealed.
¹³ Your shoots are an orchard of pomegranates with all choicest fruits, henna with nard,
¹⁴ nard and saffron, calamus and cinnamon, with all trees of frankincense, myrrh and aloes, with all chief spices—
¹⁵ a garden fountain, a well of living water, and flowing streams from Lebanon.
¹⁶ Awake, O north wind, and come, O south wind!

❞ The Song of Solomon is a genuine "spiritual" song of God's love for man, not despite the fact that it is a genuine "secular" love song, but because of it. A person loves because God loves and as God loves. His human soul is a soul awakened and loved by God.

FRANZ ROSENZWEIG (1886–1929), Jewish philosopher

❞ Song of Songs uses romantic love and marriage rather than any one of the many other human forms of love as its chosen symbol for the love of God because romantic love and marriage comprise the fullest and completest of all human loves.

PETER KREEFT

Blow upon my garden, let its fragrance be wafted abroad.
Let my beloved come to his garden, and eat its choicest fruits.

The beloved comes (Song 5:1–7)

5 ¹ I come to my garden, my sister, my bride,
I gather my myrrh with my spice, I eat my honeycomb with my
honey, I drink my wine with my milk. Eat, O friends, and drink: drink
deeply, O lovers!

² I slept, but my heart was awake. Hark! my beloved is knocking.
"Open to me, my sister, my love, my dove, my perfect one;
for my head is wet with dew, my locks with the drops of the night."

³ I had put off my garment, how could I put it on?
I had bathed my feet, how could I soil them?

⁴ My beloved put his hand to the latch,
and my heart was thrilled within me.

⁵ I arose to open to my beloved, and my hands dripped with myrrh,
my fingers with liquid myrrh, upon the handles of the bolt.

⁶ I opened to my beloved, but my beloved had turned and gone.
My soul failed me when he spoke. I sought him, but found him not;
I called him, but he gave no answer.

⁷ The watchmen found me, as they went about in the city;
they beat me, they wounded me, they took away my mantle,
those watchmen of the walls.

Franz Werfel's novel *The Song of Bernadette* ends with a touching scene: Little Sister Bernadette is waiting for death. Werfel describes how her eyes gleam once again and look for something. In the silence of Bernadette's final desire, Abbé Fèbvre recites several verses from the Song of Solomon: "I slept, but my heart was awake. Hark! My beloved is knocking. Open to me, my sister, my love, my dove, my perfect one; for my head is wet with dew, my locks with the drops of the night."

A divine flame! (Song 8:1–7)

8 ¹ O that you were like a brother to me, that nursed at my mother's breast! If I met you outside, I would kiss you, and none would despise me.

² I would lead you and bring you into the house of my mother, and into the chamber of her that conceived me. I would give you spiced wine to drink, the juice of my pomegranates.

³ O that his left hand were under my head, and that his right hand embraced me!

⁴ I adjure you, O daughters of Jerusalem, that you stir not up nor awaken love until it please.

⁵ Who is that coming up from the wilderness, leaning upon her beloved? Under the apple tree I awakened you. There your mother was in travail with you, there she who bore you was in travail.

⁶ Set me as a seal upon your heart, as a seal upon your arm; for love is strong as death, jealousy is cruel as the grave. Its flashes are flashes of fire, a most vehement flame.

⁷ Many waters cannot quench love, neither can floods drown it. If a man offered for love all the wealth of his house, it would be utterly scorned.

▶ Pomegranates are an ancient symbol for fruitfulness—full of juicy, red seeds. As at the beginning of the book, so too here the woman takes the initiative in courting for love.

▶ "As strong as death" (v. 6) means stronger than death: Someone who is a match for death overcomes it.

▶ "A most vehement flame" is a translation for a Hebrew word that occurs only once, which literally means "Yah's flame—God's flame". Now at this point in the Song of Solomon, God appears: the love between a man and a woman is at the same time a flame of God, an expression of the fire of divine love.

THE WISDOM OF

Solomon

What is perhaps the latest book of the Old Testament was written in Greek. It shows how God's spirit and wisdom fill the world. They are at work in history and in nature for the benefit of the righteous. The latter are in God's hand, even in the midst of persecution and early death (Wis 3:1; 4:7). Thus the Wisdom of Solomon overcomes the idea that associates externally visible well-being with closeness to God; it makes clear that suffering and apparent failures can also be part of the journey to him. What matters most is one's inner disposition and good heart.

▶ God can be reached, and this strong motivation opens the book. Those with responsibility ("rulers") are addressed in particular, but others are included with them.

▶ Already in the OT, God's Spirit is called "holy" in a few passages (e.g., Is 63:10f.). He is incompatible with any sort of wickedness.

❞ If I am filled with myself, married to my own ideas, … convinced that somehow I am the hub of the universe, there is of course no room in me for being filled with God, for accepting or even desiring his wisdom, for making him my center of gravity.

THOMAS DUBAY, S.M.

Exhortation to an upright life (Wis 1:1–7)

1 ¹ Love righteousness, you rulers of the earth,
  think of the Lord with uprightness,
and seek him with sincerity of heart;
² because he is found by those who do not put him to the test,
and manifests himself to those who do not distrust him.
³ For perverse thoughts separate men from God,
and when his power is tested, it convicts the foolish;
⁴ because wisdom will not enter a deceitful soul,
nor dwell in a body enslaved to sin.
⁵ For a holy and disciplined spirit will flee from deceit,
and will rise and depart from foolish thoughts,
and will be ashamed at the approach of unrighteousness.
⁶ For wisdom is a kindly spirit and will not free a blasphemer from
the guilt of his words; because God is witness of his inmost feelings,
and a true observer of his heart, and a hearer of his tongue.
⁷ Because the Spirit of the Lord has filled the world,
and that which holds all things together knows what is said.

There is an unhealthy dynamic to wanting nothing but pleasure in life. Here it leads to an attack against the righteous man.

The just man as God's son (Wis 2:6–24)

2 [6] "Come, therefore, let us enjoy the good things that exist,
and make use of the creation to the full as in youth.

[7] Let us take our fill of costly wine and perfumes,
and let no flower of spring pass by us.

[8] Let us crown ourselves with rosebuds before they wither.

[9] Let none of us fail to share in our revelry,
everywhere let us leave signs of enjoyment,
because this is our portion, and this our lot.

[10] Let us oppress the righteous poor man; let us not spare the widow nor regard the gray hairs of the aged.

[11] But let our might be our law of right,
for what is weak proves itself to be useless.

[12] "Let us lie in wait for the righteous man,
because he is inconvenient to us and opposes our actions; he reproaches us for sins against the law, and accuses us of sins against our training.

[13] He professes to have knowledge of God,
and calls himself a child of the Lord.

[14] He became to us a reproof of our thoughts;

[15] the very sight of him is a burden to us, because his manner of life is unlike that of others, and his ways are strange.

The Old Testament lament about the evil fate that befalls the "righteous" was later applied to Jesus. Countless images were produced that show the "Man of Sorrows".

▶ Righteous conduct (v. 12) is like a thorn to people who do evil. It pricks their conscience, and they try to remove it.

[16] We are considered by him as something base, and he avoids our ways as unclean;he calls the last end of the righteous happy,
and boasts that God is his father.

[17] Let us see if his words are true,
and let us test what will happen at the end of his life;

[18] for if the righteous man is God's son, he will help him,
and will deliver him from the hand of his adversaries.

[19] Let us test him with insult and torture,
that we may find out how gentle he is,
and make trial of his forbearance.

[20] Let us condemn him to a shameful death,
for, according to what he says, he will be protected."

[21] Thus they reasoned, but they were led astray,
for their wickedness blinded them,

[22] and they did not know the secret purposes of God,
nor hope for the wages of holiness,
nor discern the prize for blameless souls;

[23] for God created man for incorruption,
and made him in the image of his own eternity,

[24] but through the devil's envy death entered the world,
and those who belong to his party experience it.

B Those who passed by derided him, wagging their heads and saying, "You who would destroy the temple and build it in three days, save yourself! If you are the Son of God, come down from the cross."
Mt 27:39–40

▶ The thinking described earlier is unmasked as false. It lacks the perspective of eternity.

▶ Verse 23 refers to the creation of man in Gen 1; v. 24 alludes to the fall of the first couple in Gen 3, when they were seduced by the "serpent".

God's testing, protection, and reward for the righteous (Wis 3:1–8)

If you put a ripe bunch of grapes in the wine press, it yields a delicious juice. So too from the press of our suffering flows a wine that nourishes and strengthens the soul. All sufferings lose their bitterness when one suffers in union with the Lord.

JOHN VIANNEY, the Curé of Ars

▶ Suffering is like a refining process: it preserves what is genuine and good.

3 ¹ But the souls of the righteous are in the hand of God,
and no torment will ever touch them.
² In the eyes of the foolish they seemed to have died,
and their departure was thought to be an affliction,
³ and their going from us to be their destruction;
but they are at peace.
⁴ For though in the sight of men they were punished,
their hope is full of immortality.
⁵ Having been disciplined a little, they will receive great good,
because God tested them and found them worthy of himself;
⁶ like gold in the furnace he tried them,
and like a sacrificial burnt offering he accepted them.
⁷ In the time of their visitation they will shine forth,
and will run like sparks through the stubble.

⁸ They will govern nations and rule over peoples,
and the LORD will reign over them for ever.

An early death as sign of God's love (Wis 4:7–14)

4 ⁷ But the righteous man, though he die early, will be at rest.
⁸ For old age is not honored for length of time,
nor measured by number of years;
⁹ but understanding is gray hair for men,
and a blameless life is ripe old age.
¹⁰ There was one who pleased God and was loved by him,
and while living among sinners he was taken up.
¹¹ He was caught up lest evil change his understanding
or guile deceive his soul.
¹² For the fascination of wickedness obscures what is good,
and roving desire perverts the innocent mind.
¹³ Being perfected in a short time, he fulfilled long years;
¹⁴ for his soul was pleasing to the LORD,
therefore he took him quickly from the midst of wickedness.

The Prayer of Solomon (Wis 9:4.9–18)

9 ⁴ Give me the wisdom that sits by your throne, and do not reject me from among your servants.
⁹ With you is wisdom, who knows your works and was present when

you made the world, and who understands what is pleasing in your sight and what is right according to your commandments.

¹⁰ Send her forth from the holy heavens, and from the throne of your glory send her, that she may be with me and toil, and that I may learn what is pleasing to you.

¹¹ For she knows and understands all things, and she will guide me wisely in my actions and guard me with her glory. ...

¹⁷ Who has learned your counsel, unless you have given wisdom and sent your holy Spirit from on high?

¹⁸ And thus the paths of those on earth were set right,
and men were taught what pleases you, and were saved by wisdom.

> Grant me your grace, most merciful Jesus, "that it may be with me and may labor with me" (Wis 9:10) and continue with me to the end. Grant me always to will and desire what is most acceptable to you and pleases you best. Let your will be mine and let my will always follow yours and agree perfectly with it. Let me always will or not will the same with you, and let me not be able to will or not will otherwise than as you will or will not.
>
> **THOMAS À KEMPIS** (1380–1471), *The Imitation of Christ*, III, 15.

The third and last part of the book (Wis 11–19) outlines God's action as savior and judge, using the example of the signs and wonders in Egypt and the Exodus. Toward the beginning of it, we find statements about God and his actions, some of them unique.

God as the friend of all who live (Wis 11:22–12:2)

11 ²² Because the whole world before you is like a speck that tips the scales,

and like a drop of morning dew that falls upon the ground.
²³ But you are merciful to all, for you can do all things,
and you overlook men's sins, that they may repent.
²⁴ For you love all things that exist,
and you loathe none of the things which you have made,
for you would not have made anything if you had hated it.
²⁵ How would anything have endured if you had not willed it?
Or how would anything not called forth by you have been preserved?
²⁶ You spare all things, for they are yours, O Lord who love the living.

12 ¹ For your immortal spirit is in all things.
² Therefore you correct little by little those who trespass,
and remind and warn them of the things wherein they sin,
that they may be freed from wickedness and put their trust in you, O Lord.

19 ²² For in everything, O Lord, you have exalted and glorified your people; and you have not neglected to help them at all times and in all places.

▶ God's infinite greatness (v. 22) is another reason for his patience and kindness. These characteristics are aimed at conversion (see also 12:2) and make it possible.

▶ Since everything belongs to God, he treats it carefully and attentively. In some translations, "O Lord who love the living" reads "Friend of life", which is a unique name for God.

After a fall, stand up again right away! Do not leave the sin in your heart for one moment!
JOHN VIANNEY

▶ This verse [Wis 19:22] is perhaps chronologically the last verse of the Old Testament.

THE BOOK OF

Sirach

The book was originally written in Hebrew by one "Jesus the son of Sirach, son of Eleazar" (Sir 50:27); it was translated into Greek by a descendant. It combines the familiar Jewish traditions with the demands of a new era. Thus it testifies to the lasting value of old faith attitudes and at the same time to the need to adapt them to new and different circumstances. At the beginning of the book, it reflects generally on knowledge and wisdom:

Wisdom only with God and from him (Sir 1:1–12)

1 ¹ All wisdom comes from the Lord and is with him for ever.
² The sand of the sea, the drops of rain,
and the days of eternity—who can count them?

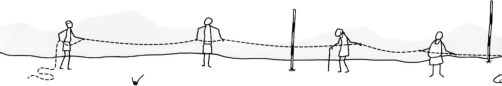

³ The height of heaven, the breadth of the earth,
the abyss, and wisdom—who can search them out?
⁴ Wisdom was created before all things,
and prudent understanding from eternity.
⁵ The source of wisdom is God's word in the highest heaven,
and her ways are the eternal commandments.
⁶ The root of wisdom—to whom has it been revealed?
Her clever devices—who knows them?
⁷ The knowledge of wisdom—to whom was it manifested?
And her abundant experience—who has understood it?
⁸ There is One who is wise, the Creator of all, the King greatly to be feared, sitting upon his throne, and ruling as God.
⁹ The Lord himself created wisdom in the holy spirit; he saw her and apportioned her, he poured her out upon all his works.
¹⁰ She dwells with all flesh according to his gift,
and he supplied her to those who love him.
¹¹ The fear of the Lord is glory and exultation,
and gladness and a crown of rejoicing.
¹² The fear of the Lord delights the heart,
and gives gladness and joy and long life.

▶ Verse 5, and also v. 7, which is omitted here, were later additions. Here Wisdom is connected also with God's revelation, as is explained in Sir 24.

▶ God does not "sit" on his wisdom; he shares it abundantly with his creation and also with us.

▶ The author of the book points out the way we can gain a share in divine wisdom. For him, the fear of the Lord is the "beginning, full measure, crown and root of wisdom" (vv. 14–20; see also Abraham in Gen 22:12).

When many things change, the question arises: What is lasting and reliable? Sirach assigns particular value to relationships and especially to friendship.

True friendship (Sir 6:14–17)

6 ¹⁴ A faithful friend is a sturdy shelter:
he that has found one has found a treasure.
¹⁵ There is nothing so precious as a faithful friend,
and no scales can measure his excellence.
¹⁶ A faithful friend is an elixir of life;
and those who fear the Lord will find him.
¹⁷ Whoever fears the Lord directs his friendship aright,
for as he is, so is his neighbor also.

▶ As with the strong woman in Prov 31, there is no material equivalent for such a constant, genuine relationship of solidarity.

99 For if I do not love them [friends] as they are, then they are not the ones whom I love, and my love is not genuine.

SIMONE WEIL

God's greatness (Sir 18:1–8, 11–14)

18 ¹ He who lives for ever created the whole universe;
² the Lord alone will be declared righteous. …
⁴ To none has he given power to proclaim his works;
and who can search out his mighty deeds?
⁵ Who can measure his majestic power?
And who can fully recount his mercies?
⁶ It is not possible to diminish or increase them,
nor is it possible to trace the wonders of the Lord.
⁷ When a man has finished, he is just beginning,
and when he stops, he will be at a loss.
⁸ What is man, and of what use is he?

B My soul magnifies the Lord … for he who is mighty has done great things for me, and holy is his name.

Lk 1:46.49 (Magnificat)

What is his good and what is his evil?…
¹¹ Therefore the Lord is patient with them
and pours out his mercy upon them.
¹² He sees and recognizes that their end will be evil;
therefore he grants them forgiveness in abundance.
¹³ The compassion of man is for his neighbor,
but the compassion of the LORD is for all living beings.
He rebukes and trains and teaches them,
and turns them back, as a shepherd his flock.
¹⁴ He has compassion on those who accept his discipline
and who are eager for his judgments.

B What is man that you are mindful of him, and the son of man that you care for him?

Ps 8:5

But when God looked at man, he was very pleased, because he had created him in his image and clothed him in his likeness, so that with the full force of his rational voice he might proclaim all the wondrous works of God. Man is indeed the perfect miraculous work of God, because God is known through him and because God made all creatures for his sake.

HILDEGARD OF BINGEN (1098–1179), Benedictine nun, mystic, and Doctor of the Church

God as just judge (Sir 35:12–20)

35 ¹⁴ Do not offer him a bribe, for he will not accept it;
and do not trust to an unrighteous sacrifice;
for the Lord is the judge,
and with him is no partiality.
¹³ He will not show partiality in the case of a poor man;
and he will listen to the prayer of one who is wronged.
¹⁴ He will not ignore the supplication of the fatherless,
nor the widow when she pours out her story.
¹⁵ Do not the tears of the widow run down her cheek
as she cries out against him who has caused them to fall?
¹⁶ He whose service is pleasing to the Lord will be accepted,

💡 God shows no partiality! Who says? How do we know that? Just look at the Acts of the Apostles 10:34–35!

↗ Lk 18:2–5: vindicating the widow

99 God the Father is generous. He comes … to be found where man passes his days in joy or in sorrow. … He chose to live in our history as it is, with all the weight of its limitations and of its tragedies. In doing so, he has demonstrated in an unequalled manner his merciful and truly loving disposition toward the human creature. He is God-with-us.

POPE FRANCIS, December 18, 2013

and his prayer will reach to the clouds.
¹⁷ The prayer of the humble pierces the clouds,
and he will not be consoled until it reaches the Lord;
he will not desist until the Most High visits him,
and the just judge executes judgment.
¹⁸ And the Lord will not delay,
neither will he be patient with them,
till he crushes the loins of the unmerciful
and repays vengeance on the nations;
till he takes away the multitude of the insolent,
and breaks the scepters of the unrighteous;
¹⁹ till he repays man according to his deeds,
and the works of men according to their devices;
till he judges the case of his people
and makes them rejoice in his mercy.
²⁰ Mercy is as welcome when he afflicts them
as clouds of rain in the time of drought.

A prayer for deliverance (Sir 36:1–15)

36 ¹ Have mercy upon us, O Lord, the God of all, and look upon us, and show us the light of your mercy;
² send fear of you upon the nations.
³ Lift up your hand against foreign nations

99 You and no other shall be my partner, said God to the people, and not because you are beautiful or great or powerful, but because I in my unsearchable freedom have chosen you to enter into love, into mutual love with me.

HANS URS VON BALTHASAR

and let them see your might.
⁴ As in us you have been sanctified before them,
so in them may you be magnified before us;
⁵ and let them know you, as we have known
that there is no God but you, O Lord. …
¹³ Have pity on the city of your sanctuary,
Jerusalem, the place of your rest.
¹⁴ Fill Zion with the celebration of your wondrous deeds,
and your temple with your glory.
¹⁵ Bear witness to those whom you created in the beginning,
and fulfil the prophecies spoken in your name.

Sirach reflects for the first time in the Bible about the relation between a human physician and God as the real physician.

The physician as God's helper (Sir 38:1–15)

▶ Illnesses were widespread in antiquity, and the average life expectancy was low. The physician's profession developed slowly at first, and his training was usually simple, too. Moreover, his relation to God as the real "physician" was not clear.

38 ¹ Honor the physician with the honor due him, according to your need of him, for the Lᴏʀᴅ created him;
² for healing comes from the Most High,
and he will receive a gift from the king.
³ The skill of the physician lifts up his head,
and in the presence of great men he is admired.
⁴ The Lord created medicines from the earth,
and a sensible man will not despise them.
⁵ Was not water made sweet with a tree

in order that his power might be known?

⁶ And he gave skill to men
that he might be glorified in his marvelous works.

⁷ By them he heals and takes away pain;

⁸ the pharmacist makes of them a compound.
His works will never be finished;
and from him health is upon the face of the earth.

⁹ My son, when you are sick do not be negligent,
but pray to the Lord, and he will heal you.

¹⁰ Give up your faults and direct your hands aright,
and cleanse your heart from all sin.

¹¹ Offer a sweet-smelling sacrifice, and a memorial portion of fine flour, and pour oil on your offering, as much as you can afford.

¹² And give the physician his place, for the Lord created him;
let him not leave you, for there is need of him.

¹³ There is a time when success lies in the hands of physicians,

¹⁴ for they too will pray to the Lord that he should grant them success in diagnosis and in healing, for the sake of preserving life.

¹⁵ He who sins before his Maker,
may he fall into the care of a physician.

▶ An allusion to Ex 15:22–26, where Moses makes bitter water drinkable in this way.

▶ Divine and human healing are not opposed to each other; they are connected.

 I am the LORD [YHWH], your healer.

Ex 15:26

 Bless the LORD, O my soul, ... who heals all your diseases.

Ps 103:2–3

▶ A warning: sins against God can have health-related consequences.

The privilege of studying God's revelation is a gift. Someone who regularly spends time with the Bible expands his horizons and grows in knowledge.

The student of the law (Sir 39:1–8)

39 ¹ On the other hand he who devotes himself to the study of the law of the Most High will seek out the wisdom of all the ancients, and will be concerned with prophecies;

² he will preserve the discourse of notable men
and penetrate the subtleties of parables;

³ he will seek out the hidden meanings of proverbs
and be at home with the obscurities of parables.

⁴ He will serve among great men and appear before rulers; he will travel through the lands of foreign nations, for he tests the good and the evil among men.

⁵ He will set his heart to rise early to seek the Lord who made him,
and will make supplication before the Most High; he will open his mouth in prayer and make supplication for his sins.

⁶ If the great Lord is willing, he will be filled with the spirit of understanding; he will pour forth words of wisdom
and give thanks to the Lord in prayer.

⁷ He will direct his counsel and knowledge rightly,
and meditate on his secrets.

⁸ He will reveal instruction in his teaching,
and will glory in the law of the Lord's covenant.

▶ Prayer is decisive for understanding the Word of God because it sets our sights on him.

The Books of the Prophets

Prophets are spokesmen for God. In their message, they convey how God sees the world and mankind. Prophets encourage and criticize, strengthen and herald new developments. In this way, they point toward deeper dimensions of our world. They stand up for truth and justice. Their criticism is often uncomfortable, especially for those in power who do not fulfill their responsibilities. They also give hope, however, when there seems to be no way out and resignation prevails.

Prophets broaden restricted perspectives and open our horizon to the workings of God. They often recognize historical events as divine intervention. Thus, for example, they see the advance of the Assyrians in the eighth century B.C. or the capture of Jerusalem by Babylonian troops in 587 B.C. (↗ 2 Kings 17) as God's response to the incorrigible sins among his people. World history thus manifests a religious dimension. The last part of the Old Testament contains the "writing prophets". In each case, a work is attributed to a person like Isaiah or Amos—in contrast to Elijah, Elisha, or Nathan, who are mentioned in the Books of Samuel and the Kings.

The first writing prophets appeared in the eighth century B.C. The most recent book, Daniel, is often thought to have originated in the second century B.C. Isaiah, Jeremiah, and Ezekiel are called the "major" prophets because of their size. They are followed by the "apocalyptic" Book of Daniel (→ the introduction to it). The twelve so-called "minor" prophets, from Hosea to Malachi, conclude the collection of books of the prophets. Although they are short, each one also conveys its own important message. Without the books of the prophets we cannot understand the New Testament or Jesus. At the heart of his message, Jesus refers to Isaiah (→ Is 61:1–2 and Lk 4:17–21). The mighty language of the prophets and their powerful images impress us even today.

THE BOOK OF

Isaiah

The name Isaiah means "YHWH is my help", and that is a theme
of the book: God grants salvation and deliverance. The prophet Isaiah lived toward the end of the eighth century before
Christ in Jerusalem, in a time when the Assyrians conquered
the Northern Kingdom of Israel (↗ 2 Kings 17), and they were
increasing pressure on the Southern Kingdom, too. The Book
of Isaiah depicts how God repeatedly helps his people in their
need, despite their transgressions, and gives them new life.

From Is 40 on, the book focuses exclusively on the postexilic
period (among the Persians, starting in 539 B.C.) with many
wonderful, luminous passages. We hear famous readings from
the Book of Isaiah in Advent (e.g., from chapters 11, 35, 40), on
Christmas (Is 9:1–6), in Lent (Is 58), on Good Friday (Is 52:13–
53:12), and during the Easter Vigil (Is 55:1–11).

Whereas everything seems to indicate that Israel's history has
irrevocably come to an end, the book offers encouragement
to expect from God a new future that is good not only for the
Jewish people but for the whole world.

For the New Testament, the Book of the Prophet Isaiah is the
most important source of expressions of the hope connected
with Jesus.

▶ God is compared to parents who desperately seek their children who have run away.

🔅 Anyone who has ever wondered where the ox and the ass in the Nativity scene come from will find the answer here (and not in the Gospel of Luke).

▶ Illnesses and injuries are images here for the state of society.

▶ "Zion" is the Temple Mount in Jerusalem; "Daughter Zion" means the population of the city, personified as a young woman. Here she is exposed to dangers, although later she is depicted as God's Bride (Is 62:5).

God's ungrateful children (Is 1:2–20)

1 ² Hear, O heavens, and give ear, O earth; for the LORD has spoken: "Sons have I reared and brought up, but they have rebelled against me.

³ The ox knows its owner, and the donkey its master's crib; but Israel does not know, my people does not understand."

⁴ Ah, sinful nation, a people laden with iniquity, offspring of evildoers, sons who deal corruptly! They have forsaken the LORD, they have despised the Holy One of Israel, they are utterly estranged.

⁵ Why will you still be struck down, that you continue to rebel?
The whole head is sick, and the whole heart faint.

⁶ From the sole of the foot even to the head, there is no soundness in it, but bruises and sores and bleeding wounds; they are not pressed out, or bound up, or softened with oil.

⁷ Your country lies desolate, your cities are burned with fire; in your very presence strangers devour your land; it is desolate, as overthrown by strangers.

⁸ And the daughter of Zion is left like a booth in a vineyard, like a lodge in a cucumber field, like a besieged city.

⁹ If the LORD of hosts had not left us a few survivors, we should have been like Sodom, and become like Gomor'rah.

❞ Share your belongings for the sake of a greater justice. Do not victimize anyone. Be a brother to all people, always take the side of the marginalized and the despised.
BROTHER ROGER SCHUTZ,
founder of Taizé

▶ God condemns their sacrifices and other forms of worship so harshly because the people commit crimes "iniquity" in v. 13; "blood" and "evildoing" in vv. 15–16).

❞ But the line that divides good from evil runs through the heart of every man.
ALEKSANDR SOLZHENITSYN
(1918–2008), Russian Nobel Prize winner for literature

▶ The colors symbolize the fact that God can forgive even the most serious guilt, free us from it, and heal us.

¹⁰ Hear the word of the LORD, you rulers of Sodom! Give ear to the teaching of our God, you people of Gomor'rah!

¹¹ "What to me is the multitude of your sacrifices? says the LORD; I have had enough of burnt offerings of rams and the fat of fed beasts; I do not delight in the blood of bulls, or of lambs, or of he-goats.

¹² "When you come to appear before me, who requires of you this trampling of my courts?

¹³ Bring no more vain offerings; incense is an abomination to me. New moon and sabbath and the calling of assemblies—I cannot endure iniquity and solemn assembly.

¹⁴ Your new moons and your appointed feasts my soul hates; they have become a burden to me, I am weary of bearing them.

¹⁵ When you spread forth your hands, I will hide my eyes from you;
even though you make many prayers, I will not listen; your hands are full of blood.

¹⁶ Wash yourselves; make yourselves clean; remove the evil of your doings from before my eyes; cease to do evil,

¹⁷ learn to do good; seek justice, correct oppression; defend the fatherless, plead for the widow.

¹⁸ "Come now, let us reason together, says the LORD: though your sins are like scarlet, they shall be as white as snow; though they are red like crimson, they shall become like wool.

¹⁹ If you are willing and obedient, you shall eat the good of the land;
²⁰ but if you refuse and rebel, you shall be devoured by the sword; for the mouth of the LORD has spoken."

Although the "faithful city" Jerusalem is ruled by murderers, whom God intends to chastise (Is 1:21–31), the city is to become a magnet for other nations:

The pilgrimage of the nations (Is 2:2–4)

2 ² It shall come to pass in the latter days that the mountain of the house of the LORD shall be established as the highest of the mountains, and shall be raised above the hills; and all the nations shall flow to it,

³ and many peoples shall come, and say: "Come, let us go up to the mountain of the LORD, to the house of the God of Jacob; that he may teach us his ways and that we may walk in his paths." For out of Zion shall go forth the law, and the word of the LORD from Jerusalem.

⁴ He shall judge between the nations and shall decide for many peoples; and they shall beat their swords into plowshares, and their spears into pruning hooks; nation shall not lift up sword against nation, neither shall they learn war any more.

▶ Isaiah repeated this passage from Mic 4:1–3, thus emphasizing how the common worship of God and the recognition of justice have positive effects on understanding among nations and peace on earth. Jerusalem plays a supporting role; to this day, countless believers from various religions look to the God who revealed himself there.

Israel does not accomplish its mission to testify to the forgiving God who loves justice. The "Song of the Vineyard" in Is 5 poignantly expresses this:

A song about God's vineyard and cries of woe (Is 5:1–24)

5 ¹ Let me sing for my beloved a love song concerning his vineyard: My beloved had a vineyard on a very fertile hill.

² He dug it and cleared it of stones, and planted it with choice vines; he built a watchtower in the midst of it, and hewed out a wine vat in it; and he looked for it to yield grapes, but it yielded wild grapes.

³ And now, O inhabitants of Jerusalem and men of Judah, judge, I beg you, between me and my vineyard.

⁴ What more was there to do for my vineyard, that I have not done in it? When I looked for it to yield grapes, why did it yield wild grapes?

⁵ And now I will tell you what I will do to my vineyard. I will remove its hedge, and it shall be devoured; I will break down its wall, and it shall be trampled down.

⁶ I will make it a waste; it shall not be pruned or hoed, and briers and thorns shall grow up; I will also command the clouds that they rain no rain upon it.

⁷ For the vineyard of the LORD of hosts is the house of Israel, and

▶ A vineyard demands a lot of work. God spared no effort on it but was disappointed.

B There was a householder who planted a vineyard, and set a hedge around it, and dug a wine press in it, and built a tower.
Mt 21:33

❞ The external deserts in the world are growing, because the internal deserts have become so vast.
POPE BENEDICT XVI, April 24, 2005

▶ The vineyard stands for the people (↗ Mt 21:33–46). The Hebrew text plays on two sets of words ("justice/bloodshed" and "righteousness/cry") in order to depict incisively how expectations of fairness are turned upside down in reality.

99 On one side of the street there are 36 upscale restaurants. If you eat there, you pay dearly. Yet over there, there is hunger. One right next to the other. And we have a tendency to get used to this. … I think the Church must increasingly set the example of rejecting all worldliness. … The Church is not an NGO but something else.

POPE FRANCIS, January 19, 2015

the men of Judah are his pleasant planting; and he looked for justice, but behold, bloodshed; for righteousness, but behold, a cry!

⁸ Woe to those who join house to house, who add field to field, until there is no more room, and you are made to dwell alone in the midst of the land. …

¹¹ Woe to those who rise early in the morning, that they may run after strong drink, who linger late into the evening till wine inflames them!

¹² They have lyre and harp, timbrel and flute and wine at their feasts; but they do not regard the deeds of the LORD, or see the work of his hands.

¹³ Therefore my people go into exile for want of knowledge; their honored men are dying of hunger, and their multitude is parched with thirst. …

²⁰ Woe to those who call evil good and good evil, who put darkness for light and light for darkness, who put bitter for sweet and sweet for bitter!

²¹ Woe to those who are wise in their own eyes, and shrewd in their own sight!

²² Woe to those who are heroes at drinking wine, and valiant men in mixing strong drink,

▶ The cries of woe are an indictment of crimes for which the wealthy (vv. 8, 12) and the powerful (v. 23) are mainly responsible. The consequences affect them (v. 24) but also the entire community (v. 13).

²³ who acquit the guilty for a bribe, and deprive the innocent of his right!

²⁴ Therefore, as the tongue of fire devours the stubble, and as dry grass sinks down in the flame, so their root will be as rottenness, and their blossom go up like dust; for they have rejected the law of the LORD of hosts, and have despised the word of the Holy One of Israel.

Given the crimes among his people, God seeks someone to proclaim his message. In the following account of his vocation, Isaiah volunteers.

▶ Seraphim are heavenly beings that stand in awe before God's greatness and therefore cover their faces and their feet.

▶ The threefold "Holy!" expresses the greatest possible holiness. The Sanctus (Holy, Holy, Holy) in the Mass quotes this passage.

Asked by the All-Holy God: Isaiah's vocation (Is 6:1–13)

6 ¹ In the year that King Uzzi'ah died I saw the Lord sitting upon a throne, high and lifted up; and his train filled the temple.

² Above him stood the seraphim; each had six wings: with two he covered his face, and with two he covered his feet, and with two he flew.

³ And one called to another and said: "Holy, holy, holy is the LORD of hosts; the whole earth is full of his glory."

⁴ And the foundations of the thresholds shook at the voice of him who called, and the house was filled with smoke.

⁵ And I said: "Woe is me! For I am lost; for I am a man of unclean lips, and I dwell in the midst of a people of unclean lips; for my eyes have seen the King, the LORD of hosts!"

⁶ Then flew one of the seraphim to me, having in his hand a burning coal which he had taken with tongs from the altar.

⁷ And he touched my mouth, and said: "Behold, this has touched your lips; your guilt is taken away, and your sin forgiven."

⁸ And I heard the voice of the Lord saying, "Whom shall I send, and who will go for us?" Then I said, "Here am I! Send me."

⁹ And he said, "Go, and say to this people: 'Hear and hear, but do not understand; see and see, but do not perceive.'

¹⁰ Make the heart of this people fat, and their ears heavy, and shut their eyes; lest they see with their eyes, and hear with their ears, and understand with their hearts, and turn and be healed."

¹¹ Then I said, "How long, O Lord!"

And he said: "Until cities lie waste without inhabitant, and houses without men, and the land is utterly desolate,

¹² and the LORD removes men far away, and the forsaken places are many in the midst of the land.

¹³ And though a tenth remain in it, it will be burned again, like a terebinth or an oak, whose stump remains standing when it is felled." The holy seed is its stump.

 No one on earth is worthy of Him, neither the saints, nor the angels nor archangels. ... Do not excuse yourselves by saying that you are miserable sinners and therefore do not dare to draw near Him. That would be like saying that you were too sick to call a doctor or to take medicine

JOHN VIANNEY

▶ Even though God knows the people and reckons that the listeners will reject it, the proclamation makes sense. The chance for a new generation is to be preserved in the "holy seed" (v. 13). God himself will again open their eyes and ears (Is 35:5) and liberate them (42:7).

The Book of Isaiah speaks repeatedly about children (as early as 1:2). Many receive symbolic names: one son of the prophet is name Shearjashub (a remnant shall return) (Is 7:3). The child of a virgin is to be named Immanuel (God is with us) (Is 7:14). Matthew recognizes the fulfilment of the prophecy in the birth of Jesus: "Behold, a virgin shall conceive and bear a son, and his name shall be called Emmanuel" (Mt 1:23).

The sign of the Lord (Is 7:10–17)

7 ¹⁰ Again the LORD spoke to A'haz, ¹¹ "Ask a sign of the LORD your God; let it be deep as Sheol or high as heaven."

¹² But A'haz said, "I will not ask, and I will not put the LORD to the test."

¹³ And he said, "Hear then, O house of David! Is it too little for you to weary men, that you weary my God also?

¹⁴ Therefore the Lord himself will give you a sign. Behold, a virgin shall conceive and bear a son, and shall call his name Imman'u-el.

¹⁵ He shall eat curds and honey when he knows how to refuse the evil and choose the good.

¹⁶ For before the child knows how to refuse the evil and choose the good, the land before whose two kings you are in dread will be deserted.

B Behold, a virgin shall conceive and bear a son, and his name shall be called Emmanuel (which means, God with us).

Mt 1:23

"God with us" was often misused as an inscription on the buckle of uniform jackets worn by soldiers as they went to war.

▶ "The day of Midian" probably alludes to Gideon's victory over the Midianites in Judg 7–8.

▶ The "boot" and the blood-stained garments symbolize military power.

[17] The LORD will bring upon you and upon your people and upon your father's house such days as have not come since the day that E'phraim departed from Judah—the king of Assyria."

A prince of peace (Is 9:1–7)

9 [1] But there will be no gloom for her that was in anguish. In the former time he brought into contempt the land of Zeb'ulun and the land of Naph'tali, but in the latter time he will make glorious the way of the sea, the land beyond the Jordan, Galilee of the nations.

[2] The people who walked in darkness have seen a great light; those who dwelt in a land of deep darkness, on them has light shined.

[3] You have multiplied the nation, you have increased its joy; they rejoice before you as with joy at the harvest, as men rejoice when they divide the spoil.

[4] For the yoke of his burden, and the staff for his shoulder, the rod of his oppressor, you have broken as on the day of Mid'ian.

[5] For every boot of the tramping warrior in battle tumult and every garment rolled in blood will be burned as fuel for the fire.

[6] For to us a child is born, to us a son is given; and the government will be upon his shoulder, and his name will be called "Wonderful Counselor, Mighty God, Everlasting Father, Prince of Peace."

" God cannot give us happiness and peace apart from himself.

C. S. LEWIS

[7] Of the increase of his government and of peace there will be no end, upon the throne of David, and over his kingdom, to establish it, and to uphold it with justice and with righteousness from this time forth and for evermore. The zeal of the LORD of hosts will do this.

Is 11 develops this proclamation with images from the plant and animal world.

▶ Jesse was the father of King David (see 1 Sam 16:1–13). The image of the "stump" foretells that the kingdom of the house of David will come to a cata-strophic end like a felled tree; the "shoot" and the "branch", on the other hand, indicate that God will grant a new beginning (↗ 2 Sam 7:16).

Justice and peace as consequences of the Spirit of God (Is 11:1–10)

11 [1] There shall come forth a shoot from the stump of Jesse, and a branch shall grow out of his roots.

[2] And the Spirit of the LORD shall rest upon him, the spirit of wis-dom and understanding, the spirit of counsel and might, the spirit of knowledge and the fear of the LORD.

[3] And his delight shall be in the fear of the LORD. He shall not judge by what his eyes see, or decide by what his ears hear;

[4] but with righteousness he shall judge the poor, and decide with equity for the meek of the earth; and he shall strike the earth with the rod of his mouth, and with the breath of his lips he shall slay the wicked.

⁵ Righteousness shall be the belt of his waist, and faithfulness the belt of his loins.

⁶ The wolf shall dwell with the lamb, and the leopard shall lie down with the kid, and the calf and the lion and the fatling together, and a little child shall lead them.

⁷ The cow and the bear shall feed; their young shall lie down together; and the lion shall eat straw like the ox.

⁸ The sucking child shall play over the hole of the asp, and the weaned child shall put his hand on the adder's den.

⁹ They shall not hurt or destroy in all my holy mountain; for the earth shall be full of the knowledge of the LORD as the waters cover the sea.

¹⁰ In that day the root of Jesse shall stand as an ensign to the peoples; him shall the nations seek, and his dwellings shall be glorious.

▶ These immortal images stand for a world in which violence, hostility, and dangers are overcome—even among men.

▶ Isaiah's visions are not just a utopia. They indicate a direction in which many people have already walked, whereby they changed the world for the better.

How peoples relate to each other and to God is a fundamental question of mankind, as is evident today also in many conflicts. The Book of Isaiah deals with it intensively, for instance in the sayings about the nations in Is 13–23. Earlier, Is 2 depicted an international pilgrimage to God in Jerusalem, where everyone wants to become acquainted with his teaching and his Law so as to create the conditions for peace. Is 25 goes even farther.

God's feast on Zion (Is 25:6–10)

25 ⁶ On this mountain the LORD of hosts will make for all peoples a feast of fat things, a feast of choice wines—of fat things full of marrow, of choice wines well refined. ⁷ And he will destroy on this mountain the covering that is cast over all peoples, the veil that is spread over all nations.

⁸ He will swallow up death for ever, and the Lord GOD will wipe away tears from all faces, and the reproach of his people he will take away from all the earth, for the LORD has spoken.

⁹ It will be said on that day, "Behold, this is our God; we have waited for him, that he might save us. This is the LORD; we have waited for him; let us be glad and rejoice in his salvation."

¹⁰ For the hand of the LORD will rest on this mountain, and Moab shall be trodden down in his place, as straw is trodden down in a dung-pit.

▶ God is like an extremely generous host: he serves the very best (v. 6). He removes the "covering" or "veil"—everything that hinders understanding among the peoples, such as ideologies and prejudices (v. 7). He tenderly comforts those who are mourning or suffering, and he even destroys death (v. 8).

99 The worst thing we do to God is leave him alone.
C. S. LEWIS

The following chapters bring many more proclamations of salvation: "Your dead shall live, their bodies shall rise. O dwellers in the dust, awake and sing for joy! For your dew is a dew of light" (Is 26:19). God once again stands up for his vineyard (Is 27:2–5, in contrast to Is 5:5–6). God will be called "your Teacher" (Is 30:20) and "our judge, ... our king [who] will save us" (33:22). The new salvation granted by God becomes ever more pronounced, quite forcefully already in Is 35 and then from Is 40 on.

God's coming transforms the world (Is 35:1–10)

35 ¹ The wilderness and the dry land shall be glad, the desert shall rejoice and blossom;

like the lily ² it shall blossom abundantly, and rejoice with joy and singing. The glory of Lebanon shall be given to it, the majesty of Car'mel and Sharon. They shall see the glory of the LORD, the majesty of our God.

³ Strengthen the weak hands, and make firm the feeble knees.

⁴ Say to those who are of a fearful heart, "Be strong, fear not! Behold, your God will come with vengeance, with the recompense of God. He will come and save you."

⁵ Then the eyes of the blind shall be opened, and the ears of the deaf unstopped;

⁶ then shall the lame man leap like a deer, and the tongue of the mute sing for joy. For waters shall break forth in the wilderness, and streams in the desert;

⁷ the burning sand shall become a pool, and the thirsty ground springs of water; the haunt of jackals shall become a swamp, the grass shall become reeds and rushes.

▶ The mountains of Lebanon and Carmel were wooded, the plain of Sharon lies on the Mediterranean Sea and is especially fertile; both are signs of God's blessings. Similar splendor is to appear in the wilderness, so that it rejoices (also vv. 6–7).

▶ Transformations in nature (water in the desert) and among men go together—creation is one. Even what is dried out and unfruitful in life will be transformed.

👤 Between the persecutions of the world and the consolations of God, the Church walks along her pilgrim way.

AUGUSTINE

⁸ And a highway shall be there, and it shall be called the Holy Way; the unclean shall not pass over it, and fools shall not err therein.

⁹ No lion shall be there, nor shall any ravenous beast come up on it; they shall not be found there, but the redeemed shall walk there.

¹⁰ And the ransomed of the LORD shall return, and come to Zion with singing; everlasting joy shall be upon their heads; they shall obtain joy and gladness, and sorrow and sighing shall flee away.

Is 36–39 repeats the story about Isaiah that is recounted in the Books of Kings (2 Kings 18:13, 17–20, 19). In it Isaiah implies the conquest of Jerusalem by the Babylonians (Is 39:5–7), which is not mentioned explicitly anywhere else in the Book of Isaiah. But the following chapters (Is 40 ff.) are concerned with comforting Zion, which presupposes the Babylonian Exile.

▶ "Warfare" can also mean "time of service", which in the Middle Ages meant the work that serfs had to perform for their landlords.

▶ "The voice of one crying in the wilderness: Prepare the way of the Lord" (Mk 1:3). The Gospels see John the Baptist as this voice in the desert.

Proclaim God's coming! (Is 40:1–11)

40 ¹ Comfort, comfort my people, says your God.
² Speak tenderly to Jerusalem, and cry to her that her warfare is ended, that her iniquity is pardoned, that she has received from the LORD's hand double for all her sins.

³ A voice cries: "In the wilderness prepare the way of the LORD, make straight in the desert a highway for our God.

⁴ Every valley shall be lifted up, and every mountain and hill be made low; the uneven ground shall become level, and the rough places a plain.

⁵ And the glory of the LORD shall be revealed, and all flesh shall see it together, for the mouth of the LORD has spoken."

⁶ A voice says, "Cry!" And I said, "What shall I cry?" All flesh is grass, and all its beauty is like the flower of the field.

⁷ The grass withers, the flower fades, when the breath of the LORD blows upon it; surely the people is grass.

⁸ The grass withers, the flower fades; but the word of our God will stand for ever.

⁹ Get you up to a high mountain, O Zion, herald of good tidings; lift up your voice with strength, O Jerusalem, herald of good tidings, lift it up, fear not; say to the cities of Judah, "Behold your God!"

¹⁰ Behold, the Lord GOD comes with might, and his arm rules for him; behold, his reward is with him, and his recompense before him.

¹¹ He will feed his flock like a shepherd, he will gather the lambs in his arms, he will carry them in his bosom, and gently lead those that are with young.

▶ Women, too, are part of this proclamation of the Good News about the coming of God. The Greek word for "[female] messenger of joy" (and "bring good tidings" in Is 61:1) is the basis for the word *evangelium*, "Gospel" (↗ Mt 11:5).

God needs people to give testimony for him. To the prophet Isaiah (see his call in Is 6) and the various speakers in Is 40 comes the symbolic figure of the Servant of God. Although he is meek and silent and must endure much, in this way he reveals God's hidden plan for the salvation of all mankind and advances it. In his person is reflected the fate of countless people who endure disadvantages and sufferings for God and for the sake of justice, among them and especially Jesus.

God's servant (Is 42:1–9)

42 ¹ Behold my servant, whom I uphold, my chosen, in whom my soul delights; I have put my Spirit upon him, he will bring forth justice to the nations.

² He will not cry or lift up his voice, or make it heard in the street;

³ a bruised reed he will not break,

and a dimly burning wick he will not quench; he will faithfully bring forth justice.

⁴ He will not fail or be discouraged till he has established justice in the earth; and the islands wait for his law.

⁵ Thus says God, the LORD, who created the heavens and stretched them out, who spread forth the earth and what comes from it, who gives breath to the people upon it and spirit to those who walk in it:

⁶ "I am the LORD, I have called you in righteousness, I have taken you by the hand and kept you; I have given you as a covenant to the people, a light to the nations,

⁷ to open the eyes that are blind, to bring out the prisoners from the dungeon, from the prison those who sit in darkness.

⁸ I am the LORD, that is my name; my glory I give to no other, nor my praise to graven images.

⁹ Behold, the former things have come to pass, and new things I now declare; before they spring forth I tell you of them."

▶ The meek appearance of the Servant corresponds to God's tenderness (↗ Is 40:11).

Sometimes I think that I really don't need God and have to solve my problems alone. Then I fall on my face and realize that I can do nothing without God. He never extinguishes the little flame in my heart, which I often treat so carelessly. I have discovered that God does not let me fall, even though I sometimes have little trust. God is someone who loves "in spite of it all".

BERNADETTE

The surprising thing about the Servant is that he himself has problems perceiving: "Who is blind but my servant, or deaf as my messenger whom I send? ... He sees many things, but does not observe them; his ears are open, but he does not hear" (Is 42:19-20). But precisely through the experience of his own suffering, he becomes able to help others in their constraints and to open their minds and hearts. The following poem shows how God stands by his Servant:

God's love song (Is 43:1-7)

43 ¹ But now thus says the LORD, he who created you, O Jacob, he who formed you, O Israel: "Fear not, for I have redeemed you; I have called you by name, you are mine.

² When you pass through the waters I will be with you; and through the rivers, they shall not overwhelm you; when you walk through fire you shall not be burned, and the flame shall not consume you.

³ For I am the LORD your God, the Holy One of Israel, your Savior. I give Egypt as your ransom, Ethiopia and Seba in exchange for you.

⁴ Because you are precious in my eyes, and honored, and I love you, I give men in return for you, peoples in exchange for your life.

⁵ Fear not, for I am with you; I will bring your offspring from the east, and from the west I will gather you;

⁶ I will say to the north, Give up, and to the south, Do not withhold; bring my sons from afar and my daughters from the end of the earth,

99 God wants every child to be happy and to smile, and his favor rests upon them. ... The child has something which must never be lacking in those who would enter the kingdom of heaven.

POPE BENEDICT XVI, *Africae munus*

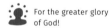 For the greater glory of God!

IGNATIUS OF LOYOLA, motto

⁷ every one who is called by my name, whom I created for my glory, whom I formed and made."

Faith in the one good God of all creation raises the problem of how to reconcile this belief with major changes in history, especially negative experiences such as suffering and injustice.

▶ The Persian King Cyrus conquered Babylon in 539 B.C. (↗ Ezra and Neh). With that began a good two centuries of lasting rule over almost the entire Near East. Cyrus receives here the title "Anointed" (= Messiah). God himself commissioned him to rule the world.

 I accept no awards in my name. I am nothing.

MOTHER TERESA

All is in God's hand (Is 45:1-8)

45 ¹ Thus says the LORD to his anointed, to Cyrus, whose right hand I have grasped, to subdue nations before him and uncover the loins of kings, to open doors before him that gates may not be closed:

² "I will go before you and level the mountains, I will break in pieces the doors of bronze and cut asunder the bars of iron,

³ I will give you the treasures of darkness and the hoards in secret places, that you may know that it is I, the LORD, the God of Israel, who call you by your name.

⁴ For the sake of my servant Jacob, and Israel my chosen, I call you by your name, I surname you, though you do not know me.

⁵ I am the LORD, and there is no other, besides me there is no God; I clothe you, though you do not know me,

⁶ that men may know, from the rising of the sun and from the west, that there is none besides me; I am the LORD, and there is no other.

⁷ I form light and create darkness, I make well-being and create woe, I am the LORD, who do all these things.

⁸ "Shower, O heavens, from above, and let the skies rain down righteousness; let the earth open, that salvation may sprout forth, and let it cause righteousness to spring up also;
I the LORD have created it.

▶ Few passages in the OT profess "monotheism" so clearly as this one (vv. 5–6, ↗ Deut 4:35).

▶ The Advent hymn, "Let the Clouds Rain Down the Just One" comes from this passage.

While God urges them to awaken, desolate conditions, disappointment, and a mood of resignation prevail among the people. Yet Zion says: "The LORD has forsaken me, my LORD has forgotten me" (Is 49:14).

God's consolation for Zion (Is 49:13–18)

49 ¹³ Sing for joy, O heavens, and exult, O earth;
break forth, O mountains, into singing!
For the LORD has comforted his people,
and will have compassion on his afflicted.
¹⁴ But Zion said, "The LORD has forsaken me,
my Lord has forgotten me."
¹⁵ "Can a woman forget her sucking child,
that she should have no compassion on the son of her womb?
Even these may forget, yet I will not forget you.

99 Thereby, [the Church] is already a spouse, by having become the mother of the children of God, who are, within her, the fruit of his grace.

LOUIS BOUYER (1913–2004), Catholic convert, priest, theologian, and author

¹⁶ Behold, I have graven you on the palms of my hands;
your walls are continually before me.
¹⁷ Your builders outstrip your destroyers,
and those who laid you waste go forth from you.
¹⁸ Lift up your eyes round about and see;
they all gather, they come to you.
As I live, says the LORD, you shall put them all on as an ornament,
you shall bind them on as a bride does.

▶ This passage addresses Jerusalem, which has been destroyed by the Babylonians but is to be rebuilt again under Persian rule.

God's Servant is sensible but not oversensitive. He can listen and console, but also endures aggression from others.

The third song of the suffering servant (Is 50:4–9)

50 ⁴ The Lord GOD has given me the tongue of those who are taught, that I may know how to sustain with a word him that is weary. Morning by morning he wakens, he wakens my ear
to hear as those who are taught.
⁵ The Lord GOD has opened my ear, and I was not rebellious, I turned not backward.
⁶ I gave my back to those who struck me, and my cheeks to those who pulled out the beard; I hid not my face from shame and spitting.
⁷ For the Lord GOD helps me; therefore I have not been confound-

O God, I need you to teach me day by day, according to each day's opportunities and needs. My ears are dull, so that I cannot hear your voice. My eyes are dim, so that I cannot see the signs of your presence. You alone can quicken my hearing and purge my sight, and cleanse and renew my heart. Teach me to sit at your feet and to hear your word. Amen.

JOHN HENRY NEWMAN

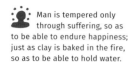

Man is tempered only through suffering, so as to be able to endure happiness; just as clay is baked in the fire, so as to be able to hold water.

AUGUSTINE

ed; therefore I have set my face like a flint, and I know that I shall not be put to shame;

⁸ he who vindicates me is near. Who will contend with me? Let us stand up together. Who is my adversary? Let him come near to me.

⁹ Behold, the Lord GOD helps me; who will declare me guilty? Behold, all of them will wear out like a garment; the moth will eat them up.

The so-called Fourth Song of the Suffering Servant brings the theme of God's Servant (↗ earlier in Is 42; 43; 49–50) to its climax. It shows how the community arrives at insight by looking at him.

God's Servant carries the community in his suffering (Is 53:1–12)

53 ¹ Who has believed what we have heard? And to whom has the arm of the LORD been revealed?

² For he grew up before him like a young plant, and like a root out of dry ground; he had no form or comeliness that we should look at him, and no beauty that we should desire him.

³ He was despised and rejected by men; a man of sorrows, and acquainted with grief; and as one from whom men hide their faces he was despised, and we esteemed him not.

⁴ Surely he has borne our griefs and carried our sorrows; yet we esteemed him stricken, struck down by God, and afflicted.

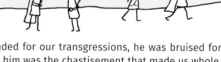

▶ The Church also says *Crucifixus etiam pro nobis* (= He was crucified for us) about Jesus Christ in the Creed.

▶ Now those in the community ("we") finally recognize that God's Servant suffered for their guilt and thereby healed them.

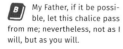

⁵ But he was wounded for our transgressions, he was bruised for our iniquities; upon him was the chastisement that made us whole, and with his stripes we are healed.

⁶ All we like sheep have gone astray; we have turned every one to his own way; and the LORD has laid on him the iniquity of us all.

⁷ He was oppressed, and he was afflicted, yet he opened not his mouth; like a lamb that is led to the slaughter, and like a sheep that before its shearers is silent, so he opened not his mouth.

⁸ By oppression and judgment he was taken away; and as for his generation, who considered that he was cut off out of the land of the living, stricken for the transgression of my people?

⁹ And they made his grave with the wicked and with a rich man in his death, although he had done no violence, and there was no deceit in his mouth.

▶ My Father, if it be possible, let this chalice pass from me; nevertheless, not as I will, but as you will.

Mt 26:39, Jesus in Gethsemane

¹⁰ Yet it was the will of the LORD to bruise him; he has put him to grief; when he makes himself an offering for sin, he shall see his offspring, he shall prolong his days; the will of the LORD shall prosper in his hand;

¹¹ he shall see the fruit of the travail of his soul and be satisfied; by his knowledge shall the righteous one, my servant, make many to be accounted righteous; and he shall bear their iniquities.

¹² Therefore I will divide him a portion with the great, and he shall divide the spoil with the strong; because he poured out his soul to death, and was numbered with the transgressors; yet he bore the sin of many, and made intercession for the transgressors.

> Unless a grain of wheat falls into the earth and dies, it remains alone; but if it dies, it bears much fruit.
>
> Jn 12:24

Is 54 places beside the Servant of God a symbolic female figure. Daughter Zion (↗ Is 2:8) is grown up here and stands for the community that worships God in the Temple in Jerusalem. She, too, experiences a fortunate turn of events in her life, as Is 55 goes on to present:

New salvation (Is 55:1–13)

55 ¹ Ho, every one who thirsts, come to the waters; and he who has no money, come, buy and eat! Come, buy wine and milk without money and without price.

² Why do you spend your money for that which is not bread, and your labor for that which does not satisfy? Listen diligently to me, and eat what is good, and delight yourselves in rich food.

³ Incline your ear, and come to me; hear, that your soul may live; and I will make with you an everlasting covenant, my steadfast, merciful love for David.

⁴ Behold, I made him a witness to the peoples, a leader and commander for the peoples.

⁵ Behold, you shall call nations that you know not, and nations that knew you not shall run to you, because of the LORD your God, and of the Holy One of Israel, for he has glorified you.

> ▶ With the paradoxical demand to "buy without money", God invites the people to receive his plenty as a gift. What he gives us is truly nourishing and contrasts with everything that we spend a lot of time and effort on but does not really make us happy.

⁶ "Seek the LORD while he may be found, call upon him while he is near;

⁷ let the wicked forsake his way, and the unrighteous man his thoughts; let him return to the LORD, that he may have mercy on him, and to our God, for he will abundantly pardon.

⁸ For my thoughts are not your thoughts, neither are your ways my ways, says the LORD.

⁹ For as the heavens are higher than the earth, so are my ways higher than your ways and my thoughts than your thoughts.

¹⁰ "For as the rain and the snow come down from heaven, and do not return there but water the earth, making it bring forth and sprout, giving seed to the sower and bread to the eater,

¹¹ so shall my word be that goes forth from my mouth; it shall not return to me empty, but it shall accomplish that which I intend, and prosper in the thing for which I sent it.

¹² "For you shall go out in joy, and be led forth in peace; the mountains and the hills before you shall break forth into singing, and all the trees of the field shall clap their hands.

¹³ Instead of the thorn shall come up the cypress; instead of the brier shall come up the myrtle; and it shall be to the LORD for a memorial, for an everlasting sign which shall not be cut off."

> 99 Whenever a community receives the message of salvation, the Holy Spirit enriches its culture with the transforming power of the Gospel. ... Christianity does not have simply one cultural expression, but rather ... will also reflect the different faces of the cultures and peoples in which it is received and takes root.
>
> **POPE FRANCIS**, *Evangelii Gaudium*, 116

> ▶ God's word not only lasts eternally (Is 40:8) but is also infinitely fruitful, like water in nature.

Good tidings (Is 61:1–3)

When God's peace has taken root in you, you will bring this peace to other people, and you will heal them of their fear of life and their doubts.

CHARBEL MAKHLOUF (1828–1889), patron saint of Lebanon

61 [1] The Spirit of the Lord GOD is upon me, because the LORD has anointed me to bring good tidings to the afflicted; he has sent me to bind up the brokenhearted, to proclaim liberty to the captives, and the opening of the prison to those who are bound;

[2] to proclaim the year of the LORD's favor, and the day of vengeance of our God; to comfort all who mourn;

[3] to grant to those who mourn in Zion—to give them a garland instead of ashes, the oil of gladness instead of mourning, the mantle of praise instead of a faint spirit; that they may be called oaks of righteousness, the planting of the LORD, that he may be glorified.

In this prayer the people confess their own guilt, but then also call upon God to intervene against their misfortune.

" The God of glory who created us and shares His life with us continually seeks us out in order to establish an everlasting bond of unconditional love.

DEACON HAROLD BURKE-SIVERS Catholic speaker and evangelist

The lament of the people (Is 63:7–64:12)

63 [7] I will recount the merciful love of the LORD, the praises of the LORD, according to all that the LORD has granted us, and the great goodness to the house of Israel which he has granted them according to his mercy, according to the abundance of his steadfast love.

▶ Concerning God's disappointment with Israel as his children, ↗ the beginning of this book (Is 1:2). "Holy Spirit" occurs in the Hebrew OT only here (vv. 10–11) and in Ps 51:11.

▶ God turns against the people (v. 10) and thus brings them back to their senses. They remember the miracles of the Exodus and dare once again to address God ("you", v. 14).

As a father pities his children, so the LORD pities those who fear him.

Ps 103:13

[8] For he said, Surely they are my people, sons who will not deal falsely; and he became their Savior.

[9] In all their affliction he was afflicted, and the angel of his presence saved them; in his love and in his pity he redeemed them; he lifted them up and carried them all the days of old.

[10] But they rebelled and grieved his holy Spirit; therefore he turned to be their enemy, and himself fought against them.

[11] Then he remembered the days of old, of Moses his servant. Where is he who brought up out of the sea the shepherds of his flock? Where is he who put in the midst of them his holy Spirit,

[12] who caused his glorious arm to go at the right hand of Moses, who divided the waters before them to make for himself an everlasting name,

[13] who led them through the depths? Like a horse in the desert, they did not stumble.

[14] Like cattle that go down into the valley, the Spirit of the LORD gave them rest. So you led your people, to make for yourself a glorious name.

[15] Look down from heaven and see, from your holy and glorious habitation. Where are your zeal and your might? The yearning of your heart and your compassion are withheld from me.

¹⁶ For you are our Father, though Abraham does not know us and Israel does not acknowledge us; you, O LORD, are our Father, our Redeemer from of old is your name.

¹⁷ O LORD, why do you make us err from your ways and harden our heart, so that we fear you not? Return for the sake of your servants, the tribes of your heritage.

¹⁸ Your holy people possessed your sanctuary a little while; our adversaries have trodden it down.

¹⁹ We have become like those over whom you have never ruled, like those who are not called by your name.

▶ Twice the people call God "our Father" (again in 64:8). This is one origin of the prayer: "Our Father who art in heaven, hallowed be thy name ..." (Mt 6:9).

💡 This is the source of the Advent hymn, "O Savior, Rend the Heavens Wide."

64 ³When you did terrible things which we looked not for, you came down, the mountains quaked at your presence.

⁴ From of old no one has heard or perceived by the ear, no eye has seen a God besides you, who works for those who wait for him.

⁵ You meet him that joyfully works righteousness, those that remember you in your ways. Behold, you were angry, and we sinned; in our sins we have been a long time, and shall we be saved?

⁶ We have all become like one who is unclean, and all our righteous deeds are like a polluted garment. We all fade like a leaf, and our iniquities, like the wind, take us away.

▶ Literally v. 4 reads: "If only you would meet someone who joyfully does justice, those who remember you on your paths!" The problem is not with God, but that all have gone astray and are far from God.

⁷ There is no one that calls upon your name, that bestirs himself to take hold of you; for you have hidden your face from us, and have delivered us into the hand of our iniquities.

⁸ Yet, O LORD, you are our Father; we are the clay, and you are our potter; we are all the work of your hand.

⁹ Be not exceedingly angry, O LORD, and remember not iniquity for ever. Behold, consider, we are all your people.

¹⁰ Your holy cities have become a wilderness, Zion has become a wilderness, Jerusalem a desolation.

¹¹ Our holy and beautiful house, where our fathers praised you, has been burned by fire, and all our pleasant places have become ruins.

¹² Will you restrain yourself at these things, O LORD? Will you keep silent, and afflict us sorely?

💡 Incredibly tense emotions: feelings of guilt and at the same time the entreaty for God finally to show some sympathy!

💡 What a beautiful image for God: an artist who deals with his material lovingly! Every being that he creates is a work of art! ↗ also Gen 2:7: "Then the Lord God formed man..."

In the concluding chapters (Is 65–66), God answers the prayer of his people. He intends to oppose injustice, to stay close to his people and grant them happiness. God even promises new heavens and a new earth (Is 65:17, ↗ Rev 21:1).

THE BOOK OF

Jeremiah

Jeremiah means "May YHWH exalt, raise up". This prayer is fitting in a time when much was sinking: the prophet Jeremiah witnesses the decline of the kingdom in Judah around 600 B.C. He lives through the conquest of Jerusalem by Babylonian troops and the destruction of the city and Temple in the year 587. When the foundations that formerly carried the community are ruined, the question arises: What is lasting?

The Book of Jeremiah (= Jer) answers this question by showing how God makes new life grow amid sorrow and loss. The prophet, too, has this experience. He is persecuted, imprisoned, threatened with death, yet God's word gains through him an unstoppable power and becomes the foundation for later generations, too. Like Jeremiah, Jesus, too, criticized powerful priests and was therefore subjected to strong pressures. Some even considered Jesus to be a new Jeremiah (Mt 16:13–14).

▶ Jeremiah's mission as "prophet for the nations" is unique and shows that God cares about all mankind.

" Each of us is the result of a thought of God. Each of us is willed, each of us is loved, each of us is necessary.

POPE BENEDICT XVI, April 24, 2005

▶ God had promised Moses that he would send a prophet like him: "I will put my words in his mouth" (Deut 18:18). Consequently, Jeremiah is presented here as the promised prophet like Moses.

▶ In Hebrew, this is a play on words between "almond tree" *(shaqed)* and "watchman" *(shoqed)*.

A special vocation (Jer 1)

1 ⁴ Now the word of the LORD came to me saying, ⁵ "Before I formed you in the womb I knew you, and before you were born I consecrated you; I appointed you a prophet to the nations."

⁶ Then I said, "Ah, Lord GOD! Behold, I do not know how to speak, for I am only a youth." ⁷ But the LORD said to me, "Do not say, 'I am only a youth'; for to all to whom I send you you shall go, and whatever I command you you shall speak.

⁸ Be not afraid of them, for I am with you to deliver you, says the LORD."

⁹ Then the LORD put forth his hand and touched my mouth; and the LORD said to me, "Behold, I have put my words in your mouth.

¹⁰ See, I have set you this day over nations and over kingdoms, to pluck up and to break down, to destroy and to overthrow, to build and to plant."

¹¹ And the word of the LORD came to me, saying, "Jeremi'ah, what do you see?" And I said, "I see a rod of almond." ¹² Then the LORD said to me, "You have seen well, for I am watching over my word to perform it."...

" So it is in the history of God's people that the genuine prophet is persecuted, even killed.

THOMAS DUBAY, S.M.

B I know your works: you are neither cold nor hot. Would that you were cold or hot! So, because you are lukewarm, and neither cold nor hot, I will spew you out of my mouth. For you say, I am rich, I have prospered, and I need nothing; not knowing that you are wretched, pitiable, poor, blind, and naked.

Rev 3:15–17

▶ God asks questions and is willing to listen to criticism. The play on words "worthlessness-worthless" alludes to 2 Kings 17:15 and thus points to the fall of the Northern Kingdom of Israel.

¹⁷ But you, gird up your loins; arise, and say to them everything that I command you. Do not be dismayed by them, lest I dismay you before them.

¹⁸ And I, behold, I make you this day a fortified city, an iron pillar, and bronze walls, against the whole land, against the kings of Judah, its princes, its priests, and the people of the land.

¹⁹ They will fight against you; but they shall not prevail against you, for I am with you, says the LORD, to deliver you."

Incomprehensible estrangement (Jer 2:1–8)

2 ¹ The word of the LORD came to me, saying, ² "Go and proclaim in the hearing of Jerusalem, Thus says the LORD, I remember the devotion of your youth, your love as a bride, how you followed me in the wilderness, in a land not sown.

³ Israel was holy to the LORD, the first fruits of his harvest. All who ate of it became guilty; evil came upon them, says the LORD."

⁴ Hear the word of the LORD, O house of Jacob, and all the families of the house of Israel. ⁵ Thus says the LORD: "What wrong did your fathers find in me that they went far from me, and went after worthlessness, and became worthless?

⁶ They did not say, 'Where is the LORD who brought us up from the land of Egypt, who led us in the wilderness, in a land of deserts and

pits, in a land of drought and deep darkness, in a land that none passes through, where no man dwells?'

⁷ And I brought you into a plentiful land to enjoy its fruits and its good things. But when you came in you defiled my land, and made my heritage an abomination.

⁸ The priests did not say, 'Where is the LORD?' Those who handle the law did not know me; the rulers transgressed against me; the prophets prophesied by Ba'al, and went after things that do not profit.

▶ The leading groups in the community, even the priests and false prophets, are chiefly responsible for the infidelity to God. "Baal" (= Lord) was a popular deity.

These accusations are typical for Jer. Many passages point out the guilt of the people; if they convert, however, Jer also promises God's renewed grace (e.g., Jer 3:1–4:4). God is profoundly moved by the sorry state of his people, as is Jeremiah:

The discourse in the Temple (Jer 7:1–11)

7 ¹ The word that came to Jeremi'ah from the LORD: ² "Stand in the gate of the LORD's house, and proclaim there this word, and say, Hear the word of the LORD, all you men of Judah who enter these gates to worship the LORD. ³ Thus says the LORD of hosts, the God of Israel, Amend your ways and your doings, and I will let you dwell

in this place. ⁴ Do not trust in these deceptive words: 'This is the temple of the LORD, the temple of the LORD, the temple of the LORD.'

⁵ "For if you truly amend your ways and your doings, if you truly execute justice one with another, ⁶ if you do not oppress the alien, the fatherless or the widow, or shed innocent blood in this place, and if you do not go after other gods to your own hurt, ⁷ then I will let you dwell in this place, in the land that I gave of old to your fathers for ever.

⁸ "Behold, you trust in deceptive words to no avail. ⁹ Will you steal, murder, commit adultery, swear falsely, burn incense to Ba'al, and go after other gods that you have not known, ¹⁰ and then come and stand before me in this house, which is called by my name, and say, 'We are delivered!'—only to go on doing all these abominations? ¹¹ Has this house, which is called by my name, become a den of robbers in your eyes? Behold, I myself have seen it, says the LORD.

Obedience, not sacrifice (Jer 7:21–26)

²¹ Thus says the LORD of hosts, the God of Israel: "Add your burnt offerings to your sacrifices, and eat the flesh.

²² For in the day that I brought them out of the land of Egypt, I did not speak to your fathers or command them concerning burnt offerings and sacrifices.

" When even one American—who has done nothing wrong—is forced by fear to shut his mind and close his mouth, then all Americans are in peril.

HARRY S. TRUMAN (1884–1972), 33rd President of the United States

 Jesus entered the temple of God and drove out all who sold and bought in the temple, and he overturned the tables of the money-changers and the seats of those who sold pigeons. He said to them, "It is written: 'My house shall be called a house of prayer'; but you make it a den of robbers."

Mt 21:12

God seeks you more than your sacrificial offering.

AUGUSTINE

Somehow all paths look right. But then there is this voice, deep inside. A thousand times already I have ignored it, especially when my ego was once again stronger than my heart. I try to learn to listen by reading the Bible daily and reflecting on it. I pray to God to keep me on his monitor whenever I stray from his path. Only with him is the fullness of joy.

NADIA

▶ It is not clear whether God is speaking here or Jeremiah. Both are dismayed and would just like to weep.

²³ But this command I gave them, 'Obey my voice, and I will be your God, and you shall be my people; and walk in all the way that I command you, that it may be well with you.' ²⁴ But they did not obey or incline their ear, but walked in their own counsels and the stubbornness of their evil hearts, and went backward and not forward.

²⁵ From the day that your fathers came out of the land of Egypt to this day, I have persistently sent all my servants the prophets to them, day after day;

²⁶ yet they did not listen to me, or incline their ear, but stiffened their neck. They did worse than their fathers.

Broken by sadness (Jer 8:21–22; 9:1–11)

8 ²¹ For the wound of the daughter of my people my heart is wounded, I mourn, and dismay has taken hold on me.

²² Is there no balm in Gilead? Is there no physician there? Why then has the health of the daughter of my people not been restored?

▶ God would rather be in the wilderness (v. 1) than surrounded by lies and crimes.

🗩 Please, do not let the terrorism of gossip be among you! Get rid of it! Let there be fraternity. And if you have something against your brother, say it to his face. … At times you may end up coming to blows, this is not a problem: this is better than the terrorism of gossip.

POPE FRANCIS, November 7, 2014

🅱 No human being can tame the tongue—a restless evil, full of deadly poison.

Jas 3:8

▶ When God "avenges himself", this is to be understood as "just compensation" (↗ Is 35:4).

9 ¹ O that my head were waters, and my eyes a fountain of tears, that I might weep day and night for the slain of the daughter of my people!

² O that I had in the desert a wayfarers' lodging place, that I might leave my people and go away from them! For they are all adulterers, a company of treacherous men.

³ They bend their tongue like a bow; falsehood and not truth has grown strong in the land; for they proceed from evil to evil, and they do not know me, says the LORD.

⁴ Let every one beware of his neighbor, and put no trust in any brother; for every brother is a supplanter, and every neighbor goes about as a slanderer.

⁵ Every one deceives his neighbor, and no one speaks the truth; they have taught their tongue to speak lies; they commit iniquity and are too weary to repent.

⁶ Heaping oppression upon oppression, and deceit upon deceit, they refuse to know me, says the LORD.

⁷ Therefore thus says the LORD of hosts: "Behold, I will refine them and test them, for what else can I do, because of my people?

⁸ Their tongue is a deadly arrow; it speaks deceitfully; with his mouth each speaks peaceably to his neighbor, but in his heart he plans an ambush for him.

⁹ Shall I not punish them for these things? says the LORD; and shall I not avenge myself on a nation such as this?

¹⁰ "Take up weeping and wailing for the mountains, and a lamentation for the pastures of the wilderness, because they are laid waste so that no one passes through, and the lowing of cattle is not heard; both the birds of the air and the beasts have fled and are gone.

¹¹ I will make Jerusalem a heap of ruins, a lair of jackals; and I will make the cities of Judah a desolation, without inhabitant."

The true basis for glory (Jer 9:23–24)

9 ²³ Thus says the LORD: "Let not the wise man glory in his wisdom, let not the mighty man glory in his might, let not the rich man glory in his riches;

²⁴ but let him who glories glory in this, that he understands and knows me, that I am the LORD who practice steadfast love, justice, and righteousness in the earth; for in these things I delight, says the LORD."

▶ God weeps and mourns over ruin and destruction.

The source of mercy never runs dry. It is man's fault if he becomes a desert.

ANTONY OF PADUA (ca. 1195–1231), Franciscan and Doctor of the Church

"Let him who boasts, boast of the Lord." For it is not the man who commends himself that is accepted, but the man whom the LORD commends.

2 Cor 10:17–18

Jer 11–20 depicts how the relationship between God and the People of Israel breaks down. "The house of Israel and the house of Judah have broken my covenant" (Jer 11:10). As a consequence, Jeremiah, too, is persecuted more and more. In the so-called confessions (five intense passages: 11:18–12:6; 15:10–21; 17:12–18; 18:18–23; 20:7–18), Jeremiah expresses his sorrows, finally, after he is imprisoned at the Temple in Jerusalem:

Jeremiah is tortured—and he prays (Jer 20:1–18)

20 ¹ Now Pashhur the priest, the son of Im'mer, who was chief officer in the house of the LORD, heard Jeremi'ah prophesying these things.

² Then Pashhur beat Jeremi'ah the prophet, and put him in the stocks that were in the upper Benjamin Gate of the house of the LORD.

³ On the next day, when Pashhur released Jeremi'ah from the stocks, Jeremi'ah said to him, "The LORD does not call your name Pashhur, but Terror on every side.

⁴ For thus says the LORD: Behold, I will make you a terror to yourself and to all your friends. They shall fall by the sword of their enemies while you look on. And I will give all Judah into the hand of the king of Babylon; he shall carry them captive to Babylon, and shall slay them with the sword.

⁵ Moreover, I will give all the wealth of the city, all its gains, all its prized belongings, and all the treasures of the kings of Judah into

▶ Jeremiah had smashed an earthen vessel and thus symbolically announced the downfall of Jerusalem (Jer 19; the drama *The Broken Jug* by Heinrich von Kleist alludes to this). As a priest and prophet, Pashhur is a "colleague" of Jeremiah.

▶ The "stocks" are an instrument of torture that confine the body in a crooked position. Jeremiah was locked in the stocks at the Benjamin Gate on the way to his hometown of Anathoth (↗ Jer 1:1) in order to ridicule him publicly.

▶ At first Jeremiah reacts to the torture by communicating to Pashhur God's judgment upon him (vv. 4–6); then in v. 7 he turns to God.

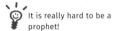 It is really hard to be a prophet!

▶ Jeremiah is in a dilemma: if he speaks, he is rejected (v. 8). If he does not speak, it tears him up inside (v. 9).

▶ "Terror … on every side" had been Jeremiah's description of Jerusalem's situation (6:25) and Pashhur's future (20:3). Now he is mocked with this exclamation.

the hand of their enemies, who shall plunder them, and seize them, and carry them to Babylon.

⁶ And you, Pashhur, and all who dwell in your house, shall go into captivity; to Babylon you shall go; and there you shall die, and there you shall be buried, you and all your friends, to whom you have prophesied falsely."

⁷ O Lord, you have deceived me, and I was deceived; you are stronger than I, and you have prevailed. I have become a laughingstock all the day; every one mocks me.

⁸ For whenever I speak, I cry out, I shout, "Violence and destruction!" For the word of the Lord has become for me a reproach and derision all day long.

⁹ If I say, "I will not mention him, or speak any more in his name," there is in my heart as it were a burning fire shut up in my bones, and I am weary with holding it in, and I cannot.

¹⁰ For I hear many whispering. Terror is on every side! "Denounce him! Let us denounce him!" say all my familiar friends, watching for my fall. "Perhaps he will be deceived, then we can overcome him, and take our revenge on him."

¹¹ But the Lord is with me as a dread warrior; therefore my persecutors will stumble, they will not overcome me. They will be greatly

▶ "Vengeance" actually means "just compensation" ↗ above at Jer 9:8 and Is 35:4).

▶ This profession of praise and trust in vv. 11–13 immediately follows the lament in vv. 7–10: in his extreme situation, Jeremiah experiences sudden shifts of emotion.

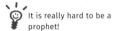 The Bible leaves nothing out. Not even brutal curses and unrealistic wishes.

shamed, for they will not succeed. Their eternal dishonor will never be forgotten.

¹² O Lord of hosts, who test the righteous, who see the heart and the mind, let me see your vengeance upon them, for to you have I committed my cause.

¹³ Sing to the Lord; praise the Lord! For he has delivered the life of the needy from the hand of evildoers.

¹⁴ Cursed be the day on which I was born! The day when my mother bore me, let it not be blessed! ¹⁵ Cursed be the man who brought the news to my father, "A son is born to you," making him very glad.

¹⁶ Let that man be like the cities which the Lord overthrew without pity; let him hear a cry in the morning and an alarm at noon,

¹⁷ because he did not kill me in the womb; so my mother would have been my grave, and her womb for ever great.

¹⁸ Why did I come forth from the womb to see toil and sorrow, and spend my days in shame?

The following chapters are filled with "words of the Lord" that came to Jeremiah. They concern the last kings of Judah (Jer 21–22), false prophets (Jer 23:9–40) like Hananiah (Jer 28), and also the death threats made against Jeremiah (Jer 26). In the center of the whole book stands God's universal judgment on all peoples (Jer 25), which begins with Jerusalem and ends with Babylon. This plan is carried out in Jer 26–52. The Babylonian troops besiege Jerusalem for the first time in 597 B.C. King Jehoiachin must surrender and is deported with most of the upper class to the region near Babylon. God addresses these people in exile through Jeremiah:

Jeremiah's letter to the exiles in Babylon (Jer 29:1–14)

29 ¹ These are the words of the letter which Jeremi'ah the prophet sent from Jerusalem to the elders of the exiles, and to the priests, the prophets, and all the people, whom Nebuchadnez'zar had taken into exile from Jerusalem to Babylon.

² This was after King Jeconi'ah, and the queen mother, the eunuchs, the princes of Judah and Jerusalem, the craftsmen, and the smiths had departed from Jerusalem.

³ The letter was sent by the hand of Ela'sah the son of Sha'phan and Gemari'ah the son of Hilki'ah, whom Zedeki'ah king of Judah sent to Babylon to Nebuchadnez'zar king of Babylon. It said: ⁴ "Thus says the LORD of hosts, the God of Israel, to all the exiles whom I have sent into exile from Jerusalem to Babylon: ⁵ Build houses and live in them; plant gardens and eat their produce.

⁶ Take wives and have sons and daughters; take wives for your sons, and give your daughters in marriage, that they may bear sons and daughters; multiply there, and do not decrease.

⁷ But seek the welfare of the city where I have sent you into exile, and pray to the LORD on its behalf, for in its welfare you will find your welfare.

⁸ For thus says the LORD of hosts, the God of Israel: Do not let your prophets and your diviners who are among you deceive you, and do not listen to the dreams which they dream, ⁹ for it is a lie which they are prophesying to you in my name; I did not send them, says the LORD.

> Good letters are like good friends.
>
> **OSCAR WILDE** (1854–1900), Irish author

🅑 Love your enemies and pray for those who persecute you.
Mt 5:44

▶ God encourages the exiles not to give up but to live their lives with hope.

▶ Other "prophets" believed in a swift return in "two years" (Jer 28:3–4): according to them, the exiles should not adapt or settle down.

¹⁰ "For thus says the LORD: When seventy years are completed for Babylon, I will visit you, and I will fulfil to you my promise and bring you back to this place.

¹¹ For I know the plans I have for you, says the LORD, plans for welfare and not for evil, to give you a future and a hope. ¹² Then you will call upon me and come and pray to me, and I will hear you. ¹³ You will seek me and find me; when you seek me with all your heart,

¹⁴ I will be found by you, says the LORD, and I will restore your fortunes and gather you from all the nations and all the places where I have driven you, says the LORD, and I will bring you back to the place from which I sent you into exile.

▶ The new Babylonian Empire lasted for about 70 years, from Nebuchadnezzar's victory at Carchemish in 605 B.C. until the entrance of the Persian King Cyrus into Babylon in 539 B.C., who then allowed the Jews to return home (↗ Ezra and 2 Chron 36:23).

▶ While far from home, the exiles can experience God's closeness in a new way. Concerning the promise of a restoration, ↗ Deut 30:3.

Jer 30–31 describe the promised improvement in their lot in six poems and several additional promises. In the first poem (with motifs from Is 43), God promises that his people will return home from their dire hardship (30:5–7). The foreign nations suffer the consequences of their crimes (v. 11; ↗ Deut 30:7). The second poem depicts how God sends healing to "wounded Zion" (vv. 12–17).

The scroll of consolation (Jer 30–31)

30 ⁵ "Thus says the LORD: We have heard a cry of panic, of terror, and no peace.

▶ God quotes a group of anxious men (see v. 6).

▶ God announces an end to the oppression by quoting Is 10:27 in v. 8.

▶ "David" here means an ideal ruler in the future (↗ Ezek 34:23–24).

Let nothing disturb you, let nothing frighten you. All things are passing away. God never changes. Patience obtains all things. Whoever has God lacks nothing; God alone suffices.

TERESA OF AVILA

⁶ Ask now, and see, can a man bear a child? Why then do I see every man with his hands on his loins like a woman in labor? Why has every face turned pale?

⁷ Alas! that day is so great there is none like it; it is a time of distress for Jacob; yet he shall be saved out of it.

⁸ "And it shall come to pass in that day, says the LORD of hosts, that I will break the yoke from off their neck, and I will burst their bonds, and strangers shall no more make servants of them. ⁹ But they shall serve the LORD their God and David their king, whom I will raise up for them.

¹⁰ "Then fear not, O Jacob my servant, says the LORD, nor be dismayed, O Israel; for behold, I will save you from afar, and your offspring from the land of their captivity. Jacob shall return and have quiet and ease, and none shall make him afraid.

¹¹ For I am with you to save you, says the LORD; I will make a full end of all the nations among whom I scattered you, but of you I will not make a full end.

I will chasten you in just measure, and I will by no means leave you unpunished ...

> The third poem (30:18–31:1) depicts the healing of the community. The so-called "covenant formula" in v. 22 shows that the relationship with God exists again, for the ruler, too (v. 21, in contrast to Jer 2:8).

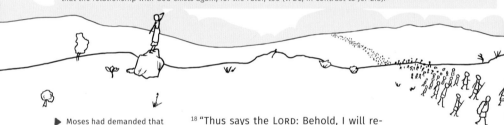

▶ Moses had demanded that a city that fell away from God should be destroyed forever (Deut 13:17); God abolishes this requirement.

❞ [W]ith Jeremiah an inward change of the whole people is the essence of the New Covenant the Lord will make in place of the Old.

AIDAN NICHOLS, O.P., (b. 1948), British Dominican priest and theologian

▶ God makes a unique declaration of love for Israel.

¹⁸ "Thus says the LORD: Behold, I will restore the fortunes of the tents of Jacob, and have compassion on his dwellings; the city shall be rebuilt upon its mound, and the palace shall stand where it used to be.

¹⁹ Out of them shall come songs of thanksgiving, and the voices of those who make merry. I will multiply them, and they shall not be few; I will make them honored, and they shall not be small.

²⁰ Their children shall be as they were of old, and their congregation shall be established before me; and I will punish all who oppress them.

²¹ Their prince shall be one of themselves, their ruler shall come forth from their midst; I will make him draw near, and he shall approach me, for who would dare of himself to approach me? says the LORD.

²² And you shall be my people, and I will be your God."

²³ Behold the storm of the LORD! Wrath has gone forth, a whirling tempest; it will burst upon the head of the wicked.

²⁴ The fierce anger of the LORD will not turn back until he has executed and accomplished the intents of his mind. In the latter days you will understand this.

31 ¹ "At that time, says the LORD, I will be the God of all the families of Israel, and they shall be my people."

² Thus says the LORD: "The people who survived the sword found grace in the wilderness; when Israel sought for rest,

³ the LORD appeared to him from afar. I have loved you with an everlasting love; therefore I have continued my faithfulness to you.

⁴ Again I will build you, and you shall be built, O virgin Israel! Again you shall adorn yourself with timbrels, and shall go forth in the dance of the merrymakers.

⁵ Again you shall plant vineyards upon the mountains of Samar'ia; the planters shall plant, and shall enjoy the fruit.

⁶ For there shall be a day when watchmen will call in the hill country of E'phraim: 'Arise, and let us go up to Zion, to the LORD our God.'"

The fifth poem leads from the Exile (v. 8) to festive joy at the common meal at the Temple in Jerusalem (vv. 12–14).

⁷ For thus says the LORD:

"Sing aloud with gladness for Jacob, and raise shouts for the chief of the nations; proclaim, give praise, and say, 'The LORD has saved his people, the remnant of Israel.'

⁸ Behold, I will bring them from the north country, and gather them from the farthest parts of the earth, among them the blind and the

▶ Ephraim acknowledges his failings and asks God for a new chance.

lame, the woman with child and her who has labor pains, together; a great company, they shall return here.

⁹ With weeping they shall come, and with consolations I will lead them back, I will make them walk by brooks of water, in a straight path in which they shall not stumble; for I am a father to Israel, and E'phraim is my first-born.

¹⁰ "Hear the word of the LORD, O nations, and declare it in the islands afar off; say, 'He who scattered Israel will gather him, and will keep him as a shepherd keeps his flock.'

¹¹ For the LORD has ransomed Jacob, and has redeemed him from hands too strong for him.

¹² They shall come and sing aloud on the height of Zion, and they shall be radiant over the goodness of the LORD, over the grain, the wine, and the oil, and over the young of the flock and the herd; their life shall be like a watered garden, and they shall languish no more.

¹³ Then shall the maidens rejoice in the dance, and the young men and the old shall be merry. I will turn their mourning into joy, I will comfort them, and give them gladness for sorrow.

¹⁴ I will feast the soul of the priests with abundance, and my people shall be satisfied with my goodness, says the LORD."

99 Let your religion be less of a theory and more of a love affair.

G.K. CHESTERTON

B May those who sow in tears reap with shouts of joy!

Ps 126:5

The sixth poem, as before, presents female and male figures alternately: Rachel, Ephraim, the virginal Israel. Women and men have equal value and joint responsibility for building up the community.

▶ Ramah was a town north of Jerusalem where people were gathered to be sent into exile (Jer 40:1). "Rachel" is the name of the favorite wife of Jacob/Israel in Gen 28–35. Here she mourns symbolically as the mother of the people over their exile.

▶ "Ephraim" is a grandson of Jacob and Rachel (Gen 41:52); he stands for the "young" people of Israel. As after the exodus from Egypt (Ex 15:20), Israel sings and dances again. The people celebrate the end of their separation from God.

💡 "My heart yearns" is literally in Hebrew "my bowels rumble."

¹⁵ Thus says the LORD: "A voice is heard in Ra'mah, lamentation and bitter weeping. Rachel is weeping for her children; she refuses to be comforted for her children, because they are not."

¹⁶ Thus says the LORD: "Keep your voice from weeping, and your eyes from tears; for your work shall be rewarded, says the LORD, and they shall come back from the land of the enemy.

¹⁷ There is hope for your future, says the LORD, and your children shall come back to their own country.

¹⁸ I have heard E'phraim bemoaning, 'You have chastened me, and I was chastened, like an untrained calf; bring me back that I may be restored, for you are the LORD my God.

¹⁹ For after I had turned away I repented; and after I was instructed, I struck my thigh; I was ashamed, and I was confounded, because I bore the disgrace of my youth.'

²⁰ Is E'phraim my dear son? Is he my darling child? For as often as I speak against him, I do remember him still. Therefore my heart yearns for him; I will surely have mercy on him, says the LORD ....

Prospects for a happy time (Jer 31:28–37)

²⁸ And it shall come to pass that as I have watched over them to pluck up and break down, to overthrow, destroy, and bring evil, so I will watch over them to build and to plant, says the LORD. ²⁹ In those

▶ Jeremiah's vocation takes a turn here for the better: God "watches" over his word (1:12), and now comes the time "to build and to plant" (↗ 1:10).

▶ In the Old Testament, only Jeremiah announces a "new covenant": Jesus repeats this at the Last Supper (Lk 22:20; 1 Cor 11:25); in Latin this becomes the New "Testament". Whereas in the Sinai Covenant (Ex 19–24) God had written his commandments on stone tablets (Ex 31:18), now he intends to inscribe them directly on the heart, so that they are "very near" (↗ Deut 30:14).

God is faithful.
1 Cor 10:13

days they shall no longer say: 'The fathers have eaten sour grapes, and the children's teeth are set on edge.'

³⁰ But every one shall die for his own sin; each man who eats sour grapes, his teeth shall be set on edge.

³¹ "Behold, the days are coming, says the LORD, when I will make a new covenant with the house of Israel and the house of Judah,

³² not like the covenant which I made with their fathers when I took them by the hand to bring them out of the land of Egypt, my covenant which they broke, and I showed myself their Master, says the LORD.

³³ But this is the covenant which I will make with the house of Israel after those days, says the LORD: I will put my law within them, and I will write it upon their hearts; and I will be their God, and they shall be my people.

³⁴ And no longer shall each man teach his neighbor and each his brother, saying, 'Know the LORD,' for they shall all know me, from the least of them to the greatest, says the LORD; for I will forgive their iniquity, and I will remember their sin no more."

³⁵ Thus says the LORD, who gives the sun for light by day and the fixed order of the moon and the stars for light by night, who stirs up the sea so that its waves roar—the LORD of hosts is his name:

[36] "If this fixed order departs from before me, says the LORD, then shall the descendants of Israel cease from being a nation before me for ever."

[37] Thus says the LORD: "If the heavens above can be measured, and the foundations of the earth below can be explored, then I will cast off all the descendants of Israel for all that they have done, says the LORD."

After the scroll of consolation, further promises of salvation follow in Jer 32–33. These passages form the heart of Jer and are the key to a correct understanding of Jerusalem's downfall (in Jer 39 and 52, → 2 Kings 25). Tearing down is a necessary prerequisite for building up. God's judgment also affects other nations (Jer 46ff.), especially the Babylonians, who had destroyed Jerusalem (Jer 50).

Babylon, too, comes to an end (Jer 50:1–10)

50 [1] The word which the LORD spoke concerning Babylon, concerning the land of the Chalde'ans, by Jeremi'ah the prophet:

▶ The capture of Babylon in 539 B.C. also meant a downfall for its gods Bel and Marduk (here called "Merodach").

[2] "Declare among the nations and proclaim, set up a banner and proclaim, conceal it not, and say: 'Babylon is taken, Bel is put to shame, Mer'odach is dismayed. Her images are put to shame, her idols are dismayed.'

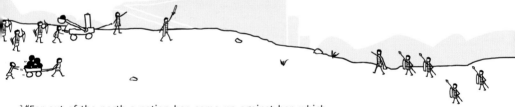

[3] "For out of the north a nation has come up against her, which shall make her land a desolation, and none shall dwell in it; both man and beast shall flee away.

[4] "In those days and in that time, says the LORD, the people of Israel and the people of Judah shall come together, weeping as they come; and they shall seek the LORD their God. [5] They shall ask the way to Zion, with faces turned toward it, saying, 'Come, let us join ourselves to the LORD in an everlasting covenant which will never be forgotten.'

[6] "My people have been lost sheep; their shepherds have led them astray, turning them away on the mountains; from mountain to hill they have gone, they have forgotten their fold. [7] All who found them have devoured them, and their enemies have said, 'We are not guilty, for they have sinned against the LORD, their true habitation, the LORD, the hope of their fathers.'

[8] "Flee from the midst of Babylon, and go out of the land of the Chalde'ans, and be as he-goats before the flock. [9] For behold, I am stirring up and bringing against Babylon a company of great nations, from the north country; and they shall array themselves against her; from there she shall be taken. Their arrows are like a skilled warrior who does not return empty-handed. [10] Chalde'a shall be plundered; all who plunder her shall be sated, says the LORD.

❝❝ Yet now, in this system devoid of ethics, at the center there is an idol and the world has become an idolater of this "god-money". Money is in command! Money lays down the law! It orders all these things that are useful to it, this idol. And what happens? To defend this idol all crowd to the center and those on the margins are put down, the elderly fall away, because there is no room for them in this world!

POPE FRANCIS, September 22, 2013

▶ The conquest of Babylon clears the way for the migration of the exiles back to Jerusalem; strengthened, they now seek God.

THE
Lamentations
OF JEREMIAH

AND THE BOOK OF
Baruch

The Book of Lamentations takes as its theme the downfall of Jerusalem. Therefore, it is closely related to the Book of Jeremiah. Five special poems, composed in alphabetical order, depict the immense sorrow that has come over the population of the city. Yet we hear also about signs of hope:

LAMENTATIONS

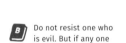

Trust God in sorrow (Lam 3:19–33)

3 ¹⁹ Remember my affliction and my bitterness, the wormwood and the gall!

²⁰ My soul continually thinks of it and is bowed down within me.

²¹ But this I call to mind, and therefore I have hope:

²² The steadfast love of the LORD never ceases, his mercies never come to an end;

²³ they are new every morning; great is your faithfulness.

²⁴ "The LORD is my portion," says my soul, "therefore I will hope in him." ²⁵ The LORD is good to those who wait for him, to the soul that seeks him.

²⁶ It is good that one should wait quietly for the salvation of the LORD.

²⁷ It is good for a man that he bear the yoke in his youth.

²⁸ Let him sit alone in silence when he has laid it on him;

²⁹ let him put his mouth in the dust—there may yet be hope;

³⁰ let him give his cheek to the one who strikes him, and be filled with insults.

³¹ For the Lord will not cast off for ever, ³² but, though he cause grief, he will have compassion according to the abundance of his steadfast love;

³³ for he does not willingly afflict or grieve the sons of men.

Do not resist one who is evil. But if any one strikes you on the right cheek, turn to him the other also.

Mt 5:39

Give me a soul that knows not boredom, grumblings, sighs, and laments, nor excess of stress, because of that obstructing thing called "I".

THOMAS MORE

▶ As though "against his innermost inclination", God allows painful events to befall men, also.

The last poem, too, is characterized by this tension between dire need and trust in God. It leads at the conclusion to a prayer:

Petitions and requests at the conclusion of the laments (Lam 5:10–22)

5 ¹⁰ Our skin is hot as an oven with the burning heat of famine.
¹¹ Women are ravished in Zion, virgins in the towns of Judah.

¹² Princes are hung up by their hands; no respect is shown to the elders.

¹³ Young men are compelled to grind at the mill; and boys stagger under loads of wood.

¹⁴ The old men have quit the city gate, the young men their music.

¹⁵ The joy of our hearts has ceased; our dancing has been turned to mourning.

¹⁶ The crown has fallen from our head; woe to us, for we have sinned!

¹⁷ For this our heart has become sick, for these things our eyes have grown dim,

¹⁸ for Mount Zion which lies desolate; jackals prowl over it.

¹⁹ But you, O LORD, reign for ever; your throne endures to all generations.

²⁰ Why do you forget us for ever, why do you so long forsake us?

²¹ Restore us to yourself, O LORD, that we may be restored! Renew our days as of old!

²² Or have you utterly rejected us? Are you exceedingly angry with us?

B How long, O LORD? Will you forget me for ever? How long will you hide your face from me? How long must I bear pain in my soul, and have sorrow in my heart all the day? How long shall my enemy be exalted over me? Consider and answer me, O LORD my God; lighten my eyes, lest I sleep the sleep of death.

Ps 13:1–3

▶ These questions at the end of Lam remain unanswered, yet those who pray trust that God's wrath is limited and will pass (3:22–33).

The Book of Baruch, like Lamentations, is thematically related to Jeremiah, because the author, Baruch (the name means "blessed"), is a confidant of that prophet (Jer 32:12) and, most importantly, takes the Exile as his theme.

BARUCH

3 ³⁵ This is our God; no other can be compared to him!
³⁶ He found the whole way to knowledge, and gave her to Jacob his servant and to Israel whom he loved.

³⁷ Afterward she appeared upon earth and lived among men.

4 ¹ She is the book of the commandments of God, and the law that endures for ever. All who hold her fast will live, and those who forsake her will die.

² Turn, O Jacob, and take her; walk toward the shining of her light.

³ Do not give your glory to another, or your advantages to an alien people.

⁴ Happy are we, O Israel, for we know what is pleasing to God.

👤 Be assured: heaven and earth shall pass away before the Lord lets you out of his sight, if you remain obedient or else have resolved to be obedient.

FRANCIS DE SALES

▶ Knowing what pleases people close to you helps to foster a successful relationship. Similarly, the Torah shows how we can please God.

Ezekiel

The name Ezekiel means "may God strengthen". Like Jeremiah, this book, too, is profoundly marked by the experience of the Babylonian Exile.

Unlike Jeremiah, the prophet Ezekiel himself is in exile. God's messages in the first part of the book mainly explain why Israel had to experience this catastrophe (Ezek 1–24); in the latter part, they present the prospect of a redemptive future (Ezek 33–48), especially in the vision of a new temple in Jerusalem (Ezek 40–48).

Ezekiel strives for an interior transformation of the individual and of the community. He emphasizes personal responsibility (Ezek 18). With the gift of a new heart and a new spirit (Ezek 36), God makes it possible for his people to become pure again and to be honestly united with him. The dead bones brought to life (Ezek 37) are an image that communicates hope: dejection and small numbers are transformed by God into new life.

The book is remarkable for its profuse visions, which lend it a sometimes mystical character. In the New Testament, the Revelation of John often harks back to Ezekiel's colorful imagery.

The vision of God's throne (Ezek 1)

▶ Ezekiel himself lives among the exiles. His message to them is credible because he shares their fate. The "thirtieth year" probably refers to Ezekiel's age; in that year he would have been permitted to begin his service as a priest (Num 4:3).

▶ King Jehoiachin was carried off in 597 B.C. (2 Kings 24:15); Ezekiel's call is therefore dated 593 B.C. The river Chebar is a tributary of the Euphrates in modern-day Iraq.

▶ In early Christianity, these four animals (↗ also Rev 4:7) became symbols of the four evangelists: the man stands for Matthew, the lion for Mark, the ox for Luke, and the eagle for John.

1 ¹ In the thirtieth year, in the fourth month, on the fifth day of the month, as I was among the exiles by the river Che'bar, the heavens were opened, and I saw visions of God. ² On the fifth day of the month (it was the fifth year of the exile of King Jehoi'achin), ³ the word of the LORD came to Ezek'iel the priest, the son of Buzi, in the land of the Chalde'ans by the river Che'bar; and the hand of the LORD was upon him there.

⁴ As I looked, behold, a stormy wind came out of the north, and a great cloud, with brightness round about it, and fire flashing forth continually, and in the midst of the fire, as it were gleaming bronze. ⁵ And from the midst of it came the likeness of four living creatures. And this was their appearance: they had the form of men, ⁶ but each had four faces, and each of them had four wings. ⁷ Their legs were straight, and the soles of their feet were like the sole of a calf's foot; and they sparkled like burnished bronze. ⁸ Under their wings on their four sides they had human hands. And the four had their faces and their wings thus: ⁹ their wings touched one another; they went every one straight forward, without turning as they went. ¹⁰ As for the likeness of their faces, each had the face of a man in front; the four had the face of a lion on the right side, the four had the

face of an ox on the left side, and the four had the face of an eagle at the back. ¹¹ Such were their faces. And their wings were spread out above; each creature had two wings, each of which touched the wing of another, while two covered their bodies. ¹² And each went straight forward; wherever the spirit would go, they went, without turning as they went. ¹³ In the midst of the living creatures there was something that looked like burning coals of fire, like torches moving back and forth among the living creatures; and the fire was bright, and out of the fire went forth lightning. ¹⁴ And the living creatures darted back and forth, like a flash of lightning.

¹⁵ Now as I looked at the living creatures, I saw a wheel upon the earth beside the living creatures, one for each of the four of them. ¹⁶ As for the appearance of the wheels and their construction: their appearance was like the gleaming of a chrysolite; and the four had the same likeness, their construction being as it were a wheel within a wheel. ¹⁷ When they went, they went in any of their four directions without turning as they went. ¹⁸ The four wheels had rims and they had spokes;and their rims were full of eyes round about. ¹⁹ And when the living creatures went, the wheels went beside them; and when the living creatures rose from the earth, the wheels rose. ²⁰ Wherever the spirit would go, they went, and the wheels rose along with them; for the spirit of the living creatures was in the wheels....

❞ A word is worth a thousand pictures.

JOSEPH FESSIO, S.J. (b. 1941), American Jesuit priest and founder and editor of Ignatius Press

▶ The many eyes (v. 18) symbolize watchful perception: they, along with the moving spirit and the light, are signs of the divine presence.

²² Over the heads of the living creatures there was the likeness of a firmament, shining like crystal, spread out above their heads. ²³ And under the firmament their wings were stretched out straight, one toward another; and each creature had two wings covering its body. ²⁴ And when they went, I heard the sound of their wings like the sound of many waters, like the thunder of the Almighty, a sound of tumult like the sound of a host; when they stood still, they let down their wings. ²⁵ And there came a voice from above the firmament over their heads; when they stood still, they let down their wings.

²⁶ And above the firmament over their heads there was the likeness of a throne, in appearance like sapphire; and seated above the likeness of a throne was a likeness as it were of a human form.

▶ Water, jewels, gold: experiences of power and beauty again point to God.

Ezekiel depicts God's "glory" in various images. The rainbow recalls God's covenant with Noah and all creation (Gen 9:13). Ezek 1 shows God as fascinating, moving, and "human".

Overcome by God's glory (Ezek 1:27–28)

²⁷ And upward from what had the appearance of his loins I saw as it were gleaming bronze, like the appearance of fire enclosed round about; and downward from what had the appearance of his loins I saw as it were the appearance of fire, and there was brightness

round about him. ²⁸ Like the appearance of the bow that is in the cloud on the day of rain, so was the appearance of the brightness round about.

Such was the appearance of the likeness of the glory of the LORD. And when I saw it, I fell upon my face, and I heard the voice of one speaking.

Ezekiel's call (Ezek 2–3)

2 ¹ And he said to me, "Son of man, stand upon your feet, and I will speak with you." ² And when he spoke to me, the Spirit entered into me and set me upon my feet; and I heard him speaking to me. ³ And he said to me, "Son of man, I send you to the sons of Israel, to a nation of rebels, who have rebelled against me; they and their fathers have transgressed against me to this very day. ⁴ The people also are impudent and stubborn: I send you to them; and you shall say to them, 'Thus says the Lord GOD.' ⁵ And whether they hear or refuse to hear (for they are a rebellious house) they will know that there has been a prophet among them. ⁶ And you, son of man, be not afraid of them, nor be afraid of their words, though briers and thorns are with you and you sit upon scorpions; be not afraid of their words, nor be dismayed at their looks, for they are a rebellious

▶ This intense experience of God overcomes Ezekiel. God wants not to frighten him, however, but rather to encounter him as a self-confident and honest man.

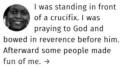

I was standing in front of a crucifix. I was praying to God and bowed in reverence before him. Afterward some people made fun of me. →

→ At first I did not know what to say, but then I defended my faith and my way of praying. Through my faith, I had the strength and the courage to confront them, even though they did not want to hear it.

VALENTINE

The Book of Ezekiel is bitter and sweet at the same time, full of painful contents, and yet in Ezekiel's mouth its message becomes "sweet as honey" (3:3). Facing up to bitter realizations is the fastest way to regain a zest for life.

99 A book must be the ax for the frozen sea within us.

FRANZ KAFKA

house. ⁷ And you shall speak my words to them, whether they hear or refuse to hear; for they are a rebellious house.

⁸ "But you, son of man, hear what I say to you; be not rebellious like that rebellious house; open your mouth, and eat what I give you." ⁹ And when I looked, behold, a hand was stretched out to me, and behold, a written scroll was in it; ¹⁰ and he spread it before me; and it had writing on the front and on the back, and there were written on it words of lamentation and mourning and woe.

3 ¹ And he said to me, "Son of man, eat what is offered to you; eat this scroll, and go, speak to the house of Israel." ² So I opened my mouth, and he gave me the scroll to eat. ³ And he said to me, "Son of man, eat this scroll that I give you and fill your stomach with it." Then I ate it; and it was in my mouth as sweet as honey....

¹² Then the Spirit lifted me up, and as the glory of the LORD arose from its place, I heard behind me the sound of a great earthquake; ¹³ it was the sound of the wings of the living creatures as they touched one another, and the sound of the wheels beside them, that sounded like a great earthquake. ¹⁴ The Spirit lifted me up and took me away, and I went in bitterness in the heat of my spirit, the hand of the LORD being strong upon me; ¹⁵ and I came to the exiles

at Tela'bib, who dwelt by the river Che'bar. And I sat there overwhelmed among them seven days....

Ezekiel is "overwhelmed" along with the exiles (Ezek 3:15) because their forced deportation was a traumatic experience. The Exile also prompted intense reflection about the question of guilt. Must we suffer because of the guilt of our forefathers? Ezekiel denies this.

▶ Prophet = hero? Ezekiel runs the risk of sinking into melancholy and depression (3:15 and other passages).

99 I do not believe in collective guilt. The guilty are guilty, but the children of the guilty are children.

ELIE WIESEL (1928–2016), Holocaust survivor

Justice and the opportunity to repent (Ezek 18)

18 ¹ The word of the LORD came to me again: ² "What do you mean by repeating this proverb concerning the land of Israel, 'The fathers have eaten sour grapes, and the children's teeth are set on edge'? ³ As I live, says the Lord GOD, this proverb shall no more be used by you in Israel. ⁴ Behold, all souls are mine; the soul of the father as well as the soul of the son is mine: the soul that sins shall die.

⁵ "If a man is righteous and does what is lawful and right—⁶ if he does not eat upon the mountains or lift up his eyes to the idols of the house of Israel, does not defile his neighbor's wife or approach a woman in her time of impurity, ⁷ does not oppress any one, but restores to the debtor his pledge, commits no robbery, gives his bread

to the hungry and covers the naked with a garment, ⁸ does not lend at interest or take any increase, withholds his hand from iniquity, executes true justice between man and man, ⁹ walks in my statutes, and is careful to observe my ordinances—he is righteous, he shall surely live, says the Lord GOD....

²¹ "But if a wicked man turns away from all his sins which he has committed and keeps all my statutes and does what is lawful and right, he shall surely live; he shall not die. ²² None of the transgressions which he has committed shall be remembered against him; for the righteousness which he has done he shall live. ²³ Have I any pleasure in the death of the wicked, says the Lord GOD, and not rather that he should turn from his way and live? ²⁴ But when a righteous man turns away from his righteousness and commits iniquity and does the same abominable things that the wicked man does, shall he live? None of the righteous deeds which he has done shall be remembered; for the treachery of which he is guilty and the sin he has committed, he shall die.

²⁵ "Yet you say, 'The way of the LORD is not just.' Hear now, O house of Israel: Is my way not just? Is it not your ways that are not just? ²⁶ When a righteous man turns away from his righteousness and

> **B** Is not this the fast that I choose: to loose the bonds of wickedness, to undo the thongs of the yoke, to let the oppressed go free, and to break every yoke? Is it not to share your bread with the hungry, and bring the homeless poor into your house; when you see the naked, to cover him, and not to hide yourself from your own flesh?
>
> Is 58:6–7

> I pray for the brother who wounded me and whom I have honestly forgiven.
>
> **POPE JOHN PAUL II** two days after the assassination attempt in May 1981, about Ali Agca, who came within a hair's breadth of killing him.

commits iniquity, he shall die for it; for the iniquity which he has committed he shall die. ²⁷ Again, when a wicked man turns away from the wickedness he has committed and does what is lawful and right, he shall save his life. ²⁸ Because he considered and turned away from all the transgressions which he had committed, he shall surely live, he shall not die....

> **B** If we say we have no sin, we deceive ourselves, and the truth is not in us.
>
> 1 Jn 1,8

Not a heart of stone, but a heart of flesh (Ezek 36)

36 ²² "Therefore say to the house of Israel, Thus says the Lord GOD: It is not for your sake, O house of Israel, that I am about to act, but for the sake of my holy name, which you have profaned among the nations to which you came. ²³ And I will vindicate the holiness of my great name, which has been profaned among the nations, and which you have profaned among them; and the nations will know that I am the LORD, says the Lord GOD, when through you I vindicate my holiness before their eyes. ²⁴ For I will take you from the nations, and gather you from all the countries, and bring you into your own land. ²⁵ I will sprinkle clean water upon you, and you shall be clean from all your uncleannesses, and from all your idols I will cleanse you. ²⁶ A new heart I will give you, and a new spirit I will put within you; and I will take out of your flesh the heart of stone

> ▶ God's holy name is profaned when Israel disobeys his commandments (↗ Lev 22:31–32). Israel has not glorified God—in contrast, God will treat his people with special generosity in order to make his name known.

> **B** Create in me a clean heart, O God, and put a new and right spirit within me.
>
> Ps 51:10

> Come, Holy Spirit, fill the hearts of your faithful and enkindle in them the fire of your love. Send forth your spirit and they shall be created, and you shall renew the face of the earth.

Ancient prayer to the Holy Spirit

> In God there is no hunger that needs to be filled, only plenteousness that desires to give.

C. S. LEWIS

and give you a heart of flesh. [27] And I will put my spirit within you, and cause you to walk in my statutes and be careful to observe my ordinances. [28] You shall dwell in the land which I gave to your fathers; and you shall be my people, and I will be your God. [29] And I will deliver you from all your uncleannesses; and I will summon the grain and make it abundant and lay no famine upon you. [30] I will make the fruit of the tree and the increase of the field abundant, that you may never again suffer the disgrace of famine among the nations....

New spirit for dead bones (Ezek 37)

37 [1] The hand of the LORD was upon me, and he brought me out by the Spirit of the LORD, and set me down in the midst of the valley; it was full of bones. [2] And he led me round among them; and behold, there were very many upon the valley; and behold, they were very dry. [3] And he said to me, "Son of man, can these bones live?" And I answered, "O Lord GOD, you know." [4] Again he said to me, "Prophesy to these bones, and say to them, O dry bones, hear the word of the LORD. [5] Thus says the Lord GOD to these bones: Behold,

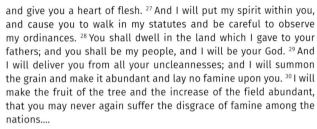

> See, this is the Church! Today, please take up the Bible at home. Open it at Chapter 37 of the Prophet Ezekiel, do not forget, and read this, it is beautiful. This is the Church, she is a masterpiece, the masterpiece of the Spirit who instills in each one the new life of the Risen One.

POPE FRANCIS, October 22, 2014

> What "graves" are there in my life from which God should bring me out?
>
> What are my "dead spots" that God wants to enliven?
>
> How can I allow myself to be "inspired" by God?

I will cause breath to enter you, and you shall live. [6] And I will lay sinews upon you, and will cause flesh to come upon you, and cover you with skin, and put breath in you, and you shall live; and you shall know that I am the LORD."

[7] So I prophesied as I was commanded; and as I prophesied, there was a noise, and behold, a rattling, and the bones came together, bone to its bone. [8] And as I looked, there were sinews on them, and flesh had come upon them, and skin had covered them; but there was no spirit in them. [9] Then he said to me, "Prophesy to the spirit, prophesy, son of man, and say to the spirit, Thus says the Lord GOD: Come from the four winds, O spirit, and breathe upon these slain, that they may live." [10] So I prophesied as he commanded me, and the spirit came into them, and they lived, and stood upon their feet, an exceedingly great host.

New hope for Israel

[11] Then he said to me, "Son of man, these bones are the whole house of Israel. Behold, they say, 'Our bones are dried up, and our hope is lost; we are clean cut off.' [12] Therefore prophesy, and say to them, Thus says the Lord GOD: Behold, I will open your graves, and raise you from your graves, O my people; and I will bring you home into the land of Israel. [13] And you shall know that I am the LORD,

when I open your graves, and raise you from your graves, O my people. [14] And I will put my Spirit within you, and you shall live, and I
will place you in your own land; then you shall know that I, the LORD,
have spoken, and I have done it, says the LORD."

Vision of the new Temple (Ezek 47)

47 [1] Then he brought me back to the door of the temple; and
behold, water was issuing from below the threshold of the
temple toward the east (for the temple faced east); and the water
was flowing down from below the right side of the threshold of the
temple, south of the altar. [2] Then he brought me out by way of the
north gate, and led me round on the outside to the outer gate, that
faces toward the east; and the water was coming out on the right
side.

[3] Going on eastward with a line in his hand, the man measured a
thousand cubits, and then led me through the water; and it was an-
kle-deep. [4] Again he measured a thousand, and led me through the
water; and it was knee-deep. Again he measured a thousand, and
led me through the water; and it was up to the loins. [5] Again he measured a thousand, and it was a river that I could not pass through,
for the water had risen; it was deep enough to swim in, a river that
could not be passed through.

▶ The region to the east of
the Temple in Jerusalem is the
Judean desert; through the new
spring it is transformed into an
orchard (v. 2).

▶ A little stream flowing
through a hot, arid environment usually dries up after a
while. God's "stream of grace",
in contrast, becomes bigger
and bigger and unstoppable,
even in the desert.

New life on the river

[6] And he said to me, "Son of man, have you seen this?"
Then he led me back along the bank of the river. [7] As I went back,
I saw upon the bank of the river very many trees on the one side
and on the other. [8] And he said to me, "This water flows toward the
eastern region and goes down into the Ar'abah; and when it enters
the stagnant waters of the sea, the water will become fresh. [9] And
wherever the river goes every living creature which swarms will live,
and there will be very many fish; for this water goes there, that the
waters of the sea may become fresh; so everything will live where
the river goes.

[10] Fishermen will stand beside the sea; from En-ge'di to En-eg'laim
it will be a place for the spreading of nets; its fish will be of very
many kinds, like the fish of the Great Sea.

[11] But its swamps and marshes will not become fresh; they are to
be left for salt. [12] And on the banks, on both sides of the river, there
will grow all kinds of trees for food. Their leaves will not wither nor
their fruit fail, but they will bear fresh fruit every month, because
the water for them flows from the sanctuary. Their fruit will be for
food, and their leaves for healing."

Everyone who is sup-
posed to bear fruit must
experience the desert.

CHARLES DE FOUCAULD

▶ The "stagnant waters of the
sea" are the Dead Sea, at the
deepest point on earth (416
meters [1365 feet] below sea
level). No fish can survive in it.

▶ The "Great Sea" is the Mediterranean—which at that time
was full of fish.

Y → 311
What are the fruits of the Holy
Spirit?

THE BOOK OF

Daniel

The events related in the Book of Daniel take place in the Babylonian and Persian period. Daniel, like Ezekiel, finds himself among the exiles. The book was completed much later, however. Like Ezekiel, Daniel has visions that apparently refer to a distant future, to the end of the world, yet in fact also interpret history up to the present day of the original readers.

The Book of Daniel was composed partly in Hebrew and partly in Aramaic; moreover the Greek translation has supplemented it with several passages (e.g., Dan 13–14). In the New Testament, the Book of Revelation continues this genre of apocalyptic literature; it is heavily influenced by Daniel.

God strengthens the body and the soul (Dan 1:1–20)

1 ¹ In the third year of the reign of Jehoi'akim king of Judah, Nebuchadnez'zar king of Babylon came to Jerusalem and besieged it. ² And the Lord gave Jehoi'akim king of Judah into his hand, with some of the vessels of the house of God; and he brought them to the land of Shi'nar, to the house of his god, and placed the vessels in the treasury of his god. ³ Then the king commanded Ash'penaz, his chief eunuch, to bring some of the people of Israel, both of the royal family and of the nobility, ⁴ youths without blemish, handsome and skilful in all wisdom, endowed with knowledge, understanding learning, and competent to serve in the king's palace, and to teach them the letters and language of the Chalde'ans. ⁵ The king assigned them a daily portion of the rich food which the king ate, and of the wine which he drank. They were to be educated for three years, and at the end of that time they were to stand before the king. ⁶ Among these were Daniel, Hanani'ah, Mish'a-el, and Azari'ah of the tribe of Judah. ⁷ And the chief of the eunuchs gave them names: Daniel he called Belteshaz'zar, Hanani'ah he called Shad'rach, Mish'a-el he called Me'shach, and Azari'ah he called Abed'nego.

⁸ But Daniel resolved that he would not defile himself with the king's rich food, or with the wine which he drank; therefore he asked

> ❝❞ Never allow yourself to be misled into remaining silent when your conscience orders you to speak. And never belong to the army of thousands upon thousands who have "fear of the world".
>
> The German author **ERNST WIECHERT** (b. 1887) was taken away by the Nazis to the concentration camp in Buchenwald. He survived and died in 1950 in Switzerland.

▶ This account makes it clear that some Jews in the Babylonian Exile studied the literature and the science of the Babylonians. Many passages in the Old Testament try to show that the God of Israel surpasses the religion and knowledge of the Babylonians (e.g., the creation account in Gen 1).

A vegetarian or even veg-an way of life in the Bible? Who would have thought? The chief of the eunuchs gave Daniel and his companions the Ten-Day Test. And see: the guys looked great afterward.

▶ The Torah contains many rules stating which foods are pure and which are impure (e.g., Deut 14). In the New Testament, these rules are abolished for Christians (Mk 7:19; Acts 10:9–16).

I would not believe if I did not realize that it is reasonable to believe.

THOMAS AQUINAS

the chief of the eunuchs to allow him not to defile himself. 9And God gave Daniel favor and compassion in the sight of the chief of the eunuchs; 10and the chief of the eunuchs said to Daniel, "I fear lest my lord the king, who appointed your food and your drink, should see that you were in poorer condition than the youths who are of your own age. So you would endanger my head with the king." 11Then Daniel said to the steward whom the chief of the eunuchs had appointed over Daniel, Hanani'ah, Mish'a-el, and Azari'ah; 12"Test your servants for ten days; let us be given vegetables to eat and water to drink. 13Then let our appearance and the appearance of the youths who eat the king's rich food be observed by you, and according to what you see deal with your servants." 14So he listened to them in this matter, and tested them for ten days. 15At the end of ten days it was seen that they were better in appearance and fatter in flesh than all the youths who ate the king's rich food. 16So the steward took away their rich food and the wine they were to drink, and gave them vegetables.

17As for these four youths, God gave them learning and skill in all letters and wisdom; and Daniel had understanding in all visions and dreams. 18At the end of the time, when the king had commanded

Of course we couldn't possibly convince anyone by ourselves. We're earthen vessels. ... We're not the ones doing the convincing. God is.

MARY BETH BONACCI, popular Catholic author and speaker

that they should be brought in, the chief of the eunuchs brought them in before Nebuchadnez'zar. 19And the king spoke with them, and among them all none was found like Daniel, Hanani'ah, Mish'a-el, and Azari'ah; therefore they stood before the king. 20And in every matter of wisdom and understanding concerning which the king inquired of them, he found them ten times better than all the magicians and enchanters that were in all his kingdom.

King Nebuchadnezzar tries to force the three young men to worship the Babylonian gods.

They say that we kings are God's images on earth. So I looked at myself in the mirror. That is not very flattering to the dear Lord.

FREDERICK II, THE GREAT (1712–1786), King of Prussia

We had reached the bottom. It is not possible to sink lower than this; no human condition is more miserable than this, nor could it →

God rescues them from the fire (Dan 3:14–24)

3 14Nebuchadnez'zar said to them, "Is it true, O Shad'rach, Me'shach, and Abed'nego, that you do not serve my gods or worship the golden image which I have set up? 15Now if you are ready when you hear the sound of the horn, pipe, lyre, trigon, harp, bagpipe, and every kind of music, to fall down and worship the image which I have made, well and good; but if you do not worship, you shall immediately be cast into a burning fiery furnace; and who is the god that will deliver you out of my hands?"

16Shad'rach, Me'shach, and Abed'nego answered the king, "O Nebuchadnez'zar, we have no need to answer you in this matter. 17If it be so, our God whom we serve is able to deliver us from the burning fiery furnace; and he will deliver us out of your hand, O king. ¹⁸ But if not, be it known to you, O king, that we will not serve your gods or worship the golden image which you have set up."

¹⁹ Then Nebuchadnez'zar was full of fury, and the expression of his face was changed against Shad'rach, Me'shach, and Abed'nego. He ordered the furnace heated seven times more than it was accustomed to be heated. ²⁰ And he ordered certain mighty men of his army to bind Shad'rach, Me'shach, and Abed'nego, and to cast them into the burning fiery furnace. ²¹ Then these men were bound in their mantles, their tunics, their hats, and their other garments, and they were cast into the burning fiery furnace. ²² Because the king's order was strict and the furnace very hot, the flame of the fire slew those men who took up Shad'rach, Me'shach, and Abed'nego. ²³ And these three men, Shad'rach, Me'shach, and Abed'nego, fell bound into the burning fiery furnace.

²⁴ And they walked about in the midst of the flames, singing hymns to God and blessing the Lord.

The monsters and the new king (Dan 7:1–14)

7 ¹ In the first year of Belshaz'zar king of Babylon, Daniel had a dream and visions of his head as he lay in his bed. Then he wrote down the dream, and told the sum of the matter. ² Daniel said, "I saw in my vision by night, and behold, the four winds of

→ conceivably be so. Nothing belongs to us any more; they have taken away our clothes, our shoes, even our hair; if we speak, they will not listen to us, and if they listen, they will not understand. They will even take away our name: and if we want to keep it, we will have to find ourselves the strength to do so, to manage somehow so that behind the name something of us, of us as we were, still remains. ...
PRIMO LEVI (1918–1987) survivor of Auschwitz

▶ "Daniel" means "God [El] has done justice for me"—which comes true in the miracle of the fiery furnace.

B Then the three, as with one mouth, praised and glorified and blessed God in the furnace, saying:
"Blessed are you, O LORD, God of our fathers, and to be praised and highly exalted for ever. And blessed is your glorious, holy name and to be highly praised and highly exalted for ever; Blessed are you in the temple of your holy glory and to be extolled and highly glorified for ever.
Blessed are you, who sit upon cherubim and look upon the deeps, and to be praised and highly exalted for ever.
Blessed are you upon the throne of your kingdom and to be extolled and highly exalted for ever.
Blessed are you in the firmament of heaven and to be sung and glorified for ever.
Bless the LORD, all works of the LORD, sing praise to him and highly exalt him for ever."

Dan 3:28–35, The hymn of the three young men in the fiery furnace

▶ Belshazzar, the last King of Babylon, was murdered in 539 B.C. (↗ Dan 5:30).

▶ Monsters have fascinated people for millennia—and to this day. In this vision, they stand for tyrannical kings/kingdoms. The four beasts are often thought to symbolize the Assyrian, the Babylonian, Persian, and Greek empires.

▶ Horns (vv. 7–8) in the Bible stand for power—and here symbolically, too, for rulers. The "fourth" horn probably refers to Antiochus IV Epiphanes, who persecuted pious Jews with particular severity and in 167 B.C. profaned the Temple in Jerusalem.

heaven were stirring up the great sea. ³ And four great beasts came up out of the sea, different from one another. ⁴ The first was like a lion and had eagles' wings. Then as I looked its wings were plucked off, and it was lifted up from the ground and made to stand upon two feet like a man; and the mind of a man was given to it. ⁵ And behold, another beast, a second one, like a bear. It was raised up on one side; it had three ribs in its mouth between its teeth; and it was told, 'Arise, devour much flesh.' ⁶ After this I looked, and behold, another, like a leopard, with four wings of a bird on its back; and the beast had four heads; and dominion was given to it. ⁷ After this I saw in the night visions, and behold, a fourth beast, terrifying and dreadful and exceedingly strong; and it had great iron teeth; it devoured and broke in pieces, and stamped the residue with its feet. It was different from all the beasts that were before it; and it had ten horns. ⁸ I considered the horns, and behold, there came up among them another horn, a little one, before which three of the first horns were plucked up by the roots; and behold, in this horn were eyes like the eyes of a man, and a mouth speaking great things.

⁹ As I looked, thrones were placed
and one that was ancient of days took his seat;
his clothing was white as snow, and the hair of his head like pure wool;

💡 Nowhere in the whole Bible except here is God depicted as an "old man".

🅱 Then they will see the Son of man coming in clouds with great power and glory.

Mk 13:26

his throne was fiery flames,
its wheels were burning fire.
¹⁰ A stream of fire issued
and came forth from before him;
a thousand thousands served him,
and ten thousand times ten thousand stood before him;
the court sat in judgment, and the books were opened.
¹¹ I looked then because of the sound of the great words which the horn was speaking. And as I looked, the beast was slain, and its body destroyed and given over to be burned with fire. ¹² As for the rest of the beasts, their dominion was taken away, but their lives were prolonged for a season and a time. ¹³ I saw in the night visions,
and behold, with the clouds of heaven
there came one like a son of man,
and he came to the Ancient of Days and was presented before him.
¹⁴ And to him was given dominion and glory and kingdom,
that all peoples, nations, and languages should serve him;
his dominion is an everlasting dominion, which shall not pass away,
and his kingdom one that shall not be destroyed.

The overwhelming apparition (Dan 10:4–19)

10 ⁴ On the twenty-fourth day of the first month, as I was standing on the bank of the great river, that is, the Tigris, ⁵ I lifted up my eyes and looked, and behold, a man clothed in linen, whose loins were belted with gold of U'phaz. ⁶ His body was like beryl, his face like the appearance of lightning, his eyes like flaming torches, his arms and legs like the gleam of burnished bronze, and the sound of his words like the noise of a multitude. ⁷ And I, Daniel, alone saw the vision, for the men who were with me did not see the vision, but a great trembling fell upon them, and they fled to hide themselves. ⁸ So I was left alone and saw this great vision, and no strength was left in me; my radiant appearance was fearfully changed, and I retained no strength. ⁹ Then I heard the sound of his words; and when I heard the sound of his words, I fell on my face in a deep sleep with my face to the ground.

¹⁰ And behold, a hand touched me and set me trembling on my hands and knees. ¹¹ And he said to me, "O Daniel, man greatly beloved, give heed to the words that I speak to you, and stand upright, for now I have been sent to you." While he was speaking this word to me, I stood up trembling. ¹² Then he said to me, "Fear not, Daniel, for

▶ The Tigris is the second large river flowing through the "land of two rivers" in modern-day Iraq.

💡 What happens when someone encounters the living God? The historian of religion Rudolf Otto (1869–1937) says that one meets the *mysterium tremendum* (the awe-inspiring mystery); at the same time, however, one may experience God as the *mysterium fascinans* (fascinating mystery).

▶ Whereas Ezekiel was simply put back on his feet (→ Ezek 2:2), the divine messenger helps Daniel to pick himself up, encouragingly addresses him as "man greatly beloved", and gives him the strength to stand up by himself.

from the first day that you set your mind to understand and humbled yourself before your God, your words have been heard, and I have come because of your words. ¹³ The prince of the kingdom of Persia withstood me twenty-one days; but Michael, one of the chief princes, came to help me, so I left him there with the prince of the kingdom of Persia ¹⁴ and came to make you understand what is to befall your people in the latter days. For the vision is for days yet to come."

¹⁵ When he had spoken to me according to these words, I turned my face toward the ground and was speechless. ¹⁶ And behold, one in the likeness of the sons of men touched my lips; then I opened my mouth and spoke. I said to him who stood before me, "O my Lord, by reason of the vision pains have come upon me, and I retain no strength. ¹⁷ How can my Lord's servant talk with my Lord? For now no strength remains in me, and no breath is left in me."

¹⁸ Again one having the appearance of a man touched me and strengthened me. ¹⁹ And he said, "O man greatly beloved, fear not, peace be with you; be strong and of good courage." And when he spoke to me, I was strengthened and said, "Let my Lord speak, for you have strengthened me."

▶ "Michael" means "who (mi) is like (ka) God (El)?" This angel stands up for God's uniqueness and has the task of protecting the people of Israel (Dan 12:1). On Michael's battle with the dragon, see Rev 12:7.

Hosea Joel
Amos Obadiah
Jonah Micah
Nahum Habakkuk
Zephaniah Haggai
Zechariah Malachi

These twelve prophets are called "minor" only because they are considerably shorter than the three "major" prophets (Isaiah, Jeremiah, and Ezekiel). They are no less significant, however. In powerful language, they testify to their particular experiences with God. The oldest of these prophets, such as Amos, Hosea, and Micah, appeared beginning in the eighth century B.C.

HOSEA

The name Hosea means "He (God) helped." God instructs him to marry a prostitute (Hos 1–3) in order to make clear God's relationship with Israel and the people's infidelity and sin. Yet God grants a way out.

▶ God speaks here about his close relationship with the people during the Exodus. Matthew applies this passage ("I called my son out of Egypt") to Jesus at his return with Mary and Joseph from Egypt (Mt 2:15).

▶ God loves Israel as much as human parents care for their children (vv. 3–4), although the people are unfaithful (v. 2).

▶ To return to Egypt means, for Israel, to become slaves again. This time the Assyrians are the rulers over Israel.

My heart recoils within me (Hos 11)

11 ¹ When Israel was a child, I loved him, and out of Egypt I called my son.

² The more I called them, the more they went from me; they kept sacrificing to the Ba'als, and burning incense to idols.

³ Yet it was I who taught E'phraim to walk, I took them up in my arms;
  but they did not know that I healed them.

⁴ I led them with cords of compassion, with the bands of love, and I became to them as one who raises an infant to his cheeks, and I bent down to them and fed them.

⁵ They shall return to the land of Egypt, and Assyria shall be their king, because they have refused to return to me.

⁶ The sword shall rage against their cities, consume the bars of their gates, and devour them in their fortresses.

⁷ My people are bent on turning away from me; so they are appointed to the yoke, and none shall remove it.

▶ The beginning of v. 7 reads literally: "My people are hung up in their alienation from me." This describes metaphorically how unreliable Israel has become because it has rejected its God.

▶ God is full of compassion for his people and ready to have mercy.

⁸ How can I give you up, O E'phraim! How can I hand you over, O Israel! How can I make you like Admah! How can I treat you like Zeboi'im! My heart recoils within me, my compassion grows warm and tender.

⁹ I will not execute my fierce anger, I will not again destroy E'phraim; for I am God and not man, the Holy One in your midst, and I will not come to destroy.

JOEL

Joel means "Jo is El", whereby Jo is an abbreviation of the biblical name for God YHWH and El means "God". God's judgment on the day of YHWH (e.g. 1:15; 2:1) shapes the message of this little book. Yet because God's people sincerely convert and turn to him, he has pity on them (Joel 2:12–21) and grants them a special blessing:

▶ "Spirit" means that which moves and animates God interiorly: he grants it to everyone abundantly, especially to young people and the elderly and even to those who are dependent (v. 28).

The outpouring of the Spirit (Joel 2:28–32)

2 ²⁸ "And it shall come to pass afterward, that I will pour out my spirit on all flesh; your sons and your daughters shall prophesy, your old men shall dream dreams, and your young men shall see visions.

²⁹ Even upon the menservants and maidservants in those days, I will pour out my spirit.

³⁰ "And I will give signs in the heavens and on the earth, blood and fire and columns of smoke. ³¹ The sun shall be turned to darkness, and the moon to blood, before the great and awesome day of the LORD comes. ³² And it shall come to pass that all who call upon the name of the LORD shall be delivered; for in Mount Zion and in Jerusalem there shall be those who escape, as the LORD has said, and among the survivors shall be those whom the LORD calls.

AMOS

Amos was actually a shepherd and came from the town of Tekoa, near Bethlehem. "The LORD took me from following the flock, and the LORD said to me, 'Go, prophesy to my people Israel'" (Amos 7:15). Amos stood up especially against social injustice and false piety. His prophecies are among the oldest in the Bible (starting around 765 B.C.).

A prophetic sermon exhorting the people (Amos 5)

5 ⁴ For thus says the LORD to the house of Israel: "Seek me and live; ⁵ but do not seek Bethel, and do not enter into Gilgal or cross over to Be'er-she'ba; for Gilgal shall surely go into exile, and Bethel shall come to nothing."

B The water that I shall give him will become in him a spring of water welling up to eternal life.

Jn 4:14, Jesus speaks to the Samaritan woman at Jacob's well

⁶ Seek the LORD and live, lest he break out like fire in the house of Joseph, and it devour, with none to quench it for Bethel,

⁷ O you who turn justice to wormwood, and cast down righteousness to the earth! ...

¹⁰ They hate him who reproves in the gate, and they abhor him who speaks the truth.

¹¹ Therefore because you trample upon the poor and take from him exactions of wheat, you have built houses of hewn stone, but you shall not dwell in them; you have planted pleasant vineyards, but you shall not drink their wine. ...

¹⁸ Woe to you who desire the day of the LORD! Why would you have the day of the LORD? It is darkness, and not light;

¹⁹ as if a man fled from a lion, and a bear met him; or went into the house and leaned with his hand against the wall, and a serpent bit him.

²⁰ Is not the day of the LORD darkness, and not light, and gloom with no brightness in it?

²¹ "I hate, I despise your feasts, and I take no delight in your solemn assemblies.

²² Even though you offer me your burnt offerings and cereal offerings, I will not accept them, and the peace offerings of your fatted beasts I will not look upon.

▶ Bethel, Gilgal, and Beersheba were famous pilgrimage places. Amos challenges the people to seek God himself diligently instead of those places.

▶ Amos attacks the wealthy who abuse their power and oppress the poor. They should not be able to enjoy their economic success.

❞ A sharing manner of life is not optional. ... Sheer justice demands equitable participation.

THOMAS DUBAY, S.M.

▶ To all external appearances pious, many hypocrites hope for the "day of the Lord" (see above in the Book of Joel). Amos destroys their illusions— that day will be bad for them.

▶ This critique of sacrifices and worship services is among the most severe in the Bible. God despises piety without justice!

²³ Take away from me the noise of your songs; to the melody of your harps I will not listen.
²⁴ But let justice roll down like waters, and righteousness like an ever-flowing stream.

OBADIAH

Obadiah, the shortest book in the Old Testament, deals with the kindred nation "Edom". This people descended from Esau, Jacob's older twin brother (Gen 25:30). Obadiah accuses the Edomites of siding with the enemies at Judah's downfall and rejoicing over it.

❞ God's judgment reveals whether or not I am in heaven, that is, whether or not heaven is in me. The judgment does not send me to heaven or hell but reveals the presence of heaven or the absence of heaven (= hell) in my soul.

PETER KREEFT

The day of the Lord Is near (Obed 12–15)

¹² But you should not have gloated over the day of your brother in the day of his misfortune; you should not have rejoiced over the people of Judah in the day of their ruin; you should not have boasted in the day of distress.
¹³ You should not have entered the gate of my people in the day of his calamity; you should not have gloated over his disaster in the

day of his calamity; you should not have looted his goods in the day of his calamity.

💡 The "Golden Rule" is: Do not do to others what you do not want someone to do to you. It is known in many very different cultures.

¹⁴ You should not have stood at the parting of the ways to cut off his fugitives; you should not have delivered up his survivors in the day of distress. ¹⁵ For the day of the LORD is near upon all the nations. As you have done, it shall be done to you, your deeds shall return on your own head.

JONAH

Jonah is the funniest book in the Bible. It ironically switches all the roles: the "unbelievers" behave quite piously, while the prophet Jonah stubbornly and bitterly will not listen to God. The name Jonah means "dove", yet he is by no means as peaceful as you would expect a dove to be.

▶ Instead of setting out for the capital of the Assyrians to the northeast, Jonah takes the opposite direction westward across the Mediterranean. Tarshish is probably located in modern-day Spain. Not until nearly the end of the book (↗ Jon 4:2) do we learn why Jonah does not want to obey.

A frustrated flight (Jon 1)

1 ¹ Now the word of the LORD came to Jonah the son of Amit'tai, saying, ² "Arise, go to Nin'eveh, that great city, and cry against it; for their wickedness has come up before me." ³ But Jonah rose to flee to Tar'shish from the presence of the LORD. He went down to Joppa and found a ship going to Tarshish; so he paid the fare, and went on board, to go with them to Tarshish, away from the presence of the LORD.

⁴ But the LORD hurled a great wind upon the sea, and there was a mighty tempest on the sea, so that the ship threatened to break up. ⁵ Then the mariners were afraid, and each cried to his god; and they threw the wares that were in the ship into the sea, to lighten it for them. But Jonah had gone down into the inner part of the ship and had lain down, and was fast asleep. ⁶ So the captain came and said to him, "What do you mean, you sleeper? Arise, call upon your god! Perhaps the god will give a thought to us, that we do not perish."

⁷ And they said to one another, "Come, let us cast lots, that we may know on whose account this evil has come upon us." So they cast lots, and the lot fell upon Jonah. ⁸ Then they said to him, "Tell us on whose account this evil has come upon us. What is your occupation? And from where do you come? What is your country? And of what people are you?" ⁹ And he said to them, "I am a Hebrew; and I fear the LORD, the God of heaven, who made the sea and the dry land." ¹⁰ Then the men were exceedingly afraid, and said to him, "What is this

▶ While the sailors are doing everything possible to save the ship, Jonah makes himself comfortable.

"" We can run away from God as a Christian, as a Catholic, and even as a priest, bishop or Pope. We can all flee from God. This is a daily temptation: not to listen to God, not to hear his voice, not to hear his promptings, his invitation in our hearts.
POPE FRANCIS, October 7, 2013

▶ The sailors realize the contradiction between Jonah's profession of faith (v. 9) and his behavior (v. 10), opposing the great God whom he professes.

that you have done!" For the men knew that he was fleeing from the presence of the LORD, because he had told them.

¹¹ Then they said to him, "What shall we do to you, that the sea may quiet down for us?" For the sea grew more and more tempestuous. ¹² He said to them, "Take me up and throw me into the sea; then the sea will quiet down for you; for I know it is because of me that this great tempest has come upon you." ¹³ Nevertheless the men rowed hard to bring the ship back to land, but they could not, for the sea grew more and more tempestuous against them. ¹⁴ Therefore they cried to the LORD, "We beg you, O LORD, let us not perish for this man's life, and lay not on us innocent blood; for you, O LORD, have done as it pleased you."

¹⁵ So they took up Jonah and threw him into the sea; and the sea ceased from its raging. ¹⁶ Then the men feared the LORD exceedingly, and they offered a sacrifice to the LORD and made vows.

▶ The "heathen" sailors carefully question Jonah (v. 8), try to protect him (v. 13), and pray to his God. They act in an exemplary way: considerate, responsible, and pious (see also v. 16).

An odd prayer (Jon 2)

2 ¹ Then Jonah prayed to the LORD his God from the belly of the fish, ² saying,

"I called to the LORD, out of my distress, and he answered me; out of the belly of Sheol I cried, and you heard my voice.

▶ "Three days" often symbolically stands for a time of transformation. It takes Jonah that long to turn to God.

▶ There was no mention earlier about Jonah's cries to God; on the contrary: while the sailors were praying, he was sleeping (1:5).

▶ Jonah twists the facts: he had commanded the sailors to throw him into the sea (1:12) and has only himself to blame for his situation.

▶ Jonah is immersed in illusions and fantasies: he waited for three days before he began to pray (v. 1). And instead of thinking about the Temple (v. 5 and v. 8), he should be setting out for Nineveh. The sailors, who believed in other gods, were faithful to Jonah and to God (1:5–16).

³ For you cast me into the deep, into the heart of the seas, and the flood was round about me; all your waves and your billows passed over me.

⁴ Then I said, 'I am cast out from your presence; how shall I again look upon your holy temple?'

⁵ The waters closed in over me, the deep was round about me; weeds were wrapped about my head

⁶ at the roots of the mountains. I went down to the land whose bars closed upon me for ever; yet you brought up my life from the Pit, O LORD my God.

⁷ When my soul fainted within me, I remembered the LORD; and my prayer came to you, into your holy temple.

⁸ Those who pay regard to vain idols forsake their true loyalty.

⁹ But I with the voice of thanksgiving will sacrifice to you; what I have vowed I will pay. Deliverance belongs to the LORD!"

¹⁰ And the LORD spoke to the fish, and it vomited out Jonah upon the dry land.

An exemplary conversion (Jon 3)

3¹ Then the word of the LORD came to Jonah the second time, saying, ² "Arise, go to Nin'eveh, that great city, and proclaim to it the message that I tell you."

³ So Jonah arose and went to Nin'eveh, according to the word of the LORD. Now Nineveh was an exceedingly great city, three days' journey in breadth.⁴ Jonah began to go into the city, going a day's journey. And he cried, "Yet forty days, and Nin'eveh shall be overthrown!"

⁵ And the people of Nin'eveh believed God; they proclaimed a fast, and put on sackcloth, from the greatest of them to the least of them.

⁶ Then tidings reached the king of Nin'eveh, and he arose from his throne, removed his robe, and covered himself with sackcloth, and sat in ashes. ⁷ And he made proclamation and published through Nin'eveh, "By the decree of the king and his nobles: Let neither man nor beast, herd nor flock, taste anything; let them not feed, or drink water, ⁸ but let man and beast be covered with sackcloth, and let them cry mightily to God; yes, let every one turn from his evil way and from the violence which is in his hands. ⁹ Who knows, God may yet repent and turn from his fierce anger, so that we perish not?"

¹⁰ When God saw what they did, how they turned from their evil way, God repented of the evil which he had said he would do to them; and he did not do it.

99 The Book of Jonah takes up problems of mission in its own way: Israel may not flee like Jonah from God's missionary commission, and above all it may not be jealous like Jonah of the Gentiles who could come to salvation.

HANS URS VON BALTHASAR

▶ Jonah's minimal proclamation contrasts with Nineveh's complete conversion. Nowhere does the Bible report that God's People Israel ever converted in a similar way. The hope that God could take back and "repent of" his threatened judgment (v. 9) recalls God's regret in Ex 32:14 (↗ also Joel 2:14).

A sulky prophet (Jon 4)

4 ¹ But it displeased Jonah exceedingly, and he was angry. ² And he prayed to the LORD and said, "I pray you, LORD, is not this what I said when I was yet in my country? That is why I made haste to flee to Tar'shish; for I knew that you are a gracious God and merciful, slow to anger, and abounding in mercy, and that you repent of evil. ³ Therefore now, O LORD, take my life from me, I beg you, for it is better for me to die than to live."

⁴ And the LORD said, "Do you do well to be angry?" ⁵ Then Jonah went out of the city and sat to the east of the city, and made a booth for himself there. He sat under it in the shade, till he should see what would become of the city.

⁶ And the Lord GOD appointed a plant, and made it come up over Jonah, that it might be a shade over his head, to save him from his discomfort. So Jonah was exceedingly glad because of the plant. ⁷ But when dawn came up the next day, God appointed a worm which attacked the plant, so that it withered. ⁸ When the sun rose, God appointed a sultry east wind, and the sun beat upon the head of Jonah so that he was faint; and he asked that he might die, and said, "It is better for me to die than to live."

> 99 He who takes pity on himself and is moved by his own pain at once loses the boon it offers.
>
> **HENRI CARDINAL DE LUBAC**

▶ Only here (v. 2) does Jonah state the reason for his flight. The fact that God has mercy on the enemy, too, grieves him so much that he no longer wants to live (v. 3).

▶ Jonah answers like a sulky child. He is driven to and fro by his feelings, dependent on externals like shade or heat. →

⁹ But God said to Jonah, "Do you do well to be angry for the plant?" And he said, "I do well to be angry, angry enough to die."

¹⁰ And the LORD said, "You pity the plant, for which you did not labor, nor did you make it grow, which came into being in a night, and perished in a night. ¹¹ And should not I pity Nin'eveh, that great city, in which there are more than a hundred and twenty thousand persons who do not know their right hand from their left, and also much cattle?"

→ They preoccupy him so much that he lets his life be defined by them. The fact that God cares about the happiness of entire nations makes him angry and argumentative.

▶ God has compassion on men and animals. Obviously it is much harder to lead the prophet to insight and conversion than all Nineveh.

MICAH

Micah means "Who is like (you)?" It is an abbreviation of the name Michael ("Who is like God?" ↗ Dan 10:13). Just as severely as Amos, he criticizes social and religious problems, but the concluding message of the book is conciliatory.

God as a forgiving shepherd (Mic 7:14–20)

7 ¹⁴ Shepherd your people with your staff, the flock of your inheritance, who dwell alone in a forest in the midst of a garden land;

let them feed in Bashan and Gilead as in the days of old.

¹⁵ As in the days when you came out of the land of Egypt I will show them marvelous things.

▶ As "shepherd", God has responsibility and cares for his people. Bashan and Gilead are fruitful regions east of the Jordan. As in the earliest days when the chosen people occupied the land →

→ (→ the Book of Joshua), this region, too, should belong to Israel again.

▶ Israel has been oppressed by foreign nations, but now it hopes for a backlash (vv. 16–17). In it God should become universally recognized, too.

▶ "Who is a God like you?" plays on the prophet's name. There is no one to compare with God because he forgives sin!

¹⁶ The nations shall see and be ashamed of all their might; they shall lay their hands on their mouths; their ears shall be deaf; ¹⁷ they shall lick the dust like a serpent, like the crawling things of the earth; they shall come trembling out of their strongholds, they shall turn in dread to the LORD our God, and they shall fear because of you. ¹⁸ Who is a God like you, pardoning iniquity and passing over transgression for the remnant of his inheritance? He does not retain his anger for ever because he delights in mercy. ¹⁹ He will again have compassion upon us, he will tread our iniquities under foot. You will cast all our sins into the depths of the sea. ²⁰ You will show faithfulness to Jacob and mercy to Abraham, as you have sworn to our fathers from the days of old.

NAHUM

Nahum means "consoled". This Scripture is leveled at the Assyrian capital, Nineveh, and aims to console the land of Judah, which for a long time has suffered under the pitiless threat of the Assyrians.

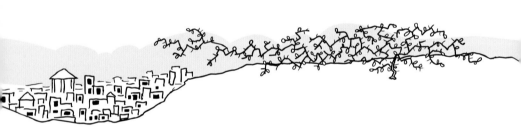

▶ "Vengeance" actually means just compensation. It means here that God is taking action against the brutal, violent rule of the world power Assyria.

▶ "Slow to anger" alludes to the central passage Ex 34:6–7.

▶ These powerful images are not supposed to make God frightening but are intended, rather, to give hope that God can subdue even the most terrible human powers.

A God of just compensation! (Nahum 1:1–10; 2:1)

1 ¹ An oracle concerning Nin'eveh. The book of the vision of Na'hum of El'kosh. ² The LORD is a jealous God and avenging, the LORD is avenging and wrathful; the LORD takes vengeance on his adversaries and keeps wrath for his enemies. ³ The LORD is slow to anger and of great might, and the LORD will by no means clear the guilty. His way is in whirlwind and storm, and the clouds are the dust of his feet. ⁴ He rebukes the sea and makes it dry, he dries up all the rivers; Bashan and Carmel wither, the bloom of Lebanon fades. ⁵ The mountains quake before him, the hills melt; the earth is laid waste before him, the world and all that dwell therein. ⁶ Who can stand before his indignation? Who can endure the heat of his anger? His wrath is poured out like fire, and the rocks are broken asunder by him. ⁷ The LORD is good, a stronghold in the day of trouble; he knows those who take refuge in him. ⁸ But with an overflowing flood he will make a full end of his adversaries, and will pursue his enemies into darkness.

⁹ What do you plot against the LORD? He will make a full end; he will not take vengeance twice on his foes.

¹⁰ Like entangled thorns they are consumed, like dry stubble....

2 The shatterer has come up against you. Man the ramparts; watch the road; gird your loins; collect all your strength.

The laughing angel of Rheims Cathedral

HABAKKUK

Like Nahum, Habakkuk, too, confronts a destructive world power—in his case, though, the Babylonians (Hab 1:6). At the beginning, the short book describes the horrible threat (Hab 1), but it ends with a psalm in which God intervenes as savior (Hab 3). The verse Hab 2:4 is famous (the righteous shall live by his faith) because Paul cited it (Rom 1:17; Gal 3:11).

A prophet cries for help (Hab 1:1–12)

1 ¹ The oracle of God which Habak'kuk the prophet saw.

² O LORD, how long shall I cry for help, and you will not hear? Or cry to you "Violence!" and you will not save?

³ Why do you make me see wrongs and look upon trouble? Destruction and violence are before me; strife and contention arise.

▶ The prophet reproaches God (1:2–3) but at the same time has confidence (1:12). We, too, are allowed to tell God quite honestly what is on our hearts, even contradictory moods and thoughts.

⁴ So the law is slacked and justice never goes forth. For the wicked surround the righteous, so justice goes forth perverted.

⁵ Look among the nations, and see; wonder and be astounded. For I am doing a work in your days that you would not believe if told.

⁶ For behold, I am rousing the Chalde'ans, that bitter and hasty nation, who march through the breadth of the earth, to seize habitations not their own.

⁷ Dread and fearsome are they; their justice and dignity proceed from themselves.

⁸ Their horses are swifter than leopards, more fierce than the evening wolves; their horsemen press proudly on. Yes, their horsemen come from afar; they fly like an eagle swift to devour.

⁹ They all come for violence; terror of them goes before them. They gather captives like sand.

¹⁰ At kings they scoff, and of rulers they make sport. They laugh at every fortress, for they heap up earth and take it.

¹¹ Then they sweep by like the wind and go on, guilty men, whose own might is their god!

¹² Are you not from everlasting, O LORD my God, my Holy One? We shall not die. O LORD, you have ordained them as a judgment; and you, O Rock, have established them for chastisement.

💡 "Legal positivism" regards what is defined by an authority or majority as the only "law". The German philosopher Robert Spaemann says that if there were "no natural law, then it would be impossible to argue at all about questions of justice".

▶ "Chaldeans" refers to the Babylonian Empire (↗ 2 Kings 25).

💡 The philosopher Friedrich Nietzsche mocked Christianity on account of its compassion and sympathy with the weak. Someone who believes in God sees that we are all little in God's sight but have also received dignity (↗ Ps 8, Gen 1:27).

ZEPHANIAH

Zephaniah means "Ya (= God) sheltered" (→ Ps 27:5). This short book succinctly combines many prophetic themes: judgment and hope for Judah and for foreign nations. In the third and final chapter, these themes reach a climax:

99 It is easier to build a city in the sky than a state without God.

PLATO

The divine fire purifies. After a "heated interval", one sees things more clearly and can express them more plainly and honestly.

▶ The "rivers of Ethiopia" (in Hebrew, "Kush", v. 10) are mainly the Blue and White Nile (today in Ethiopia and Sudan). This region was perceived as the most remote end of the inhabited world.

Hope for the unity of mankind (Zeph 3:1–2, 8–18)

3 ¹ Woe to her that is rebellious and defiled, the oppressing city! ² She listens to no voice, she accepts no correction. She does not trust in the LORD, she does not draw near to her God....

⁸ "Therefore wait for me," says the LORD, "for the day when I arise as a witness. For my decision is to gather nations, to assemble kingdoms, to pour out upon them my indignation, all the heat of my anger; for in the fire of my jealous wrath all the earth shall be consumed.

⁹ "Yes, at that time I will change the speech of the peoples to a pure speech, that all of them may call on the name of the LORD and serve him with one accord.

¹⁰ From beyond the rivers of Ethiopia my suppliants, the daughter of my dispersed ones, shall bring my offering.

99 If detachment is one-half of what readiness for the kingdom means, humility is the other. Unless we are converted and become as little as a child, there is no possibility of getting to God.

THOMAS DUBAY, S.M.

99 Perhaps the most exciting invitation [to joy] is that of the prophet Zephaniah, who presents God with his people in the midst of a celebration overflowing with the joy of salvation. I find it thrilling to read this text.

POPE FRANCIS, EG 45

¹¹ "On that day you shall not be put to shame because of the deeds by which you have rebelled against me; for then I will remove from your midst your proudly exultant ones, and you shall no longer be haughty in my holy mountain.

¹² For I will leave in the midst of you a people humble and lowly. They shall seek refuge in the name of the LORD,

¹³ those who are left in Israel; they shall do no wrong and utter no lies, nor shall there be found in their mouth a deceitful tongue. For they shall pasture and lie down, and none shall make them afraid."

¹⁴ Sing aloud, O daughter of Zion; shout, O Israel! Rejoice and exult with all your heart, O daughter of Jerusalem!

¹⁵ The LORD has taken away the judgments against you, he has cast out your enemies. The King of Israel, the LORD, is in your midst; you shall fear evil no more.

¹⁶ On that day it shall be said to Jerusalem: "Do not fear, O Zion; let not your hands grow weak.

¹⁷ The LORD, your God, is in your midst, a warrior who gives victory; he will rejoice over you with gladness, he will renew you in his love; he will exult over you with loud singing

¹⁸ as on a day of festival.

HAGGAI

Next after Zephaniah comes the short Book of Haggai, which is about the rebuilding of the Temple in Jerusalem in the Persian era (after the destruction by the Babylonians in 587 B.C., → the Books of Ezra and Nehemiah). This happened under the Persian King Darius I, who started his reign in 522 B.C. Under his supreme rule, Zerubbabel was the highest-ranking official in Jerusalem. He was a grandson of Jehoiachin, the last king of Judah, who had been taken into exile (→ 2 Kings 24:15; 1 Chron 3:17–19).

The call to build the Temple (Hag 1:1–14)

1 ^{1} In the second year of Dari'us the king, in the sixth month, on the first day of the month, the word of the LORD came by Hag'gai the prophet to Zerub'babel the son of She-al'ti-el, governor of Judah, and to Joshua the son of Jehoz'adak, the high priest, ^{2} "Thus says the LORD of hosts: This people say the time has not yet come to rebuild the house of the LORD." ^{3} Then the word of the LORD came by Hag'gai the prophet, ^{4} "Is it a time for you yourselves to dwell in your paneled houses, while this house lies in ruins? ^{5} Now therefore thus says the LORD of hosts: Consider how you have fared. ^{6} You have sown much, and harvested little; you eat, but you never have enough; you drink, but you never have your fill; you clothe yourselves, but no one is warm; and he who earns wages earns wages to put them into a bag with holes.

Haggai is not a special case. In 1206, Francis of Assisi, kneeling before a crucifix, also heard a voice say: "Go and repair my house, which, as you see, is completely in ruins." At first, Francis took the matter literally, obtained stones and mortar, and restored the little Church of San Damiano. Later he understood that God had called him to preserve his whole Church from interior decay.

^{7} "Thus says the LORD of hosts: Consider how you have fared. ^{8} Go up to the hills and bring wood and build the house, that I may take pleasure in it and that I may appear in my glory, says the LORD. ^{9} You have looked for much, and behold, it came to little; and when you brought it home, I blew it away. Why? says the LORD of hosts. Because of my house that lies in ruins, while you busy yourselves each with his own house. ^{10} Therefore the heavens above you have withheld the dew, and the earth has withheld its produce. ^{11} And I have called for a drought upon the land and the hills, upon the grain, the new wine, the oil, upon what the ground brings forth, upon men and cattle, and upon all their labors."
^{12} Then Zerub'babel the son of She-al'ti-el, and Joshua the son of Jehoz'adak, the high priest, with all the remnant of the people, obeyed the voice of the LORD their God, and the words of Hag'gai the prophet, as the LORD their God had sent him; and the people feared before the LORD. ^{13} Then Hag'gai, the messenger of the LORD, spoke to the people with the LORD's message, "I am with you, says the LORD." ^{14} And the LORD stirred up the spirit of Zerub'babel the son of She-al'ti-el, governor of Judah, and the spirit of Joshua the son of Jehoz'adak, the high priest, and the spirit of all the remnant of the people; and they came and worked on the house of the LORD of hosts, their God. ...

▶ From time immemorial, God's Spirit has moved people to overcome convenience and selfishness and to commit themselves to valuable concerns.

ZECHARIAH

The following, considerably longer Book of Zechariah, too, dates back to the Persian period (→ Zech 1:1, in reference to the Persian King Darius I). "Zechariah" means "Ya (= God) remembered." The visions in this book recall those of Ezekiel and Daniel.

A holy mountain for all nations (Zech 8:1–8)

8 ¹ And the word of the LORD of hosts came to me, saying, ²"Thus says the LORD of hosts: I am jealous for Zion with great jealousy, and I am jealous for her with great wrath.

³ Thus says the LORD: I will return to Zion, and will dwell in the midst of Jerusalem, and Jerusalem shall be called the faithful city, and the mountain of the LORD of hosts, the holy mountain.

⁴ Thus says the LORD of hosts: Old men and old women shall again sit in the streets of Jerusalem, each with staff in hand for very age.

⁵ And the streets of the city shall be full of boys and girls playing in its streets.

⁶ Thus says the LORD of hosts: If it is marvelous in the sight of the remnant of this people in these days, should it also be marvelous in my sight, says the LORD of hosts?

⁷ Thus says the LORD of hosts: Behold, I will save my people from the east country and from the west country;

⁸ and I will bring them to dwell in the midst of Jerusalem; and they shall be my people and I will be their God, in faithfulness and in righteousness."

▶ Concerning the "covenant formula" in v. 8, ↗ Jer 30:22.

Many nations stream toward Jerusalem (Zech 8:18–23)

¹⁸ And the word of the LORD of hosts came to me, saying, ¹⁹"Thus says the LORD of hosts: The fast of the fourth month, and the fast of the fifth, and the fast of the seventh, and the fast of the tenth, shall be to the house of Judah seasons of joy and gladness, and cheerful feasts; therefore love truth and peace.

²⁰ "Thus says the LORD of hosts: Peoples shall yet come, even the inhabitants of many cities; ²¹ the inhabitants of one city shall go to another, saying, 'Let us go at once to entreat the favor of the LORD, and to seek the LORD of hosts; I am going.' ²² Many peoples and strong nations shall come to seek the LORD of hosts in Jerusalem, and to entreat the favor of the LORD. ²³ Thus says the LORD of hosts: In those days ten men from the nations of every tongue shall take hold of the robe of a Jew, saying, 'Let us go with you, for we have heard that God is with you.'"

▶ The idea of a "pilgrimage of the nations" (v. 20) to Jerusalem comes from Mic 4:2 and Is 2:3.

99 The domain of the Messianic king is no longer a specific country that would later necessarily be separated from other countries and hence, inevitably, would take a stance against them. His country is the earth, the whole world. He creates unity in the multiplicity of cultures, overcoming every boundary.

POPE BENEDICT XVI, April 9, 2006

Zion's king of peace (Zech 9:9–10)

9 ⁹ Rejoice greatly, O daughter of Zion! Shout aloud, O daughter of Jerusalem! Behold, your king comes to you; triumphant and victorious is he, humble and riding on a donkey, on a colt the foal of a donkey.

¹⁰ I will cut off the chariot from E'phraim and the war horse from Jerusalem; and the battle bow shall be cut off, and he shall command peace to the nations;

his dominion shall be from sea to sea, and from the River to the ends of the earth.

▶ Whereas horses were used as mounts in combat and as status symbols, donkeys served peaceful purposes as the beasts of burden of lowly people.

MALACHI

Malachi means "my messenger". The book, written in the style of a polemic, advocates taking both Temple worship and social justice seriously. This last book of the Old Testament in Christian editions of the Bible ends with a powerful prospect:

Jubilation over the Sun of justice (Mal 3:14–15; 4:1–2)

3 ¹⁴ You have said, 'It is vain to serve God. What is the good of our keeping his charge or of walking as in mourning before the LORD

B Do not say, "I will repay evil"; wait for the LORD, and he will help you.

Prov 20:22

of hosts? ¹⁵ Henceforth we deem the arrogant blessed; evildoers not only prosper but when they put God to the test they escape.' "...

4 ¹ "For behold, the day comes, burning like an oven, when all the arrogant and all evildoers will be stubble; the day that comes shall burn them up, says the LORD of hosts, so that it will leave them neither root nor branch.

² But for you who fear my name the sun of righteousness shall rise, with healing in its wings. You shall go forth leaping like calves from the stall.

▶ The image of the winged sun was used often in ancient Egypt as a symbol for divine protection. Here, the divine sun brings justice and healing.

The coming day (Mal 4:3–6)

³ And you shall tread down the wicked, for they will be ashes under the soles of your feet, on the day when I act, says the LORD of hosts.

⁴ "Remember the law of my servant Moses, the statutes and ordinances that I commanded him at Horeb for all Israel.

⁵ "Behold, I will send you Eli'jah the prophet before the great and awesome day of the LORD comes.

⁶ And he will turn the hearts of fathers to their children and the hearts of children to their fathers, lest I come and strike the land with a curse."

▶ These final verses of the Books of the Prophets and of the Old Testament refer to Moses (Ex-Deut) and Elijah (↗ 1 Kings 17–2 Kings 2). Jesus meets both men at the Transfiguration (↗ Mk 9:2–8; Mt 17:1–8; Lk 9:28–36). This makes visible the fact that Jesus is in dialogue and in agreement with the major figures of the Old Testament.

The New Testament

The New Testament is the second part of the Christian Bible. It was written because something new happened: Jesus came into the world. What he did and suffered had to be told. The faith that he had risen from the dead had to be expressed. Through Jesus and his call to discipleship and the mission of his disciples, the Church came about. How it all began with the Church is described in the New Testament.

At the beginning of the early Christian tradition stands oral proclamation. But then they start to write. The apostle Paul composed letters in order to reach the communities that he had founded when he could not be with them personally. The Gospels were written so as to keep the memory of Jesus alive.

The written word helps to bridge the distances between places and times. Thus the knowledge about who Jesus is and how the Church came into being can be handed down from generation to generation.

The written word, however, comes alive over and over again. What happened then, in the fullness of time (Gal 4:4), remains of current interest. It is important "today"—always and in all ages. In this way Jesus interpreted the Word of God in the synagogue of his hometown, Nazareth, after he had read from the Book of the Prophet Isaiah: "Today this Scripture has been fulfilled in your hearing" (Lk 4:21). Here and now, also, it is important to discover the living Spirit of God in the written characters of Sacred Scripture. Then reading the Bible becomes a faith experience.

Throughout the New Testament, the Old Testament is presupposed. It is called "Scripture" or "the Scriptures". It is considered sacred. It is the basis of the New Testament. For Jesus and the apostles, it is clear that God's story with humanity and his people does not begin just with the coming of the Messiah; it begins with creation and the call of Israel to give God glory among the nations. That is why the New Testament cannot be understood without the Old Testament. The converse is true also: the Old Testament can be understood in a new way if it is read in the light that proceeds from Jesus Christ.

> **B** Do not think that I have come to abolish the law and the prophets; I have come not to abolish them but to fulfil them. For truly, I say to you, till heaven and earth pass away, not an iota, not a dot, will pass from the law until all is accomplished. Whoever then relaxes one of the least of these commandments and teaches men so, shall be called least in the kingdom of heaven; but he who does them and teaches them shall be called great in the kingdom of heaven.
>
> Mt 5:17–19

REVELATION

The New Testament begins with the four Gospels: according to Matthew, according to Mark, according to Luke, and according to John. The Gospels tell about Jesus: his life, his death, and his Resurrection. That is why they stand at the head of the New Testament.

After the Gospels come the Acts of the Apostles. This book tells how the first disciples carried out Jesus' commission: "You shall be my witnesses in Jerusalem and in all Judea and Samaria and to the end of the earth" (Acts 1:8). In the history of the Church, the story of Jesus continues—to this day.

The Acts of the Apostles are followed by the letters of the apostles. They call for and promote the building up of the Church. They provide a polyphonic witness to the faith. They show how God's Word moved the first Christian communities. They very frankly address difficulties in finding the right way. But they point to a direction that is valid even today.

The New Testament ends with the Revelation of John. It is a prophetic Scripture. It offers a prospect of the new heaven and the new earth. In the heavenly Jerusalem, a new Paradise comes about. In this Paradise, the promise by which all live in their faith will be perfectly fulfilled.

The Gospels

The Gospels tell the story of Jesus. Gospel means "Good-spell", the Old English equivalent of the Greek word *Evangelion*, "Good news". According to the New Testament, there is basically only one Gospel. For there is only one God, and his Word, which Jesus proclaims, is infinitely good.

But God's Gospel must be proclaimed by men in their own words. At the beginning of the New Testament stand four of these testimonies. They all refer to the one Gospel. That is why, since the earliest days of Christianity, they have borne the titles: the Gospel according to Matthew, the Gospel according to Mark, the Gospel according to Luke, and the Gospel according to John.

All the Gospels were written by Christians who believed in the Resurrection of Jesus and therefore told about his life. The Gospels are based on ancient oral tradition and eyewitness tesimony. They depict Jesus in such a way as to make clear not only his past but also his present significance.

Later, still more Gospels were written. But only the four according to Matthew, Mark, Luke, and John were included in the Bible. They are the oldest and most important testimonies about Jesus. They are the ones that were recognized as authentic everywhere, then as now.

All the Gospels have many things in common, especially the first three. But they also have their own peculiarities, especially the fourth. They show Jesus from different sides. This is an invitation to become better and better acquainted with Jesus.

This Bible focuses on Matthew, because it became the first in the sequence of Gospels and over the centuries also acquired great significance. Typical excerpts from the Gospels of Mark and Luke are presented in this Bible. More extensive passages are given from the Gospel of John, which has distinctive features not found in the other three Gospels.

Anyone who wants to read all four Gospels must look to a complete Bible. He will be rewarded with a wealth of testimonies about Jesus.

THE GOSPEL ACCORDING TO

Matthew

The New Testament begins with the Gospel according to Matthew. According to tradition, its author is the tax-collector Matthew, whom Jesus himself called to discipleship (Mt 9:9).

The Gospel of Matthew begins with a genealogy of Jesus, a summary history of Israel. This genealogy anchors the New Testament in the Old Testament.

The Gospel of Matthew ends with the commission by the risen Lord to call all nations to discipleship. This commission opens up the story of Jesus for the history of the Church—"to the close of the age", in other words, until the end of the world (Mt 28:20).

Jesus is a member of God's People Israel. He brings God's salvation to all peoples. He is "Emmanuel—God with us" (Is 7:14, Mt 1:23).

The evangelist tells the story of Jesus' ministry and suffering. This story does not end with the Cross. It begins anew with the Resurrection of Jesus from the dead. In the light of Easter morning, everyone should recognize that Jesus is the Son of God; he fulfills God's will "on earth as it is in heaven" (Mt 6:10).

The Christian community in Matthew lives in close contact with Judaism. It debates with the Pharisees about the correct interpretation of the Law. Through its orientation to Jesus, it brings the Judeo-Christian heritage into the Church.

THE PREHISTORY (MT 1:1–2:23)

Jesus' roots (Mt 1:1–17)

▶ Jesus' genealogy shows where Jesus comes from and who he is. David is the great king of Israel. Hope in redemption is connected with him. Abraham is the forefather of Israel. He received God's promise that he would be a blessing for all nations (Gen 12:3). Jesus fulfills this promise. He is the Messiah of Israel, who brings salvation to all peoples.

1 ¹ The book of the genealogy of Jesus Christ, the son of David, the son of Abraham.
² Abraham was the father of Isaac, and Isaac the father of Jacob, and Jacob the father of Judah and his brothers, ³ and Judah the father of Per'ez and Ze'rah by Ta'mar, and Perez the father of Hezron, and Hezron the father of Ram, ⁴ and Ram the father of Ammin'adab, and Amminadab the father of Nahshon, and Nahshon the father of Salmon, ⁵ and Salmon the father of Boaz by Ra'hab, and Boaz the father of O'bed by Ruth, and Obed the father of Jesse, ⁶ and Jesse the father of David the king. And David was the father of Solomon by the wife of Uri'ah, ⁷ and Solomon the father of Rehobo'am, and Rehoboam the father of Abi'jah, and Abijah the father of Asa, ⁸ and Asa the father of Jehosh'aphat, and Jehoshaphat the father of Jo'ram, and Joram the father of Uzzi'ah, ⁹ and Uzzi'ah the father of Jo'tham, and Jotham the father of A'haz, and Ahaz the father of Hezeki'ah, ¹⁰ and Hezeki'ah the father of Manas'seh, and Manasseh the father of Amos, and Amos the father of Josi'ah, ¹¹ and Josi'ah the father of Jechoni'ah and his brothers, at the time of the deportation to Babylon. ¹² And after the deportation to Babylon: Jechoni'ah was the father of She-al'ti-el, and She-alti-

▶ Five women are mentioned: Tamar (↗ Gen 38), Rahab (↗ Josh 2), Ruth (↗ Ruth), Solomon's mother, Bathsheba (↗ 2 Sam 11; 1 Kings 1)—and, last but not least, Mary.

▶ There is a gap in Jesus' genealogy. The chain of who-fathered-whom ends with Joseph. How does Jesus fit into the salvation history of Israel from the time of Abraham and David? The answer is given in the Nativity Gospel of Matthew: Jesus is the Son of God, born of the Virgin Mary.

el the father of Zerub'babel, ¹³ and Zerub'babel the father of Abi'ud, and Abiud the father of Eli'akim, and Eliakim the father of A'zor, ¹⁴ and A'zor the father of Za'dok, and Zadok the father of A'chim, and Achim the father of Eli'ud, ¹⁵ and Eli'ud the father of Elea'zar, and Eleazar the father of Matthan, and Matthan the father of Jacob, ¹⁶ and Jacob the father of Joseph the husband of Mary, of whom Jesus was born, who is called Christ. ¹⁷ So all the generations from Abraham to David were fourteen generations, and from David to the deportation to Babylon fourteen generations, and from the deportation to Babylon to the Christ fourteen generations.

▶ Matthew recounts the birth of Jesus from Joseph's point of view. The Gospel of Luke gives Mary's perspective (Lk 1–2). It also contains the Nativity Gospel that is proclaimed in the liturgy (Lk 2:1–20).

Who Jesus is (Mt 1:18–25)

¹⁸ Now the birth of Jesus Christ took place in this way. When his mother Mary had been betrothed to Joseph, before they came together she was found to be with child of the Holy Spirit; ¹⁹ and her husband Joseph, being a just man and unwilling to put her to shame, resolved to send her away quietly. ²⁰ But as he considered this, behold, an angel of the Lord appeared to him in a dream, saying, "Joseph, son of David, do not fear to take Mary your wife, for that which is conceived in her is of the Holy Spirit; ²¹ she will bear a son, and you shall call his name Jesus, for he will save his people from their sins." ²² All this took place to fulfil what the Lord had spoken by the prophet:

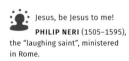

Jesus, be Jesus to me!
PHILIP NERI (1505–1595), the "laughing saint", ministered in Rome.

[23] "Behold, a virgin shall conceive and bear a son, and his name shall be called Emmanuel"(which means, God with us).
[24] When Joseph woke from sleep, he did as the angel of the Lord commanded him; he took his wife,[25] but knew her not until she had borne a son; and he called his name Jesus.

 "Jesus" in English is "God saves."

We saw His star (Mt 2:1–12)

2 [1] Now when Jesus was born in Bethlehem of Judea in the days of Herod the king, behold, Wise Men from the East came to Jerusalem, saying, [2] "Where is he who has been born king of the Jews? For we have seen his star in the East, and have come to worship him." [3] When Herod the king heard this, he was troubled, and all Jerusalem with him; [4] and assembling all the chief priests and scribes of the people, he inquired of them where the Christ was to be born. [5] They told him, "In Bethlehem of Judea; for so it is written by the prophet:

[6] 'And you, O Bethlehem, in the land of Judah, are by no means least among the rulers of Judah; for from you shall come a ruler who will govern my people Israel.'"

▶ The story of Jesus plays out from the very start in a worldwide context. The wise men come with the wisdom of the East to Israel and, with the help of Israel's Bible (↗ Mic 5:1 f.), find their way to Bethlehem. There they worship the Child with his Mother.

99 The birthday of the Lord is the birthday of freedom.
POPE LEO I (ca 400–461)

[7] Then Herod summoned the Wise Men secretly and ascertained from them what time the star appeared; [8] and he sent them to Bethlehem, saying, "Go and search diligently for the child, and when you have found him bring me word, that I too may come and worship him." [9] When they had heard the king they went their way; and behold, the star which they had seen in the East went before them, till it came to rest over the place where the child was. [10] When they saw the star, they rejoiced exceedingly with great joy; [11] and going into the house they saw the child with Mary his mother, and they fell down and worshiped him. Then, opening their treasures, they offered him gifts, gold and frankincense and myrrh. [12] And being warned in a dream not to return to Herod, they departed to their own country by another way.

99 Songs of thankfulness and praise, / Jesus, Lord, to You we raise, / Manifested by the star / To the sages from afar, / Branch of royal David's stem, / In Your birth at Bethlehem, / Praises be to You addressed, / God in man made manifest.
CHRISTOPHER WORDSWORTH (1807–1885), from a hymn for Epiphany

In flight (Mt 2:13–15)

[13] Now when they had departed, behold, an angel of the Lord appeared to Joseph in a dream and said, "Rise, take the child and his mother, and flee to Egypt, and remain there till I tell you; for Herod is about to search for the child, to destroy him." [14] And he rose and took the child and his mother by night, and departed to Egypt, [15] and remained there until the death of Herod. This was to fulfil what the Lord had spoken by the prophet, "Out of Egypt have I called my son."

In 2014, ISIS soldiers marked the doors of Christians in Mosul with the Arabic letter "N", which stands for "Nazarenes". All Christians living there had to leave their homes.

The massacres of the children in Bethlehem (Mt 2:16–18)

▶ Herod was a cruel despot, and so he also had potential successors from his own family executed. The murder of the innocent children in Bethlehem recalls the persecution of the Jews and points ahead to the Passion of Christ. In many countries, a new wave of terror and violence does not stop even at children and youngsters.

¹⁶ Then Herod, when he saw that he had been tricked by the Wise Men, was in a furious rage, and he sent and killed all the male children in Bethlehem and in all that region who were two years old or under, according to the time which he had ascertained from the Wise Men. ¹⁷ Then was fulfilled what was spoken by the prophet Jeremiah:

¹⁸ "A voice was heard in Ra'mah, wailing and loud lamentation, Rachel weeping for her children; she refused to be consoled, because they were no more."

Jesus comes to Nazareth (Mt 2:19–23)

99 The flight into Egypt caused by Herod's threat shows us that God is present where man is in danger, where man is suffering, where he is fleeing, where he experiences rejection and abandonment; but God is also present where man dreams, where he hopes to return in freedom to his homeland.

POPE FRANCIS, December 29, 2013

¹⁹ But when Herod died, behold, an angel of the Lord appeared in a dream to Joseph in Egypt, saying, ²⁰ "Rise, take the child and his mother, and go to the land of Israel, for those who sought the child's life are dead." ²¹ And he rose and took the child and his mother, and went to the land of Israel. ²² But when he heard that Archela'us reigned over Judea in place of his father Herod, he was afraid to go there, and being warned in a dream he withdrew to the district of Galilee. ²³ And he went and dwelt in a city called Nazareth, that what was spoken by the prophets might be fulfilled. "He shall be called a Nazarene."

JESUS BEGINS HIS PUBLIC MINISTRY (MT 3,1–4,11)

John the Baptist: Repent! (Mt 3:1–12)

▶ Luke's Gospel relates the miraculous birth of the Baptist, which is intertwined with the birth of Jesus (Lk 1).

3 ¹ In those days came John the Baptist, preaching in the wilderness of Judea, ² "Repent, for the kingdom of heaven is at hand." ³ For this is he who was spoken of by the prophet Isaiah when he said,

"The voice of one crying in the wilderness: Prepare the way of the Lord, make his paths straight."

▶ John is dressed like Elijah (1 Kings 1:8). Elijah is supposed to return, to prepare Israel for its encounter with God (Mal 3:1, 23–24).

⁴ Now John wore a garment of camel's hair, and a leather belt around his waist; and his food was locusts and wild honey. ⁵ Then went out to him Jerusalem and all Judea and all the region about the Jordan, ⁶ and they were baptized by him in the river Jordan, confessing their sins.

▶ John preaches judgment. He proclaims that God's wrath is righteous. But he also points to a way out: there is the opportunity for repentance. Baptism in the Jordan forgives sins; it prepares for the "mightier one". John is the precursor of Jesus.

⁷ But when he saw many of the Pharisees and Sad'ducees coming for baptism, he said to them, "You brood of vipers! Who warned you to flee from the wrath to come? ⁸ Bear fruit that befits repentance, ⁹ and do not presume to say to yourselves, 'We have Abraham as our father'; for I tell you, God is able from these stones to raise up children to Abraham. ¹⁰ Even now the axe is laid to the root of the trees; every tree therefore that does not bear good fruit is cut down and thrown into the fire.

¹¹ "I baptize you with water for repentance, but he who is coming after me is mightier than I, whose sandals I am not worthy to carry; he will baptize you with the Holy Spirit and with fire. ¹² His winnowing fork is in his hand, and he will clear his threshing floor and gather his wheat into the granary, but the chaff he will burn with unquenchable fire."

The baptism of Jesus (Mt 3:13–17)

¹³ Then Jesus came from Galilee to the Jordan to John, to be baptized by him. ¹⁴ John would have prevented him, saying, "I need to be baptized by you, and do you come to me?" ¹⁵ But Jesus answered him, "Let it be so now; for thus it is fitting for us to fulfil all righteousness." Then he consented. ¹⁶ And when Jesus was baptized, he went up immediately from the water, and behold, the heavens were opened and he saw the Spirit of God descending like a dove, and alighting on him; ¹⁷ and behold, a voice from heaven, saying, "This is my beloved Son, with whom I am well pleased."

> He became what we are, so that he could make us what he is.
>
> **ATHANASIUS THE GREAT** (ca. 298–373), Doctor of the Church

Diabolical temptations (Mt 4:1–11)

4 ¹ Then Jesus was led up by the Spirit into the wilderness to be tempted by the devil. ² And he fasted forty days and forty nights, and afterward he was hungry. ³ And the tempter came and said to him, "If you are the Son of God, command these stones to become loaves of bread." ⁴ But he answered, "It is written,

> "Devil" means literally: the one who confuses. He tries to deflect Jesus from his path.

'Man shall not live by bread alone, but by every word that proceeds from the mouth of God.' "

⁵ Then the devil took him to the holy city, and set him on the pinnacle of the temple,⁶and said to him, "If you are the Son of God, throw yourself down; for it is written,

'He will give his angels charge of you,' and 'On their hands they will bear you up, lest you strike your foot against a stone.' "

⁷ Jesus said to him, "Again it is written, 'You shall not tempt the Lord your God.' " ⁸ Again, the devil took him to a very high mountain, and showed him all the kingdoms of the world and the glory of them; ⁹ and he said to him, "All these I will give you, if you will fall down and worship me." ¹⁰ Then Jesus said to him, "Begone, Satan! for it is written,

'You shall worship the Lord your God and him only shall you serve.' "

¹¹ Then the devil left him, and behold, angels came and ministered to him.

> We surrender to instincts of flesh and blood, overcome by disgust for the spiritual life; we fall into all the illusions of naturalism, and we call this "Christianity incarnate". ... What a beautiful plan for Christianity incarnate Satan presented to Jesus, in the desert! Jesus preferred a Christianity crucified.
>
> **HENRI CARDINAL DE LUBAC**

THE MINISTRY OF JESUS IN GALILEE (MT 4:12–17:999)

Jesus begins with his proclamation (Mt 4:12–17)

¹² Now when he heard that John had been arrested, he withdrew into Galilee; ¹³ and leaving Nazareth he went and dwelt in Ca-

> Jesus got a rather late start. He lived for thirty years with his parents, only to become then in only three years the best documented figure in the ancient world. There are more testimonies about Jesus than about almost any other figure in antiquity.

▶ Zebulon and Naphtali are the names of two tribes of Israel that settled in the north of the Holy Land (see map p. 83).

(see map p. 83)

> No great Christian evangelist has been known for relying only on actions to the exclusion of words.

KARL KEATING

> Do you know what the best method of evangelizing a young person is? Another young person. That is the way that you must follow!

POPE FRANCIS, June 9, 2014

▶ Right at the beginning of his ministry, Jesus calls his first disciples—literally "pupils"—to follow him. He wants to spread the Good News that the kingdom of heaven is near. That is why he makes fishermen fishers of men. They are supposed to cast their nets to win other people to the faith. To do that, they must follow Jesus and learn from him.

▶ The Sermon on the Mount is the first of Jesus' great discourses in which he summarizes his proclamation. Jesus addresses it to his disciples; but he speaks in such a way that all those who are at the foot of the mountain can hear him. They should be able to decide freely to put their faith in Jesus' words.

per'na-um by the sea, in the territory of Zeb'ulun and Naph'tali, [14] that what was spoken by the prophet Isaiah might be fulfilled: [15] "The land of Zeb'ulun and the land of Naph'tali, toward the sea, across the Jordan, Galilee of the Gentiles—[16] the people who sat in darkness have seen a great light, and for those who sat in the region and shadow of death light has dawned." [17] From that time Jesus began to preach, saying, "Repent, for the kingdom of heaven is at hand."

Fishermen become fishers of men (Mt 4:18–22)

[18] As he walked by the Sea of Galilee, he saw two brothers, Simon who is called Peter and Andrew his brother, casting a net into the sea; for they were fishermen. [19] And he said to them, "Follow me, and I will make you fishers of men." [20] Immediately they left their nets and followed him. [21] And going on from there he saw two other brothers, James the son of Zeb'edee and John his brother, in the boat with Zebedee their father, mending their nets, and he called them. [22] Immediately they left the boat and their father, and followed him.

People come in droves to Jesus (Mt 4:23–25)

[23] And he went about all Galilee, teaching in their synagogues and preaching the gospel of the kingdom and healing every disease and every infirmity among the people. [24] So his fame spread throughout all Syria, and they brought him all the sick, those afflicted with various diseases and pains, demoniacs, epileptics, and paralytics, and he healed them. [25] And great crowds followed him from Galilee and the Decap'olis and Jerusalem and Judea and from beyond the Jordan.

THE SERMON ON THE MOUNT (5:1–7:29)

5 [1] Seeing the crowds, he went up on the mountain, and when he sat down his disciples came to him. [2] And he opened his mouth and taught them, saying:

The Beatitudes (Mt 5:3–12)

[3] "Blessed are the poor in spirit, for theirs is the kingdom of heaven.

[4] "Blessed are those who mourn, for they shall be comforted.

[5] "Blessed are the meek, for they shall inherit the earth.

[6] "Blessed are those who hunger and thirst for righteousness, for they shall be satisfied.

⁷ "Blessed are the merciful, for they shall obtain mercy.

⁸ "Blessed are the pure in heart, for they shall see God.

⁹ "Blessed are the peacemakers, for they shall be called sons of God.

¹⁰ "Blessed are those who are persecuted for righteousness' sake, for theirs is the kingdom of heaven.

¹¹ "Blessed are you when men revile you and persecute you and utter all kinds of evil against you falsely on my account. ¹² Rejoice and be glad, for your reward is great in heaven, for so men persecuted the prophets who were before you.

> Reflection on the beatitudes cannot be solely a matter of the mind; it must transform the depths of our hearts. This can only occur through prayer.
> **ROBERT SPITZER, S.J.**

Salt of the earth, light of the world (Mt 5:13–16)

¹³ "You are the salt of the earth; but if salt has lost its taste, how shall its saltiness be restored? It is no longer good for anything except to be thrown out and trodden under foot by men.

¹⁴ "You are the light of the world. A city set on a hill cannot be hidden. ¹⁵ Nor do men light a lamp and put it under a bushel, but on a stand, and it gives

▶ A beatitude is a blessing—and more than that. Someone who is "blessed" is more than happy. The blessed are filled with God's joy.

light to all in the house. ¹⁶ Let your light so shine before men, that they may see your good works and give glory to your Father who is in heaven.

Heavenly justice (Mt 5:17-20)

¹⁷ "Do not think that I have come to abolish the law and the prophets; I have come not to abolish them but to fulfil them. ¹⁸ For truly, I say to you, till heaven and earth pass away, not an iota, not a dot, will pass from the law until all is accomplished. ¹⁹ Whoever then relaxes one of the least of these commandments and teaches men so, shall be called least in the kingdom of heaven; but he who does them and teaches them shall be called great in the kingdom of heaven. ²⁰ For I tell you, unless your righteousness exceeds that of the scribes and Pharisees, you will never enter the kingdom of heaven.

 Despite all the suffering and incredibly threatening circumstances in the world, this passage gives me the confidence that a life of faith can be an example for others. I often get the feeling that many efforts for peaceful coexistence and respectful treatment of people and the environment simply make no impression. Yet these sentences from the Bible tell us not to let ourselves get discouraged. Every one of us can be a light in the world.

CHRISTIAN

You shall not kill—not even with words (Mt 5:21–26)

²¹ "You have heard that it was said to the men of old, 'You shall not kill; and whoever kills shall be liable to judgment.' ²² But I say to you that every one who is angry with his brother shall be liable to judgment; whoever insults his brother shall be liable to the council, and whoever says, 'You fool!' shall be liable to the hell of fire. ²³ So if you are offering your gift at the altar, and there remember that your

▶ Jesus makes a declaration of principle. He speaks with authority. But he does not speak ill of the Old Testament Law or of the prophets of Israel. He concentrates on the will of God, who has in mind what is best for us.

When you free your soul from hatred you make peace with God and you make peace with your neighbors.

CATHERINE OF SIENA

Adultery begins in the head. Jesus criticizes the look with which a man desires to take possession of a woman.

▶ Jesus is speaking metaphorically. He does not want people to maim themselves but, rather, to know what matters in life.

brother has something against you, ²⁴ leave your gift there before the altar and go; first be reconciled to your brother, and then come and offer your gift. ²⁵ Make friends quickly with your accuser, while you are going with him to court, lest your accuser hand you over to the judge, and the judge to the guard, and you be put in prison; ²⁶ truly, I say to you, you will never get out till you have paid the last penny.

Being faithful (Mt 5:27–30)

²⁷ "You have heard that it was said, 'You shall not commit adultery.' ²⁸ But I say to you that every one who looks at a woman lustfully has already committed adultery with her in his heart.

²⁹ If your right eye causes you to sin, pluck it out and throw it away; it is better that you lose one of your members than that your whole body be thrown into hell.

³⁰ And if your right hand causes you to sin, cut it off and throw it away; it is better that you lose one of your members than that your whole body go into hell.

Until death do us part (Mt 5:31–32)

³¹ "It was also said, 'Whoever divorces his wife, let him give her a certificate of divorce.' ³² But I say to you that every one who divorces

▶ These words were spoken in an age when only men had a right to divorce. What was "unchastity"? Many scholars say it refers to a certain kind of invalid union. Because that union was invalid, ending it was not the same as ending a marriage. Jesus stands up for the indissolubility of marriage (↗ Mt 19:3–12; 1 Mk 10:1–10).

his wife, except on the ground of unchastity, makes her an adulteress; and whoever marries a divorced woman commits adultery.

Let your yes mean yes, and your no mean no (Mt 5:33–37)

³³ "Again you have heard that it was said to the men of old, 'You shall not swear falsely, but shall perform to the Lord what you have sworn.' ³⁴ But I say to you, Do not swear at all, either by heaven, for it is the throne of God, ³⁵ or by the earth, for it is his footstool, or by Jerusalem, for it is the city of the great King. ³⁶ And do not swear by your head, for you cannot make one hair white or black.

³⁷ Let what you say be simply 'Yes' or 'No'; anything more than this comes from the Evil One.

Breaking the vicious circle of violence (Mt 5:38–42)

³⁸ "You have heard that it was said, 'An eye for an eye and a tooth for a tooth.' ³⁹ But I say to you, Do not resist one who is evil. But if any one strikes you on the right cheek, turn to him the other also; ⁴⁰ and if any one would sue you and take your coat, let him have your cloak as well; ⁴¹ and if any one forces you to go one mile, go with him two miles. ⁴² Give to him who begs from you, and do not refuse him who would borrow from you.

One cannot live a trial life or die a trial death. One cannot love on a trial basis or accept a person on trial and for a limited time.

POPE JOHN PAUL II, November 15, 1980

Love knows no boundaries (Mt 5:43–48)

⁴³ "You have heard that it was said, 'You shall love your neighbor and hate your enemy.' ⁴⁴ But I say to you, Love your enemies and pray for those who persecute you, ⁴⁵ so that you may be sons of your Father who is in heaven; for he makes his sun rise on the evil and on the good, and sends rain on the just and on the unjust.

⁴⁶ For if you love those who love you, what reward have you? Do not even the tax collectors do the same? ⁴⁷ And if you salute only your brethren, what more are you doing than others? Do not even the Gentiles do the same? ⁴⁸ You, therefore, must be perfect, as your heavenly Father is perfect.

Donate—but honestly! (Mt 6:1–4)

6 ¹ "Beware of practicing your piety before men in order to be seen by them; for then you will have no reward from your Father who is in heaven.

² "Thus, when you give alms, sound no trumpet before you, as the hypocrites do in the synagogues and in the streets, that they may be praised by men. Truly, I say to you, they have their reward. ³ But when you give alms, do not let your left hand know what your right

When I get into an argument with people or am down in the dumps, I always try first to get a moment of peace and quiet. Often I simply go for a walk. Then that does me a lot of good. After a while, I have the courage to ask for forgiveness. I sense: Jesus is the one who is giving me strength and courage.
NICO

❞ Love is the only force capable of transforming an enemy into a friend.
MARTIN LUTHER KING
(1929–1968), American minister and human-rights activist

▶ Alms are donations for the needy.

hand is doing, ⁴ so that your alms may be in secret; and your Father who sees in secret will reward you.

Pray, but how? The Our Father (Mt 6:5–15)

⁵ "And when you pray, you must not be like the hypocrites; for they love to stand and pray in the synagogues and at the street corners, that they may be seen by men. Truly, I say to you, they have their reward. ⁶ But when you pray, go into your room and shut the door and pray to your Father who is in secret; and your Father who sees in secret will reward you.

⁷ "And in praying do not heap up empty phrases as the Gentiles do; for they think that they will be heard for their many words. ⁸ Do not be like them, for your Father knows what you need before you ask him. ⁹ Pray then like this:
Our Father who art in heaven,
Hallowed be thy name.
¹⁰ Thy kingdom come.
Thy will be done,
On earth as it is in heaven.
¹¹ Give us this day our daily bread;
¹² And forgive us our trespasses,
As we forgive those who trespass against us;

▶ A synagogue is a Jewish house of prayer and gathering.

❞ One thing that is not being tried in any particularly enthusiastic way by people who call themselves Catholics is Catholicism.
BENEDICT GROESCHEL, C.F.R.
1933–2014), American Franciscan priest and author

💡 Again and again John Vianney, the saintly Curé of Ars, came into his church and saw an old farmer who sat there for hours praying. The farmer looked very happy as he did so. The Curé of Ars asked him: "Tell me, how do you pray?" The farmer replied: "I look at HIM, and HE looks at me. That is enough."

¹³ And lead us not into temptation,
But deliver us from evil.
¹⁴ For if you forgive men their trespasses, your heavenly Father also will forgive you; ¹⁵ but if you do not forgive men their trespasses, neither will your Father forgive your trespasses.

Fasting, yes; sadness, no (Mt 6:16–18)

¹⁶ "And when you fast, do not look dismal, like the hypocrites, for they disfigure their faces that their fasting may be seen by men. Tru-ly, I say to you, they have their reward.¹⁷ But when you fast, anoint your head and wash your face,¹⁸ that your fasting may not be seen by men but by your Father who is in secret; and your Father who sees in secret will reward you.

What is truly valuable (Mt 6:19–24)

¹⁹ Do not lay up for yourselves treasures on earth, where moth and rust consume and where thieves break in and steal, ²⁰ but lay up for yourselves treasures in heaven, where neither moth nor rust con-sumes and where thieves do not break in and steal. ²¹ For where your treasure is, there will your heart be also.

²² "The eye is the lamp of the body. So, if your eye is sound, your

▶ Jesus is making a point dra-matically. He chooses drastic images so that we might open our eyes to the evil in our own heart and fight against sin.

99 [Through bodily fasting] you give us strength to purify our hearts, to control our desires, and so to serve you in freedom.

Preface II for Lent

 I always like to plan everything down to the smallest detail. But many things simply cannot be planned. In that case it always comforts me to know that God already knows why things turn out one way or another. (Christina)

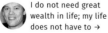 I do not need great wealth in life; my life does not have to →

whole body will be full of light; ²³ but if your eye is not sound, your whole body will be full of darkness. If then the light in you is dark-ness, how great is the darkness!

²⁴ "No one can serve two masters; for either he will hate the one and love the other, or he will be devoted to the one and despise the other. You cannot serve God and mammon.

Do not worry (Mt 6:25–34)

²⁵ "Therefore I tell you, do not be anxious about your life, what you shall eat or what you shall drink, nor about your body, what you shall put on. Is not life more than food, and the body more than clothing? ²⁶ Look at the birds of the air: they neither sow nor reap nor gather into barns, and yet your heavenly Father feeds them. Are you not of more value than they? ²⁷ And which of you by being anxious can add one cubit to his span of life? ²⁸ And why are you anxious about clothing? Consider the lilies of the field, how they grow; they neither toil nor spin; ²⁹ yet I tell you, even Solomon in all his glory was not clothed like one of these. ³⁰ But if God so clothes the grass of the field, which today is alive and tomorrow is thrown into the oven, will he not much more clothe you, O you of little faith? ³¹ Therefore do not be anxious, saying, 'What shall we eat?' or 'What shall we drink?' or 'What shall we wear?' ³² For the Gentiles seek all

these things; and your heavenly Father knows that you need them all. ³³ But seek first his kingdom and his righteousness, and all these things shall be yours as well.

³⁴ "Therefore do not be anxious about tomorrow, for tomorrow will be anxious for itself. Let the day's own trouble be sufficient for the day.

→ revolve around how to become richer or more powerful. Ultimately it depends on God, who supports and guides my life. (George)

CHRISTINA & GEORGE

Do not write other people off (Mt 7:1–5)

7 ¹ "Judge not, that you be not judged. ² For with the judgment you pronounce you will be judged, and the measure you give will be the measure you get. ³ Why do you see the speck that is in your brother's eye, but do not notice the log that is in your own eye? ⁴ Or how can you say to your brother, 'Let me take the speck out of your eye,' when there is the log in your own eye? ⁵ You hypocrite, first take the log out of your own eye, and then you will see clearly to take the speck out of your brother's eye.

📖 Cast all your anxieties on him, for he cares about you.

1 Pet 5:7

▶ Jesus is not criticizing the administration of justice. He is opposed to people condemning other people because they disapprove of their behavior. The final judgment belongs to God alone.

No pearls before swine (Mt 7:6)

⁶ "Do not give dogs what is holy; and do not throw your pearls before swine, lest they trample them under foot and turn to attack you.

💡 Dogs did not matter much; swine were regarded as unclean animals. A list of unclean animals can be found in Lev 3:11.

Pray with great confidence (Mt 7:7–11)

⁷ "Ask, and it will be given you; seek, and you will find; knock, and it will be opened to you. ⁸ For every one who asks receives, and he who seeks finds, and to him who knocks it will be opened. ⁹ Or what man of you, if his son asks him for bread, will give him a stone? ¹⁰ Or if he asks for a fish, will give him a serpent? ¹¹ If you then, who are evil, know how to give good gifts to your children, how much more will your Father who is in heaven give good things to those who ask him!

🍷 → 486, 487
Why should we petition God?
Why should we petition God for other people?

▶ The Golden Rule is known in many cultures. Since antiquity it has been traditional in India and China, Persia, Egypt, and Greece. In the Sermon on the Mount, it is a bridge from the Gospel to the wisdom of the nations.

The Golden Rule of getting along with others (Mt 7:12)

¹² So whatever you wish that men would do to you, do so to them; for this is the law and the prophets.

Choose the right way (Mt 7:13–14)

¹³ "Enter by the narrow gate; for the gate is wide and the way is easy, that leads to destruction, and those who enter by it are many. ¹⁴ For the gate is narrow and the way is hard, that leads to life, and those who find it are few.

📖 I call heaven and earth to witness against you this day, that I have set before you life and death, blessing and curse; therefore choose life, that you and your descendants may live.

Deut 30:19

I try with all my heart to know the Father's will for my life and to do the works that God prepared for me in advance. I try to get rid of my old assurances and to build my life on Jesus. I face big challenges because of the decisions that I must make. I get help from personal conversation with God and also from advice from my brothers and sisters in Christ.

MICHAELA

By their fruits you will know them (Mt 7:15–23)

15 "Beware of false prophets, who come to you in sheep's clothing but inwardly are ravenous wolves. 16 You will know them by their fruits. Are grapes gathered from thorns, or figs from thistles? 17 So, every sound tree bears good fruit, but the bad tree bears evil fruit. 18 A sound tree cannot bear evil fruit, nor can a bad tree bear good fruit. 19 Every tree that does not bear good fruit is cut down and thrown into the fire. 20 Thus you will know them by their fruits.

21 "Not every one who says to me, 'Lord, Lord,' shall enter the kingdom of heaven, but he who does the will of my Father who is in heaven. 22 On that day many will say to me, 'Lord, Lord, did we not prophesy in your name, and cast out demons in your name, and do many mighty works in your name?' 23 And then will I declare to them, 'I never knew you; depart from me, you evildoers.'

Do not build on sand (Mt 7:24–27)

24 "Every one then who hears these words of mine and does them will be like a wise man who built his house upon the rock; 25 and the rain fell, and the floods came, and the winds blew and beat upon that house, but it did not fall, because it had been founded on the rock. 26 And every one who hears these words of mine and does not

" But what does it mean to build a house on the rock? Building on the rock means, first of all, to build on Christ and with Christ.

POPE BENEDICT XVI, May 27, 2006

do them will be like a foolish man who built his house upon the sand; 27 and the rain fell, and the floods came, and the winds blew and beat against that house, and it fell; and great was the fall of it."

Jesus makes an impression (Mt 7:28)

28 And when Jesus finished these sayings, the crowds were astonished at his teaching, 29 for he taught them as one who had authority, and not as their scribes.

The Sermon on the Mount is followed by a series of Jesus' miracles. In Matthew, they are called mighty works, because they prove the power of Jesus over sickness and want, over guilt and sin. The Sermon on the Mount showed that Jesus is a master of the word. Now the evangelist shows that Jesus follows up words with deeds.

MIRACLE AFTER MIRACLE (MT 8:1–9:34)

A leper is made clean (Mt 8:1–4)

8 1 When he came down from the mountain, great crowds followed him; 2 and behold, a leper came to him and knelt before him, saying, "Lord, if you will, you can make me clean." 3 And he stretched out his hand and touched him, saying, "I will; be clean." And imme-

diately his leprosy was cleansed. ⁴ And Jesus said to him, "See that you say nothing to any one; but go, show yourself to the priest, and offer the gift that Moses commanded, for a proof to the people."

A pagan comes to the faith (Mt 8:5–13)

⁵ As he entered Caper'na-um, a centurion came forward to him, begging him ⁶ and saying, "Lord, my servant is lying paralyzed at home, in terrible distress." ⁷ And he said to him, "I will come and heal him." ⁸ But the centurion answered him, "Lord, I am not worthy to have you come under my roof; but only say the word, and my servant will be healed. ⁹ For I am a man under authority, with soldiers under me; and I say to one, 'Go,' and he goes, and to another, 'Come,' and he comes, and to my slave, 'Do this,' and he does it." ¹⁰ When Jesus heard him, he marveled, and said to those who followed him, "Truly, I say to you, not even in Israel have I found such faith. ¹¹ I tell you, many will come from east and west and sit at table with Abraham, Isaac, and Jacob in the kingdom of heaven, ¹² while the sons of the kingdom will be thrown into the outer darkness; there men will

▶ "Leprosy" is an infectious skin disease that according to Old Testament Law made a person "unclean". A "leprous" person is not allowed to participate in the life of God's people (Lev 13–14).

▶ Before Communion everyone makes this statement his own: "Lord, I am not worthy that you should enter under my roof, but only say the word and my soul shall be healed."

▶ The unusual thing about this healing is that the centurion is not a Jew, but a pagan. Jesus crosses over a boundary. He brings the Kingdom of God to the pagans, too.

weep and gnash their teeth." ¹³ And to the centurion Jesus said, "Go; let it be done for you as you have believed." And the servant was healed at that very moment.

Peter's mother-in-law is cured (Mt 8:14–15)

¹⁴ And when Jesus entered Peter's house, he saw his mother-in-law lying sick with a fever; ¹⁵ he touched her hand, and the fever left her, and she rose and served him.

All that came were healed (Mt 8:16–17)

¹⁶ That evening they brought to him many who were possessed with demons; and he cast out the spirits with a word, and healed all who were sick. ¹⁷ This was to fulfil what was spoken by the prophet Isaiah, "He took our infirmities and bore our diseases."

Jesus demands all or nothing (Mt 8:18–22)

¹⁸ Now when Jesus saw great crowds around him, he gave orders to go over to the other side. ¹⁹ And a scribe came up and said to him, "Teacher, I will follow you wherever you go." ²⁰ And Jesus said to him, "Foxes have holes, and birds of the air have nests; but the Son of man has nowhere to lay his head." ²¹ Another of the disciples said

Y → 240–242
How was "sickness" interpreted in the Old Testament? Why did Jesus show so much interest in the sick? Why should the Church take special care of the sick?

▶ The believer has sufficient motive for believing, for he is moved by the authority of Divine teaching confirmed by miracles, and, what is more, by the inward instinct of the Divine invitation: hence, he does not believe lightly.

THOMAS AQUINAS

▶ This is a very hard saying. Burying one's parents is the last service that children must perform for them. Jesus is very deliberately being provocative. He wants to make clear what deserves priority: the new life. It comes about by following Jesus.

to him, "Lord, let me first go and bury my father." [22] But Jesus said to him, "Follow me, and leave the dead to bury their own dead."

Jesus rescues his disciples (Mt 8:23–27)

[23] And when he got into the boat, his disciples followed him. [24] And behold, there arose a great storm on the sea, so that the boat was being swamped by the waves; but he was asleep. [25] And they went and woke him, saying, "Save us, Lord; we are perishing." [26] And he said to them, "Why are you afraid, O men of little faith?" Then he rose and rebuked the winds and the sea; and there was a great calm. [27] And the men marveled, saying, "What sort of man is this, that even winds and sea obey him?"

Jesus delivers from demons (Mt 8:28–34)

[28] And when he came to the other side, to the country of the Gad'arenes, two demoniacs met him, coming out of the tombs, so fierce that no one could pass that way. [29] And behold, they cried out, "What have you to do with us, O Son of God? Have you come here to torment us before the time?" [30] Now a herd of many swine was feeding at some distance from them.

[31] And the demons begged him, "If you cast us out, send us away into the herd of swine." [32] And he said to them, "Go." So they came

out and went into the swine; and behold, the whole herd rushed down the steep bank into the sea, and perished in the waters. [33] The herdsmen fled, and going into the city they told everything, and what had happened to the demoniacs. [34] And behold, all the city came out to meet Jesus; and when they saw him, they begged him to leave their neighborhood.

Jesus forgives sins (Mt 9:1–8)

9 [1] And getting into a boat he crossed over and came to his own city. [2] And behold, they brought to him a paralytic, lying on his bed; and when Jesus saw their faith, he said to the paralytic, "Take heart, my son; your sins are forgiven." [3] And behold, some of the scribes said to themselves, "This man is blaspheming." [4] But Jesus, knowing their thoughts, said, "Why do you think evil in your hearts? [5] For which is easier, to say, 'Your sins are forgiven,' or to say, 'Rise and walk'? [6] But that you may know that the Son of man has authority on earth to forgive sins"—he then said to the paralytic—"Rise, take up your bed and go home." [7] And he rose and went home. [8] When the crowds saw it, they were afraid, and they glorified God, who had given such authority to men.

Jesus, the physician (Mt 9:9–13)

[9] As Jesus passed on from there, he saw a man called Matthew sitting at the tax office; and he said to him, "Follow me." And he rose and followed him.

Someone who has faith does not tremble. He does not act rashly, he is not pessimistic, he does not lose his nerve.

POPE JOHN XXIII

▶ For the people of Jesus' time, possession was a terrible experience: an inexplicable illness, against which no one could do anything—only God. Jesus has power over evil spirits.

¹⁰ And as he sat at table in the house, behold, many tax collectors and sinners came and sat down with Jesus and his disciples. ¹¹ And when the Pharisees saw this, they said to his disciples, "Why does your teacher eat with tax collectors and sinners?" ¹² But when he heard it, he said, "Those who are well have no need of a physician, but those who are sick. ¹³ Go and learn what this means, 'I desire mercy, and not sacrifice.' For I came not to call the righteous, but sinners."

> Tradition regards this Matthew as the author of the Gospel.

> The Pharisees criticize Jesus because he does not shun sinners. They fear that he does not distinguish between good and evil. They think that bad company spoils morals. They do not see that Jesus' holiness is contagious. He makes the sick healthy and sinners just.

New wine in new wineskins (Mt 9:14–17)

¹⁴ Then the disciples of John came to him, saying, "Why do we and the Pharisees fast, but your disciples do not fast?" ¹⁵ And Jesus said to them, "Can the wedding guests mourn as long as the bridegroom is with them? The days will come, when the bridegroom is taken away from them, and then they will fast.

> The bridegroom stands for Jesus. His bride is Israel, Daughter Zion.

¹⁶ And no one puts a piece of unshrunk cloth on an old garment, for the patch tears away from the garment, and a worse tear is made. ¹⁷ Neither is new wine put into old wineskins; if it is, the skins burst, and the wine is spilled, and the skins are destroyed; but new wine is put into fresh wineskins, and so both are preserved."

A girl is brought back to life, and a woman is healed (Mt 9:18–26)

¹⁸ While he was thus speaking to them, behold, a ruler came in and knelt before him, saying, "My daughter has just died; but come and lay your hand on her, and she will live." ¹⁹ And Jesus rose and followed him, with his disciples. ²⁰ And behold, a woman who had suffered from a hemorrhage for twelve years came up behind him and touched the fringe of his garment; ²¹ for she said to herself, "If I only touch his garment, I shall be made well." ²² Jesus turned, and seeing her he said, "Take heart, daughter; your faith has made you well." And instantly the woman was made well. ²³ And when Jesus came to the ruler's house, and saw the flute players, and the crowd making a tumult, ²⁴ he said, "Depart; for the girl is not dead but sleeping." And they laughed at him. ²⁵ But when the crowd had been put outside, he went in and took her by the hand, and the girl arose.

²⁶ And the report of this went through all that district.

> Why do you rely on yourself and are thus unable to stand? Cast yourself on him! And do not fear, he will not give way and let you fall! No, cast yourself confidently on him; he will catch you and heal you.
>
> AUGUSTINE

> Jesus does not heal automatically. He wants to awaken the people's faith through his healings, too. The one who believes can be healed. The woman becomes a model for faith.

Jesus restores sight (Mt 9:27–31)

²⁷ And as Jesus passed on from there, two blind men followed him, crying aloud, "Have mercy on us, Son of David." ²⁸ When he entered the house, the blind men came to him; and Jesus said to them, "Do you believe that I am able to do this?" They said to him, "Yes, Lord." ²⁹ Then he touched their eyes, saying, "According to your faith let it be done to you." ³⁰ And their eyes were opened. And Jesus sternly

> "Son of David" is a title for the Messiah, the Christ. The "Son of David" helps—that is the hope of the blind men, whom no one else can help.

charged them, "See that no one knows it." [31] But they went away and spread his fame through all that district.

The mute can speak again (Mt 9:32–34)

[32] As they were going away, behold, a mute demoniac was brought to him. [33] And when the demon had been cast out, the mute man spoke; and the crowds marveled, saying, "Never was anything like this seen in Israel." [34] But the Pharisees said, "He casts out demons by the prince of demons."

Next in the Gospel of Matthew comes the mission of the disciples, who like Jesus are supposed to proclaim the Gospel (Mt 9:35—11:1). After a few examples show how differently people react to the proclamation (Mt 11:2—12:50), Jesus gives a second major discourse. In parables he explains what is happening with the spread of the Good News.

PARABLES OF THE KINGDOM OF HEAVEN (MT 13:1–53)

▶ A parable is a story in images. Jesus relates incidents from people's everyday lives. They are supposed to discover God in this life and hope in him beyond this life.

All's well that ends well (Mt 13:1–9)

13 [1] That same day Jesus went out of the house and sat beside the sea. [2] And great crowds gathered about him, so that he got into a boat and sat there; and the whole crowd stood on the beach. [3] And he told them many things in parables, saying: "A sow-

er went out to sow. [4] And as he sowed, some seeds fell along the path, and the birds came and devoured them. [5] Other seeds fell on rocky ground, where they had not much soil, and immediately they sprang up, since they had no depth of soil, [6] but when the sun rose they were scorched; and since they had no root they withered away. [7] Other seeds fell upon thorns, and the thorns grew up and choked them. [8] Other seeds fell on good soil and brought forth grain, some a hundredfold, some sixty, some thirty. [9] He who has ears, let him hear."

Why parables? (Mt 13:10–17)

[10] Then the disciples came and said to him, "Why do you speak to them in parables?" [11] And he answered them, "To you it has been given to know the secrets of the kingdom of heaven, but to them it has not been given. [12] For to him who has will more be given, and he will have abundance; but from him who has not, even what he has will be taken away. [13] This is why I speak to them in parables, because seeing they do not see, and hearing they do not hear, nor do they understand. [14] With them indeed is fulfilled the prophecy of Isaiah which says:

'You shall indeed hear but never understand, and you shall indeed see but never perceive.

¹⁵ For this people's heart has grown dull, and their ears are heavy of hearing, and their eyes they have closed, lest they should perceive with their eyes, and hear with their ears, and understand with their heart, and turn for me to heal them.'

¹⁶ But blessed are your eyes, for they see, and your ears, for they hear. ¹⁷ Truly, I say to you, many prophets and righteous men longed to see what you see, and did not see it, and to hear what you hear, and did not hear it.

▶ Jesus' parables are not complicated. You can quickly understand the story that they tell. But someone who really wants to understand a parable has to relate it to his own life. That is difficult. Jesus speaks about this difficulty in the words of the prophet Isaiah. God closes the ears of those who do not want to hear.

There will be problems, but … (Mt 13:18–23)

¹⁸ "Hear then the parable of the sower. ¹⁹ When any one hears the word of the kingdom and does not understand it, the Evil One comes and snatches away what is sown in his heart; this is what was sown along the path. ²⁰ As for what was sown on rocky ground, this is he who hears the word and immediately receives it with joy; ²¹ yet he has no root in himself, but endures for a while, and when tribulation or persecution arises on account of the word, immediately he falls away. ²² As for what was sown among thorns, this is he who hears the word, but the cares of the world and the delight in riches choke the word, and it proves unfruitful. ²³ As for what was sown on good soil, this is he who hears the word and understands it; he indeed bears

▶ The interpretation (vv. 18–23) connects the parable of the sower with the experiences that Jesus and his disciples have on their mission. They must be ready for failures. But they do not have to become discouraged: in the end the harvest will be abundant.

fruit, and yields, in one case a hundredfold, in another sixty, and in another thirty."

Do not pull up the weeds too soon (Mt 13:24–30)

²⁴ Another parable he put before them, saying, "The kingdom of heaven may be compared to a man who sowed good seed in his field; ²⁵ but while men were sleeping, his enemy came and sowed weeds among the wheat, and went away. ²⁶ So when the plants came up and bore grain, then the weeds appeared also. ²⁷ And the servants of the householder came and said to him, 'Sir, did you not sow good seed in your field? How then has it weeds?' ²⁸ He said to them, 'An enemy has done this.' The servants said to him, 'Then do you want us to go and gather them?' ²⁹ But he said, 'No; lest in gathering the weeds you root up the wheat along with them. ³⁰ Let both grow together until the harvest; and at harvest time I will tell the reapers, Gather the weeds first and bind them in bundles to be burned, but gather the wheat into my barn.' "

A little mustard seed of hope (Mt 13:31–32)

³¹ Another parable he put before them, saying, "The kingdom of heaven is like a grain of mustard seed which a man took and sowed in his field; ³² it is the smallest of all seeds, but when it has grown

 My faith had developed in very different ways in various phases of my life. In the parable of the sower, I recognize my own faith journey. At one moment my faith is mighty; I can feel its strong roots. Then again it lies uncovered on the rocky ground, quite unprotected and threatened. The parable gives me courage to keep working at my story with God.

CHRISTA

▶ God is the judge—he alone. No human being, and no disciple, can replace him. Jesus does not describe evil in flattering words. But the most important task of his disciples is to allow time and to make room for people to be able to repent.

it is the greatest of shrubs and becomes a tree, so that the birds of the air come and make nests in its branches."

Just a little can change everything (Mt 13:33)

[33] He told them another parable. "The kingdom of heaven is like leaven which a woman took and hid in three measures of meal, till it was all leavened."

Parables tell of mysteries (Mt 13:34–35)

[34] All this Jesus said to the crowds in parables; indeed he said nothing to them without a parable. [35] This was to fulfil what was spoken by the prophet:

"I will open my mouth in parables, I will utter what has been hidden since the foundation of the world."

At the end the weeds must go (Mt 13:36–43)

[36] Then he left the crowds and went into the house. And his disciples came to him, saying, "Explain to us the parable of the weeds of the field." [37] He answered, "He who sows the good seed is the Son of man; [38] the field is the world, and the good seed means the sons of the kingdom; the weeds are the sons of the evil one, [39] and the enemy

who sowed them is the devil; the harvest is the close of the age, and the reapers are angels. [40] Just as the weeds are gathered and burned with fire, so will it be at the close of the age. [41] The Son of man will send his angels, and they will gather out of his kingdom all causes of sin and all evildoers, [42] and throw them into the furnace of fire, where there will be weeping and gnashing of teeth. [43] Then the righteous will shine like the sun in the kingdom of their Father. He who has ears, let him hear.

My treasure! My pearl! (Mt 13:44–46)

[44] "The kingdom of heaven is like treasure hidden in a field, which a man found and covered up; then in his joy he goes and sells all that he has and buys that field.

[45] "Again, the kingdom of heaven is like a merchant in search of fine pearls, [46] who, on finding one pearl of great value, went and sold all that he had and bought it.

Many fish go into the net (Mt 13:47–50)

[47] "Again, the kingdom of heaven is like a net which was thrown into the sea and gathered fish of every kind; [48] when it was full, men drew it ashore and sat down and sorted the good into vessels

---

> The Church started very small and insignificant. But through faith and perseverance in love, it grew into a worldwide family of believers.

STEVE RAY

▶ Leaven is a combination of lactic bacteria and yeast fungus. If even a small amount of leaven is mixed into normal dough, the whole mass of dough changes within a short time. It becomes airy, aromatic, tastier, more easily digestible, and longer lasting.

> On the day of the Last Judgment, they will not ask us what we read but what we did; they will not ask how eloquently we spoke but how piously we lived.

THOMAS À KEMPIS (1380–1471), author of *The Imitation of Christ*

Blessed is the man who trusts in the LORD, whose trust is the LORD.

Jer 17:7

We receive from God as much as we hope for from him.

THÉRÈSE OF LISIEUX

but threw away the bad. ⁴⁹ So it will be at the close of the age. The angels will come out and separate the evil from the righteous, ⁵⁰ and throw them into the furnace of fire, where there will be weeping and gnashing of teeth.

The disciples ought to understand (Mt 13:51–53)

⁵¹ "Have you understood all this?" They said to him, "Yes." ⁵² And he said to them, "Therefore every scribe who has been trained for the kingdom of heaven is like a householder who brings out of his treasure what is new and what is old."

⁵³ And when Jesus had finished these parables, he went away from there.

▶ The parable is an image for the Last Judgment. God is just. He distinguishes exactly between good and evil. That is why there is no salvation without judgment. But the judgment exists for the sake of salvation.

Y → 163
What is the Last Judgment?

▶ There is no contradiction between faith and knowledge. Faith seeks understanding. Thinking benefits from faith.

THE DISCIPLES GO TO THE SCHOOL OF JESUS (MT 16:13–17:9)

Matthew goes on to tell how Jesus spreads the Good News by word and deed (Mt 14:1—16:12). His disciples are with him. They continue to go to the school of faith.

Peter professes his faith in the Messiah— and still has a lot to learn (Mt 16:13–20)

16 ¹³ Now when Jesus came into the district of Caesare'a Phil-ip'pi, he asked his disciples, "Who do men say that the Son of man is?" ¹⁴ And they said, "Some say John the Baptist, others say Eli'jah, and others Jeremiah or one of the prophets." ¹⁵ He said to them, "But who do you say that I am?" ¹⁶ Simon Peter replied, "You are the Christ, the Son of the living God." ¹⁷ And Jesus answered him, "Blessed are you, Simon Bar-Jona! For flesh and blood has not re-vealed this to you, but my Father who is in heaven. ¹⁸ And I tell you, you are Peter, and on this rock I will build my Church, and the gates of Hades shall not prevail against it. ¹⁹ I will give you the keys of the kingdom of heaven, and whatever you bind on earth shall be bound in heaven, and whatever you loose on earth shall be loosed in heaven." ²⁰ Then he strictly charged the disciples to tell no one that he was the Christ.

Jesus will suffer and rise from the dead (Mt 16:21–23)

²¹ From that time Jesus began to show his disciples that he must go to Jerusalem and suffer many things from the elders and chief priests and scribes, and be killed, and on the third day be raised. ²² And Peter took him and began to rebuke him, saying, "God forbid,

❝❝ Tradition is handing on the fire, not worshipping the ashes.

GUSTAV MAHLER (1860–1911), Austrian composer

▶ The "Church" is the commu-nion of believers. She stands on the foundation of the Rock, Peter. For Peter is the pre-eminent disciple of Jesus. He professes his faith: Jesus is the Christ. That is the fundamental profession of the Church to this day. He has the power of the keys: "To bind" and "to loose" refer to the forgiveness of sins and the power to declare au-thoritative teaching. According to Mt 18:18, the whole commu-nity is involved.

▶ The contrast could not be starker: Peter, after professing his faith, gets in Jesus' way. He thinks in human terms. He does not want Jesus to die. He has to learn that Jesus walks the way of suffering. This way leads to the Resurrection.

Lord! This shall never happen to you." [23] But he turned and said to Peter, "Get behind me, Satan! You are a hindrance to me; for you are not on the side of God, but of men."

Discipleship: a matter of life and death (Mt 16:24–28)

[24] Then Jesus told his disciples, "If any man would come after me, let him deny himself and take up his cross and follow me. [25] For whoever would save his life will lose it, and whoever loses his life for my sake will find it. [26] For what will it profit a man, if he gains the whole world and forfeits his life? Or what shall a man give in return for his life? [27] For the Son of man is to come with his angels in the glory of his Father, and then he will repay every man for what he has done. [28] Truly, I say to you, there are some standing here who will not taste death before they see the Son of man coming in his kingdom."

 I do not like the crosses in my life. But I know that I have the privilege of carrying them with me. And I know that they are making me strong. In difficult, bitter moments, my strength increases. I am closer to Jesus. My rough edges are smoothed down. And so I tell myself: Don't run away when Golgotha comes. Embrace it!

NICO

He was transfigured before their eyes (Mt 17:1–9)

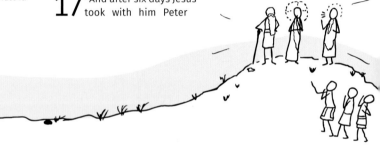

17 [1] And after six days Jesus took with him Peter

▶ Moses and Elijah represent the Old Testament and God's People Israel.

99 When one has the grace to live a strong experience of God, it is as if one is experiencing something like what happened to the disciples during the Transfiguration: a momentary foretaste of what will constitute the happiness of Paradise.

POPE BENEDICT XVI, March 12, 2006

and James and John his brother, and led them up a high mountain apart. [2] And he was transfigured before them, and his face shone like the sun, and his garments became white as light. [3] And behold, there appeared to them Moses and Eli'jah, talking with him. [4] And Peter said to Jesus, "Lord, it is well that we are here; if you wish, I will make three booths here, one for you and one for Moses and one for Eli'jah." [5] He was still speaking, when behold, a bright cloud overshadowed them, and a voice from the cloud said, "This is my beloved Son, with whom I am well pleased; listen to him." [6] When the disciples heard this, they fell on their faces, and were filled with awe. [7] But Jesus came and touched them, saying, "Rise, and have no fear." [8] And when they lifted up their eyes, they saw no one but Jesus only.

[9] And as they were coming down the mountain, Jesus commanded them, "Tell no one the vision, until the Son of man is raised from the dead."

JESUS COMES TO JERUSALEM (MT 21:1–22:14)

Matthew continues his account with two further announcements of Jesus' suffering and Resurrection (Mt 17:22–23; 20:17–19). He records the difficulties that his disciples had in understanding this way. But Jesus remains with them and takes them with him to Jerusalem.

Jesus enters the city (Mt 21:1–11)

21 ¹ And when they drew near to Jerusalem and came to Beth'phage, to the Mount of Olives, then Jesus sent two disciples, ² saying to them, "Go into the village opposite you, and immediately you will find a donkey tied, and a colt with her; untie them and bring them to me. ³ If any one says anything to you, you shall say, 'The Lord has need of them,' and he will send them immediately." ⁴ This took place to fulfil what was spoken by the prophet, saying,

⁵ "Tell the daughter of Zion,
Behold, your king is coming to you,
  humble, and mounted on a donkey,
and on a colt, the foal of a donkey."

⁶ The disciples went and did as Jesus had directed them; ⁷ they brought the donkey and the colt, and put their garments on them, and he sat on them. ⁸ Most of the crowd spread their garments on the road, and others cut branches from the trees and spread them on the road. ⁹ And the crowds that went before him and that followed him shouted, "Hosanna to the Son of David! Blessed is he who comes in the name of the Lord! Hosanna in the highest!" ¹⁰ And when he entered Jerusalem, all the city was stirred, saying, "Who is this?"

▶ Jesus enters the City of God as a royal Messiah. His power, however, is not based on violence. Jesus is a peacemaker. He follows the path of humility and submission. That is why death has no power over him.

▶ "Hosanna" is a Hebrew word meaning: "God, help!" But in Jesus' day, it was also a cry of jubilation.

¹¹ And the crowds said, "This is the prophet Jesus from Nazareth of Galilee."

The Temple, a house of prayer (Mt 21:12–17)

¹² And Jesus entered the temple of God and drove out all who sold and bought in the temple, and he overturned the tables of the money-changers and the seats of those who sold pigeons. ¹³ He said to them, "It is written, 'My house shall be called a house of prayer'; but you make it a den of robbers."

¹⁴ And the blind and the lame came to him in the temple, and he healed them. ¹⁵ But when the chief priests and the scribes saw the wonderful things that he did, and the children crying out in the temple, "Hosanna to the Son of David!" they were indignant; ¹⁶ and they said to him, "Do you hear what these are saying?" And Jesus said to them, "Yes; have you never read, 'Out of the mouths of babies and infants you have brought perfect praise'?"

¹⁷ And leaving them, he went out of the city to Beth'any and lodged there.

▶ The services of the merchants and money-changers were used so that the sacrifices could be offered correctly. They worked in the "outer court".

Faith can move mountains (Mt 21:18–22)

¹⁸ In the morning, as he was returning to the city, he was hungry. ¹⁹ And seeing a fig tree by the wayside he went to it, and found

▶ This story is a parable being related. The dried-up fig tree foretells the destruction of Jerusalem, which occurred in A.D. 70.

Υ → 21, 22
Faith—what is it?
How does one go about
believing?

▶ Prayer in faith is answered—in a marvelous way. And if not? Then God has something else, something bigger and better in mind—even if I do not understand it.

A man came to our house and said, "My only child is dying! The doctor has prescribed a medicine that you can only get in England." While we were talking, a man came in with a basket of medicines. I looked at that basket of medicines: right on the top was the very medicine the first man needed for his dying child! There are millions of children in the world, and God is concerned with that little child in the slums of Calcutta. To send that man at that very moment! To put the medicine right on the top, so I could see it!

MOTHER TERESA

nothing on it but leaves only. And he said to it, "May no fruit ever come from you again!" And the fig tree withered at once. ²⁰ When the disciples saw it they marveled, saying, "How did the fig tree wither at once?" ²¹ And Jesus answered them, "Truly, I say to you, if you have faith and never doubt, you will not only do what has been done to the fig tree, but even if you say to this mountain, 'Be taken up and cast into the sea,' it will be done. ²² And whatever you ask in prayer, you will receive, if you have faith."

Jesus claims his authority (Mt 21:23–27)

²³ And when he entered the temple, the chief priests and the elders of the people came up to him as he was teaching, and said, "By what authority are you doing these things, and who gave you this authority?" ²⁴ Jesus answered them, "I also will ask you a question; and if you tell me the answer, then I also will tell you by what authority I do these things. ²⁵ The baptism of John, where was it from? From heaven or from men?" And they argued with one another, "If we say, 'From heaven,' he will say to us, 'Why then did you not believe him?' ²⁶ But if we say, 'From men,' we are afraid of the multitude; for all hold that John was a prophet." ²⁷ So they answered Jesus, "We do not know." And he said to them, "Neither will I tell you by what authority I do these things.

❝❞ Agnostics, who are constantly exercised by the question of God, those who long for a pure heart but suffer on account of their sin, are closer to the Kingdom of God than believers whose life of faith is "routine" and who regard the Church merely as an institution, without letting it touch their hearts, or letting the faith touch their hearts.

POPE BENEDICT XVI, September 25, 2011

▶ This parable of Jesus alludes to the Song of the Vineyard in Is 5. The vineyard stands for Israel, the people of God. We can recognize Jesus in the beloved son who is sent as the final messenger. He is killed by the vinedressers. But the vineyard remains. However, it needs good laborers. Jesus wants to recruit them.

It depends on action (Mt 21:28–32)

²⁸ "What do you think? A man had two sons; and he went to the first and said, 'Son, go and work in the vineyard today.' ²⁹ And he answered, 'I will not'; but afterward he repented and went. ³⁰ And he went to the second and said the same; and he answered, 'I go, sir,' but did not go. ³¹ Which of the two did the will of his father?" They said, "The first." Jesus said to them, "Truly, I say to you, the tax collectors and the harlots go into the kingdom of God before you. ³² For John came to you in the way of righteousness, and you did not believe him, but the tax collectors and the harlots believed him; and even when you saw it, you did not afterward repent and believe him.

Murder in the vineyard (Mt 21:33–46)

³³ "Hear another parable. There was a householder who planted a vineyard, and set a hedge around it, and dug a wine press in it, and built a tower, and leased it to tenants, and went into another country. ³⁴ When the season of fruit drew near, he sent his servants to the tenants, to get his fruit; ³⁵ and the tenants took his servants and beat one, killed another, and stoned another. ³⁶ Again he sent other servants, more than the first; and they did the same to them. ³⁷ Afterward he sent his son to them, saying, 'They will respect my son.' ³⁸ But when the tenants saw the son, they said to themselves, 'This is

the heir; come, let us kill him and have his inheritance.' ³⁹ And they took him and cast him out of the vineyard, and killed him. ⁴⁰ When therefore the owner of the vineyard comes, what will he do to those tenants?" ⁴¹ They said to him, "He will put those wretches to a miserable death, and lease the vineyard to other tenants who will give him the fruits in their seasons."

⁴² Jesus said to them, "Have you never read in the Scriptures:
'The very stone which the builders rejected
has become the cornerstone;
this was the Lord's doing,
and it is marvelous in our eyes'?
⁴³ Therefore I tell you, the kingdom of God will be taken away from you and given to a nation producing the fruits of it. ⁴⁴ And he who falls on this stone will be broken to pieces; but when it falls on any one, it will crush him."

⁴⁵ When the chief priests and the Pharisees heard his parables, they perceived that he was speaking about them. ⁴⁶ But when they tried to arrest him, they feared the multitudes, because they held him to be a prophet.

A prophet has no honor in his own country.
Jn 4:44

▶ The "cornerstone" is the most important stone for the equilibrium of a house. It dictates the whole process of construction.

No one chooses a vocation himself; he receives it and must strive to recognize it. One must lend an ear to God's voice in order to discern the signs of his will. And once his will is known, one must do it, whatever it may be, whatever the cost.

CHARLES DE FOUCAULD

Celebrating a wedding (Mt 22:1–14)

22 ¹ And again Jesus spoke to them in parables, saying, ² "The kingdom of heaven may be compared to a king who gave a marriage feast for his son, ³ and sent his servants to call those who were invited to the marriage feast; but they would not come. ⁴ Again he sent other servants, saying, 'Tell those who are invited, Behold, I have made ready my dinner, my oxen and my fat calves are killed, and everything is ready; come to the marriage feast.' ⁵ But they made light of it and went off, one to his farm, another to his business, ⁶ while the rest seized his servants, treated them shamefully, and killed them. ⁷ The king was angry, and he sent his troops and destroyed those murderers and burned their city. ⁸ Then he said to his servants, 'The wedding is ready, but those invited were not worthy. ⁹ Go therefore to the streets, and invite to the marriage feast as many as you find.' ¹⁰ And those servants went out into the streets and gathered all whom they found, both bad and good; so the wedding hall was filled with guests.

¹¹ "But when the king came in to look at the guests, he saw there a man who had no wedding garment; ¹² and he said to him, 'Friend, how did you get in here without a wedding garment?' And he was speechless. ¹³ Then the king said to the attendants, 'Bind him hand and foot, and cast him into the outer darkness, where there will be

▶ These two parables belong together. The first speaks about the unexpected good fortune of being able to celebrate the king's wedding, although they were not actually invited. The second warns, however: No one should feel overly secure. The important thing is to prove worthy of the celebration. All the guests—except one—did so despite the surprising invitation.

▶ The host is not unjust. All the other guests are well dressed; only the one man is not. If need be, the master of the house would have helped him by providing nice clothing. Apparently the banquet was not important enough to him.

weeping and gnashing of teeth.' ¹⁴ For many are called, but few are chosen."

Matthew follows this with a series of controversies touching on important questions in the life of faith: paying taxes (Mt 22:15–22), the resurrection of the dead (Mt 22:23–33), the greatest Commandment (Mt 22:34–40), and the Messiah (Mt 22:41–46). Afterward, Jesus gives another major discourse. It begins with multiple "woes" aimed at the scribes and Pharisees, who interpret the Law too narrowly (Mt 23); it continues with a prophecy of the end times (Mt 23); and it ends with three parables: the ten virgins (Mt 25:1–13), the talents (Mt 25:14–30), and the judgment of the world (Mt 25:31–46).

Let deeds speak (Mt 25:31–46)

▶ The right hand is considered the good side, the left as the bad.

💡 This parable places before our eyes the "works of mercy": feeding the hungry, giving drink to the thirsty, sheltering strangers, clothing the naked, caring for the sick, visiting the imprisoned, burying the dead.

25 ³¹ "When the Son of man comes in his glory, and all the angels with him, then he will sit on his glorious throne. ³² Before him will be gathered all the nations, and he will separate them one from another as a shepherd separates the sheep from the goats, ³³ and he will place the sheep at his right hand, but the goats at the left. ³⁴ Then the King will say to those at his right hand, 'Come, O blessed of my Father, inherit the kingdom prepared for you from the foundation of the world; ³⁵ for I was hungry and you gave me food, I was thirsty and you gave me drink, I was a stranger and you welcomed

💡 One day Mother Teresa brought a woman in off the street. Her body was filthy, with open wounds and maggots. Mother Teresa patiently bathed her and washed her wounds. The woman kept screaming insults and swear words at her. Mother Teresa just smiled. Finally the woman murmured: "Why does she do this? Who taught her this?" She simply answered: "My God taught me." When the woman asked who this God is, Mother Teresa kissed her on the forehead and said: "You know my God. My God's name is Love."

me, ³⁶ I was naked and you clothed me, I was sick and you visited me, I was in prison and you came to me.' ³⁷ Then the righteous will answer him, 'Lord, when did we see you hungry and feed you, or thirsty and give you drink? ³⁸ And when did we see you a stranger and welcome you, or naked and clothe you? ³⁹ And when did we see you sick or in prison and visit you?' ⁴⁰ And the King will answer them, 'Truly, I say to you, as you did it to one of the least of these my brethren, you did it to me.'

⁴¹ Then he will say to those at his left hand, 'Depart from me, you cursed, into the eternal fire prepared for the devil and his angels; ⁴² for I was hungry and you gave me no food, I was thirsty and you gave me no drink, ⁴³ I was a stranger and you did not welcome me, naked and you did not clothe me, sick and in prison and you did not visit me.' ⁴⁴ Then they also will answer, 'Lord, when did we see you hungry or thirsty or a stranger or naked or sick or in prison, and did not minister to you?'

⁴⁵ Then he will answer them, 'Truly, I say to you, as you did it not to one of the least of these, you did it not to me.' ⁴⁶ And they will go away into eternal punishment, but the righteous into eternal life."

JESUS' PASSION AND RESURRECTION (MT 26:1–28-20)

Jesus must die (Mt 26:1–5)

26 ¹ When Jesus had finished all these sayings, he said to his disciples, ² "You know that after two days the Passover is coming, and the Son of man will be delivered up to be crucified." ³ Then the chief priests and the elders of the people gathered in the palace of the high priest, who was called Cai'aphas, ⁴ and took counsel together in order to arrest Jesus by stealth and kill him. ⁵ But they said, "Not during the feast, lest there be a tumult among the people."

A woman anoints Jesus (Mt 26:6–13)

⁶ Now when Jesus was at Beth'any in the house of Simon the leper, ⁷ a woman came up to him with an alabaster jar of very expensive ointment, and she poured it on his head, as he sat at table. ⁸ But when the disciples saw it, they were indignant, saying, "Why this waste? ⁹ For this ointment might have been sold for a large sum, and given to the poor." ¹⁰ But Jesus, aware of this, said to them, "Why do

There is no saying anywhere in the Gospel that had a greater influence on me and changed my life more deeply than this one: "Whatsoever you do for the least of my brothers, you do it for me." When I reflect that these words came from the mouth of Jesus and that it is the same mouth that says: "This is my Body, this is my Blood," then I see clearly that I am called to seek and to love Jesus above all in these least ones.

CHARLES DE FOUCAULD

you trouble the woman? For she has done a beautiful thing to me. ¹¹ For you always have the poor with you, but you will not always have me. ¹² In pouring this ointment on my body she has done it to prepare me for burial. ¹³ Truly, I say to you, wherever this gospel is preached in the whole world, what she has done will be told in memory of her."

▶ The woman gave a sign. Jesus is the Anointed One. The Anointed One is the Messiah, in Greek: the Christ. He will die. But his death will bring eternal life. That is why the woman is remembered in the proclamation of the Gospel.

Judas betrays Jesus (Mt 26:14–16)

¹⁴ Then one of the Twelve, who was called Judas Iscariot, went to the chief priests ¹⁵ and said, "What will you give me if I deliver him to you?" And they paid him thirty pieces of silver. ¹⁶ And from that moment he sought an opportunity to betray him.

❞ Am I like Judas, who feigns love and then kisses the Master in order to hand him over, to betray him?

POPE FRANCIS, April 13, 2014

The Passover meal is prepared (Mt 26:17–19)

¹⁷ Now on the first day of Unleavened Bread the disciples came to Jesus, saying, "Where will you have us prepare for you to eat the Passover?" ¹⁸ He said, "Go into the city to such a one, and say to him, 'The Teacher says, My time is at hand; I will keep the Passover at your house with my disciples.' " ¹⁹ And the disciples did as Jesus had directed them, and they prepared the Passover.

▶ The Feast of Unleavened Bread is the Passover meal, at which Israel's emigration from Egypt is celebrated (Ex 12). The Passover meal should be eaten in the city of Jerusalem.

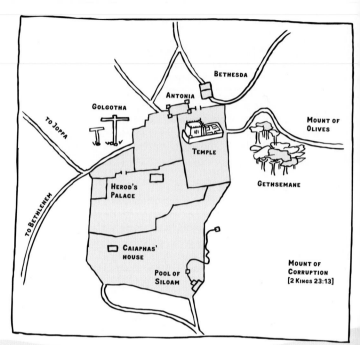

JERUSALEM
AT THE TIME OF
JESUS

Y → 99, 216
What happened at the Last Supper?
In what way is Christ there when the Eucharist is celebrated?

B For I received from the Lord what I also delivered to you, that the Lord Jesus on the night when he was betrayed took bread, and when he had given thanks, he broke it, and said, "This is my body which is for you. Do this in remembrance of me." In the same way also the chalice, after supper, saying, "This chalice is the new covenant in my blood. Do this, as often as you drink it, in remembrance of me."

1 Cor 11:23–25

Friends leave a sign behind, maybe a ring, but Christ leaves us His Body and His Blood, His Soul and His Divinity, Himself, without keeping anything back.

BERNARDINE OF SIENA
(1380–1444), Italian saint

The Last Supper (Mt 26:20–29)

²⁰ When it was evening, he sat at table with the twelve disciples; ²¹ and as they were eating, he said, "Truly, I say to you, one of you will betray me." ²² And they were very sorrowful, and began to say to him one after another, "Is it I, Lord?" ²³ He answered, "He who has dipped his hand in the dish with me, will betray me. ²⁴ The Son of man goes as it is written of him, but woe to that man by whom the Son of man is betrayed! It would have been better for that man if he had not been born." ²⁵ Judas, who betrayed him, said, "Is it I, Master?" He said to him, "You have said so."

²⁶ Now as they were eating, Jesus took bread, and blessed, and broke it, and gave it to the disciples and said, "Take, eat; this is my body." ²⁷ And he took a chalice, and when he had given thanks he gave it to them, saying, "Drink of it, all of you; ²⁸ for this is my blood of the covenant, which is poured out for many for the forgiveness of sins. ²⁹ I tell you I shall not drink again of this fruit of the vine until that day when I drink it new with you in my Father's kingdom."

The disciples will desert Jesus (Mt 26:30–35)

³⁰ And when they had sung a hymn, they went out to the Mount of Olives. ³¹ Then Jesus said to them, "You will all fall away because of me this night; for it is written, 'I will strike the shepherd, and the

sheep of the flock will be scattered.' ³² But after I am raised up, I will go before you to Galilee." ³³ Peter declared to him, "Though they all fall away because of you, I will never fall away." ³⁴ Jesus said to him, "Truly, I say to you, this very night, before the cock crows, you will deny me three times." ³⁵ Peter said to him, "Even if I must die with you, I will not deny you." And so said all the disciples.

Jesus prays for his life (Mt 26:36-46)

³⁶ Then Jesus went with them to a place called Gethsem'ane, and he said to his disciples, "Sit here, while I go over there and pray." ³⁷ And taking with him Peter and the two sons of Zeb'edee, he began to be sorrowful and troubled. ³⁸ Then he said to them, "My soul is very sorrowful, even to death; remain here, and watch with me." ³⁹ And going a little farther he fell on his face and prayed, "My Father, if it be possible, let this chalice pass from me; nevertheless, not as I will, but as you will." ⁴⁰ And he came to the disciples and found them sleeping; and he said to Peter, "So, could you not watch with me one hour? ⁴¹ Watch and pray that you may not enter into temptation; the spirit indeed is willing, but the flesh is weak." ⁴² Again, for the second time, he went away and prayed, "My Father, if this cannot

▶ Judas betrayed Jesus. The original Greek text reads: "handed over". The New Testament uses that same word to say that God the Father "gave up" his Son Jesus (e.g., Gal 1:4). In this terminology, the mystery of redemption becomes evident: Judas brought ruin upon himself. But God makes the best out of the evil. Men want to get hold of Jesus. But Jesus makes himself totally God's gift to mankind.

▶ Gethsemane in English is: olive press. The name goes with the olive trees on the Mount of Olives.

▶ The chalice is an image for suffering.

pass unless I drink it, your will be done." ⁴³ And again he came and found them sleeping, for their eyes were heavy. ⁴⁴ So, leaving them again, he went away and prayed for the third time, saying the same words. ⁴⁵ Then he came to the disciples and said to them, "Are you still sleeping and taking your rest? Behold, the hour is at hand, and the Son of man is betrayed into the hands of sinners. ⁴⁶ Rise, let us be going; see, my betrayer is at hand."

▶ Jesus teaches us to pray in the Our Father: "Thy will be done" (Mt 6:10). In his most difficult hour, he makes this petition his own. He does not seek death. But he is ready to walk the way of suffering.

The Betrayal and Arrest of Jesus (Mt 26:47–56)

⁴⁷ While he was still speaking, Judas came, one of the Twelve, and with him a great crowd with swords and clubs, from the chief priests and the elders of the people. ⁴⁸ Now the betrayer had given them a sign, saying, "The one I shall kiss is the man; seize him." ⁴⁹ And he came up to Jesus at once and said, "Hail, Master!"And he kissed him. ⁵⁰ Jesus said to him, "Friend, why are you here?" Then they came up and laid hands on Jesus and seized him. ⁵¹ And behold, one of those who were with Jesus stretched out his hand and drew his sword, and struck the slave of the high priest, and cut off his ear. ⁵² Then Jesus said to him, "Put your sword back into its place; for all who take the sword will perish by the sword. ⁵³ Do you think that I cannot appeal to my Father, and he will at once send me more than twelve legions of angels? ⁵⁴ But how then should the Scriptures be fulfilled, that it must be so?" ⁵⁵ At that hour Jesus said to the crowds, "Have you

❞ Judas told those with him that the man he should kiss was the one they should seize. The word he used for "kiss" applied to the somewhat sketchy embrace normal where the kiss is equivalent to a handshake. But the kiss he actually gave the Lord he was betraying was (as Mark and Matthew tell us) the kiss of warmest devotion: and one marvels at the nerve of the man who so soon after would be driven by remorse to hang himself.

FRANK SHEED, (1897–1981), Catholic writer, publisher, and speaker

Sometimes people treat me badly, and then I always ask myself how I should react. Often I have found that it may start to get even worse if I react angrily right away but that it goes well when I try to listen to Jesus first.

JOHN

▶ Caiaphas was high priest from A.D. 18–36. As such, he was also president of the Sanhedrin, the parliament and tribunal of Jerusalem.

▶ Jesus is found guilty of blasphemy. Yet he defends God's authority. He is the Son of man, who puts God's dominion into action.

come out as against a robber, with swords and clubs to capture me? Day after day I sat in the temple teaching, and you did not seize me. ⁵⁶ But all this has taken place, that the Scriptures of the prophets might be fulfilled." Then all the disciples deserted him and fled.

Jesus is interrogated by the Sanhedrin (Mt 26:57–68)

⁵⁷ Then those who had seized Jesus led him to Cai'aphas the high priest, where the scribes and the elders had gathered. ⁵⁸ But Peter followed him at a distance, as far as the courtyard of the high priest, and going inside he sat with the guards to see the end.

⁵⁹ Now the chief priests and the whole council sought false testimony against Jesus that they might put him to death, ⁶⁰ but they found none, though many false witnesses came forward. At last two came forward ⁶¹ and said, "This fellow said, 'I am able to destroy the temple of God, and to build it in three days.'" ⁶² And the high priest stood up and said, "Have you no answer to make? What is it that these men testify against you?" ⁶³ But Jesus was silent. And the high priest said to him, "I adjure you by the living God, tell us if you are the Christ, the Son of God." ⁶⁴ Jesus said to him, "You have said so. But I tell you, hereafter you will see the Son of man seated at the

▶ Jesus is accused of being a blasphemer, of laying claim to a divine role. In fact, though, Jesus is the one who gives honor to God by professing that he is sent. He is the Son of God, who has come to proclaim and to bring about God's dominion.

Peter is the Rock that wobbles but does not fall, because Jesus holds him steady.

▶ Is the denial of Jesus by Peter a less serious sin than his betrayal by Judas? But Peter does not despair. After his Resurrection, Jesus will again make him his disciple.

right hand of Power, and coming on the clouds of heaven." ⁶⁵ Then the high priest tore his robes, and said, "He has uttered blasphemy. Why do we still need witnesses? You have now heard his blasphemy. ⁶⁶ What is your judgment?" They answered, "He deserves death."

⁶⁷ Then they spat in his face, and struck him; and some slapped him, ⁶⁸ saying, "Prophesy to us, you Christ! Who is it that struck you?"

Peter denies Jesus (Mt 26:69–75)

⁶⁹ Now Peter was sitting outside in the courtyard. And a maid came up to him, and said, "You also were with Jesus the Galilean." ⁷⁰ But he denied it before them all, saying, "I do not know what you mean." ⁷¹ And when he went out to the porch, another maid saw him, and she said to the bystanders, "This man was with Jesus of Nazareth." ⁷² And again he denied it with an oath, "I do not know the man." ⁷³ After a little while the bystanders came up and said to Peter, "Certainly you are also one of them, for your accent betrays you." ⁷⁴ Then he began to invoke a curse on himself and to swear, "I do not know the man." And immediately the cock crowed. ⁷⁵ And Peter remembered the saying of Jesus, "Before the cock crows, you will deny me three times." And he went out and wept bitterly.

Jesus is handed over to Pilate (Mt 27:1–2)

27 [1] When morning came, all the chief priests and the elders of the people took counsel against Jesus to put him to death; [2] and they bound him and led him away and delivered him to Pilate the governor.

▶ Pontius Pilate was the Roman governor in Judea from A.D. 26 to 36. Only the emperor's representative could pass judgment on a serious crime and declare a death sentence.

Judas puts an end to his life (Mt 27:3–10)

[3] When Judas, his betrayer, saw that he was condemned, he repented and brought back the thirty pieces of silver to the chief priests and the elders, [4] saying, "I have sinned in betraying innocent blood." They said, "What is that to us? See to it yourself." [5] And throwing down the pieces of silver in the temple, he departed; and he went and hanged himself. [6] But the chief priests, taking the pieces of silver, said, "It is not lawful to put them into the treasury, since they are blood money." [7] So they took counsel, and bought with them the potter's field, to bury strangers in. [8] Therefore that field has been called the Field of Blood to this day. [9] Then was fulfilled what had been spoken by the prophet Jeremiah, saying, "And they took the thirty pieces of silver, the price of him on whom a price had been set by some of the sons of Israel, [10] and they gave them for the potter's field, as the Lord directed me."

💡 What were 30 pieces of silver worth? Hard to say. In Jesus' day you could buy a slave for that much money.

Pilate condemns Jesus to death (Mt 27:11–26)

[11] Now Jesus stood before the governor; and the governor asked him, "Are you the King of the Jews?" Jesus said to him, "You have said so." [12] But when he was accused by the chief priests and elders, he made no answer. [13] Then Pilate said to him, "Do you not hear how many things they testify against you?" [14] But he gave him no answer, not even to a single charge; so that the governor wondered greatly.

[15] Now at the feast the governor was accustomed to release for the crowd any one prisoner whom they wanted. [16] And they had then a notorious prisoner, called Barab'bas. [17] So when they had gathered, Pilate said to them, "Whom do you want me to release for you, Barab'bas or Jesus who is called Christ?" [18] For he knew that it was out of envy that they had delivered him up. [19] Besides, while he was sitting on the judgment seat, his wife sent word to him, "Have nothing to do with that righteous man, for I have suffered much over him today in a dream." [20] Now the chief priests and the elders persuaded the people to ask for Barab'bas and destroy Jesus. [21] The governor again said to them, "Which of the two do you want me to release for you?" And they said, "Barab'bas." [22] Pilate said to them, "Then what shall I do with Jesus who is called Christ?" They all said, "Let him be crucified." [23] And he said, "Why, what evil has he done?" But they shouted all the more, "Let him be crucified."

99 In this story of Good Friday it is the best things in the world that are at their worst. That is what really shows us the world at its worst. It was, for instance, the priests of a true monotheism and the soldiers of an international civilization.

G.K. CHESTERTON

▶ Jesus does not get a fair trial. Pilate recognizes his innocence but still hands him over to be crucified. Jesus was condemned as "King of the Jews". Allegedly he incited a rebellion against the Romans. In truth he brought the Kingdom of God to earth.

The people take the responsibility that Pilate wants to shirk. They seem to be firmly convinced that Jesus is guilty. But the blood that is supposed to "be upon" them is the blood that Jesus "poured out for the forgiveness of sins" (Mt 26:26).

²⁴ So when Pilate saw that he was gaining nothing, but rather that a riot was beginning, he took water and washed his hands before the crowd, saying, "I am innocent of this righteous man's blood; see to it yourselves." ²⁵ And all the people answered, "His blood be on us and on our children!" ²⁶ Then he released for them Barab'bas, and having scourged Jesus, delivered him to be crucified.

What sort of king! (Mt 27:27–31a)

²⁷ Then the soldiers of the governor took Jesus into the praetorium, and they gathered the whole battalion before him. ²⁸ And they stripped him and put a scarlet robe upon him, ²⁹ and plaiting a crown of thorns they put it on his head, and put a reed in his right hand. And kneeling before him they mocked him, saying, "Hail, King of the Jews!" ³⁰ And they spat upon him, and took the reed and struck him on the head. ³¹ᵃ And when they had mocked him, they stripped him of the robe, and put his own clothes on him.

A "battalion" is a troop of Roman soldiers. As a rule it was made up of anywhere from 500 to 1,000 men.

Jesus is crucified (Mt 27:32–44)

³² As they were marching out, they came upon a man of Cyre'ne, Simon by name; this man they compelled to carry his cross. ³³ And

We too can be toward others like Pilate, who did not have the courage to go against the tide to save Jesus' life, and instead washed his hands.

POPE FRANCIS, July 27, 2013

How important is Jesus to me? Is he really my King and my Lord?

The place of execution was located in front of the gates of the city, in keeping with Jewish law. Today the Church of the Holy Sepulcher and Resurrection is in the middle of the old city of Jerusalem.

when they came to a place called Gol'gotha (which means the place of a skull), ³⁴ they offered him wine to drink, mingled with gall; but when he tasted it, he would not drink it. ³⁵ And when they had crucified him, they divided his garments among them by casting lots; ³⁶ then they sat down and kept watch over him there. ³⁷ And over his head they put the charge against him, which read, "This is Jesus the King of the Jews." ³⁸ Then two robbers were crucified with him, one on the right and one on the left. ³⁹ And those who passed by derided him, wagging their heads ⁴⁰ and saying, "You who would destroy the temple and build it in three days, save yourself! If you are the Son of God, come down from the cross." ⁴¹ So also the chief priests, with the scribes and elders, mocked him, saying, ⁴² "He saved others; he cannot save himself. He is the King of Israel; let him come down now from the cross, and we will believe in him. ⁴³ He trusts in God; let God deliver him now, if he desires him; for he said, 'I am the Son of God.'" ⁴⁴ And the robbers who were crucified with him also reviled him in the same way.

Anyone who loves would like to become like the beloved; that is the secret of my life. I have lost my heart to this Jesus of Nazareth, who 1900 years ago was crucified; my whole life long I am trying to become like him.

CHARLES DE FOUCAULD

Jesus dies on the cross (Mt 27:45–56)

⁴⁵ Now from the sixth hour there was darkness over all the land until the ninth hour. ⁴⁶ And about the ninth hour Jesus cried with a loud voice, "Eli, Eli, la'ma sabach'-tha'ni?" that is, "My God, my God,

The sixth hour is 12:00 noon; the ninth hour is 3:00 P.M.

why have you forsaken me?" ⁴⁷ And some of the bystanders hearing it said, "This man is calling Eli'jah." ⁴⁸ And one of them at once ran and took a sponge, filled it with vinegar, and put it on a reed, and gave it to him to drink. ⁴⁹ But the others said, "Wait, let us see whether Eli'jah will come to save him." ⁵⁰ And Jesus cried again with a loud voice and yielded up his spirit.

⁵¹ And behold, the curtain of the temple was torn in two, from top to bottom; and the earth shook, and the rocks were split; ⁵² the tombs also were opened, and many bodies of the saints who had fallen

> Holy Mother, pierce me through, / in my heart each wound renew / of my Savior crucified. / Let me share with you his pain, / who for all our sins was slain, / who for me in torments died.

From the **STABAT MATER** by the Franciscan friar Jacopone da Todi (d. 1306).

THE SEVEN WORDS OF JESUS ON THE CROSS

My God, my God, why have you forsaken me?
Mk 15:34; Mt 27:46

Father, forgive them; for they know not what they do.
Lk 23:34

Truly, I say to you, today you will be with me in Paradise.
Lk 23:43

Father, into your hands I commit my spirit!
Lk 23:46

Woman, behold your son! Behold your mother!
Jn 19:26

I thirst.
Jn 19:28

It is finished.
Jn 19:30

asleep were raised, ⁵³ and coming out of the tombs after his resurrection they went into the holy city and appeared to many. ⁵⁴ When the centurion and those who were with him, keeping watch over Jesus, saw the earthquake and what took place, they were filled with awe, and said, "Truly this was the Son of God!"

▶ Jesus' last word on the Cross, according to Mt, is a prayer in the words of Ps 22:1. This prayer is the complaint of a suffering just man. He cries out to God in his need because only he can help.

> At evening, when the breeze was cool / the Fall of Adam was revealed; / At evening it was trampled by the Savior. / At evening Noah's dove returned, / bringing an olive leaf with it. / O wondrous time! O evening hour! / A peace treaty has now been made with God, / for Jesus accomplished his cross. / His body comes to rest. / Ah, my dear soul, go now and beg, / And let them give the dead Jesus to you: / O salutary, exquisite keepsake!

PICANDER (Christian Friedrich Henrici, 1700–1764) a hymn incorporated into Bach's *Saint Matthew Passion*

▶ Usually crucified criminals were buried secretly in the ground; Jesus gets an honorable tomb.

55 There were also many women there, looking on from afar, who had followed Jesus from Galilee, ministering to him; 56 among whom were Mary Mag'dalene, and Mary the mother of James and Joseph, and the mother of the sons of Zeb'edee.

Jesus is buried (Mt 27:57–61)

57 When it was evening, there came a rich man from Arimathe'a, named Joseph, who also was a disciple of Jesus. 58 He went to Pilate and asked for the body of Jesus. Then Pilate ordered it to be given to him. 59 And Joseph took the body, and wrapped it in a clean linen shroud, 60 and laid it in his own new tomb, which he had hewn in the rock; and he rolled a great stone to the door of the tomb, and departed. 61 Mary Mag'dalene and the other Mary were there, sitting opposite the tomb.

The tomb is heavily guarded (Mt 27:62–66)

62 Next day, that is, after the day of Preparation, the chief priests and the Pharisees gathered before Pilate 63 and said, "Sir, we remember how that impostor said, while he was still alive, 'After three days I will rise again.' 64 Therefore order the tomb to be made secure

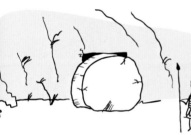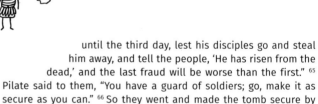

▶ While all the disciples abandoned Jesus, the women from Galilee remain faithful to Jesus. They follow Jesus and imitate him.

until the third day, lest his disciples go and steal him away, and tell the people, 'He has risen from the dead,' and the last fraud will be worse than the first." 65 Pilate said to them, "You have a guard of soldiers; go, make it as secure as you can." 66 So they went and made the tomb secure by sealing the stone and setting a guard.

The tomb Is empty (Mt 28:1–8)

> The assumption that the apostles were deceivers is thoroughly absurd. Think it through to the end and imagine these twelve men, how they gathered after the death of Jesus Christ and formed a conspiracy to claim that he had risen. ... Think it through!

BLAISE PASCAL (1623–1662), French philosopher

28 1 Now after the sabbath, toward the dawn of the first day of the week, Mary Mag'dalene and the other Mary went to see the tomb. 2 And behold, there was a great earthquake; for an angel of the Lord descended from heaven and came and rolled back the stone, and sat upon it. 3 His appearance was like lightning, and his clothing white as snow. 4 And for fear of him the guards trembled and became like dead men. 5 But the angel said to the women, "Do not be afraid; for I know that you seek Jesus who was crucified. 6 He is not here; for he has risen, as he said. Come, see the place where he lay. 7 Then go quickly and tell his disciples that he has risen from the dead, and behold, he is going before you to Galilee; there you will see him. Behold, I have told you." 8 So they departed quickly from the tomb with fear and great joy, and ran to tell his disciples.

Jesus appears to the women (Mt 28:9–10)

⁹ And behold, Jesus met them and said, "Hail!" And they came up and took hold of his feet and worshiped him. ¹⁰ Then Jesus said to them, "Do not be afraid; go and tell my brethren to go to Galilee, and there they will see me."

Y → 104
Can you be a Christian without believing in the Resurrection of Christ?

The high priests try to hush up the story (Mt 28:11–15)

¹¹ While they were going, behold, some of the guard went into the city and told the chief priests all that had taken place. ¹² And when they had assembled with the elders and taken counsel, they gave a sum of money to the soldiers ¹³ and said, "Tell people, 'His disciples came by night and stole him away while we were asleep.' ¹⁴ And if this comes to the governor's ears, we will satisfy him and keep you out of trouble." ¹⁵ So they took the money and did as they were directed; and this story has been spread among the Jews to this day.

All people can become disciples (Mt 28:16–20)

¹⁶ Now the eleven disciples went to Galilee, to the mountain to which Jesus had directed them. ¹⁷ And when they saw him they worshiped him; but some doubted. ¹⁸ And Jesus came and said to them, "All authority in heaven and on earth has been given to me. ¹⁹ Go therefore and make disciples of all nations, baptizing them in the name of the Father and of the Son and of the Holy Spirit, ²⁰ teaching them to observe all that I have commanded you; and behold, I am with you always, to the close of the age."

▶ The women from Galilee, who followed Jesus to the foot of the Cross and know where he is buried, find the tomb empty. Afterward they are the first to see the Risen Lord. Jesus makes them messengers for those whom he will send as apostles into the whole world.

▶ The claim that the disciples had made off with the body is quite ancient. Matthew tells the true story: Jesus rose from the dead.

▶ In Galilee Jesus started to proclaim the Good News of God's heavenly kingdom. Therefore in Galilee begins also the proclamation of his Resurrection. In this proclamation, everything that Jesus taught comes true.

Mark

WELCOME TO
THE BEAUTIFUL
TOWN OF

NAZARETH

The Gospel of Mark is the shortest of all the Gospels. It focuses on two main themes: the public ministry and the public suffering of Jesus. The Gospel shows, in the light of the Easter faith, that these two things go together. Jesus laid down his life for his message—and his message is embodied by Jesus himself, by his life and his death.

Anyone who wants to understand where Jesus' authority comes from must look at the helplessness of the Crucified; and anyone who wants to know what the Cross means must begin in Galilee with the Good News of the Kingdom of God (Mk 1:14f.).

Tradition attributes this Gospel to John Mark, a disciple of Peter. Today it is often regarded as the oldest Gospel.

At one point, the evangelist directly addresses those for whom he is writing: "Let the reader understand" (Mk 13:14). That is a motto for the whole Bible.

Mark begins his history of Jesus with John the Baptist and the baptism of Jesus in the Jordan. He describes how Jesus proclaims the Good News in word and deed: "The time is fulfilled, and the kingdom of God is at hand" (Mk 1:15). Typical elements of Jesus' teaching are his parables. The evangelist groups them together as examples of Jesus' preaching:

JESUS IN GALILEE (MK 6:1–56)

Disbelief in Nazareth (Mk 6:1–6a)

6 ¹He went away from there and came to his own country; and his disciples followed him. ²And on the sabbath he began to teach in the synagogue;

and many who heard him were astonished, saying, "Where did this man get all this? What is the wisdom given to him? What mighty works are wrought by his hands! ³Is not this the carpenter, the son of Mary and brother of James and Joses and Judas and Simon, and are not his sisters here with us?"

And they took offense at him.

⁴And Jesus said to them, "A prophet is not without honor, except in his own country, and among his own kin, and in his own house."

What is disbelief? The inability or unwillingness to imagine how close God can come to us.

▶ The "brothers" and "sisters" of Jesus are his relatives: they belong to his extended family.

⁵And he could do no mighty work there, except that he laid his hands upon a few sick people and healed them. ⁶ᵃAnd he marveled because of their unbelief.

The journeys of the disciples (Mk 6:6b–13)

⁶And he went about among the villages teaching.

⁷And he called to him the Twelve, and began to send them out two by two, and gave them authority over the unclean spirits. ⁸He charged them to take nothing for their journey except a staff; no bread, no bag, no money in their belts; ⁹but to wear sandals and not put on two tunics.

¹⁰And he said to them, "Where you enter a house, stay there until you leave the place. ¹¹And if any place will not receive you and they refuse to hear you, when you leave, shake off the dust that is on your feet for a testimony against them."

¹²So they went out and preached that men should repent. ¹³And they cast out many demons, and anointed with oil many that were sick and healed them.

▶ In Nazareth, Jesus is sent away. But he does not take offense or give up but rather extends his ministry. He sends out his disciples. For all people are supposed to hear the Good News in high-fidelity audio. The disciples are supposed to say and do precisely what he says and does—so that those who encounter only his disciples and not Jesus himself will be at no disadvantage whatsoever. On their missionary journey, the disciples are supposed to share the poverty of Jesus himself—and thereby give to the people to whom they are sent the opportunity to do a good deed and offer hospitality.

A false follower (Mk 6:14–29)

¹⁴King Herod heard of it; for Jesus' name had become known. Some said, "John the Baptist has been raised from the dead; that is why these powers are at work in him." ¹⁵But others said, "It is Eli'jah." And

▶ This Herod is a son of the tyrant who murdered children (Mt 2:16–18).

> As a result of the confidence in science that is one of the hallmarks of our time, ever-changing images of the historical Jesus form the opinions of "men" while barring the entrance to faith with the categorical claim that reason is autonomous.
>
> **JOSEPH CARDINAL RATZINGER/ POPE BENEDICT XVI**, *On the Way to Jesus Christ* (2003)

▶ Herodias had obtained a divorce in order to marry Herod, her brother-in-law. The scandal is mentioned not only in the New Testament but also in the Jewish historical records of antiquity. There is no Jewish parallel to the "Dance of the Veils".

others said, "It is a prophet, like one of the prophets of old." ¹⁶ But when Herod heard of it he said, "John, whom I beheaded, has been raised."

The murder of John the Baptist (Mk 6:17–29)

¹⁷ For Herod had sent and seized John, and bound him in prison for the sake of Hero'di-as, his brother Philip's wife; because he had married her. ¹⁸ For John said to Herod, "It is not lawful for you to have your brother's wife."

¹⁹ And Hero'di-as had a grudge against him, and wanted to kill him. But she could not, ²⁰ for Herod feared John, knowing that he was a righteous and holy man, and kept him safe. When he heard him, he was much perplexed; and yet he heard him gladly.

²¹ But an opportunity came when Herod on his birthday gave a banquet for his courtiers and officers and the leading men of Galilee. ²² For when Hero'di-as' daughter came in and danced, she pleased Herod and his guests; and the king said to the girl, "Ask me for whatever you wish, and I will grant it."

²³ And he vowed to her, "Whatever you ask me, I will give you, even half of my kingdom." ²⁴ And she went out, and said to her mother,

The death of John the Baptist, precursor of the Savior, also testifies that earthly existence is not an absolute good; what is more important is remaining faithful to the word of the Lord even at the risk of one's life.

POPE JOHN PAUL II, *Evangelium vitae*, 47

▶ Jesus took breaks: time for God, time for himself, time for his disciples. These times of rest are important: Sunday, a time to pray, a time to reflect.

"What shall I ask?" And she said, "The head of John the Baptist." ²⁵ And she came in immediately with haste to the king, and asked, saying, "I want you to give me at once the head of John the Baptist on a platter." ²⁶ And the king was exceedingly sorry; but because of his oaths and his guests he did not want to break his word to her. ²⁷ And immediately the king sent a soldier of the guard and gave orders to bring his head. He went and beheaded him in the prison, ²⁸ and brought his head on a platter, and gave it to the girl; and the girl gave it to her mother.

²⁹ When his disciples heard of it, they came and took his body, and laid it in a tomb.

Rest along the way (Mk 6:30–32)

³⁰ The apostles returned to Jesus, and told him all that they had done and taught. ³¹ And he said to them, "Come away by yourselves to a lonely place, and rest a while." For many were coming and going, and they had no leisure even to eat.

³² And they went away in the boat to a lonely place by themselves.

Five loaves and two fish—and Jesus (Mk 6:33–44)

³³ Now many saw them going, and knew them, and they ran there on foot from all the towns, and got there ahead of them. ³⁴ As he landed

he saw a great throng, and he had compassion on them, because they were like sheep without a shepherd; and he began to teach them many things.

[35] And when it grew late, his disciples came to him and said, "This is a lonely place, and the hour is now late; [36] send them away, to go into the country and villages round about and buy themselves something to eat." [37] But he answered them, "You give them something to eat." And they said to him, "Shall we go and buy two hundred denarii worth of bread, and give it to them to eat?" [38] And he said to them, "How many loaves have you? Go and see." And when they had found out, they said, "Five, and two fish."

[39] Then he commanded them all to sit down by companies upon the green grass. [40] So they sat down in groups, by hundreds and by fifties.

[41] And taking the five loaves and the two fish he looked up to heaven, and blessed, and broke the loaves, and gave them to the disciples to set before the people; and he divided the two fish among them all. [42] And they all ate and were satisfied. [43] And they took up twelve baskets full of broken pieces and of the fish. [44] And those who ate the loaves were five thousand men.

The "breaking of the bread" refers to the Eucharist. Two thousand years later, we continue to relive that primordial image of the Church. At every celebration of the Eucharist, we are spiritually brought back to the paschal →

An apparition (Mk 6:45–52)

[45] Immediately he made his disciples get into the boat and go before him to the other side, to Beth-sa'ida, while he dismissed the crowd. [46] And after he had taken leave of them, he went up on the mountain to pray.

[47] And when evening came, the boat was out on the sea, and he was alone on the land. [48] And he saw that they were distressed in rowing, for the wind was against them. And about the fourth watch of the night he came to them, walking on the sea. He meant to pass by them, [49] but when they saw him walking on the sea they thought it was a ghost, and cried out; [50] for they all saw him, and were terrified. But immediately he spoke to them and said, "Take heart, it is I; have no fear."

[51] And he got into the boat with them and the wind ceased. And they were utterly astounded, [52] for they did not understand about the loaves, but their hearts were hardened.

The work continues (Mk 6:53–56)

[53] And when they had crossed over, they came to land at Gennes'aret, and moored to the shore. [54] And when they got out of the boat, immediately the people recognized him, [55] and ran about the whole neighborhood and began to bring sick people on their pallets to any place where they heard he was.

→ Triduum: to the events of the evening of Holy Thursday, to the Last Supper and to what followed it.

POPE JOHN PAUL II, Encyclical *Ecclesia de Eucharistia*

▶ The disciples are important. They have little. But Jesus makes sure that they can draw from his fullness.

▶ In the fullest sense of the word, only God can say "I", because only he is in no way defined by others. This "I" of God is manifested in the Person of Jesus.

B The LORD passed before him, and proclaimed, "The LORD, the LORD, a God merciful and gracious, slow to anger, and abounding in mercy and faithfulness.

Ex 34:6

> **I invite all Christians, everywhere, at this very moment, to a renewed personal encounter with Jesus Christ, or at least an openness to letting him encounter them; I ask all of you to do this unfailingly each day.**
>
> **POPE FRANCIS**, *Evangelii Gaudium*, 3

▶ Tyre is located outside of Galilee in modern-day Lebanon.

▶ Jesus insists on Israel's prerogative; nothing must be taken away from the Jews when he turns to the pagans.

⁵⁶ And wherever he came, in villages, cities, or country, they laid the sick in the market places, and begged him that they might touch even the fringe of his garment; and as many as touched it were made well.

An impossible healing (Mk 7:24–30)

7 ²⁴ And from there he arose and went away to the region of Tyre and Sidon. And he entered a house, and would not have any one know it; yet he could not be hidden. ²⁵ But immediately a woman, whose little daughter was possessed by an unclean spirit, heard of him, and came and fell down at his feet. ²⁶ Now the woman was a Greek, a Syrophoeni'cian by birth. And she begged him to cast the demon out of her daughter. ²⁷ And he said to her, "Let the children first be fed, for it is not right to take the children's bread and throw it to the dogs." ²⁸ But she answered him, "Yes, Lord; yet even the dogs under the table eat the children's crumbs." ²⁹ And he said to her, "For this saying you may go your way; the demon has left your daughter." ³⁰ And she went home, and found the child lying in bed, and the demon gone.

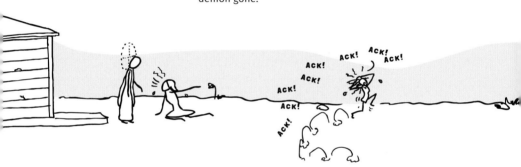

💡 Jesus lets her negotiate with him. The woman's arguments are convincing.

▶ The Decapolis ("Ten Cities") is a pagan territory across the Jordan River, in modern-day Jordan.

▶ "Ephphatha" is Aramaic, Jesus' mother tongue.

▶ Jesus does not want people to rejoice over him too soon: He still has a long road ahead of him. But the enthusiasm is uncontrollable.

A miracle at the side of the road (Mk 7:31–37)

³¹ Then he returned from the region of Tyre, and went through Sidon to the Sea of Galilee, through the region of the Decap'olis. ³² And they brought to him a man who was deaf and had an impediment in his speech; and they begged him to lay his hand upon him. ³³ And taking him aside from the multitude privately, he put his fingers into his ears, and he spat and touched his tongue; ³⁴ and looking up to heaven, he sighed, and said to him, "Eph'phatha," that is, "Be opened." ³⁵ And his ears were opened, his tongue was released, and he spoke plainly. ³⁶ And he charged them to tell no one; but the more he charged them, the more zealously they proclaimed it. ³⁷ And they were astonished beyond measure, saying, "He has done all things well; he even makes the deaf hear and the mute speak."

THE WAY OF SERVICE (MK 10:32–45)

A word against fear (Mk 10:32–34)

10 ³² And they were on the road, going up to Jerusalem, and Jesus was walking ahead of them; and they were amazed, and those who followed were afraid. And taking the Twelve again, he began to tell them what was to happen to him, ³³ saying, "Behold, we are going up to Jerusalem; and the Son of man will be delivered to the chief priests and the scribes, and they will condemn him to death, and deliver him to the Gentiles; ³⁴ and they will mock him, and spit upon him, and scourge him, and kill him; and after three days he will rise."

▶ Jesus knows what awaits him. He does not seek suffering, but he does accept it, because he connects it with God.

Ambition (Mk 10:35–40)

³⁵ And James and John, the sons of Zeb'edee, came forward to him, and said to him, "Teacher, we want you to do for us whatever we ask of you." ³⁶ And he said to them, "What do you want me to do for you?" ³⁷ And they said to him, "Grant us to sit, one at your right hand and one at your left, in your glory." ³⁸ But Jesus said to them, "You do not know what you are asking. Are you able to drink the chalice that I drink, or to be baptized with the baptism with which I am baptized?" ³⁹ And they said to him, "We are able." And Jesus said to them, "The chalice that I drink you will drink; and with the baptism with which I am baptized, you will be baptized; ⁴⁰ but to sit at my right hand or at my left is not mine to grant, but it is for those for whom it has been prepared."

😊 Jesus' career takes a nose dive—right into our hearts. That is also the way of discipleship: getting down on our knees before God and giving the poor a helping hand.

▶ The chalice is the cup of suffering that God hands to Jesus (↗ Mk 14:36). Baptism here is an image for the death that leads to life (↗ Rom 6:3–4).

The lower place is higher (Mk 10:41–45)

⁴¹ And when the ten heard it, they began to be indignant at James and John. ⁴² And Jesus called them to him and said to them, "You know that those who are supposed to rule over the Gentiles lord it over them, and their great men exercise authority over them. ⁴³ But it shall not be so among you; but whoever would be great among you must be your servant, ⁴⁴ and whoever would be first among you must be slave of all. ⁴⁵ For the Son of man also came not to be served but to serve, and to give his life as a ransom for many."

▶ In those days, a ransom had to be paid in order to buy the freedom of a slave. Jesus frees sinners by giving up his life for them.

The fruit of love is service. The fruit of service is peace.
MOTHER TERESA OF CALCUTTA

Mark relates how Jesus walks to his death in order to perform this service to the very end. Toward the end of the Gospel, we find the Easter message: "He is going before you to Galilee; there you will see him, as he told you" (Mk 16:7).

THE GOSPEL ACCORDING TO

Luke

The Gospel of Luke is the first part of a two-volume work. The second part is the Acts of the Apostles (Acts 1:1f.). The two parts are closely related: in the Gospel, Luke describes how Jesus calls disciples, who spread the Good News farther. In the Acts of the Apostles, he then relates how in the early Church the message of Jesus acquired new importance and was understood in light of the Resurrection.

In the prologue of his Gospel, Luke describes precisely his viewpoint, method, and purpose (Lk 1:1–4). He himself is not a disciple of Jesus, but he repeats the testimony of those who were "eyewitnesses and ministers of the word", primarily the twelve apostles. He carefully tested all the traditions as to their quality and selected only the best. He tries to convince "Theophilus"—in English, "God's friend"—that in his catechesis he has found the right approach to the faith and then to show him how he can continue along the path of discipleship.

Luke begins with the Gospel of Jesus' childhood, of which the Christmas story is one part. He recorded many of the most famous parables. He also gave an especially colorful account of the Easter Gospel.

This Bible offers a small selection from these parts. You can find much more if you read the whole Gospel in an unabridged Bible.

Luke, "the physician" (Col 4:14), is closely connected with Paul in the Church's tradition. In his Gospel, Luke shows above all how Jesus goes in search of people who have gone astray. "The Son of man came to seek and to save the lost" (Lk 19:10).

The Birth of John the Baptist Foretold (Lk 1:5–25)

1 [5] In the days of Herod, king of Judea, there was a priest named Zechari'ah, of the division of Abi'jah; and he had a wife of the daughters of Aaron, and her name was Elizabeth. [6] And they were both righteous before God, walking in all the commandments and ordinances of the Lord blamelessly. [7] But they had no child, because Elizabeth was barren, and both were advanced in years.

[8] Now while he was serving as priest before God when his division was on duty, [9] according to the custom of the priesthood, it fell to him by lot to enter the temple of the Lord and burn incense. [10] And the whole multitude of the people were praying outside at the hour of incense. [11] And there appeared to him an angel of the Lord standing on the right side of the altar of incense. [12] And Zechari'ah was troubled when he saw him, and fear fell upon him. [13] But the angel said to him, "Do not be afraid, Zechari'ah, for your prayer is heard, and your wife Elizabeth will bear you a son, and you shall call his name John.

[14] And you will have joy and gladness,
and many will rejoice at his birth;
[15] for he will be great before the Lord,

▶ Infertility was seen as a punishment from God, with the blame falling upon the woman in doubtful cases. Recall the promise of the birth of Isaac (Gen 18) and the prayer of Hanna that God would give her a son (1 Sam 1).

99 We are all tempted because the law of our spiritual life, our Christian life is a struggle: a struggle. That's because the Prince of this world, Satan, doesn't want our holiness, he doesn't want us to follow Christ."

POPE FRANCIS, April 11, 2014

▶ According to the Old Testament (v. 16) this is the mission of Elijah when he comes again to prepare the way of the Messiah (cf. Mal 3:23-24 –Old Testament prophecy ends with these words).

☺ Zechariah doubts—Mary believes. Zechariah loses his speech—Mary blossoms.

God has placed you in this world to use his goodness for you, by giving you his grace and his glory. For this he has given you the understanding to know him, the memory to remember him, the will to love him, the imagination to represent to yourself his blessings, the eyes to see the wonders of his work, the tongue to praise him.

FRANCIS DE SALES

and he shall drink no wine nor strong drink,
and he will be filled with the Holy Spirit,
even from his mother's womb.
[16] And he will turn many of the sons of Israel to the Lord their God, [17] and he will go before him in the spirit and power of Eli'jah,
to turn the hearts of the fathers to the children,
and the disobedient to the wisdom of the just,
to make ready for the Lord a people prepared."
[18] And Zechari'ah said to the angel, "How shall I know this? For I am an old man, and my wife is advanced in years." [19] And the angel answered him, "I am Gabriel, who stand in the presence of God; and I was sent to speak to you, and to bring you this good news. [20] And behold, you will be silent and unable to speak until the day that these things come to pass, because you did not believe my words, which will be fulfilled in their time." [21] And the people were waiting for Zechari'ah, and they wondered at his delay in the temple. [22] And when he came out, he could not speak to them, and they perceived that he had seen a vision in the temple; and he made signs to them and remained mute. [23] And when his time of service was ended, he went to his home.

[24] After these days his wife Elizabeth conceived, and for five months she hid herself, saying, [25] "Thus the Lord has done to me in the days when he looked on me, to take away my reproach among men."

The Birth of Jesus Foretold (Lk 1:26–38)

26 In the sixth month the angel Gabriel was sent from God to a city of Galilee named Nazareth, 27 to a virgin betrothed to a man whose name was Joseph, of the house of David; and the virgin's name was Mary. 28 And he came to her and said, "Hail, full of grace, the Lord is with you!" 29 But she was greatly troubled at the saying, and considered in her mind what sort of greeting this might be. 30 And the angel said to her," Do not be afraid, Mary, for you have found favor with God. 31 And behold, you will conceive in your womb and bear a son, and you shall call his name Jesus.

32 He will be great, and will be called the Son of the Most High; and the Lord God will give to him the throne of his father David, 33 and he will reign over the house of Jacob for ever; and of his kingdom there will be no end."

34 And Mary said to the angel, "How can this be, since I have no husband?" 35 And the angel said to her, "The Holy Spirit will come upon you, and the power of the Most High will overshadow you; therefore the child to be born will be called holy, the Son of God. 36 And behold, your kinswoman Elizabeth in her old

Scientists estimate that around 108 billion people have lived on earth. Of all these, one opened the great door to God. It was Mary, when the Lord of heaven and earth wanted to become man. She answered with her great 'Yes'. Out of pure love, nothing else.

▶ Evolution does not produce a Messiah. Jesus is God's Son from eternity but born of the Virgin Mary (cf. Mt 1:23). She is his mother—and the mother of all who believe.

Though modest silence is pleasing, dutiful speech is now more necessary. Open your heart to faith, O blessed Virgin, your lips to praise, your womb to the Creator.

BERNARD OF CLAIRVAUX

age has also conceived a son; and this is the sixth month with her who was called barren. 37 For with God nothing will be impossible." 38 And Mary said, "Behold, I am the handmaid of the Lord; let it be to me according to your word." And the angel departed from her.

Mary Visits Elizabeth (Lk 1:39–45)

39 In those days Mary arose and went with haste into the hill country, to a city of Judah, 40 and she entered the house of Zechari'ah and greeted Elizabeth. 41 And when Elizabeth heard the greeting of Mary, the child leaped in her womb; and Elizabeth was filled with the Holy Spirit 42 and she exclaimed with a loud cry, "Blessed are you among women, and blessed is the fruit of your womb! 43 And why is this granted me, that the mother of my Lord should come to me? 44 For behold, when the voice of your greeting came to my ears, the child in my womb leaped for joy. 45 And blessed is she who believed that there would be a fulfilment of what was spoken to her from the Lord."

I praise God: the Magnificat (Lk 1:46–55)

46 And Mary said, "My soul magnifies the Lord,
47 and my spirit rejoices in God my Savior,
48 for he has regarded the low estate of his handmaiden.
For behold, henceforth all generations will call me blessed;

And the angel simply takes off! Mary is alone with this mass of info. She has to figure it out all alone. I imagine this in real time: there was no one she could speak to. Eventually to Joseph, but...

SANDRA

▶ The Magnificat is a New Testament psalm. The whole history of the people of God takes on new meaning in relation to Mary. A revolution begins: the poor get what is rightfully theirs. It is God's revolution. Its leader is Jesus.

⁴⁹ for he who is mighty has done great things for me, and holy is his name.
⁵⁰ And his mercy is on those who fear him from generation to generation.
⁵¹ He has shown strength with his arm, he has scattered the proud in the imagination of their hearts,
⁵² he has put down the mighty from their thrones, and exalted those of low degree;
⁵³ he has filled the hungry with good things, and the rich he has sent empty away.
⁵⁴ He has helped his servant Israel, in remembrance of his mercy,
⁵⁵ as he spoke to our fathers, to Abraham and to his posterity for ever."
⁵⁶ And Mary remained with her about three months, and returned to her home.

The Birth of John the Baptist (Lk 1:57–79)

1 ⁵⁷ Now the time came for Elizabeth to be delivered, and she gave birth to a son. ⁵⁸ And her neighbors and kinsfolk heard that the Lord had shown great mercy to her, and they rejoiced with her. ⁵⁹ And on the eighth day they came to circumcise the child; and they would

have named him Zechari'ah after his father, ⁶⁰ but his mother said, "Not so; he shall be called John." ⁶¹ And they said to her, "None of your kindred is called by this name." ⁶² And they made signs to his father, inquiring what he would have him called. ⁶³ And he asked for a writing tablet, and wrote, "His name is John." And they all marveled. ⁶⁴ And immediately his mouth was opened and his tongue loosed, and he spoke, blessing God. ⁶⁵ And fear came on all their neighbors. And all these things were talked about through all the hill country of Judea; ⁶⁶ and all who heard them laid them up in their hearts, saying, "What then will this child be?" For the hand of the Lord was with him.
⁶⁷ And his father Zechari'ah was filled with the Holy Spirit, and prophesied, saying,
⁶⁸ "Blessed be the Lord God of Israel,
for he has visited and redeemed his people,
⁶⁹ and has raised up a horn of salvation for us
in the house of his servant David,
⁷⁰ as he spoke by the mouth of his holy prophets from of old,
⁷¹ that we should be saved from our enemies,
and from the hand of all who hate us;
⁷² to perform the mercy promised to our fathers,
and to remember his holy covenant,
⁷³ the oath which he swore to our father Abraham, ⁷⁴ to grant us

The story of Jesus begins long before his birth—and it is not over to this day.

I am God Almighty; walk before me, and be blameless. And I will make my covenant between me and you, and will multiply you exceedingly.

Gen 17:1–2

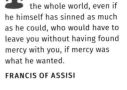

that we, being delivered from the hand of our enemies,
might serve him without fear,
[75] in holiness and righteousness before him all the days of our life.
[76] And you, child, will be called the prophet of the Most High;
for you will go before the Lord to prepare his ways,
[77] to give knowledge of salvation to his people
in the forgiveness of their sins,
[78] through the tender mercy of our God,
when the day shall dawn upon us from on high
[79] to give light to those who sit in darkness and in the shadow of
death, to guide our feet into the way of peace."

There can be no one in the whole world, even if he himself has sinned as much as he could, who would have to leave you without having found mercy with you, if mercy was what he wanted.

FRANCIS OF ASSISI

CHRISTMAS—AND AFTERWARDS (LK 2:1–52)

The whole world is on the move (Lk 2:1–3)

2 [1] In those days a decree went out from Caesar Augustus that all the world should be enrolled. [2] This was the first enrollment, when Quirin'ius was governor of Syria. [3] And all went to be enrolled, each to his own city.

Jesus is born in Bethlehem (Lk 2:4–7)

[4] And Joseph also went up from Galilee, from the city of Nazareth, to Judea, to the city of David, which is called Bethlehem, because he was of the house and lineage of David, [5] to be enrolled with Mary his betrothed, who was with child.
[6] And while they were there, the time came for her to be delivered. [7] And she gave birth to her first-born son and wrapped him in swaddling cloths, and laid him in a manger, because there was no place for them in the inn.

▶ Taxation was a tool of political power. Augustus sets the whole world in motion. But only one journey is earth-shaking: Joseph and Mary travel to Bethlehem.

The shepherds in the fields hear the Good News (Lk 2:8–14)

[8] And in that region there were shepherds out in the field, keeping watch over their flock by night. [9] And an angel of the Lord appeared to them, and the glory of the Lord shone around them, and they were filled with fear. [10] And the angel said to them, "Be not afraid; for behold, I bring you good news of a great joy which will come to all the people; [11] for to you is born this day in the city of David a Savior, who is Christ the Lord. [12] And this will be a sign for you: you will find a baby wrapped in swaddling cloths and lying in a manger." [13] And suddenly there was with the angel a multitude of the heavenly host praising God and saying,

▶ Shepherds are simple folk who practice David's profession in the City of David.

" May the light of this day enter our hearts, brighten and warm our homes, bring calm and hope to our cities, and give peace to the world.

POPE BENEDICT XVI, Christmas 2008

Jesus, what made you so little? Love!

BERNHARD OF CLAIRVAUX

 Dear Mother of God, I find that I am more fortunate than you. For I have you as a mother. ... Now you are the Mother of God, but you gave us this Jesus wholly and entirely. ... So we are richer than you, for we possess Jesus and you too belong to us.

THÉRÈSE OF LISIEUX

[14] "Glory to God in the highest,
and on earth peace among men with whom he is pleased!"

The shepherds go to the crib (Lk 2:15–20)

[15] When the angels went away from them into heaven, the shepherds said to one another, "Let us go over to Bethlehem and see this thing that has happened, which the Lord has made known to us." [16] And they went with haste, and found Mary and Joseph, and the baby lying in a manger. [17] And when they saw it they made known the saying which had been told them concerning this child; [18] and all who heard it wondered at what the shepherds told them. [19] But Mary kept all these things, pondering them in her heart. [20] And the shepherds returned, glorifying and praising God for all they had heard and seen, as it had been told them.

Jesus is circumcised according to Jewish custom and is brought to the Temple. There he is awaited by Simeon and Anna—two elderly people who have remained young at heart, because they have not given up hope in God's salvation. Simeon intones a third song of praise: the *Nunc dimittis*.

I thank you (Lk 2:29-32)

[29] "Lord, now let your servant depart in peace,
according to your word;
[30] for my eyes have seen your salvation
[31] which you have prepared in the presence of all peoples,
[32] a light for revelation to the Gentiles,
and for glory to your people Israel."

Luke ends the so-called Infancy Narrative with an episode that depicts the twelve-year-old Jesus; according to the Jewish understanding of that time, he is a youth on the threshold of being an adult.

The pupil as teacher (Lk 2:41–52)

▶ At the age of 12, Jesus is no longer a little child. He knows where he belongs. He walks his own way. His parents have yet to learn this.

💡 If there had been an emergency call number back then, Joseph certainly would have grabbed his cell phone.

[41] Now his parents went to Jerusalem every year at the feast of the Passover. [42] And when he was twelve years old, they went up according to custom; [43] and when the feast was ended, as they were returning, the boy Jesus stayed behind in Jerusalem. His parents did not know it, [44] but supposing him to be in the company they went a day's journey, and they sought him among their kinsfolk and acquaintances; [45] and when they did not find him, they returned to Jerusalem, seeking him. [46] After three days they found him in the temple, sitting among the teachers, listening to them and asking them questions; [47] and all who heard him were amazed at his understanding and his

answers. ⁴⁸ And when they saw him they were astonished; and his mother said to him, "Son, why have you treated us so? Behold, your father and I have been looking for you anxiously." ⁴⁹ And he said to them, "How is it that you sought me? Did you not know that I must be in my Father's house?" ⁵⁰ And they did not understand the saying which he spoke to them. ⁵¹ And he went down with them and came to Nazareth, and was obedient to them; and his mother kept all these things in her heart.

⁵² And Jesus increased in wisdom and in stature, and in favor with God and man.

"Children and fools speak the truth!" Again and again I am impressed by children's trust in God. My sister was once worried about a friend and prayed together with her children for him. But she could not stop worrying about her friend. The children just said: "But we have entrusted him to God!"

MARIA

Luke—like Matthew—tells about the preaching of John the Baptist and the baptism of Jesus in the Jordan, but also about the temptation of Jesus in the desert. Then the evangelist depicts how Jesus began the public proclamation of his Gospel in his hometown.

NOW IT STARTS (LK 4:16–30)

Jesus reads the Bible (Lk 4:16–21)

4 ¹⁶ And he came to Nazareth, where he had been brought up; and he went to the synagogue, as was his custom, on the sabbath day. And he stood up to read; ¹⁷ and there was given to him the book of the prophet Isaiah. He opened the book and found the place where it was written,

¹⁸ "The Spirit of the Lord is upon me,
because he has anointed me to preach good news to the poor.
He has sent me to proclaim release to the captives
and recovering of sight to the blind,
to set at liberty those who are oppressed,
¹⁹ to proclaim the acceptable year of the Lord."

²⁰ And he closed the book, and gave it back to the attendant, and sat down; and the eyes of all in the synagogue were fixed on him. ²¹ And he began to say to them, "Today this Scripture has been fulfilled in your hearing."

▶ Jesus begins his public preaching with a reading from the Bible in the house of God. That is no coincidence. He shows where his roots are and what path he intends to walk.

" How I would like a Church which is poor and for the poor!
POPE FRANCIS, March 16, 2013

Jesus gives the shortest sermon in the world (v. 21): "Today!" Now is the time, now is the hour—for Jesus is there, the Messiah. Everyone must listen to him—even today.

Being critical—but real (Lk 4:22–27)

²² And all spoke well of him, and wondered at the gracious words which proceeded out of his mouth; and they said, "Is not this Joseph's son?" ²³ And he said to them, "Doubtless you will quote to me

Often I have a problem with people close to me. I cannot appreciate my neighbors very well. →

→ The people in Jesus' hometown were probably very close to him. I think that for them he was always the young man whom they had known since he was a little boy. That is why it was difficult for them to recognize him as the Son of God, even when he worked miracles.

RUTH

this proverb, 'Physician, heal yourself; what we have heard you did at Caper'na-um, do here also in your own country.' ²⁴ And he said, "Truly, I say to you, no prophet is acceptable in his own country. ²⁵ But in truth, I tell you, there were many widows in Israel in the days of Eli'jah, when the heaven was shut up three years and six months, when there came a great famine over all the land; ²⁶ and Eli'jah was sent to none of them but only to Zar'ephath, in the land of Si'don, to a woman who was a widow. ²⁷ And there were many lepers in Israel in the time of the prophet Eli'sha; and none of them was cleansed, but only Na'aman the Syrian."

A threat and an escape (Lk 4:28–30)

▶ Jesus is not deterred by the protest and goes his own way. The scene at the mountain of Nazareth already foreshadows the rocks of Golgotha: Jesus will die, but he does not remain in the tomb.

²⁸ When they heard this, all in the synagogue were filled with wrath. ²⁹ And they rose up and put him out of the city, and led him to the brow of the hill on which their city was built, that they might throw him down headlong. ³⁰ But passing through the midst of them he went away.

Luke follows this with several accounts in which Jesus acts as a rescuer, a savior, and a physician, who sets people free.

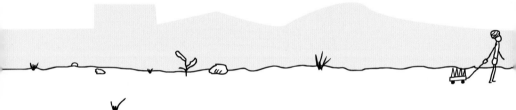

Y → 90, 91
Did Jesus work miracles, or are they just pious tales?
But why did Jesus work miracles?

B And they were astonished beyond measure, saying, "He has done all things well; he even makes the deaf hear and the mute speak."

Mk 7:37

▶ Without her son, the mother, a widow, would have been defenseless. Jesus awakens the young man from the dead, not only in order to prove his divine power, but also in order to help the woman.

A resurrection at midday (Lk 7:11–17)

7 ¹¹ Soon afterward he went to a city called Na'in, and his disciples and a great crowd went with him. ¹² As he drew near to the gate of the city, behold, a man who had died was being carried out, the only son of his mother, and she was a widow; and a large crowd from the city was with her.

¹³ And when the Lord saw her, he had compassion on her and said to her, "Do not weep." ¹⁴ And he came and touched the bier, and the bearers stood still. And he said, "Young man, I say to you, arise."

¹⁵ And the dead man sat up, and began to speak. And he gave him to his mother.

¹⁶ Fear seized them all; and they glorified God, saying, "A great prophet has arisen among us!" and "God has visited his people!" ¹⁷ And this report concerning him spread through the whole of Judea and all the surrounding country.

A question for Jesus—and an answer contained in it (Lk 7:18–23)

¹⁸ The disciples of John told him of all these things. ¹⁹ And John, calling to him two of his disciples, sent them to the Lord, saying, "Are you he who is to come, or shall we look for another?" ²⁰ And when the men had come to him, they said, "John the Baptist has sent us to you, saying, 'Are you he who is to come, or shall we look for anoth-

er?'" ²¹ In that hour he cured many of diseases and plagues and evil spirits, and on many that were blind he bestowed sight.

²² And he answered them, "Go and tell John what you have seen and heard: the blind receive their sight, the lame walk, lepers are cleansed, and the deaf hear, the dead are raised up, the poor have good news preached to them.

²³ And blessed is he who takes no offense at me."

▶ John must have known the answer: After all, he is a prophet! But he, too, must ask. For Jesus is greater than any human thought. The New Testament does not conceal the question. Anyone who reads it today must give an answer, too.

Beyond sensationalism begins faith (Lk 7:24–27)

²⁴ When the messengers of John had gone, he began to speak to the crowds concerning John: "What did you go out into the wilderness to behold? A reed shaken by the wind? ²⁵ What then did you go out to see? A man clothed in soft raiment? Behold, those who are gorgeously apparelled and live in luxury are in kings' courts. ²⁶ What then did you go out to see? A prophet?

Yes, I tell you, and more than a prophet. ²⁷ This is he of whom it is written,

'Behold, I send my messenger before your face,
who shall prepare your way before you.'

▶ Jesus lets deeds speak. He answers with precisely the things that John's disciples can see and hear. But with his answer, he places it in the light of Isaiah's prophecy. Thus it becomes clear: in Jesus is fulfilled what God intends for mankind.

John is the greatest—and quite small (Lk 7:28–30)

²⁸ I tell you, among those born of women none is greater than John; yet he who is least in the kingdom of God is greater than he."

²⁹ (When they heard this all the people and the tax collectors justified God, having been baptized with the baptism of John;

³⁰ but the Pharisees and the lawyers rejected the purpose of God for themselves, not having been baptized by him.)

Religiously tone deaf? Help is on the way (Lk 7:31–32)

³¹ "To what then shall I compare the men of this generation, and what are they like?

³² They are like children sitting in the market place and calling to one another,

'We piped to you, and you did not dance;
we wailed, and you did not weep.'

▶ On account of a court intrigue, he was beheaded and his head presented on a silver platter: John the Baptist, the great precursor of Jesus.

In a bad mood? Jesus is able to celebrate (Lk 7:33–35)

³³ For John the Baptist has come eating no bread and drinking no wine; and you say, 'He has a demon.' ³⁴ The Son of man has come eating and drinking; and you say, 'Behold, a glutton and a drunkard, a friend of tax collectors and sinners!' ³⁵ Yet wisdom is justified by all her children."

Got sins? There is forgiveness (Lk 7:36–50)

▶ Some tried to discredit Jesus because he did not keep his distance from sinners. But that is his mission: he brings God's light into the darkness.

³⁶ One of the Pharisees asked him to eat with him, and he went into the Pharisee's house, and sat at table.

▶ The woman knows how important forgiveness is, because she has committed sins, but she does not despair.

³⁷ And behold, a woman of the city, who was a sinner, when she learned that he was sitting at table in the Pharisee's house, brought an alabaster flask of ointment, ³⁸ and standing behind him at his feet, weeping, she began to wet his feet with her tears, and wiped them with the hair of her head, and kissed his feet, and anointed them with the ointment.

³⁹ Now when the Pharisee who had invited him saw it, he said to himself, "If this man were a prophet, he would have known who and what sort of woman this is who is touching him, for she is a sinner."

⁴⁰ And Jesus answering said to him, "Simon, I have something to say to you." And he answered, "What is it, Teacher?"

▶ The woman is incredibly brave. She stakes everything on one action. She loves Jesus— and expects only criticism in return.

⁴¹ "A certain creditor had two debtors; one owed five hundred denarii, and the other fifty. ⁴² When they could not pay, he forgave them both. Now which of them will love him more?"

▶ A parable clarifies the situation. Jesus is a teacher. He wants to convince. Simon just has to add one and one.

⁴³ Simon answered, "The one, I suppose, to whom he forgave more." And he said to him, "You have judged rightly."

⁴⁴ Then turning toward the woman he said to Simon, "Do you see this woman? I entered your house, you gave me no water for my feet, but she has wet my feet with her tears and wiped them with her hair.

My Lord and my God, take from me everything that distances me from you. My Lord and my God, give me everything that brings me closer to you. My Lord and my God, detach me from myself and give my all to you.

Prayer of St. **NICHOLAS OF FLÜE** (1417–1487)

⁴⁵ You gave me no kiss, but from the time I came in she has not ceased to kiss my feet. ⁴⁶ You did not anoint my head with oil, but she has anointed my feet with ointment. ⁴⁷ Therefore I tell you, her sins, which are many, are forgiven, for she loved much; but he who is forgiven little, loves little." ⁴⁸ And he said to her, "Your sins are forgiven." ⁴⁹ Then those who were at table with him began to say among themselves, "Who is this, who even forgives sins?"

⁵⁰ And he said to the woman, "Your faith has saved you; go in peace."

▶ The accusation is dangerous: the forgiveness of sins is God's prerogative (↗ Mk 2:1–12).

The company of Jesus (Lk 8:1–3)

8 ¹ Soon afterward he went on through cities and villages, preaching and bringing the good news of the kingdom of God. And the Twelve were with him, ² and also some women who had been

healed of evil spirits and infirmities: Mary, called Mag'dalene, from whom seven demons had gone out,[3] and Jo-an'na, the wife of Chuza, Herod's steward, and Susanna, and many others, who provided for them out of their means.

THE GOOD SAMARITAN (LK 10:25–37)

Loving God and Neighbor (Lk 10:25–28)

10 [25] And behold, a lawyer stood up to put him to the test, saying, "Teacher, what shall I do to inherit eternal life?"

[26] He said to him, "What is written in the law? What do you read there?"

[27] And he answered, "You shall love the Lord your God with all your heart, and with all your soul, and with all your strength, and with all your mind; and your neighbor as yourself."

[28] And he said to him, "You have answered right; do this, and you will live."

Being a neighbor to others (Lk 10:29–37)

[29] But he, desiring to justify himself, said to Jesus, "And who is my neighbor?"

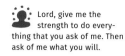
Lord, give me the strength to do everything that you ask of me. Then ask of me what you will.

AUGUSTINE

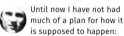
When all is said and done, it is … the Church, starting with Jesus Himself, who offers women true freedom.

TERESA TOMEO

Until now I have not had much of a plan for how it is supposed to happen: to love God with all my whole heart, all my strength, and all my mind. Still, I have understood that, just as in the natural life, it has to do with getting to know the person first! And that depends on spending as much time as possible with him. Doing everything with him. →

[30] Jesus replied, "A man was going down from Jerusalem to Jericho, and he fell among robbers, who stripped him and beat him, and departed, leaving him half dead. [31] Now by chance a priest was going down that road; and when he saw him he passed by on the other side. [32] So likewise a Levite, when he came to the place and saw him, passed by on the other side.

[33] But a Samaritan, as he journeyed, came to where he was; and when he saw him, he had compassion, [34] and went to him and bound up his wounds, pouring on oil and wine; then he set him on his own beast and brought him to an inn, and took care of him. [35] And the next day he took out two denarii and gave them to the innkeeper, saying, 'Take care of him; and whatever more you spend, I will repay you when I come back.'

[36] Which of these three, do you think, proved neighbor to the man who fell among the robbers?"

[37] He said, "The one who showed mercy on him." And Jesus said to him, "Go and do likewise."

→ Taking him seriously and honoring him in a very practical way by my behavior. When I feel like it and also when it is sometimes more difficult!

GEORGE

▶ The priest and the Levite should have helped. There is no excuse for them. The Samaritan is the one from whom the lawyer would least have expected a positive reaction, because Jews and Samaritans were enemies.

Jesus asks questions like Socrates: having studied the Scriptures, the lawyer himself knows the correct answer best: it is written in the Law and in his heart.

Because Jesus himself acts as the merciful Samaritan does, he meets not only with much approval but also with rejection from those who think that he is not holy enough if he bothers about sinners. Jesus answers by telling parables.

LOST! BUT FOUND! (LK 15:1–32)

Jesus in bad company? (Lk 15:1–2)

15 [1] Now the tax collectors and sinners were all drawing near to hear him. [2] And the Pharisees and the scribes murmured, saying, "This man receives sinners and eats with them."

The Good Shepherd (Lk 15:3–7)

[3] So he told them this parable: [4] "What man of you, having a hundred sheep, if he has lost one of them, does not leave the ninety-nine in the wilderness, and go after the one which is lost, until he finds it? [5] And when he has found it, he lays it on his shoulders, rejoicing. [6] And when he comes home, he calls together his friends and his neighbors, saying to them, 'Rejoice with me, for I have found my sheep which was lost.'

[7] Just so, I tell you, there will be more joy in heaven over one sinner who repents than over ninety-nine righteous persons who need no repentance.

Since the days of the early Church, Jesus has been depicted as the "Good Shepherd".

> There is nothing more beautiful than to be surprised by the Gospel, by the encounter with Christ. There is nothing more beautiful than to know Him and to speak to others of our friendship with Him.

POPE BENEDICT XVI, at the beginning of his pontificate, April 24, 2005

The woman who rejoices (Lk 15:8–10)

[8] "Or what woman, having ten silver coins, if she loses one coin, does not light a lamp and sweep the house and seek diligently until she finds it? [9] And when she has found it, she calls together her friends and neighbors, saying, 'Rejoice with me, for I have found the coin which I had lost.'

[10] Just so, I tell you, there is joy before the angels of God over one sinner who repents."

The son who loses his way (Lk 15:11–16)

[11] And he said, "There was a man who had two sons; [12] and the younger of them said to his father, 'Father, give me the share of property that falls to me.' And he divided his living between them.

[13] Not many days later, the younger son gathered all he had and took his journey into a far country, and there he squandered his property in loose living. [14] And when he had spent everything, a great famine arose in that country, and he began to be in want. [15] So he went and joined himself to one of the citizens of that country, who sent him into his fields to feed swine. [16] And he would gladly have fed on the pods that the swine ate; and no one gave him anything.

> The younger son thought he could find fun and freedom by leaving his father, but instead he was reduced to poverty and humiliation—feeding pigs and even envying the pigs! It is an image of life apart from God.

DR. MARY HEALY, Scripture scholar and popular author

▶ It was unusual and even disgraceful for a son to demand his share of an inheritance before his father's death. The trouble is made worse when he squanders the money.

▶ Someone who was herding swine had sunk as low as it gets. Consuming pork was considered in the Old Testament to be a sign of apostasy. To this day, Jews and Muslims eat no pork.

Heartfelt repentance (Lk 15:17–20)

¹⁷ But when he came to himself he said, 'How many of my father's hired servants have bread enough and to spare, but I perish here with hunger! ¹⁸ I will arise and go to my father, and I will say to him, "Father, I have sinned against heaven and before you; ¹⁹ I am no longer worthy to be called your son; treat me as one of your hired servants." ' ²⁰ And he arose and came to his father.

The love that makes you alive (Lk 15:20–24)

But while he was yet at a distance, his father saw him and had compassion, and ran and embraced him and kissed him. ²¹ And the son said to him, 'Father, I have sinned against heaven and before you; I am no longer worthy to be called your son.' ²² But the father said to his servants, 'Bring quickly the best robe, and put it on him; and put a ring on his hand, and shoes on his feet; ²³ and bring the fatted calf and kill it, and let us eat and make merry; ²⁴ for this my son was dead, and is alive again; he was lost, and is found.'

And they began to make merry.

Sinning is like driving in the wrong direction at very high speed. You may have only one opportunity to avoid a crash: turn the car around and drive in the other direction!

YOUCAT UPDATE! GO TO CONFESSION

▶ Without repentance, there is no forgiveness. But the father's love is greater than the son's contrition.

Y → 338
What is grace??

"Sometimes we celebrate Easter in the middle of the day." That happens here. The father's love makes everything new.

What about the older brother? (Lk 15:25–32)

²⁵ "Now his elder son was in the field; and as he came and drew near to the house, he heard music and dancing. ²⁶ And he called one of the servants and asked what this meant. ²⁷ And he said to him, 'Your brother has come, and your father has killed the fatted calf, because he has received him safe and sound.' ²⁸ But he was angry and refused to go in.

His father came out and entreated him, ²⁹ but he answered his father, 'Behold, these many years I have served you, and I never disobeyed your command; yet you never gave me a kid, that I might make merry with my friends. ³⁰ But when this son of yours came, who has devoured your living with harlots, you killed for him the fatted calf!'

³¹ And he said to him, 'Son, you are always with me, and all that is mine is yours. ³² It was fitting to make merry and be glad, for this your brother was dead, and is alive; he was lost, and is found.'"

▶ "A man had two sons", so the parable began. The second part is as important as the first. The reconciliation in the father's house is not a matter of course. Will the older brother join the celebration? The parable is open-ended. The question is for all who can identify with him because they obediently remained at home.

God forgives a repentant sinner his sins faster than a mother can pull her child out of the fire.

JOHN VIANNEY

Death and Resurrection mark the story of Jesus himself. Luke enriches the Easter Gospel with an account in which both the sorrow and the gladness of faith find expression, the memory of Jesus and openness to the future of the Church.

TO EMMAUS AND BACK (LK 24:13–35)

A journey full of sadness (Lk 24:13–16)

▶ It was about ten kilometers [6.2 miles], or a two hours' walk.

24 [13] That very day two of them were going to a village named Emma'us, about seven miles from Jerusalem, [14] and talking with each other about all these things that had happened. [15] While they were talking and discussing together, Jesus himself drew near and went with them. [16] But their eyes were kept from recognizing him.

" We too can see Jesus "in the breaking of the Bread" (the Eucharist).

DR. TIM GRAY

A conversation about disappointments (Lk 24:17–24)

▶ Sometimes Cleopas is identified with Clopas, the husband of one of the women at the foot of the Cross (according to Jn 19:25).

[17] And he said to them, "What is this conversation which you are holding with each other as you walk?" And they stood still, looking sad. [18] Then one of them, named Cle'opas, answered him, "Are you the only visitor to Jerusalem who does not know the things that have happened there in these days?"

[19] And he said to them, "What things?"

▶ The risen Jesus is like a good pastor: He walks along the way with them; he asks the reason for their grief; he listens; he interprets what happened in the light of the Bible; he remains with the two disciples—and he breaks bread with them.

And they said to him, "Concerning Jesus of Nazareth, who was a prophet mighty in deed and word before God and all the people, [20] and how our chief priests and rulers delivered him up to be condemned to death, and crucified him. [21] But we had hoped that he was the one to redeem Israel. Yes, and besides all this, it is now the third day since this happened. [22] Moreover, some women of our company amazed us. They were at the tomb early in the morning [23] and did not find his body; and they came back saying that they had even seen a vision of angels, who said that he was alive. [24] Some of those who were with us went to the tomb, and found it just as the women had said; but him they did not see."

A hope-filled discussion of Scripture (Lk 24:25–27)

[25] And he said to them, "O foolish men, and slow of heart to believe all that the prophets have spoken! [26] Was it not necessary that the Christ should suffer these things and enter into his glory?"

[27] And beginning with Moses and all the prophets, he interpreted to them in all the Scriptures the things concerning himself.

Rembrandt: Christ with the disciples on the road to Emmaus

A common meal (Lk 24:28–31)

[28] So they drew near to the village to which they were going. He appeared to be going further, [29] but they constrained him, saying, "Stay

with us, for it is toward evening and the day is now far spent." So he went in to stay with them. ³⁰ When he was at table with them, he took the bread and blessed and broke it, and gave it to them. ³¹ And their eyes were opened and they recognized him; and he vanished out of their sight.

A journey full of joy (Lk 24:32–35)

³² They said to each other, "Did not our hearts burn within us while he talked to us on the road, while he opened to us the Scriptures?"

³³ And they rose that same hour and returned to Jerusalem; and they found the Eleven gathered together and those who were with them, ³⁴ who said, "The Lord has risen indeed, and has appeared to Simon!"

³⁵ Then they told what had happened on the road, and how he was known to them in the breaking of the bread.

> The Gospel of Luke ends with the promise of the Holy Spirit to the disciples and Jesus' Ascension. This is precisely where the Acts of the Apostles begins. In the New Testament, however, the Gospel according to John follows first.

▶ Why did Jesus "have to" suffer? Not because God is so cruel that he wanted to see blood before he would be gracious. But, rather, because redemption was accomplished in the midst of havoc, where evil was rampant, and because Jesus does not react to violence with violence but, rather, with love.

99 Jesus said, "You foolish men!" (He never said that to women, by the way.) "So slow to believe the full message of the prophets!" Are we also not slow, when we take ourselves so seriously? Whatever I'm thinking, it's gospel truth. If I'm feeling something, it has to be right. We're no different from these disciples going to Emmaus.

MOTHER ANGELICA (1923–2016), American Franciscan nun and foundress of EWTN

B Christ died for our sins in accordance with the Scriptures. He was buried, he was raised on the third day in accordance with the Scriptures, and he appeared to Cephas, then to the Twelve.

1 Cor 15:3-5

THE GOSPEL ACCORDING TO

John

Since ancient times, the Gospel according to John has been giv-
en a special preminence. It intends to promote friendship with
Jesus (Jn 15:12–17). It speaks a simple language but goes deep.
It begins with a prayer: God's Eternal Word was made flesh in
Jesus Christ (Jn 1:1–18). It makes it clear to the readers that it
means to promote faith: "Now Jesus did many other signs in the
presence of the disciples, which are not written in this book; but
these are written that you may believe that Jesus is the Christ,
the Son of God, and that believing you may have life in his
name" (Jn 20:30–31).

The evangelist makes it clear in his book that Jesus is one with
God (Jn 10:30). His word is "God's word" (Jn 14:10); his work is
"God's work" (Jn 5:36); he is God's image. In him we can tell who
God is (Jn 14:2–7) and who man is (→ Jn 19:5).

John tells about seven "signs" that Jesus performs: visible traces
of grace. He tells about the washing of the feet and about the
long conversations of Jesus with his disciples. He wants to
remove their fear before his death and give them hope in the
new life from the Resurrection. The following excerpts from the
Gospel of John focus on these signs and the farewell discourses,
which end in the high-priestly prayer.

▶ The Greek reads "the Logos". God's Word is "logical"; it makes sense.

👤 The darker it becomes around us here, the more we must open our hearts for the light from above.
EDITH STEIN

▶ This hymn of faith goes back to the story of creation (Gen 1) and before that. Jesus did not become God's Son at some particular point; on the contrary, he is the Son of God from the beginning; he became man in order to bring God to mankind. That is why we can say in faith: In Jesus we can read the meaning of all creation and of all history.

▶ The "Prologue" is followed by the story of how John the Baptist prepares people for the Messiah and how Jesus finds his first disciples (Jn 1:19–51).

▶ "Flesh" here means: totally a man, from his birth to his death.

❞ As we wait for heaven, we are like twins still in their mother's womb. "Soon we will see our mother", says the one twin. "Who put that idea in your head? How could there be such a thing as a mother? We are well looked after here", says the other. It is similar with faith: we cannot see God and yet are surrounded by him.
ROBERT SPAEMANN reflecting on a story by Henri J. M. Nouwen

The hymn about the beginning: God becomes man (Jn 1:1–18)

1 ¹ In the beginning was the Word, and the Word was with God, and the Word was God.
² He was in the beginning with God;
³ all things were made through him,
and without him was not anything made that was made.
⁴ In him was life, and the life was the light of men.
⁵ The light shines in the darkness,
and the darkness has not overcome it.
⁶ There was a man sent from God, whose name was John.
⁷ He came for testimony, to bear witness to the light, that all might believe through him.
⁸ He was not the light, but came to bear witness to the light.
⁹ The true light that enlightens every man
was coming into the world.
¹⁰ He was in the world,
and the world was made through him,
yet the world knew him not.
¹¹ He came to his own home,
and his own people received him not.

¹² But to all who received him,
who believed in his name,
he gave power to become children of God;
¹³ who were born, not of blood
nor of the will of the flesh
nor of the will of man, but of God.
¹⁴ And the Word became flesh
and dwelt among us, full of grace and truth;
we have beheld his glory,
glory as of the only-begotten Son from the Father.
¹⁵ (John bore witness to him, and cried, "This was he of whom I said, 'He who comes after me ranks before me, for he was before me.'")
¹⁶ And from his fulness have we all received,
grace upon grace.
¹⁷ For the law was given through Moses;
grace and truth came through Jesus Christ.
¹⁸ No one has ever seen God;
the only-begotten Son, who is in the bosom of the Father,
he has made him known.

The Prologue is followed by the story of how John the Baptist prepares people for the Messiah and how Jesus finds his first disciples (Jn 1:19–51).

The wedding feast at Cana (Jn 2:1–12)

2 ¹ On the third day there was a marriage at Cana in Galilee, and the mother of Jesus was there; ² Jesus also was invited to the marriage, with his disciples. ³ When the wine failed, the mother of Jesus said to him, "They have no wine." ⁴ And Jesus said to her, "O woman, what have you to do with me? My hour has not yet come." ⁵ His mother said to the servants, "Do whatever he tells you."

⁶ Now six stone jars were standing there, for the Jewish rites of purification, each holding twenty or thirty gallons. ⁷ Jesus said to them, "Fill the jars with water." And they filled them up to the brim. ⁸ He said to them, "Now draw some out, and take it to the steward of the feast." So they took it. ⁹ When the steward of the feast tasted the water now become wine, and did not know where it came from (though the servants who had drawn the water knew), the steward of the feast called the bridegroom ¹⁰ and said to him, "Every man serves the good wine first; and when men have drunk freely, then the poor wine; but you have kept the good wine until now."

▶ Mary mediates between Jesus and the people: she makes the concern of the newlyweds her own and instructs the servants to obey Jesus. Tradition has always seen in this a symbolic description of the role that Mary plays in God's plan of salvation. Jesus fulfills her request.

💡 Imagine that the guests have to drink tea for the rest of the feast! No, that just will not do!

POPE FRANCIS, February 14, 2014, to young couples preparing for their wedding

¹¹ This, the first of his signs, Jesus did at Cana in Galilee, and manifested his glory; and his disciples believed in him.

¹² After this he went down to Caper'na-um, with his mother and his brethren and his disciples; and there they stayed for a few days.

▶ According to the Gospel of John, Jesus performs seven "signs". All of them illustrate the fact that God gives mankind eternal life and already allows us to have a taste of it here on earth.

John goes on to tell about the cleansing of the Temple (Jn 2:13–22), about a nighttime conversation in Jerusalem with Nicodemus, a Jewish ruler, about birth to eternal life (Jn 3:1–21), and about a noonday conversation with a Samaritan woman at Jacob's well about true worship of God (Jn 4:1–42).

The healing of a child (Jn 4:43–54)

4 ⁴³ After the two days he departed to Galilee. ⁴⁴ For Jesus himself testified that a prophet has no honor in his own country. ⁴⁵ So when he came to Galilee, the Galileans welcomed him, having seen all that he had done in Jerusalem at the feast, for they too had gone to the feast.

⁴⁶ So he came again to Cana in Galilee, where he had made the water wine. And at Caper'na-um there was an official whose son was ill. ⁴⁷ When he heard that Jesus had come from Judea to Galilee, he went and begged him to come down and heal his son, for he was at the point of death. ⁴⁸ Jesus therefore said to him, "Unless you see signs and wonders you will not believe." ⁴⁹ The official said to him, "Sir, come down before my child dies."

▶ The man worked for the tetrarch, or minor governor, of Galilee, Herod Antipas (Lk 3:1).

> Jesus said, "My Father works until now; and I work." There is an air of equality about this bracketing himself with God which is quite unmistakable and could only be maddening. God "works"—creates, conserves in existence the beings he has created, exercises his providence—ceaselessly, on the Sabbath as at all times. When good is to be done, his Son is no more bound by times and seasons than he.

FRANK SHEED

▶ The father does all he can for his sick child—very good. Jesus prevents his death—even better. The son loves and the father believes—that is the whole Gospel in miniature.

⁵⁰ Jesus said to him, "Go; your son will live." The man believed the word that Jesus spoke to him and went his way. ⁵¹ As he was going down, his servants met him and told him that his son was living. ⁵² So he asked them the hour when he began to mend, and they said to him, "Yesterday at the seventh hour the fever left him." ⁵³ The father knew that was the hour when Jesus had said to him, "Your son will live"; and he himself believed, and all his household.

⁵⁴ This was now the second sign that Jesus did when he had come from Judea to Galilee.

Jesus heals a lame man (Jn 5:1–17)

5 ¹ After this there was a feast of the Jews, and Jesus went up to Jerusalem.

² Now there is in Jerusalem by the Sheep Gate a pool, in Hebrew called Beth-za'tha, which has five porticoes. ³ In these lay a multitude of invalids, blind, lame, paralyzed.

⁵ One man was there, who had been ill for thirty-eight years. ⁶ When Jesus saw him and knew that he had been lying there a long time, he said to him, "Do you want to be healed?" ⁷ The sick man answered him, "Sir, I have no man to put me into the pool when the water is troubled, and while I am going another steps

down before me." ⁸ Jesus said to him, "Rise, take up your pallet, and walk." ⁹ And at once the man was healed, and he took up his pallet and walked.

▶ Jesus heals the man on his own, in the power of God himself. He does not rely on the healing water. Nor does he take away anyone else's place. He needs only to speak the word, and the man is healed.

▶ On the Sabbath, work was not allowed (↗ Ex 20:8–10; Deut 5:12–15). God himself rests (↗ Gen 2:1–4). But he keeps the world alive. Jesus does that, too, by healing on the Sabbath.

Now that day was the sabbath. ¹⁰ So the Jews said to the man who was cured, "It is the sabbath, it is not lawful for you to carry your pallet." ¹¹ But he answered them, "The man who healed me said to me, 'Take up your pallet, and walk.'" ¹² They asked him, "Who is the man who said to you, 'Take up your pallet, and walk'?" ¹³ Now the man who had been healed did not know who it was, for Jesus had withdrawn, as there was a crowd in the place. ¹⁴ Afterward, Jesus found him in the temple, and said to him, "See, you are well! Sin no more, that nothing worse befall you." ¹⁵ The man went away and told the Jews that it was Jesus who had healed him. ¹⁶ And this was why the Jews persecuted Jesus, because he did this on the sabbath. ¹⁷ But Jesus answered them, "My Father is working still, and I am working." ¹⁸ This was why the Jews sought all the more to kill him, because he not only broke the sabbath but also called God his Father, making himself equal with God.

A big argument about healing on the Sabbath: Jesus is accused of usurping God's authority (Jn 5:18). That is why he explains in a long discourse that he acts with the full authority of God and that he worked this sign of healing precisely so that people might know that in Jesus they have encountered God himself (Jn 5:19–47).

Jesus feeds the people (Jn 6:1–15)

6 ¹ After this Jesus went to the other side of the Sea of Galilee, which is the Sea of Tibe'ri-as.

² And a multitude followed him, because they saw the signs which he did on those who were diseased. ³Jesus went up into the hills, and there sat down with his disciples. ⁴Now the Passover, the feast of the Jews, was at hand.

⁵ Lifting up his eyes, then, and seeing that a multitude was coming to him, Jesus said to Philip, "How are we to buy bread, so that these people may eat?" ⁶ This he said to test him, for he himself knew what he would do. ⁷ Philip answered him, "Two hundred denarii would not buy enough bread for each of them to get a little."

⁸ One of his disciples, Andrew, Simon Peter's brother, said to him, ⁹ "There is a lad here who has five barley loaves and two fish; but what are they among so many?"

¹⁰ Jesus said, "Make the people sit down." Now there was much grass in the place; so the men sat down, in number about five thousand. ¹¹ Jesus then took the loaves, and when he had given thanks, he distributed them to those who were seated; so also the fish, as much as they wanted.

 The one who started this miracle of the loaves was a youngster who generously offered his own food. I, too, have a share in God's power to work in the world; I can help start a miracle. To do that, though, I must offer myself to God and take a concrete step. In that way God's power becomes visible among people. I just have to start.

ANGELIKA

¹² And when they had eaten their fill, he told his disciples, "Gather up the fragments left over, that nothing may be lost." ¹³ So they gathered them up and filled twelve baskets with fragments from the five barley loaves, left by those who had eaten.

¹⁴ When the people saw the sign which he had done, they said, "This is indeed the prophet who is to come into the world!"

¹⁵ Perceiving then that they were about to come and take him by force to make him king, Jesus withdrew again to the hills by himself.

▶ Jesus does not perform a magic trick. He prays. This is his union with God the Father. From this union comes all life.

☺ The true king hangs on the Cross.

Jesus walks on water (Jn 6:16–21)

¹⁶ When evening came, his disciples went down to the sea, ¹⁷ got into a boat, and started across the sea to Caper'na-um. It was now dark, and Jesus had not yet come to them. ¹⁸ The sea rose because a strong wind was blowing.

¹⁹ When they had rowed about three or four miles, they saw Jesus walking on the sea and drawing near to the boat. They were frightened, ²⁰ but he said to them, "It is I; do not be afraid." ²¹ Then they were glad to take him into the boat, and immediately the boat was at the land to which they were going.

▶ The Greek text says that the distance was "twenty-five or thirty *stadia*"; each *stadion* was about 200 meters. The disciples were therefore 5 or 6 kilometers [roughly 3 or 4 miles] from the shore.

☺ "Fear not!" This occurs 365 times in the Bible. Once for every day in the year.

Next there is an important discussion in the synagogue of Capernaum (Jn 6:22-59): Jesus intends to show the people who want to satisfy their earthly hunger that they are hungry for God and that he is the only one who can satisfy this hunger: "...I am the bread of life; he who comes to me shall not hunger, and he who believes in me shall never thirst."(Jn 6:35). And later, more emphatically, "...Truly, truly, I say to you, unless you eat the flesh of the Son of man and drink his blood, you have no life in you; he who eats my flesh and drinks my blood has eternal life, and I will raise him up at the last day.(Jn: 6:53) Even within the circle of his followers, there is division and some of his followers walk away (Jn 6:60-71), Jesus asks the remaining disciples if they will go away too, but Peter says: "Lord, to whom shall we go? You have the words of eternal life" (Jn 6:68). After this crisis, John the Evangelist relates how Jesus proclaims God's Word again in Jerusalem and starts bitter debates about his preaching and his person. He reveals himself as the light of the world (Jn 8:12). We recommend that you read the whole discourse in full in an unabridged Bible.

Jesus heals a man who was blind from birth (Jn 9:1–7)

▶ The disciples are caught up in the popular notion that a sick person is being punished for his own sin or that of his Jesus himself, however, makes it clear: that is a false conclusion; God wants the blind man to live, and he wants him to be healed.

9 [1] As he passed by, he saw a man blind from his birth. [2] And his disciples asked him, "Rabbi, who sinned, this man or his parents, that he was born blind?" [3] Jesus answered, "It was not that this man sinned, or his parents, but that the works of God might be made manifest in him. [4] We must work the works of him who sent me, while it is day; night comes, when no one can work. [5] As long as I am in the world, I am the light of the world."

99 No one is so blind as those that will not see.

JONATHAN SWIFT (1667–1745), Irish author

[6] As he said this, he spat on the ground and made clay of the spittle and anointed the man's eyes with the clay, [7] saying to him, "Go, wash in the pool of Silo'am" (which means Sent). So he went and washed and came back seeing.

A bitter argument follows, and the healed man and his parents are drawn into it (Jn 9:6–34). The argument revolves around Jesus' relationship to God (Jn 9:35–41). He himself reveals that he is the Good Shepherd, who is one with the Father (Jn 10).

Jesus awakens Lazarus from the dead (Jn 11:1–44)

▶ The awakening of Lazarus is the seventh and greatest "sign" of Jesus. It reveals that Jesus not only will raise the dead at the end of all time, but that he already brings about eternal life here and now: in the indestructible love of God, which is accepted in faith.

11 [1] Now a certain man was ill, Laz'arus of Beth'any, the village of Mary and her sister Martha. [2] It was Mary who anointed the Lord with ointment and wiped his feet with her hair, whose brother Laz'arus was ill. [3] So the sisters sent to him, saying, "Lord, he whom you love is ill." [4] But when Jesus heard it he said, "This illness is not unto death; it is for the glory of God, so that the Son of God may be glorified by means of it."

[5] Now Jesus loved Martha and her sister and Laz'arus. [6] So when he heard that he was ill, he stayed two days longer in the place where he was. [7] Then after this he said to the disciples, "Let us go into Judea again."

⁸ The disciples said to him, "Rabbi, the Jews were but now seeking to stone you, and are you going there again?" ⁹ Jesus answered, "Are there not twelve hours in the day? If any one walks in the day, he does not stumble, because he sees the light of this world. ¹⁰ But if any one walks in the night, he stumbles, because the light is not in him."

¹¹ Thus he spoke, and then he said to them, "Our friend Laz'arus has fallen asleep, but I go to awake him out of sleep." ¹² The disciples said to him, "Lord, if he has fallen asleep, he will recover." ¹³ Now Jesus had spoken of his death, but they thought that he meant taking rest in sleep. ¹⁴ Then Jesus told them plainly, "Laz'arus is dead; ¹⁵ and for your sake I am glad that I was not there, so that you may believe. But let us go to him." ¹⁶ Thomas, called the Twin, said to his fellow disciples, "Let us also go, that we may die with him."

¹⁷ Now when Jesus came, he found that Laz'arus had already been in the tomb four days. ¹⁸ Beth'any was near Jerusalem, about two miles off, ¹⁹ and many of the Jews had come to Martha and Mary to console them concerning their brother. ²⁰ When Martha heard

▶ Judea is the territory around Jerusalem. Bethany is about 3 kilometers [2 miles] distant from Jerusalem.

Lazarus was not just seemingly dead. He really had died. That is also why Lazarus raised from the dead was not a zombie but a genuine man.

that Jesus was coming, she went and met him, while Mary sat in the house. ²¹ Martha said to Jesus, "Lord, if you had been here, my brother would not have died. ²² And even now I know that whatever you ask from God, God will give you." ²³ Jesus said to her, "Your brother will rise again."

²⁴ Martha said to him, "I know that he will rise again in the resurrection at the last day." ²⁵ Jesus said to her, "I am the resurrection and the life; he who believes in me, though he die, yet shall he live, ²⁶ and whoever lives and believes in me shall never die. Do you believe this?" ²⁷ She said to him, "Yes, Lord; I believe that you are the Christ, the Son of God, he who is coming into the world." ²⁸ When she had said this, she went and called her sister Mary, saying quietly, "The Teacher is here and is calling for you."

²⁹ And when she heard it, she rose quickly and went to him. ³⁰ Now Jesus had not yet come to the village, but was still in the place where Martha had met him. ³¹ When the Jews who were with her in the house, consoling her, saw Mary rise quickly and go out, they followed her, supposing that she was going to the tomb to weep there. ³² Then Mary, when she came where Jesus was and saw him, fell at his feet, saying to him, "Lord, if you had been here, my brother would not have died." ³³ When Jesus saw her weeping, and the Jews who came with her also weeping, he was deeply moved in spirit and troubled;

▶ In Jesus' time, everyone was convinced that after three days a person was certainly dead.

▶ Martha, full of sorrow and anxiety, goes out to meet Jesus. She is drawn by Jesus into a discussion of faith. In several steps, Martha is led to a deep profession of faith. She is a decisive witness to God's Word—out of love for her brother and out of friendship with Jesus.

❞ Jesus wept: tears, not of despair, but of love and sympathy for Lazarus and his family. This small narrative detail points to an awesome theological mystery: Jesus, who became man in every respect except sin, experienced a full range of human emotions.

SCOTT HAHN and **CURTIS MITCH**
Ignatius Catholic Study Bible

▶ Jesus shows emotions. Death does not leave him unmoved. He intends to show that death does not have the final word. That is why he will call Lazarus back from the tomb.

99 Today I invite you to think for a moment, in silence, here: where is my interior necrosis? Where is the dead part of my soul? Where is my tomb? Think, for a short moment, all of you in silence. Let us think: what part of the heart can be corrupted because of my attachment to sin, one sin or another? And to remove the stone, to take away the stone of shame and allow the Lord to say to us, as he said to Lazarus: "Come out!"

POPE FRANCIS, April 6, 2014

[34] and he said, "Where have you laid him?" They said to him, "Lord, come and see." [35] Jesus wept. [36] So the Jews said, "See how he loved him!" [37] But some of them said, "Could not he who opened the eyes of the blind man have kept this man from dying?"

[38] Then Jesus, deeply moved again, came to the tomb; it was a cave, and a stone lay upon it. [39] Jesus said, "Take away the stone." Martha, the sister of the dead man, said to him, "Lord, by this time there will be an odor, for he has been dead four days." [40] Jesus said to her, "Did I not tell you that if you would believe you would see the glory of God?" [41] So they took away the stone.

And Jesus lifted up his eyes and said, "Father, I thank you that you have heard me. [42] I knew that you always hear me, but I have said this on account of the people standing by, that they may believe that you sent me."

[43] When he had said this, he cried with a loud voice, "Laz'arus, come out." [44] The dead man came out, his hands and feet bound with bandages, and his face wrapped with a cloth. Jesus said to them, "Unbind him, and let him go."

To the **FOOTWASHING**

John then recounts how it was just this raising of Lazarus from the dead that led the Sanhedrin to decide to kill Jesus (Jn 11:45-53). But Jesus appears in and around Jerusalem to conclude his public proclamation.

THE WAY OF THE PASSION INTO ETERNAL LIFE (JN 13:1–21:25)

Jesus washes the feet of his disciples (Jn 13:1–20)

▶ The Jewish feast of Passover corresponds to the Christian celebration of Easter.

☀ Washing another person's feet is a respectful service that slaves often performed.

13 [1] Now before the feast of the Passover, when Jesus knew that his hour had come to depart out of this world to the Father, having loved his own who were in the world, he loved them to the end.

[2] And during supper, when the devil had already put it into the heart of Judas Iscariot, Simon's son, to betray him, [3] Jesus, knowing that the Father had given all things into his hands, and that he had come from God and was going to God, [4] rose from supper, laid aside his garments, and tied a towel around himself. [5] Then he poured water into a basin, and began to wash the disciples' feet, and to wipe them with the towel that was tied around him.

[6] He came to Simon Peter; and Peter said to him, "Lord, do you wash my feet?" [7] Jesus answered him, "What I am doing you do not know now, but afterward you will understand." [8] Peter said to him, "You shall never wash my feet." Jesus answered him, "If I do not

wash you, you have no part in me." [9] Simon Peter said to him, "Lord, not my feet only but also my hands and my head!" [10] Jesus said to him, "He who has bathed does not need to wash, except for his feet, but he is clean all over; and you are clean, but not all of you."

[11] For he knew who was to betray him; that was why he said, "You are not all clean."

[12] When he had washed their feet, and taken his garments, and resumed his place, he said to them, "Do you know what I have done to you? [13] You call me Teacher and Lord; and you are right, for so I am. [14] If I then, your Lord and Teacher, have washed your feet, you also ought to wash one another's feet. [15] For I have given you an example, that you also should do as I have done to you. [16] Truly, truly, I say to you, a servant is not greater than his master; nor is he who is sent greater than he who sent him. [17] If you know these things, blessed are you if you do them.

[18] I am not speaking of you all; I know whom I have chosen; it is that the Scripture may be fulfilled, 'He who ate my bread has lifted his heel against me.' [19] I tell you this now, before it takes place, that when it does take place you may believe that I am he. [20] Truly, truly, I say to you, he who receives any one whom I send receives me; and he who receives me receives him who sent me."

▶ In conversation with Peter, Jesus interpreted the washing of the feet as a sign of the communication of salvation. He is the *diákonos*, or servant, who by laying down his life frees the disciples from the "filth" of sin and gives them the "purity" of eternal life. In conversation with his disciples, Jesus portrays himself afterward as a model: in following Jesus, they should serve one another: they should help one another to be freed from sin and to enter more deeply into communion with God and with one another.

▶ An allusion to the betrayer, Judas Iscariot.

Jesus identifies the traitor (Jn 13:21–30)

[21] When Jesus had thus spoken, he was troubled in spirit, and testified, "Truly, truly, I say to you, one of you will betray me." [22] The disciples looked at one another, uncertain of whom he spoke. [23] One of his disciples, whom Jesus loved, was lying close to the breast of Jesus;

[24] so Simon Peter beckoned to him and said, "Tell us who it is of whom he speaks." [25] So lying thus, close to the breast of Jesus, he said to him, "Lord, who is it?" [26] Jesus answered, "It is he to whom I shall give this morsel when I have dipped it." So when he had dipped the morsel, he gave it to Judas, the son of Simon Iscariot. [27] Then after the morsel, Satan entered into him. Jesus said to him, "What you are going to do, do quickly." [28] Now no one at the table knew why he said this to him. [29] Some thought that, because Judas had the money box, Jesus was telling him, "Buy what we need for the feast"; or, that he should give something to the poor. [30] So, after receiving the morsel, he immediately went out; and it was night.

❞ No sin is too great to be forgiven! The fact that we have a troubled past must not frighten us away. It becomes a piece of jewelry if we give it to God so as to receive the consolation of forgiveness.
ALBINO LUCIANI (Pope John Paul I) (1912–1978)

▶ Judas' betrayal is not explained. His motives remain in obscurity. God made the best out of human guilt: deliverance from evil.

The commandment of love (Jn 13:31–35)

[31] When he had gone out, Jesus said, "Now is the Son of man glorified, and in him God is glorified;

[32] if God is glorified in him, God will also glorify him in himself, and glorify him at once. [33] Little children, yet a little while I am with

▶ Jesus is the Son of man. His glorification is the honor that is bestowed on him by the Resurrection—for the salvation of all mankind.

▶ The commandment of love is already recorded in the Old Testament. What is new is its application to the community of disciples (↗ 1 Jn 2:7–11; 4:7–21).

you. You will seek me; and as I said to the Jews so now I say to you, 'Where I am going you cannot come.'

³⁴ A new commandment I give to you, that you love one another; even as I have loved you, that you also love one another. ³⁵ By this all men will know that you are my disciples, if you have love for one another."

Peter will deny Jesus (Jn 13:36–38)

▶ Here Jesus alludes to Peter's martyrdom (↗ Jn 21:19f.).

³⁶ Simon Peter said to him, "Lord, where are you going?" Jesus answered, "Where I am going you cannot follow me now; but you shall follow afterward." ³⁷ Peter said to him, "Lord, why can I not follow you now? I will lay down my life for you."

³⁸ Jesus answered, "Will you lay down your life for me? Truly, truly, I say to you, the cock will not crow, till you have denied me three times.

JESUS' FAREWELL TO HIS DISCIPLES (JN 14)

Jesus goes to the Father (Jn 14:1–7)

▶ God's house with many rooms—that is an ancient image for the fullness of eternal life.

14 ¹ "Let not your hearts be troubled; believein God, believe also in me.² In my Father's house are many rooms; if it were not

▶ Jesus not only speaks the truth: he stands up for it with his whole person. He does not just promise life but gives it. That is why he is not *a* way but *the* Way. God's love is unconditional—and Jesus stands up for this truth with his life; he gives his word that it is so. His way excludes no one but, rather, leads everyone to God.

so, would I have told you that I go to prepare a place for you?³And when I go and prepare a place for you, I will come again and will take you to myself, that where I am you may be also.⁴And you know the way where I am going."

⁵ Thomas said to him, "Lord, we do not know where you are going; how can we know the way?"

⁶ Jesus said to him, "I am the way, and the truth, and the life; no one comes to the Father, but by me.

⁷ If you had known me, you would have known my Father also; henceforth you know him and have seen him."

Jesus unites his disciples with God (Jn 14:8–14)

▶ The "greater" works are those of the mission that will be performed after Easter—and to this day—throughout the world in order to win souls for Jesus in the power of the Spirit and through him for God.

⁸ Philip said to him, "Lord, show us the Father, and we shall be satisfied." ⁹ Jesus said to him, "Have I been with you so long, and yet you do not know me, Philip? He who has seen me has seen the Father; how can you say, 'Show us the Father'? ¹⁰ Do you not believe that I am in the Father and the Father is in me? The words that I say to you I do not speak on my own authority; but the Father who dwells in me does his works. ¹¹ Believe me that I am in the Father and the Father is in me; or else believe me for the sake of the works themselves.

EIGHT "I AM" SAYINGS OF JESUS

I am the bread of life. Jn 6:35

I am the light of the world. Jn 8:12

Before Abraham was, I am. Jn 8:58

I am the door. Jn 10:7,9

I am the good shepherd. Jn 10:11,14

I am the resurrection
and the life. Jn 11:25

I am the way, and the truth,
and the life. Jn 14:6

I am the true vine. Jn 15:1

¹² "Truly, truly, I say to you, he who believes in me will also do the works that I do; and greater works than these will he do, because I go to the Father. ¹³ Whatever you ask in my name, I will do it, that the Father may be glorified in the Son; ¹⁴ if you ask anything in my name, I will do it.

Jesus promises his disciples the Holy Spirit (Jn 14:15–20)
¹⁵ "If you love me, you will keep my commandments.¹⁶And I will ask the Father, and he will give you another Counselor, to be with you for ever, ¹⁷ even the Spirit of truth, whom the world cannot receive, because it neither sees him nor knows him; you know him, for he dwells with you, and will be in you.
¹⁸ "I will not leave you desolate; I will come to you. ¹⁹ Yet a little while, and the world will see me no more, but you will see me; because I live, you will live also. ²⁰ In that day you will know that I am in my Father, and you in me, and I in you.

It's about Love (Jn 14:21–26)
²¹ He who has my commandments and keeps them, he it is who loves me; and he who loves me will be loved by my Father, and I will love him and manifest myself to him." ²² Judas (not Iscariot) said to

▶ The "Paraclete"—a Greek term that also means the "Comforter" or the "Advocate"—is a great help for the disciples in the world. He reminds them of Jesus (Jn 14:26), enables them to bear witness (Jn 15:26f.), and guides them "into all the truth" (Jn 16:13).

I once had the pleasure of traveling through the mountains with a monk. As we marveled at the landscape, he commented: What must it be like in heaven, if there is such beauty already on earth? That really made me think. If God gives us such gifts even here, what will heaven look like?

ROY

▶ The "ruler of this world" is the devil, whom Jesus drives out of the world (Jn 12:31f.).

him, "Lord, how is it that you will manifest yourself to us, and not to the world?" 23 Jesus answered him, "If a man loves me, he will keep my word, and my Father will love him, and we will come to him and make our home with him. 24 He who does not love me does not keep my words; and the word which you hear is not mine but the Father's who sent me.

25 "These things I have spoken to you, while I am still with you. 26 But the Counselor, the Holy Spirit, whom the Father will send in my name, he will teach you all things, and bring to your remembrance all that I have said to you.

Peace I Leave with You (Jn 14:27–31)

27 Peace I leave with you; my peace I give to you; not as the world gives do I give to you. Let not your hearts be troubled, neither let them be afraid.

28 You heard me say to you, 'I go away, and I will come to you.' If you loved me, you would have rejoiced, because I go to the Father; for the Father is greater than I. 29 And now I have told you before it takes place, so that when it does take place, you may believe. 30 I will no longer talk much with you, for the ruler of this world is coming. He has no power over me; 31 but I do as the Father has commanded me, so that the world may know that I love the Father. Rise, let us go from here.

Another very important farewell discourse follows, which examines in greater depth the theme of the first. Be sure to read Jn 15-16 in an unabridged Bible.

THE HIGH-PRIESTLY PRAYER (JN 17:1–26)

▶ The "world" is God's creation, but it is also a place of resistance against God and goodness. Jesus comes not from the world but from God; he does not remain in the world but goes to the Father. The disciples live in the world.

▶ Jesus is a priest. He reconciled mankind with God. That is why he prays for the salvation of the world.

The beginning of the prayer (Jn 17:1–4)

17 1 When Jesus had spoken these words, he lifted up his eyes to heaven and said, "Father, the hour has come; glorify your Son that the Son may glorify you, 2 since you have given him power over all flesh, to give eternal life to all whom you have given him. 3 And this is eternal life, that they know you the only true God, and Jesus Christ whom you have sent. 4 I glorified you on earth, having accomplished the work which you gave me to do.

Jesus Prays for Himself (Jn 17:5–8)

5 and now, Father, glorify me in your own presence with the glory which I had with you before the world was made.

6 "I have manifested your name to the men whom you gave me out of the world; they were yours, and you gave them to me, and they have kept your word. 7 Now they know that everything that you have given me is from you; 8 for I have given them the words which you gave me, and they have received them and know in truth that I came

from you; and they have believed that you sent me.

Jesus prays for his disciples (Jn 17:9–19)

⁹ I am praying for them; I am not praying for the world but for those whom you have given me, for they are yours;

¹⁰ all mine are yours, and yours are mine, and I am glorified in them. ¹¹ And now I am no more in the world, but they are in the world, and I am coming to you.

Holy Father, keep them in your name, which you have given me, that they may be one, even as we are one. ¹² While I was with them, I kept them in your name, which you have given me; I have guarded them, and none of them is lost but the son of perdition, that the Scripture might be fulfilled.

¹³ But now I am coming to you; and these things I speak in the world, that they may have my joy fulfilled in themselves. ¹⁴ I have given them your word; and the world has hated them because they are not of the world, even as I am not of the world. ¹⁵ I do not pray that you should take them out of the world, but that you should keep them from the evil one. ¹⁶ They are not of the world, even as I am not of the world.

¹⁷ Sanctify them in the truth; your word is truth. ¹⁸ As you sent me

> 99 In order to accomplish her true task adequately, the Church must constantly renew the effort to detach herself from the "worldliness" of the world. In this she follows the words of Jesus: "They are not of the world, even as I am not of the world" (Jn 17:16). … When the Church becomes less worldly, her missionary witness shines more brightly. Once liberated from her material and political burdens, the Church can reach out more effectively and in a truly Christian way to the whole world, she can be truly open to the world.
>
> **POPE BENEDICT XVI**, speech in Freiburg, September 24, 2011

▶ "The son of perdition" refers to Judas Iscariot (Jn 13:18, 27, 29).

into the world, so I have sent them into the world. ¹⁹ And for their sake I consecrate myself, that they also may be consecrated in truth.

Jesus prays for all believers (Jn 17:20–26)

²⁰ "I do not pray for these only, but also for those who believe in me through their word, ²¹ that they may all be one; even as you, Father, are in me, and I in you, that they also may be in us, so that the world may believe that you have sent me. ²² The glory which you have given me I have given to them, that they may be one even as we are one, ²³ I in them and you in me, that they may become perfectly one, so that the world may know that you have sent me and have loved them even as you have loved me.

²⁴ Father, I desire that they also, whom you have given me, may be with me where I am, to behold my glory which you have given me in your love for me before the foundation of the world. ²⁵ O righteous Father, the world has not known you, but I have known you; and these know that you have sent me. ²⁶ I made known to them your name, and I will make it known, that the love with which you have loved me may be in them, and I in them."

💡 To sanctify = to make holy. Jesus prays to the Father for a sort of update to our interior software.

> 99 During the Second World War, as bombs were hailing down on us, we opened at random the little Gospel book that we had brought with us into the air-raid shelter and found the passage in Jesus' Testament: "That all may be one, as you, Father, are in me and I am in you." Until then these words had been practically unknown to us. Now they lit up before us like stars. We sensed that we had been born for this! … We were certain that God wanted to make a divine adventure out of our lives.
>
> **CHIARA LUBICH** (1920–2008), founder of the Focolare Movement

💡 "I love you", God says to me—and to you—and to us and to all people. I have only to answer: "Yes, I love you, too." Then everything is good.

In John's Gospel, the account of the Passion comes next, which shows many similarities with the Passion narratives of the Synoptic Gospels, Matthew, Mark, and Luke, but also numerous differences (Jn 18:1—19:42).

▶ The first day of the week
is Sunday, the day after the
Sabbath.

▶ The "other disciple" is the
"disciple whom Jesus loved"
(↗ Jn 13:23).

THE EASTER GOSPEL (JN 20:1–21:25)

The race to the empty tomb (Jn 20:1–10)

20 ¹ Now on the first day of the week, Mary Mag'dalene came to the tomb early, while it was still dark, and saw that the stone had been taken away from the tomb.

² So she ran, and went to Simon Peter and the other disciple, the one whom Jesus loved, and said to them, "They have taken the Lord out of the tomb, and we do not know where they have laid him."

³ Peter then came out with the other disciple, and they went toward the tomb. ⁴ They both ran, but the other disciple outran Peter and reached the tomb first; ⁵ and stooping to look in, he saw the linen cloths lying there, but he did not go in.

⁶ Then Simon Peter came, following him, and went into the tomb; he saw the linen cloths lying, ⁷ and the napkin, which had been on his head, not lying with the linen cloths but rolled up in a place by itself.

⁸ Then the other disciple, who reached the tomb first, also went in, and he saw and believed; ⁹ for as yet they did not know the Scrip-

▶ Faith is a path. At the empty
tomb, the beloved disciple,
unlike Peter, comes to believe
already. But he still needs the
sight of the relics. Faith that is
founded on Sacred Scripture
is deeper.

▶ The most obvious explanation for the empty tomb is that
someone removed the body.
Mary Magdalene is not satisfied
with that, however, but asks.

ture, that he must rise from the dead. ¹⁰ Then the disciples went back to their homes.

Jesus appears to Mary Magdalene (Jn 20:11–18)

¹¹ But Mary stood weeping outside the tomb, and as she wept she stooped to look into the tomb; ¹² and she saw two angels in white, sitting where the body of Jesus had lain, one at the head and one at the feet. ¹³ They said to her, "Woman, why are you weeping?" She said to them, "Because they have taken away my Lord, and I do not know where they have laid him."

¹⁴ Saying this, she turned round and saw Jesus standing, but she did not know that it was Jesus. ¹⁵ Jesus said to her, "Woman, why are you weeping? Whom do you seek?" Supposing him to be the garden-er, she said to him, "Sir, if you have carried him away, tell me where you have laid him, and I will take him away."

¹⁶ Jesus said to her, "Mary." She turned and said to him in Hebrew, "Rab-bo'ni!" (which means Teacher).

¹⁷ Jesus said to her, "Do not hold me, for I have not yet ascended to the Father; but go to my brethren and say to them, I am ascending to my Father and your Father, to my God and your God."

¹⁸ Mary Mag'dalene went and said to the disciples, "I have seen the Lord"; and she told them that he had said these things to her.

Jesus sends his disciples (Jn 20:19–23)

¹⁹ On the evening of that day, the first day of the week, the doors being shut where the disciples were, for fear of the Jews, Jesus came and stood among them and said to them, "Peace be with you." ²⁰ When he had said this, he showed them his hands and his side. Then the disciples were glad when they saw the Lord. ²¹ Jesus said to them again, "Peace be with you. As the Father has sent me, even so I send you." ²² And when he had said this, he breathed on them, and said to them, "Receive the Holy Spirit. ²³ If you forgive the sins of any, they are forgiven; if you retain the sins of any, they are retained."

Jesus leads Thomas to believe (Jn 20:24–29)

²⁴ Now Thomas, one of the Twelve, called the Twin, was not with them when Jesus came. ²⁵ So the other disciples told him, "We have seen the Lord." But he said to them, "Unless I see in his hands the

▶ The recognition scene is very carefully and intensively depicted. There is no spectacle. Jesus calls Mary by her name, and in that way she can recognize him and become an apostle to the apostles.

▶ The mission of the disciples, which Jesus began by sending them out before Easter, is continued after Easter. Jesus himself gives his Spirit to his disciples. They are to free people from their sins but also to call injustice clearly by its name.

print of the nails, and place my finger in the mark of the nails, and place my hand in his side, I will not believe." ²⁶ Eight days later, his disciples were again in the house, and Thomas was with them. The doors were shut, but Jesus came and stood among them, and said, "Peace be with you." ²⁷ Then he said to Thomas, "Put your finger here, and see my hands; and put out your hand, and place it in my side; do not be faithless, but believing." ²⁸ Thomas answered him, "My Lord and my God!" ²⁹ Jesus said to him, "You have believed because you have seen me. Blessed are those who have not seen and yet believe."

A stage direction from the evangelist (Jn 20:30–31)

³⁰ Now Jesus did many other signs in the presence of the disciples, which are not written in this book; ³¹ but these are written that you may believe that Jesus is the Christ, the Son of God, and that believing you may have life in his name.

The miraculous catch of fish (Jn 21:1–14)

21 ¹ After this Jesus revealed himself again to the disciples by the Sea of Tibe′ri-as; and he revealed himself in this way. ² Simon Peter, Thomas called the Twin, Nathan′a-el of Cana in Gal-

▶ The Gospel does not say whether Thomas actually touched Jesus. It records Jesus' willingness. As risen Lord, he still bears the marks of the wounds. The Cross is not a thing of the past; it remains in the present. The risen crucified Lord is the one who leads Thomas to believe.

Y → 21, 22
Faith—what is it? How does one go about believing?

▶ Even though no one can see the risen Lord in the flesh now, we can read the Gospel and in that way come to believe.

When you pray, you speak to God. When you read the Bible, God speaks to you.

AUGUSTINE

" Yesterday I celebrated the 60th anniversary of the day when I heard Jesus' voice in my heart. I am telling you this not so that you will make me a cake here, no. ... →

→ Why? Because I feel like Tarzan and I feel strong enough to go ahead? No, I have not re-gretted it because always, even at the darkest moments, the moments of sin and moments of frailty, moments of failure, I have looked at Jesus and trusted in him and he has not deserted me.

POPE FRANCIS to the young people of Sardinia, September 22, 2013

▶ Peter is asked three times about his love for Jesus because he denied him three times (Jn 18:12–27).

ilee, the sons of Zeb'edee, and two others of his disciples were to-gether. ³ Simon Peter said to them, "I am going fishing." They said to him, "We will go with you." They went out and got into the boat; but that night they caught nothing.

⁴ Just as day was breaking, Jesus stood on the beach; yet the disci-ples did not know that it was Jesus. ⁵ Jesus said to them, "Children, have you any fish?" They answered him, "No." ⁶ He said to them, "Cast the net on the right side of the boat, and you will find some." So they cast it, and now they were not able to haul it in, for the quantity of fish.

⁷ That disciple whom Jesus loved said to Peter, "It is the Lord!" When Simon Peter heard that it was the Lord, he put on his clothes, for he was stripped for work, and sprang into the sea. ⁸ But the oth-er disciples came in the boat, dragging the net full of fish, for they were not far from the land, but about a hundred yards off.

⁹ When they got out on land, they saw a charcoal fire there, with

fish lying on it, and bread. ¹⁰ Jesus said to them, "Bring some of the fish that you have just caught." ¹¹ So Simon Peter went aboard and hauled the net ashore, full of large fish, a hundred and fifty-three of them; and although there were so many, the net was not torn.

¹² Jesus said to them, "Come and have breakfast." Now none of the disciples dared ask him, "Who are you?" They knew it was the Lord. ¹³ Jesus came and took the bread and gave it to them, and so with the fish.

¹⁴ This was now the third time that Jesus was revealed to the disci-ples after he was raised from the dead.

Do you love me? (Jn 21:15–19)

¹⁵ When they had finished breakfast, Jesus said to Simon Peter, "Simon, son of John, do you love me more than these?" He said to him, "Yes, Lord; you know that I love you." He said to him, "Feed my lambs." ¹⁶ A second time he said to him, "Simon, son of John, do you love me?" He said to him, "Yes, Lord; you know that I love you." He said to him, "Tend my sheep." ¹⁷ He said to him the third time, "Si-mon, son of John, do you love me?"

Peter was grieved because he said to him the third time, "Do you love me?" And he said to him, "Lord, you know everything; you know that I love you." Jesus said to him, "Feed my sheep." [18] Truly, truly, I say to you, when you were young, you fastened your own belt and walked where you would; but when you are old, you will stretch out your hands, and another will fasten your belt for you and carry you where you do not wish to go." [19] (This he said to show by what death he was to glorify God.) And after this he said to him, "Follow me."

What becomes of the beloved disciple? (Jn 21:20–23)

[20] Peter turned and saw following them the disciple whom Jesus loved, who had lain close to his breast at the supper and had said, "Lord, who is it that is going to betray you?" [21] When Peter saw him, he said to Jesus, "Lord, what about this man?" [22] Jesus said to him, "If it is my will that he remain until I come, what is that to you? Follow me!"

[23] The saying spread abroad among the brethren that this disciple

There is only one thing to do on this earth: love Jesus with all the strength of our heart and save souls for him, so that he will be loved.

THÉRÈSE OF LISIEUX

Jesus is the Good Shepherd (Jn 10). He appoints Peter to pasture his flock. Peter is to make sure that they remain the flock of Jesus Christ.

was not to die; yet Jesus did not say to him that he was not to die, but, "If it is my will that he remain until I come, what is that to you?"

The conclusion of the Gospel (Jn 21:24–25)

[24] This is the disciple who is bearing witness to these things, and who has written these things; and we know that his testimony is true.

[25] But there are also many other things which Jesus did; were every one of them to be written, I suppose that the world itself could not contain the books that would be written.

For me, Jesus is my God, Jesus my life, Jesus my only love, Jesus my All in all, Jesus my One and Only. Jesus, I love you with my whole heart, with my whole being.

MOTHER TERESA

You do not have to become a martyr in order to be a witness to the faith.

THE

Acts of the Apostles

The Acts of the Apostles is Luke's second book, after the Gospel
(Acts 1:1). Luke relates how the early Church fulfilled Jesus'
commission step by step (Acts 1:8). It begins with the mission
in Jerusalem. It begins on the Feast of Pentecost. It quickly
meets with resistance but does not let that stop it. Then Philip
travels the road to the Samaritans, the sworn enemies who are
supposed to become brethren in faith.

Afterward paths open up to far-off pagans. Peter is the first to
baptize someone who is not Jewish: the centurion Cornelius in
Caesarea. Then Barnabas and Paul begin a systematic mission
among the nations outside of Israel. Some in the Church object.
But at the Council of the Apostles (Acts 15), the obstacles to
their work are cleared away. Paul decisively follows this approval to its logical conclusions. Although he himself was once a
persecutor of the Church, now he becomes a preacher of the
Gospel even in Rome.

The Acts of the Apostles shows us in snapshots how turbulently
the Church grew. At first there were only a few who came to
believe in Jesus Christ. But then there were more and more of
them—to this day.

Foreword (Acts 1:1–3)

1 ¹ In the first book, O Theoph'ilus, I have dealt with all that Jesus began to do and teach, ² until the day when he was taken up, after he had given commandment through the Holy Spirit to the apostles whom he had chosen. ³ To them he presented himself alive after his passion by many proofs, appearing to them during forty days, and speaking of the kingdom of God.

PREPARATION FOR THE MISSION (ACTS 1:4-8)

The commission to go forth (Acts 1:4–8)

⁴ And while staying with them he charged them not to depart from Jerusalem, but to wait for the promise of the Father, which, he said, "you heard from me, ⁵ for John baptized with water, but before many days you shall be baptized with the Holy Spirit."

⁶ So when they had come together, they asked him, "Lord, will you at this time restore the kingdom to Israel?" ⁷ He said to them, "It is not for you to know times or seasons which the Father has fixed by his own authority. ⁸ But you shall receive power when the Holy Spirit has come upon you; and you shall

be my witnesses in Jerusalem and in all Judea and Samar'ia and to the end of the earth."

Jesus' Ascension into heaven (Acts 1:9–11)

⁹ And when he had said this, as they were looking on, he was lifted up, and a cloud took him out of their sight.

¹⁰ And while they were gazing into heaven as he went, behold, two men stood by them in white robes, ¹¹ and said, "Men of Galilee, why do you stand looking into heaven? This Jesus, who was taken up from you into heaven, will come in the same way as you saw him go into heaven."

The expectant early Christian community (Acts 1:12–14)

¹² Then they returned to Jerusalem from the mount called Olivet, which is near Jerusalem, a sabbath day's journey away;

¹³ and when they had entered, they went up to the upper room, where they were staying, Peter and John and James and Andrew, Philip and Thomas, Bartholomew and Matthew, James the son of Alphae'us and Simon the Zealot and Judas the son of James. ¹⁴ All these with one accord devoted themselves to prayer, together with the women and Mary the mother of Jesus, and with his brethren.

💡 40—an awesome number! 40 days have passed since Easter morning. For 40 days Jesus fasts in the desert. The Lenten season before Easter lasts 40 days, and the people of Israel wandered for 40 years in the desert after their Exodus from Egypt. The number 40 designates times of trial and testing—times in which something great is being prepared.

Matthias becomes the twelfth apostle (Acts 1:15–26)

¹⁵ In those days Peter stood up among the brethren (the company of persons was in all about a hundred and twenty), and said, ¹⁶ "Brethren, the Scripture had to be fulfilled, which the Holy Spirit spoke beforehand by the mouth of David, concerning Judas who was guide to those who arrested Jesus. ¹⁷ For he was numbered among us, and was allotted his share in this ministry. ¹⁸ (Now this man bought a field with the reward of his wickedness; and falling headlong he burst open in the middle and all his bowels gushed out. ¹⁹ And it became known to all the inhabitants of Jerusalem, so that the field was called in their language Akel'dama, that is, Field of Blood.) ²⁰ For it is written in the book of Psalms,

'Let his habitation become desolate,
    and let there be no one to live in it'; and 'His office let another take.'

²¹ So one of the men who have accompanied us during all the time that the Lord Jesus went in and out among us, ²² beginning from the baptism of John until the day when he was taken up from us—one of these men must become with us a witness to his resurrection."

²³ And they put forward two, Joseph called Barsab'bas, who was surnamed Justus, and Matthi'as. ²⁴ And they prayed and said, "Lord, you know the

💡 12—another awesome number. There are 12 months in a year, 12 constellations in the sky. Israel is a people made up of 12 tribes. The Church has 12 apostles. The dozen is completed—history can begin.

❞ The apostles had to take their first steps without Jesus being present the way he was in his ministry. But he promised to empower them with the Holy Spirit, and that their witness would reach the ends of the earth. We, too, must take our first steps →

hearts of all men, show which one of these two you have chosen ²⁵ to take the place in this ministry and apostleship from which Judas turned aside, to go to his own place." ²⁶ And they cast lots for them, and the lot fell on Matthi'as; and he was enrolled with the eleven apostles.

PENTECOST (ACTS 2:1–47)

The descent of the Holy Spirit (Acts 2:1–13)

2 ¹ When the day of Pentecost had come, they were all together in one place. ² And suddenly a sound came from heaven like the rush of a mighty wind, and it filled all the house where they were sitting. ³ And there appeared to them tongues as of fire, distributed and resting on each one of them. ⁴ And they were all filled with the Holy Spirit and began to speak in other tongues, as the Spirit gave them utterance.

⁵ Now there were dwelling in Jerusalem Jews, devout men from every nation under heaven. ⁶ And at this sound the multitude came together, and they were bewildered, because each one heard them speaking in his own language. ⁷ And they were amazed and wondered, saying, "Are not all these who are speaking Galileans? ⁸ And how is it that we hear, each of us in his own native language? ⁹ Par'thians and Medes and E'lamites and residents of Mesopota'mia,

→ in sharing our Faith, and Jesus will empower us with the Holy Spirit as well.
JIMMY AKIN, (b. 1965), author and Catholic apologist

▶ Drawing lots (v. 26) signifies that God himself should make the final decision. The Twelve represent the entire people of God.

▶ Pentecost (in English: fifty) originally referred to the Jewish "Feast of Weeks" (Shavuot), 50 days after the feast of Passover (Ex 34:22; Deut 16:10). The Feast of Weeks commemorates the giving of the Ten Commandments on Mount Sinai. Pentecost is celebrated by Christians to commemorate the descent of the Holy Spirit on the early Church, which happened during the Jewish celebration commemorating God's establishment of the Covenant People of Israel.

Judea and Cappado'cia, Pontus and Asia, ¹⁰ Phryg'ia and Pamphyl'ia, Egypt and the parts of Libya belonging to Cyre'ne, and visitors from Rome, both Jews and proselytes, ¹¹ Cretans and Arabians, we hear them telling in our own tongues the mighty works of God." ¹² And all were amazed and perplexed, saying to one another, "What does this mean?" ¹³ But others mocking said, "They are filled with new wine."

Peter's Pentecost sermon (Acts 2:14–36)

¹⁴ But Peter, standing with the Eleven, lifted up his voice and addressed them, "Men of Judea and all who dwell in Jerusalem, let this be known to you, and give ear to my words.

¹⁵ For these men are not drunk, as you suppose, since it is only the third hour of the day; ¹⁶ but this is what was spoken by the prophet Joel:

¹⁷ 'And in the last days it shall be, God declares,
that I will pour out my Spirit upon all flesh,
and your sons and your daughters shall prophesy,
and your young men shall see visions,
and your old men shall dream dreams;
¹⁸ yes, and on my menservants and my maidservants in those days
I will pour out my Spirit; and they shall prophesy.

> ▶ The Gospel can be proclaimed and understood equally well in all the languages in the world. The miracle of Pentecost is the fact that the Holy Spirit brings about this understanding. The disciples can express themselves in such a way that the Jews from all over the world understand them in their native language.

> ▶ In his sermon, Peter clarifies the situation. He cites the promise of the prophet Joel, that all the children of Israel will be able to speak prophetically, and explains that this promise is now fulfilled because Jesus is risen from the dead.

Я задаволены!* 私も**

* I am fulfilled!
** Me too!

> Since I had the privilege of learning that on Pentecost the nation of Israel was born and received the Ten Commandments and that on Pentecost the Christian community was born and God's Spirit was poured out, I began to understand what it means to worship our Father in Spirit and in Truth. What a wonderful journey of discovery back to the People of Israel and to the origins of our faith! It is not always easy to go beyond what you are used to, but worthwhile, because it is so unimaginably deep and far-reaching—into eternity.
>
> **MICHAEL**

> ▶ Pilate and his soldiers are described as lawless because they do not obey God's Law.

¹⁹ And I will show wonders in the heaven above
and signs on the earth beneath,
blood, and fire, and vapor of smoke;
²⁰ the sun shall be turned into darkness
and the moon into blood,
before the day of the Lord comes,
the great and manifest day.
²¹ And it shall be that whoever calls on the name of the Lord shall be saved.'

²² "Men of Israel, hear these words: Jesus of Nazareth, a man attested to you by God with mighty works and wonders and signs which God did through him in your midst, as you yourselves know— ²³ this Jesus, delivered up according to the definite plan and foreknowledge of God, you crucified and killed by the hands of lawless men.

²⁴ But God raised him up, having loosed the pangs of death, because it was not possible for him to be held by it. ²⁵ For David says concerning him,
'I saw the Lord always before me,
for he is at my right hand that I may not be shaken;
²⁶ therefore my heart was glad, and my tongue rejoiced;

moreover my flesh will dwell in hope.

[27] For you will not abandon my soul to Hades,
nor let your Holy One see corruption.

[28] You have made known to me the ways of life;
you will make me full of gladness with your presence.'

[29] "Brethren, I may say to you confidently of the patriarch David that he both died and was buried, and his tomb is with us to this day. [30] Being therefore a prophet, and knowing that God had sworn with an oath to him that he would set one of his descendants upon his throne, [31] he foresaw and spoke of the resurrection of the Christ, that he was not abandoned to Hades, nor did his flesh see corruption.

[32] This Jesus God raised up, and of that we all are witnesses.

[33] Being therefore exalted at the right hand of God, and having received from the Father the promise of the Holy Spirit, he has poured out this which you see and hear.

[34] For David did not ascend into the heavens; but he himself says, 'The Lord said to my Lord, Sit at my right hand,

[35] till I make your enemies a stool for your feet.'

[36] Let all the house of Israel therefore know assuredly that God has made him both Lord and Christ, this Jesus whom you crucified."

> Holy Spirit, Lord of Light,
> From the clear celestial height.
> Thy pure beaming radiance give.

Come, thou Father of the poor,
Come, with treasures which endure;
Come, thou Light of all that live!

Thou, of all consolers best,
Thou, the soul's delightful guest,
Dost refreshing peace bestow.

Thou in toil art comfort sweet;
Pleasant coolness in the heat;
Solace in the midst of woe.

Light immortal, Light divine,
Visit thou these hearts of thine,
And our inmost being fill.

If thou take thy grace away,
Nothing pure in man will stay;
All his good is turned to ill.

Heal our wounds, our strength renew;
On our dryness pour thy dew,
Wash the stains of guilt away. →

The first baptisms (Acts 2:37–41)

[37] Now when they heard this they were cut to the heart, and said to Peter and the rest of the apostles, "Brethren, what shall we do?"

[38] And Peter said to them, "Repent, and be baptized every one of you in the name of Jesus Christ for the forgiveness of your sins; and you shall receive the gift of the Holy Spirit. [39] For the promise is to you and to your children and to all that are far off, every one whom the Lord our God calls to him."

[40] And he testified with many other words and exhorted them, saying, "Save yourselves from this crooked generation." [41] So those who received his word were baptized, and there were added that day about three thousand souls.

The life of the early Christian community (Acts 2:42–47)

[42] And they held steadfastly to the apostles' teaching and fellowship, to the breaking of the bread and to the prayers.

[43] And fear came upon every soul; and many wonders and signs were done through the apostles.

[44] And all who believed were together and had all things in common; [45] and they sold their possessions and goods and distributed them to all, as any had need. [46] And day by day, attending the

→Bend the stubborn heart and will;
Melt the frozen, warm the chill;
Guide the steps that go astray.

Thou, on us who evermore
Thee confess and thee adore,
With thy sevenfold gifts descend.

Give us comfort when we die;
Give us life with thee on high;
Give us joys that never end. AMEN.

From the Pentecost Sequence by the English Cardinal **STEPHEN LANGTON** (ca. 1150–1228)

▶ The Church to this day is made up of these four elements: The teaching of the apostles makes the Gospel of Jesus present; the community combines love of God and love of neighbor; "breaking bread" is a short expression for the Eucharistic celebration; prayer is the language of faith, with a special reference to the Psalms.

They say that a policeman is your friend and helper. That is right, in some respects, but our true friend and helper in any situation in life is the Holy Spirit. I would not want to live without him. He is the perfect helper, full of strength and life. I love him very much.

WALTER

temple together and breaking bread in their homes, they partook of food with glad and generous hearts, ⁴⁷ praising God and having favor with all the people. And the Lord added to their number day by day those who were being saved.

Luke then describes how Peter and the other apostles proclaim the Gospel in Jerusalem (Acts 4:1—5:42). They meet with much success, but also strong resistance. Stephen becomes the first martyr (Acts 6:8—8:1a). He is falsely accused, but forgives his murderers (Acts 7:60). A persecution of the early Christian community follows, in which Saul/ Paul, too, is actively involved (Acts 8:1–3). Luke next relates the missionary activities of the deacon Philip. He brings the Samaritans (Acts 8:4–25) and the Ethiopian eunuch (Acts 8:26–40) to the faith.

THE CONVERSION OF SAUL (ACTS 9:1–31)

▶ Saul is his Jewish name; Paul, his Roman name.

9 ¹ But Saul, still breathing threats and murder against the disciples of the Lord, went to the high priest ² and asked him for letters to the synagogues at Damascus, so that if he found any belonging to the Way, men or women, he might bring them bound to Jerusalem.

Day and night, [the nuns] prayed before the Blessed Sacrament for the conversion of the Nazis. ... Soon we had a dozen convents in North Africa praying and making sacrifices for our [prison] camp. In the face of such storming of heaven, many men lost all resistance, expelled the unbelief and paganism of the Nazi credo from their hearts, and accepted belief in God; after some months of prodding they came to confession and received their second First Holy Communion.

GEREON KARL GOLDMANN O.F.M. (1916–2003), German Franciscan priest, former German soldier and Nazi resistance fighter

▶ Tarsus is Paul's hometown.

The vision of the risen Lord (Acts 9:3–9)

³ Now as he journeyed he approached Damascus, and suddenly a light from heaven flashed about him. ⁴ And he fell to the ground and heard a voice saying to him, "Saul, Saul, why do you persecute me?" ⁵ And he said, "Who are you, Lord?" And he said, "I am Jesus, whom you are persecuting; ⁶ but rise and enter the city, and you will be told what you are to do."

⁷ The men who were traveling with him stood speechless, hearing the voice but seeing no one.

⁸ Saul arose from the ground; and when his eyes were opened, he could see nothing; so they led him by the hand and brought him into Damascus. ⁹ And for three days he was without sight, and neither ate nor drank.

The Lord prepares Ananias (Acts 9:10–16)

¹⁰ Now there was a disciple at Damascus named Anani'as. The Lord said to him in a vision, "Ananias."

And he said, "Here I am, Lord."

¹¹ And the Lord said to him, "Rise and go to the street called Straight, and inquire in the house of Judas for a man of Tarsus named Saul; for behold, he is praying, ¹² and he has seen a man named Anani'as come in and lay his hands on him so that he might regain his sight."

¹³ But Anani'as answered, "Lord, I have heard from many about this man, how much evil he has done to your saints at Jerusalem; ¹⁴ and here he has authority from the chief priests to bind all who call upon your name." ¹⁵ But the Lord said to him, "Go, for he is a chosen instrument of mine to carry my name before the Gentiles and kings and the sons of Israel; ¹⁶ for I will show him how much he must suffer for the sake of my name."

Paul's baptism (Acts 9:17–20)

¹⁷ So Anani'as departed and entered the house. And laying his hands on him he said, "Brother Saul, the Lord Jesus who appeared to you on the road by which you came, has sent me that you may regain your sight and be filled with the Holy Spirit." ¹⁸ And immediately something like scales fell from his eyes and he regained his sight. Then he rose and was baptized, ¹⁹ and took food and was strengthened.

For several days he was with the disciples at Damascus. ²⁰ And in the synagogues immediately he proclaimed Jesus, saying, "He is the Son of God."

> Lord, make me an instrument of Thy peace;
> Where there is hatred, let me sow love;
> Where there is injury, pardon;
> Where there is error, the truth;
> Where there is doubt, the faith;
> Where there is despair, hope;
> Where there is darkness, light;
> And where there is sadness, joy.
> O Divine Master,
> Grant that I may not so much seek
> To be consoled, as to console;
> To be understood, as to understand;
> To be loved as to love.
> For it is in giving that we receive;
> It is in pardoning that we are pardoned;
> And it is in dying that we are born to eternal life. Amen.
>
> The Peace Prayer

Last-minute rescue (Acts 9:21–25)

²¹ And all who heard him were amazed, and said, "Is not this the man who made havoc in Jerusalem of those who called on this name? And he has come here for this purpose, to bring them bound before the chief priests?" ²² But Saul increased all the more in strength, and confounded the Jews who lived in Damascus by proving that Jesus was the Christ.

²³ When many days had passed, the Jews plotted to kill him, ²⁴ but their plot became known to Saul. They were watching the gates day and night, to kill him; ²⁵ but his disciples took him by night and let him down over the wall, lowering him in a basket..

 Is there any evidence that I am a believer?

Is my life any different from the mainstream?

Have I ever spoken with my friends about God?

What would I have to change in my life if God were to play the principal role in it?

The persecutor is persecuted (Acts 9:26–31)

²⁶ And when he had come to Jerusalem he attempted to join the disciples; and they were all afraid of him, for they did not believe that he was a disciple. ²⁷ But Barnabas took him, and brought him to the apostles, and declared to them how on the road he had seen the Lord, who spoke to him, and how at Damascus he had preached boldly in the name of Jesus.

²⁸ So he went in and out among them at Jerusalem, ²⁹ preaching boldly in the name of the Lord. And he spoke and disputed against the Hellenists; but they were seeking to kill him. ³⁰ And when the

> Jesus does not want any admirers; he can do without them, but not without followers.
>
> **SØREN KIERKEGAARD**

Ƴ → 122–123
Why does God want there to be a Church?
What is the task of the Church?

brethren knew it, they brought him down to Caesare'a, and sent him off to Tarsus.
[31] So the Church throughout all Judea and Galilee and Samar'ia had peace and was built up; and walking in the fear of the Lord and in the comfort of the Holy Spirit it was multiplied.

Luke tells how Peter was led by the Holy Spirit to baptize the first Gentile, the centurion Cornelius (Acts 10–11). After that he reports on the increasingly critical situation in Jerusalem (Acts 12).

THE FIRST MISSIONARY JOURNEY (ACTS 13:1–14:28)

Barnabas and Saul are sent forth (Acts 13:1–3)

▶ Syrian Antioch is one of the most important communities in the history of early Christianity.

13 [1] Now in the Church at Antioch there were prophets and teachers, Barnabas, Symeon who was called Ni'ger, Lucius of Cyre'ne, Man'a-en a member of the court of Herod the tetrarch, and Saul.
[2] While they were worshiping the Lord and fasting, the Holy Spirit said, "Set apart for me Barnabas and Saul for the work to which I have called them." [3] Then after fasting and praying they laid their hands on them and sent them off.

The first stops on the journey (Acts 13:4–13)

▶ Seleucia is the port city of Antioch. Cyprus is a large Greek island. Salamis and Pathos are cities on Cyprus.

99 He who does not recognize that he is full of vanity, ambition, weakness, misery, and injustice is very blind. And more so if, after recognizing this, he does not want to be freed from these vices.

BLAISE PASCAL

▶ The proconsul is the chief administrator, the emperor's representative in the province.

▶ Perga belongs to the province of Pamphylia and is located on the mainland of Asia Minor in modern-day Turkey.

[4] So, being sent out by the Holy Spirit, they went down to Seleu'cia; and from there they sailed to Cyprus.
[5] When they arrived at Sal'amis, they proclaimed the word of God in the synagogues of the Jews. And they had John to assist them. [6] When they had gone through the whole island as far as Pa'phos, they came upon a certain magician, a Jewish false prophet, named Bar-Jesus. [7] He was with the proconsul, Sergius Paulus, a man of intelligence, who summoned Barnabas and Saul and sought to hear the word of God. [8] But El'ymas the magician (for that is the meaning of his name) withstood them, seeking to turn away the proconsul from the faith. [9] But Saul, who is also called Paul, filled with the Holy Spirit, looked intently at him [10] and said, "You son of the devil, you enemy of all righteousness, full of all deceit and villainy, will you not stop making crooked the straight paths of the Lord? [11] And now, behold, the hand of the Lord is upon you, and you shall be blind and unable to see the sun for a time." Immediately mist and darkness fell upon him and he went about seeking people to lead him by the hand. [12] Then the proconsul believed, when he saw what had occurred, for he was astonished at the teaching of the Lord.
[13] Now Paul and his company set sail from Pa'phos, and came to Perga in Pamphyl'ia. And John left them and returned to Jerusalem.

Sermon in Antioch of Pisidia (Acts 13:14–42)

[14] They passed on from Perga and came to Antioch of Pisid'ia. And on the sabbath day they went into the synagogue and sat down. [15] After the reading of the law and the prophets, the rulers of the synagogue sent to them, saying, "Brethren, if you have any word of exhortation for the people, say it."

[16] So Paul stood up, and motioning with his hand said: "Men of Israel, and you that fear God, listen.

[17] The God of this people Israel chose our fathers and made the people great during their stay in the land of Egypt, and with uplifted arm he led them out of it. [18] And for about forty years he bore with them in the wilderness. [19] And when he had destroyed seven nations in the land of Canaan, he gave them their land as an inheritance, for about four hundred and fifty years. [20] And after that he gave them judges until Samuel the prophet. [21] Then they asked for a king; and God gave them Saul the son of Kish, a man of the tribe of Benjamin, for forty years. [22] And when he had removed him, he raised up David to be their king; of whom he testified and said, 'I have found in David, the son of Jesse, a man after my heart, who will do all my will.' [23] Of this man's posterity God has brought to Israel a Savior, Jesus, as he promised.

▶ Antioch in Pisidia (v. 14) is not Syrian Antioch but, rather, the capital of another Roman province bordering Pamphylia to the north.

▶ Paul traces the salvation history of Israel, incorporates the story of Jesus in it, and concludes with a demand for conversion. It is unclear, though, what effect his sermon will have.

B Bear fruits that befit repentance, and do not begin to say to yourselves, "We have Abraham as our father"; for I tell you, God is able from these stones to raise up children to Abraham.

Lk 3:8

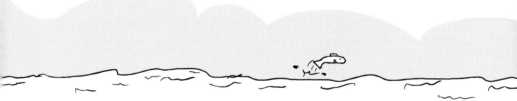

[24] Before his coming John had preached a baptism of repentance to all the people of Israel. [25] And as John was finishing his course, he said, 'What do you suppose that I am? I am not he. No, but after me one is coming, the sandals of whose feet I am not worthy to untie.'

[26] "Brethren, sons of the family of Abraham, and those among you that fear God, to us has been sent the message of this salvation. [27] For those who live in Jerusalem and their rulers, because they did not recognize him nor understand the utterances of the prophets which are read every sabbath, fulfilled these by condemning him. [28] Though they could charge him with nothing deserving death, yet they asked Pilate to have him killed. [29] And when they had fulfilled all that was written of him, they took him down from the tree, and laid him in a tomb.

[30] But God raised him from the dead; [31] and for many days he appeared to those who came up with him from Galilee to Jerusalem, who are now his witnesses to the people. [32] And we bring you the good news that what God promised to the fathers, [33] this he has fulfilled to us their children by raising Jesus; as also it is written in the second psalm,

'You are my Son,
today I have begotten you.'

[34] And as for the fact that he raised him from the dead, no more to return to corruption, he spoke in this way,

B Even now the axe is laid to the root of the trees; every tree therefore that does not bear good fruit is cut down and thrown into the fire.

Lk 3:9

▶ Those who fear God are Gentiles who believe in the one God, the God of Israel, but have not fully converted to Judaism.

Y → 17
What significance does the Old Testament have for Christians?

AQUILEIA

DALMATIA

ITALY

SARDINIA

ROME

PUTEOLI

CORSICA

MACEDONIA

PHI
AMPHIPOLIS
APPOLONIA
THESSALONICA
BEROEA

MESSINA   RHEGIUM

SICILY

SYRACUSE

CORINTH

CARTHAGE

MALTA

MEDITERRAN

CYRENE

AFRICA

THE JOURNEYS OF PAUL

—————— First Journey

– – – – – Second Journey

· · · · · · · Third Journey

||||||||||||| As a prisoner to Rome

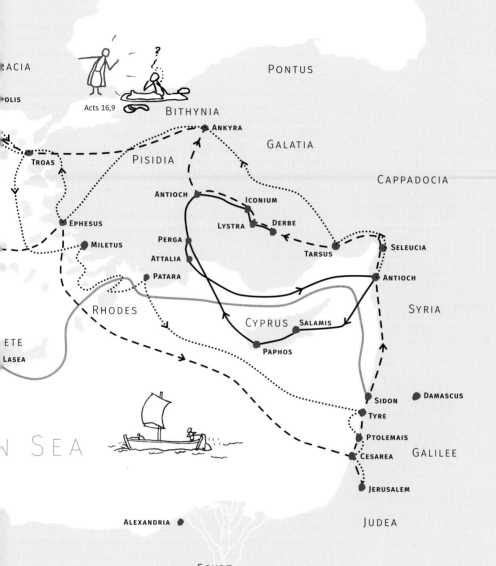

RACIA

OLIS

PONTUS

Acts 16,9

BITHYNIA

GALATIA

TROAS

PISIDIA

CAPPADOCIA

Ankyra

ANTIOCH

ICONIUM

EPHESUS

LYSTRA

DERBE

SELEUCIA

MILETUS

PERGA

TARSUS

ATTALIA

ANTIOCH

PATARA

RHODES

SYRIA

CYPRUS

SALAMIS

ETE

PAPHOS

LASEA

DAMASCUS

SIDON

TYRE

N SEA

PTOLEMAIS

GALILEE

CESAREA

JERUSALEM

ALEXANDRIA

JUDEA

EGYPT

> The Easter Resurrection was the final proof that God's love in man and for man had won the final victory over sin and death. For the worst thing that sin could do is not to bomb cities and kill a fellow-man; it is to crucify God. Having done this and lost, it would never do anything as bad again. Having been conquered at its strongest point, evil must now remain eternally defeated.
>
> **FULTON J. SHEEN** (1895–1979)
> Archbishop

▶ Paul reads the Bible of Israel, the Old Testament, with the eyes of Christian faith. For him, the key to understanding it is the fact that Jesus is the promised Messiah. Anyone who believes in him receives the forgiveness of sins. This means that he is made just.

▶ "Proselytes" in the Greek text are Gentiles who have converted to Judaism.

'I will give you the holy and sure blessings of David.'

[35] Therefore he says also in another psalm,

'You will not let your Holy One see corruption.'

[36] For David, after he had served the counsel of God in his own generation, fell asleep, and was laid with his fathers, and saw corruption; [37] but he whom God raised up saw no corruption. [38] Let it be known to you therefore, brethren, that through this man forgiveness of sins is proclaimed to you, [39] and by him every one that believes is freed from everything from which you could not be freed by the law of Moses. [40] Beware, therefore, lest there come upon you what is said in the prophets:

[41] 'Behold, you scoffers, and wonder, and perish;

for I do a deed in your days,

a deed you will never believe, if one declares it to you.'"

[42] As they went out, the people begged that these things might be told them the next sabbath.

The formation of a small Christian community (Acts 13:43–52)

[43] And when the meeting of the synagogue broke up, many Jews and devout converts to Judaism followed Paul and Barnabas, who spoke to them and urged them to continue in the grace of God.

Sometimes I run away and shut the door of my heart against goodness and truth. I can sense the truth within me; the Lord is calling me to share in his joy. He says that we should live and that we should have genuine joy. It is so simple: he is calling me to be full of joy and to make others happy.

IVAN

▶ This is a gesture of leave-taking that indicates that the person wants to take nothing along with him from those who drive him away (↗ Lk 9:5; 10:11).

[44] The next sabbath almost the whole city gathered together to hear the word of God. [45] But when the Jews saw the multitudes, they were filled with jealousy, and contradicted what was spoken by Paul, and reviled him. [46] And Paul and Barnabas spoke out boldly, saying, "It was necessary that the word of God should be spoken first to you. Since you thrust it from you, and judge yourselves unworthy of eternal life, behold, we turn to the Gentiles. [47] For so the Lord has commanded us, saying,

'I have set you to be a light for the Gentiles,

that you may bring salvation to the uttermost parts of the earth.'"

[48] And when the Gentiles heard this, they were glad and glorified the word of God; and as many as were ordained to eternal life believed. [49] And the word of the Lord spread throughout all the region. [50] But the Jews incited the devout women of high standing and the leading men of the city, and stirred up persecution against Paul and Barnabas, and drove them out of their district. [51] But they shook off the dust from their feet against them, and went to Ico'nium. [52] And the disciples were filled with joy and with the Holy Spirit.

Quarrel of Paul and Barnabas (Acts 14:1–7)

14 [1] Now at Ico'nium they entered together into the Jewish synagogue, and so spoke that a great company believed, both of Jews and of Greeks. [2] But the unbelieving Jews stirred up the

Gentiles and poisoned their minds against the brethren. ³ So they remained for a long time, speaking boldly for the Lord, who bore witness to the word of his grace, granting signs and wonders to be done by their hands. ⁴ But the people of the city were divided; some sided with the Jews, and some with the apostles. ⁵ When an attempt was made by both Gentiles and Jews, with their rulers, to molest them and to stone them, ⁶ they learned of it and fled to Lystra and Der′be, cities of Lycao′nia, and to the surrounding country; ⁷ and there they preached the gospel.

A misunderstanding is cleared up (Acts 14:8–18)
⁸ Now at Lystra there was a man sitting, who could not use his feet; he was a cripple from birth, who had never walked. ⁹ He listened to Paul speaking; and Paul, looking intently at him and seeing that he had faith to be made well, ¹⁰ said in a loud voice, "Stand upright on your feet." And he sprang up and walked. ¹¹ And when the crowds saw what Paul had done, they lifted up their voices, saying in Lycao′nian, "The gods have come down to us in the likeness of men!" ¹² Barnabas they called Zeus, and Paul, because he was the chief

▶ The next stops, Iconium, Lystra, and Derbe, lead step by step out of Greek-speaking territory.

A funny story: a huge cult on account of one little miracle! Paul sets their standards straight.

Paul enters into "dialogue" with the cultural and religious values of different peoples. To the Lyca-onians, who practiced a cosmic religion, →

speaker, they called Hermes. ¹³ And the priest of Zeus, whose temple was in front of the city, brought oxen and garlands to the gates and wanted to offer sacrifice with the people. ¹⁴ But when the apostles Barnabas and Paul heard of it, they tore their garments and rushed out among the multitude, crying, ¹⁵ "Men, why are you doing this? We also are men, of like nature with you, and bring you good news, that you should turn from these vain things to a living God who made the heaven and the earth and the sea and all that is in them. ¹⁶ In past generations he allowed all the nations to walk in their own ways; ¹⁷ yet he did not leave himself without witness, for he did good and gave you from heaven rains and fruitful seasons, satisfying your hearts with food and gladness." ¹⁸ With these words they scarcely restrained the people from offering sacrifice to them.

Rescued from mortal danger (Acts 14:19–20)
¹⁹ But Jews came there from Antioch and Ico′nium; and having per-suaded the people, they stoned Paul and dragged him out of the city, supposing that he was dead. ²⁰ But when the disciples gathered about him, he rose up and entered the city; and on the next day he went on with Barnabas to Derbe.

→ he speaks of religious expe-riences related to the cosmos. With the Greeks he discusses philosophy and quotes their own poets (cf. Acts 17:18, 26–28). The God whom Paul wishes to reveal is already present in their lives; indeed, this God has created them and mysteriously guides nations and history.
POPE JOHN PAUL II, Encyclical *Redemptoris Missio*, 25

We labor, working with our own hands. When reviled, we bless; when persecuted, we endure; when slandered, we try to conciliate; we have become, and are now, as the refuse of the world, the dregs of all things.
1 Cor 4:12–13

> Persecutions break out. The Church presents to the world a hitherto unheard-of spectacle. She does not answer violence with violence.

CHARLES JOURNET (1891–1975), Swiss Catholic theologian and cardinal

▶ The apostles organize the newly founded communities. They need ministries. So "elders" (presbyters, and hence "priests") are appointed.

As the rain and the snow come down from heaven, and do not return there but water the earth, making it bring forth and sprout, ... so shall my word be that goes forth from my mouth; it shall not return to me empty, but it shall accomplish that which I intend.

Is 55:10–11

The return to Antioch (Acts 14:21–28)

²¹ When they had preached the gospel to that city and had made many disciples, they returned to Lystra and to Ico'nium and to Antioch, ²² strengthening the souls of the disciples, exhorting them to continue in the faith, and saying that through many tribulations we must enter the kingdom of God. ²³ And when they had appointed elders for them in every church, with prayer and fasting, they committed them to the Lord in whom they believed.

²⁴ Then they passed through Pisid'ia, and came to Pamphyl'ia. ²⁵ And when they had spoken the word in Perga, they went down to Attali'a; ²⁶ and from there they sailed to Antioch, where they had been commended to the grace of God for the work which they had fulfilled.

²⁷ And when they arrived, they gathered the Church together and declared all that God had done with them, and how he had opened a door of faith to the Gentiles. ²⁸ And they remained no little time with the disciples.

THE COUNCIL OF APOSTLES IN JERUSALEM (ACTS 15:1–35)

▶ The Council of the Apostles is one of the most important events in early Christianity. Paul, too, records it (Gal 2:1–11). Essentially it was about the question of whether all Gentiles had to become Jews first in order to be able to become Christians. Consequently, though, it was also about whether baptism is sufficient to start out on the path to everlasting life or whether men had to be circumcised, also. Finally Peter and Paul prevailed, having stood up for the power of the Spirit and the freedom of faith.

Come to me, all who labor and are heavy laden, and I will give you rest. ... For my yoke is easy, and my burden is light.

Mt 11:28,30

A dispute (Acts 15: 1–5)

15 ¹ But some men came down from Judea and were teaching the brethren, "Unless you are circumcised according to the custom of Moses, you cannot be saved." ² And when Paul and Barnabas had no small dissension and debate with them, Paul and Barnabas and some of the others were appointed to go up to Jerusalem to the apostles and the elders about this question. ³ So, being sent on their way by the Church, they passed through both Phoeni'cia and Samar'ia, reporting the conversion of the Gentiles, and they gave great joy to all the brethren.

⁴ When they came to Jerusalem, they were welcomed by the Church and the apostles and the elders, and they declared all that God had done with them.

⁵ But some believers who belonged to the party of the Pharisees rose up, and said, "It is necessary to circumcise them, and to charge them to keep the law of Moses."

Peter relates his experience (Acts 15:6–11)

⁶ The apostles and the elders were gathered together to consider this matter. ⁷ And after there had been much debate, Peter rose and said to them, "Brethren, you know that in the early days God made

choice among you, that by my mouth the Gentiles should hear the word of the gospel and believe. [8] And God who knows the heart bore witness to them, giving them the Holy Spirit just as he did to us; [9] and he made no distinction between us and them, but cleansed their hearts by faith. [10] Now therefore why do you make trial of God by putting a yoke upon the neck of the disciples which neither our fathers nor we have been able to bear? [11] But we believe that we shall be saved through the grace of the Lord Jesus, just as they will.".

Barnabas and Paul tell their story (Acts 15:12)

[12] And all the assembly kept silence; and they listened to Barnabas and Paul as they related what signs and wonders God had done through them among the Gentiles.

James interprets the experience in light of the Bible (Acts 15:13–18)

[13] After they finished speaking, James replied, "Brethren, listen to me. [14] Symeon has related how God first visited the Gentiles, to take out of them a people for his name. [15] And with this the words of the prophets agree, as it is written,

[16] 'After this I will return,
and I will rebuild the dwelling of David, which has fallen;
I will rebuild its ruins,
and I will set it up,
[17] that the rest of men may seek the Lord,
and all the Gentiles who are called by my name,
[18] says the Lord, who has made these things known from of old.'

James suggests a solution (Acts 15:19–21)

[19] Therefore my judgment is that we should not trouble those of the Gentiles who turn to God, [20] but should write to them to abstain from the pollutions of idols and from unchastity and from what is strangled and from blood.

[21] For from early generations Moses has had in every city those who preach him, for he is read every sabbath in the synagogues."

A decision Is made (Acts 15:22–29)

[22] Then it seemed good to the apostles and the elders, with the whole Church, to choose men from among them and send them to Antioch with Paul and Barnabas. They sent Judas called Barsab'bas,

> "This is Peter's ongoing mission: to ensure that the Church is never identified with a single nation, with a single culture or with a single State but is always the Church of all; to ensure that she reunites humanity over and above every boundary and, in the midst of the divisions of this world, makes God's peace present, the reconciling power of his love.
>
> **POPE BENEDICT XVI,** June 29, 2008

▶ In the Church there was a dispute over whether the Gentiles had to become Jews first in order to be able then to be Christians. Barnabas and Paul are for the "shortest path". Peter is on their side. That is why they can both tell the story of their missionary journey (Acts 13–14). This convinces all that pagans are welcome in the Church. Only faith matters.

 There is neither Jew nor Greek, there is neither slave nor free, there is neither male nor female; for you are all one in Christ Jesus.

Gal 3:28

▶ This is a question of basic purity laws that should clarify the profession of faith in the one God in a pagan environment. Above all, they are supposed to regulate the coexistence of Jewish Christians and Gentile Christians in one community.

▶ The early Christian community in Jerusalem establishes peace in the young Church through a groundbreaking decision. No one needs to become a Jew first in order to be able to become a Christian. But the Gentile Christians should be considerate of the Jews. That is a model for resolving conflict even today.

99 The apostles saw in their decision the decision of the Holy Spirit. You can be confident that the Spirit is speaking when the Church's speaking. ... So what do you think of that? Do you trust the Church? Do you believe it to be true yourselves?

CHARLES CHAPUT O.F.M., (1944), Archbishop of Philadelphia

and Silas, leading men among the brethren, ²³ with the following letter: "The brethren, both the apostles and the elders, to the brethren who are of the Gentiles in Antioch and Syria and Cili'cia, greeting.

²⁴ Since we have heard that some persons from us have troubled you with words, unsettling your minds, although we gave them no instructions, ²⁵ it has seemed good to us in assembly to choose men and send them to you with our beloved Barnabas and Paul, ²⁶ men who have risked their lives for the sake of our Lord Jesus Christ. ²⁷ We have therefore sent Judas and Silas, who themselves will tell you the same things by word of mouth. ²⁸ For it has seemed good to the Holy Spirit and to us to lay upon you no greater burden than these necessary things: ²⁹ that you abstain from what has been sacrificed to idols and from blood and from what is strangled and from unchastity. If you keep yourselves from these, you will do well. Farewell."

The Council's decision is relayed to the communities (Acts 15:30–35)

³⁰ So when they were sent off, they went down to Antioch; and having gathered the congregation together, they delivered the letter. ³¹ And when they read it, they rejoiced at the exhortation. ³² And Ju-

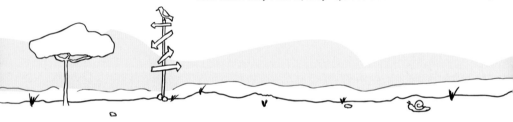

das and Silas, who were themselves prophets, exhorted the brethren with many words and strengthened them. ³³ And after they had spent some time, they were sent off in peace by the brethren to those who had sent them.

³⁵ But Paul and Barnabas remained in Antioch, teaching and preaching the word of the Lord, with many others also.

THE SECOND MISSIONARY JOURNEY OF PAUL (ACTS 15:36–18:22)

Paul and Barnabas go their separate ways (Acts 15:36–41)

³⁶ And after some days Paul said to Barnabas, "Come, let us return and visit the brethren in every city where we proclaimed the word of the Lord, and see how they are."

³⁷ And Barnabas wanted to take with them John called Mark. ³⁸ But Paul thought best not to take with them one who had withdrawn from them in Pamphyl'ia, and had not gone with them to the work.

³⁹ And there arose a sharp contention, so that they separated from each other; Barnabas took Mark with him and sailed away to Cyprus, ⁴⁰ but Paul chose Silas and departed, being commended by the brethren to the grace of the Lord. ⁴¹ And he went through Syria and Cili'cia, strengthening the churches.

Fire in his hand: Barnabas

▶ There were quarrels in the early Church, too. But they were also able to unite. The rule applies here: March separately, strike in unison. The Gospel is proclaimed in many ways. Paul pushes on especially far with his mission.

Paul gains a coworker, Timothy (Acts 16:1–5)

16 [1] And he came also to Derbe and to Lystra. A disciple was there, named Timothy, the son of a Jewish woman who was a believer; but his father was a Greek. [2] He was well spoken of by the brethren at Lystra and Ico'nium. [3] Paul wanted Timothy to accompany him; and he took him and circumcised him because of the Jews that were in those places, for they all knew that his father was a Greek.

[4] As they went on their way through the cities, they delivered to them for observance the decisions which had been reached by the apostles and elders who were at Jerusalem. [5] So the churches were strengthened in the faith, and they increased in numbers daily.

Paul's vision of the man of Macedonia (Acts 16:6–10)

[6] And they went through the region of Phry'gia and Galatia, having been forbidden by the Holy Spirit to speak the word in Asia. [7] And when they had come opposite My'sia, they attempted to go into Bithyn'ia, but the Spirit of Jesus did not allow them; [8] so, passing by My'sia, they went down to Troas.

[9] And a vision appeared to Paul in the night: a man of Macedonia was standing pleading with him and saying, "Come over to Macedonia and help us."

▶ Timothy becomes Paul's star pupil. Because he has a Jewish mother, Paul has him circumcised. In that way he can proclaim the Gospel without denying his Jewish roots.

❞ Today's youth will become tomorrow's leaders. That's what happened with Timothy, a young companion of St. Paul who later became a bishop to whom the Apostle wrote two of his epistles in the New Testament.
STEVE RAY

❞ The deeper truth is that reform, if it is real reform, is an exercise of love.
RICHARD JOHN NEUHAUS
(1936–2009), Catholic priest and writer

[10] And when he had seen the vision, immediately we sought to go on into Macedonia, concluding that God had called us to preach the gospel to them.

▶ Macedonia is a part of Greece. Its capital is Thessalonica, today Thessaloniki.

Paul founds a community in Philippi (Acts 16:11–15)

[11] Setting sail therefore from Troas, we made a direct voyage to Sam'othrace, and the following day to Ne-ap'olis,

[12] and from there to Philip'pi, which is the leading city of the district of Macedonia, and a Roman colony. We remained in this city some days;

[13] and on the sabbath day we went outside the gate to the riverside, where we supposed there was a place of prayer;and we sat down and spoke to the women who had come together. [14] One who heard us was a woman named Lydia, from the city of Thyati'ra, a seller of purple goods, who was a worshiper of God. The Lord opened her heart to listen to what was said by Paul. [15] And when she was baptized, with her household, she begged us, saying, "If you have judged me to be faithful to the Lord, come to my house and stay." And she prevailed upon us.

▶ Philippi was a foundation of the Romans. The Philippians therefore regard themselves as Roman citizens.

▶ Lydia is the first Christian woman in Europe. She is from Thyatira, a city in modern-day Turkey (↗ Rev 2:18–29). She was a God-fearer, i.e., a Gentile who sympathized with Judaism. The first Christian community in Europe gathered at her house.

Paul delivers a slave girl from an evil spirit (Acts 16:16–21)

[16] As we were going to the place of prayer, we were met by a slave girl who had a spirit of divination and brought her owners much

Being a Christian was never so dangerous as today. Never before have so many Christians been discriminated against, threatened, and persecuted. Worldwide as many as 100 million Christians are affected, and the trend is increasing. Christians are not the only ones to be disadvantaged on account of their faith; worldwide, however, they suffer the most from religious persecution. Although the right to religious freedom has been recognized internationally for decades as a fundamental human right, people are prevented from practicing their faith, and in a whole series of countries there are serious violations of freedom of religion.

gain by soothsaying. ¹⁷ She followed Paul and us, crying, "These men are servants of the Most High God, who proclaim to you the way of salvation." ¹⁸ And this she did for many days. But Paul was annoyed, and turned and said to the spirit, "I charge you in the name of Jesus Christ to come out of her." And it came out that very hour.

¹⁹ But when her owners saw that their hope of gain was gone, they seized Paul and Silas and dragged them into the market place before the rulers; ²⁰ and when they had brought them to the magistrates they said, "These men are Jews and they are disturbing our city. ²¹ They advocate customs which it is not lawful for us Romans to accept or practice."

Paul is thrown into prison for no reason (Acts 16:22–24)

²² The crowd joined in attacking them; and the magistrates tore the garments off them and gave orders to beat them with rods. ²³ And when they had inflicted many blows upon them, they threw them into prison, charging the jailer to keep them safely. ²⁴ Having received this charge, he put them into the inner prison and fastened their feet in the stocks.

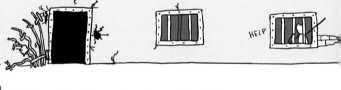

▶ The song of Paul and Silas in jail has a parallel in the Old Testament: the story of the three Jewish men, Hananiah, Azariah, and Mishael, who in Dan 3 refused to worship the golden image of Nebuchadnezzar and therefore were thrown into the fiery furnace but emerged from it unharmed. The song of praise of the three men is recited in the Church's Liturgy of the Hours.

Paul is set free from prison (Acts 16:25–26)

²⁵ But about midnight Paul and Silas were praying and singing hymns to God, and the prisoners were listening to them,

²⁶ and suddenly there was a great earthquake, so that the foundations of the prison were shaken; and immediately all the doors were opened and every one's chains were unfastened.

The prison guard comes to the faith (Acts 16:27–34)

²⁷ When the jailer woke and saw that the prison doors were open, he drew his sword and was about to kill himself, supposing that the prisoners had escaped.

²⁸ But Paul cried with a loud voice, "Do not harm yourself, for we are all here."

²⁹ And he called for lights and rushed in, and trembling with fear he fell down before Paul and Silas, ³⁰ and brought them out and said, "Men, what must I do to be saved?"

³¹ And they said, "Believe in the Lord Jesus, and you will be saved, you and your household." ³² And they spoke the word of the Lord to him and to all that were in his house.

³³ And he took them the same hour of the night, and washed their wounds, and he was baptized at once, with all his family. ³⁴ Then he brought them up into his house, and set food before them; and he rejoiced with all his household that he had believed in God.

Paul insists on his rights (Acts 16:35–40)

[35] But when it was day, the magistrates sent the police, saying, "Let those men go."

[36] And the jailer reported the words to Paul, saying, "The magistrates have sent to let you go; now therefore come out and go in peace."

[37] But Paul said to them, "They have beaten us publicly, uncondemned, men who are Roman citizens, and have thrown us into prison; and do they now cast us out secretly? No! let them come themselves and take us out."

[38] The police reported these words to the magistrates, and they were afraid when they heard that they were Roman citizens;

[39] so they came and apologized to them. And they took them out and asked them to leave the city.

[40] So they went out of the prison, and visited Lydia; and when they had seen the brethren, they exhorted them and departed.

Early Christian baptistry in Emmaus Nicopolis

Paul founds the Church of Thessalonica (Acts 17:1–10a)

17 [1] Now when they had passed through Amphip′olis and Apol-lo′nia, they came to Thessaloni′ca, where there was a syn-

agogue of the Jews. [2] And Paul went in, as was his custom, and for three weeks he argued with them from the Scriptures, [3] explaining and proving that it was necessary for the Christ to suffer and to rise from the dead, and saying, "This Jesus, whom I proclaim to you, is the Christ."

[4] And some of them were persuaded, and joined Paul and Silas; as did a great many of the devout Greeks and not a few of the leading women.

[5] But the Jews were jealous, and taking some wicked fellows of the rabble, they gathered a crowd, set the city in an uproar, and attacked the house of Jason, seeking to bring them out to the people. [6] And when they could not find them, they dragged Jason and some of the brethren before the city authorities, crying, "These men who have turned the world upside down have come here also, [7] and Jason has received them; and they are all acting against the decrees of Caesar, saying that there is another king, Jesus."

[8] And the people and the city authorities were disturbed when they heard this. [9] And when they had taken security from Jason and the rest, they let them go.

[10a] The brethren immediately sent Paul and Silas away by night to Beroe′a.

Y → 194–202
The Sacrament of Baptism

▶ Christians were soon considered public enemy Number One because they openly professed their faith. In doing so, they demystified the Roman State. The emperor was only a man. He had to render justice and support the poor. In truth, though, Christians are not insurrectionists. They are like the yeast that leavens the whole dough.

Several years ago I became acquainted with a Jesuit priest who so enthusiastically and vividly told me about God that →

→ I was speechless. He said that God is alive, he is passionate and congenial, he is interested in me, he is full of love for mankind, and many other things. I let myself in for this adventure with Jesus. The priest did not promise too much. Knowing God as Father, friend, lover, consoler, provider is wonderful. I would like to know him even better and make him known. He fills up the deep hole within me with love, reconciliation, acceptance, and appreciation. And he is able to make something beautiful and valuable out of the worst experiences.

WOLFGANG

Paul founds a community in Bereoa (Acts 17:10–15)

10b and when they arrived they went into the Jewish synagogue. 11 Now these Jews were more noble than those in Thessaloni'ca, for they received the word with all eagerness, examining the Scriptures daily to see if these things were so. 12 Many of them therefore believed, with not a few Greek women of high standing as well as men. 13 But when the Jews of Thessaloni'ca learned that the word of God was proclaimed by Paul at Beroe'a also, they came there too, stirring up and inciting the crowds. 14 Then the brethren immediately sent Paul off on his way to the sea, but Silas and Timothy remained there. 15 Those who conducted Paul brought him as far as Athens; and receiving a command for Silas and Timothy to come to him as soon as possible, they departed.

Paul debates religion in Athens (Acts 17:16–21)

16 Now while Paul was waiting for them at Athens, his spirit was provoked within him as he saw that the city was full of idols. 17 So he argued in the synagogue with the Jews and the devout persons, and in the market place every day with those who chanced to be there.

▶ Epicureans and Stoics are philosophical schools that criticize the popular cult of the gods.

▶ There is some danger in this charge, because the great philosopher Socrates had been sentenced to death on account of an accusation that he was introducing foreign deities.

▶ Paul shows the Athenians a way leading from the worship of many gods to the worship of the one God. Even now they worship God, but as an unknown god. Paul makes this God known to them. He is the Creator, who cannot be equated with the things of this world and does not need sacrifices. The philosophers with whom he is debating can agree with →

18 Some also of the Epicurean and Stoic philosophers met him. And some said, "What would this babbler say?" Others said, "He seems to be a preacher of foreign divinities"—because he preached Jesus and the resurrection. 19 And they took hold of him and brought him to the Are-op'agus, saying, "May we know what this new teaching is which you present? 20 For you bring some strange things to our ears; we wish to know therefore what these things mean." 21 Now all the Athenians and the foreigners who lived there spent their time in nothing except telling or hearing something new.

Paul gives an introduction to the Christian faith (Acts 17:22–31)

22 So Paul, standing in the middle of the Are-op'agus, said: "Men of Athens, I perceive that in every way you are very religious. 23 For as I passed along, and observed the objects of your worship, I found also an altar with this inscription, 'To an unknown god.' What therefore you worship as unknown, this I proclaim to you. 24 The God who made the world and everything in it, being Lord of heaven and earth, does not live in shrines made by man, 25 nor is he served by human hands, as though he needed anything, since he himself gives to all men life and breath and everything. 26 And he made from one every nation of men to live on all the face of the earth, having determined allotted periods and the boundaries of their habitation, 27 that they should seek God, in the hope that they

might feel after him and find him. Yet he is not far from each one of us, ²⁸ for

'In him we live and move and have our being';
as even some of your poets have said,
'For we are indeed his offspring.'

²⁹ Being then God's offspring, we ought not to think that the Deity is like gold, or silver, or stone, a representation by the art and imagination of man. ³⁰ The times of ignorance God overlooked, but now he commands all men everywhere to repent, ³¹ because he has fixed a day on which he will judge the world in righteousness by a man whom he has appointed, and of this he has given assurance to all men by raising him from the dead."

Mixed reactions (Acts 17:32–34)
³² Now when they heard of the resurrection of the dead, some mocked; but others said, "We will hear you again about this."³³So Paul went out from among them. ³⁴ But some men joined him and believed, among them Dionys'ius the Are-op'agite and a woman named Dam'aris and others with them.

→ him this far. A genuine question of faith, though, is the Resurrection of Jesus from the dead.

> The pagan Western world was seeking God. That's why it found God and was converted. The modern world can be reconverted too. All it has to do is seek, as honestly and humbly as the ancient Greeks, and the story of Acts can come alive again.

PETER KREEFT

Paul comes to Corinth (Acts 18:1–4)

18 ¹ After this he left Athens and went to Corinth. ² And he found a Jew named Aqui'la, a native of Pontus, lately come from Italy with his wife Priscilla, because Claudius had commanded all the Jews to leave Rome.

And he went to see them; ³ and because he was of the same trade he stayed with them, and they worked, for by trade they were tentmakers. ⁴ And he argued in the synagogue every sabbath, and persuaded Jews and Greeks.

In Corinth a Christian community is formed (Acts 18:5–11)
⁵ When Silas and Timothy arrived from Macedonia, Paul was occupied with preaching, testifying to the Jews that the Christ was Jesus. ⁶ And when they opposed and reviled him, he shook out his garments and said to them, "Your blood be upon your heads! I am innocent. From now on I will go to the Gentiles."
⁷ And he left there and went to the house of a man named Titius Justus, a worshiper of God; his house was next door to the synagogue.
⁸ Crispus, the ruler of the synagogue, believed in the Lord, together with all his household; and many of the Corinthians hearing Paul believed and were baptized. ⁹ And the Lord said to Paul one night in a vision, "Do not be afraid, but speak and do not be silent; ¹⁰ for I am

▶ That happened in A.D. 48. A little later Paul arrives in Corinth.

> Neither the praise of men nor the fear of men should motivate us.

Motto of Blessed Bishop **CLEMENS AUGUST VON GALEN** (1878–1946). Hitler hated the "Lion of Münster", who had publicly preached against the euthanasia campaign of the Nazis and had denounced them as murderers. The *Führer* wanted him killed but feared the loss of the whole region because of the bishop's immense popularity.

B Preach the word, be urgent in season and out of season, convince, rebuke, and exhort, be unfailing in patience and in teaching.

2 Tim 4:2

▶ Through an inscription in the Greek Temple of Delphi, we know that in A.D. 51/52 or 52/53 Gallio was proconsul in Corinth, the capital of Achaia.

❝❞ The Church is by her very nature missionary. She exists so that every one can encounter Jesus.

POPE FRANCIS, July 17, 2014

▶ Cenchreae is a port city of Corinth. The vow is the Nazirite vow (↗ Num 6). It underscores his religious seriousness.

Y → 49
Does God guide the world and my life?

💡 Paul is said to have traveled 17,000 kilometers [10,500 miles] in his missionary journeys. Of course in the Roman Empire he also had a well-developed network of 200,000 kilometers [124,000 miles] of roads available.

with you, and no man shall attack you to harm you; for I have many people in this city." ¹¹ And he stayed a year and six months, teaching the word of God among them.

Paul is accused but is released (Acts 18:12–17)

¹² But when Gallio was proconsul of Acha'ia, the Jews made a united attack upon Paul and brought him before the tribunal, ¹³ saying, "This man is persuading men to worship God contrary to the law." ¹⁴ But when Paul was about to open his mouth, Gallio said to the Jews, "If it were a matter of wrongdoing or vicious crime, I should have reason to bear with you, O Jews; ¹⁵ but since it is a matter of questions about words and names and your own law, see to it yourselves; I refuse to be a judge of these things." ¹⁶ And he drove them from the tribunal. ¹⁷ And they all seized Sos'thenes, the ruler of the synagogue, and beat him in front of the tribunal. But Gallio paid no attention to this.

Paul returns from his missionary journey (Acts 18:18–22)

¹⁸ After this Paul stayed many days longer, and then took leave of the brethren and sailed for Syria, and with him Priscilla and Aqui'la. At Cen'chre-ae he cut his hair, for he had a vow. ¹⁹ And they came to Ephesus, and he left them there; but he himself went into the

synagogue and argued with the Jews. ²⁰ When they asked him to stay for a longer period, he declined; ²¹ but on taking leave of them he said, "I will return to you if God wills," and he set sail from Ephesus. ²² When he had landed at Caesare'a, he went up and greeted the Church, and then went down to Antioch.

Luke next tells about another of Paul's journeys to the communities that he has founded (Acts 18:23—21:17). When he comes back to Jerusalem again, he is arrested (Acts 21:18–22:29). He has to defend himself before the council and the chief priests (Acts 22:30—23:11) and before various Roman officials (Acts 23:12—26:32). But he is not acquitted. Therefore he appeals to the emperor. So he comes to Rome, but as a prisoner. Rescued from a violent storm at sea (Acts 27:14–26), he reaches Rome. There he is under house arrest, but he can proclaim the Gospel (Acts 28:11–31).

Paul in Rome (Acts 28:16–31)

28 ¹⁶ And when we came into Rome, Paul was allowed to stay by himself, with the soldier that guarded him. ¹⁷ After three days he called together the local leaders of the Jews; and when they had gathered, he said to them, "Brethren, though I had done nothing against the people or the customs of our fathers, yet I was delivered prisoner from Jerusalem into the hands of the Romans. ¹⁸ When they had examined me, they wished to set me at liberty, because there was no reason for the death penalty in my case. ¹⁹ But when the Jews objected, I was compelled to appeal to

Peter, the fisherman from the Sea of Galilee, and Paul, the learned Pharisee from Cilicia (in what is today Turkey), labored at the end of their lives in the capital of the world, Rome. The Acts of the Apostles reports nothing about the end of Paul of Tarsus, but the First Letter of Clement (ca. A.D. 90–100) does, although it was not included in the Bible: "Because of jealousy and envy, the greatest and most righteous pillars of the faith were persecuted and fought to the death."

Caesar—though I had no charge to bring against my nation. ²⁰ For this reason therefore I have asked to see you and speak with you, since it is because of the hope of Israel that I am bound with this chain."

²¹ And they said to him, "We have received no letters from Judea about you, and none of the brethren coming here has reported or spoken any evil about you. ²² But we desire to hear from you what your views are; for with regard to this sect we know that everywhere it is spoken against."

²³ When they had appointed a day for him, they came to him at his lodging in great numbers. And he expounded the matter to them from morning till evening, testifying to the kingdom of God and try-

▶ Paul is a Jew. His profession of faith in Jesus does not change that. Therefore he seeks dialogue. There will be debates. But there are also worthwhile conversations about the faith.

🙶 It is mainly the deeds of a love so noble that lead many to put a brand upon us. "See", they say, "how they love one another and how they →

ing to convince them about Jesus both from the law of Moses and from the prophets. ²⁴ And some were convinced by what he said, while others disbelieved. ²⁵ So, as they disagreed among themselves, they departed, after Paul had made one statement: "The Holy Spirit was right in saying to your fathers through Isaiah the prophet:

²⁶ 'Go to this people, and say,
You shall indeed hear but never understand,
and you shall indeed see but never perceive.
²⁷ For this people's heart has grown dull,
and their ears are heavy of hearing,
and their eyes they have closed;
lest they should perceive with their eyes,
and hear with their ears,
and understand with their heart,
and turn for me to heal them.'

²⁸ Let it be known to you then that this salvation of God has been sent to the Gentiles; they will listen." [²⁹]

³⁰ And he lived there two whole years at his own expense, and welcomed all who came to him, ³¹ preaching the kingdom of God and teaching about the Lord Jesus Christ quite openly and unhindered.

→ are ready even to die for one another."
TERTULLIAN (ca. 160–220), Early Christian writer, from Carthage

▶ The so-called "obduracy" of Israel does not mean that the Jews are rejected. Rather, Paul, citing the prophet Isaiah, sees Providence at work—God will also find his very own way of saving Israel (↗ Rom 11:26).

▶ The "Kingdom of God" is the main theme of Jesus' preaching. Paul holds fast to this belief at all times and combines it with his proclamation of Jesus as the Messiah.

The Letters

As an appendix to the Acts of the Apostles, the New Testament includes a whole series of letters written by the apostles. It starts with the letters of Paul. Then come the "Catholic letters" of James, Peter, John, and Jude. (They have been regarded as addressed to a more general audience than Paul's letters. They have been called "Catholic" in the sense of "universal".)

The apostles are among the most important figures in the early period of Christianity. They were all active as missionaries; they all worked also, though, in building up the Church. Their letters are building blocks for the foundation of the Church of all ages.

The letters are addressed either to specific communities in the mission territories or else to whole mission regions, sometimes also to individual persons.

The letters proclaim the Gospel by addressing the first members of the communities directly about their faith. They deal with their questions; they try to help them to find their path of faith; they criticize and encourage.

The New Testament letters are like a window through which we can observe the life of the earliest Christian communities. They are like a treasure chest in which the oldest professions of the faith are preserved. But they are also like a mirror in which all Christians to this day can find their own questions about the faith and their own courage to believe.

In this Bible, only a few letters can be presented. They should whet your appetite for more. They are letters that record and inspire deep faith experiences.

Apostle Paul

Many letters from Paul were included in the New Testament. He wrote them over the course of his missionary work so that the Christian communities might develop further in their faith.

The Letters of the apostle Paul have a threefold key significance.

First, they are the oldest testimonies about the early Church. They were written by an author who was very close to the situations of the original Christian communities. They are like windows through which we can look at the liturgy and everyday lives, the professions of faith and the charity, the social challenges, and the religious orientations of the first Christians.

Second, the letters of the apostle Paul are literary masterpieces. These letters are full of deep religious fervor and great clarity of thought. Paul brings himself in fully as a person—and he demands much of his readers. He wants them to catch the joy of faith.

Third, the letters are outstanding witnesses to early Christian theology. They are a treasure chest full of faith testimonies and an intellectual gateway. They show that faith provides food for thought and that faith benefits from reasonable reflection.

The letters have some passages that are rough going (see 2 Pet 3:16, "there are some things in them hard to understand"). But they reward careful reading.

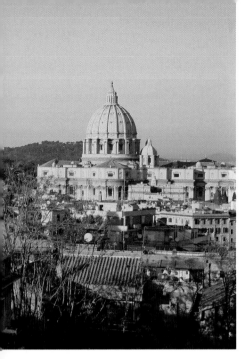

THE LETTER TO THE ROMANS

Paul writes his longest and most important letter to the Christians in Rome, the capital of the Roman Empire. At that time, Rome was the largest city in the world. Paul wants to convince the Romans to support him on his missionary journey to Spain. He knows, though, that many criticize him personally and his efforts for the Gentile missions. He wants to persuade the Romans. That is why he takes a wide theological perspective and presents many facets of the Gospel, the Good News of God that saves all who have faith in it (Rom 1:16–17). One high point is what he says about the working of the Holy Spirit in those who believe.

In the Letter to the Romans, Paul establishes, first, that no one can be justified through "works of the law" but only through "faith in Jesus" Christ (Rom 3:26, 28). The great example of this is Abraham (Rom 4). After that, the apostle shows what a life of faith looks like: the significance of the reconciliation that God grants (Rom 5), of the baptism that all believers have received (Rom 6), and of the gift of the Spirit that makes them new men and women (Rom 8).

💡 Faith creates certainty. The best is yet to come— because God himself is coming.

Y → 337
How are we saved?

Y → 68
Original sin? What does the Fall of Adam and Eve have to do with us?

▶ Paul recalls the story of Adam (↗ Gen 1, 2). He says: Adam's sin, wanting to be like God, is the sin of all of us.

The great reconciliation (Rom 5:9–11)

⁹ Since, therefore, we are now justified by his blood, much more shall we be saved by him from the wrath of God. ¹⁰ For if while we were enemies we were reconciled to God by the death of his Son, much more, now that we are reconciled, shall we be saved by his life. ¹¹ Not only so, but we also rejoice in God through our Lord Jesus Christ, through whom we have now received our reconciliation.

Human guilt (Rom 5:12–14)

¹² Therefore as sin came into the world through one man and death through sin, and so death spread to all men because all men sinned—¹³ sin indeed was in the world before the law was given, but sin is not counted where there is no law.

¹⁴ Yet death reigned from Adam to Moses, even over those whose sins were not like the transgression of Adam, who was a type of the one who was to come.

Grace is much stronger than sin (Rom 5:15)

¹⁵ But the free gift is not like the trespass. For if many died through one man's trespass, much more have the grace of God and the free gift in the grace of that one man Jesus Christ abounded for many.

▶ We are responsible for our personal sins. Grace, however, comes from God. That is why grace is much stronger than sin. It creates new life.

Adam is weak; Christ is strong (Rom 5:16–19)

¹⁶ And the free gift is not like the effect of that one man's sin. For the judgment following one trespass brought condemnation, but the free gift following many trespasses brings justification. ¹⁷ If, because of one man's trespass, death reigned through that one man, much more will those who receive the abundance of grace and the free gift of righteousness reign in life through the one man Jesus Christ.

¹⁸ Then as one man's trespass led to condemnation for all men, so one man's act of righteousness leads to acquittal and life for all men. ¹⁹ For as by one man's disobedience many were made sinners, so by one man's obedience many will be made righteous.

He became what we are, so that he could make us what he is.

ATHANASIUS THE GREAT

▶ Several times Paul repeats this difference. The one Adam causes many to be sinners, because they commit sins of their own. But the one Christ, the second Adam, makes all believers just, so that they might perform works of justice. What could be better than that?

The Law cannot save, but grace can (Rom 5:20–21)

²⁰ Law came in, to increase the trespass; but where sin increased, grace abounded all the more, ²¹ so that, as sin reigned in death,

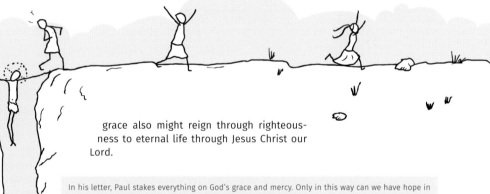

grace also might reign through righteousness to eternal life through Jesus Christ our Lord.

In his letter, Paul stakes everything on God's grace and mercy. Only in this way can we have hope in eternal life. But what about our own lives? Some raise the objection: Does it not matter, then, how one lives and whether one obeys God's commandments? Paul corrects this misunderstanding.

A misunderstanding is cleared up (Rom 6:1–2)

6 ¹ What shall we say then? Are we to continue in sin that grace may abound? ² By no means! How can we who died to sin still live in it?

Through Baptism Comes New Life (Rom 6:3–5)

³ Do you not know that all of us who have been baptized into Christ Jesus were baptized into his death? ⁴ We were buried therefore with him by baptism into death, so that as Christ was raised from the dead by the glory of the Father, we too might walk in newness of life. ⁵ For if we have been united with him in

▶ Baptism is the sacrament of a new beginning: dying with Christ and rising again with him. The visible sign is the water that is poured over the candidate or in which he is immersed. The invisible effect is membership in the family of Jesus, which must be manifested in new behavior.

a death like his, we shall certainly be united with him in a resurrection like his.

To die and to live with Christ (Rom 6:6–11)

[6] We know that our former man was crucified with him so that the sinful body might be destroyed, and we might no longer be enslaved to sin. [7] For he who has died is freed from sin.

[8] But if we have died with Christ, we believe that we shall also live with him. [9] For we know that Christ being raised from the dead will never die again; death no longer has dominion over him. [10] The death he died he died to sin, once for all, but the life he lives he lives to God. [11] So you also must consider yourselves dead to sin and alive to God in Christ Jesus.

Fighting for justice (Rom 6:12–14)

[12] Let not sin therefore reign in your mortal bodies, to make you obey their passions. [13] Do not yield your members to sin as instruments of wickedness, but yield yourselves to God as men who have

The words "All must die" are bitter. Great sweetness, however, follows on the heels of this bitterness. For dying unites us with God.

FRANCIS DE SALES

▶ "Once and for all"—there is only one baptism (Eph 4:5), because Jesus lived and died only once and was raised from the dead. Baptism has lasting validity. It is not a provisional arrangement. But its significance has to be discovered.

Faith means being able to fight. With no weapons except love.

been brought from death to life, and your members to God as instruments of righteousness. [14] For sin will have no dominion over you, since you are not under law but under grace.

Free from sin (Rom 6:15–18)

[15] What then? Are we to sin because we are not under law but under grace? By no means! [16] Do you not know that if you yield yourselves to any one as obedient slaves, you are slaves of the one whom you obey, either of sin, which leads to death, or of obedience, which leads to righteousness?

[17] But thanks be to God, that you who were once slaves of sin have become obedient from the heart to the standard of teaching to which you were committed, [18] and, having been set free from sin, have become slaves of righteousness.

Free to serve God and neighbor (Rom 6:19–23)

[19] I am speaking in human terms, because of your natural limitations. For just as you once yielded your members to impurity and to greater and greater iniquity, so now yield your members to righteousness for sanctification.

[20] When you were slaves of sin, you were free in regard to righteousness. [21] But then what return did you get from the things of which you are now ashamed? The end of those things is death. [22] But

HE loves as Love, HE knows as Truth, HE judges as Justice, HE reigns as Majesty; HE rules as the Kingdom, HE protects as Savior, HE works as Might, HE reveals as Light, HE helps as Grace. What, then, is God? The final destination for all and salvation for the elect.

BERNARD OF CLAIRVAUX

▶ "Slaves of sin"—that is sheer imprisonment, because one becomes the plaything of one's own desires. "Slaves of righteousness"—that is sheer freedom, because now all of life gains meaning.

❞ We need to remember that Catholic teaching is not an "ideal" to be attained by the few, but a way of life that can and should be lived by all of us.

ARCHBISHOP CHARLES CHAPUT

now that you have been set free from sin and have become slaves of God, the return you get is sanctification and its end, eternal life. [23] For the wages of sin is death, but the free gift of God is eternal life in Christ Jesus our Lord.

Sin is sick and makes people sick. Wanting to live is only human, but not at the expense of others.

In Rom 7, Paul reflects on why the "Law" cannot save sinful man. He shows at the beginning of chapter 8 that salvation comes through Jesus Christ. Then he writes again about the working of the Holy Spirit.

The Spirit who gives life (Rom 8:11–13)

8 [11] If the Spirit of him who raised Jesus from the dead dwells in you, he who raised Christ Jesus from the dead will give life to your mortal bodies also through his Spirit who dwells in you.

[12] So then, brethren, we are debtors, not to the flesh, to live according to the flesh—[13] for if you live according to the flesh you will die, but if by the Spirit you put to death the deeds of the body you will live.

The Spirit who teaches us to pray (Rom 8:14–17)

[14] For all who are led by the Spirit of God are sons of God. [15] For you did not receive the spirit of slavery to fall back into fear, but you have received the spirit of sonship. When we cry, "Abba! Father!" [16] it is the Spirit himself bearing witness with our spirit that we are children of God, [17] and if children, then heirs, heirs of God and fellow heirs with Christ, provided we suffer with him in order that we may also be glorified with him.

The Spirit who gives hope (Rom 8:18–25)

[18] I consider that the sufferings of this present time are not worth comparing with the glory that is to be revealed to us. [19] For the creation waits with eager longing for the revealing of the sons of God; [20] for the creation was subjected to futility, not of its own will but by the will of him who subjected it in hope; [21] because the creation itself will be set free from its bondage to decay and obtain the glorious liberty of the children of God. [22] We know that the whole creation has been groaning with labor pains together until now; [23] and not only the creation, but we ourselves, who have the first fruits of the Spirit, groan inwardly as we wait for adoption as sons, the redemption of our bodies. [24] For in this hope we were saved. Now hope that is seen is not hope. For who hopes for what he sees? [25] But if we hope for what we do not see, we wait for it with patience.

> Lord, Holy Spirit, here we are, burdened with sin, yet specially gathered in your Name. Come into our midst, be among us, pour yourself out into our hearts! Teach us what we should do, show us where we should go, tell us what we must achieve in order to please you in all things through your help. Let ignorance not mislead us, let human applause not seduce us, let corruption and false considerations not ruin us. Let us never stray from what is true. Amen.

This prayer was recited by the Council Fathers at the First Vatican Council (1869–1871)

B I wait for the LORD, my soul waits, and in his word I hope; my soul waits for the LORD more than watchmen for the morning.

Ps 130:5–6

My past no longer troubles me; it belongs to the divine mercy. My future does not yet trouble me; it belongs to Divine Providence. What concerns and challenges me is today. But it belongs to God's grace and to the submission of my good will.

FRANCIS DE SALES

The Spirit who helps us in our weakness (Rom 8:26–27)

26 Likewise the Spirit helps us in our weakness; for we do not know how to pray as we ought, but the Spirit himself intercedes for us with sighs too deep for words. 27 And he who searches the hearts of men knows what is the mind of the Spirit, because the Spirit intercedes for the saints according to the will of God.

The Spirit who leads people to Jesus (Rom 8:28–30)

28 We know that in everything God works for good with those who love him, who are called according to his purpose. 29 For those whom he foreknew he also predestined to be conformed to the image of his Son, in order that he might be the first-born among many brethren.

30 And those whom he predestined he also called; and those whom he called he also justified; and those whom he justified he also glorified.

God who is for us (Rom 8:31–39)

31 What then shall we say to this? If God is for us, who is against us? 32 He who did not spare his own Son but gave

I am totally glad that Jesus Christ will be my judge and no one else. I am not afraid; nothing can separate us, not even my faults. That makes the battle with myself and my bad habits and big weaknesses much easier. As long as I remain with him, I have already won the battle. Whatever happens, I am on the winning side. So I keep a deep inner equilibrium, whatever happens.

FLÁVIO

▶ Paul was a poet, too. The faith inspired his best thoughts and verses. Here he writes a love song to God. It can have only one theme: the love of God himself.

him up for us all, will he not also give us all things with him?

33 Who shall bring any charge against God's elect? It is God who justifies;

34 who is to condemn? Is it Christ Jesus, who died, yes, who was raised from the dead, who is at the right hand of God, who indeed intercedes for us?

35 Who shall separate us from the love of Christ? Shall tribulation, or distress, or persecution, or famine, or nakedness, or peril, or sword? 36 As it is written,

"For your sake we are being killed all the day long;
we are regarded as sheep to be slaughtered."

37 No, in all these things we are more than conquerors through him who loved us.

38 For I am sure that neither death, nor life, nor angels, nor principalities, nor things present, nor things to come, nor powers, 39 nor height, nor depth, nor anything else in all creation, will be able to separate us from the love of God in Christ Jesus our Lord.

THE FIRST LETTER TO THE CORINTHIANS

The Letter to the Romans is followed by two Letters to the Corinthians. This community was going through an especially turbulent time. There was a lot of quarreling in the Church, but also with the apostle. Finally, the Gospel of peace prevails. The First Letter to the Corinthians answers questions from the Church. Paul grapples intensely with the life of the community. He is critical but wants to help the Christians to discover their talents and to incorporate them into the life of the Church.

The gift of the Holy Spirit (1 Cor 12:1–11)

12 ¹ Now concerning spiritual gifts, brethren, I do not want you to be uninformed. ² You know that when you were heathen, you were led astray to mute idols, however you may

have been moved. ³ Therefore I want you to understand that no one speaking by the Spirit of God ever says "Jesus be cursed!" and no one can say "Jesus is Lord " except by the Holy Spirit.

⁴ Now there are varieties of gifts, but the same Spirit;

⁵ and there are varieties of service, but the same Lord;

⁶ and there are varieties of working, but it is the same God who inspires them all in every one.

⁷ To each is given the manifestation of the Spirit for the common good. ⁸ To one is given through the Spirit the utterance of wisdom, and to another the utterance of knowledge according to the same Spirit, ⁹ to another faith by the same Spirit, to another gifts of healing by the one Spirit, ¹⁰ to another the working of miracles, to another prophecy, to another the ability to distinguish between spirits, to another various kinds of tongues, to another the interpretation of tongues.

¹¹ All these are inspired by one and the same Spirit, who apportions to each one individually as he wills.

One Body with Many Members (1 Cor 12:12–27)

¹² For just as the body is one and has many members, and all the members of the body, though many, are one body, so it is with

▶ "Jesus is Lord" is a very short profession of faith. "Lord" in Greek is *Kyrios*. This was the name for God used by the Jews who spoke Greek. The profession therefore says: Jesus is God.

▶ The Greek word for "gift of grace" is *charisma*.

▶ Paul does not make a complete list but just mentions good examples. The one Spirit gives many gifts because there are many tasks and many people who come forward. "Speaking in tongues" is ecstatic prayer in a language that others do not understand. Therefore it requires interpretation.

▶ With the image of the Church as the Body of Christ, Paul makes two things clear. First: the many members all belong to the one Body; so they can be used only if they do not separate themselves from the Body. Second: the Body is made up of many members; it is healthy only when it has all its members. Even those who are seemingly weak are important; those who seem strong must place themselves at the service of the weak and of the Body as a whole.

🙶 All the baptized, whatever their position in the Church or their level of instruction in the faith, are agents of evangelization, and it would be insufficient to envisage a plan of evangelization to be carried out by professionals while the rest of the faithful would simply be passive recipients.

POPE FRANCIS, *Evangelii Gaudium*, 120

Christ. ¹³ For by one Spirit we were all baptized into one body—Jews or Greeks, slaves or free—and all were made to drink of one Spirit.

¹⁴ For the body does not consist of one member but of many. ¹⁵ If the foot should say, "Because I am not a hand, I do not belong to the body," that would not make it any less a part of the body. ¹⁶ And if the ear should say, "Because I am not an eye, I do not belong to the body," that would not make it any less a part of the body. ¹⁷ If the whole body were an eye, where would be the hearing? If the whole body were an ear, where would be the sense of smell? ¹⁸ But as it is, God arranged the organs in the body, each one of them, as he chose. ¹⁹ If all were a single organ, where would the body be?

²⁰ As it is, there are many parts, yet one body. ²¹ The eye cannot say to the hand, "I have no need of you," nor again the head to the feet, "I have no need of you." ²² On the contrary, the parts of the body which seem to be weaker are indispensable, ²³ and those parts of the body which we think less honorable we invest with the greater honor, and our unpresentable parts are treated with greater modesty, ²⁴ which our more presentable parts do not require. But God has so composed the body, giving the greater honor to the inferior part, ²⁵ that there may be no discord in the body, but that the members may have the same care for one another. ²⁶ If one member suffers, all suffer together; if one member is honored, all rejoice together.

²⁷ Now you are the body of Christ and individually members of it.

🙶 What I want you to understand is that you have great dignity because you are a child of God.

MOTHER ANGELICA

 Love ... Sharing faith, praying together, interceding for others. Together hoping in God and going boldly into the world. Making love grow through works of charity. Serving each other and making everyday life better. Deliberately spending time together. Admitting our faults and forgiving each other—every evening, even if it was only something trivial. Being best friends. Caring about my appearance for my spouse's sake. Accepting and honoring the other as a gift and God's masterpiece.

MARIE AND CORNELIUS

The tasks in the Church (1 Cor 12:28–31)

²⁸ And God has appointed in the Church first apostles, second prophets, third teachers, then workers of miracles, then healers, helpers, administrators, speakers in various kinds of tongues.

²⁹ Are all apostles? Are all prophets? Are all teachers? Do all work miracles? ³⁰ Do all possess gifts of healing? Do all speak with tongues? Do all interpret? ³¹ But earnestly desire the higher gifts.

And I will show you a still more excellent way.

But the greatest of these is love (1 Cor 13:1–13)

13 ¹ If I speak in the tongues of men and of angels, but have not love, I am a noisy gong or a clanging cymbal.

² And if I have prophetic powers, and understand all mysteries and all knowledge, and if I have all faith, so as to remove mountains, but have not love, I am nothing.

³ If I give away all I have, and if I deliver my body to be burned, but have not love, I gain nothing.

⁴ Love is patient and kind; love is not jealous or boastful;

⁵ it is not arrogant or rude. Love does not insist on its own way; it is not irritable or resentful;

⁶ it does not rejoice at wrong, but rejoices in the right.

⁷ Love bears all things, believes all things, hopes all things, endures all things.

⁸ Love never ends; as for prophecies, they will pass away; as for tongues, they will cease; as for knowledge, it will pass away.

⁹ For our knowledge is imperfect and our prophecy is imperfect; ¹⁰ but when the perfect comes, the imperfect will pass away.

¹¹ When I was a child, I spoke like a child, I thought like a child, I reasoned like a child; when I became a man, I gave up childish ways.

¹² For now we see in a mirror dimly, but then face to face.

Now I know in part; then I shall understand fully, even as I have been fully understood.

¹³ So faith, hope, love abide, these three; but the greatest of these is love.

▶ It is about God's love in the hearts of men. The "Hymn of Love" is the favorite passage of many couples who are getting married, because they recognize in their love a glimmer of divine love. Paul, though, wrote the hymn to teach that life in the Church is defined, not by competition, but by mutual concern and support. Marriage is an especially beautiful opportunity for this.

At the conclusion, Paul reminds the Corinthians of the Gospel with which their faith began.

The Gospel of Life (1 Cor 15:3–11)

15 ³ For I delivered to you as of first importance what I also received, that Christ died for our sins in accordance with the Scriptures, ⁴ that he was buried, that he was raised on the third day in accordance with the Scriptures, ⁵ and that he appeared to Ce'phas, then to the Twelve.

" Having charity, we have God in us. So the life of charity, the life of union with God, is no different from eternal life.

HENRI CARDINAL LUBAC, S.J.

⁶ Then he appeared to more than five hundred brethren at one time, most of whom are still alive, though some have fallen asleep. ⁷ Then he appeared to James, then to all the apostles. ⁸ Last of all, as to one untimely born, he appeared also to me.

⁹ For I am the least of the apostles, unfit to be called an apostle, because I persecuted the Church of God. ¹⁰ But by the grace of God I am what I am, and his grace toward me was not in vain. On the contrary, I worked harder than any of them, though it was not I, but the grace of God which is with me. ¹¹ Whether then it was I or they, so we preach and so you believed.

B If Christ has not been raised, your faith is futile and you are still in your sins.

1 Cor 15:17

THE SECOND LETTER TO THE CORINTHIANS

The Second Letter to the Corinthians looks back at disagreements between the apostle and his community and rejoices over the reconciliation between them.

> **"** Here we can begin to see that true freedom is not merely the ability to make choices. It's found in the ability to consistently make good choices—virtuous choices—that enable us to live our relationships with excellence.
>
> **DR. EDWARD SRI**

God wants us to be free (2 Cor 3:17–4:2)

3 [17] Now the Lord is the Spirit, and where the Spirit of the Lord is, there is freedom. [18] And we all, with unveiled face, beholding the glory of the Lord, are being changed into his likeness from one degree of glory to another; for this comes from the Lord who is the Spirit.

4 [1] Therefore, having this ministry by the mercy of God, we do not lose heart. [2] We have renounced disgraceful, underhanded ways; we refuse to practice cunning or to tamper with God's word, but by

> The weakest person is the one who can have the greatest hope for the greatest graces, because God adapts to human misery.
>
> **THÉRÈSE OF LISIEUX**

> God would be unjust and cruel if he intended to hold us to a commandment that we cannot keep.
>
> **AUGUSTINE**

the open statement of the truth we would commend ourselves to every man's conscience in the sight of God.

The image of God—right in front of our eyes (2 Cor 4:3–6)

[3] And even if our gospel is veiled, it is veiled only to those who are perishing. [4] In their case the god of this world has blinded the minds of the unbelievers, to keep them from seeing the light of the gospel of the glory of Christ, who is the likeness of God. [5] For what we preach is not ourselves, but Jesus Christ as Lord, with ourselves as your servants for Jesus' sake. [6] For it is the God who said, "Let light shine out of darkness," who has shone in our hearts to give the light of the knowledge of the glory of God in the face of Christ.

Our treasure in fragile vessels (2 Cor 4:7–10)

[7] But we have this treasure in earthen vessels, to show that the transcendent power belongs to God and not to us. [8] We are afflicted in every way, but not crushed; perplexed, but not driven to despair; [9] persecuted, but not forsaken; struck down, but not destroyed; [10] always carrying in the body the death of Jesus, so that the life of Jesus may also be manifested in our bodies.

Our new life—out of death (2 Cor 4:11–15)

¹¹ For while we live we are always being given up to death for Jesus' sake, so that the life of Jesus may be manifested in our mortal flesh. ¹² So death is at work in us, but life in you.

¹³ Since we have the same spirit of faith as he had who wrote, "I believed, and so I spoke," we too believe, and so we speak, ¹⁴ knowing that he who raised the Lord Jesus will raise us also with Jesus and bring us with you into his presence. ¹⁵ For it is all for your sake, so that as grace extends to more and more people it may increase thanksgiving, to the glory of God.

The invisible—in our sight (2 Cor 4:16–18)

¹⁶ So we do not lose heart. Though our outer man is wasting away, our inner man is being renewed every day. ¹⁷ For this slight momentary affliction is preparing for us an eternal weight of glory beyond all comparison, ¹⁸ because we look not to the things that are seen but to the things that are unseen; for the things that are seen are transient, but the things that are unseen are eternal.

God's tent—our home (2 Cor 5:1–4)

5 ¹ For we know that if the earthly tent we live in is destroyed, we have a building from God, a house not made with hands, eternal

> **"** All the elements of this life—the sorrows, the joys, the setbacks, the trials—combine with the grace of God to mold and form us into His Image. ... Whatever capacity for love the soul has grown to at death will determine its glory and joy in Heaven.
>
> **MOTHER ANGELICA**

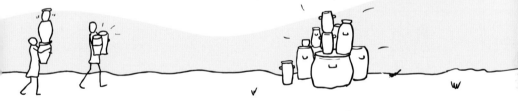

in the heavens. ² Here indeed we groan, and long to put on our heavenly dwelling, ³ so that by putting it on we may not be found naked. ⁴ For while we are still in this tent, we sigh with anxiety; not that we would be unclothed, but that we would be further clothed, so that what is mortal may be swallowed up by life.

God's Spirit—we are on the way (2 Cor 5:5–9)

⁵ He who has prepared us for this very thing is God, who has given us the Spirit as a guarantee.

⁶ So we are always of good courage; we know that while we are at home in the body we are away from the Lord, ⁷ for we walk by faith, not by sight. ⁸ We are of good courage, and we would rather be away from the body and at home with the Lord. ⁹ So whether we are at home or away, we make it our aim to please him.

For Christians, it is quite normal to feel a bit "homeless": in front of the television, in a casino, in the company of bad friends. "Our commonwealth is in heaven" (↗ Phil 3:20).

▶ A lot of things in the world are imperfect. But there is one great big plus: the Holy Spirit. All who believe have received him. But he works outside the Church, too.

▶ To be a Christian means to hope. There is no need to fear death. Awaiting us beyond this earthly life is not nothing, but heaven.

THE LETTER OF PAUL TO THE GALATIANS

The Letter to the Galatians is addressed to Christians who lived in a region in modern-day Turkey. The word "Galatians" is derived from "Celts". They were migrants who had settled long before.

In a harsh conflict with missionary competitors, Paul stands up for the Christians' freedom. He shows that faith in Jesus is what "justifies" someone, in other words, fixes his relationship to God, thanks to God's grace. This faith is extremely active. It is "working through love" (Gal 5:6).

▶ Circumcision is a sign of faith for Jewish men (→ Rom 4:11). Gentile Christians do not need it. Anyone who requires it acts as though baptism were not enough. That was one of the major conflicts in early Christianity. Paul prevailed. Only in that way could a universal Church come about.

▶ That is a key element in being a Christian: faith is active. Love does not just happen somehow; it goes together with faith from the start.

▶ Paul may have been a Jewish missionary before his conversion.

▶ The Cross is a scandal (↗ 1 Cor 1:23) because it is an instrument of torture.

A necessary warning (Gal 5:1–4)

5 ¹ For freedom Christ has set us free; stand fast therefore, and do not submit again to a yoke of slavery.
² Now I, Paul, say to you that if you receive circumcision, Christ will be of no advantage to you. ³ I testify again to every man who receives circumcision that he is bound to keep the whole law. ⁴ You are severed from Christ, you who would be justified by the law; you have fallen away from grace.

Great confidence (Gal 5:5–11)

⁵ For through the Spirit, by faith, we wait for the hope of righteousness. ⁶ For in Christ Jesus neither circumcision nor uncircumcision is of any avail, but faith working through love.
⁷ You were running well; who hindered you from obeying the truth? ⁸ This persuasion is not from him who called you. ⁹ A little leaven leavens all the dough.
¹⁰ I have confidence in the Lord that you will take no other view than mine; and he who is troubling you will bear his judgment, whoever he is. ¹¹ But if I, brethren, still preach circumcision, why am I still persecuted? In that case the stumbling block of the cross has been removed.

Freedom—an opportunity for love (Gal 5:13–15)

¹³ For you were called to freedom, brethren; only do not use your freedom as an opportunity for the flesh, but through love be servants of one another. ¹⁴ For the whole law is fulfilled in one word, "You shall love your neighbor as yourself." ¹⁵ But if you bite and devour one another take heed that you are not consumed by one another.

The Holy Spirit is active against selfishness (Gal 5:16–21)

¹⁶ But I say, walk by the Spirit, and do not gratify the desires of the flesh. ¹⁷ For the desires of the flesh are against the Spirit, and the desires of the Spirit are against the flesh; for these are opposed to each other, to prevent you from doing what you would. ¹⁸ But if you are led by the Spirit you are not under the law.

¹⁹ Now the works of the flesh are plain: immorality, impurity, licentiousness, ²⁰ idolatry, sorcery, enmity, strife, jealousy, anger, selfishness, dissension, party spirit, ²¹ envy, drunkenness, carousing, and the like. I warn you, as I warned you before, that those who do such things shall not inherit the kingdom of God.

The French printmaker Honoré Daumier (1808–1879) pointedly caricatured the secret vices of his contemporaries. The antidote is prescribed by the American civil rights leader and pastor Martin Luther King: "Let no man pull you low enough to hate him."

Y → 120, 311
What does the Holy Spirit do in my life?
What are the fruits of the Holy Spirit?

The fruit of the spirit: love (Gal 5:22–26)

²² But the fruit of the Spirit is love, joy, peace, patience, kindness, goodness, faithfulness,
²³ gentleness, self-control; against such there is no law.
²⁴ And those who belong to Christ Jesus have crucified the flesh with its passions and desires.
²⁵ If we live by the Spirit, let us also walk by the Spirit. ²⁶ Let us have no self-conceit, no provoking of one another, no envy of one another.

▶ The Cross of Jesus is a death that leads to life. So, too, according to Paul, overcoming oneself is the path to self-fulfillment. Anyone who loves as Jesus did becomes a new man—in the Holy Spirit.

The law of Christ: forgiveness (Gal 6:1–2)

6 ¹ Brethren, if a man is overtaken in any trespass, you who are spiritual should restore him in a spirit of gentleness. Look to yourself, lest you too be tempted.
² Bear one another's burdens, and so fulfil the law of Christ.

💡 "Fraternal correction" is a term for the Christian way of helping someone else find the right path discreetly and lovingly.

▶ Christ's law is the Commandment of Love.

THE LETTER TO THE EPHESIANS

The Letter to the Ephesians meditates on the mystery of the Church, in which God's peace can be experienced. It begins with a hymn in praise of the grace of God, who has led Christians to the faith in the Church.

Praised be God (Eph 1:3–14)

1 ³ Blessed be the God and Father of our Lord Jesus Christ, who has blessed us in Christ with every spiritual blessing in the heavenly places,

⁴ even as he chose us in him before the foundation of the world, that we should be holy and blameless before him.

⁵ He destined us in love to be his sons through Jesus Christ, according to the purpose of his will,

> We need not, I suppose, rush out into every thunderstorm declaring ... the praise of the Lord just because it is sprinkling. Yet we are somehow dull if the thought never occurs to us.
>
> **JAMES SCHALL, S.J.** (b. 1928), American Jesuit priest, theologian, and political philosopher

> God is not an unknown Person, a hypothesis perhaps about the very beginning of the cosmos. God is flesh and blood. He is one of us. We know him by his Face, by his Name. He is Jesus Christ who speaks to us in the Gospel. He is both man and God. And being God, he chose man to enable us to choose God. Thus, we must enter into the knowledge of Jesus and then friendship with him in order to walk with him.
>
> **POPE BENEDICT XVI**, February 7, 2008

⁶ to the praise of his glorious grace which he freely bestowed on us in the Beloved.

⁷ In him we have redemption through his blood, the forgiveness of our trespasses, according to the riches of his grace

⁸ which he lavished upon us.

⁹ For he has made known to us in all wisdom and insight the mystery of his will,

according to his purpose which he set forth in Christ

¹⁰ as a plan for the fulness of time, to unite all things in him, things in heaven and things on earth.

¹¹ In him, according to the purpose of him who accomplishes all things according to the counsel of his will,

¹² we who first hoped in Christ have been destined and appointed to live for the praise of his glory.

¹³ In him you also, who have heard the word of truth, the gospel of your salvation, and have believed in him, were sealed with the promised Holy Spirit,

¹⁴ who is the guarantee of our inheritance until we acquire possession of it, to the praise of his glory.

Come, Holy Spirit, into your Church (Eph 1:15–23)

¹⁵ For this reason, because I have heard of your faith in the Lord Jesus and your love toward all the saints, ¹⁶ I do not cease to give thanks for you, remembering you in my prayers, ¹⁷ that the God of our Lord Jesus Christ, the Father of glory, may give you a spirit of wisdom and of revelation in the knowledge of him,

¹⁸ having the eyes of your hearts enlightened, that you may know what is the hope to which he has called you, what are the riches of his glorious inheritance in the saints, ¹⁹ and what is the immeasurable greatness of his power in us who believe, according to the working of his great might

²⁰ which he accomplished in Christ when he raised him from the dead and made him sit at his right hand in the heavenly places, ²¹ far above all rule and authority and power and dominion, and above every name that is named, not only in this age but also in that which is to come;

²² and he has put all things under his feet and has made him the head over all things for the Church, ²³ which is his body, the fulness of him who fills all in all.

Let no one ever come to you without leaving better and happier. Be the living expression of God's kindness: kindness in your face, kindness in your eyes, kindness in your smile, kindness in your warm greeting. In the slums we are the light of God's kindness for the poor. To the children, to the poor, to all who suffer and are lonely, always give a happy smile.

MOTHER TERESA

In the middle of the letter, the Ephesians are reminded of the Gospel with which their faith began.

We are baptized (Eph 4:1–6)

4 ¹ I therefore, a prisoner for the Lord, beg you to walk in a manner worthy of the calling to which you have been called,

² with all lowliness and meekness, with patience, forbearing one another in love, ³ eager to maintain the unity of the Spirit in the bond of peace.

⁴ There is o n e body and o n e Spirit, just as you were called to the o n e hope that belongs to your call, ⁵ o n e Lord, o n e faith, o n e baptism,

⁶ o n e God and Father of us all, who is above all and through all and in all.

▶ The Church is one, because there is only one God. Baptism creates the connection. The unity of the Church is not uniformity but, rather, a communion of many quite different people who all together stake their whole life on God.

Jesus Christ is our Lord (Eph 4:7–10)

⁷ But grace was given to each of us according to the measure of Christ's gift. ⁸ Therefore it is said,

"When he ascended on high he led a host of captives,
and he gave gifts to men."

⁹ (In saying, "He ascended," what does it mean but that he had also descended into the lower parts of the earth? ¹⁰ He who descended is he who also ascended far above all the heavens, that he might fill all things.)

▶ Jesus, glorified at God's right hand, is the same one who lived on earth and died. That is why he uses his position as the risen Lord to continue distributing God's gifts and blessings.

THE LETTER TO THE PHILIPPIANS

Paul writes the Letter to the Philippians from prison. Although innocent of any crime, he has been arrested merely because he proclaimed the Gospel. He does not know whether he will be set free or sentenced to death. He rejoices over the strong support of the community in Philippi and with this letter means to thank them for their help. But he also wants to share his own faith with the Philippians and to warn them not to go down the wrong path. Although Paul is looking death in the eye, he sees reason for profound joy, for he knows that Jesus Christ is at his side.

▶ The custom then in writing a letter was for the sender to name himself first. Paul founded the community in Philippi (↗ Acts 16:11–40); Timothy is one of his most important coworkers. For Paul, the "saints" are all the members of the community, because they are all united with God through baptism. The "bishops" and "deacons" are members of the community's leadership team.

▶ Here the "day of Jesus Christ" (v. 6) is the last day of Christ's Second Coming.

99 The judgment of Christ will bring to light who has believed and lived the Gospel and who has not. The Gospels make it clear that the believer has already been judged favorably and so has nothing whatever to fear. ...

KENNETH BAKER, S.J. (1929), American Jesuit priest and theologian

Address and greeting (Phil 1:1–2)

1 ¹ Paul and Timothy, servants of Christ Jesus,
To all the saints in Christ Jesus who are at Philip'pi, with the bishops and deacons: ² Grace to you and peace from God our Father and the Lord Jesus Christ.

The apostle's thanks and intercession (Phil 1:3–11)

³ I thank my God in all my remembrance of you, ⁴ always in every prayer of mine for you all making my prayer with joy, ⁵ thankful for your partnership in the gospel from the first day until now. ⁶ And I am sure that he who began a good work in you will bring it to completion at the day of Jesus Christ. ⁷ It is right for me to feel this way about you all, because I hold you in my heart, for you are all partakers with me of grace, both in my imprisonment and in the defense and confirmation of the gospel. ⁸ For God is my witness, how I yearn for you all with the affection of Christ Jesus.

⁹ And it is my prayer that your love may abound more and more, with knowledge and all discernment. ¹⁰ so that you may approve what is excellent, and may be pure and blameless for the day of Christ, ¹¹ filled with the fruits of righteousness which come through Jesus Christ, to the glory and praise of God.

Paul proclaims the Gospel—and not everyone likes it (Phil 1:12–19)

¹² I want you to know, brethren, that what has happened to me has really served to advance the gospel, ¹³ so that it has become known throughout the whole praetorian guard and to all the rest that my imprisonment is for Christ; ¹⁴ and most of the brethren have been made confident in the Lord because of my imprisonment, and are much more bold to speak the word of God without fear.

¹⁵ Some indeed preach Christ from envy and rivalry, but others from good will. ¹⁶ The latter do it out of love, knowing that I am put here for the defense of the gospel; ¹⁷ the former proclaim Christ out of partisanship, not sincerely but thinking to afflict me in my imprisonment. ¹⁸ What then? Only that in every way, whether in pretense or in truth, Christ is proclaimed; and in that I rejoice.

¹⁹ Yes, and I shall rejoice. For I know that through your prayers and the help of the Spirit of Jesus Christ this will turn out for my deliverance.

▶ The title "brethren" in the New Testament letters means both men and women equally.

▶ The *praetorium* is the political center of the city where Paul was detained, either in Rome or in Ephesus.

When you merely pray, then you pray for yourself alone. But when you pray for everyone, then everyone prays for you.
AMBROSE OF MILAN (340–397), Doctor of the Church

The apostle's great hope in life and in death: to be with Christ (Phil 1:20–26)

²⁰ ...as it is my eager expectation and hope that I shall not be at all ashamed, but that with full courage now as always Christ will be honored in my body, whether by life or by death. ²¹ For to me to live is Christ, and to die is gain. ²² If it is to be life in the flesh, that means fruitful labor for me. Yet which I shall choose I cannot tell. ²³ I am hard pressed between the two. My desire is to depart and be with Christ, for that is far better.

²⁴ But to remain in the flesh is more necessary on your account. ²⁵ Convinced of this, I know that I shall remain and continue with you all, for your progress and joy in the faith, ²⁶ so that in me you may have ample cause to glory in Christ Jesus, because of my coming to you again.

The Apostle's Exhortation: Do Not Let Yourselves Be Frightened (Phil 1:27–30)

²⁷ Only let your manner of life be worthy of the gospel of Christ, so that whether I come and see you or am absent, I may hear of you that you stand firm in one spirit, with one mind striving side by side for the faith of the gospel, ²⁸ and not frightened in anything by your opponents. This is a clear omen to them of their destruction, but of

? Do I let myself be intimidated when faith in God is ridiculed? Or am I a "fighter", as Paul was?

▶ Paul has to be prepared for the possibility that he will be killed on account of his faith.

▶ "In Christ": for Paul that is the place where he wants to live and die. "In Christ" means: in the love, in the community, in the friendship that Christ freely gives. The risen Jesus is like a house in which one can live (↗ 2 Cor 5:1–4), like clothing that one puts on (Gal 3:26 ff.), like a second skin into which one can slip (↗ 1 Cor 15:48f.).

your salvation, and that from God. [29] For it has been granted to you that for the sake of Christ you should not only believe in him but also suffer for his sake, [30] engaged in the same conflict which you saw and now hear to be mine.

Stick together! (Phil 2:1–4)

2 [1] So if there is any encouragement in Christ, any incentive of love, any participation in the Spirit, any affection and sympathy, [2] complete my joy by being of the same mind, having the same love, being in full accord and of one mind. [3] Do nothing from selfishness or conceit, but in humility count others better than yourselves. [4] Let each of you look not only to his own interests, but also to the interests of others.

The hymn of faith in Jesus Christ (Phil 2:5–11)

[5] Have this mind among yourselves, which was in Christ Jesus, [6] who, though he was in the form of God, did not count equality with God a thing to be grasped, [7] but emptied himself, taking the form of a servant, being born in the likeness of men. [8] And being found in human form he humbled himself and became obedient unto death, even death on a cross.

[9] Therefore God has highly exalted him and bestowed on him the name which is above every name, [10] that at the name of Jesus every knee should bow, in heaven and on earth and under the earth, [11] and every tongue confess that Jesus Christ is Lord, to the glory of God the Father.

Rely on God (Phil 2:12–18)

[12] Therefore, my beloved, as you have always obeyed, so now, not only as in my presence but much more in my absence, work out your own salvation with fear and trembling; [13] for God is at work in you, both to will and to work for his good pleasure. [14] Do all things without grumbling or questioning, [15] that you may be blameless and innocent, children of God without blemish in the midst of a crooked and perverse generation, among whom you shine as lights in the world, [16] holding fast the word of life, so that in the day of Christ I may be proud that I did not run in vain or labor in vain. [17] Even if I am to be poured as a libation upon the sacrificial offering of your faith, I am glad and rejoice with you all. [18] Likewise you also should be glad and rejoice with me.

I know that it is true that nothing great is done without suffering, without humiliation, and that all things are possible by means of it.

JOHN HENRY NEWMAN

" You all know how deeply the community of faith has been wounded recently through the attacks of the evil one, through the penetration of sin itself into the interior, yes, into the heart of the Church. Do not make that an excuse to flee from the face of God! You yourselves are the Body of Christ, the Church! Bring the undiminished fire of your love into this Church whose countenance has so often been disfigured by man.

POPE BENEDICT XVI, in the Foreword to YOUCAT

▶ The great hymn of faith traces the whole way of Jesus: from heaven to earth and back again. He was God, but he gave everything away. He shared the life of men; he suffered death on the Cross. But God the Father did not leave him in the tomb. He exalted him above all people and all things. Everyone should and will call him Lord. Then God's glory and man's salvation are perfected. The hymn is sung to this day in the liturgy. It ends with a fundamental profession of the faith: "Jesus Christ is Lord" (↗ 1 Cor 12:3).

If you want to have eternal joy, cling to the one who is eternal.

AUGUSTINE

Paul cares about his people: Timothy (Phil 2:19–24)

[19] I hope in the Lord Jesus to send Timothy to you soon, so that I may be cheered by news of you. [20] I have no one like him, who will be genuinely anxious for your welfare. [21] They all look after their own interests, not those of Jesus Christ. [22] But Timothy's worth you know, how as a son with a father he has served with me in the gospel. [23] I hope therefore to send him just as soon as I see how it will go with me; [24] and I trust in the Lord that shortly I myself shall come also.

Epaphroditus, the messenger from Philippi (Phil 2:25–30)

[25] I have thought it necessary to send to you Epaphrodi'tus my brother and fellow worker and fellow soldier, and your messenger and minister to my need, [26] for he has been longing for you all, and has been distressed because you heard that he was ill. [27] Indeed he was ill, near to death. But God had mercy on him, and not only on him but on me also, lest I should have sorrow upon sorrow. [28] I am the more eager to send him, therefore, that you may rejoice at seeing him again, and that I may be less anxious. [29] So receive him in the Lord with all joy; and honor such men, [30] for he nearly died for the work of Christ, risking his life to complete your service to me.

I would like to proclaim the Gospel on all five continents at the same time, to the most remote islands. ... I would like to be a missionary, not just for a few years: I would like to have been one from the beginning of the world and remain one until the end of time.

THÉRÈSE OF LISIEUX spent her whole adult life in the cloister. In 1927 she was named "Patroness of the Missions".

The era of Jesus, the era of the Church, is the missionary era. Our faith is in touch with Jesus only if we understand and live it as missionaries, only if we truly desire that all flesh shall see the salvation of God.

CARDINAL JOSEPH RATZINGER
Co-Workers of the Truth (1992)

Rejoice! (Phil 3:1)

3 [1] Finally, my brethren, rejoice in the Lord. To write the same things to you is not irksome to me, and is safe for you.

Paul criticizes his opponents (Phil 3:2–4)

[2] Look out for the dogs, look out for the evil-workers, look out for those who mutilate the flesh.

[3] For we are the true circumcision, who worship God in spirit,and glory in Christ Jesus, and put no confidence in the flesh. [4] Though I myself have reason for confidence in the flesh also. If any other man thinks he has reason for confidence in the flesh, I have more.

Paul describes his journey to faith (Phil 3:5–11)

[5] [I was] circumcised on the eighth day, of the people of Israel, of the tribe of Benjamin, a Hebrew born of Hebrews; as to the law a Pharisee, [6] as to zeal a persecutor of the Church, as to righteousness under the law blameless. [7] But whatever gain I had, I counted as loss for the sake of Christ. [8] Indeed I count everything as loss because of the surpassing worth of knowing Christ Jesus my Lord. For his sake I have suffered the loss of all things, and count them as refuse, in order that I may gain Christ [9] and be found in him, not having a righteousness of my own, based on law, but that which is through faith

Give me ten unselfish people, and that is enough for me; with them I can convert the whole world.

PHILIP NERI (1515–1595), Italian saint who started a new movement of faith, especially in Rome

Paul can be polemical, too. He does show in Rom 4:11 that he has great respect for circumcision ("seal of righteousness"), but here he takes to task those who focus on externals instead of conversion of the heart.

Paul grew up as a Jew. Everything changed for him through his encounter with Jesus Christ (↗ Gal 1:13–16). He recognized him.

I will never forget how I gave my life to Jesus. I was reading the story of Pentecost in the Bible, and it became clear to me that the same Holy Spirit who gave the apostles strength to do great things also wanted me to do great things in my life. Then I knew that it would be the greatest adventure simply to give my life to Jesus.

KARA

Paul is athletic. He compares himself with a marathon runner. The course is long. You need good training. But the goal is rewarding. Therefore Paul is motivated.

in Christ, the righteousness from God that depends on faith; [10] that I may know him and the power of his resurrection, and may share his sufferings, becoming like him in his death, [11] that if possible I may attain the resurrection from the dead.

Paul is still journeying (Phil 3:12-14)

[12] Not that I have already obtained this or am already perfect; but I press on to make it my own, because Christ Jesus has made me his own. [13] Brethren, I do not consider that I have made it my own; but one thing I do, forgetting what lies behind and straining forward to what lies ahead, [14] I press on toward the goal for the prize of the upward call of God in Christ Jesus.

The Philippians should come along (Phil 3:15–21)

[15] Let those of us who are mature be thus minded; and if in anything you are otherwise minded, God will reveal that also to you. [16] Only let us hold true to what we have attained.

[17] Brethren, join in imitating me, and mark those who so walk as you have an example in us. [18] For many, of whom I have often told you and now tell you even with tears, walk as enemies of the cross

of Christ. [19] Their end is destruction, their god is the belly, and they glory in their shame, with minds set on earthly things. [20] But our commonwealth is in heaven, and from it we await a Savior, the Lord Jesus Christ, [21] who will change our lowly body to be like his glorious body, by the power which enables him even to subject all things to himself.

A graffito from a sports arena in ancient Rome shows a crucified man with a donkey's head. The caricature is captioned: "Alexamenos worships his god", and thus mocks a Christian who reverences as God a criminal who was executed on the Cross.

Ɏ → 342
Are we all supposed to become "saints"?

The Philippians have to stick together (Phil 4:1–3)

4 [1] Therefore, my brethren, whom I love and long for, my joy and crown, stand firm in this way in the Lord, my beloved.

[2] I entreat Eu-o'dia and I entreat Syn'tyche to agree in the Lord. [3] And I also ask you, who are a true co-worker, help these women, for they have labored side by side with me in the gospel together with Clement and the rest of my fellow workers, whose names are in the book of life.

Once again: There is reason for joy (Phil 4:4–9)

[4] Rejoice in the Lord always; again I will say, Rejoice. [5] Let all men know your forbearance. The Lord is at hand. [6] Have no anxiety about anything, but in everything by prayer and supplication with thanksgiving let your requests be made known to God. [7] And the peace of God, which passes all understanding, will keep your hearts and your minds in Christ Jesus.

⁸ Finally, brethren, whatever is true, whatever is honorable, whatever is just, whatever is pure, whatever is lovely, whatever is gracious, if there is any excellence, if there is anything worthy of praise, think about these things. ⁹ What you have learned and received and heard and seen in me, do; and the God of peace will be with you.

Acknowledgment of the Philippians' Gifts (Phil 4:10–20)

¹⁰ I rejoice in the Lord greatly that now at length you have revived your concern for me; you were indeed concerned for me, but you had no opportunity. ¹¹ Not that I complain of want; for I have learned, in whatever state I am, to be content. ¹² I know how to be abased, and I know how to abound; in any and all circumstances I have learned the secret of facing plenty and hunger, abundance and want. ¹³ I can do all things in him who strengthens me.

¹⁴ Yet it was kind of you to share my trouble. ¹⁵ And you Philippians yourselves know that in the beginning of the gospel, when I left Macedonia, no church entered into partnership with me in giving and receiving except you only; ¹⁶ for even in Thessaloni'ca you sent me help once and again. ¹⁷ Not that I seek the gift; but I seek the fruit which increases to your credit. ¹⁸ I have received full payment,

> " The joy of the Gospel fills the hearts and lives of all who encounter Jesus. Those who accept his offer of salvation are set free from sin, sorrow, inner emptiness and loneliness. With Christ joy is constantly born anew. ... There are Christians whose lives seem like Lent without Easter. I realize of course that joy is not expressed the same way at all times in life.
>
> **POPE FRANCIS,** *Evangelii Gaudium,* 1.6

▶ The Philippians have organized a campaign to show solidarity with their imprisoned apostle.

and more; I am filled, having received from Epaphrodi'tus the gifts you sent, a fragrant offering, a sacrifice acceptable and pleasing to God. ¹⁹ And my God will supply every need of yours according to his riches in glory in Christ Jesus. ²⁰ To our God and Father be glory for ever and ever. Amen.

Final Greetings and Benediction (Phil 4:21–23)

²¹ Greet every saint in Christ Jesus. The brethren who are with me greet you. ²² All the saints greet you, especially those of Caesar's household.

²³ The grace of the Lord Jesus Christ be with your spirit.

> I don't think there is anyone who needs God's help and grace as much as I do. Sometimes I feel so helpless and weak. I think that is why God uses me. Because I cannot depend on my own strength, I rely on him 24 hours a day. My secret is simple: I pray. I love to pray. The urge to pray is always in me. Prayer enlarges the heart until it is ready to receive God's gift of himself. We so much want to pray correctly, but then we fail. If you want to pray better, pray more. If we want to be able to love, we must pray.
>
> **MOTHER TERESA**

▶ Caesar's household is the palace or a government building. Some of the employees had become Christian.

THE LETTER TO THE COLOSSIANS

The Letter to the Colossians criticizes an esoteric "philosophy" that gives the impression that faith in Christ has to be supplemented by special penitential practices of the Old Testament and mystical worship of the angels. Paul, on the contrary, expresses the conviction that God, through Jesus Christ, did everything, more than enough for the salvation of mankind. He encourages the community to live their faith in God in the midst of the world. The world is not a prison. It is a gift from God, which should be accepted in faith and handed on in love.

Lord Jesus Christ,
eternal Son of the eternal Father,
born of the Virgin Mary, we pray you:
reveal to us again and again
the mystery of God, so that in you,
in your divine Person,
in the warmth of your humanity,
in the love of your Heart,
we can recognize the image
of the invisible God.
Heart of Jesus, in which the whole fullness of divinity dwells!
Heart of Jesus, from whose fullness we have all received,
King and center of all hearts
for all eternity! Amen.

Prayer of **POPE JOHN PAUL II**

The Supremacy of Christ (Col 1:15–20)

1 ¹⁵ He is the image of the invisible God, the first-born of all creation;
¹⁶ for in him all things were created,
in heaven and on earth,
visible and invisible,
whether thrones or dominions or principalities or authorities—
all things were created through him and for him.
¹⁷ He is before all things,
and in him all things hold together.
¹⁸ He is the head of the body, the Church;
he is the beginning, the first-born from the dead,
that in everything he might be pre-eminent.
¹⁹ For in him all the fulness of God was pleased to dwell,
²⁰ and through him to reconcile to himself all things,
whether on earth or in heaven,
making peace by the blood of his cross.

The Colossians—once and now (Col 1:21–23)

²¹ And you, who once were estranged and hostile in mind, doing evil deeds, ²² he has now reconciled in his body of flesh by his death, in order to present you holy and blameless and irreproachable before him, ²³ provided that you continue in the faith, stable and steadfast, not shifting from the hope of the gospel which you heard, which has been preached to every creature under heaven, and of which I, Paul, became a minister.

Paul: for Christ in the Church (Col 1:24–29)

²⁴ Now I rejoice in my sufferings for your sake, and in my flesh I complete what is lacking in Christ's afflictions for the sake of his body, that is, the Church, ²⁵ of which I became a minister according to the divine office which was given to me for you, to make the word of God fully known, ²⁶ the mystery hidden for ages and generations but now made manifest to his saints. ²⁷ To them God chose to make known how great among the Gentiles are the riches of the glory of this mystery, which is Christ in you, the hope of glory. ²⁸ Him we proclaim, warning every man and teaching every man in all wisdom, that we may

" The Colossians, like all who have been reconciled and believe, should feel obliged to the Son: to his Cross, to his blood, to his *death*. … When he willed to sacrifice, he selected his own body. … He did it for the Colossians as well as for everyone else.

ADRIENNE VON SPEYR (1902–1967), Swiss mystic, Catholic convert, writer, and physician

▶ It is not that Christ did not do more than enough for the salvation of mankind through his life and death. But what he did for us must be made present again and again. This happens through the apostle's ministry. His suffering in prison confirms the meaning of his mission.

present every man mature in Christ. ²⁹ For this I toil, striving with all the energy which he mightily inspires within me.

The Church—Rooted in Christ (Col 2:1–7)

2 ¹ For I want you to know how greatly I strive for you, and for those at La-odice'a, and for all who have not seen my face, ² that their hearts may be encouraged as they are knit together in love, to have all the riches of assured understanding and the knowledge of God's mystery, of Christ, ³ in whom are hidden all the treasures of wisdom and knowledge.

⁴ I say this in order that no one may delude you with beguiling speech. ⁵ For though I am absent in body, yet I am with you in spirit, rejoicing to see your good order and the firmness of your faith in Christ.

⁶ As therefore you received Christ Jesus the Lord, so live in him, ⁷ rooted and built up in him and established in the faith, just as you were taught, abounding in thanksgiving.

" My suffering can further the salvation of others as well as my own. Suffering in the present helps in the application of the graces won for us by Christ on the Cross. By offering up my suffering in union with Christ's, I raise my suffering to a new level of significance. Suffering becomes holy.

DAVID CURRIE, Catholic convert from Evangelicalism, author, and lecturer

▶ Laodicea is a nearby city in Colossae.

▶ Rooted in Christ: Jesus is like the soil from which a plant draws water and nutrients. So it can and should be with the faithful in the Church.

THE FIRST LETTER TO THE THESSALONIANS

Next come two Letters to the Thessalonians. Both letters deal intensively with questions about the future: How much time does mankind have? How can the time be used to the best advantage?

The First Letter to the Thessalonians, which many scholars consider the oldest writing in the New Testament, is an expression of joy that the community, which is being persecuted fiercely, is withstanding the pressure and has developed well. In this letter, Paul emphasizes the great triad of Christian life: faith—love—hope (1 Thess 1:3; 5:8). Faith stands at the beginning, for first God's Word must be proclaimed and accepted. Then comes love, because being a Christian happens in the middle of life. Lastly there is hope: If God is coming, then that makes everything else better.

99 The great misfortune of this world, the great misery of this age, is not that there are godless people but, rather, that we are such mediocre Christians.

GEORGES BERNANOS

Being Christian is a lighthouse project. The people of Jesus should be "light of the world" (Mt 5:14). No secret back-room strategies! Nothing that needs to avoid the light of the world! Transparency, please!

Man needs three things for salvation: to know what he should believe, to know what he should desire, and to know what he should do.

THOMAS AQUINAS

Faith is enlightenment (1 Thess 5:1–10)

5 ¹ But as to the times and the seasons, brethren, you have no need to have anything written to you. ² For you yourselves know well that the day of the Lord will come like a thief in the night. ³ When people say, "There is peace and security," then sudden destruction will come upon them as labor pains come upon a woman with child, and there will be no escape. ⁴ But you are not in darkness, brethren, for that day to surprise you like a thief. ⁵ For you are all sons of light and sons of the day; we are not of the night or of darkness. ⁶ So then let us not sleep, as others do, but let us keep awake and be sober.

⁷ For those who sleep sleep at night, and those who get drunk are drunk at night.

⁸ But, since we belong to the day, let us be sober, and put on the breastplate of faith and love, and for a helmet the hope of salvation.

⁹ For God has not destined us for wrath, but to obtain salvation through our Lord Jesus Christ, ¹⁰ who died for us so that whether we wake or sleep we might live with him.

THE SECOND LETTER
TO THE THESSALONIANS

The Second Letter to the Thessalonians deals with the problem that the Second Coming of Jesus Christ, which many believers expected in the immediate future, has not yet occurred.

The standing of Christians (2 Thess 2:13–15)

2 ¹³ But we are bound to give thanks to God always for you, brethren beloved by the Lord, because God chose you from the beginning to be saved through sanctification by the Spirit and belief in the truth. ¹⁴ To this he called you through our gospel, so that you may obtain the glory of our Lord Jesus Christ. ¹⁵ So then, brethren, stand firm and hold to the traditions which you were taught by us, either by word of mouth or by letter.

The apostle prays for the community (2 Thess 2:16–17)

¹⁶ Now may our Lord Jesus Christ himself, and God our Father, who loved us and gave us eternal comfort and good hope through grace, ¹⁷ comfort your hearts and establish them in every good work and word.

The community prays for the apostle (2 Thess 3:1–5)

3 ¹ Finally, brethren, pray for us, that the word of the Lord may speed on and triumph, as it did among you, ² and that we may be delivered from wicked and evil men; for not all have faith. ³ But the Lord is faithful; he will strengthen you and guard you from evil. ⁴ And we have confidence in the Lord about you, that you are doing and will do the things which we command. ⁵ May the Lord direct your hearts to the love of God and to the steadfastness of Christ.

Warning against Idleness (2 Thess 3:9–12)

⁹ It was not because we have not that right, but to give you in our conduct an example to imitate. ¹⁰ For even when we were with you, we gave you this command: If any one will not work, let him not eat. ¹¹ For we hear that some of you are walking in idleness, mere busybodies, not doing any work. ¹² Now such persons we command and exhort in the Lord Jesus Christ to do their work in quietness and to earn their own living.

▶ You are allowed to pray for yourself—especially if you are being persecuted on account of the faith. According to the Sermon on the Mount, however, you should also pray for your persecutors (↗ Mt 5:43–48).

 Do you love me?
Jn 21:15

Three times Jesus asks Peter this question. Peter, the man who denied Jesus three times. He asks me the same question.

▶ Paul was a laborer. Not all people have a job. But those who work must not be ashamed of their work and should be appreciated.

THE FIRST LETTER TO TIMOTHY

Next in the New Testament there are three "Pastoral Letters" to Timothy and Titus. They focus on the major task of equipping the Church with the ministry of the bishop, the elders (presbyters), and the deacons for the time after the death of the apostle.

The First Letter to Timothy is addressed to the apostle Paul's prize pupil. Timothy is still young. Yet he already has a very important duty in the Church. He must take care that "sound" teaching keeps the faith from becoming sick. Paul wants to strengthen his backbone. Timothy should take him as a model. He must be trustworthy. That is why he must know what he believes and live what he teaches.

▶ This refers to esoteric myths (v. 7) that falsify the core of the Gospel.

Y → 356
Is esotericism, as found, for example, in New Age beliefs, compatible with the Christian faith?

▶ The faithful are those who already know that God's plan is for all mankind.

99 You yourselves are the Body of Christ, the Church! Bring the undiminished fire of your love into this Church whose countenance has so often been disfigured by man. "Never flag in zeal, be aglow with the Spirit, serve the Lord!" (Rom 12:11).

Appeal by **POPE BENEDICT XVI** to young people in his Foreword to YOUCAT

Faith is athletic (1 Tim 4:6–11)

4 ⁶ If you put these instructions before the brethren, you will be a good minister of Christ Jesus, nourished on the words of the faith and of the good doctrine which you have followed. ⁷ Have nothing to do with godless and silly myths. Train yourself in godliness; ⁸ for while bodily training is of some value, godliness is of value in every way, as it holds promise for the present life and also for the life to come.
⁹ The saying is sure and worthy of full acceptance.
¹⁰ For to this end we toil and strive,because we have our hope set on the living God, who is the Savior of all men, especially of those who believe.
¹¹ Command and teach these things.

The Church is young (1 Tim 4:12–14)

¹² Let no one despise your youth, but set the believers an example in speech and conduct, in love, in faith, in purity. ¹³ Till I come, attend to the public reading of Scripture, to preaching, to teaching. ¹⁴ Do not neglect the gift you have, which was given you by prophetic utterance when the elders laid their hands upon you.

THE SECOND LETTER TO TIMOTHY

The Second Letter to Timothy has the tone of a farewell. Paul senses that he will die. He instructs Timothy to work for the continued life and growth of the Church. Paul will die, but Jesus Christ lives, and the apostle's teaching remains relevant.

Set a clear course (2 Tim 3:10–13)

3 ¹⁰ Now you have observed my teaching, my conduct, my aim in life, my faith, my patience, my love, my steadfastness, ¹¹ my persecutions, my sufferings, what befell me at Antioch, at Ico'nium, and at Lystra, what persecutions I endured; yet from them all the Lord rescued me. ¹² Indeed all who desire to live a godly life in Christ Jesus will be persecuted, ¹³ while evil men and impostors will go on from bad to worse, deceivers and deceived.

Knowing where we come from (2 Tim 3:14–17)

¹⁴ But as for you, continue in what you have

▶ Apostolic succession is a distinctive characteristic of the Church. Here is the core of it: Doctrine is not newly invented but, rather, grows out of tradition; and those who teach authoritatively (the bishops) are united with one another and with their predecessors in a close union established by the Holy Spirit.

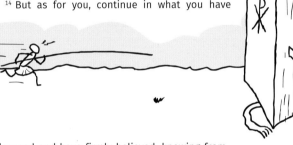

learned and have firmly believed, knowing from whom you learned it ¹⁵ and how from childhood you have been acquainted with the Sacred Writings which are able to instruct you for salvation through faith in Christ Jesus.

¹⁶ All Scripture is inspired by God and profitable for teaching, for reproof, for correction, and for training in righteousness, ¹⁷ that the man of God may be complete, equipped for every good work.

▶ This is an important statement about the Bible as Sacred Scripture. It is not a dead letter, but a living Spirit; it must be interpreted in the community of the faithful. Preaching must be binding and comprehensible. That is the Alpha and Omega for the Church.

Advance courageously (2 Tim 4:1–4)

¹ I charge you in the presence of God and of Christ Jesus who is to judge the living and the dead, and by his appearing and his kingdom: ² preach the word, be urgent in season and out of season, convince, rebuke, and exhort, be unfailing in patience and in teaching.

³ For the time is coming when people will not endure sound teaching, but having itching ears they will accumulate for themselves teachers to suit their own likings, ⁴ and will turn away from listening to the truth and wander into myths.

❝❞ May the world of our time … receive the good news not from evangelizers who are dejected, discouraged, impatient or anxious, but from ministers of the Gospel whose lives glow with fervor, who have first received the joy of Christ.
POPE FRANCIS,
Evangelii Gaudium, 10

THE LETTER TO TITUS

The Letter to Titus, addressed to another promising pupil of the apostle, encourages him to proclaim a faith that is not sick but sound, because it relies on God.

 Grace "trains" a Christian. For it is not something foreign to believers but, rather, makes them new men and new women, who learn what God plans for them.

He who made you also knows what he wants to do with you.

AUGUSTINE

As though transformed (Tit 2:11–15)

2 ¹¹ For the grace of God has appeared for the salvation of all men, ¹² training us to renounce irreligion and worldly passions, and to live sober, upright, and godly lives in this world, ¹³ awaiting our blessed hope, the appearing of the glory of our great God and Savior Jesus Christ.

As hoped for (Tit 2:14–15)

¹⁴ who gave himself for us to redeem us from all iniquity and to purify for himself a people of his own who are zealous for good deeds.

But when the time had fully come, God sent forth his Son, born of woman, born under the law, to redeem those who were under the law, so that we might receive adoption as sons.

Gal 4:4–5

The Catholic lives with two lives simultaneously, a natural life and a supernatural "life". As birth has brought him into a natural order, so baptism has brought him into a supernatural order of existence.

MSGR. RONALD KNOX

 Ignorance of Scripture is ignorance of Christ.

JEROME (347–419)

¹⁵ Declare these things; exhort and reprove with all authority. Let no one disregard you.

After a short transition, the Letter recounts the Nativity Gospel in its own words.

Maintain Good Deeds (Tit 3:4–8)

3 ⁴ but when the goodness and loving kindness of God our Savior appeared, ⁵ he saved us, not because of deeds done by us in righteousness, but in virtue of his own mercy, by the washing of regeneration and renewal in the Holy Spirit, ⁶ which he poured out upon us richly through Jesus Christ our Savior, ⁷ so that we might be justified by his grace and become heirs in hope of eternal life. ⁸ The saying is sure

⁸ The saying is sure. I desire you to insist on these things, so that those who have believed in God may be careful to apply themselves to good deeds; these are excellent and profitable to men.

THE LETTER TO PHILEMON

At the end of Paul's Letters is a short message to Philemon, in which Paul appeals for the emancipation of a slave who turned to him for help. Probably Paul wrote this letter during one of his stays in prison: he had been arrested on account of the faith.

Heartfelt thanks (Philem 4–7)

[4] I thank my God always when I remember you in my prayers, [5]because I hear of your love and of the faith which you have toward the Lord Jesus and all the saints, [6] and I pray that the sharing of your faith may promote the knowledge of all the good that is ours in Christ. [7] For I have derived much joy and comfort from your love, my brother, because the hearts of the saints have been refreshed through you.

▶ Philemon is an exemplary Christian, devoted to works of charity; now he should prove his generosity when it is a question of his own life.

A good word (Philem 9–12)

Yet for love's sake I prefer to appeal to you—I, Paul, an ambassador and now a prisoner also for Christ Jesus— [10] I appeal to you for my child, Ones'imus, whose father I have become in my imprisonment. [11] (Formerly he was useless to you, but now he is indeed useful to you and to me.) [12] I am sending him back to you, sending my very heart.

▶ Paul baptized the slave in prison.

▶ Onesimus in English is "useful". Paul wants him to be useful to the Church, no longer as a slave, but as a free collaborator.

A good idea (Philem 13–16)

[13] I would have been glad to keep him with me, in order that he might serve me on your behalf during my imprisonment for the gospel; [14] but I preferred to do nothing without your consent in order that your goodness might not be by compulsion but of your own free will.

[15] Perhaps this is why he was parted from you for a while, that you might have him back for ever, [16] no longer as a slave but more than a slave, as a beloved brother, especially to me but how much more to you, both in the flesh and in the Lord.

▶ This is revolutionary: The slave as a brother. That is precisely the idea of baptism (↗ Gal 3:28).

A good name (Philem 17–18)

[17] So if you consider me your partner, receive him as you would receive me. [18] If he has wronged you at all, or owes you anything, charge that to my account. [19] I, Paul, write this with my own hand, I will repay it—to say nothing of your owing me even your own self.

▶ Here the letter becomes like a guarantee: Paul accepts responsibility for whatever Philemon demands. But Philemon will renounce his supposed rights to Onesimus as a slave because he knows how much he owes Paul.

THE LETTER OF PAUL TO THE HEBREWS

The Letter to the Hebrews plays a special role. It follows the Letters of Paul because it is stylistically and theologically related to them. But it does not note who the sender is; it was not composed by Paul himself but by an unknown author who was likewise a great theologian. The letter resembles a written sermon about Jesus, who as High Priest reconciled mankind with God once and for all by offering his own life as a sacrifice. Being a priest means being a mediator between God and men. Jesus is God's Word among men, and he is the "pioneer and perfecter of our faith" (Heb 12:2), who brings all who follow him out of this world to God, into the heavenly sanctuary.

▶ The high priest of Jerusalem was the head of the Temple. He was in charge of offering sacrifices. Jesus is not one of these high priests. He is "great": he comes from God himself. He does not slaughter an animal to offer sacrifice but gives his own life for mankind.

" The ministers of the Gospel must be people who can warm the hearts of the people, who walk through the dark night with them, who know how to dialogue and to descend themselves into their people's night, into the darkness, but without getting lost.

POPE FRANCIS, September 21, 2013

▶ A mediator must know both sides: God's and mankind's. In Jesus the two come together.

Able to sympathize (Heb 4:14–16)

4 ¹⁴ Since then we have a great high priest who has passed through the heavens, Jesus, the Son of God, let us hold fast our confession. ¹⁵ For we have not a high priest who is unable to sympathize with our weaknesses, but one who in every respect has been tempted as we are, yet without sinning. ¹⁶ Let us then with confidence draw near to the throne of grace, that we may receive mercy and find grace to help in time of need.

To deal gently (Heb 5:1–3)

5 ¹ For every high priest chosen from among men is appointed to act on behalf of men in relation to God, to offer gifts and sacrifices for sins. ² He can deal gently with the ignorant and wayward, since he himself is beset with weakness. ³ Because of this he is bound to offer sacrifice for his own sins as well as for those of the people.

To be called (Heb 5:4–6)

⁴ And one does not take the honor upon himself, but he is called by God, just as Aaron was.
⁵ So also Christ did not exalt himself to be made a high priest, but was appointed by him who said to him,

"You are my Son,
today I have begotten you";
⁶ as he says also in another place,
"You are a priest for ever,
according to the order of Melchiz'edek."

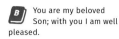

You are my beloved
Son; with you I am well
pleased.

Mk 1:11

▶ According to the Gospels,
this verse was spoken at the
baptism of Jesus in the Jordan
(↗ Mt 3:17).

To be obedient (Heb 5:7–10)

⁷ In the days of his flesh, Jesus offered up prayers and supplications, with loud cries and tears, to him who was able to save him from death, and he was heard for his godly fear.

⁸ Although he was a Son, he learned obedience through what he suffered; ⁹ and being made perfect he became the source of eternal salvation to all who obey him, ¹⁰ being designated by God a high priest according to the order of Melchiz'edek.

▶ In Gethsemane Jesus prayed
for his life—but entrusted
himself entirely to God (↗ Mt
26:36–46).

After the writer of the letter explains in detail how Christ as High Priest puts an end to worship with bloody sacrifices by offering himself as a sacrifice, i.e., voluntarily interceding with his life for the lives of all men, he comes to speak about the consequences of it for the faith. The prospects are magnificent. But the demands are great. At the conclusion of the letter, there is a glimpse of the horizon: we are destined for heaven.

The Sinai effect (Heb 12:18–21)

12 ¹⁸ For you have not come to what may be touched, a blazing fire, and darkness, and gloom, and a tempest, ¹⁹ and the sound of a trumpet, and a voice whose words made the hearers entreat that no further messages be spoken to them. ²⁰ For they could not endure the order that was given, "If even a beast touches the mountain, it shall be stoned." ²¹ Indeed, so terrifying was the sight that Moses said, "I tremble with fear."

Access to heaven on earth (Heb 12:22–24)

²² But you have come to Mount Zion and to the city of the living God, the heavenly Jerusalem, and to innumerable angels in festal gathering, ²³ and to the assembly of the first-born who are enrolled in heaven, and to a judge who is God of all, and to the spirits of just men made perfect, ²⁴ and to Jesus, the mediator of a new covenant, and to the sprinkled blood that speaks more graciously than the blood of Abel.

The peak experience
on Mount Sinai was
life-changing. How much more
intense, then, is a look into
open heaven!

Stay together (Heb 13:1–2)

13 ¹ Let brotherly love continue. ² Do not neglect to show hospitality to strangers, for thereby some have entertained angels unawares.

99 Angels don't always
inspire fear. Sometimes
they disguise themselves as
humans.

PETER KREEFT

THE

Catholic
Letters

The "Catholic" Letters are as a rule not addressed to an individual community but, rather, to larger regions. "Catholic" means: general, universal. These letters, which follow the Letters of Paul and Hebrews, are "catholic" because they intend to speak to the whole Church. They hold the faithful of very different languages and nations together. They show how deeply united they are with Christ and how unified they are with one another because of this.

The names of the authors—James, Peter, John, and Jude—are familiar from the story of Jesus and the original Christian community. The first three are the apostles who, according to the Letter to the Galatians, recognized Paul at the Council of the Apostles as a colleague having equal authority in the college of the apostles; Paul calls them the "pillars" of the Church (Gal 2:9). There is also Jude, a brother of James.

The "Catholic Letters" are still highly relevant today. They say that there is only one Church because there is only one God. All Christians throughout the world are baptized; they all bear the name of the one "Christ", Jesus of Nazareth. they are called to live out this faith. The Catholic Letters, like the Letters of Paul, give them a handy compass: They themselves must walk, but they find their orientation if they bring with them the momentum of the beginnings.

THE LETTER OF JAMES

The Letter of James is a critical warning to the first Christians. The letter is written in the style of the Old Testament prophets. It renews their critique of social injustice. The rich must stand up for the poor; otherwise, their faith is lip service.

Pay no attention to externals (Jas 2:1–5)

2 ¹ My brethren, show no partiality as you hold the faith of our Lord Jesus Christ, the Lord of glory. ² For if a man with gold rings and in fine clothing comes into your assembly, and a poor man in shabby clothing also comes in, ³ and you pay attention to the one who wears the fine clothing and say, "Have a seat here, please," while you say to the poor man, "Stand there," or, "Sit at my feet," ⁴ have you not made distinctions among yourselves, and become judges with evil thoughts?

▶ The "honorable name" (v. 7) is the Name of Christ. Those who are baptized bear this name.

❞ What do hypocrites do? They make themselves out to be good. They mask their faces like a holy picture: they pray looking up to heaven to be seen. They feel that they are more righteous than others; they look down on others. This is hypocrisy. And the Lord says no to it. No one should feel self-righteous. We all need to be justified, and the only one who justifies us is Jesus Christ.

POPE FRANCIS, March 18, 2014

💡 What is the particular temptation of the pious? Hypocrisy.

⁵ Listen, my beloved brethren. Has not God chosen those who are poor in the world to be rich in faith and heirs of the kingdom which he has promised to those who love him?

The poor are Number One (Jas 2:6–9)

⁶ But you have dishonored the poor man. Is it not the rich who oppress you, is it not they who drag you into court? ⁷ Is it not they who blaspheme that honorable name by which you are called?

⁸ If you really fulfill the royal law, according to the Scripture, "You shall love your neighbor as yourself," you do well. ⁹ But if you show partiality, you commit sin, and are convicted by the law as transgressors.

No one needs lip service (Jas 2:14–17)

¹⁴ What does it profit, my brethren, if a man says he has faith but has not works? Can his faith save him?

¹⁵ If a brother or sister is poorly clothed and in lack of daily food, ¹⁶ and one of you says to them, "Go in peace, be warmed and filled," without giving them the things needed for the body, what does it profit? ¹⁷ So faith by itself, if it has no works, is dead.

THE FIRST LETTER OF PETER

The First Letter of Peter is addressed to Christians who live as "strangers" in the "dispersion", the "Diaspora". They are a small minority, discriminated against on account of their faith. These believers, however, must not lose courage and should see even in their suffering an opportunity to discover the faith and to witness to it. They are challenged to give a public "account" of their reasons for hope (1 Pet 3:15). A Christian way of life has the greatest persuasive power: no crazy speculations, no retreat from the world, no cheap adaptation to what others are saying, but rather concentration on their own strengths. And that means: on Jesus Christ.

The address (1 Pet 1:1–2)

1 ¹ Peter, an apostle of Jesus Christ,
To the exiles of the Dispersion in Pontus, Galatia, Cappado'cia, Asia, and Bithyn'ia, ² chosen and destined by God the Father and sanctified by the Spirit for obedience to Jesus Christ and for sprinkling with his blood:
May grace and peace be multiplied to you.

▶ These regions are located in modern-day Turkey. In them Christianity spread very quickly. The Acts of the Apostles tells how it all began (Acts 13–20). The First Letter of Peter says it can continue.

First: Thank God for everything (1 Pet 1:3–12)

³ Blessed be the God and Father of our Lord Jesus Christ! By his great mercy we have been born anew to a living hope through the resurrection of Jesus Christ from the dead, ⁴ and to an inheritance which is imperishable, undefiled, and unfading, kept in heaven for you, ⁵ who by God's power are guarded through faith for a salvation ready to be revealed in the last time.

▶ New birth is an image for baptism (1 Pet 2:2).

⁶ In this you rejoice,though now for a little while you may have to suffer various trials, ⁷ so that the genuineness of your faith, more precious than gold which though perishable is tested by fire, may redound to praise and glory and honor at the revelation of Jesus Christ. ⁸ Without having seen him you love him; though you do not now see him you believe in him and rejoice with unutterable and exalted joy. ⁹ As the outcome of your faith you obtain the salvation of your souls.

▶ A trial is a test. God gives Christians an opportunity to prove themselves. And if it does not work out? Then God is still there and picks up those who fall.

▶ This refers to the Old Testament prophets.

📖 Blessed are those who have not seen and yet believe.

Jn 20:29

▶ Peter looks back at the time before his conversion. The letter looks at things in black-and-white contrasts in order to emphasize how great God's grace is.

💡 How wonderful it is to be able to believe. Someone who believes has the greatest view of the world and the best outlook on the world.

[10] The prophets who prophesied of the grace that was to be yours searched and inquired about this salvation; [11] they inquired what person or time was indicated by the Spirit of Christ within them when predicting the sufferings of Christ and the subsequent glory. [12] It was revealed to them that they were serving not themselves but you, in the things which have now been announced to you by those who preached the good news to you through the Holy Spirit sent from heaven, things into which angels long to look.

Then: Recognize your own vocation (1 Pet 1:13–17)

[13] Therefore gird up your minds, be sober, set your hope fully upon the grace that is coming to you at the revelation of Jesus Christ. [14] As obedient children, do not be conformed to the passions of your former ignorance, [15] but as he who called you is holy, be holy yourselves in all your conduct; [16] since it is written, "You shall be holy, for I am holy." [17] And if you invoke as Father him who judges each one impartially according to his deeds, conduct yourselves with fear throughout the time of your exile.

▶ Jesus is compared to a sacrificial lamb: he is innocent. But he sheds his blood, not in order to take revenge on his killers, but to redeem all mankind.

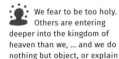 We fear to be too holy. Others are entering deeper into the kingdom of heaven than we, ... and we do nothing but object, or explain away, or criticize, or make excuses, or wonder.

BLESSED JOHN HENRY NEWMAN

99 The miraculous thing about miracles is that they do sometimes happen.

G.K. CHESTERTON

As though newborn (1 Pet 1:18–25)

[18] You know that you were ransomed from the futile ways inherited from your fathers, not with perishable things such as silver or gold, [19] but with the precious blood of Christ, like that of a lamb without blemish or spot. [20] He was destined before the foundation of the world but was made manifest at the end of the times for your sake. [21] Through him you have confidence in God, who raised him from the dead and gave him glory, so that your faith and hope are in God.

[22] Having purified your souls by your obedience to the truth for a sincere love of the brethren, love one another earnestly from the heart. [23] You have been born anew, not of perishable seed but of imperishable, through the living and abiding word of God; [24] for
"All flesh is like grass
and all its glory like the flower of grass.
The grass withers, and the flower falls,
[25] but the word of the Lord abides for ever."
That word is the good news which was preached to you.

Coming to Jesus (1 Pet 2:1–8)

2 [1] So put away all malice and all guile and insincerity and envy and all slander. [2] Like newborn infants, long for the pure spiritual

milk, that by it you may grow up to salvation; ³ for you have tasted the kindness of the Lord.

⁴ Come to him, to that living stone, rejected by men but in God's sight chosen and precious; ⁵ and like living stones be yourselves built into a spiritual house, to be a holy priesthood, to offer spiritual sacrifices acceptable to God through Jesus Christ. ⁶ For it stands in Scripture:

"Behold, I am laying in Zion a stone, a cornerstone chosen and precious,
and he who believes in him will not be put to shame."

⁷ To you therefore who believe, he is precious, but for those who do not believe,

"The very stone which the builders rejected has become the cornerstone,"

⁸ and "A stone that will make men stumble, a rock that will make them fall";

for they stumble because they disobey the word, as they were destined to do.

God gave me the gift of life. He forgives me my faults. He is always kind to me. He gives me strength and fresh courage to live. God consoles me whenever I am sad. He knows me. He looks at me with love.

STEPHANIE

▶ The cornerstone that gives support to the foundation is Jesus Christ.

▶ This means the Temple, the house of God that is built, not of stones, but of believers. The "spiritual sacrifices" are their prayers and liturgies.

Belonging to the people of God (1 Pet 2:9–10)

⁹ But you are a chosen race, a royal priesthood, a holy nation, God's own people,that you may declare the wonderful deeds of him who called you out of darkness into his marvelous light. ¹⁰ Once you were no people but now you are God's people; once you had not received mercy but now you have received mercy.

Social solidarity (1 Pet 2:11–17)

¹¹ Beloved, I beg you as aliens and exiles to abstain from the passions of the flesh that wage war against your soul. ¹² Maintain good conduct among the Gentiles, so that in case they speak against you as wrongdoers, they may see your good deeds and glorify God on the day of visitation.

¹³ Be subject for the Lord's sake to every human institution,whether it be to the emperor as supreme, ¹⁴ or to governors as sent by him to punish those who do wrong and to praise those who do right. ¹⁵ For it is God's will that by doing right you should put to silence the ignorance of foolish men. ¹⁶ Live as free men, yet without using your freedom as a pretext for evil; but live as servants of God. ¹⁷ Honor all men. Love the brotherhood. Fear God. Honor the emperor.

▶ All the people of God have a threefold dignity: they are elected, because God calls them; they are kings and priests, because God allows them to share in his power and grace; they are holy, because they belong to God.

▶ The day of visitation is the last day of the Last Judgment.

▶ Christians are a small minority who suffer from persecutions. But they know that there must be a political order that serves justice. In any case: no king and no emperor is God.

Slaves, too, belong to the Church (1 Pet 2:18–25)

[18] Servants, be submissive to your masters with all respect, not only to the kind and gentle but also to the overbearing. [19] For one is approved if, mindful of God, he endures pain while suffering unjustly. [20] For what credit is it, if when you do wrong and are beaten for it you take it patiently? But if when you do right and suffer for it you take it patiently, you have God's approval.

[21] For to this you have been called, because Christ also suffered for you, leaving you an example, that you should follow in his steps. [22] He committed no sin;
no guile was found on his lips.
[23] When he was reviled, he did not revile in return;
when he suffered, he did not threaten;
but he trusted to him who judges justly.
[24] He himself bore our sins in his body on the tree,
that we might die to sin and live to righteousness.
By his wounds you have been healed.
[25] For you were straying like sheep,
but have now returned to the Shepherd
and Guardian of your souls.

▶ Enslaved men and women had an especially hard time. They had scarcely any rights. However, they should not despair in their suffering. For Jesus, too, suffered. He died the death of a slave. The letter portrays Jesus with the features of the suffering Servant of God (Is 53), whose story is proclaimed in the reading on Good Friday.

❞ We're free only to the extent that we unburden ourselves of our own willfulness and practice the art of living according to God's plan. When we do this, when we choose to live according to God's intentions for us, then—and only then—will we be truly free.

ARCHBISHOP CHARLES CHAPUT O.F.M.

▶ Peter discusses the mutual respect Christian wives and husbands should have for one another as "joint heirs of the grace of life" (1 Pet 3:7).

❞ A Church without women is like the college of the apostles without Mary. The role of women in the Church is not simply maternity, to be mothers, but much greater: it is precisely to be the icon of →

Living as husband and wife (1 Pet 3:1–7)

3 [1] Likewise you wives, be submissive to your husbands, so that some, though they do not obey the word, may be won without a word by the behavior of their wives, [2] when they see your reverent and chaste behavior. [3] Let not yours be the outward adorning with braiding of hair, decoration of gold, and wearing of robes, [4] but let it be the hidden person of the heart with the imperishable jewel of a gentle and quiet spirit, which in God's sight is very precious. [5] So once the holy women who hoped in God used to adorn themselves and were submissive to their husbands, [6] as Sarah obeyed Abraham, calling him lord. And you are now her children if you do right and let nothing terrify you.

[7] Likewise you husbands, live considerately with your wives, bestowing honor on the woman as the weaker sex, since you are joint heirs of the grace of life, in order that your prayers may not be hindered.

Being unified (1 Pet 3:8–12)

[8] Finally, all of you, have unity of spirit, sympathy, love of the brethren, a tender heart and a humble mind. [9] Do not return evil for evil or reviling for reviling; but on the contrary bless, for to this you have been called, that you may obtain a blessing. [10] For

"He that would love life
and see good days,
let him keep his tongue from evil
and his lips from speaking guile;
¹¹ let him turn away from evil and do right;
let him seek peace and pursue it.
¹² For the eyes of the Lord are upon the righteous,
and his ears are open to their prayer.
But the face of the Lord is against those that do evil."

Give witness (1 Pet 3:13–16)

¹³ Now who is there to harm you if you are zealous for what is right? ¹⁴ But even if you do suffer for righteousness' sake, you will be blessed. Have no fear of them, nor be troubled, ¹⁵ but in your hearts reverence Christ as Lord. Always be prepared to make a defense to any one who calls you to account for the hope that is in you, yet do it with gentleness and reverence; ¹⁶ and keep your conscience clear, so that, when you are abused, those who revile your good behavior in Christ may be put to shame.

→ the Virgin, of Our Lady; the one who helps make the Church grow!

POPE FRANCIS, on the return flight from Rio de Janeiro, July 28, 2013

The LORD bless you and keep you: The LORD make his face to shine upon you, and be gracious to you: The LORD lift up his countenance upon you, and give you peace.

Num 6:24–26
(The Aaronic Blessing)

In all of Sacred Scripture, there is no stronger link to reason than 1 Pet 3:15. Believing means putting the brain in gear!

Following Jesus (1 Pet 3:17–22)

¹⁷ For it is better to suffer for doing right, if that should be God's will, than for doing wrong. ¹⁸ For Christ also died for sins once for all, the righteous for the unrighteous, that he might bring us to God, being put to death in the flesh but made alive in the spirit; ¹⁹ in which he went and preached to the spirits in prison, ²⁰ who formerly did not obey, when God's patience waited in the days of Noah, during the building of the ark, in which a few, that is, eight persons, were saved through water. ²¹ Baptism, which corresponds to this, now saves you, not as a removal of dirt from the body but as an appeal to God for a clear conscience, through the resurrection of Jesus Christ, ²² who has gone into heaven and is at the right hand of God, with angels, authorities, and powers subject to him.

You need to know your faith with that same precision with which an IT specialist knows the inner workings of a computer. You need to understand it like a good musician knows the piece he is playing. Yes, you need to be more deeply rooted in the faith than the generation of your parents so that you can engage the challenges and temptations of this time with strength and determination.

POPE BENEDICT XVI, Foreword to YOUCAT

Beginning a new life (1 Pet 4:1–6)

4 ¹ Since therefore Christ suffered in the flesh, arm yourselves with the same thought, for whoever has suffered in the flesh has ceased from sin, ² so as to live for the rest of the time in the flesh no longer by human passions but by the will of God. ³ Let the time

▶ Jesus "descended into hell", into the realm of the dead. For he conquered death in all its forms. Therefore he also brings life to those who died long before Christ.

that is past suffice for doing what the Gentiles like to do, living in licentiousness, passions, drunkenness, revels, carousing, and lawless idolatry. ⁴ They are surprised that you do not now join them in the same wild debauchery, and they abuse you; ⁵ but they will give account to him who is ready to judge the living and the dead. ⁶ For this is why the gospel was preached even to the dead, that though judged in the flesh like men, they might live in the spirit like God.

Making good use of the time (1 Pet 4:7–11)

⁷ The end of all things is at hand; therefore keep sane and sober for your prayers. ⁸ Above all hold unfailing your love for one another, since love covers a multitude of sins. ⁹ Practice hospitality ungrudgingly to one another. ¹⁰ As each has received a gift, employ it for one another, as good stewards of God's varied grace: ¹¹ whoever speaks, as one who utters oracles of God; whoever renders service, as one who renders it by the strength which God supplies; in order that in everything God may be glorified through Jesus Christ. To him belong glory and dominion for ever and ever. Amen.

> "Woulda, coulda, shoulda." Isn't it true that many people find themselves saying those words near the end of their lives as they look back and survey all the lost opportunities they let slip away to be good, loving, forgiving, compassionate, faithful, honorable, selfless, and kind? But by then, it's too late.
> **PATRICK MADRID,** (1960), American Catholic author and radio talk show host

▶ The best protection against persecution is a convincing Christian life-style. It is not a guarantee. But someone who lives out his faith in truth, love, and mercy can be persuasive.

Withstanding trials (1 Pet 4:12–19)

¹² Beloved, do not be surprised at the fiery ordeal which comes upon you to prove you, as though something strange were happening to you. ¹³ But rejoice in so far as you share Christ's sufferings, that you may also rejoice and be glad when his glory is revealed. ¹⁴ If you are reproached for the name of Christ, you are blessed, because the spirit of glory and of God rests upon you. ¹⁵ But let none of you suffer as a murderer, or a thief, or a wrongdoer, or a mischief-maker; ¹⁶ yet if one suffers as a Christian, let him not be ashamed, but under that name let him glorify God. ¹⁷ For the time has come for judgment to begin with the household of God; and if it begins with us, what will be the end of those who do not obey the gospel of God? ¹⁸ And

"If the righteous man is scarcely saved,
where will the impious and sinner appear?"

¹⁹ Therefore let those who suffer according to God's will do right and entrust their souls to a faithful Creator.

In bringing about the Redemption through suffering, Christ *has* also *raised human suffering to the level of the Redemption.* Thus each man, in his suffering, can also become a sharer in the redemptive suffering of Christ.
JOHN PAUL II, *Salvifici doloris,* 19

Tending the Flock of Christ (1 Pet 5:1–5)

5 ¹ So I exhort the elders among you, as a fellow elder and a witness of the sufferings of Christ as well as a partaker in the glory that is to be revealed. ² Tend the flock of God that is your charge,

not by constraint but willingly, not for shameful gain but eagerly, [3] not as domineering over those in your charge but being examples to the flock. [4] And when the chief Shepherd is manifested you will obtain the unfading crown of glory. [5] Likewise you that are younger be subject to the elders. Clothe yourselves, all of you, with humility toward one another, for "God opposes the proud, but gives grace to the humble."

 As long as there is still time, let us visit Christ, heal Christ, feel Christ, clothe Christ, shelter Christ, honor Christ.

GREGORY NAZIANZEN (330–390), Doctor of the Church

Trust in God (1 Pet 5:6–11)

[6] Humble yourselves therefore under the mighty hand of God, that in due time he may exalt you. [7] Cast all your anxieties on him, for he cares about you. [8] Be sober, be watchful. Your adversary the devil prowls around like a roaring lion, seeking some one to devour. [9] Resist him, firm in your faith, knowing that the same experience of suffering is required of your brotherhood throughout the world. [10] And after you have suffered a little while, the God of all grace, who has called you to his eternal glory in Christ, will himself restore, establish, and strengthen you. [11] To him be the dominion for ever and ever. Amen.

▶ The elders (presbyters; priests) are the supervisors of the Christian community.

❞ Be shepherds, with the "smell of the sheep", as shepherds among your flock, fishers of men.

POPE FRANCIS, March 28, 2013

▶ "The chief Shepherd" (v. 4) means Jesus (↗ 1 Pet 2:25).

In conclusion: best wishes (1 Pet 5:12–14)

[12] By Silva'nus, a faithful brother as I regard him, I have written briefly to you, exhorting and declaring that this is the true grace of God; stand fast in it. [13] She who is at Babylon, who is likewise chosen, sends you greetings; and so does my son Mark. [14] Greet one another with the kiss of love.

Peace to all of you that are in Christ.

❞ **Anxieties-Casting Contract** between Jesus Christ and you, according to 1 Pet 5:7, "Cast all your anxieties on him, for he cares about you."
1. I write down my anxieties and hand them over to Jesus Christ.
2. He takes them and assumes responsibility for the best possible solution.
3. An unlimited number of anxieties may be transferred.
4. Any attempt to break this contract and to take the anxieties back should be prevented by the following prayer: "I thank you, Lord, for taking my anxieties. I trust that you will help and support me. Amen."

Internet

THE SECOND LETTER OF PETER

The Second Letter of Peter grapples with the problem that earthly time is being drawn out much longer than many expected; its answer has to do with God's measure of time, which surpasses all worldly notions.

A theological meltdown (2 Pet 1:3–4)

1 [3] His divine power has granted to us all things that pertain to life and godliness, through the knowledge of him who called us to his own glory and excellence, [4] by which he has granted to us his precious and very great promises, that through these you may escape from the corruption that is in the world because of passion, and become partakers of the divine nature.

A powerful chain reaction (2 Pet 1:5–7)

[5] For this very reason make every effort to supplement your faith with virtue,

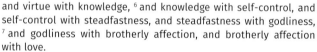

and virtue with knowledge, [6] and knowledge with self-control, and self-control with steadfastness, and steadfastness with godliness, [7] and godliness with brotherly affection, and brotherly affection with love.

A story about heaven and earth (2 Pet 1:16–18)

[16] For we did not follow cleverly devised myths when we made known to you the power and coming of our Lord Jesus Christ, but we were eyewitnesses of his majesty. [17] For when he received honor and glory from God the Father and the voice was borne to him by the Majestic Glory, "This is my beloved Son, with whom I am well pleased," [18] we heard this voice borne from heaven, for we were with him on the holy mountain.

A book of life (2 Pet 1:19–21)

[19] And we have the prophetic word made more sure. You will do well to pay attention to this as to a lamp shining in a dark place, until the day dawns and the morning star rises in your hearts. [20] First of all you must understand this, that no prophecy of Scripture is a matter of one's own interpretation, [21] because no prophecy ever came by the impulse of man, but men moved by the Holy Spirit spoke from God.

▶ For even if man fails, God still remains at his side and carries him through the crisis.

▶ This means: on earth (↗ 2 Cor 5).

B After six days Jesus took with him Peter and James and John, and led them up a high mountain apart by themselves; and he was transfigured before them, and his garments became glistening, intensely white, as no fuller on earth could bleach them.

Mk 9:2–3

THE LETTERS OF JOHN

The three Letters of John are closely related to the Gospel of John. They resemble especially the farewell discourses (Jn 14–16) that Jesus gave to his disciples in the Upper Room after washing their feet (Jn 13), and the high-priestly prayer (Jn 17). The common element is meditation on the love of God, which has shown its human face in Jesus Christ. Jesus is a man of flesh and blood; yet he is also the Son of God, the Word of God made flesh (Jn 1:14). Some tried to separate these two poles. The Letters of John keep them together. They see threats of a division in the Christian community because of different beliefs. That is why they exalt love: it comes from God, and it must profoundly shape the life of the faithful.

THE FIRST LETTER OF JOHN

Overcoming sin (1 Jn 3:5–8)

3 ⁵ You know that he appeared to take away sins, and in him there is no sin. ⁶ Any one who abides in him does not sin; any one who sins has not seen him, nor has he known him.

⁷ Little children, let no one deceive you. He who does right is righteous, as he is righteous. ⁸ He who commits sin is of the devil; for the devil has sinned from the beginning. The reason the Son of God appeared was to destroy the works of the devil.

Someone who practices mental prayer does not remain long in sin. For he will either repent or quit praying, because prayer and sin cannot exist side by side.

TERESA OF AVILA

A clear criterion: justice (1 Jn 3:9–10)

⁹ Any one born of God does not commit sin; for God's seed abides in him, and he cannot sin because he is born of God.

¹⁰ By this it may be seen who are the children of God, and who are the children of the devil: whoever does not do right is not of God, nor he who does not love his brother.

▶ God's seed is God's Word, which puts down roots and bears fruit, as in the parable of the sower (↗ Mt 13:1–9).

Loving our brothers and sisters (1 Jn 3:11–15)

¹¹ For this is the message which you have heard from the beginning, that we should love one another, ¹² and not be like Cain who was of the Evil One and murdered his brother. And why did he murder him?

▶ This fratricide (↗ Gen 4:1–16) is a sinister sign of what should not happen in the world, yet does over and over again.

▶ Love excludes no one. But it must always begin with our neighbor: The person whom I see is the one whom I should love. It starts in the Church.

Because his own deeds were evil and his brother's righteous.

¹³ Do not wonder, brethren, that the world hates you. ¹⁴ We know that we have passed out of death into life, because we love the brethren. He who does not love remains in death. ¹⁵ Any one who hates his brother is a murderer, and you know that no murderer has eternal life abiding in him.

... as Jesus did (1 Jn 3:16–18)

¹⁶ By this we know love, that he laid down his life for us; and we ought to lay down our lives for the brethren.

¹⁷ But if any one has the world's goods and sees his brother in need, yet closes his heart against him, how does God's love abide in him?

¹⁸ Little children, let us not love in word or speech but in deed and in truth.

💡 Love is precious. It costs something, but whoever invests in love can count on the best return on investment in heaven or on earth: God's friendship, deep interior peace, and the satisfaction of being on the right track.

No fear of the future (1 Pet 3:19–22)

¹⁹ By this we shall know that we are of the truth, and reassure our hearts before him ²⁰ whenever our hearts condemn us; for God is greater than our hearts, and he knows everything. ²¹ Beloved, if our hearts do not condemn us, we have confidence before God; ²² and

▶ God is the truth of our life. Someone who believes knows this.

" God's love is greater than our sins, and it can overcome our distrust of him, if we let it.

DR. TIM GRAY

we receive from him whatever we ask, because we keep his commandments and do what pleases him.

The fundamental commandment: faith and love (1 Jn 3:23–24)

²³ And this is his commandment, that we should believe in the name of his Son Jesus Christ and love one another, just as he has commanded us. ²⁴ All who keep his commandments abide in him, and he in them. And by this we know that he abides in us, by the Spirit which he has given us.

" Just as faith is a principle of understanding, so obedience must be a principle of freedom.

HENRI CARDINAL DE LUBAC

Being critical (1 Jn 4:1–3)

4 ¹ Beloved, do not believe every spirit, but test the spirits to see whether they are of God; for many false prophets have gone out into the world.

² By this you know the Spirit of God: every spirit which confesses that Jesus Christ has come in the flesh is of God,

▶ It seems so simple to separate Jesus from God. But that is when the problems really start. All our hope depends on the fact that Jesus of Nazareth is the Son of God.

³ and every spirit which does not confess Jesus is not of God. This is the spirit of antichrist, of which you heard that it was coming, and now it is in the world already.

We say what we believe (1 Jn 4:4–6)

[4] Little children, you are of God, and have overcome them; for he who is in you is greater than he who is in the world. [5] They are of the world, therefore what they say is of the world, and the world listens to them. [6] We are of God. Whoever knows God listens to us, and he who is not of God does not listen to us. By this we know the spirit of truth and the spirit of error.

We love because we are loved (1 Jn 4:7–10)

[7] Beloved, let us love one another; for love is of God, and he who loves is born of God and knows God. [8] He who does not love does not know God; for God is love. [9] In this the love of God was made manifest among us, that God sent his only-begotten Son into the world, so that we might live through him. [10] In this is love, not that we loved God but that he loved us and sent his Son to be the expiation for our sins.

▶ The "world" here is a sound-proof space that is shut off from God's Word.

 The Church's ever-increasing self-awareness and its struggle to model itself on Christ's ideal can only result in its acting and thinking quite differently from the world around it, which it is nevertheless striving to influence.

POPE PAUL VI., Encyclical *Ecclesiam suam* (1964), 56

God is genuinely courteous.

The First Letter of John is a long theological meditation on God's love, which became man in Jesus Christ. The letter is the companion piece to the Gospel of John. "God is love": the letter is able to go clearly and concisely to the heart of biblical theology (1 Jn 4:8–16).

The Mystery of Faith (1 Jn 4:11–14)

[11] Beloved, if God so loved us, we also ought to love one another. [12] No man has ever seen God; if we love one another, God abides in us and his love is perfected in us. [13] By this we know that we abide in him and he in us, because he has given us of his own Spirit. [14] And we have seen and testify that the Father has sent his Son as the Savior of the world.

Remaining in God's love (1 Jn 4:15–16)

[15] Whoever confesses that Jesus is the Son of God, God abides in him, and he in God. [16] So we know and believe the love God has for us. God is love, and he who abides in love abides in God, and God abides in him.

▶ God's love is a gift that we should share with others.

 If I believe that God is love (and I do), this includes a wonderful mission: I have the privilege of being a witness to this love—in my family, among friends, at work, even while taking out the trash. Whatever I tackle and try to do as carefully and joyfully as I can, is a lifelong mission. And a great one, too!

CHRISTOPHER

If I had recognized sooner that the tiny castle of my soul sheltered such a great King, I would not have left him alone so often.

TERESA OF AVILA

Be not afraid (1 Jn 4:17–18)

¹⁷ In this is love perfected with us, that we may have confidence for the day of judgment, because as he is so are we in this world. ¹⁸ There is no fear in love, but perfect love casts out fear. For fear has to do with punishment, and he who fears is not perfected in love.

Receiving love—giving love (1 Jn 4:19–21)

¹⁹ We love, because he first loved us. ²⁰ If any one says, "I love God," and hates his brother, he is a liar; for he who does not love his brother whom he has seen, cannot love God whom he has not seen. ²¹ And this commandment we have from him, that he who loves God should love his brother also.

Signs of love (1 Jn 5:1–5)

5 ¹ Every one who believes that Jesus is the Christ has been born of God, and every one who loves the parent loves the one begotten by him. ² By this we know that we love the children of God, when we love God and obey his commandments. ³ For this is the love of God, that we keep his commandments. And his commandments are not burdensome. ⁴ For whatever is born of God overcomes the world; and this is the victory that overcomes the world, our faith. ⁵ Who is it that overcomes the world but he who believes that Jesus is the Son of God?

THE SECOND LETTER OF JOHN

The Second Letter of John is a short message with a warning against false doctrines that do not take the Gospel of God's love seriously.

He has showed you, O man, what is good; and what does the LORD require of you but to do justice, and to love kindness, and to walk humbly with your God?

Mic 6:8

Only love matters (2 Jn 6)

⁶ And this is love, that we follow his commandments; this is the commandment, as you have heard from the beginning, that you follow love.

THE THIRD LETTER OF JOHN

The Third Letter of John sides in internal Church conflicts with the theology of the Gospel of John.

Do not be overcome by evil, but overcome evil with good.

Rom 12:21

Doing good (3 Jn 11)

¹¹ Beloved, do not imitate evil but imitate good. He who does good is of God; he who does evil has not seen God.

THE LETTER OF JUDE

The Letter of Jude reflects a harsh day of reckoning with heresies. The writer assumes that the readers of the letter know what his opponents are teaching, and therefore it is not clear today what that was. Probably it concerned fundamental questions of how to live out the faith in the world.

The letter was not written by Judas Iscariot, the betrayer of Jesus. The Jude of this letter is, rather, "the brother of James" and thus a relative of Jesus (↗ Mk 6:3; Mt 13:55).

Look out! (Jude 17–19)

[17] But you must remember, beloved, the predictions of the apostles of our Lord Jesus Christ; [18] they

said to you, "In the last time there will be scoffers, following their own ungodly passions." [19] It is these who set up divisions, worldly people, devoid of the Spirit.

Pray! (Jude 20–21)

[20] But you, beloved, build yourselves up on your most holy faith; pray in the Holy Spirit; [21] keep yourselves in the love of God; wait for the mercy of our Lord Jesus Christ unto eternal life.

Be merciful! (Jude 22–23)

[22] And convince some, who doubt; [23] save some, by snatching them out of the fire; on some have mercy with fear, hating even the garment spotted by the flesh.

Glory to God alone (Jude 24–25)

[24] Now to him who is able to keep you from falling and to present you without blemish before the presence of his glory with rejoicing, [25] to the only God, our Savior through Jesus Christ our Lord, be glory, majesty, dominion, and authority, before all time and now and for ever. Amen.

 Blessed is the man who walks not in the counsel of the wicked, nor stands in the way of sinners, nor sits in the seat of scoffers.

Ps 1:1

 The best prayer is the one that contains the most love.

CHARLES DE FOUCAULD

 Be imitators of God, as beloved children. And walk in love, as Christ loved us and gave himself up for us, a fragrant offering and sacrifice to God. But immorality and all impurity or covetousness must not even be named among you, as is fitting among saints.

Eph 5:1–3

THE REVELATION OF

John

The last book of the Bible was written by a Christian prophet. John had a vision on the island of Patmos and wrote it down. He was persecuted on account of his faith, probably during the reign of the Roman Emperor Domitian (A.D. 81–96).

The book is fascinating and equally controversial. It has often been used to calculate the date of the end of the world. That is a misuse of Scripture. In fact, John looks into the abyss of human suffering, but he also looks into the heights of heavenly glory. The two are united by Jesus Christ. He came from heaven to bring about the Kingdom of God. Thanks to him, the world does not end in a sea of violence but is transformed into the world as God intends it.

Prelude (Rev 1:1–3)

1 ¹ The revelation of Jesus Christ, which God gave him to show to his servants what must soon take place; and he made it known by sending his angel to his servant John, ² who bore witness to the word of God and to the testimony of Jesus Christ, even to all that he saw.

³ Blessed is he who reads aloud the words of the prophecy, and blessed are those who hear, and who keep what is written therein; for the time is near.

▶ God the Father reveals to Jesus, the Son of God, the great plan of how he will save the world. John is initiated into this plan. He is supposed to write down what God has shown to him, so that all can know it.

The Beginning of a Letter (Rev 1:4–8)

⁴ John to the seven churches that are in Asia:

Grace to you and peace from him who is and who was and who is to come, and from the seven spirits who are before his throne, ⁵ and from Jesus Christ the faithful witness, the first-born of the dead, and the ruler of kings on earth.

To him who loves us and has freed us from our sins by his blood ⁶ and made us a kingdom, priests to his God and Father, to him be glory and dominion for ever and ever. Amen. ⁷ Behold, he is coming with the clouds, and every eye will see him, every one who pierced him; and all tribes of the earth will wail on account of him. Even so. Amen.

▶ Asia is a region in today's western Turkey, with Ephesus as its center (↗ Rev 2–3).

B This chalice which is poured out for you is the new covenant in my blood.
Lk 22:20

▶ Alpha and omega are the first and last letters of the Greek alphabet.

The "seer" of Patmos

▶ All seven churches are located in the area surrounding Ephesus in modern-day Turkey.

⁸ "I am the Alpha and the Omega," says the Lord God, who is and who was and who is to come, the Almighty.

John is commissioned (Rev 1:9–20)

⁹ I John, your brother, who share with you in Jesus the tribulation and the kingdom and the patient endurance, was on the island called Patmos on account of the word of God and the testimony of Jesus. ¹⁰ I was in the Spirit on the Lord's day, and I heard behind me a loud voice like a trumpet ¹¹ saying, "Write what you see in a book and send it to the seven churches, to Ephesus and to Smyrna and to Per'gamum and to Thyati'ra and to Sardis and to Philadelphia and to La-odice'a."

¹² Then I turned to see the voice that was speaking to me, and on turning I saw seven golden lampstands, ¹³ and in the midst of the lampstands one like a Son of man, clothed with a long robe and with a golden sash across his chest;

¹⁴ his head and his hair were white as white wool, white as snow; his eyes were like a flame of fire, ¹⁵ his feet were like burnished bronze, refined as in a furnace, and his voice was like the sound of many waters; ¹⁶ in his right hand he held seven stars, from his mouth issued a sharp two-edged

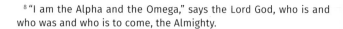

▶ The images show the Son of man as a royal high priest. He has God's full authority; he reconciles mankind with God.

sword, and his face was like the sun shining in full strength.

¹⁷ When I saw him, I fell at his feet as though dead. But he laid his right hand upon me, saying, "Fear not, I am the first and the last, ¹⁸ and the living one; I died, and behold I am alive for evermore, and I have the keys of Death and Hades.

¹⁹ Now write what you see, what is and what is to take place hereafter.

▶ Every church has a guardian angel in heaven.

²⁰ As for the mystery of the seven stars which you saw in my right hand, and the seven golden lampstands, the seven stars are the angels of the seven churches and the seven lampstands are the seven churches.

Next come the seven messages to the seven churches (Rev 2:1—3:22), which show how great a challenge it was to keep the faith in the midst of a crisis in society.

▶ Heaven opens, and John is allowed to look in. At the center is God's throne. Everything proceeds from him; everything leads to him. These are human images that the prophet sees, but they convey an impression of the heavenly glory.

THE VISION OF THE BEGINNING (REV 4:1–5:14)

The open door (Rev 4:1)

4 ¹ After this I looked, and behold, in heaven an open door! And the first voice, which I had heard speaking to me like a trumpet, said, "Come up here, and I will show you what must take place after this."

A glimpse of heaven (Rev 4:2–7)

² At once I was in the Spirit, and behold, a throne stood in heaven, with one seated on the throne! ³ And he who sat there appeared like jasper and carnelian, and round the throne was a rainbow that looked like an emerald.

⁴ Round the throne were twenty-four thrones, and seated on the thrones were twenty-four elders, clothed in white garments, with golden crowns upon their heads.

⁵ From the throne issue flashes of lightning, and voices and peals of thunder, and before the throne burn seven torches of fire, which are the seven spirits of God;

⁶ and before the throne there is as it were a sea of glass, like crystal.

And round the throne, on each side of the throne, are four living creatures, full of eyes in front and behind:

⁷ the first living creature like a lion, the second living creature like an ox, the third living creature with the face of a man, and the fourth living creature like a flying eagle.

Thrice holy (Rev 4:8–11)

⁸ And the four living creatures, each of them with six wings, are full of eyes all round and within, and day and night they never cease to sing,

"Holy, holy, holy, is the Lord God Almighty,
who was and is and is to come!"

⁹ And whenever the living creatures give glory and honor and thanks to him who is seated on the throne, who lives for ever and ever, ¹⁰ the twenty-four elders fall down before him who is seated on the throne and worship him who lives for ever and ever; they cast their crowns before the throne, singing,

¹¹ "Worthy are you, our Lord and God,
to receive glory and honor and power,
for you created all things,
and by your will they existed and were created."

The scroll with the seven seals (Rev 5:1–4)

5 ¹ And I saw in the right hand of him who was seated on the throne a scroll written within and on the back, sealed with seven seals;

² and I saw a strong angel proclaiming with a loud voice, "Who is worthy to open the scroll and break its seals?"

³ And no one in heaven or on earth or under the earth was able to open the scroll or to look into it,

⁴ and I wept much that no one was found worthy to open the scroll or to look into it.

> A man can no more diminish God's glory by refusing to worship Him than a lunatic can put out the sun by scribbling the word "darkness" on the walls of his cell
>
> **C. S. LEWIS**

▶ The twenty-four elders, the seven fiery torches, and the four living creatures are Old Testament images from the prophets Isaiah, Ezekiel, and Daniel, which are combined in a new way in the Revelation to John. Later the four living creatures became symbols of the evangelists: Mark, the lion; Luke, the ox; Matthew, the man; John, the eagle.

▶ This is the beating heart of the Revelation to John (↗ Is 6:3). The Holy God is the Creator and Redeemer; to him belong past, present, and future.

▶ In heaven, the Kingdom of God is perfect; on earth, it has yet to prevail. The future is clear: God prevails. It has been revealed to the prophet.

 The scroll with the seven seals is the screenplay of salvation history.

▶ The course of history is determined by who can open the book. No one can do it: no man and no angel. Only Jesus, depicted under the image of the Lamb that was slain.

▶ The Lion is an awesome image of hope in the Messiah.

The Lion... (Rev 5:5)

⁵ Then one of the elders said to me, "Weep not; behold, the Lion of the tribe of Judah, the Root of David, has conquered, so that he can open the scroll and its seven seals."

... as a Lamb (Rev 5:6–7)

⁶ And between the throne and the four living creatures and among the elders, I saw a Lamb standing, as though it had been slain, with seven horns and with seven eyes,which are the seven spirits of God sent out into all the earth;

⁷ and he went and took the scroll from the right hand of him who was seated on the throne.

▶ The strong Lion is a weak Lamb. For the victory over evil is won precisely in the death of Jesus, who rose from the dead. Therefore the Lamb, which still bears a mortal wound, is "standing"—just like the risen Lord, who, according to the Gospel of John, still bore the wounds of his Passion (↗ Jn 20:20, 24–29).

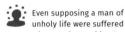 Even supposing a man of unholy life were suffered to enter heaven, he would not be happy there. None but the holy can look upon the Holy One; without holiness no man can endure to see the Lord.

JOHN HENRY NEWMAN

The new song (Rev 5:8–10)

⁸ And when he had taken the scroll, the four living creatures and the twenty-four elders fell down before the Lamb, each holding a harp, and with golden bowls full of incense, which are the prayers of the saints;

⁹ and they sang a new song, saying,
"Worthy are you to take the scroll
and to open its seals,
for you were slain
and by your blood you ransomed men for God
from every tribe and tongue and people and nation,

▶ The faithful are the people of God. Jesus is their King, their Priest, and their Prophet. They acquire a share of his power, his saving mission, and his wisdom.

¹⁰ and have made them a kingdom
and priests to our God,
and they shall reign on earth."

Heavenly Praise (Rev 5:11–14)

¹¹ Then I looked, and I heard around the throne and the living creatures and the elders the voice of many angels, numbering myriads of myriads and thousands of thousands, ¹² saying with a loud voice, "Worthy is the Lamb who was slain, to receive power and wealth and wisdom and might and honor and glory and blessing!"

¹³ And I heard every creature in heaven and on earth and under the earth and in the sea, and all therein, saying, "To him who sits upon the throne and to the Lamb be blessing and honor and glory and might for ever and ever!"

¹⁴ And the four living creatures said, "Amen!" and the elders fell down and worshiped.

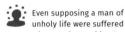 It benefits us to praise the one whom we love; if we praise him who is all-good, we ourselves become better. And since he knows that it benefits us if we love him, he makes himself lovable through his own praise, which explains to us why he is lovable. Thus he enlivens our hearts for his praise, and he fills his servants with his spirit so that they might praise him.

AUGUSTINE

The opening of the seals begins a threefold cascade of visions. They show the downfall of evil in the world. People must suffer much, even the just. But God's dominion prevails—for the salvation of all mankind.

The new heaven and the new earth (Rev 21:1–8)

21 ¹ Then I saw a new heaven and a new earth; for the first heaven and the first earth had passed away, and the sea was no more.

² And I saw the holy city, new Jerusalem, coming down out of heaven from God, prepared as a bride adorned for her husband;

³ and I heard a great voice from the throne saying, "Behold, the dwelling of God is with men. He will dwell with them, and they shall be his people, and God himself will be with them; ⁴ he will wipe away every tear from their eyes, and death shall be no more, neither shall there be mourning nor crying nor pain any more, for the former things have passed away."

⁵ And he who sat upon the throne said, "Behold, I make all things new." Also he said, "Write this, for these words are trustworthy and true."

⁶ And he said to me, "It is done! I am the Alpha and the Omega, the beginning and the end. To the thirsty I will give water without price from the fountain of the water of life. ⁷ He who conquers shall have this heritage, and I will be his God and he shall be my son. ⁸ But as for the cowardly, the faithless, the polluted, as for murderers, for-

▶ The words about the tears that will be wiped away and about death that will be no more are traditionally quoted in obituary notices and on prayer cards commemorating the deceased. When a person dies, it really is an all-or-nothing proposition. Those who believe can hope that everything will be all right at the end, even though here we must say many bitter farewells and walk through many valleys of tears.

B Every one who drinks of this water will thirst again, but whoever drinks of the water that I shall give him will never thirst.

Jesus in Jn 4:13–14

nicators, sorcerers, idolaters, and all liars, their lot shall be in the lake that burns with fire and brimstone, which is the second death."

The City of God (Rev 21:9–11)

⁹ Then came one of the seven angels who had the seven bowls full of the seven last plagues, and spoke to me, saying, "Come, I will show you the Bride, the wife of the Lamb."

¹⁰ And in the Spirit he carried me away to a great, high mountain, and showed me the holy city Jerusalem coming down out of heaven from God, ¹¹ having the glory of God, its radiance like a most rare jewel, like a jasper, clear as crystal.

The walls and gates (Rev 21:12–21)

¹² It had a great, high wall, with twelve gates, and at the gates twelve angels, and on the gates the names of the twelve tribes of the sons of Israel were inscribed; ¹³ on the east three gates, on the north three gates, on the south three gates, and on the west three gates. ¹⁴ And the wall of the city had twelve foundations, and on them the twelve names of the twelve apostles of the Lamb.

¹⁵ And he who talked to me had a measuring rod of gold to measure the city and its gates and walls.

▶ The city is symbolized as a woman. She is the personification of the people of God: Daughter Zion becomes the Bride of the Messiah. The city is the heavenly Jerusalem.

They are badly mistaken who think that union with God consists of ecstasies, delights, and spiritual consolations. It consists solely of the abandonment of our will to God, provided that this abandonment is complete.

TERESA OF AVILA

▶ The dimensions are the ideal dimensions of the heavenly city according to the vision of the prophet Ezekiel (↗ Ezek 40).

> You have a thousand wounds, from which flows your mercy, and you bless all your enemies. You bless even those who no longer know it. The world's mercy is your runaway daughter, and all human law has received a share of yours. All human wisdom has learned from you. You are the hidden writing beneath all their signs. You are the hidden stream in the depths of their waters.

GERTRUD VON LE FORT (1876–1971), "Hymns to the Church"

[16] The city lies foursquare, its length the same as its breadth; and he measured the city with his rod, twelve thousand stadia; its length and breadth and height are equal. [17] He also measured its wall, a hundred and forty-four cubits by a man's measure, that is, an angel's.

[18] The wall was built of jasper, while the city was pure gold, clear as glass.

[19] The foundations of the wall of the city were adorned with every jewel; the first was jasper, the second sapphire, the third agate, the fourth emerald, [20] the fifth onyx, the sixth carnelian, the seventh chrysolite, the eighth beryl, the ninth topaz, the tenth chrysoprase, the eleventh jacinth, the twelfth amethyst.

[21] And the twelve gates were twelve pearls, each of the gates made of a single pearl, and the street of the city was pure gold, transparent as glass.

A city without a temple, but with God (Rev 21:22–23)

[22] And I saw no temple in the city, for its temple is the Lord God the Almighty and the Lamb. [23] And the city has no need of sun or moon to shine upon it, for the glory of God is its light, and its lamp is the Lamb.

▶ The precious materials and beauty of the city reflect its heavenly splendor. Jewels in antiquity had a highly symbolic value. They reflect the harmony of the cosmos.

 The Church is the mother of the living.

AMBROSE OF MILAN

> The Church is an ever-ancient woman and yet an ever-youthful bride. She is the Mother of Christians—and she is my mother. You don't attack my mom and get away with it!

PATRICK MADRID

No one can have God as his Father unless he has the Church as his Mother.

CYPRIAN OF CARTHAGE (d. 258), bishop and martyr

Open gates for all nations (Rev 21:24–27)

[24] By its light shall the nations walk; and the kings of the earth shall bring their glory into it, [25] and its gates shall never be shut by day—and there shall be no night there;

[26] they shall bring into it the glory and the honor of the nations. [27] But nothing unclean shall enter it, nor any one who practices abomination or falsehood, but only those who are written in the Lamb's book of life.

A paradise in the city (Rev 22:1–5)

22 [1] Then he showed me the river of the water of life, bright as crystal, flowing from the throne of God and of the Lamb [2] through the middle of the street of the city; also, on either side of the river, the tree of life with its twelve kinds of fruit, yielding its fruit each month; and the leaves of the tree were for the healing of the nations.

[3] There shall no more be anything accursed, but the throne of God and of the Lamb shall be in it, and his servants shall worship him;

[4] they shall see his face, and his name shall be on their foreheads. [5] And night shall be no more; they need no light of lamp or sun, for the Lord God will be their light, and they shall reign for ever and ever.

Conclusion of the book—and of the whole Bible (Rev 22:6–21)

⁶ And he said to me, "These words are trustworthy and true. And the Lord, the God of the spirits of the prophets, has sent his angel to show his servants what must soon take place. ⁷ And behold, I am coming soon."

Blessed is he who keeps the words of the prophecy of this book.

⁸ I John am he who heard and saw these things. And when I heard and saw them, I fell down to worship at the feet of the angel who showed them to me; ⁹ but he said to me, "You must not do that! I am a fellow servant with you and your brethren the prophets, and with those who keep the words of this book. Worship God."

¹⁰ And he said to me, "Do not seal up the words of the prophecy of this book, for the time is near. ¹¹ Let the evildoer still do evil, and the filthy still be filthy, and the righteous still do right, and the holy still be holy."

¹² "Behold, I am coming soon, bringing my recompense, to repay every one for what he has done. ¹³ I am the Alpha and the Omega, the first and the last, the beginning and the end."

▶ The conclusion has the format of a dialogue. God speaks through an angel. The prophet listens and answers for the whole Church.

❞ If you were to die tonight and stand before God, and He were to ask you, "Why should I take you to Heaven?" What would you say?

PETER KREEFT

❞ When we are immersed in the perfect love of the Trinity and all others in the Kingdom of Heaven, there can be no alienation from self →

¹⁴ Blessed are those who wash their robes, that they may have the right to the tree of life and that they may enter the city by the gates. ¹⁵ Outside are the dogs and sorcerers and fornicators and murderers and idolaters, and every one who loves and practices falsehood.

¹⁶ "I Jesus have sent my angel to you with this testimony for the churches. I am the root and the offspring of David, the bright morning star."

¹⁷ The Spirit and the Bride say, "Come." And let him who hears say, "Come." And let him who is thirsty come, let him who desires take the water of life without price.

¹⁸ I warn every one who hears the words of the prophecy of this book: if any one adds to them, God will add to him the plagues described in this book, ¹⁹ and if any one takes away from the words of the book of this prophecy, God will take away his share in the tree of life and in the holy city, which are described in this book.

²⁰ He who testifies to these things says, "Surely I am coming soon." Amen. Come, Lord Jesus!

²¹ The grace of the Lord Jesus be with all the saints. Amen.

→ or others—no emptiness, no darkness, no negation, no loneliness, no pain that arises out of egocentricity, narcissism, or evil. We are in complete harmony with self and others and at peace with self and others; this perfect harmony and peace may be described as perfect home. This is our true calling, what the unconditionally loving God has prepared for us—what we were created for.

ROBERT SPITZER, S.J.

📖 I am the way, and the truth, and the life; no one comes to the Father, but by me.

Jn 14:6

Instructions for Use

 Here a Scripture passage from another book is cited that offers a deeper insight into the passage you are reading.

 The Bible is full of surprises and often full of humor, too. When you see this sign, a light will go on or there will be some fun.

 This sign stands for helpful explanations from scriptural scholarship. There are many passages in Sacred Scripture that seem obscure to today's readers. Then, too, one would often simply read past certain passages unless there were an indication of why they were so important.

 Saints interpreted the Bible by their lives. Many of them even gave their lives for the truth of the faith. What they have to say often comes from their prayer and meditation.

 Testimonies by young people show how the Word of God moved them and changed their lives.

 Millions of people have read the Bible and grappled with it. Original quotations by Christians and non-Christians bring to light the relevance and power of God's Word.

 God's Word challenges us and changes us. Where especially important questions come up, you find them under this sign.

 When you see this sign, you can look up the topic in YOUCAT, the Youth Catechism of the Catholic Church. There you will find in question-and-answer format the basics that a Catholic Christian must know. The Church's knowledge of the faith is drawn from the original document of faith, Sacred Scripture. Readers who want very precise information can look it up in the Cathechism of the Catholic Church, the great reference work of Church teaching.

Index of Names

Index of Subjects

Я задаволены!*

(`ỏ`

Scripture Index

This Bible cites some important Scripture passages as cross-references; they are found on the following pages:

Maps and Diagrams

Citations from Contemporary German Literature

Martin Buber, *Die Erzählungen der Chassidim* (Zürich: Manesse Verlage, 1949; Munich: Random House, 2014), 166; Jörg Sieger (www.joerg-sieger.de), 38; Silja Walter, *Gesamtausgabe*, vol. 2 (Freiburg/Switzerland: Paulusverlag, 2000), 407.

Photographs

Basical Augsburg 250/251; Bernadette Baumgartner 199; Christa Berger 269; Fouda Bienvenu 247; Martine Boutros 10/11; Cécile Brûlon 164; Laura Carlos 217; Jürgen Erhard 303; Francisco Eugenio 226; www.fahrbuch.de 130; Wolfgang Fässler 332, 345; Michaela Gassner 264; Maddy Giesbrecht 359; Dominique Haas 12/13, 16/17, 34, 54, 74, 78/79, 80, 90, 118, 128, 142, 286, 362, 382, 387; Julia Hiemetzberger 215; Annelies Kammerer 137; Katharina Kiechle 132; Christoph Kraus 397; Stephanie Kriz 389; Michael Langer 61, 368, 374; Jeronimo Lauricio 182; Emilie Leclerc 259; Ruth Leitner 300; Alexander von Lengerke 140/141, 161, 178, 252, 273, 354; Christian Lesch 259; Nicola Majnaric 30; Zoran Marincic 83; Angelika Mayer 313; Tobias Mayer 94; Wolfgang Moroder 186; Gertrud Nemeth 268; Sandra Pantenburg 295; pfarre-mittergrabern.at 289; Claudio Peri © dpa 265; © Rheinisches Bildarchiv Köln, rba_c024166 329; Michaela Ruhnke 43; Nadia Savitri Meinar 200, 384; Raphael Schadt 162; Michael Scharf 218, 234; Joachim Schäfer, Ökumenisches Heiligenlexikon 177; Max Schmid 18, 326, 350/351, 380, 381; Marie und Cornelius von Schönau 360; Georg und Christina Schreyer 72, 262; Nils Schubert 395; Luc Serafin 50, 62, 89, 104, 122, 136, 152, 155, 163, 168, 172, 175, 176, 180, 184, 188/189, 190, 195, 198, 199, 202, 204, 206, 220, 228, 237, 242, 302, 308, 319, 323, 352, 364, 366, 367, 375, 376, 377, 378, 379, 383, 386, 389, 392, 394, 399, 400; Clara Steber 173, 210, 223, 280, 299, 330, 338, 358, 372; Raphael Steber 150, 320; Martin Stiglmayr 49; Nico Sucker 261, 272; Roswitha Völker 65; Peter Paul van Voorst 69; Dimitry Vrubel 279; Thorsten Wulff, mit freundlicher Unterstützung von Johannes Kneifel und dem Verlag Wunderlich 332

Public Domain Sources:
Korea.net, CC BY-SA 2.0, https://commons.wikimedia.org/wiki/File%3APope_Francis_Korea_Haemi_Castle_19_(cropped).jpg 6; Novica Nakov, CC BY-SA 2.0, http://commons.
wikimedia.org/wiki/Category:Icons_of_Michael?uselang=de#mediaviewer/File:Icon_14.
jpg 233; Alex Proimos, CC BY 2.0, https://commons.wikimedia.org/wiki/File%3ALending_
an_Ear_(7085965167).jpg 47; Bracha L. Ettinger, CC BY-SA 2.5, https://commons.
wikimedia.org/wiki/File%3AEmmanuel_Levinas.jpg 134; Falk2, Wikimedia Commons,
lizensiert unter: CC BY-SA 3.0, http://commons.wikimedia.org/wiki/File%3AX1.27_
Kloster_Rus%C3%A1nu.jpg 264; Zvi Harduf via the PikiWiki – Israel free image collection
project, CC BY 2.5, http://commons.wikimedia.org/wiki/File%3APikiWiki_Israel_14320_
Wildlife_and_Plants_of_Israel.JPG 227; Daniel Ortmann, CC BY-SA 2.5, https://commons.
wikimedia.org/wiki/File%3ACistern_getting_water.jpg 132; Joop van Bilsen / Anefo,
CC-BY-SA 3.0, https://commons.wikimedia.org/wiki/File%3AMartin_Buber_1963c.jpg 166;
Bundesarchiv, Bild 146-1987-074-16, CC-BY-SA 3.0, https://commons.wikimedia.org/
wiki/File%3ABundesarchiv_Bild_146-1987-074-16%2C_Dietrich_Bonhoeffer.jpg 159;
Jakob Lazarus, CC BY-SA 3.0, http://commons.wikimedia.org/wiki/File:Holy_Paraclete_
Dove.jpg 358; Bundesarchiv, B 145 Bild-F059404-0019 / Schaack, Lothar / CC-BY-SA 3.0,
https://commons.wikimedia.org/wiki/File%3ABundesarchiv_B_145_Bild-F059404-
0019%2C_Bundespr%C3%A4sident_empf%C3%A4ngt_Papst_Johannes_Paul_II..jpg 225;
Dirk D., CC BY-SA 3.0, https://commons.wikimedia.org/wiki/File%3ABethlehem_-_Stern_
von_Bethlehem_in_der_Geburtsgrotte.jpg 292; Lilly M, CC BY-SA 3.0, https://commons.
wikimedia.org/wiki/File%3AEquus_asinus_Kadzid%C5%82owo_002.jpg 273; Museo de
Almeria, CC BY-SA 3.0, https://commons.wikimedia.org/wiki/File%3ABuen_PastorMuseo.
jpg 304; Andreas Praefcke, CC BY 3.0; https://commons.wikimedia.org/wiki/File%3AMer-
azhofen_Pfarrkirche_Hochaltar_Relief_Kanaan-Kundschafter.jpg 59; Presidência da
Republica/Roberto Stuckert Filho (Agência Brasil), CC BY 3.0, http://commons.wikimedia.
org/wiki/File%3AFrancisco_(20-03-2013).jpg 101; Sailko, CC BY-SA 3.0, https://commons.
wikimedia.org/wiki/File%3AJacopo_filippo_argenta_e_martino_da_modena%2C_grad-
uale_XIII%2C_1480-1500_ca%2C_13%2C2_geremia.jpg 209; Abraham Sobkowski OFM,
CC-BY-SA-3.0, http://commons.wikimedia.org/wiki/Jerusalem?uselang=de#mediaviewer/
File:Zion_Gate.JPG 117; Volodymyr D-k, CC BY-SA 3.0, http://commons.wikimedia.org/
wiki/File%3AFalling_of_Lenin_in_Khmelnytskyi_park.jpg 65; Manfred Werner – Tsui, CC
BY-SA 3.0, https://commons.wikimedia.org/wiki/ File%3AEM-Qualifikationss-
piel_%C3%96sterreich-Russland_2014-11-15_003_David_Alaba.jpg 361; http://images.
google.de/imgres?imgurl=http%3A%2F%2Fuploads0.wikiart.org%2Fimages%2Fgus-
tave-dore%2Fthe-new-jerusalem.jpg&imgrefurl=http%3A%2F%2Fwww.wikiart.
org%2Fen%2Fgustave-dore%2Fthe-new-jerusalem&h=722&w=533&tb-
nid=A7kJQ7zvAKq3vM%3A&docid=PK8kVuSo0UgsGM&ei=mWlhVtmnHceBU5WJieAG&tb-
m=isch&client=safari&iact=rc&uact=3&dur=865&page=1&start=0&ndsp=65&ved=0a-
hUKEwiZ2Mis_sHJAhXHwBQKHZVRAmwQrQMIOzAK, PD 246; Côme Duhey, PD, https://
commons.wikimedia.org/wiki/File%3AComeduhey_bapteme_du_christ.jpg 257;
Hochschul- und Landesbibliothek Fulda, PD, https://commons.wikimedia.org/wiki/
File%3AWeltchronik_Fulda_Aa88_087r_detail.jpg 66; https://upload.wikimedia.org/
wikipedia/commons/7/7a/Léon_Bloy_1887.jpg, PD 157; Museum of Fine Arts, Boston,
PD, https://commons.wikimedia.org/wiki/File%3ASchmerzensmann.jpg 181; Ökumenisches Heiligenlexikon, PD, https://commons.wikimedia.org/wiki/File%3ASaint_Edith_
Stein.jpg 160; Frederick Richard Pickersgill, PD, http://commons.wikimedia.org/wiki/
File%3AFoster_Bible_Pictures_0084-1_Rahab_Helping_the_Two_Israelite_Spies.jpg 78;
Andreas Praefcke, PD, http://commons.wikimedia.org/wiki/Category:Naaman?use-
lang=de#mediaviewer/File:Enamel_plaque_Naaman_BM.jpg 113; http://www.zeno.org/
nid/20004244982, PD 109; J.L. Raab, PD, https://upload.wikimedia.org/wikipedia/
commons/c/cc/Immanuel_Kant_%28portrait%29.jpg 154; Zénaïde Alexeïevna Ragozin,
PD, https://commons.wikimedia.org/wiki/File%3ABabylons_h%C3%A6ngende_haver.png
173; Remiel at en.wikipedia, PD, http://commons.wikimedia.org/wiki/File%3AStPaul_El-
Grecojpg 335; Samuelson, PD, https://commons.wikimedia.org/wiki/File%3AEbensee_
concentration_camp_prisoners_1945.jpg, 146/147; Avishai Teicher, PD, http://commons.
wikimedia.org/wiki/File%3ABaptistry_in_Emmaus_Nicopolis%2C_Israel.jpg 345; Vassil,
PD, https://commons.wikimedia.org/wiki/File%3AAnge_au_sourire.jpg 243; https://
commons.wikimedia.org/wiki/File:Petrus_et_Paulus_4th_century_etchin.JPG, PD 349;
http://commons. wikimedia.org/wiki/File%3AThe_child_Samuel_tells_Eli_about_God's_
displeasure_with_him._Wellcome_V0034309.jpg, PD 92; http://commons.wikimedia.org/
wiki/File%3ATeresa_of_%C3%81vila.jpg, PD 395; http://commons.wikimedia.org/wiki/
File%3ASimone_Weil_1921.jpg, PD 396; http://commons.wikimedia.org/wiki/
Category:New_Jerusalem?uselang=de#mediaviewer/File:BambergApocalypseFoli-
o055rNew_Jerusalem.JPG, PD 406; https://commons.wikimedia.org/wiki/File%3ACre-

Links to the licensing contracts
http://creativecommons.org/licenses/by-sa/2.0/legalcode
http://creativecommons.org/licenses/by-sa/2.5/legalcode
http://creativecommons.org/licenses/by-sa/3.0/de/legalcode
http://creativecommons.org/publicdomain/zero/1.0/legalcode

Acknowledgments

The YOCAT Foundation thanks all the volunteers who helped create this youth bible.

Thanks to all the young people who gave their witness or sent in photos for the bible.

Thanks to the participants of YOUDEPRO 2015: Kara Logan, Sharon Murphy, Nadia Nicole, Vallentine Onundo, Ivan Vrlic.

Thanks to the participants of YOUDEPRO 2014: Martine Boutros, Jerônimo Lauricio, Nicolas Lázaro, Jomar Luciano, Cyriac Panackal, Johann Rhee.

Thanks to the students of the Religion Institute of the Ecclesiastical Teachers' College in Vienna/Krems: Christa Berger, David Hadl, Stefanie Kriz, Ruth Leitner, Christian Lesch, Nicola Majnaric, Zoran Marincic, Angelika Mayer, Martin Mayerhofer, Clemens Moser, Gertrud Nemeth, Martin Stiglmayr, Birgit Szokoll, Roswitha Völker.

Thanks to the participants of the Bible Week: Michaela Kofler, Ruth Leitner, Clemens Moser, Alexander Saller, Benjamin Schiedler, Nico Sucker.

Thanks to the collaborators from the Augsburg House of Prayer: Jürgen Erhard, Wolfgang Fässler, Michael Franz, Michaela Gassner, Raphael Schadt.

Thanks to Flávio Amaral, Bernadette Baumgartner, Magnus Eble, Isabel Meuser, Christoph Kraus, Tobias E. Mayer, Sandra Pantenburg, Michaela Runke, Maria Scheckenbach, Christiana and Georg Schreyer, Marie and Cornelius von Schönau.

Thanks to the Emmanuel Community and to the participants of the Desert Retreat, especially Dominique Haas.

Thanks to the BASICAL Team from the Augsburg Diocese with Florian Markter and Ulrike Zengerle.

Thanks to Cécile Brûlon, Laura Carlos, Francisco Eugenio, Katharina Kiechle, Emilie Leclerc, Luzia Mayer, Nadia Nicole, Michael Scharf, Max Schmid, Nils Shubert, Luc Serafin, Raphael Steber, Peter Paul van Voorst.

Thanks to all whom we inadvertently left out.

Notes

Notes

Notes

Notes

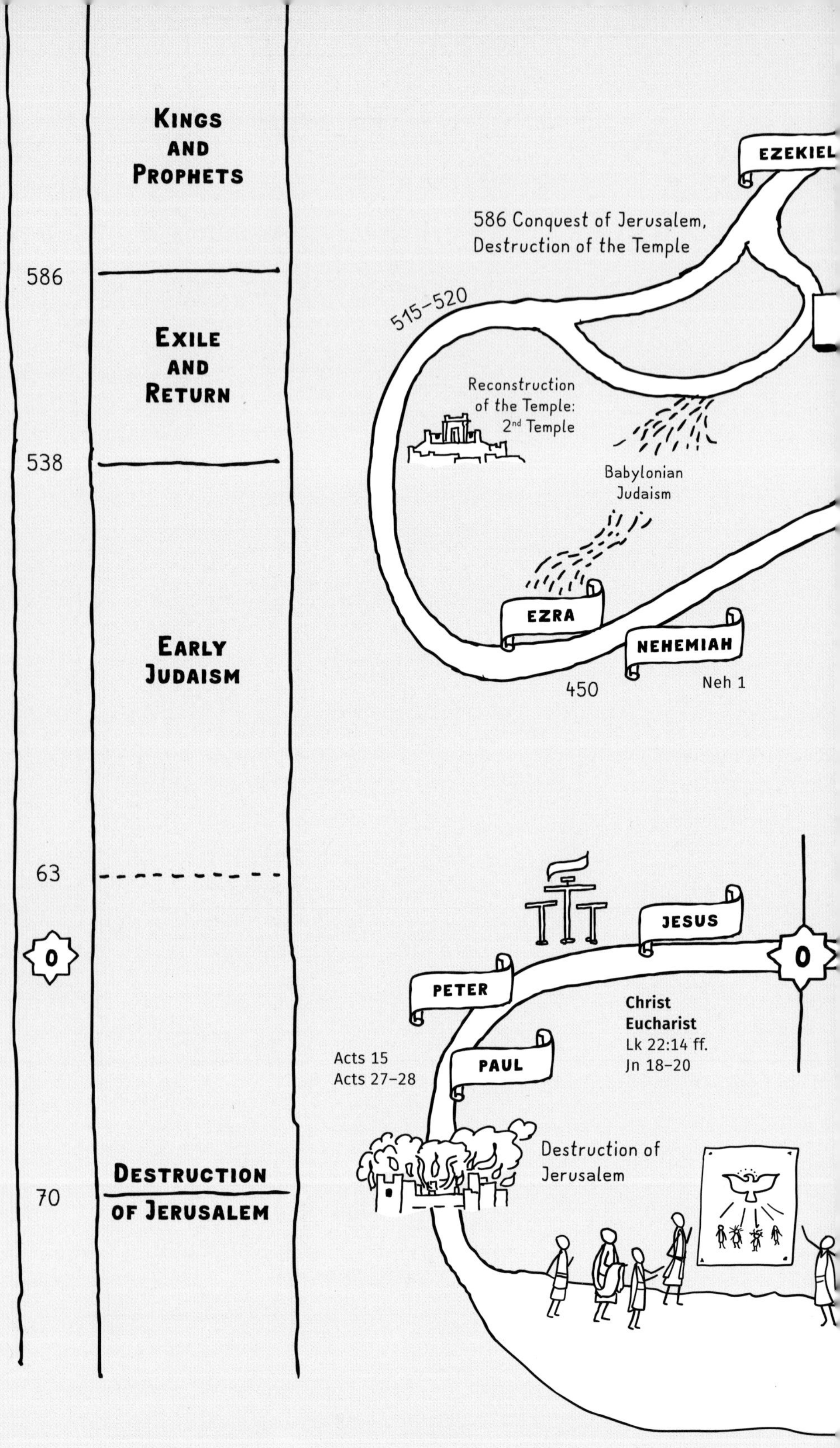

KINGS
AND
PROPHETS

586

EXILE
AND
RETURN

538

EARLY
JUDAISM

63

0

70

DESTRUCTION
OF JERUSALEM

EZEKIEL

586 Conquest of Jerusalem,
Destruction of the Temple

515–520

Reconstruction
of the Temple:
2nd Temple

Babylonian
Judaism

EZRA

NEHEMIAH

450   Neh 1

JESUS

PETER

Christ
Eucharist
Lk 22:14 ff.
Jn 18–20

Acts 15
Acts 27–28

PAUL

Destruction of
Jerusalem

0

Original graphics by Robert Saam

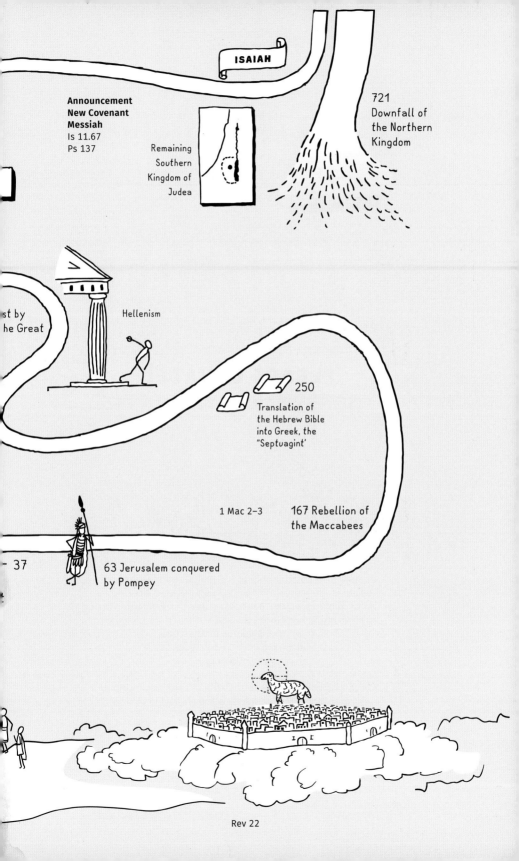

ISAIAH

**Announcement
New Covenant
Messiah**
Is 11.67
Ps 137

Remaining
Southern
Kingdom of
Judea

721
Downfall of
the Northern
Kingdom

st by
he Great

Hellenism

250
Translation of
the Hebrew Bible
into Greek, the
"Septuagint"

1 Mac 2–3

167 Rebellion of
the Maccabees

– 37

63 Jerusalem conquered
by Pompey

Rev 22

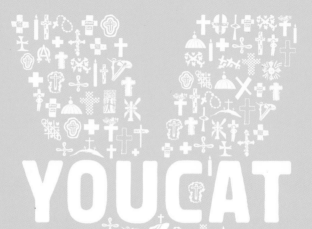

YOUCAT

PLEASE DONATE!

Through distributed profits of its publication projects and donations, the non-profit YOUCAT Foundation gGmbH promotes projects of the new evangelization worldwide, in which young people are encouraged to discover the Christian faith as the foundation for their lives.
Scheibenwandstr. 3 | D–83229 Aschau
www.youcat.org

You can support the work of the YOUCAT Foundation with a monetary donation that will be acknowledged in writing.

Deutsche Bank AG
BLZ: 720 700 24, Account # 031 888 100
IBAN: DE13 7207 0024 0031 8881 00, BIC: DEUTDEDB720